Differential
Psychology

THE MACMILLAN COMPANY
NEW YORK · CHICAGO
DALLAS · ATLANTA · SAN FRANCISCO
LONDON · MANILA
IN CANADA
BRETT-MACMILLAN LTD.
GALT, ONTARIO

Differential Psychology

INDIVIDUAL AND GROUP DIFFERENCES IN BEHAVIOR

Third Edition

ANNE ANASTASI

*Professor of Psychology
Graduate School,
Fordham University*

New York
THE MACMILLAN COMPANY

Preface

It is an exciting experience to revise a book which first appeared two decades earlier. In the process, one is made vividly aware of intervening progress in the particular specialty, in the field as a whole, and even—to some extent—in contemporary culture. The development of more effective research methodologies, the rapid accumulation of fresh data, and the emergence of new theories represent only the more obvious changes. Equally noteworthy are the subtler modifications in relative emphasis on different topics and in forms of expression within a field. A social psychologist, anthropologist, or linguist might find fruitful data for content analysis in this area. Even a comparative study of the phraseology and lingo employed in reporting essentially the same points would be of interest. When undertaking a revision, the author who is sensitive to developments around him soon finds himself writing a substantially new book.

Psychology is growing too rapidly to permit the revision of a textbook by simple accrual. As content accumulates, the need for selectivity, assimilation, and organization rises sharply. Accordingly, although about half of the material reported in the present edition is new, its introduction has been accomplished without lengthening the book. In fact, the number of chapters has been reduced from 24 in the second edition to 18 in the present revision, with some corresponding shortening in the book as a whole. The primary purpose of such condensation has been to focus attention more clearly upon important concepts, basic methodological problems, and major findings. The present length of the book is also more suitable for one-semester courses.

Specifically, the historical introduction and the discussion of psychological testing have been condensed; biological and psychological factors in simple behavior development have been brought together in one comprehensive chapter on the methodology of heredity-environment research (Ch. 4); the material on effects of practice has been combined with that on schooling and intelligence in a single chapter on training and individual differences;

v

all family resemblance studies, including those on twins and foster children, have been treated in one chapter; the two chapters on sex differences have been condensed into one chapter; and the number of chapters on race differences has been reduced from three to two.

The chapter on physique and behavior has been placed earlier in the book because of its fundamental importance in any consideration of the etiology of behavioral differences. For similar reasons, the chapter on social class differences now precedes those on race differences. Among the topics which have been considerably expanded or introduced for the first time in the present edition may be mentioned: effects of early experience upon subsequent behavior, the role of physiological factors in behavior, long-range studies of population changes, longitudinal follow-ups of children and adults, intellectual functioning in maturity and old age, age differences in personality traits, applications of factor analysis, development of multiple aptitude batteries and the profile approach in the measurement of individual differences, the relation of perception and personality, the nature of creativity, and research on culture and personality in the study of national and ethnic groups. The present edition has again drawn extensively upon recent findings in biology, anthropology, and sociology. Increasing use has also been made of research conducted in European countries.

While keeping abreast of the many changes in the field, the present revision retains the fundamental objectives of the two earlier editions. First, differential psychology is presented, not as a separate field of psychology, but as one approach to the understanding of behavior. Its fundamental questions are no different from those of general psychology. It is apparent that if we can explain why individuals react differently from one another, we shall have gone far toward understanding why each individual reacts as he does. The data of differential psychology should thus help to clarify the basic mechanisms of behavior. It is primarily from this point of view that the problems of individual and group differences are surveyed in the present text.

A second aim of the book has been to coordinate the various topics which have usually been joined together loosely under the caption of "individual differences." The rapid growth of differential psychology has resulted in an increasing specialization of interest among research workers and a frequent disregard of the broader implications of the data. The mutual interrelation of the various problems has often been obscured by the accumulation of data at a more rapid pace than they could comfortably be assimilated. For this reason, the writer has endeavored to bear constantly in mind the interrelationships among different types of investigations and has attempted to present a systematic organization and integration of the material. No chapter stands alone. Each is related to what precedes it and to what is to follow.

Thirdly, it has been the author's aim to report the major problems of differential psychology in a form readily comprehensible to the college student. An attempt has been made to present the material clearly and simply, while avoiding the errors of significant omission and falsification which so frequently characterize popularization. An understanding of the basic concepts and major findings within any area need not be limited to those who have mastered its specialized techniques. At the same time, the present book is not intended to be a literature survey. First and foremost, it is a textbook designed to develop in the student the intellectual skills needed for understanding and evaluating the data of differential psychology. Throughout the book, special emphasis has been placed upon the examination of common pitfalls and sources of error in the interpretation of obtained results. The student is thus provided with certain tools whereby he may evaluate for himself a set of data with which he is confronted. This would seem to be far more important than the mere presentation of a body of facts. The development of critical ability and of a dispassionate and objective attitude toward human behavior is more urgently needed today than ever before.

It is a pleasure to acknowledge the cooperation of several colleagues and associates in the preparation of this book. Dr. John P. Foley, Jr., who was a co-author of the second edition, found it impossible to participate in the same capacity in the present revision, owing to the pressure of other professional responsibilities. His collaboration in the earlier edition, however, represents a lasting contribution to the book. In addition, he found time for a critical reading of at least half of the present manuscript. Sincere thanks are extended to the instructors of courses in Differential Psychology who kindly responded to an inquiry regarding desirable revisions in the text. Some of the respondents sent a wealth of additional material in the form of student reactions, reports of unpublished research, and personal reprints. All the questionnaire returns proved extremely helpful in the preparation of the present revision. The writer is likewise indebted to Professor Dorothea McCarthy, of the Department of Psychology, Fordham University, for many valuable suggestions. Appreciation is due to Dr. Norman L. Munn and to the Houghton Mifflin Company for their courtesy in providing a glossy print of Figure 24B, which is based on material originally published in an article by D. C. Pease and R. F. Baker in *Science* but no longer available in reproducible form. Finally, grateful acknowledgment is made to the following members of the Fordham University library staff for their efficient and gracious assistance in bibliographic matters: Miss Elizabeth Rumics, Head of Reader Services, Miss Adelaide Rodriguez, Reference Librarian, and Miss Margaret Tighe, Assistant in Reference and Circulation.

A.A.

Contents

CHAPTER 1

Origins of Differential Psychology

Man has always been aware of differences among his fellow beings. He has, to be sure, entertained various theories, beliefs, or superstitions concerning the causes of such differences, and has interpreted them differently according to his own traditional background. But at all times he seems to have accepted the fact of their existence. Among the earliest records of human activity there is evidence that individual differences were recognized and utilized. In pre-literate cultures, the artist, the medicine man, and the tribal chief are examples of persons who displayed special talents or personality characteristics. At any level of cultural development, specialization of labor itself implies a tacit assumption of differences among people.

Nor is the recognition of individual differences limited to the human species. Instances from animal behavior can readily be found. The acceptance of certain individuals as "leaders" by herds of elephants, buffaloes, and similar gregarious animals has been widely discussed in the literature of both fact and fiction. The frequently described "pecking hierarchy" of chickens is another case in point. A definite relationship of social domination is often displayed by chickens in the barnyard, this fighting or pecking behavior usually centering about the acquisition of food. In such cases, A will attack B, although the reverse will not occur. Violent conflicts often ensue when the authority of the chief pecker in the group is disputed. These and many other examples illustrate the prevalence of differential responses to individuals within one's own group.

The objective and quantitative investigation of individual differences in behavior is the domain of differential psychology. What is the nature and extent of such differences? What can be discovered about their causes? How are the differences affected by training, growth, physical conditions? In what

1

manner are the differences in various traits related to one another, or organized? These are some of the fundamental questions raised by differential psychology which will be treated in the first part of the present book.

Differential psychology is also concerned with an analysis of the nature and characteristics of major traditional groupings, such as the subnormal and the genius, the sexes, and racial, national, and cultural groups. This provides the subject matter of the last seven chapters. The study of such group differences serves a threefold purpose. First, certain groups are recognized and responded to as such in contemporary society. It is therefore of practical concern to learn as much as possible about the nature of such groups. Information of this sort may in turn modify the popular percept of these groups and may ultimately contribute toward the improvement of intergroup relations.

Second, the comparative investigation of different groups should help to clarify the fundamental problems of individual differences in general. In such groups we can see the principles of individual differences in operation and can note their effects. Group differences in behavior, when considered in conjunction with other concomitant differences among the groups, furnish an excellent available means of analyzing the causes of human variability.

Third, the comparison of a psychological phenomenon as it occurs in different groups may contribute toward a clearer understanding of the phenomenon itself. The findings of general psychology, when tested in widely varying groups, are sometimes found to be not so general as was supposed. To study a phenomenon in all its varied manifestations is to have a better grasp of its essential nature.

Notwithstanding the early and widespread recognition of individual differences in the practical adjustments of everyday life, the systematic investigation of such differences is a relatively recent development in psychology. We may therefore begin by considering the conditions that led up to modern differential psychology.

INDIVIDUAL DIFFERENCES IN EARLY PSYCHOLOGICAL THEORY [1]

One of the earliest instances of the explicit recognition of individual differences is to be found in the *Republic* of Plato. A fundamental aim of

[1] To supplement the brief historical sketch of the study of individual differences given in the present and following sections, the reader is referred to any of the standard works on the history of psychology, such as Boring (7), Murphy (23), and Rand (28).

The numbers in parentheses here and throughout the book refer to the numbered References at the end of the respective chapter.

Plato's ideal state was, in fact, the assignment of individuals to the special tasks for which they were suited. In Book II of the *Republic* appeared the following statement: ". . . no two persons are born exactly alike, but each differs from each in natural endowments, one being suited for one occupation and another for another" (11, p. 60). Plato, moreover, proposed a series of "actions to perform" for use as tests of military aptitude to select the soldiers of his ideal state. Designed to sample the various traits considered essential for military prowess, these "actions" represent the first systematically described aptitude test on record.

Nor did the versatile genius of Aristotle overlook individual variation. His writings devoted considerable space to group differences, including species, racial, social, and sex differences in mental and moral traits. In many of his works there is also an implicit assumption of individual differences, although Aristotle did not provide any extensive treatment of these differences as such. One gets the impression that he regarded the existence of individual variation as too obvious to require special mention. That he attributed such differences at least in part to innate factors seems to be indicated by a number of statements such as the following:

Perhaps, then, someone may say, "Since it is in my power to be just and good, if I wish I shall be the best of all men." This, of course, is not possible. . . . For he who wills to be best will not be so, unless Nature also be presupposed (29, *Magna Moralia*, 1187ᵇ).

Throughout the several *Ethics* of Aristotle, there appear passages that imply individual variation. The following statement, for example, leaves little doubt regarding Aristotle's position on this point:

After these distinctions we must notice that in everything continuous and divisible there is excess, deficiency, and the mean, and these in relation to one another or in relation to us, e.g., in the gymnastic or medical arts, and in those of building and navigation, and in any sort of action, alike scientific and non-scientific, skilled and unskilled (29, *Ethica Eudemia*, 1220ᵇ).

Aristotle then proceeded to describe the characteristics of men possessing an excess or a deficient amount of various traits such as irascibility, audacity, shamelessness, and others.

In the Scholasticism of the Middle Ages, individual differences received relatively little attention. Philosophical generalizations regarding the nature of mind were formulated largely through theoretical rather than empirical means. The observation of individuals thus played little or no part in the development of such doctrines. Of particular interest for differential psychology is the "faculty psychology" advanced by St. Augustine and St. Thomas

Aquinas. Such "faculties" as "memory," "imagination," and "will" have been regarded by some as the precursors of the traits and factors currently identified through statistical analysis of test scores. These recently determined factors, however, differ in a number of important ways from the rationally derived faculties of Scholastic philosophy.

The many varieties of Associationism which flourished from the seventeenth to the nineteenth centuries likewise had little to say about individual differences. It was with the elaborate mechanics whereby ideas became associated, giving rise to complex mental processes, that the associationists were primarily concerned. Their statements were general principles with no allowance for individual variation. Bain, the last of the so-called pure associationists, did, however, give some attention to individual differences in his writings. The following passage is taken from his book on *The Senses and the Intellect* (1855): "There is a natural force of adhesiveness, specific to each constitution, and distinguishing one individual from another. This property, like almost every other assignable property of human nature, I consider to be unequally distributed" (3, p. 237).

A simultaneous development in educational theory should probably be included at this point. In the writings and practices of a group of "naturalist" educators of the late eighteenth and early nineteenth centuries, including Rousseau, Pestalozzi, Herbart, and Froebel, there is evident a definite shift of interest to the individual child. Educational policies and methods were to be determined, not by external criteria, but by direct observation of the child and his capacities. Emphasis, however, was still placed on observation of the individual as representative of individuals in general, rather than as distinct from other individuals. Although statements can be found in the writings of these educators to the effect that individuals differ and that their education should be adapted to these differences, still the emphasis is laid more heavily upon free, "natural" education in contrast to externally imposed procedures, rather than upon individual differences themselves. The term "individual" is often used to mean simply "human nature."

THE PERSONAL EQUATION IN ASTRONOMY

Curiously enough, the first systematic measurements of individual differences were undertaken not in psychology but in the much older science of astronomy. In 1796, Maskelyne, the astronomer royal at the Greenwich Observatory, dismissed Kinnebrook, his assistant, because the latter observed the times of stellar transits nearly a second later than he did. The method employed at the time to make such observations was the "eye and ear" method. This method involved not only coordination of visual and auditory impressions, but also rather complex spatial judgments. The observer noted the time to a second on the clock, then began to count seconds with the heard beats of the clock, at the same time watching the star as it crossed the field of the telescope. He noted the position of the star at the last beat of the clock just before it reached the "critical" line in the field; then, similarly, he noted its position with the first beat immediately after it had crossed that line. From these observations, an estimate was made in tenths of a second of the exact time when the star crossed the critical line. This was the accepted procedure and was regarded as accurate to one- or two-tenths of a second.

In 1816 Bessel, astronomer at Königsberg, read of the Kinnebrook incident in a history of the Greenwich Astronomical Observatory, and became interested in measuring what came to be known as the "personal equation" of different observers. Originally, the personal equation referred to the difference in seconds between the estimates of two observers. Bessel collected and published data on several trained observers, and pointed out not only the presence of such a personal equation or error when comparing any two observers, but also the variability in the equation from time to time. This represents the first published record of quantitative data on individual differences.

Many astronomers followed up Bessel's measurements. In the latter half of the nineteenth century, with the introduction of chronographs and chronoscopes, it became possible to measure the personal equation of a given observer without reference to any other observer. The attempt was made to reduce all observations to their objectively correct values without reference to a system of time based upon one observer as a standard. Astronomers also undertook an analysis of the various conditions that affected the size of the personal equation. It was this latter problem, rather than the measurement of individual differences, which was taken up by the early experimental psychologists in their studies of "reaction time."

RISE OF EXPERIMENTAL PSYCHOLOGY

During the latter half of the nineteenth century, psychology began to venture away from its armchair and enter the laboratory. Most of the early experimental psychologists were physiologists whose experiments gradually came to take on a psychological tinge. As a result, both the viewpoints and the methods of physiology were frequently carried over directly into the infant science of psychology. In 1879, Wilhelm Wundt established the first laboratory of experimental psychology at Leipzig. Experiments of a psychological nature had been performed previously by Weber, Fechner, Helmholtz, and others, but Wundt's laboratory was the first to be devoted exclusively to psychology and to offer facilities for training students in the methods of the new science. Consequently it exerted a profound influence upon the development of early experimental psychology. Students from many nations were attracted to Wundt's laboratory and, upon their return, established similar laboratories in their own countries.

The problems investigated in these early laboratories testify to the close kinship of experimental psychology with physiology. The study of visual and auditory sensation, reaction time, psychophysics, and association constituted nearly the entire field of experimentation. It was characteristic of the early experimental psychologists either to ignore individual differences or to regard them simply as chance "errors." The greater the individual variation in a phenomenon, the less accurate would be the generalizations regarding its nature. The extent of individual differences thus represented the "probable error" to be expected in the application of general laws of psychology.

It is apparent that the rise of experimental psychology shifted the emphasis away from—rather than toward—the study of individual differences. Its major contribution to the development of a differential psychology is to be found in the demonstration that psychological phenomena are amenable to objective and even quantitative investigation, that psychological theories can be tested by actual data, that psychology, in short, could become an empirical science. Such a step was required before theories about the individual could be replaced by studies on individual differences.

CONTRIBUTIONS OF BIOLOGICAL SCIENCE

During the late nineteenth century, biology made rapid strides under the impetus of Charles Darwin's formulation of the doctrine of evolution. A by-product of this doctrine was the rise to prominence of the comparative viewpoint, which involves the observation of similar phenomena in different species. In the effort to test some of the implications of evolutionary theory, Darwin and a number of his contemporaries amassed the first large body of data on animal behavior. Beginning with anecdotal material and field observations, this search led eventually to the highly controlled animal experiments of the twentieth century. Differential psychology has profited in many ways from such investigations of animal behavior. Examples of relevant types of research, to be considered more fully in Chapter 4, include the study of developmental sequences in the effort to discover principles of behavior development; the exploration of anatomical and other organic changes that parallel changes in behavior; and the many experiments on the effect of controlled environmental factors upon subsequent behavior.

Of particular importance to differential psychology is the work of the English biologist Francis Galton, one of Darwin's most eminent followers. It was Galton who first attempted to apply the evolutionary principles of variation, selection, and adaptation to the study of human individuals. Galton's scientific pursuits were many and varied, but they were unified by his underlying interest in the study of heredity. In 1869, he published a book entitled *Hereditary Genius* in which, by the application of the now well-known family history method, he tried to demonstrate the inheritance of specific talents in various fields of work (cf. Ch. 9 for fuller report). Two similar books followed, one on *English Men of Science* (1874), the other on *Natural Inheritance* (1889).

In connection with his study of human heredity, it soon became apparent to Galton that related and unrelated individuals must be measured, objectively and in large numbers, in order to discover the degrees of resemblance among them. For this purpose, he devised numerous tests and measures, and in 1882 established his famous anthropometric laboratory at South Kensington Museum in London. There, for the payment of a small fee, individuals could be tested in sensory discrimination, motor capacities, and other simple processes.

Through the measurement of sensory processes, Galton hoped to arrive at an estimate of the subject's intellectual level. In the *Inquiries into Human Faculty,* a collection of miscellaneous essays published in 1883, he wrote: "The only information that reaches us concerning outward events appears to pass through the avenue of our senses; and the more perceptive the senses are of difference, the larger is the field upon which our judgment and intelligence can act" (13, p. 27). And again, on the basis of findings on the inferior sensitivity of idiots, he observed that sensory discriminative capacity "would on the whole be highest among the intellectually ablest" (13, p. 29). For this reason, measures of sensory capacity, such as vision and hearing, constituted a relatively large portion of the tests which Galton constructed and employed. Among these tests may be mentioned the Galton bar for visual discrimination of length, the Galton whistle for determination of the highest audible pitch, and kinesthetic discrimination tests based on the arrangement of a series of weights, as well as tests of strength of movement, speed of simple reactions, and many others of a similar nature. Galton also initiated the use of free association tests, a technique that was subsequently adopted and further developed by Wundt. Galton's study of individual and group differences in mental imagery was another of his pioneer efforts. It represented the first extensive application of questionnaire methods in psychology.

Another prominent influence in shaping differential psychology is to be found in the development of the modern science of genetics. The rediscovery of Mendel's laws of heredity in 1900 led to vigorous experimentation on the mechanism of heredity. The highly successful research on the inheritance of physical traits in animals, of which the work on the fruit fly *Drosophila* is the outstanding example, has been reflected in differential psychology in a number of ways. First, it contributed to the clarification and refinement of the concept of heredity. Second, it provided a variety of genetic models in terms of which behavior data could be examined. Third, it led directly to animal experimentation on selective breeding and cross-breeding for psychological characteristics (cf. Ch. 4). Finally, the development of human genetics has suggested methods for the statistical analysis of family resemblances and differences, which have been extensively applied to psychological data (cf. Ch. 9).

GROWTH OF STATISTICAL METHOD

One of the chief research tools of differential psychology is statistical analysis. Galton was keenly aware of the need for specialized statistical techniques to process the data of individual differences that he gathered. Accordingly, he set about to adapt a number of mathematical procedures for this purpose. Among the principal statistical problems with which Galton was concerned were those of the normal distribution curve (cf. Ch. 2) and of correlation. In reference to the latter, he carried out much of the spade work and evolved an index which eventually came to be known as the coefficient of correlation. It was his student Karl Pearson, however, who later worked out the mathematical details of correlation theory. Pearson, too, was responsible for developing and systematizing what until recently constituted nearly the whole field of statistics.

Still another British statistician whose contributions significantly affected the subsequent course of statistics was R. A. Fisher. Working primarily within the area of agricultural research, Fisher derived a number of new statistical techniques which have proved extremely useful in many other fields, including psychology, and have opened up vast new possibilities for data analysis. His name has been most closely associated with analysis of variance, a technique that permits the simultaneous investigation of the effects of several variables in a single experiment.

An intelligent interpretation of almost any study in differential psychology requires an understanding of certain fundamental statistical concepts. It is beyond the scope of the present book to describe computational procedures, or even to discuss statistical concepts at any length. Many excellent books are available in the field of psychological statistics, and the student is urged to consult them for fuller details.[2] It may be advantageous at this point, nevertheless, to summarize the essential meaning of two statistical concepts that are of paramount importance in differential psychology, namely, statistical significance and correlation.

Statistical Significance. The question of statistical significance refers primarily to the extent to which similar results would be expected if an investigation were to be repeated. How likely is it that, in another investigation of the same problem, the original conclusion would be reversed? This is obviously a fundamental question to ask about any study. One reason for expecting a certain amount of change in the results is to be found in sampling error. This "chance error," or source of uncontrolled fluctuations in the data, arises from the fact that any one investigator employs only a *sample* of the total possible *population* with which he is concerned.

If, for example, an investigator wants to know the mean height of 8-year-old American boys, he might measure 500 8-year-old boys distributed over the country. Theoretically, he should try to get a truly random sample for this purpose. Thus if he had the name of every 8-year-old boy, he might draw lots until he had accumulated 500 names. Or he might arrange the names alphabetically and choose every tenth one. A random sample is one in which every individual has an equal chance of being included. This condition implies that every choice is independent of every other. For instance, if a sampling procedure were followed whereby the selection of an individual precluded the choice of any of his relatives, the resulting sample would not be truly random.

In actual practice, the investigator would probably assemble a representative sample by making certain that his group was distributed in the same way as the total population of 8-year-old American boys with respect to such factors as urban-rural ratio, section of country, socioeconomic level of neighborhood, type of school, and the like. In any event, the mean height of the sample would be taken as the best approximation of the population

[2] A few short, elementary introductions to psychological statistics have been published, of which Garrett (14) is a recent example. For more detailed coverage and more advanced treatment, the reader is referred to such standard texts as Garrett (15), Guilford (18), and McNemar (21).

mean. The two measures would not, however, be identical. Nor would the
same mean be obtained in another random sample of 500 8-year-old American boys. It is these chance fluctuations in results from one random sample
to another that constitute what is known as "sampling error."

There is still another way in which chance errors may affect our results.
If we measure the running speed of a group of children and then repeat
these measurements on the same group another day, we shall probably
arrive at a slightly different mean speed on the two occasions. It may happen
that a number of the children were tired when tested on the first day, but
were in top condition on the second occasion. In the course of repeated
measurements over many occasions, these chance errors would balance out.
But the results of any one day's observations may be too high or too low.
In this case, we can think of the single day's results as a sampling of
measures out of the entire "population" of measures that could be obtained
on the same group.

Both types of chance errors can be estimated by applying statistical
measures of *reliability*. Formulas are available for computing the reliability
of means, of differences between means, of variability measures, of correlations, and of many other indices. By these procedures, we can predict the
probable limits within which our results may fluctuate because of chance
errors. As might be expected, an important element in all these formulas
is the number of cases in the sample. Other things being equal, the larger
the sample the more stable will be the results, since in large groups chance
errors tend to cancel out.

One of the most common applications of such reliability measures in
differential psychology concerns the significance of the difference between
two sets of scores. Is the obtained difference large enough to fall beyond the
probable limits of chance fluctuation? If the answer is yes, we conclude that
the difference is statistically significant.

Suppose that a group of women average 8 points higher than a group of
men on a verbal comprehension test. To evaluate the significance of this
difference, we compute what is known as a *t* ratio.[3] By reference to a table
of *t*, we can look up the probability that a difference as large as or larger
than the obtained difference of 8 points in favor of either group could have
resulted by chance. Suppose we find that this probability (or *P* value) is 1
out of 100 ($P = .01$). This means that if there were no sex difference in
verbal comprehension in the entire population and if we were to draw 100

---

[3] In earlier studies, the "critical ratio" was most commonly used for this purpose.
Although differing in certain details, both are interpreted in essentially the same way.
Moreover, with large groups (100 or more cases), the results obtained by the two
techniques do not vary appreciably.

random samples of men and women from that population, only once would we find a mean difference as large as 8. We therefore say that the obtained sex difference is "significant at the .01 level." Such a statement is an expression of the confidence that can be put in our conclusion. Thus if the investigator concluded that his results demonstrate a sex difference, his chances of being wrong are 1 out of 100. Conversely, his chances of being right are, of course, 99 out of 100. Another frequently reported confidence level is $P = .05$. This means that there are 5 chances out of 100 of being in error, and 95 chances out of 100 of being correct.

Another type of problem in which we need a t ratio, with its P value, is one involving the effect of some experimental condition, such as the administration of vitamin tablets, upon test performance. Does the group that received the vitamin perform significantly better than the control group which was given only a placebo, or control tablet? Is the mean difference between the two groups large enough to reach the .01 level of confidence? Or could such a difference result by chance more than once out of 100 times?

Still another example is provided by the retesting of the same subjects before and after some interpolated experience, such as a special training program. Again we need to know whether the gains shown by the group are large enough to fall outside of the expected chance results.

It might be added that the P value need not—and rarely does—fall exactly on the designated limits, such as .05, .01, or .001. If, for example, the investigator is willing to accept the .01 level of confidence, it means that he will draw a conclusion when the chances of its being wrong are *one or less* out of 100. Hence it is customary to report the P values in the form of $P < .05$ or $P < .01$. This may be read: the chances that the conclusion is in error are less than 5 out of 100 or less than one out of 100, respectively.

Correlation.   Another statistical concept with which the student of differential psychology should be familiar is that of correlation. By this term is meant the degree of relationship or correspondence between two sets of measures. For example, we may want to know the relationship between the scores obtained by the same individuals on two different tests, such as a numerical reasoning and a mechanical comprehension test. Or the problem may be to find the degree of correspondence between the scores of related persons, such as fathers and sons, on the same test. In another investigation, it may be a question of correlating the scores of the identical subjects on the same test administered on different occasions, such as before and after a practice period. There are obviously many problems in differential psychology that call for this type of analysis.

The most common measure of correlation is the Pearson product-moment correlation coefficient, conventionally designated by the symbol *r*. This coefficient provides a single index of the amount and direction of correlation present within the whole group. It can vary from +1.00 (a perfect positive correlation), through 0, to −1.00 (a perfect negative or inverse correlation).

A +1.00 correlation means that the individual receiving the highest score in one set of measures also receives the highest score in the other set, the one who is second best in the first is second best in the second, etc., each person's relative standing in the two measures being identical. A −1.00 correlation, on the other hand, indicates that the highest score in one measure is paired off with the lowest in the other, a corresponding perfect reversal occurring throughout the group. A zero correlation signifies no relationship at all between the two sets of scores, or the sort of arrangement that would result if the scores were shuffled and paired off at random. The same interpretations apply, of course, when the scores of different persons, such as fathers and sons, have been correlated. For example, a +1.00 correlation would signify that the highest-scoring father in the group had the highest-scoring son, the second-highest-scoring father had the second-highest-scoring son, and so forth.

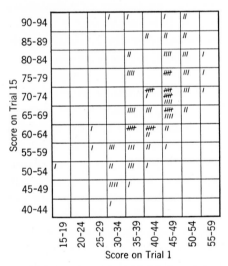

Fig. 1. Bivariate Distribution of 114 Subjects on Initial and Final Trials of a Hidden Words Test: Correlation = .82. (Unpublished data from Anastasi, 1.)

The sign of the correlation coefficient, whether positive or negative, indicates the direction of relationship. A negative correlation signifies an inverse relation between the variables. The numerical size of the coefficient represents the closeness or degree of correspondence. The correlations found in psychological research are almost never numerically equal to 1.00. In other words, correlation is not perfect (in either direction), but reflects some individual variation within the group. What we generally find is a tendency for the high scorers in one variable to score high in the other, with a certain number of individual exceptions within the group. Numerically, the resulting correlation coefficient will have some value between 0 and 1.00.

An example of a relatively high positive correlation is given in Figure 1. This figure shows a "bivariate distribution," or distribution in two variables.

The first variable (plotted on the baseline) represents scores on the first trial of a Hidden Words test, in which the subjects were to underline every four-letter English word they located in a page of pied type. The second variable (plotted on the vertical axis) refers to the scores obtained by the same subjects on another form of the same test administered in trial 15. Each tally mark in the diagram shows the score of one of the 114 subjects on both trial 1 and trial 15. For example, one subject whose initial score fell between 15 and 19 achieved a final score between 50 and 54. When the Pearson correlation coefficient between these two sets of scores was computed, it proved to be .82.

Without going into computational details, we may simply note that this correlational technique is based upon each individual's deviation from the group mean in the two variables. Thus if all individuals had fallen equally far above or below the group mean on both the initial and final trials, the correlation would have been $+1.00$. It will be seen that Figure 1 does not show such perfect correspondence. At the same time, the tally marks do tend to cluster along a diagonal from the lower left to the upper right corner. Such a bivariate distribution indicates a high positive correlation, there being no individuals scoring very low on the initial and very high on the final trial, or very high on the initial and very low on the final trial. What the coefficient of .82 actually indicates is that the subjects tended to maintain the same relative standing in the group at the beginning and end of practice.

Knowing the number of cases from which a correlation was computed, we can also evaluate the statistical significance of the obtained r by the methods cited in the earlier part of this section. Thus with 114 cases, an r of .82 is found to be significant at the .001 level. This statement means that, if the two sets of scores were actually uncorrelated (i.e., $r = 0$), then a correlation as high as .82 or higher would result by chance less than once out of 1000 times. We can thus be highly confident that the variables are actually correlated.

In addition to the Pearson r, there are other methods of measuring correlation, suitable for use in special situations. For example, when subjects have been ranked or when they have been classified into a few discrete categories, in one or both traits, the correlation between the traits can still be found by appropriate formulas. The resulting coefficients are also expressed numerically on a scale ranging from 0 to 1.00 and can be interpreted in approximately the same way as a Pearson r.

The rapidly growing field of statistics has contributed many concepts and techniques to differential psychology besides those of statistical significance and correlation. These two have been singled out at this point because they will be encountered early in our discussion and will recur in connection with almost every topic. Other important statistical procedures will be introduced in relation to specific topics. For example, distribution curves and measures of variability will be considered in Chapter 2. Similarly, techniques of factor analysis, representing a further analysis of correlation coefficients, will be cited in connection with the research on trait organization (Ch. 10).

THE TESTING MOVEMENT IN PSYCHOLOGY

Of equal importance with statistics as a tool of differential psychology is psychological testing.[4] We have already identified the early beginnings of the testing movement in the pioneer research of Galton with simple sensori-motor tests. Another outstanding contributor to the development of psychological testing was the American psychologist James McKeen Cattell. In Cattell we find a convergence of two parallel movements: the rise of experimental psychology and the measurement of individual differences. For his doctorate at Leipzig under Wundt, Cattell prepared a dissertation on individual differences in reaction time. He subsequently spent some time lecturing in England, where his interest in individual differences was bolstered by contact with Galton. Upon returning to America, Cattell was active both in the establishment of laboratories for experimental psychology and in the spread of the testing movement.

Early Mental Tests. In an article written by Cattell in 1890 (9), the term "mental test" was used for the first time in the psychological literature. This article described a series of tests which were being administered annually to college students in the effort to determine their intellectual level. The tests, which had to be given individually, included measures of muscular strength, speed of movement, sensitivity to pain, keenness of vision and of hearing, weight discrimination, reaction time, memory, and the like. In his choice of tests, Cattell shared Galton's view that a measure of intellectual functioning could be obtained through tests of sensory discrimination and reaction time. Cattell's preference for such tests was also strengthened by his belief that simple functions could be measured with precision, in contrast to more complex functions, whose objective measurement looked like a well-nigh hopeless task at the time.

Cattell's tests were typical of those to be found in a number of test series

[4] For a more detailed treatment of the rise of the testing movement, as well as for an introduction to the field of psychological testing, the student is referred to any recent text on psychological testing, such as Anastasi (2).

which appeared during the last decade of the nineteenth century. Some efforts to tap more complex psychological functions may nevertheless be noted in the inclusion of tests of reading, verbal association, memory, and simple arithmetic (22, 30). Such tests were administered to school children, college students, and miscellaneous adults. At the Columbian Exposition held in Chicago in 1893, Jastrow set up an exhibit at which visitors were invited to take tests of sensory, motor, and simple perceptual processes and to compare their skill with the norms (cf. 26 ,27). A few attempts to evaluate such early tests yielded very discouraging results. The individual's performance showed little correspondence from one test to another (30, 37), and it exhibited little or no correlation with independent estimates of intellectual level as determined by teachers' ratings (6, 16) or academic grades (37).

A number of similar test series were assembled by European psychologists of the period, including Oehrn (25), Kraepelin (20), and Ebbinghaus (12) in Germany, and Guicciardi and Ferrari (17) in Italy. In an article published in France in 1895, Binet and Henri (4) criticized most of the available test series as being too largely sensory and as concentrating unduly on simple, specialized abilities. They further maintained that, in the measurement of more complex functions, a high degree of precision is not needed, since individual differences are larger in these functions. Partly to meet these objections, Binet and Henri proposed a new series of tests, covering such functions as memory, imagination, attention, comprehension, suggestibility, and esthetic appreciation. In these tests may be recognized the trends that were eventually to lead to the development of the famous Binet "intelligence tests."

Intelligence Tests. In 1904, the French Minister of Public Instruction appointed a commission to study the problem of retardation among public school children. As a direct outgrowth of his work for this commission, Binet, in collaboration with Simon, prepared the first intelligence scale designed to yield an over-all index of the individual's level of intellectual functioning (5). In 1908 appeared Binet's first revision of this scale, in which the tests were grouped into age levels on the basis of empirical tryouts. For example, in the 3-year level were placed all tests that normal 3-year-olds could pass, in the 4-year level all tests passed by normal 4-year-olds, and so on to age 13. A child's score on the scale is then reported as a "mental age," i.e., the age of normal children whose performance he equals.

Even prior to the 1908 revision, the Binet-Simon tests attracted wide attention among psychologists throughout the world. Translations and adaptations appeared in many languages. In America, a number of different revisions were prepared, the most famous of which is that developed under the direction of Terman at Stanford University, known as the Stanford-Binet (34). It was in this scale that the Intelligence Quotient (IQ), or ratio between mental age and chronological age, was first introduced. The current revision of this scale, often referred to as the Terman-Merrill Scale (35), is still one of the most widely used individual tests of intelligence.

Group Testing. Another important milestone in the progress of psychological testing is to be found in the development of group scales. The Binet scales and others patterned after them are known as "individual tests" in the sense that only one subject can be tested at a time. Moreover, these tests are of such a nature that a highly trained examiner is required to administer them. Large-scale testing is not feasible under these conditions. The advent of group intelligence scales was probably the chief factor in the popularization of psychological testing. Group tests are not only adapted to the simultaneous testing of large groups, but their administration and scoring are also simplified.

The impetus for the development of group tests was furnished in 1917 by the urgent need for testing over one and one-half million men in the United States Army during World War I. A quick, rough classification of recruits in respect to intelligence was required for many military purposes. Army psychologists met this problem by constructing two group scales, known as the Army Alpha and the Army Beta. The former was prepared for general use. The latter was a nonlanguage scale designed for testing illiterates and foreign-born draftees who were not sufficiently familiar with English.

Later Developments. The years since World War I witnessed a phenomenal rise in the number of available tests, the employment of increasingly varied techniques, and the application of tests to many different aspects of behavior. Group intelligence scales were constructed for all ages and types of subjects, from kindergarten children to graduate students. Soon they were supplemented by tests of *special aptitudes,* such as musical or mechanical abilities. A more recent development has been the appearance of *multiple factor batteries.* These batteries were a natural outgrowth of research on trait organization, to be considered in Chapters 10 and 11. Essentially, in place of a single global score such as an IQ, the multiple factor batteries provide a profile of scores on a number of major aptitudes.

Another parallel development has been the extension of psychological testing to *nonintellectual traits,* through the use of personality inventories, projective techniques, and other devices. Beginning in World War I with Woodworth's Personal Data Sheet, this type of testing has grown rapidly to include measures of interests, attitudes, emotional adjustment, and social traits. Although a tremendous amount of energy and inventiveness has gone into the preparation of tests for these purposes, the success attained to date does not yet equal that of aptitude tests.

Test Concepts. As in the case of statistics, there are certain basic concepts relating to psychological tests with which the student of differential psychology should be familiar. One of these is the concept of *norms*. No score on a psychological test has meaning until it is compared with the test norms. Such norms are gathered in the process of standardizing a new test, by giving the test to a large group of subjects representative of the population for which the test is designed. The performance of this group then serves as a standard in terms of which any individual's score can be evaluated. Norms may be expressed in a number of different ways, such as mental ages, percentiles, or standard scores. But all enable the examiner to "place" the subject in reference to the standardization sample. Is his test performance equal to the group average? Is he above or below the average, and if so how far?

Another important concept is that of *test reliability*. By this is meant the consistency of a test. If an individual were retested on a different day or with an alternate form of the same test, how far would his score vary? Reliability is usually determined by correlating the scores obtained by the same persons on two occasions. It will be noted that test reliability depends upon one of the types of chance errors described in an earlier section. Test reliability, however, is concerned with the effect of such chance errors on the relative standing of the individual on successive tests. It does not deal with the effect of these errors on means and other group results.

One of the most fundamental questions that needs to be asked about any psychological test concerns its *validity*, i.e., the degree to which the test actually measures what it purports to measure. Validity may be investigated by checking test scores against many kinds of independently obtained data, such as school records, indices of job success, or leadership ratings.

Data on test norms, reliability, and validity should be gathered while the test is in an experimental form, prior to its release for general use. Available tests differ considerably in the extent to which they meet desirable specifications in these regards, as well as in the fullness with which the necessary information is reported. In an effort to improve and systematize this situation, the American Psychological Association issued in 1954 a set of

Technical Recommendations for Psychological Tests and Diagnostic Techniques (39). Different types of norms, ways of measuring reliability and validity, and other problems relevant to the evaluation of tests are discussed. The reader who may wish further orientation regarding current thinking about psychological tests is urged to consult this publication.

EMERGENCE OF DIFFERENTIAL PSYCHOLOGY

At the turn of the century, differential psychology had begun to assume definite shape. In 1895 Binet and Henri pubiished an article entitled *La psychologie individuelle* (4), which represented the first systematic analysis of the aims, scope, and methods of differential psychology. Their opening sentence reflected the status of this branch of psychology at the time. It read, "We broach here a new subject, difficult and as yet very meagerly explored" (4, p. 411). Binet and Henri put forth as the two major problems of differential psychology, first, the study of the nature and extent of individual differences in psychological processes; and second, the discovery of the interrelationships of mental processes within the individual, so that we may arrive at a classification of traits and determine which are the more basic functions.

In 1900 appeared the first edition of Stern's book on differential psychology, *Über Psychologie der individuellen Differenzen* (32). Part I dealt with the nature, problems, and methods of differential psychology. Within the scope of this branch of psychology Stern included differences among individuals as well as among racial and cultural groups, occupational and social levels, and the two sexes. The fundamental problem of differential psychology he characterized as threefold. First, what is the nature and extent of differences in the psychological life of individuals and groups? Second, what factors determine or affect these differences? In this connection he mentioned heredity, climate, social or cultural level, training, adaptation, etc. Third, how are the differences manifested? Can they be detected by such indices as handwriting, facial conformation, etc.? Stern also included a discussion of the concepts of psychological type, individuality, and normality and abnormality. Under the methods of differential psychology, he gave an evaluation of introspection, objective observation, the use of material from history and poetry, the study of culture, quantitative testing, and experiment. Part II contains a general discussion and some data on individual differences in various psychological traits, from simple sensory capacities to more complex mental processes and emotional characteristics. Stern's book appeared in a highly revised and enlarged edition in 1911, and again in 1921, under the title of *Die Differentielle Psychologie in ihren methodischen Grundlagen* (33).

In America, committees were being appointed to investigate testing methods and to sponsor the accumulation of data on individual differences. At its 1895 meeting, the American Psychological Association appointed a committee "to consider the feasibility of cooperation among the various psychological laboratories in the collection of mental and physical statistics" (10, p. 619). The following year, the American Association for the Advancement of Science established a standing committee to organize an ethnographic survey of the white population in the United States. Cattell, one of the members of this committee, pointed out the importance of including psychological tests in this survey and suggested that its work be coordinated with that proposed by the American Psychological Association (10, pp. 619–620).

Application of the newly devised tests to various groups was also getting under way. Kelly (19) in 1903 and Norsworthy (24) in 1906 compared normal and feebleminded children on sensorimotor and simple mental tests. Their findings highlighted the continuous gradation in ability which exists between these groups, suggesting that feeblemindedness does not constitute a distinct category. In 1903 appeared Thompson's *The Mental Traits of Sex* (36), the result of several years' testing of men and women with a variety of tests. This represents the first comprehensive investigation of psychological sex differences.

Tests of sensory acuity, motor capacities, and a few simple mental processes were also being administered for the first time to various racial groups. A few scattered investigations appeared before 1900. In 1904 Woodworth (38) and Bruner (8) tested several primitive groups at the St. Louis Exposition. In the same year appeared Spearman's original article putting forth his Two-Factor theory of mental organization and introducing a statistical technique for investigating the problem (31). With this publication, Spearman opened up the field of research on trait relationships and paved the way for current factor analysis.

SUMMARY

It is apparent that shortly after 1900 the foundations had been laid for virtually every branch of differential psychology. Influences that helped to shape this new field may be found in the philosophical writings of pre-experimental psychologists, in the early attempts of astronomers to obtain precise measurements of individual differences in reaction time, in the rise of experimental method in psychology, in certain important developments within the fields of biology and statistics, and in the mental testing movement.

The directions in which modern differential psychology has grown have also been determined in part by what has been happening in such related fields as biology and statistics, as well as by the subsequent progress of psychological testing. To these contemporary influences should be added the contributions of anthropology and social psychology, two areas that have many points of contact with differential psychology today. The relation of differential psychology to the latter disciplines will become more evident after a reading of later chapters dealing with group differences and cultural influences.

In statistical method, the contributions of such pioneers as Galton, Pearson, and Fisher have provided the differential psychologist with efficient techniques for analyzing his data. Among the most important statistical concepts utilized in differential psychology are those of statistical significance and correlation. The mental testing movement, which also traces its origins to the work of Galton, was advanced by the subsequent contributions of Cattell, Binet, Terman, and the army psychologists of World War I who prepared the first group scales of intelligence. Later stages involved the development of special aptitude tests, multiple factor batteries, and measures of nonintellectual traits. The major test concepts with which the student should be familiar include norms, reliability, and validity.

REFERENCES

1. Anastasi, Anne. Practice and variability. *Psychol. Monogr.*, 1934, 45, No. 5.
2. Anastasi, Anne. *Psychological testing.* N.Y.: Macmillan, 1954.
3. Bain, A. *The senses and the intellect.* London: Parker, 1855.
4. Binet, A., and Henri, V. La psychologie individuelle. *Année psychol.*, 1895, 2, 411–463.
5. Binet, A., and Simon, Th. Méthodes nouvelles pour le diagnostic du niveau intellectuel des anormaux. *Année psychol.*, 1905, 11, 191–244.
6. Bolton, T. L. The growth of memory in school children. *Amer. J. Psychol.*, 1891–92, 4, 362–380.
7. Boring, E. G. *A history of experimental psychology.* (Rev. Ed.) N.Y.: Appleton-Century-Crofts, 1950.
8. Bruner, F. G. The hearing of primitive peoples. *Arch. Psychol.*, 1908, No. 11.
9. Cattell, J. McK. Mental tests and measurements. *Mind*, 1890, 15, 373–380.
10. Cattell, J. McK., and Farrand, L. Physical and mental measurements of the students of Columbia University. *Psychol. Rev.*, 1896, 3, 618–648.

11. Davies, J. L., and Vaughan, D. J. (Transs.) *The republic of Plato.* N.Y.: Burt, 19——.
12. Ebbinghaus, H. Über eine neue Methode zur Prüfung geistiger Fähigkeiten und ihre Anwendung bei Schulkindern. *Z. Psychol.,* 1897, 13, 401–459.
13. Galton, F. *Inquiries into human faculty and its development.* London: Macmillan, 1883.
14. Garrett, H. E. *Elementary statistics.* N.Y.: Longmans, Green, 1956.
15. Garrett, H. E. *Statistics in psychology and education.* (5th Ed.) N.Y.: Longmans, Green, 1958.
16. Gilbert, J. A. Researches on the mental and physical development of school children. *Stud. Yale psychol. Lab.,* 1894, 2, 40–100.
17. Guicciardi, G., and Ferrari, G. C. I testi mentali per l'esame degli alienati. *Riv. sper. freniat.,* 1896, 22, 297–314.
18. Guilford, J. P. *Fundamental statistics in psychology and education.* (3rd Ed.) N.Y.: McGraw-Hill, 1956.
19. Kelly, R. L. Psychophysical tests of mentally deficient children. *Psychol. Rev.,* 1903, 10, 345–373.
20. Kraepelin, E. Der psychologische Versuch in der Psychiatrie. *Psychol. Arbeit.,* 1895, 1, 1–91.
21. McNemar, Q. *Psychological statistics.* (2nd Ed.) N.Y.: Wiley, 1955.
22. Münsterberg, H. Zur Individualpsychologie. *Zbl. Nervenheilk. Psychiat.,* 1891, 14, 196–198.
23. Murphy, G. *An historical introduction to modern psychology.* (Rev. Ed.) N.Y.: Harcourt, Brace, 1949.
24. Norsworthy, Naomi. The psychology of mentally deficient children. *Arch. Psychol.,* 1906, No. 1.
25. Oehrn, A. *Experimentelle Studien zur Individualpsychologie.* Dorpater disser., 1889 (also publ. in *Psychol. Arbeit.,* 1895, 1, 92–152).
26. Peterson, J. *Early conceptions and tests of intelligence.* Yonkers-on-Hudson, N.Y.: World Book Co., 1926.
27. Philippe, J. Jastrow—exposition d'anthropologie de Chicago—tests psychologiques, etc. *Année psychol.,* 1894, 1, 522–526.
28. Rand, B. *The classical psychologists.* N.Y.: Houghton Mifflin, 1912.
29. Ross, W. D. (Ed.) *The works of Aristotle.* Vol. 9. Oxford: Clarendon Press, 1915.
30. Sharp, Stella E. Individual psychology: a study in psychological method. *Amer. J. Psychol.,* 1898–99, 10, 329–391.
31. Spearman, C. "General intelligence" objectively determined and measured. *Amer. J. Psychol.,* 1904, 15, 201–293.
32. Stern, W. *Über Psychologie der individuellen Differenzen (Ideen zur einer "Differentielle Psychologie").* Leipzig: Barth, 1900.
33. Stern, W. *Die differentielle Psychologie in ihren methodischen Grundlagen.* Leipzig: Barth, 1921.
34. Terman, L. M. *The measurement of intelligence.* Boston: Houghton Mifflin, 1916.
35. Terman, L. M., and Merrill, Maud A. *Measuring intelligence.* Boston: Houghton Mifflin, 1937.

36. Thompson, Helen B. *The mental traits of sex*. Chicago: Univer. Chicago Press, 1903.
37. Wissler, C. The correlation of mental and physical traits. *Psychol. Monogr.*, 1901, 3, No. 16.
38. Woodworth, R. S. Race differences in mental traits. *Science*, N.S., 1910, 31, 171–186.
39. Technical recommendations for psychological tests and diagnostic techniques *Psychol. Bull.*, 1954, 51, No. 2, Part 2.

CHAPTER 2

Distribution and Extent
of Individual Differences

In popular speech, people are often classified as "haves" and "have-nots." Jones can write, Smith cannot. Helen has a talent for music, Doris for painting, Dick for mathematics, and Sam for organizing people. Such characterizations are based on arbitrary cut-off points, dictated by practical demands. In order to choose music as a vocation, or even a serious avocation, for example, an individual must have a certain minimum of musical talent. If his degree of musical ability falls below that minimum, he is not regarded as a "musical person." We are accustomed to describing the individual in terms of his *outstanding* assets and liabilities, and simply ignoring the traits in which he rates close to the average. Hence we label Mr. Black as a creative thinker, Miss Wentworth as a good mixer, and Mr. Doe as a poor sport. We do not ordinarily refer to Mr. Black as a medium sport, to Miss Wentworth as an average creative thinker, and to Mr. Doe as a mediocre mixer!

Sharp, qualitative distinctions among people are encountered every day. Closer observation reveals, however, that all individuals are distributed along a continuous scale in every characteristic. In other words, people do not fall into clearly differentiated types. Differences among people are a matter of *degree*. It is in this sense that individual differences are said to be quantitative rather than qualitative.

It might be argued that there are at least a few characteristics which a person may either have or not have, and that in this respect we may speak of qualitative differences. The classical examples are such sensory handicaps as loss of vision or of hearing. Here, it would seem, are traits characterized by presence or absence: a person can see or he cannot see; he can hear or he cannot hear. This, too, turns out to be a purely conventional and practical distinction. Anyone who has visited a school for the blind knows that

23

there are many degrees of blindness, and that not all those classified as blind are totally blind. The everyday working definition of blindness is any *degree* of visual deficiency too serious to permit normal activity. The same is obviously true of deafness and any other sensory disorder. Between the empirically established "normal" vision or hearing and what is classed as blindness or deafness there is to be found a continuous gradation of minor deficiencies. It should be added that the existence of a trait in zero degree, as in total blindness, is not inconsistent with the quantitative view of individual differences. The latter implies only that there be intermediate degrees rather than simple presence or absence.

DISTRIBUTION OF INDIVIDUAL DIFFERENCES

Since individual differences are quantitative in the above sense, we may now ask how the varying degrees of each trait are distributed among people. Are individuals scattered uniformly over the entire range or do they cluster at one or more points? What are the relative frequencies with which different degrees of a trait occur? These questions can best be answered by an examination of frequency distributions and frequency graphs.

Like all statistical devices, the frequency distribution is a means of summarizing and organizing quantitative facts in order to facilitate their understanding and to bring out significant trends. Scores on a test, or any other set of measures, are grouped into class-intervals, and the number of cases falling within each interval is tabulated. An example of a frequency distribution is given in Table 1. This shows the scores of 1000 college students on a code-learning test, in which one set of nonsense syllables was to be substituted for another. The scores, showing number of correct syllables substituted during a two-minute trial, ranged from 8 to 52. They have been grouped into class-intervals of 4 points each, beginning with 52–55 at the top of the distribution and extending down to 8–11. The column headed "Frequency" in Table 1 gives the number of persons whose scores fell within each of these class-intervals. For example, one person scored between 52 and 55, one between 48 and 51, 20 between 44 and 47, and so on. It is evident that we can get a clearer idea of the test performance of this group by looking at such a distribution than we could have obtained through an examination of the original list of 1000 scores.

The facts brought out by a frequency distribution can be even more readily perceived if presented pictorially by means of a frequency graph. Figure 2 shows the data of Table 1 in graphic form. The baseline or horizontal axis gives the scores, grouped into class-intervals; the vertical

Table 1

FREQUENCY DISTRIBUTION OF SCORES
OF 1000 COLLEGE STUDENTS ON A
CODE-LEARNING TEST

(From Anastasi, 2, p. 34)

CLASS-INTERVAL	FREQUENCY
52–55	1
48–51	1
44–47	20
40–43	73
36–39	156
32–35	328
28–31	244
24–27	136
20–23	28
16–19	8
12–15	3
8–11	2
	N = 1000

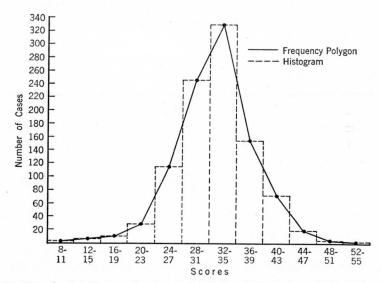

Fig. 2. Distribution Curves: Frequency Polygon and Histogram. (Data from Table 1.)

axis refers to the frequency or number of cases falling within each class-interval.

The graph has been plotted in two ways, both forms being in common use. One graph is a *frequency polygon,* in which the number of individuals within each interval is indicated by a point, centrally located in respect to the class-interval; the successive points are then joined by straight lines. The other graph is obtained by erecting a column or rectangle over each class-interval, the height of the column depending upon the number of cases in that interval. This type of graph is known as a *histogram*. If we look, for example, at the class-interval 44–47 in Table 1, we find 20 cases scoring within its limits. Accordingly, in Figure 2 a dot has been placed across from 20 and above the midpoint of the interval marked 44–47. This gives us one of the points used in plotting the frequency polygon. In the case of the histogram, the same 20 cases are represented by a column extending across the 44–47 interval and reaching up to 20 along the vertical axis.

We may describe the group further by reporting some measure of *central tendency*. If we want a single most typical or representative score to characterize the group as a whole, the measure of central tendency will provide such a score. One of the best known of these measures is the average, obtained by adding all the scores and dividing the sum by the number of cases. The more precise name for this measure is arithmetic mean—often referred to simply as the mean.

Another measure of central tendency often used in psychology is the median. This is the middlemost score, when all scores have been arranged in order of size. For large groups, it is much easier to compute the median directly from the frequency distribution. In this case we find a median point, which bisects the distribution in such a way that half the cases fall above it and half below it. Still another measure of central tendency sometimes encountered in psychological studies is the mode, or most frequent score. Again this may be found from a frequency distribution by taking the midpoint of the class-interval having the largest frequency. It may be noted that the mode corresponds to the highest point on the graph. For the distribution given in Table 1 and Figure 2, the mean is 32.37, the median 32.46, and the mode 33.5.

THE NORMAL CURVE

The reader will already have noticed certain characteristics of the distribution presented in Table 1 and Figure 2. The majority of cases cluster in the center of the range and as the extremes are approached there is a gradual and continuous tapering off. The curve shows no gaps or breaks; no clearly separated classes can be discerned. The curve is also bilaterally symmetrical; that is, if it should be divided by a vertical line through the center, the two halves so obtained would be nearly identical. This distribution curve resembles the bell-shaped "normal curve," the type most commonly found in the measurement of individual differences. A theoretically determined, perfect normal curve is illustrated in Figure 3.

The concept of the normal curve is an old one in statistics. It first became familiar as the *normal probability curve*. The probability of an event is its expected frequency of occurrence in a very large number of observations. This probability is represented by a ratio or fraction, the numerator of which is the expected outcome, and the denominator the total possible outcomes. Thus the probability or chances

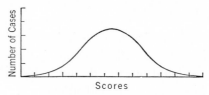

Fig. 3.   Normal Probability Curve.

that, when two coins are tossed, only heads will come up is one out of four, or ¼. This follows from the fact that the only possible combinations of heads (H) and tails (T) that can occur when two coins fall are the following four: HH, HT, TH, TT. Just one of these four, HH, contains only heads. Similarly, the probability of two tails is ¼, and that of one head and one tail is two out of four, or ½. If the number of coins is increased, say to 100, so that the number of possible combinations becomes very large, we can still determine mathematically the chances of occurrence of any one combination, such as all heads or 20 heads and 80 tails. These probabilities, or expected frequencies of occurrence, can be plotted graphically by the same method outlined above for plotting scores. The curve obtained when the number of coins is very large will be the bell-shaped normal probability curve.

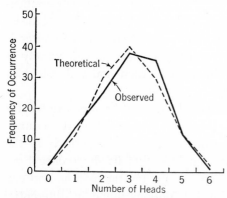

Fig. 4.   Theoretical and Observed Distributions of Number of Heads in 128 Throws of Six Coins. (Data from Guilford, 10, p. 119.)

In Figure 4 will be found the theoretical and obtained frequency curves showing number of heads in 128 throws of six coins. In each throw, the number of heads falling uppermost could, of course, vary from 0 to 6. The most frequent combination is that containing 3 heads (and 3 tails). The frequencies decrease progressively from this point as the number of heads drops below 3 or rises above 3. In Figure 4, the theoretically computed probabilities are shown in the broken-line graph, while the frequencies actually obtained in 128 successive throws of the six coins are given in the solid-line graph. It will be noted that the expected and obtained results agree rather closely. The larger the number of observations (or throws), the closer will be this agreement.

As the number of coins in the above illustration increases, the theoretically expected distribution curve approaches the normal probability curve. The results obtained by tossing coins or throwing dice are said to depend on "chance." By this is meant that the outcome is determined by a large number of independent factors whose influence has not been analyzed. The height from which a coin or die is thrown, its weight and size, the twist of the hand employed, and many other similar factors determine which particular face will fall uppermost in any one throw. The normal probability curve was first developed by the mathematicians Laplace and Gauss in connection with games of chance, the distribution of errors of observations, and other types of chance variations.

It was the nineteenth-century Belgian statistician Adolph Quetelet who first applied normal probability theory to the distribution of human characteristics (cf. 4). Quetelet noticed that certain human measurements, such as the heights and chest girths of army conscripts, were distributed according to the bell-shaped probability curve. From the approximate applicability of this curve to human variability data, he theorized that such human variability occurred when nature aimed at an "ideal" or norm, but fell short of the mark by differing amounts. In somewhat different terms, it may be argued that people's heights, weights, or intelligence test performance depend upon a very large number of independent factors, so that the end result will be distributed according to the law of chance. Quetelet's applications of the normal curve were adopted and carried forward by Galton, whose contributions to differential psychology were discussed in Chapter 1. In Galton's hands, the normal probability curve was put to a wide variety of uses, many of them centering about the quantification and refinement of data on individual and group differences.

The distribution reproduced in Table 1 and Figure 2 has been tested for "normality" by the application of appropriate mathematical procedures. Despite its minor irregularities, it does not deviate significantly from the normal probability curve. We can thus conclude that its divergence from normality is within the range expected from sampling fluctuation, and can treat it as a normal curve. Many of the distributions found in differential psychology likewise fit the mathematical specifications of a normal curve, especially when they are obtained through the use of carefully constructed measuring instruments with large representative groups. In other instances, the distribution may resemble a normal curve only roughly. Such distributions exhibit at least continuity and approximate symmetry, in the sense of having the largest clustering of persons near the center of the range and a gradual tapering off toward the extremes.

In Figures 5 to 10 will be found examples of distribution curves obtained for a wide variety of human characteristics. These distributions were chosen principally because they are based on large, representative samples, most of them including 1000 or more cases. Two curves plotted with smaller groups

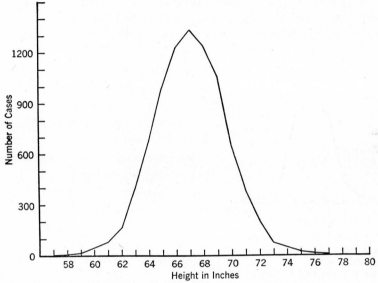

Fig. 5. Distribution of Height of 8585 English-Born Men. (From Yule and Kendall, 34, p. 95.)

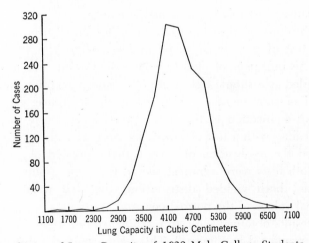

Fig. 6. Distribution of Lung Capacity of 1633 Male College Students. (From Harris *et al.*, 12, p. 94.)

have been included to illustrate the distribution of a physiological and a personality characteristic, respectively, since in these areas data on large groups are relatively scarce.

An example of the distribution of a purely structural trait is furnished in Figure 5, which shows the *height* in inches of 8585 English-born men. It will be seen that the graph approximates the mathematical normal curve to a remarkably close degree. Figure 6 presents the frequency curve of a more functional, physiological trait, *lung capacity*. This is the total volume of air, measured in cubic centimeters, that can be expelled from the lungs after a maximal inspiration. The measurements from which the curve is plotted were made on 1633 male college students. The general correspondence to the normal curve is again apparent.

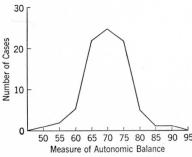

Fig. 7. Distribution of Mean Estimates of Autonomic Balance for 87 Children between the Ages of 6 and 12. (From Wenger and Ellington, 33, p. 252.)

Figure 7 is concerned with a physiological measure which is believed to have some relationship to emotional and personality characteristics. It shows the distribution of 87 children in a composite measure of *"autonomic balance."* High scores in this measure indicate a functional predominance of the parasympathetic division of the autonomic nervous system; low scores, a functional predominance of the sympathetic division. To psychologists, the autonomic nervous system has been of special interest because of its role in emotional behavior.

The graph reproduced in Figure 8 illustrates the distribution of performance on a test of *perceptual speed and accuracy*. The score is the total number of A's in a page of pied type cancelled in one minute. This is generally regarded as a simple test of attention and perception, although speed and control of movement are also involved. Reference may likewise be made in this connection to the data reported previously in Table 1 and Figure 2, dealing with a test of *simple learning*. It will be recalled that this test required the application of a code that consisted of paired nonsense syllables. Both tests were administered to the same group of 1000 college students, and both yielded distributions that fell within the expected mathematical values of the normal curve.

Typical results obtained with an *intelligence test* administered to a large sample are presented in Figure 9. This figure gives the distribution of the IQ's of 2904 children between the ages of 2 and 18 on the 1937 revision of the Stanford-Binet. Reference to the graph will show that the largest percentage of cases received IQ's in the middlemost class-interval, from 95 to 104. The percentage tapers off gradually until only a small fraction of 1 per cent is found with IQ's between 35 and 44, and between 165 and 174. Institutionalized feebleminded subjects were not included in this distribution, the

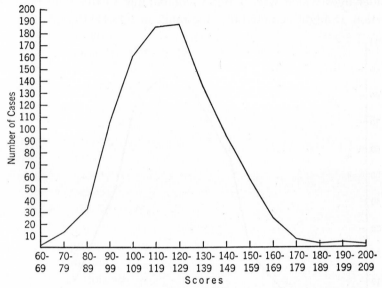

Fig. 8. Number of A's Cancelled in One Minute by 1000 College Students. (From Anastasi, 2, p. 32.)

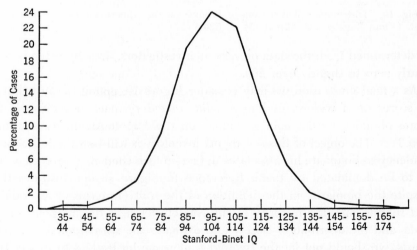

Fig. 9. Stanford-Binet IQ's of a Representative Sample of 2904 Children between the Ages of 2 and 18. (From Terman and Merrill, 27, p. 37.)

sampling also being restricted in certain other ways. Thus the group consisted entirely of American-born white subjects, with a somewhat greater
proportion of urban residents than is found in the total population of the
country. The major portion of the sampling was composed of elementary
school children, an effort having been made to secure groups at the younger
and older ages which were roughly comparable to the elementary school
population. It might be noted that the range of IQ's for the total population,

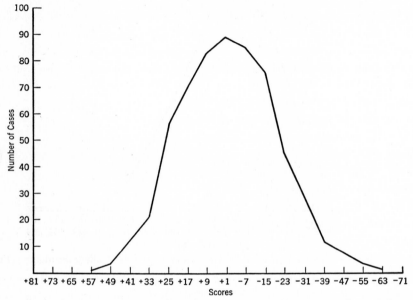

Fig. 10. Distribution of 600 College Women on the Allport Ascendance-Submission
Test. (From Ruggles and Allport, 24, p. 520.)

as determined from the data of various investigators, actually extends from
nearly zero to slightly over 200.

As a final illustration we may consider Figure 10, giving the distribution
of scores on a widely used *personality inventory*. The graph shows the
scores obtained by 600 college women on the Allport Ascendance-Submission Test. The object of this self-report inventory is to assess the individual's
tendency to dominate his associates in face-to-face contacts of everyday life,
or to be dominated by them. Reference to Figure 10 demonstrates that,
despite the bipolarity in the definition of the trait (in terms of ascendance
and submission), the majority of subjects cluster near the midpoint of the
scale, and the distribution closely approximates the normal curve. In other
words, we should not let the twofold trait name mislead us to expect that

individuals can be classified into the ascendant and the submissive. Like other measurable human characteristics, this personality trait reveals a continuous gradation, with the largest number of persons manifesting intermediate reactions.

CONDITIONS THAT AFFECT THE SHAPE
OF THE DISTRIBUTION CURVE

It should not be assumed from the examples cited in the preceding section that all distributions obtained in differential psychology fit the normal curve. There are many other possible types of frequency distributions, several of which could be readily illustrated with real data gathered on some human trait. Distribution curves may vary from mathematical "normality" in two major ways, namely, skewness and de-

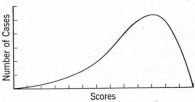

Fig. 11. A Skewed Distribution.

gree of flatness (technically called "kurtosis"). A *skewed distribution* is one in which the peak, or mode, is displaced to right or left of center. Such a distribution lacks the bilateral symmetry of the normal curve. In Figure 11 will be found an illustration of a skewed curve, with a piling up of scores at the upper end of the distribution.

Another way in which a distribution may diverge from normality is in its *degree of peakedness or flatness*. Figure 12 shows two curves, one more peaked and the other flatter than the theoretical normal curve. In the former

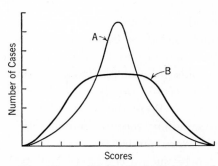

Fig. 12. A Highly Peaked (A) and a Relatively Flat (B) Distribution.

(curve A), there is an excessive piling up of cases at the center, with relatively few persons at the extremes of the scale. In the latter (curve B), the cases are spread more uniformly over a large portion of the range. An extreme type of flattened graph is represented by a *rectangular distribution*, in which the relative frequencies of all degrees of deviation from the center are identical. In this case, subjects would be distributed uniformly over the entire scale. A *multimodal curve* may be considered as still another variation in the peakedness of a distribution. As its name suggests, this type of curve has more than one mode, or peak. Individuals would thus cluster at two or more different points on the scale. The peaks may be equally high, or there may be a major peak and one or more minor ones.

Distribution curves that deviate significantly from normality and exhibit one or more of the characteristics described above occur from time to time under certain conditions. A knowledge of these conditions is essential for the proper interpretation of frequency distributions. The major factors that may influence the shape of the distribution curve include inadequacies of sampling, the use of faulty or inappropriate measuring instruments, and certain factors that operate directly upon the trait under investigation. In the following sections, we shall examine each of these three types of conditions in turn.

Sampling.   It would be possible to obtain any conceivable type of distribution by deliberately choosing subjects to fit the pattern. There would, of course, be no object to such a procedure. Similar variations may occur, however, through the operation of selective factors which may have been overlooked by the investigator. Whenever a curve deviates significantly from normality, the adequacy of the sampling ought therefore to be examined.

Skewness may result, for example, from the inclusion within a single distribution of two normally distributed groups that differ pronouncedly in both mean and range. This effect is illustrated in Figure 13. In Graph A are given the separate distribution curves of the two groups, one of which has a lower mean as well as a narrower scatter of scores than the other. Graph B shows the definitely skewed curve which is obtained when both groups are combined and plotted as one distribution.

A multimodal curve can also be obtained if the sampling tested is not chosen at random from the general population, but consists of individuals selected from widely differing levels and combined into a single group. A group consisting of 5-year-olds and 10-year-olds, for example, would present a definitely bimodal distribution in intelligence test scores, as well as in height, weight, and many other characteristics. Were the intervening age groups from 6 to 9 to be included in this sampling, the distribution would take on the appearance of the normal bell-shaped curve.

The production of a bimodal distribution by such a combination of two widely separated groups is illustrated in Figure 14. It will be noted that the overlapping between the two separate groups is slight. When the overlapping is large, as in the case of adjacent age groups, the resulting combined curve will be normal and unimodal.

Other peculiarities that may result from sampling include excessive flatness of the distribution curve (approximating a rectangular distribution), or its reverse, excessive peakedness. The latter might occur, for example, if the sampling is exceptionally homogeneous. Finally, it should be noted that an unlimited number of minor irregularities and variations in distribution curves may occur through the use of small groups. Curves plotted from a small number of cases usually present an uneven, jagged appearance, since

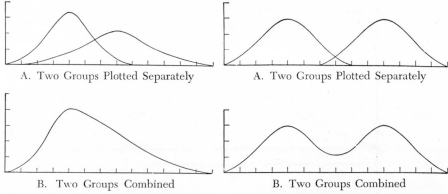

A. Two Groups Plotted Separately   A. Two Groups Plotted Separately

B. Two Groups Combined   B. Two Groups Combined

Fig. 13. Skewness Resulting from the Combination of Groups with Different Means and Ranges.   **Fig. 14.** Bimodality Resulting from the Combination of Two Groups with Widely Separated Means.

individual exceptions loom relatively large. In general, the larger the sampling, the "smoother" will be the distribution curve.

Measuring Instrument. Several characteristics of the tests or other measuring instruments employed in gathering data may likewise affect the shape of the resulting distribution curve. Thus if the *range of difficulty* covered by the test items is restricted at the upper or lower levels, a skewed curve may be artifically produced. Such a distribution will be obtained when any test is given to a group for which it is not suited. For example, if an intelligence test designed for grades 3 to 8 were administered to a college class, the large majority of subjects would score very near the maximum, and the number of cases would drop rapidly as the scores decreased. Similarly, if one of the many tests constructed for use on college freshmen were given to elementary school children, there would be a marked piling up of scores near the zero end of the scale, and the distribution would be equally asymmetrical.

Obviously these data could not be taken to mean that intelligence is not normally distributed among school children or college students. Such skewed distributions result from the fact that the difficulty range of the test does not extend far enough in the upper or lower direction. In the one case, all of those subjects who have more than a certain minimum of the ability tested will make a perfect or nearly perfect score, whereas if the test had included more difficult items, these subjects would have scattered over a wide range. This is illustrated in Figure 15, the solid line showing the actual distribution of ability in the group, and the broken line the curve that would result from the use of a test with a low "ceiling." In a similar manner, a piling up

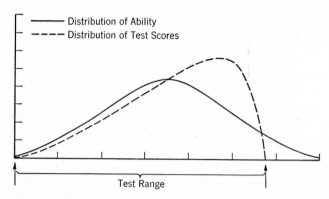

Fig. 15.   Skewness Resulting from Inadequate Test Ceiling.

of zero or very low scores will occur when the test is too difficult for the group. In choosing a test for a given group, therefore, care must be taken to ensure that the subjects have sufficient leeway at both ends of the scale. The highest and lowest scores obtained should be a considerable distance from zero and perfect scores, respectively.

An actual example of the effect of using a test with insufficient range at the low end of the scale is to be found in Figure 16. The data for this distribution were gathered in the 1947 Scottish Survey, in which an effort was made to test every 11-year-old child born in Scotland. This survey represents one of the most extensive sampling projects ever undertaken. A total of 70,805 children was included, a sampling the authors describe as complete except for the children whose sensory or motor handicaps precluded the valid administration of the test, those school children who were absent on the day of testing, and a few children attending certain private schools for whom the necessary background data could not be obtained. It is estimated that the sample tested represented approximately 88 per cent of all 11-year-old Scottish children at the time. All subjects were given a specially developed 45-minute group intelligence test, including two pages of pictorial and five pages of verbal items.

The distribution of verbal scores is given in Figure 16. Although on the whole this distribution shows a clustering of scores at the center and a progressive decrease in frequency as the extremes are approached, a number of irregularities can be noted. Inadequate coverage at the low end of the scale is strongly suggested by an examination of the test itself. The fact that 13.9 per cent of the cases fell in the class-interval 0–9 further indicates that the zero point of the test was probably set too high for the population under consideration. With the inclusion of more easy items, these cases would very

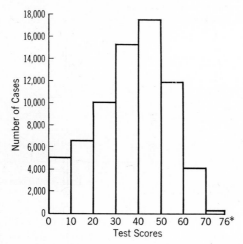

* The last class-interval does not cover 10 points, since the maximum score on the test was 76.

Fig. 16. Distribution of Scores of 70,805 11-year-old Scottish Children on a Verbal Group Test of Intelligence. (Data from Scottish Council for Research in Education, 25, p. 82.)

likely have distributed themselves over several class-intervals below the present zero of the test.

It can also be readily demonstrated that *inequality of units* in the measuring instrument can distort a frequency distribution in various ways. A good illustration is furnished by data collected on visual acuity by means of two tests (28). The frequency distributions of the same group of 226 persons on each of these tests are shown in Parts A and B of Figure 17, respectively. Graph A is a sharply peaked and skewed curve obtained with the familiar Snellen chart, in which the subject's visual acuity index is based upon the smallest row of letters he can read at a standard distance of 20 feet. Thus an individual who at 20 feet can see no more than the letters that the average person reads at 50 feet is said to have 20/50 vision. Normal vision obviously corresponds to a 20/20 index. An index such as 20/15 indicates better-than-average vision. Because of the particular choice of letter sizes in this test, not all acuity levels are sampled to an equal degree, the poorer acuity levels being represented by more items than the average or superior acuity levels. In other words, the differences in difficulty level between successive rows of letters are not equal; there are larger "gaps" in difficulty level in the center and upper portions of the acuity scale than in the lower portion.

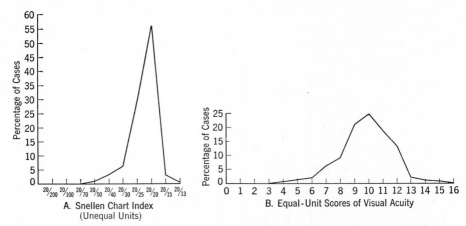

Fig. 17.   Effect of Inequality of Scale Units upon Distribution Curves: Distributions of 226 Persons on Two Tests of Visual Acuity. (From Tiffin and Wirt, 28, p. 77.)

This inequality of units can be illustrated by a comparison of the items or units on the Snellen chart with those on an equal-unit scale of visual acuity, as shown below (28, p. 77):

Equal-Unit Acuity Scale	1	2	3	4	5	6	7	8	9	10	11	12	13	14	15
Snellen Chart	$\frac{20}{200}$	$\frac{20}{100}$	$\frac{20}{70}$	$\frac{20}{50}$	$\frac{20}{40}$		$\frac{20}{30}$	$\frac{20}{25}$		$\frac{20}{20}$			$\frac{20}{15}$		$\frac{20}{13}$

The distribution of the scores of the same group of 226 persons on the equal-unit acuity test is given in Part B of Figure 17. It will be noted that this graph approximates a normal curve much more closely than does the distribution of unequal-unit scores.

Other types of deviation from a normal curve may also arise from inequality of scale units. Suppose that in the above example there had been thorough item coverage at the two ends of the scale, but gaps produced by a shortage of appropriate items at the intermediate difficulty levels. The result might have been a distribution with two peaks, since persons belonging in the center would tend to cluster at the closest available levels.

It is well to bear this effect in mind when considering results obtained with tests of certain personality characteristics, such as introversion-extroversion. Being defined in bipolar terms, such traits may have been sampled more thoroughly in their extreme manifestations, while their intermediate degrees may have insufficient coverage. Such a test would thus have poorer discriminative value and larger gaps between units in the center of the range than at the extremes. As a result, a slight bimodality could easily occur simply from the peculiarities of the measuring instrument, regardless of the distribution of the behavior itself. Similarly, by increasing the relative number of items at the extremes of a scale, a normal distribution of scores may be transformed into a relatively flat or even into a rectangular distribution.

It should be apparent by now that the scale of measurement may affect the form of the distribution curve in many ways. Strictly speaking, it is impossible to determine the actual distribution of a variable unless we have an equal-unit scale for measuring it. But the only methods now available for developing equal units in psychological tests are themselves based upon the assumption that the trait under consideration is normally distributed! To inquire what is the "actual" distribution of a psychological trait thus constitutes, at least for the present, a meaningless question.

In the process of test construction, the normal curve is treated as a methodological problem, rather than as an empirically observed fact. Whenever a non-normal distribution is obtained in the standardization group, the usual response is to set to work revising the test. Most tests have thus been deliberately adjusted so as to yield a distribution that approximates the normal curve in the population for which they were designed. Items are dropped or added, others are shifted up or down in the scale, scoring "weights" of different responses are altered, and other similar adjustments are made until the desired approximation to normality is attained. To say, then, that a given distribution is normal may simply mean that the process of test standardization was meticulously executed. Conversely, to say that a given distribution is *not* normal may mean only that the construction of the test was crude, or that the test was applied to a group for which it was unsuitable.

There are several reasons why the test constructor and the research worker in differential psychology usually seek normality of distribution. If some assumption regarding the distribution of a human trait must be made, that of the normal curve would seem to be the most plausible in the majority of situations. The known complexity and multiplicity of factors determining each individual's standing in any trait would lead us to expect the trait to be distributed in accordance with the normal probability law. Moreover, the distribution of physical traits, which are measured in terms of equal units such as inches or pounds, regularly yield normal curves. A further reason for seeking conformity to the normal curve is that normally dis tributed data are amenable to many types of statistical analyses not other wise applicable. It should be noted, however, that for certain special pur poses other types of distributions may be preferable and are accordingly employed.

Special Factors. Deviations from the normal curve may also result from conditions that affect the traits themselves, rather than from characteristics of the sampling or of the measuring instrument. One example is provided by the so-called *J-curve hypothesis of social conformity*, first proposed by Allport (1). This curve, named after its resemblance to the letter J, may be re garded as a highly skewed curve, with the majority of people falling at that end which represents complete or nearly complete conformity to the socially ac cepted standard of behavior. A favorite illustration of such J-curves is found in the reactions of motorists or pedestrians to various traffic regulations, such as stopping for traffic lights, stopping at in tersections, or driving within the proper traffic lane. Other examples of "conform ing behavior" to which the J-curve has been applied include certain religious practices, such as time of arrival at serv ices, participation in group singing, and the like.

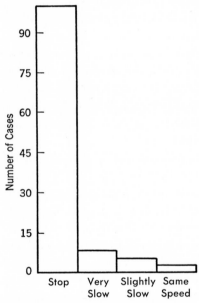

Fig. 18. J-Curve of Motorists' Be-havior at an Intersection with No Cross-Traffic but with Red Signal Light and Traffic Officer. (From All-port, 1, p. 144.)

Typical J-curves are reproduced in Figures 18 and 19. The first shows the distribution of the responses of 102 motorists at an intersection with no cross-traffic approaching, but with a red signal light and a traffic officer. It will be noted that over 90 per cent of the cases observed came to a full stop. Of the remaining small percentage, a few slowed down markedly, still fewer slowed down slightly, and a very small number continued at the same speed. In this case it can be argued that, if left to their own devices, motorists might exhibit behavior that would follow roughly a normal dis tribution. But the introduction of such "social constraints" as traffic regulations, signal lights, and a policeman serves to pull the distribution into a J-curve.

It should be noted that the location of the peak depends upon the point in the scale at which the socially imposed behavior falls. The extreme or true J-curve is not necessarily obtained in all situations involving social conformity. Thus the degree to which urban adults in America partake of alcoholic beverages would probably show a peak, not at either extreme, but at an intermediate point corresponding to "moderate social drinking." This point probably represents maximum conformity to the practices of the group, but it does not represent either a maximum or a minimum in terms of drinking behavior. It is not the J-curve itself that is important, but rather the fact that variations in the distribution curve may be introduced by social conformity. The J-curve is only a special instance of the effects of this type of "loading" factor. It may also be added parenthetically that the curve in Figure 18 is actually a reversed J and may be more accurately described as an L-curve. But it has become conventional to refer to all such highly skewed curves as J-curves, regardless of whether the peak is at the extreme right or left. The direction of the scale could, of course, be arbitrarily reversed, so that the peak would fall at the right.

A somewhat different application of the J-curve concept is given in a more recent investigation of adolescent behavior toward age peers (20). In this study, 629 junior high school students were given the names of their classmates (average class size being 35.5) with the instructions to write the numbers 1 to 5 next to each name to indicate the following reactions, respectively: "would like to have as very, very best friends," "good friends," "not friends but OK," "don't know them," and "other people in the room." For purposes of tabulation, the investigator combined the first two ratings under "acceptance," the last two under "isolation or rejection," and labeled the middle rating "passive acceptance or tolerance." The resulting distributions are portrayed in Figure 19. The two graphs in Part A show the ratings given by boys to other boys and to girls in their classrooms. Corresponding graphs for the girls are to be found in Part B. According to the investigator, these graphs indicate conformity to the mores of prepubescent and pubescent boys and girls in our culture, in so far as they reflect widespread acceptance of age-and-sex peers, combined with a tendency to avoid the opposite sex, this tendency being stronger in boys than in girls.

A word of caution should be added regarding the interpretation of J-curves. We cannot, of course, argue directly from the shape of the curve to the causes of the behavior in question. As has been noted in the preceding section, the nature of the measuring scale may affect the shape of the curve.

By cutting off a scale at its center, for example, we can obtain a J-curve from a normally distributed variable. Like any other frequency distribution, the J-curve must be examined in the light of the adequacy of the measuring scale, the sampling procedures followed in choosing subjects, and other conditions that may have influenced the form of the distribution.

Another factor that may produce a frequency distribution resembling a J-curve is sheer *rarity* of the phenomenon under consideration. When the

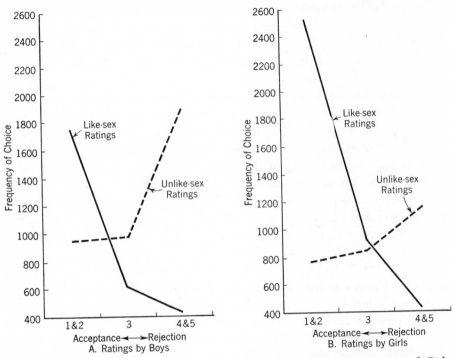

Fig. 19. J-Curves Showing Acceptance of Age Peers by Adolescent Boys and Girls. (Data from Pepinsky, 20, p. 536.)

total frequency of occurrence of an event in the sample of observations is small, its expected chance distribution is a skewed curve known to statisticians as the Poisson distribution. The greater the rarity of the phenomenon, the more skewed will be this distribution. One of the best illustrations of this type of distribution in psychology is provided by the frequency of accidents among individuals (3, 18). For example, if 200 persons have a total of 100 accidents during a given period, the expected chance distribution is as follows: 121 persons will have no accident; 61 will have 1; 15 will have 2; and 3 will have 3 accidents each (cf. 3, pp. 456–457).

This type of distribution is illustrated in Figure 20A, which shows the actual number of accidents sustained by 59 streetcar motormen during a one-month period. It might be argued that what we have here is a J-curve, in which the peak falls on complete conformity to prescribed safety rules, with its resulting record of no accidents. Or we might try to explain the form of this distribution in terms of some other hypothesis, such as the presence of a small group of "accident-prone" men. But a look at the other graphs in Figure 20 suggests that the major factor was in reality an artifact of the particular observational sample employed. If we extend our observa-

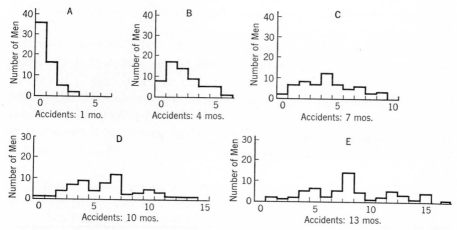

Fig. 20. Distribution of Accidents by 59 Streetcar Motormen for Various Periods of Time. (By permission from *Personnel and Industrial Psychology* by E. E. Ghiselli and C. W. Brown, Copyright, 1955, McGraw-Hill Book Company, Inc., p. 343.)

tions on the same 59 motormen from a one-month to a 13-month period, we obtain the distribution shown in Figure 20E. Although exhibiting several minor irregularities, this distribution is certainly not a J-curve, its peak falling approximately at the center of the range. As the length of the observation period increases, the total number of accidents in our sample of 59 men increases, and consequently the distribution becomes progressively less skewed.

A final illustration of special factors that may influence the form of the distribution curve is to be found in the operation of certain *pathological conditions*. There is some evidence to suggest, for example, that the IQ distribution in the total population shows an excess of very low IQ's over what would be expected in a normal curve (cf. 23). In one carefully conducted survey on a nearly complete sample of children born within a four-year period in the city of Bath, England, the proportion of cases with IQ's below 45 was about 18 times as large as would be expected in a normal distribution (23).

The most plausible explanation for such a deviation from normality would seem to be that secondary factors, such as disease or pathological conditions, increase the relative proportion of feebleminded persons from that which would be expected by chance (cf., e.g., 22). It will be recalled that a normal distribution will be obtained if the variable being measured is the composite result of a very large number of independent and equally weighted factors. Considering the extremely large number of both hereditary and environmental factors that contribute to the development of intelligence in the general population, it is reasonable to expect IQ's to distribute themselves in accordance with the normal curve. Certain low-grade forms of feeblemindedness, however, appear to result from single-factor rather than multiple-factor causation. In other words, some pathological conditions (arising from either heredity or environment) may lead directly to extreme degrees of feeblemindedness, regardless of any concomitant factors that would otherwise have determined the individual's intellectual level. Hence at the low end of the distribution, these single-factor cases are added on to the multiple-factor cases that would be expected by chance in a normal curve.

It should be added parenthetically that the available data concerning the lower end of the distribution of intellectual level, as well as the interpretation of such data, are still highly tentative. They are here cited only as an illustration of the possible effect of pathological conditions upon the form of distribution curves.

To sum up: if we begin with the expectation that distribution curves will, in general, resemble the normal curve, any deviation from normality becomes a problem for investigation. Such an approach to the form of the distribution should prove fruitful in revealing the operation of factors that merit study in their own right. For example, a significant deviation from normality may indicate that the test ceiling is too low, that its zero point is too high, or that certain portions of the difficulty range are inadequately covered by the available test items. Again, some hitherto unsuspected selective factor operating in the sample under investigation may become apparent. Finally, the shape of the obtained distribution may furnish a clue to an important influence which modifies the trait itself in such a way as to alter the distribution curve. In other words, any significant deviation from normality should serve as a signal to alert the investigator to the need for further inquiry.

MEASURING THE EXTENT OF VARIABILITY

In addition to the form of the distribution curve, another question which may be raised pertains to the extent of variability from person to person. How large are individual differences? An obvious answer might be given in terms of the *range* between the highest and lowest scores. But this is a crude measure of the extent of variability, since it is based on only two scores and may be unduly altered by the addition or removal of a single extreme case. The most precise measure of variability for most purposes is the *standard deviation* (SD). In computing it, we begin by finding the difference between each person's score and the group mean. These differences are then squared and the squares are averaged; the standard deviation is simply the square root of this average squared difference.[1]

Among the many reasons for the superiority of the standard deviation as a measure of variability is its utilization of every individual in the group. The SD also has a number of important statistical properties, especially when it is computed for a normally distributed variable. For example, in a normal distribution with a mean of 40 and an SD of 5, we know that between the scores of 35 and 45 (i.e., within a distance of 1 SD on either side of the mean) there are approximately two thirds of the cases (68 per cent). And within ±3 SD of the mean, or between 25 and 55, will be found nearly the entire group (99.7 per cent). The SD has many applications in psychological statistics, which we need not consider for the present purpose. It is apparent, however, that one of its uses is to provide a measure of the extent of individual differences, or variability, within a group of people in a particular set of scores.

Suppose, now, that we want to compare variability in different traits. Do individuals differ more in physical or in psychological traits? Are differences larger in intellectual or in emotional characteristics? To questions such as these, we can only reply categorically that there is no answer. In fact, the question of the extent of human variability itself is meaningless, unless formulated in more specific terms.

The first problem that confronts us when trying to compare variability in different traits is that of the measuring scale utilized for each of the traits, i.e., the *units* in which the measurements are reported. That the particular scale employed affects the amount of variability found is easily

[1] In terms of conventional symbols, $SD = \sqrt{\dfrac{\Sigma(X - M)^2}{N}}$

demonstrated. If the height of buildings in one city is measured in feet and in another city in yards, the buildings in the former city will seem to vary among themselves three times as much as in the latter, even though the actual range in height may be identical in the two cities. Fortunately, feet can be translated into yards and vice versa. But this cannot be done with the units of psychological tests. The number of problems correctly solved on an arithmetic test cannot be transmuted into the same kind of units as words in an analogies test.

The only solution offered so far for this difficulty is the use of measures of *relative variability*, which are based on ratios. One such measure, the coefficient of variation, was introduced by Pearson. It is found by dividing the standard deviation by the mean of the group. For the same purpose, Wechsler (32) proposed the range ratio, obtained by dividing the highest by the lowest measure in the group. Before computing this ratio, however, Wechsler excludes from the distribution the upper and lower .1 per cent (or one per thousand) on the grounds that such extreme scores are more likely to represent pathological deviations or to have been affected by gross errors of measurement. After surveying many available distributions of human traits by this method, Wechsler concludes, for example, that the tallest man is about 1.28 times as tall as the shortest; that body weight at birth varies in the ratio of 2.38:1; that the range ratio for memory span for digits among adult men is 2.50:1; and that the corresponding ratio for Binet mental ages among 9-year-old British children is 2.30:1.

When applied to scores on psychological tests, such ratios are of questionable meaning. The difficulty arises from the fact that most psychological test scores are not expressed in terms of equal-unit scales or measured from an absolute zero point.[2] For example, it cannot be assumed that repeating an 8-digit list correctly is exactly twice as difficult as recalling a 4-digit list—it is probably considerably more than twice as difficult. Thus if the highest score in the group were 8 and the lowest 4, this would not mean that the retentive power of the top scorer was twice as great as that of the poorest, as is suggested by the above range ratio. Similarly, the difference between a mental age of 3 and one of 4 is larger than that between a mental age of 11 and one of 12.

Ratios are likewise inapplicable to scales that begin at an arbitrary zero point, as is true of most psychological tests. For example, a group of 200 10-year-old children obtained scores ranging from 15 to 54 on a vocabulary test. The range ratio computed by Wechsler (32, p. 171) from these data is

---

[2] For a good introduction to different types of scales, their implications, and the arithmetic processes suitable to each type, cf. Stevens (26), pp. 21–30.

3.60:1. If, however, the zero point of this test had been lowered by adding 20 easy words that every child in the group could define, each score would have been raised by 20 points. As a result, the range ratio would now drop to 74:35, or 2.1:1. In short, because of the characteristics of the measuring scales, we cannot perform all the same operations with psychological test scores as we can with such physical scales as inches or pounds. Since the ratios obtained with available test scores are unstable and uninterpretable, they cannot be used to compare the extent of human variability in different traits.

Further difficulties appear as the whole question of human variability is examined more closely. Does a meaningful estimate of "human variability" include *all* mankind? Or should at least the clearly pathological extremes be excluded? If so, where should the line be drawn between a typical human group and an abnormal deviant? We have seen that Wechsler (32), in computing his range ratio, draws this line so as to exclude the highest and lowest thousandth of each distribution. One could, of course, argue for other limits, depending upon the purposes of the survey. Moreover, it is conceivable that the line should logically be drawn at different points for different traits.

Similarly, we may ask which factors should be held constant in measuring variability in any one trait. How homogeneous should the group be? The inclusion of children of different age levels would certainly increase the extent of variation in most traits. If only the range of individual differences within a fairly homogeneous population is desired, the difficulty of defining the required degree of homogeneity is encountered. Many traits are influenced by the socioeconomic level in which the individual is reared. Should conditions of this sort also be held constant? Should members of different ethnic stocks be included when determining the extent of human variability in such traits as stature, body weight, and similar physical dimensions?

We may conclude from this analysis that the question of the extent of individual differences cannot be answered unless put in very specific terms. The population must be defined in detail and the nature of the trait measured must be made clear, especially by indicating which conditions are to be held constant and which will be allowed to vary. Obviously all hereditary and environmental conditions that affect a given trait cannot be held constant; otherwise variation would disappear completely.

Absolute or abstract statements about the extent of human variability in such psychological traits as memory or mathematical aptitude are bound to be meaningless. Nor is it possible, with available instruments, to compare variability in different traits. At the same time, we should recognize that for practical purposes meaningful statements can be made about the extent of individual differences within a specified frame of reference. For instance, we can talk about the range of ability within a typical schoolroom, in terms of familiar age or grade norms. One survey showed that, for classes in which no grouping on the basis of ability had occurred, the mental age range was five years at the primary level, six years at the intermediate, and more than eight years at the high school level (5). This means that within, let us say, a fifth-grade classroom, the dullest child may be the intellectual equal of the average 8-year-old, while the brightest may reach the level of the typical 14-year-old.

Such differences are naturally reflected in schoolwork, as is borne out by any survey with achievement tests. These tests are objective, standardized examinations on school subjects, the scores usually being expressed in terms of grade norms. In one study conducted in New York City public schools, for example, the achievement test performance of pupils who had attended school for seven semesters ranged from the first-grade level to the ninth-grade level (cf. 14). Statements such as the above are of practical value and can be interpreted in terms of familiar frames of reference. Similarly, it would interest a teacher or school principal to learn that, although two sixth-grade classes have the same mean IQ of 110, the SD of the IQ distribution is 15 in one class and only 10 in the other. From this it would be evident that wider individual differences in school performance should be expected in the first than in the second class, and teaching procedures could be adapted accordingly.

UNIVERSALITY OF INDIVIDUAL DIFFERENCES

Individual differences are by no means confined to the human species. On the contrary, variation from individual to individual is observable throughout the animal scale. To be sure, superficial acquaintance often creates the impression of close similarity or even identity among the members of any group. But closer familiarity never fails to reveal individual differences among them. To most people, all cats may seem to behave "just like cats"—and this sentiment may be mutual! To the pet owner, however, each cat displays an unmistakable individuality of his own.

Quite understandably, the earliest reports of individual differences among animals dealt with extreme deviates, the "geniuses" of the animal kingdom. One of the most famous and best authenticated of such cases is that of "Fellow," a German shepherd dog (30, 31). Unlike many other performing dogs, Fellow was observed by psychologists under carefully controlled conditions. This animal learned to respond correctly to a large variety of verbal commands, having associated approximately 400 words with the appropriate objects and actions. Of special interest is the fact that Fellow gave the right responses even when the same command was expressed in different words, or when the same words were incorporated in different commands. It was established, moreover, that he was able to respond to the words themselves, even when gestures and other secondary cues were ruled out by placing him behind a screen.

Other examples of dogs that have been successfully taught to perform intricate tasks and respond to a wide variety of complex cues can be readily cited. Two major examples are provided by the "Seeing Eye" dogs, which are trained to lead the blind, and the "canine corps," effectively utilized for military purposes in both world wars. Nor are such illustrations limited to dogs. Chimpanzees have been taught to carry out a number of special activities, such as skating, riding a bicycle, eating with knife and fork, and unlocking doors. Mention should also be made of performing circus animals of all sorts, especially "musical" sea lions.

With the growth of comparative psychology and the development of controlled, laboratory measurement of animal behavior, the evidence for individual differences has progressed beyond the stage of anecdotal observation and isolated case studies. Every laboratory investigation employing more than one subject has revealed individual differences. Animal psychologists have not as a rule been concerned with the measurement of variability, so that data on this problem are usually mentioned only incidentally and frequently are not given in quantitative form. Whenever such data are reported, however, the range of performance in a randomly selected group is surprisingly large. Wide individual variation has been found in every phase of behavior investigated, such as the amount of general spontaneous activity, the relative strength of drives, emotionality, speed of movement, quickness of learning simple tasks, and behavior in more complex problem-solving situations.

Similarly, individual differences have been observed in every kind of animal, from simple unicellular organisms to anthropoid apes. In one investigation on a species of protozoa, for example, wide individual variations were found in the speed of establishing a conditioned reaction to light. The procedure involved the repeated paired presentation of a tactile and a light stimulus, until the light alone evoked the response originally given to the tactile stimulus. The number of trials, or repetitions, required to condition different subjects ranged from 79 to 284, with a mean of 138.5

(cf. 21, p. 308). Individual differences were likewise noted among paramecia in the rate of learning to escape from a tube, some animals failing
to learn at all (8). In another series of experiments on paramecia, the animals differed in their tendencies to group themselves into compact masses
or to swim freely, as well as in their tendencies to enter or not enter solutions of food-water to which small quantities of foreign chemicals had been
added (7).

More recently, Hirsch and Tryon (15) have developed ingenious techniques for obtaining reliable measures of individual differences in a number
of behavior functions in simple organisms. Their procedure has been applied
in particular to research on the role of heredity in the behavior of the fruit
fly *Drosophila*. Such research will be considered in Chapter 4. For the
present, however, it is of interest to note the wide individual differences
found in the initial part of these experiments. In one such study, the number
of times individuals flew upward into a test tube during 15 trials ranged
from 0 to 15. In other words, when given 15 opportunities to fly into the
upper test tube, some fruit flies did so every time, and some never did.
The rest of the subjects distributed themselves over every other possible
"score" between these two extremes.

By far the most popular experimental animal is, of course, the white rat.
The picture of a rat running a maze for the enlightenment of psychologists
has by now become a familiar stereotype. Of the many studies showing
individual differences in rat learning, one illustration will suffice. In an
experiment also to be reported more fully in Chapter 4, Tryon (29) put
142 rats through 19 trials in a maze. During each trial, the number of times
the rat entered any blind alley was recorded as his error score. The total
number of such errors during the 19 trials ranged from 7 to 214 in the case
of different subjects.

A relatively extensive set of data on individual differences in animal learning is provided by a series of research projects conducted during the 1930's
at the Columbia University laboratory of comparative psychology. Small
samples of guinea pigs, albino rats, common short-haired cats, and two
species of monkeys were tested with the same type of "problem box," in
which a series of steps of increasing complexity was presented to the animal.
The box, which is illustrated in Figure 21, consisted essentially of an outer
and an inner cage, the latter containing the incentive which the animal obtained at the completion of each successful trial. In the outer cage were
three plates on which the animal had to step in a given order before the
door to the incentive compartment was opened. The problem in Step I
consisted simply in stepping on the first plate to the right as the animal

entered the box. The other steps involved touching plates 1 and 2; 1, 2, and 3; 1, 2, 3, and back to 2; 1, 2, 3, 2, 1; and so on to other combinations.

Although these problem box studies were conducted mainly to determine the highest number of steps that any animal within a given species could master, the data yield striking evidence of individual differences within each species. Not only the number of trials required to learn each step, but also the number of steps that could be learned, differed from individual to individual. Table 2 brings together some of the relevant data, including the range in number of steps learned by each species, the number of individuals learning Step I, and the mean,

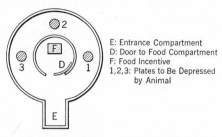

E: Entrance Compartment
D: Door to Food Compartment
F: Food Incentive
1,2,3: Plates to Be Depressed by Animal

Fig. 21. Diagram of Problem Box Used in Columbia University Studies of Animal Learning. (From Fjeld, 6, p. 403.)

range, and SD of the number of trials required to learn Step I. The latter data have been reported only for Step I, since this was the only step learned by at least some members of all groups.

Table 2

INDIVIDUAL AND GROUP DIFFERENCES IN ANIMAL LEARNING AS MEASURED BY A PROBLEM BOX

(Data from Fjeld, 6, p. 528, and Koch, 16, pp. 186, 208)

TYPE OF ANIMAL	NO. OF CASES	NO. LEARNING STEP I	TRIALS TO LEARN STEP I			RANGE IN STEPS LEARNED
			Mean	Range	SD	
Guinea pigs	30	16	185.50	53–407	176.28	0–1
Albino rats	35	24	221.04	30–453	125.26	0–2
Cats	62	62	46.69*	9–136	25.28	3–7
Monkeys (Rhesus)	17	17	162.47	19–310	94.36	2–22
Monkeys (Cebus)	6	6	137.17	42–327	108.41	5–15

* In the study on cats, the problem set in Step I was simpler, the animal being allowed to step on *any* one of the three plates. The data for Step I on this group are therefore not directly comparable to those on the other species.

Reference to Table 2 shows that, among the guinea pigs, some were unable to learn even Step I, while others succeeded; among the rats, some learned 2 steps, some 1, and a few none; among the cats, the range is from

3 to 7 steps; among the rhesus monkeys 2 to 22, and among the cebus 5 to 15. Thus variability was so large that an individual could easily be found in a "higher" species who was unable to learn as much as a given individual in a "lower" species. The results appear even more striking when we examine the number of trials required to learn Step I. For example, the best guinea pig and the best rat learned this step in fewer trials than did the poorest monkeys of both species. Such *overlapping* of distributions that differ in central tendency is an important concept in all group comparisons and one to which we shall return frequently when discussing human studies.

Although the largest number of animal studies have been concerned with learning of one sort or another, data are also available on individual differences in other psychological characteristics. In the area of emotional and motivational traits, studies on white rats have revealed distinct individual differences in manifestations of fearfulness and aggressiveness, in exploratory behavior, and in strength of the sex drive (cf. 11). In all these traits, research has demonstrated sufficient "situational generality" to permit the characterization of each individual's behavior in the trait as a whole. For example, rats tested under four different conditions tended to display a relatively consistent degree of aggressiveness. Similar results were obtained in the case of the other traits mentioned above.

Illustrative data on a higher species are provided by a preliminary study of "temperament" in the chimpanzee, described by Hebb (13). Observations were made in situations that permitted the chimpanzee to respond to men or to inanimate objects. When carefully defined categories were applied in classifying the animal's behavior in terms of friendliness, aggressiveness, avoidance, etc., wide individual differences were found which could be measured with acceptable reliability. Nissen (19) has likewise reported on the wide individual differences among 57 chimpanzees housed at the Yerkes Laboratory of Primate Biology, in Orange Park, Florida. Marked diversities were observed in almost all behavior functions, including gait, grooming, food preferences and eating habits, emotional expression, excitability, speed and accuracy of learning various tasks, use of tools, and social interaction with other chimpanzees and with humans.

An interesting example of the normal distribution curve in a behavioral trait in animals is to be found in the photograph and accompanying curve reproduced in Figure 22. The photograph shows horses on the race track just before the finish. The relative position of the horses furnishes a vivid demonstration of the normal distribution of racing performance. A few are in the lead, an equally small number lag behind, and the majority is scattered in intermediate positions. The graph is a frequency curve of the "racing capacity" of the same horses, computed by a standardized formula.

The illustrations cited will suffice to suggest that individual differences are the rule whenever the behavior of living things has been measured. The precise figures given to indicate variability do not matter. They cannot tell us the extent of variability in different species in any absolute sense. Nor

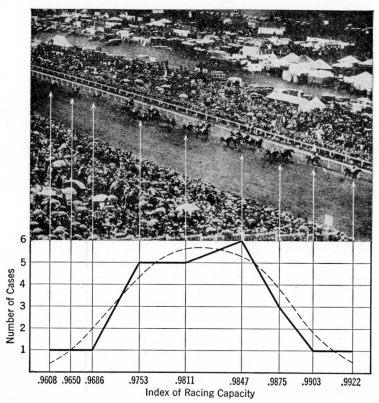

Fig. 22. A Normal Distribution Curve of Racing Capacity, Showing the Field of 24 Horses Nearing the Line at Epsom Downs. (After Laughlin, 17, p. 215.)

do they permit us to make general comparisons, any more than we can compare human variability in different traits. The particular scores and other measures given are expressed in units that are specific to the test or other observational device employed. The data do show beyond question, however, that members of the same species differ among themselves in behavior traits and that such differences are large enough to lead to overlap in the distribution of individuals from even widely separated species.

SUMMARY

Individual differences are quantitative, not qualitative. Differences among persons are a matter of degree. Frequency distributions for most traits show a clustering of individuals near the center of the range and a gradual decrease in number of cases as the extremes are approached. Such a distribution may be represented graphically as either a frequency polygon or a histogram. It can be further described by computing measures of central tendency (mean, median, or mode) and measures of variability, such as the range or the standard deviation. Many distribution curves of physical or psychological traits closely approximate the normal probability curve.

Distributions that differ from the normal curve in skewness, peakedness (kurtosis), or other characteristics may be obtained for a number of reasons. Among the major factors affecting the shape of the distribution curve are: sampling irregularities; characteristics of the measuring instrument, such as inadequacy of difficulty range and inequality of test units; and special conditions that influence the traits themselves. Illustrations of the latter conditions were considered in connection with the J-curve hypothesis of social conformity, the Poisson distribution of rare events, and the increase in frequencies at the low end of the range arising from the operation of pathological conditions.

Absolute statements regarding the extent of variability in different traits are meaningless for several reasons, chief among which are lack of comparable units and of absolute zero points in psychological scales. For practical purposes, the extent of individual differences within specific groups in concretely defined characteristics can be reported in terms of a given frame of reference. But general statements about the range of human variability in different traits cannot be meaningfully made.

Individual differences are universal throughout the animal scale. Any investigation of animal behavior, from simple unicellular organisms to anthropoid apes, reveals wide individual differences in performance. So large are these differences that overlapping of distributions is observed even when widely separated species are compared.

REFERENCES

1. Allport, F. H. The J-curve hypothesis of conforming behavior. *J. soc. Psychol.*, 1934, 5, 141–183.
2. Anastasi, Anne. Practice and variability. *Psychol. Monogr.*, 1934, 45, No. 5.
3. Blum, M. L. *Industrial psychology and its social foundations.* (Rev. Ed.) N.Y.: Harper, 1956.

4. Boring, E. G. *A history of experimental psychology.* (Rev. Ed.) N.Y.: Appleton-Century-Crofts, 1950.

5 Cook, W. W. Individual-trait differences in public schools with implications for school organization and curriculum development. *Teach. Coll. J.,* 1947, 19, 56–57, 67–70.

6. Fjeld, Harriet A. The limits of learning ability in rhesus monkeys. *Genet. Psychol. Monogr.,* 1934, 15, 369–537.

7. French, J. W. Individual differences in paramecium. *J. comp. Psychol.,* 1940, 30, 451–456.

8. French, J. W. Trial and error learning in paramecium. *J. exp. Psychol.,* 1940, 26, 609–613.

9. Ghiselli, E. E., and Brown, C. W. *Personnel and industrial psychology.* N.Y.: McGraw-Hill, 1955.

10. Guilford, J. P. *Fundamental statistics in psychology and education.* (3rd Ed.) N.Y.: McGraw-Hill, 1956.

11. Hall, C. S. Individual differences. In C. P. Stone (Ed.), *Comparative psychology.* (3rd Ed.) N.Y.: Prentice-Hall, 1951. Pp. 363–387.

12. Harris, J. A., Jackson, C. M., Paterson, D. G., and Scammon, R. L. *The measurement of man.* Minneapolis: Univer. Minn. Press, 1930.

13. Hebb, D. O. Temperament in chimpanzees: I. Method of analysis. *J. comp. physiol. Psychol.,* 1949, 42, 192–206.

14. Hildreth, Gertrude H. Individual differences. In W. S. Munroe (Ed.), *Encyclopedia of educational research.* (Rev. Ed.). N.Y.: Macmillan, 1950. Pp. 564–571.

15. Hirsch, J., and Tryon, R. C. Mass screening and reliable individual measurement in the experimental behavior genetics of lower organisms. *Psychol. Bull.,* 1956, 53, 402–410.

16. Koch, A. M. The limits of learning ability in cebus monkeys. *Genet. Psychol. Monogr.,* 1935, 17, 165–234.

17. Laughlin, H. H. Racing capacity in the thoroughbred horse. *Sci. Mon.,* 1934, 38, 210–222, 310–321.

18. Mintz, A., and Blum, M. A re-examination of the accident-proneness concept. *J. appl. Psychol.,* 1949, 33, 195–211.

19. Nissen, H. W. Individuality in the behavior of chimpanzees. *Amer. Anthropologist,* 1956, 58, 407–413.

20. Pepinsky, Pauline N. The J-curve re-visited. *J. abnorm. soc. Psychol.,* 1951, 46, 534–538.

21. Razran, G. Conditioned responses in animals other than dogs. *Psychol. Bull.,* 1933, 30, 261–324.

22. Roberts, J. A. Fraser. The genetics of mental deficiency. *Eugen. Rev.,* 1952, 44, 71–83.

23. Roberts, J. A. Fraser, Norman, R. M., and Griffiths, Ruth. Studies on a child population. IV. The form of the lower end of the frequency distribution of Stanford-Binet intelligence quotients and the fall of low intelligence quotients with advancing age. *Ann. Eugen.,* 1938, 8, 319–336.

24. Ruggles, R., and Allport, G. W. Recent applications of the A-S Reaction Study. *J. abnorm. soc. Psychol.,* 1939, 34, 518–528.

25. Scottish Council for Research in Education. *The trend of Scottish intelligence.* London: Univer. London Press, 1949.

26. Stevens, S. S. Mathematics, measurement, and psychophysics. In S. S. Stevens (Ed.), *Handbook of experimental psychology.* N.Y.: Wiley, 1951. Pp. 1–49.

27. Terman, L. M., and Merrill, Maud A. *Measuring intelligence.* Boston: Houghton Mifflin, 1937.

28. Tiffin, J., and Wirt, S. E. Determining visual standards for industrial jobs by statistical methods. *Trans. Amer. Acad. Opthal. Otolaryng.,* 1945, 50, 72–93.

29. Tryon, R. C. Genetic differences in maze-learning ability in rats. *39th Yearb., Nat. Soc. Stud. Educ.,* 1940, Part I, 111–119.

30. Warden, C. J. The ability of "Fellow," famous German shepherd dog, to understand language. *J. genet. Psychol.,* 1928, 35, 330–331.

31. Warden, C. J., and Warner, L. H. The sensory capacities and intelligence of dogs, with a report on the ability of the noted dog "Fellow" to respond to verbal stimuli. *Quart. Rev. Biol.,* 1928, 3, 1–28.

32. Wechsler, D. *The range of human capacities.* (Rev. Ed.) Baltimore: Williams & Wilkins, 1952.

33. Wenger, M. A., and Ellington, M. The measurement of autonomic balance in children: method and normative data. *Psychosom. Med.,* 1943, 5, 241–253.

34. Yule, G. U., and Kendall, M. G. *An introduction to the theory of statistics.* (13th Ed.) London: Griffin, 1949.

CHAPTER *3*

Heredity and Environment:
Basic Concepts

Why do individuals differ from one another? What are the factors that produce variation? These questions have stimulated lengthy discussion and led to lively controversy. Besides its fundamental theoretical importance, the problem of the causation of individual differences has far-reaching practical significance in many fields. Any activity designed to improve behavior development must be based upon an understanding of the factors that influence such development. Underlying all educational methods are implicit assumptions regarding the causes of individual differences. Similarly, the answers to many questions relating to vocational choices and opportunities, group relations, and social structure depend upon a knowledge of what causes psychological differences between persons of different age or sex, between ethnic or national groups, or between socioeconomic levels.

THE NATURE OF HEREDITY [1]

The basis of individual differences is to be found in each individual's hereditary background and in the environmental conditions under which he has developed. Let us first consider what, specifically, is meant by "heredity." It should be borne in mind, of course, that as herein used the term "heredity" signifies biological heredity. It is only figuratively that we speak of "social heredity," as in such expressions as "the cultural heritage

[1] To fill out the brief sketch of the mechanism of heredity which follows, the reader is urged to consult any recent text on genetics, such as Sinnott, Dunn, and Dobzhansky (22), Snyder and David (23), or Winchester (26). An excellent summary of current developments in genetics, prepared by a group of experts, is to be found in Dunn (9). For a popularized and very readable account of the field, see Scheinfeld (21).

57

of the twentieth century" or the "inheritance of the family fortune." So-called social inheritance actually falls under the heading of environmental influences.

Basically, an individual's heredity consists of the specific *genes* which he receives from each parent at conception. To call a certain influence, factor, or characteristic "hereditary" should thus mean that it can ultimately be traced to the presence of a particular gene or combination of genes. The genes are grouped into *chromosomes,* or "colored bodies," so named because they become visible within the cell nucleus when the cell is stained with certain dyes for observation. Chromosomes occur in pairs, the two members of each pair being similar in appearance and function. The number of chromosomes in each cell is, in general, constant within each species, but differs from one species to another. Each human cell, for example, contains 46 chromosomes (23 pairs); in each cell of the mosquito, there are 6 (3 pairs); and in each cell of a certain species of crayfish, there are 200 (100 pairs).

Fig. 23.   Human Chromosomes as Seen Under a Microscope: magnified 3600 times. (From Evans and Swezy, 10.)

Chromosomes are visible under a microscope, appearing as rodlike, sausage-shaped, or V-shaped bodies (cf. Fig. 23). The genes within each chromosome, however, are so minute as to be generally invisible, even with a high-power microscope. Through the observation of giant chromosomes which have been discovered within the salivary glands of certain species of flies, it has proved possible to examine the internal structure of chromosomes more fully under the microscope. Although in volume they are from 1000 to 2000 times larger, in other essential characteristics these giant chromosomes are like those found in other body cells. Figure 24 shows a segment of such a giant chromosome from the salivary glands of the fruit fly *Drosophila melanogaster.* The first part of this figure contains a photograph taken under a high-power microscope; the second part presents an electron micrograph, with a magnification of 26,000. The particles visible in the latter view are believed to be genes. Those within any one section or band of the chromosome appear to be uniform in size and shape, but differ from the particles in other bands (19).

Every individual begins life at conception as a single cell, the fertilized ovum. This cell divides into two daughter cells, each of which again divides, and so on, until the billions of cells making up the mature organism have developed. During this process of cell division, known as *mitosis,* every chromosome within the cell nucleus is duplicated by splitting longitudinally along its entire length. Each cell resulting from this division receives an identical set of chromosomes. All cells in the body thus have *identical heredity.* That some develop into eye cells, others into skin, bone,

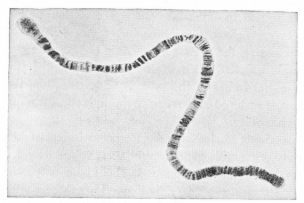

A. Photograph under High-Power Microscope.

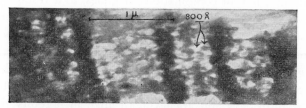

B. Electron Micrograph of Very Small Segment (Magnified 26,000 times).

Fig. 24. Portions of Giant Chromosome from the Salivary Gland of the Fruit Fly. (From Painter, 18, p. 464, and Pease and Baker, 19, p. 9.)

or any of the other varieties of body cells depends upon the influence of the *cellular environment.* Such conditions as gravity, pressure, availability of oxygen and other chemicals, and electrical fields operate differentially upon individual cells, depending on the position of the cell in relation to other cells. Technically, this means that "differential gradients" of development are established, such as surface-interior, dorso-ventral, or antero-posterior gradients. Following initial cell differentiation, the genes interact with the cellular environment in various ways in the subsequent specialized development of different cells.

When the individual attains sexual maturity, a different type of cell division occurs in the formation of the specialized reproductive cells, the ova of the female and the spermatozoa of the male. This process is known as *meiosis,* or reduction division, since the chromosomes in each reproductive cell are reduced to one-half the original number. Instead of duplicating, as they do in mitosis, the two chromosomes in each pair separate, one going to each daughter cell. It should be noted that in this type of cell division each cell may receive a different combination of chromosomes, since the chromosomes in each pair *assort at random.* Moreover, the chromosomes are not always segregated as units into the different daughter cells, but segments of one chromosome may combine with segments of another ("crossing over"), thus increasing the variety of possible combinations of genes in the individual daughter cells. When the ovum of the mother unites with the spermatozoon of the father in the process of fertilization, the full number of chromosomes is restored and remains through the subsequent mitosis of the developing offspring.

The hereditary basis for individual differences is furnished by the almost unlimited variety of possible gene combinations which may occur, especially in such a complex organism as man. It should be noted, first, that even simple human characteristics generally depend upon the combined influence of large numbers of genes. Second, the individual germ cells of each parent organism contain different combinations of genes, as a result of the process of reduction division. Third, the cells of two organisms, the mother and the father, combine to produce the new organism, thereby further increasing the variety of possible gene combinations. It should thus be apparent that no two *siblings* (i.e., brothers or sisters) will have identical heredity. The same is true of *fraternal twins,* who, although born at the same time, develop from separate germ cells and are no more alike in heredity than ordinary siblings. Fraternal twins may be of the same or opposite sex, and may be quite unlike in appearance. *Identical twins,* on the other hand, develop from the division of a single fertilized ovum and therefore have identical sets of genes. Such individuals are complete duplicates as far as heredity is concerned.

The simplest illustration of the mechanism of heredity is furnished by *unit factors,* which depend upon a single pair of genes. An example of such a unit factor is albinism, or absence of pigmentation in the eyes, hair, and skin. If the individual received a gene for albinism from each of his parents (cc), he will himself be an albino. Individuals with two genes for normal color (CC) will have normal pigmentation. Both of these individuals are described as *homozygous* with respect to albinism. This simply means that the fertilized ovum, or zygote, from which such individuals developed received like genes for albinism or for normal coloring from both parents.

If an individual received the gene for albinism from one parent and the gene for normal coloring from the other parent (Cc), he is said to be *heterozygous* in this characteristic. Such an individual will show normal coloring, since normal coloring is *dominant* and albinism is *recessive*. In other words, albinism, being a recessive factor, appears only when the individual has received the recessive gene for albinism from each parent. The heterozygous individual (Cc), although himself normal in coloring, nevertheless carries the recessive gene for albinism, which he may in turn transmit to his offspring.

Other unit factors exhibit no dominance. An example is to be found in the coloring of poultry. Black and splashed-white fowls result from a pair of genes, neither of which is dominant. Crossbreeding these two varieties of poultry will produce offspring of a third color, known as "Blue Andalusians," unlike either parent.

It should be added that, at least in the case of some factors now considered to be dominant-recessive, further research may reveal no dominance (cf. 6). In a dominant-recessive trait, the heterozygote is of course indistinguishable from one of the homozygotes. But such a situation may in reality reflect only our present state of ignorance regarding the differentiating features of the heterozygote. With the development and application of more searching techniques of analysis, differences may be revealed. In the case of pathological conditions, for example, the heterozygote may exhibit a mild form of disorder, detectable by improved methods. Or the heterozygous condition may be identifiable through detailed chemical analyses or other refined procedures. Even when the distinction between the heterozygous and homozygous conditions has no practical significance within the life of the individual organism, it provides useful information regarding the hereditary factors which the individual is in a position to transmit to his offspring.

The sex of an individual is itself determined by a pair of chromosomes, known as the sex chromosomes, and designated X and Y. If the child receives an X chromosome from each parent, it will be a female; if one X and one Y chromosome are received, a male will result. From its mother, the child can receive only X chromosomes; while the father can pass on either an X or a Y. The Y chromosome is relatively small and is believed to contain very few genes. Such a Y chromosome may be seen in Figure 23, where it has been appropriately labeled. According to present genetic knowledge, it is actually the interaction of certain genes in the X chromosomes with genes in the other chromosomes that determines the individual's sex. Every individual is believed to possess all the genes necessary for both sexes.

But the presence of the two X chromosomes leads to the development of the female sex characteristics and the suppression of the male. When there is a single X chromosome, on the other hand, the male characteristics will develop.

Certain genes occurring in the X chromosome account for *sex-linked* characteristics, a number of which have been identified. Among the best known are color-blindness and hemophilia (excessive and continued bleeding due to lack of normal blood coagulation). Both of these conditions depend upon a recessive gene carried in the X chromosome. If a daughter inherits this factor from one parent only, the dominant normal gene in the other X chromosome will prevent the appearance of the defect. Thus a girl will show the defect only if she inherits the defective gene from both parents. In the case of a boy who receives an X chromosome with the defective gene, on the other hand, the defect will invariably appear, since there is no corresponding normal gene in the Y chromosome. Consequently, such characteristics are more common among males than among females.

Certain other factors, such as baldness, are *sex-influenced*, i.e., they behave as dominants in one sex and as recessives in the other. Thus baldness will develop in a male if the gene for baldness was transmitted by either parent. In the female, it will develop only if genes for baldness were received from both parents. Still other factors, known as *sex-limited*, are present in both sexes, but their expression is inhibited in one sex by the presence of the sex hormones. Many of the physical differences between the sexes are probably based upon this type of factor. Destruction or improper functioning of the endocrine sex glands can thus bring about changes in the development of these characteristics. An example of such a sex-limited trait is beardedness in men.

It should be noted that whenever a characteristic depends upon a single pair of unit factors, the result will be distinctly identifiable types which differ qualitatively from each other. Most traits, however, depend upon *multiple factors*, the number of resulting combinations increasing rapidly as the number of contributing factors increases.[2] With even a relatively small number of contributing factors, the resulting individual differences are quantitative and their distribution may approximate the normal curve. Body height is an illustration of such a multiple-factor characteristic in the human.

In the case of certain multiple-factor characters, the appearance or non-appearance of the character itself may depend upon a unit factor. In other

---

[2] In this connection, some geneticists speak of *"major genes,"* which operate as unit factors in producing a recognizable effect, and *"polygenes,"* which contribute to the composite development of multiple-factor traits. The same gene may, of course, act as a major gene in the etiology of one trait and as a polygene in the etiology of another.

words, the operation of the multiple factors is itself dependent upon the presence of a specific gene, which may thus be regarded as a *limiting condition*. The illustration of albinism may again serve in this connection. It is now known that the determination of human eye color depends upon the presence of several pairs of genes. Different combinations of such genes produce the almost continuous gradations of observable eye color. If, however, an individual has received the unit factor for albinism from both parents (cc), he will be an albino regardless of what combination of eye-color genes he may have. The latter are rendered inoperative in the determination of his eye color by the presence of the pair of genes for albinism. Similarly, the spotted coat found in certain breeds of cattle results from a single recessive factor. But the degree of spotting varies along a virtually continuous scale and depends upon a number of modifying multiple factors. This type of relationship is especially relevant to the possible role of heredity in the development of some psychological characteristics. We shall, in fact, have occasion to refer to it again in our discussion of certain types of feeble-mindedness (cf. Ch. 12).

Finally, mention should be made of the concept of *"genic balance."* For purposes of analysis, the geneticist must necessarily study the influence of particular genes upon the development of each characteristic. We must remember, however, that every characteristic actually results from the interaction of *all* the genes that the individual has inherited. Snyder and David (23, p. 251) summarize the contemporary viewpoint of geneticists on this point as follows:

A gene always exerts its effect in the presence of other genes; hence has arisen the idea of genic balance, by which is meant that any character is the result of the entire gene complex acting in a given environment. Variations in a character may be produced by variations in a single gene, but always in the presence of the rest of the genes.

THE NATURE OF ENVIRONMENT

The concept of environment also requires clarification. The popular definition of environment is a geographical or residential one. A child is commonly said to have a "poor environment," for example, because he lives in the slums. Or his "environment" is characterized as a French village, an American small town, or a Welsh mining community. Psychologically, such descriptions of environment are highly inadequate. It cannot be concluded, for example, that an 8-year-old boy and his 5-year-old brother standing in the same room at the same time have identical psychological environments even at that moment. The very fact that the current environment of the former includes the presence of a younger sibling and that of the latter the presence of an older sibling constitutes a significant psychological difference. Moreover, the differing backgrounds of past experience of the two siblings will in turn cause a difference in what each gets out of the present situation. One point is obvious from this illustration: the fact that two children have been brought up in the same home is no indication that they have had identical psychological environments.

Psychologically, environment consists of the sum total of the stimulation the individual receives from conception until death. This is an active concept of environment, i.e., the physical presence of objects does not in itself constitute environment unless the objects serve as *stimuli* for the individual (cf. 15, 27). This definition is also more inclusive than the popular one, covering all forms of stimulation and extending over the entire life cycle.

The importance of the *prenatal environment* in determining the individual's development has been repeatedly demonstrated. Variations in diet and nutrition, glandular secretions, and other physical conditions of the mother, for example, may exert a profound and lasting influence upon the development of the embryo. That the structural development of the organism is definitely influenced by early environmental factors is clearly indicated by a number of experimentally induced alterations in lower animals.

For example, in the fruit fly, a defective gene causes the animal to produce "reduplicated legs," i.e., certain joints of the legs, or entire legs, are doubled. Although the inheritance of this defective gene has been definitely traced, this characteristic will not appear under certain environmental conditions (14). When animals known to have the defective gene are kept at a sufficiently warm temperature, the additional leg or joint will not develop. Successive generations bred under these conditions will have a normal appearance. If, however, any of their offspring are allowed to develop in colder temperatures, the defect will reappear. This furnishes a definite illustration of the fact that even a clearly demonstrable "inherited defect" will only develop under certain environmental conditions.

Experimentally produced "monsters" represent further examples of the influence of prenatal environment (24, Ch. 6 and 7). In experiments on fish eggs, "siamese-twin" fish have been produced by artificially inhibiting or slowing down the rate of development at an early age through low temperature, insufficient oxygen, or ultraviolet rays. In some cases, one twin is much smaller than the other and is deformed, the larger twin being a perfectly normal fish. Similarly, two-headed monsters have been produced among tadpoles and several species of fish by the application of various chemical or mechanical stimuli.

Fundamental variations in the number and position of the eyes of minnows have likewise been artificially induced. If the eggs of the minnow are allowed to develop in sea water to which has been added an excess of magnesium chloride, peculiar eye conditions will appear in a large majority of the embryos. Instead of the usual two eyes, many will develop a centrally placed "cyclopean" eye, so named after the one-eyed Cyclops of mythology. Others may show a single lateral eye, placed to the right or left of the head. Or the two eyes may be abnormally close together. Some of these artificially produced monsters are shown in Figure 25.

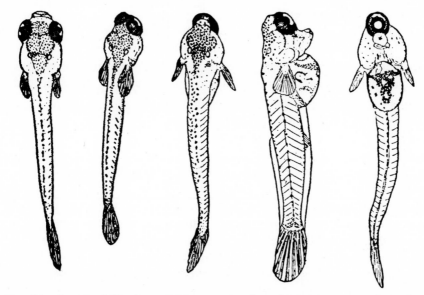

Fig. 25.   One-Eyed "Cyclopean" Minnows Resulting from Environmental Conditions. (From Stockard, 24, p. 109.)

Other physical or chemical agents may be employed to produce the same anomalies of development. The primary determining factor in the development of a particular abnormality seems to be the stage at which the agent is introduced, rather than the nature of the specific agent employed. The essential effect is a change in the rate of development, which alters the balance of growth among the different parts of the organism. In commenting on these experiments, Stockard wrote (24, pp. 109–110):

In other words, the genetic composition of these fishes causes them to develop two eyes in normal sea-water, but the same genetic composition gives rise to a single cyclopean eye when an excess of magnesium chloride is added to the sea-water. If sea-water normally had the composition which causes fish to develop with the cyclopean eye, and an experimenter should develop the eggs of fish in a solution of the same composition as our ordinary sea-water, he would find them giving rise to fish with two lateral eyes instead of the median one, and these two-eyed specimens would appear to this imaginary investigator as monsters.

Thus we cannot even speak of certain structural characteristics as being "normal" for a given species and fixed by hereditary constitution. If the environment in which the organisms develop were to undergo a change of a more or less permanent nature, a different set of characteristics would come to be considered normal. Similarities of development are attributable to common exposure to an essentially similar environment as much as to the possession of common genes.

A large body of data is being accumulated on the effects of radiation on prenatal development (20). Most of this research has so far been conducted on the rat. Results show that exposure to radiation during the embryonic stage produces a variety of morphological abnormalities, including drastic alterations in cranial and skeletal development.

Observations on various species have also demonstrated considerable *behavior development* during prenatal life, as well as the influence of specific conditions of the prenatal environment upon such development (cf. 5). The "zero point" of behavior falls well before birth, the "behavior age" or "mental age" at birth varying widely from species to species (5). Stages of motor development have been clearly established in the embryos of many animals. Sensitivity to various types of stimuli has also been noted early in prenatal life. Hence the fact that various functions may have been exercised before birth cannot be ignored in the study of subsequent behavior development. The possibility of conditioning to changes in temperature, pressure, and other stimuli in the prenatal environment must likewise be taken into account. Investigation of prenatal learning opens an interesting field of research into the origins of behavior.

Finally, it should be noted that, with increasing precision of definition, the concept of environment has gradually broadened, and that it has also become less sharply distinguishable from the concept of heredity. The popular identification of environment with "external" and heredity with "internal" influences has had to be discarded in the light of increasing knowledge of the operation of heredity and environment. In the preceding section, reference has already been made to *intercellular environment*, i.e., the environment consisting of surrounding bodily cells, in which each individual cell develops. The important role of this cellular environment in the establishment of gradients and in other developmental processes is now recognized.

Carrying the analysis still further, we should also consider the *intracellular environment*. It is obvious that the genes exert their influence in an environment consisting of the cytoplasm of the cell. The role of the intracellular environment is especially important after some differentiation has occurred in the process of cell division. Cells that contain identical genes but different cytoplasmic structure will differ in their ultimate development. Geneticists have proposed that genes may operate as enzymes or catalysts, inducing chemical changes in the cytoplasm without themselves becoming altered. The enzymatic action of a particular gene may produce different results (or no result at all), depending upon the specific chemicals in the cytoplasm of a particular cell. This theory does not preclude the possibility that genes may also exert their influence in other ways. It should be added that each gene should likewise be regarded as operating in an environment of other genes within any one cell. This mutual interdependence of genes is what is meant by the concept of genic balance, discussed in the preceding section.

From a slightly different angle, mention may be made of the fact that genes themselves, the essential element in any definition of heredity, are not completely impervious to environmental influences. Experiments have demonstrated that genes can be modified under the influence of such factors as X-rays, cosmic rays, ultraviolet rays, temperature changes, and certain chemicals such as mustard gas (cf. 7, Ch. 2). Since the genes themselves are affected, the changes produced by these agents are not only manifested in the immediate offspring but are transmissible to future generations. In such cases, a hereditary variant, or *mutation*, arises under the influence of an environmental factor. These environmental influences appear to be unspecific, however, in the sense that they stimulate or increase the frequency of gene change, but do not determine the nature of the change.

INTERACTION OF HEREDITY AND ENVIRONMENT

The early concept of "instinct," still prevalent in much popular thinking, implied the existence of behavior that is wholly hereditary.[3] The classification of behavior into "instincts" and "habits," corresponding to "native behavior" and "acquired behavior," respectively, assumed the *exclusive*

---

[3] For an analysis of many fallacies inherent in the traditional usage of the concept of instinct, cf. Ginsberg (11). Much of the content of the present section is based on an article by Anastasi and Foley (1).

operation of either heredity or environment within a given activity. Such a theory, implying the hereditary transmission of behavior functions as such, finds no support in modern genetics. It is now recognized that every trait of the individual and every reaction that he manifests depend both upon his heredity and upon his environment. Although commonly admitted to be untenable, the belief that psychological characteristics can be separated into those that are inherited and those that are acquired is implied in various loosely expressed generalizations about the inheritance of behavior characteristics. Discussions regarding the "inheritance" of intelligence, special talents, or insanity, for example, frequently leave the impression that the inheritance of the behavior itself was meant. Upon careful consideration, however, it is apparent that hereditary and environmental factors cannot be sorted out in such a fashion, nor can behavior be divided into that which is inherited and that which is acquired.

A second possible way in which the heredity-environment relationship may be conceived is in terms of *additive contribution.* According to this view, both heredity and environment contribute to all behavior development, and the resulting behavior characteristics can be analyzed into the *sum* of hereditary and environmental influences. That heredity and environment contribute jointly to the development of behavior is undoubtedly the most widely held view, but the additive assumption regarding their operation is rarely expressed as such. Just this assumption, however, underlies attempts that have been made to determine the proportional contribution of heredity and environment to the development of particular behavior characteristics.[4] A statement that "heredity contributes 75 per cent and environment 25 per cent to the development of intelligence," for example, would illustrate this additive approach. It might be noted that the same investigators who have offered such estimates of proportional contribution have occasionally argued against the additive view of heredity and environment, apparently unaware of the inconsistency in this procedure (cf. e.g., Burks, 3, 4).

The most widely accepted view of the heredity-environment relationship is that of *interaction.* This means primarily that the effects of hereditary and environmental factors are not cumulative or additive, but rather that the nature and extent of the influence of each type of factor depend upon the contribution of the other. In other words, any one environmental factor will exert a *different influence* depending upon the specific hereditary material upon which it operates. Similarly, any hereditary factor will operate

[4] An extensive analysis of the implications of the concept of "proportional contribution," as applied to the heredity-environment problem, is to be found in Loevinger (16).

differently under different environmental conditions. It is apparent that any estimate of *the* proportional contribution of a hereditary or environmental factor is inconsistent with this viewpoint, since the proportion would vary as either hereditary or environmental factors varied. To the question, "What is the relative contribution of heredity and environment to individual differences in, let us say, IQ?" there would thus be an infinite number of possible answers.

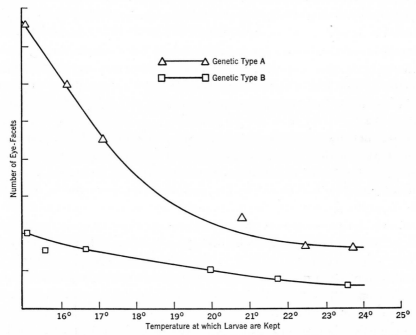

Fig. 26. An Illustration of the Interaction of Hereditary and Environmental Factors: Number of Eye Facets in *Drosophila* as a Function of Genetic Constitution and of Temperature. (From Hogben, 13, p. 96.)

As an illustration of this point we may consider first a nonpsychological characteristic whose heredity is known. The number of facets in the eyes of the fruit fly *Drosophila* has been found to vary widely in several types which differ in their gene constitution. The temperature at which the larvae are kept also determines the actual number of eye facets that develop. The interaction of these two factors, hereditary and environmental, is illustrated in Figure 26. This graph shows the effect of temperature upon the number of eye facets in two types of individuals differing in genetic constitution, which for convenience have been designated "genetic type A" and "genetic type B" on the graph. It will be noted that the *form of the curve* differs for genetic types A and B. The difference in number of eye facets between the two genetic types was much greater at 16° than at 25°. Conversely, the effect of temperature was greater on one genetic type than on the other. Thus, a "different difference" resulted from environmental changes when operating on individuals of different heredity; and a "different difference" resulted from hereditary variations when operating in different environments. The "ratio" of hereditary and environmental contributions would thus vary as either factor varied.[5]

The operation of a similar type of heredity-environment relationship can readily be recognized in the development of many familiar human characteristics. If we ask, for example, to what extent body weight depends upon such environmental factors as diet and exercise and to what extent it depends upon hereditary factors, no single answer can be given for all individuals or all environmental conditions. Because of differences in hereditary factors, the body weight of certain individuals is more susceptible to differences in diet, exercise, etc., than that of other individuals. In the former type of person, the contribution of heredity is smaller. Thus, the proportional contribution of heredity and environment to body weight may itself be determined by hereditary factors, and may vary from person to person. The proportional contribution of heredity and environment may likewise be altered by variations on the environmental side, such as the absolute amount of food intake. Thus when the total amount of food intake is low, as in a near-starvation diet, body weight undoubtedly depends to a much greater extent upon differences in the amount of food. When the total food intake is large, individual differences in body weight are probably much less dependent upon diet.

In the case of behavioral traits, it is even more futile to seek for a single figure to express the relative contribution of heredity and environment. Suppose we are asked, "How much do heredity and environment contribute to the development of intelligence?" In answering this question, we might consider first Tommy, a child with an IQ of 40. His mental deficiency, we learn, can be traced to impaired brain development resulting from a metabolic disorder, which is in turn attributable to a single recessive gene. Since this hereditary disorder sets such narrow limits to intellectual development, our conclusion would be that Tommy's intellectual level depends very largely upon his heredity.

Next let us look at Jim, whose IQ is also 40. But in his case the intellectual backwardness is traceable to a prenatal cerebral injury, which also sets very

[5] For other illustrations, cf. Haldane (12) and Hogben (13).

narrow limits to his possible intellectual development. In this case, the child's present intelligence is very largely the result of an environmental factor, the injury sustained prior to birth. Then there is Bill, whose similar IQ of 40 results from the fact that he lives in an isolated mountain community and never went to school. This child's present intellectual development would again be attributed very largely to environment. But it is obvious that the implications of such a conclusion are very different for Bill and for Jim. For one thing, the chances for future improvement look much more hopeful for Bill than for Jim.

For our last illustration, let us journey to an imaginary land, where we meet a boy named Blix, whose IQ is likewise 40. Blix is blue-eyed, and in his land there is an ancient decree that no blue-eyed child may attend school or receive instruction from anyone. Now, since eye color is rigidly determined by hereditary factors, we can draw the conclusion that, for Blix, intelligence was largely the result of heredity. Certain geneticists would argue for such an interpretation of the IQ of 40 obtained by Blix (cf., e.g., 8, p. 147). And logically, the interpretation is quite defensible. In the land of Blix, the genes for blue eyes inevitably predispose the individual to intellectual backwardness. In another environment, to be sure, they might have the opposite effect, or no effect at all, upon his intellectual development. But genes always operate within a specific environment. And between genes and complex human behavior there are many intermediate steps at which effects may vary tremendously from one environment to another.

Let us consider another kind of example involving intelligence test scores. Suppose we find a 10-point difference in IQ between two identical twins reared in separate foster homes (A and B), and a 30-point difference in IQ between two unrelated children, one reared in foster home A and the other in foster home B. Can we argue that the 10-point difference between the identical twins measures the "differentiating effect" of these two home environments, and that the 30-point difference between the unrelated children can therefore be analyzed into 10 points attributable to environment and 20 points attributable to heredity? Could we conclude that, in so far as these cases show, heredity is twice as important as environment in the production of individual differences in IQ? If we follow the concept of interaction, the answer to both questions is "No." Actually, a very slight hereditary difference between the two unrelated children may have greatly augmented the difference between the effective environments of the two foster homes. The difference in environmental stimulation between the two homes would thus have been much greater for the unrelated children than for the identical twins. No simple subtraction of the end products could disentangle the relative contribution of the factors whose initial interaction led to the obtained difference in IQ.

All the examples of interaction that have been discussed—the eye facets of the fruit fly, as well as the hypothetical examples of body weight and IQ— illustrate the *interdependence* of heredity and environment, which is fundamental to the concept of interaction. To summarize, interdependence means that the contribution of any given environmental factor to a particular trait depends upon the individual's specific hereditary background; and conversely, the contribution of any given hereditary factor depends upon the specific environmental conditions within which it operates.

Another implication of the concept of interaction is that the heredity-environment relationship can be more accurately likened to the arithmetic operation of *multiplication* [6] than to that of addition. The individual's characteristics may be conceived as the product, rather than the sum, of the hereditary and environmental factors. Under these conditions, a slight difference in environment, in combination with a slight difference in heredity, may ultimately lead to a very large difference in the resulting characteristic. We must envisage such a "multiplication" of influences as occurring successively in the individual's development, each new "product" being itself the basis for further multiplication in an ever-widening radius. Thus a slight initial difference between two individuals may launch them on two widely diverging paths of development.

Still another implication of the concept of interaction should be recognized. Any estimate of the relative contribution of hereditary and environmental factors to individual differences obviously depends upon the *range* or extent of both hereditary and environmental differences within the population under consideration. For example, susceptibility to diphtheria has been shown to depend upon a recessive hereditary factor, and immunity upon a corresponding dominant factor (23, pp. 416–417). This disease will not be contracted, however, without infection by the diphtheria bacillus. If, now, we consider a population all of whom have inherited susceptibility, then individual differences in the development of the disease could be attributed entirely to the environmental differences, i.e., exposure to infection. On the other hand, in a population in which all are equally exposed to the bacillus, any individual differences would be attributable to differences in heredity, i.e., whether the dominant gene for immunity was present. To

[6] To speak of hereditary and environmental factors as being multiplied is obviously an oversimplification, although helpful in visualizing the relationships involved. The actual mathematical function by which hereditary and environmental contributions combine is unknown and may well differ from one specific characteristic to another.

the question, "What proportion of the variance in the development of diphtheria is attributable to heredity?" opposite answers would be reached in these two populations. Similarly, a wide variety of intermediate answers could be reached in other populations, depending upon the relative frequency of exposure and the relative frequency of individuals with the dominant gene for diphtheria immunity in each population.

Throughout this discussion, the terms "heredity" and "environment" have been used without qualifications for the sake of brevity. It should not be concluded, however, that they refer to single entities or forces. Both heredity and environment are general names for *complex manifolds of many specific influences.* In the development of the individual, interaction occurs *within* as well as *between* the specific factors in each of the two categories. To speak of all the thousands of genes, each with its specific chemical and other properties, as though they represented a single force, operating as a unit to stimulate development in a particular direction, is highly misleading. It is even more clearly apparent that "environment" is not an entity which can be contrasted or juxtaposed with "heredity." Cellular environment, radiation effects upon genes, birth injuries, educational history, and socioeconomic level can scarcely be treated as a single influence!

POPULAR MISCONCEPTIONS REGARDING HEREDITY AND ENVIRONMENT

A number of misconceptions regarding the operation of heredity and environment are still prevalent in popular thought. We shall examine briefly some of the most common of these erroneous beliefs, in order to clear the way for further analysis of the heredity-environment problem.

Hereditary versus Inborn. One of the most common sources of confusion in discussions of heredity and environment is that between "hereditary" and "inborn." The popular belief that whatever is present at birth is necessarily inherited is bolstered by the lack of precision in terminology. The dictionary definitions of such terms as "hereditary," "inborn," "innate," "congenital," and "native" are difficult to differentiate. Certainly the terms are often used interchangeably, in the scientific as well as the popular literature. The scientist usually employs all or most of them as synonymous with "hereditary." The layman, on the other hand, frequently interprets all these terms with reference to birth, a reference that is obviously present in the root of such words as "inborn," "native," and "innate."

It is, of course, just as incorrect to regard the influence of heredity in the development of any trait as ceasing at birth as it is to date the onset of environmental influences from birth. Hereditary factors may affect the development of the individual long after birth and, in fact, throughout the life span. Inherited susceptibility to various diseases, for example, may not be manifested until well past middle age. Even the age at which a person dies may be determined partly by hereditary factors, as suggested by the observation that longevity tends to run in families. Hereditary influences may thus become manifest for the first time at any age. That environmental influences begin to operate long before birth has already been indicated in the discussion of prenatal environment. The influences of heredity and environment are co-extensive in time. Birth is not to be regarded as either a beginning or an end in the operation of these factors, but as one event in a developmental continuum which for the individual begins at conception and ends at death.

Resemblance to Parents.   Another popular fallacy is the belief that heredity implies parental resemblance, and vice versa. Both sides of this proposition can be shown to be false. That heredity need not result in the resemblance of offspring to immediate forebears is apparent from a consideration of the mechanism of heredity. The genes are continuous from generation to generation. They are not "produced" by the individual parents, but are simply transmitted by them to their offspring. Thus the individual inherits not only from his parents but also from all his direct ancestors. A characteristic that has remained latent for many generations may become manifest because of a particular combination of genes, e.g., two recessives. The result will be an individual unlike his parents or immediate forebears in some one respect. Instances of this sort are common in family histories. One of the most familiar illustrations is that of two brown-eyed parents having a blue-eyed child, through the combination of two recessive "blue-eye" genes in the offspring. In such cases, heredity actually serves to make the child unlike his parents.

The converse proposition, that parent-child resemblance is necessarily indicative of heredity, is equally untenable. Such resemblances may have developed through the many environmental contacts and similarities of parent and child, both prenatally (in relation to the mother) and postnatally. Not only are parents and children exposed to more nearly similar environments than are unrelated individuals, but they constitute in part each other's environment. Thus mutual influence as well as common stimulation may serve to produce resemblances. For these reasons no parent-child likeness can be attributed to hereditary factors without further analysis of its development.

Inheritance of Acquired Characteristics.   The Lamarckian hypothesis of the inheritance of acquired characteristics has found no support either in the experimental findings of genetics or in the data of embryology regarding the mechanism of heredity. Yet the popular belief persists that parents may transmit to their offspring physical as well as psychological characteristics which the parents have developed through training or experience. For example, the opinion may be expressed that if the parents attend college, their children will as a result "inherit" superior mental ability; or that if the parents engage in athletic activities, their children will have stronger muscles. Statements are also made to the effect that the parents' acquired fears, interests, prejudices, ethical or esthetic standards, mechanical skills, and the like, may be inherited by the offspring.

The truth of the matter is, of course, that only conditions which act directly upon the genes are transmissible to the offspring. It is theoretically possible, to be sure, that certain activities of the parents may bring about the operation of effective physical agents upon the genes. Exposure to radiation would be an example. The action of various types of radiation in producing gene modifications, or mutations, was mentioned in an earlier section. Genes are, however, extremely stable, and the agents that affect them very few. Certain other agents, such as alcohol, may injure the cytoplasm of the reproductive cells, thus affecting the development of the immediate offspring, but will still produce no inheritable change which might be transmitted to subsequent generations. Such direct physical effects on genes or cytoplasm are, however, a far cry from the "transmission" of an interest in the classics or a taste for non-objective paintings!

"Maternal Impressions." An even more naïve notion pertains to the influence of the mother's experiences during pregnancy upon the characteristics of the child. Under this heading would be included popular explanations of "birthmarks," as well as certain related beliefs such as the superstition that a man may have bushy eyebrows because his mother was frightened during pregnancy by a shaggy-haired Airedale! Another favorite illustration is that of the mother who attends lectures, concerts, and recitals during pregnancy in order that her child may acquire a desire for "culture." All such beliefs are now in the category of superstitions and old wives' tales.

The only prenatal influences the mother's activities can exert upon the developing offspring are indirect, biochemical effects. Thus certain toxic materials, disease bacteria, or any other agents carried by the blood stream can be transmitted by the mother to the embryo or fetus. Similarly, the mother's general level of metabolism, her nutrition, and her endocrine balance may exert considerable influence upon the development of the embryo. It follows that excessive emotional excitement during pregnancy, for example, may have an indirect effect upon the developing child, as a result of chemical changes in the maternal blood stream. But there is certainly no basis for expecting specific fears or other experiences of the mother to have a specific physical or psychological effect upon the embryo.

Heredity, Environment, and Modifiability.   Still another common misconception pertains to the modifiability of characteristics attributable to hereditary or to environmental factors. On the one hand, there is a belief that if a hereditary origin is discovered for a given condition, nothing—or very little—can be done to improve it. This is certainly not true. Hereditary diseases, for example, are neither inevitable nor incurable. They can be prevented and they respond to therapy. Traits that have a hereditary basis are responsive to such environmental factors as diet, exercise, or education. There are very few hereditary characteristics that cannot be altered by any known environmental factors. The blood groups and eye color are among such rare characteristics in man.

On the other hand, there is a corresponding belief that a characteristic or difference between individuals that is attributable to environment is easily changed, evanescent, superficial, and even perhaps a little "unreal." Such a belief is equally false. It is easy to demonstrate that environmentally produced differences are just as "real" as those traceable to heredity. Environmental differences cannot be ignored, nor can they be easily wiped out. Conversely, it would be incorrect to assume that any characteristic which resists change is necessarily hereditary. Feeblemindedness resulting from prenatal brain damage, although environmentally caused, is very resistant to improvement. Similarly, the type of training and other experiences which an individual has had during his first twenty years of life cannot be cancelled out by a relatively brief subsequent experience or educational opportunity.

"STRUCTURAL" AND "FUNCTIONAL" CHARACTERISTICS

Up to this point, we have been discussing the operation of hereditary and environmental factors in general, without special reference to psychology. We may now turn to a consideration of the applications of these concepts to psychological phenomena. The proper domain of psychology is the behavior of individuals. Structural characteristics are important in this connection in so far as they impose certain limitations upon the development of behavior. A cat cannot learn to fly because it has no wings. If a child has a defective thyroid, his movements will be slow and sluggish, and his general behavior dull and stupid. For the development of certain types of behavior, vocal organs, hands, and a human nervous system are essential prerequisites. The nature and development of bodily structures obviously play a part in determining the characteristics of behavior.

The presence of certain structural characteristics should, however, be regarded as a necessary but not a sufficient condition for the development of any specific type of behavior. In other words, the presence of all the structural prerequisites does not in itself ensure that the given behavior will appear. It also follows that the absence of a given type of behavior does not necessarily imply a structural deficiency, nor do behavior variations necessarily imply corresponding structural variations. Except for individuals with gross pathological defects, the structural equipment of most persons is such as to permit an almost unlimited variety of behavior development.

Much confusion and controversy in discussions of heredity and environment in psychology arise from a failure to distinguish between behavior characteristics and structural characteristics. Statements regarding the "inheritance" of feeblemindedness, musical talent, mathematical aptitude, or criminal tendencies are at best highly misleading.[7] Certainly, no one expects disembodied functions as such to be mysteriously transmitted through the genes. The genes are specific chemical substances which, through many successive interactions with other substances in their environment, eventually bring about the development of the structures making up the individual. No "potentialities," "tendencies," "influences," "determiners," or other similar abstractions can be discovered in the genes!

What, then, can be said regarding the role of heredity in *behavior?* Above all, it is clear that hereditary factors cannot affect behavior directly, but only indirectly through the structural equipment of the individual. The immediate question thus resolves itself into a consideration of the role of structural characteristics in behavior development.[8] In what way are given behavior characteristics related to *structural conditions,* such as glandular defects, pathological brain conditions, chemical composition of the blood, and the like, and in what way are they related to *functional conditions,* i.e., the individual's previous reactional biography?

When a specific structural condition is found to be associated with a given behavior characteristic, then the question of heredity and environment can be raised. If, for instance, a particular behavior deficiency is shown to be regularly associated with a certain brain condition, this condition may in turn be traceable to the presence or absence of a specific gene or combi-

---

[7] In many instances, of course, they are completely unfounded. But at this stage we are not considering the factual material.

[8] For a fuller elaboration of this point, cf. Anastasi and Foley (1).

nation of genes. On the other hand, the brain condition may result from physical or chemical characteristics of the prenatal environment, from birth injuries, or from other environmental factors.

A single defective gene may prevent normal brain development and thereby lead to a form of feeblemindedness. In such a case, this particular type of feeblemindedness would appear as a simple Mendelian unit in genetic studies of family pedigrees. Findings such as these would not, however, justify the assertion that "feeblemindedness" is a simple Mendelian recessive, as was proposed in some of the older psychological writings. In the first place, such a finding does not imply that only one gene is required for normal mental development. Undoubtedly many genes contribute to the structural development necessary for "intelligence." The substitution of one specific gene may, nevertheless, prevent the effect of the others from being manifested in the usual way. Hence a particular defect in a structural characteristic may be transmitted as a Mendelian unit, although the characteristic itself depends upon the combined effect of a large number of genes. In the second place, the presence of all the required genes would not ensure normal intelligence. Intellectual development—as all psychological development—depends upon the individual's reactional biography, that is, upon what he does with his structural equipment.

A word should be added regarding the use of the terms "structural" and "functional" in the present context. Each of these words has undoubtedly acquired many meanings that are not here intended. "Structural" was chosen as a convenient designation for what has been variously called organic, somatic, or physiogenic. It includes anatomical, physiological, and biochemical factors that influence behavior development. In the present sense, structural etiology can itself be investigated at different levels, ranging from gross anatomy to intracellular and molecular properties. The term "functional," on the other hand, is used to mean behavioral, experiential, psychogenic, or psychological etiology. Functional causation in this sense refers to the influence of the earlier psychological responses of the organism upon present behavior.

THE CONCEPT OF "UNLEARNED BEHAVIOR"

One application of the distinction between structural and functional etiology is to be found in the concept of "unlearned behavior." Among the criteria for the identification of such unlearned behavior that have been proposed from time to time may be mentioned: universality within a species, uniformity among different members of the species, sudden appearance without subsequent change, uniformity of developmental sequences in those cases in which change does occur, and "adaptiveness" or effectiveness far in excess of that which could reasonably be expected from the animal's own learning. Objections have been raised to each of these criteria (cf. 17, Ch. 3), the principal criticism being that behavior which meets any or all of these specifications can and does at times develop through learning.

The only completely dependable criterion of unlearned behavior is the demonstrated absence of the opportunity to learn. On the basis of this criterion, instances of unlearned behavior have been reported for various species, the clearest illustrations being furnished by the behavior of certain insects. In such cases, highly uniform and complex series of activities are performed despite the fact that the animal has had no previous contact with other members of the species or with the objects toward which the behavior is manifested. In many such species the parents die or abandon the eggs long before they are hatched. Thus the offspring have no opportunity to learn by observing the parent's behavior, nor does the parent have any opportunity to observe the effect of its preparatory activities upon the offspring.

A favorite illustration of such unlearned behavior is the pollinating behavior of the yucca moth. As soon as this insect emerges from its chrysalis, it travels to a yucca flower, from which it obtains pollen. It then finds another yucca flower, where it deposits its eggs as well as the newly gathered pollen, following a highly stereotyped sequence of reactions. The fertilized ovules of the flower, which result from this pollination, provide food for the yucca larvae when they emerge from the eggs four or five days later. In commenting on the unlearned nature of this pollinating behavior, Stone (25) has written:

> The adult does not partake of the pollen it has gathered and probably obtains no nourishment at all from the plant while performing this round of complicated activities. . . . The adult insect does not learn this complicated series of acts through imitation of its parents, long since dead, or from contemporaries, for its visual receptors do not provide the kind of vision necessary to the human concept of visual guidance. Most action systems of larvae are totally unlike those of adults, and the activities are even performed with different appendages; the body of the larva that descends the silken thread to bury itself in the ground is dedifferentiated and resynthesized during the resting state; and a prolonged interval of time, the winter season, intervenes between the last act of the larva and the first of the adult. In view of these facts, no concept of memory or transfer of training supported by experimental evidence can be invoked to account for the behavior of the yucca moth (25, p. 33).

A word of caution should be added regarding the general application of the basic criterion of unlearned behavior. Learning does not necessarily imply prior exposure to identical stimuli or exercise of the identical function. In fact, in so far as the perception of the stimuli and the nature of the responses are expected to change in the course of learning, it can be argued that learning never involves prior exercise of the identical function. Thus in determining whether or not there has been opportunity for previous learning, we must look for evidence of preliminary learning of related or similar activities which might constitute adequate preparation for the behavior in question. This point will be considered more fully in Chapter 4, in connection with an analysis of the data that have been gathered on this question.

Truly unlearned behavior can only mean behavior that is determined wholly by the structural characteristics of the organism, such that the mere presence of the necessary structures at a certain stage of development ensures the appearance of the behavior in question. Merely to say that a certain type of behavior is unlearned, however, is no answer to the question of how it develops. Such a statement only reformulates the problem, so that the question still remains to be answered. The answer now calls for knowledge of what structural factors determine such behavior and how they operate. To prove that behavior is unlearned, i.e., *not* learned, is a negative finding, which furnishes no positive information. It does not in itself tell us how the behavior develops. To call such unlearned behavior "instinctive," "innate," or "hereditary" simply obfuscates the problem, because these terms seem to suggest positive explanations or active processes, whereas *in this case they are being used only as synonyms for the negative term "unlearned."*

Moreover, it is incorrect to regard unlearned behavior as hereditary. In the first place, behavior cannot be inherited as such. It is only structural characteristics which can be directly influenced by the genes. In the second place, the structural conditions that determine such unlearned behavior may themselves result from either hereditary or environmental factors, or varying combinations of the two (cf. 2).

Similar difficulties arise from the common use of the term *"maturation"* in psychological writings. In discussions of the origin of behavior, a distinction is usually made between development through learning and development through maturation. The latter refers to the sudden appearance of a certain type of behavior, regardless of the previous activities of the organism, as soon as the requisite stage of structural development is attained. While the distinction may be theoretically sound, the use of the term "maturation" in this connection frequently creates misleading impressions. For instance, it tends to suggest a positive process of behavior development, without making it sufficiently clear that it is the structures that are developing. Moreover, certain writers who use the term "maturation" easily slip into the implication that such behavior results from an "unfolding of potentialities" which were present in the genes, and that it is therefore inherited.

Unlearned behavior has been traditionally subdivided into such categories as tropism, reflex, and instinct. These distinctions are not sharply drawn. Some writers have, in fact, used one or another of these terms exclusively to designate all unlearned behavior. The most common usage, however, is to designate as *tropistic* any behavior that is primarily an orienting (turning, approach, withdrawal) response of the entire organism toward a stimulus, such a response being essentially "forced" by the physical and chemical properties of the stimulus and of the reacting organism. An example is the turning and bending of plants toward the sun or other source of light. "*Reflex*" generally refers to a specific response of a part of the organism to a particular form of stimulation. The term is usually applied only to organisms that have a synaptic nervous system. The structural basis of the reflex is the "reflex arc," consisting of receptor, neurones, and effector. Two examples in man are the patellar reflex, or "knee jerk," and the pupillary reflex, or contraction and expansion of the pupil as intensity of illumination changes.

The term "*instinct*" has been used with more varied meanings, although nearly all its definitions imply a greater complexity of behavior than is represented by either "tropism" or "reflex." Some writers use the term to refer to a chain or integration of reflexes, as illustrated by the complex stereotyped sequences of unlearned activities observed in certain insects, such as the yucca moth cited above. Others employ the term in a vaguer sense to mean a relatively rough framework within which considerable variability of specific behavior may occur. In such definitions, instinct is often related to physiological needs, such as the need for food or water, and to the presence of hormones. It is this latter, less specific use of the term "instinct" that has opened the way for many unbridled leaps into an improbable terrain. It is here, for example, that one finds discussions of gregarious or collecting "instincts" and the like. Not only have the structural properties leading to gregariousness or collecting behavior never been identified or even vaguely guessed, but the nature of this behavior is also such as to make the search for its structural correlates appear futile and meaningless.

It is undoubtedly true that isolated instances of behavior can be found which clearly fit the definitions of tropism, reflex, or instinct. On the other hand, most behavior—human or infrahuman—cannot be classified into any one of these categories. Certain segments or aspects of a complex activity could probably be described as tropistic, reflexive, instinctive, or learned, the activity itself including more than one of these various components.

It would seem, moreover, that these terms, as well as the term "maturation," lend themselves too readily to misunderstanding and unwarranted implications. To say that a given activity or a particular component of an activity is unlearned (provided it has been conclusively demonstrated to be unlearned) is certainly a more precise and objective description of the actual observations. To call such an activity structurally determined adds to the observation the only possible source of the occurrence of such behavior. At the same time, the designation "structurally determined" centers attention on the question that logically follows, namely, what structures are involved and how do they bring about such behavior?

THE MEASUREMENT OF "CAPACITY"

Another area of psychology in which confusions regarding heredity and environment are likely to arise is that of the interpretation of psychological tests. Persons unfamiliar with the way in which psychological tests are developed and used sometimes expect such tests to measure "native intelligence," "innate capacities," "hereditary predispositions of personality," and the like. By now it should be apparent that such expectations are sheer nonsense.

Between the biochemical properties of genes—which constitute the individual's heredity—and the complex functions subsumed under the headings of intelligence and personality there intervene a vast number of steps. At each step there occur intricate interactions involving environmental conditions—past and present—as well as any relevant indirect effects of specific genes. The end product reflects a multiplicity of influences, structural and functional, hereditary and environmental.

Every psychological test measures a sample of the individual's behavior. No test provides any special devices or "tricks" for penetrating beyond behavior or for eliminating the subject's past experiences. All conditions influencing behavior will inevitably be reflected in test scores. In so far as performance on a given test correlates with performance in other situations, the test can serve in diagnosing or predicting behavior. It is in this sense only that a psychological test can be said to measure "capacity" or "potentiality."

For example, we may be able to construct a test that will predict how well high school freshmen can learn French, before they have even begun the study of French. We would thus be testing the student's capacity for learning French rather than his present knowledge of the language. Such capacity, however, would be tested by determining how well the individual performs certain necessary prerequisite functions and how effectively he learns vocabulary and grammatical rules similar to those he will be taught in French classes. In other words, we would use the students' present performance in relevant tasks to predict how well each would do when taught a new language.

It is well to remember that whenever the terms "capacity" and "potentiality" are employed in reference to psychological tests, they are to be interpreted in the above sense of prediction. No psychological test measures genes! To ask that it do so simply reflects a misconception of the nature of heredity and of its role in behavior.

SUMMARY

Heredity consists of the sum total of genes that are transmitted to the individual by his two parents at conception. Every individual receives different combinations of genes, the only exception being identical twins. Throughout the life span of the individual organism, his genes interact with environmental factors. Environment is a very broad concept, ranging from the intracellular and intercellular environment within the organism itself, to the manifold external influences that impinge upon it from conception to death. An individual's environment includes all stimuli to which he responds. Hence the effective environments of two persons will differ, even if both persons are placed in identical surroundings. The environments of two siblings reared in the same home, for example, differ in many important ways.

The more we learn about the operation of heredity and environment, the more we realize that they are inextricably intertwined. Heredity sets certain limits within which the organism may develop. In the case of complex human psychological traits, these limits are for most persons so wide as to permit almost unlimited variation. Moreover, to ask how much of an intellectual or personality trait depends upon heredity and how much upon environment is a meaningless question, since it can have as many answers as there are individuals. The question should be reformulated in terms, not of how much, but of how. What we need to know is the *modus operandi*—the way in which specific hereditary and environmental factors operate in producing specific differences in behavior.

There are a number of popular misconceptions regarding the operation of heredity and environment. All that is present at birth is not necessarily hereditary, since prenatal environment may influence basic structural and behavioral characteristics of the organism. Similarly, hereditary influences may first become manifested long after birth. Resemblance to parents may depend upon either heredity or environment. Dissimilarities between parents and children may likewise result from either type of factor. Acquired characteristics of the parents cannot be transmitted to the offspring by heredity. And the only ways in which the mother's activities during pregnancy can affect the developing offspring are through biochemical and other physical agents acting upon the embryo or fetus. Finally, it is incorrect to assume that conditions which have a hereditary origin are unchangeable or irremediable in the individual organism, or conversely that all environmentally produced differences are readily susceptible to change.

Since the influence of heredity upon behavior must always be indirect, an important intermediate question concerns the "structural" (anatomical-physiological-biochemical) conditions which set limits to behavior development. Such structural conditions can in turn be traced to the operation of both hereditary and environmental factors.

"Unlearned behavior," when conclusively demonstrated to have developed in the absence of relevant learning, is behavior that is wholly determined by the structural properties of the organism. The term "maturation" has been used to refer to the appearance of a certain type of behavior as soon as the necessary stage of structural development has been reached. Unlearned behavior has been classified into tropisms, reflexes, and instincts. These terms, especially "maturation" and "instinct," must be used with caution in order to avoid unwarranted implications. Psychological tests do not measure "native capacities." To expect them to do so reflects a misconception of the nature of heredity and of its interaction with environment.

In conclusion, it should be remembered that heredity and environment are not unitary influences, but abstractions. Each covers a vast multitude of different factors, all interacting with one another in ever-growing complexity throughout the life of the individual. Except for certain pathological deviants, every human being possesses the structural prerequisites for an almost infinite variety of behavioral development. Human evolution has moved in the direction of broadening the limits of variation set by heredity and thus making man's behavior increasingly dependent upon environmental conditions. Modern man does not have a gene for learning calculus or for appreciating abstract art. What he does have is a genetic constitution that frees him—to an unprecedented degree—from hereditary restrictions on much of his behavior and which permits well-nigh inconceivable latitude for the operation of environmental factors.

From the brief sketch given in this chapter, it should be apparent that the heredity-environment problem is by no means a simple one. Alluring generalizations can only mislead in a topic that is intrinsically complex. If this discussion has given the reader some conception of the complexity of the heredity-environment relationship, it has served its purpose well. Moreover, if the reader has come to recognize the importance of careful use of terms, to distinguish between superstition and established fact, and to follow deductions logically and objectively in the heredity-environment area, he will have made significant strides in his thinking. An honest, forthright recognition of the complexity and inherent difficulties of the problem, as well as the limitations of our present knowledge in this field, is to be preferred to a list of comfortable oversimplifications.

REFERENCES

1. Anastasi, Anne, and Foley, J. P., Jr. A proposed reorientation in the heredity-environment controversy. *Psychol. Rev.*, 1948, 55, 239–249.
2. Beach, F. A. The descent of instinct. *Psychol. Rev.*, 1955, 62, 401–410.
3. Burks, Barbara S. Statistical hazards in nature-nurture investigations. *27th Yearb., Nat. Soc. Stud. Educ.*, 1928, Part I, 9–33.
4. Burks, Barbara S. The relative influence of nature and nurture upon mental development; a comparative study of foster parent-foster child resemblance and true parent-true child resemblance. *27th Yearb., Nat. Soc. Stud. Educ.*, 1928, Part I, 219–316.
5. Carmichael, L. The onset and early development of behavior. In L. Carmichael (Ed.), *Manual of child psychology.* (Rev. Ed.) N.Y.: Wiley, 1954. Pp. 60–185.
6. Cotterman, C. W. Regular two-allele and three-allele phenotype systems. Part I. *Amer. J. hum. Genet.*, 1953, 5, 193–235.
7. Dobzhansky, Th. *Genetics and the origin of species.* (3rd Ed.) N.Y.: Columbia Univer. Press, 1951.
8. Dobzhansky, Th. The genetic nature of differences among men. In S. Persons (Ed.), *Evolutionary thought in America.* New Haven: Yale Univer. Press, 1950. Pp. 86–155.
9. Dunn, L. C. (Ed.) *Genetics in the 20th century.* N.Y.: Macmillan, 1951.
10. Evans, H. M., and Swezy, Olive. The chromosomes in man: sex and somatic. *Mem., Univer. Calif.*, 1929, 9, No. 1.
11. Ginsberg, A. A reconstructive analysis of the concept "instinct." *J. Psychol.*, 1952, 33, 235–277.
12. Haldane, J. B. S. The interaction of nature and nurture. *Ann. Eugen.*, 1946, 3, 197–205.
13. Hogben, L. *Nature and nurture.* London: Allen and Unwin, 1939.
14. Hoge, M. A. The influence of temperature on the development of a Mendelian character. *J. exp. Zool.*, 1915, 18, 241–285.
15. Kantor, J. R. *The principles of psychology.* Vol. I. N.Y.: Knopf, 1924.
16. Loevinger, Jane. On the proportional contributions of differences in nature and in nurture to differences in intelligence. *Psychol. Bull.*, 1943, 40, 725-756.

17. Munn, N. L. *The evolution and growth of human behavior.* Boston: Houghton Mifflin, 1955.
18. Painter, T. S. Salivary chromosomes and the attack on the genes. *J. Hered.,* 1934, 25, 464–476.
19. Pease, D. C., and Baker, R. F. Preliminary investigations of chromosomes and genes with the electron microscope. *Science,* 1949, 109, 8–10, 22.
20. Russell, Liane B. The effects of radiation on mammalian prenatal development. In A. Hollaender (Ed.), *Radiation biology.* Vol. I. N.Y.: McGraw-Hill, 1954. Pp. 861–918.
21. Scheinfeld, A. *You and heredity.* (Rev. Ed.) Philadelphia: Lippincott, 1951.
22. Sinnott, E. W., Dunn, L. C., and Dobzhansky, Th. *Principles of genetics.* (4th Ed.) N.Y.: McGraw-Hill, 1950.
23. Snyder, L. H. and David, P. R. *The principles of heredity.* (5th Ed.) Boston: Heath, 1957.
24. Stockard, C. R. *The physical basis of personality.* N.Y.: Norton, 1931.
25. Stone, C. P. Maturation and "instinctive" functions. In C. P. Stone (Ed.), *Comparative psychology.* (3rd Ed.) N.Y.: Prentice-Hall, 1951. Pp. 30–61.
26. Winchester, A. M. *Genetics.* Boston: Houghton Mifflin, 1951.
27. Woodworth, R. S. Heredity and environment: a critical survey of recently published material on twins and foster children. *Soc. Sci. Res. Coun. Bull.* 1941, No. 47.

CHAPTER 4

Heredity and Environment: Methodology

Psychologists have utilized a wide variety of procedures in their efforts to disentangle the complex hereditary and environmental factors that underlie behavior development. Few if any approaches, taken individually, can give conclusive answers. Each has its own peculiar advantages and limitations. Our understanding of the origins of behavioral differences is most likely to be advanced through the integration of results from different types of studies.

The chief difficulty confronting the investigator in this area is that of isolating the contributions of hereditary and environmental factors. As in all experimental design, the essential prerequisite is the control of conditions in such a way that comparisons can be made among groups or subgroups that vary in a *single factor*. Since in most investigations on individual or group differences many hereditary and environmental factors vary simultaneously, the results are often incapable of definitive interpretation.

If heredity can be assumed to be constant, as in the case of identical twins, then differences can be attributed unambiguously to environment. Similarly, if environment is held constant, any observed differences must be the result of heredity. In the light of what was said in Chapter 3 regarding the nature of effective environment, however, it is obviously extremely difficult to hold environment constant for two individuals, especially in the case of human subjects. A few of the techniques employed clearly make no attempt to separate hereditary and environmental factors, and consequently yield results that are at best descriptive, rather than explanatory. On the other hand, certain approaches permit some identification of hereditary or environmental factors which contribute to individual differences in specific traits.

In evaluating each method, we should bear in mind the nature of the problem, as outlined in the preceding chapter. Essentially, we are not asking whether a trait depends on heredity or environment. Nor is it a question of arriving at a generalized estimate of the proportional contribution of heredity and environment. Rather, the problem is one of discovering the *modus operandi* of hereditary and environmental factors in the development of behavioral differences. We want to know in what ways different factors contribute and how they combine to yield the observed results. The role of structural, or organic, conditions in behavior development is also relevant, since it is only through such structural characteristics that heredity can affect behavior.

Almost any study in differential psychology can contribute to an analysis of the origins of behavioral differences. In this sense, the present chapter could include all that follows in the entire book. Certain techniques, however, have been specially designed and utilized for the direct study of heredity and environment. They are the methods traditionally associated with the heredity-environment problem in psychology. Under this heading, we may recognize five major approaches, which will be discussed in the following sections. They include: selective breeding for psychological characteristics, normative developmental studies of behavior, the investigation of structural factors in behavior development, research on the effects of prior experience upon behavior, and statistical analyses of family resemblances and differences.

SELECTIVE BREEDING

The experimental breeding of animals selected on the basis of behavior characteristics is a recent application by psychologists of the technique of selective breeding long in use by geneticists. This is the basic method of genetics for the study of the inheritance of any characteristic. Through several refinements of this method, geneticists have succeeded in analyzing the hereditary basis of many structural characteristics and even in constructing theoretical "gene maps" for certain species. The present applications of selective breeding to behavior phenomena, however, are far from reaching such refinements. All that these studies have achieved to date is to effect, through successive generations of selective breeding, the development of two strains which differ significantly in a given behavior characteristic. Following the establishment of the contrasted strains, a beginning has been made in the search for possible structural bases for such behavior differences between strains.

One of the most extensive of these investigations employing selective breeding is that conducted by Tryon (85, 86) on maze learning in white rats. An initial group of 142 rats was given 19 trials in running a maze, and the number of "errors," i.e., entrances into blind alleys, was determined for each animal. On the basis of these error scores, a group of the brightest and a group of the dullest rats were selected for experimental mating. The "bright" rats in this parent generation (P) were mated with each other, and the "dull" were likewise mated together. This procedure was followed through 18 filial generations (F1 to F18). In each successive generation, the "brightest" rats in the bright strain were selected in terms of maze performance and were bred together, the "dullest" in the dull strain being similarly selected and interbred. Environmental conditions, such as food, lighting, temperature, and living quarters, were kept constant for all rats in the different generations.

The effect of such selective breeding upon the maze performance of each successive generation is illustrated in Figure 27. It will be noted that the distributions of the

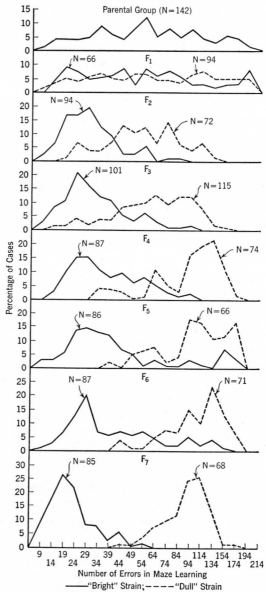

Fig. 27. Effect of Selective Breeding for Maze Performance. (From Tryon, 86, p. 113.)

bright and dull strains gradually separate until there is virtually no over-lapping between them when the F7 generation is reached. Beyond the seventh generation, the additional effects of selective breeding were negligible. When rats from the bright and dull groups were interbred, a distribution similar to that of the original parental group resulted, most of the animals now obtaining intermediate scores, with relatively few at the dull

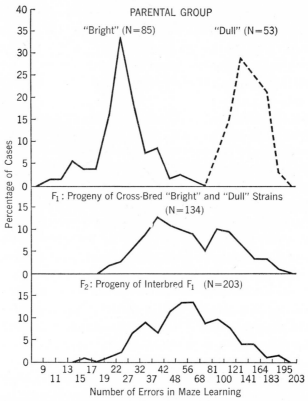

Fig. 28. Effect of Cross-Breeding Rats from "Maze-Bright" and "Maze-Dull" Strains. (From Tryon, 86, p. 115.)

and bright extremes. The distributions of the bright and dull parental groups and of two cross-bred filial generations are given in Figure 28. Tryon concluded that the results of this cross-breeding experiment were consistent with the hypothesis of multiple-factor inheritance. Hall (34) has pointed out, however, that if the strains had been pure at the time of cross-breeding, the first-generation progeny (F1) should have shown uniform maze performance, while their offspring (F2) should have exhibited a wide range of scores. The fact that the F1 cross-bred generation displayed wide individual differences in maze performance thus indicates failure to achieve homozygosity and makes the genetic interpretation of results more difficult.

Subsequent research by Tryon and others has sought to discover in what ways the maze-bright rats differed from the maze-dull. It soon became apparent that the difference was not to be found in "intelligence" or even in general learning capacity, since the maze-dull rats equaled or excelled the maze-bright in other types of learning tasks. In a follow-up of Tryon's investigation, Searle (68) obtained 30 measures on samples of rats from both strains. Analysis of results suggested that the maze-bright rats were "characteristically food driven, economical of distance, low in motivation to escape from water, and timid in response to open spaces," while the maze-dull were "relatively disinterested in food, average or better in water motivation, and timid of mechanical apparatus features" (68, p. 323). It would thus seem that the two strains differed in emotional and motivational factors, rather than in ability.

More recently, strains of maze-bright and maze-dull rats have been successfully bred by other investigators (37, 43, 71, 83). Some progress has also been made in identifying structural differences between the strains. Glandular conditions, body size, brain size, and factors related to health, vigor, and strength of the hunger drive have appeared as possible bases for the strain differences in maze learning. Comparisons of the physical characteristics of the contrasted strains have sometimes yielded inconsistent results, one investigator finding a significant difference in a particular physical characteristic, while another finds no difference in the same characteristic. These inconsistencies are not, however, unexpected if activities such as maze learning are influenced by a *multiplicity of structural conditions*. For example, if we suppose that maze learning can be facilitated by six different structural factors (a, b, c, d, e, and f), an individual experimenter who selects good maze performers in the parental generation may get rats which by chance excel in four of these six relevant structural characteristics (a, b, c, and d). The extensive inbreeding that follows in successive generations will augment *these particular structural differences,* since in effect the experimenter was selecting the animals in terms of these characteristics even though he may have been unaware of it. By the same token, another investigator who singles out his "maze-bright" rats for mating may be selecting them in terms of structural characteristics d, e, and f. In that case, successive generations of selective breeding will produce strains differentiated in d, e, and f, but not in a, b, and c.

Selective breeding has likewise been carried out with respect to such characteristics as amount of spontaneous activity (3, 63) and emotionality

(33) in rats. One investigation (35) suggested certain relationships between the traits that were selectively bred and other behavior characteristics. For example, the relatively unemotional, "fearless" rats also showed higher activity level and more aggressiveness than the relatively emotional strains.

A highly significant development in behavior genetics is to be found in the research conducted by Hirsch and Tryon on lower organisms (45). These investigators have worked out techniques for obtaining reliable measures of individual differences in behavior among such organisms as the fruit fly *Drosophila*. It is thus possible to capitalize on the mass of available genetic knowledge regarding the morphology of *Drosophila*, as well as on such other advantages as the brief time span between generations and the abundance of progeny. Through the use of the newly developed procedures, Hirsch and Tryon have already succeeded in producing strains of fruit flies that are positively or negatively geotropic, respectively, as well as others that are positively or negatively phototropic. In the former case, one strain tends to fly upward, the other downward when released in a vertical maze. In the latter, one tends to fly toward a source of light, the other away from it. The possibilities this type of research opens up may be partly visualized when it is noted that all these strain differentiations were accomplished in the course of a few months, in contrast to the eleven years required for Tryon's original rat-breeding project.

A somewhat different approach is represented by the study of behavior differences between existing strains of animals that were not selectively bred for psychological characteristics. One such study on three inbred strains of mice revealed significant differences in fighting behavior among the strains (64). Several research projects of this type have been conducted with dogs by Stockard (77) and more recently by Scott and Fuller at the Jackson Memorial Laboratory (25, 65, 66, 67). Different breeds and cross-breeds of dogs have been found to vary significantly in a number of learning tasks, as well as in emotional responses, activity level, and social behavior toward other dogs and toward their human associates. As in the studies on rats, it again appears likely that the differences in learning ability "are produced by differences in emotional, motivational, and peripheral processes, and that genetically caused differences in central processes may be either slight or nonexistent" (66, p. 225). Certain breed differences in physiological characteristics, which may in turn be related to the observed behavioral differences, were likewise found in the research on dogs.

In much of the work on all animal forms studied so far, the functioning of the endocrine glands appears to be a promising source of the observed strain differences in behavior. Whether strain differences in properties of the brain or other parts of the nervous system are involved remains an unanswered question at this time (cf. 34). In interpreting the results of selective breeding experiments, consideration should also be given to the following methodological difficulty noted by Hall:

The transmission of a trait from generation to generation may appear to be genetic, whereas in reality it is due to an extragenic factor. The mode of transmission may be some prenatal or postnatal influence of the mother on the young. The prenatal influence may be determined by transplanting the fertilized egg to a host mother of a different strain. The postnatal influence can be investigated by placing the neonates with a foster mother (34, p. 309).

To date, very few investigators have attempted to apply these controls. At the same time, there is considerable evidence (to be discussed in a later section) to indicate that all forms of behavior for which selective breeding has been carried out are distinctly modifiable by early environmental influences.

NORMATIVE DEVELOPMENTAL STUDIES

Another source of data regarding etiological factors in behavior is to be found in observations of the normal course of behavior development. What information can such an approach provide regarding the interaction of hereditary and environmental factors? By and large, investigators utilizing these procedures have looked for evidence of *maturation*. It will be recalled that maturation refers to unlearned behavior, that is, functions that appear when the prerequisite stage of structural development is reached, as contrasted with those that require specific exercise or learning. In so far as hereditary factors influence such structural development, therefore, they can be said to enter into the development of the behavior functions in question.

In the analysis of normative developmental data, the two conditions cited most frequently in support of a maturation hypothesis are *sudden emergence* of functions and *sequential patterning* of development. Thus it is argued that behavior which appears suddenly, in more or less final form, when the organism has reached a certain age must be unlearned. The uniformity of developmental stages, or sequential patterning, in any particular function has likewise been regarded as a criterion of unlearned behavior, on the grounds that opportunities for learning are likely to vary from one individual to another and could not result in such a consistent succession of like stages.

There is now available a large body of observational data on behavior development in a wide variety of animal forms—from salamander to man.

The relative simplicity of processes in lower forms facilitates the recognition of essential principles of development, whose applicability to higher forms can then be more readily investigated. Similarly, some of the most significant observations have been made at the prenatal level, partly because of the greater simplicity of behavior at this level and partly because environmental diversities and opportunities for learning are not so great as during postnatal life. To be sure, the process of behavior development continues throughout life and should include any decline in functioning which may appear in older adulthood. Since age changes in older children and adults will be considered in a later chapter (Ch. 8), however, the present discussion will be limited to the prenatal period,[1] infancy, and early childhood.

A thorough survey of investigations on prenatal behavior development in both human and subhuman species can be found in Carmichael (9). A briefer summary is given by Munn (60, Ch. 6). These sources also provide an introduction to the specialized techniques which have been developed for observing prenatal behavior in man and animals, together with a critical evaluation of such procedures. Among the classic investigations in this area may be mentioned those of Coghill (10) on the salamander, Coronios (11) on the cat, Kuo (52, 53, 54, 55) on the chick, and Carmichael (7) on the guinea pig. An outstanding recent contribution is the moving picture recording of behavior in the human fetus by Hooker (47).

The data on postnatal behavior development in animals have been brought together by Cruikshank (12). Observations on the human neonate are summarized by Pratt (61). The study of behavior development in the human infant and child constitutes a large part of the content of child psychology. Results have been reported in many published sources. The most intensive analyses of such child development data from the viewpoint of the maturation hypothesis have been carried out by Gesell and his co-workers at the Yale University Clinic of Child Development (cf. 28, 29, 30). Over the years, this group of research workers has gathered large quantities of data on the normal course of development in infancy and childhood. From these data, Gesell and his associates have prepared normative schedules showing the age at which specific changes occur in many functions. Their observations are based on carefully worked out procedures, including the use of standardized toys, cribs, chairs, and other equipment, as well as

[1] The terms "germinal," "embryonic," "fetal," and "neonatal" refer to successive stages prior to and immediately following birth. In man, for example, the germinal stage lasts for about two weeks after fertilization; from that time until the age of two months, the organism is known as an embryo, and from two months until birth, as a fetus. Between birth and approximately one month of postnatal age, the child is commonly known as a neonate. The duration of these stages, of course, varies in different species.

one-way vision screens, moving picture photography, and other refinements.

In all species investigated, there is clear evidence that behavior begins well before birth. In the human fetus, for example, responses to tactual stimuli have been reported as early as the eighth week of life. It is believed that all receptors are capable of functioning before birth, although vision, taste, smell, and temperature are unlikely to be stimulated because of the uniformity and other conditions of prenatal environment. Several types of motor responses have been identified in human fetuses from the age of eight weeks on. By the fourth month, nearly all the reflexes of the newborn can be elicited. Moreover, a number of human fetal responses appear to be the precursors of later behavior. Among these are crying, sucking, and eye reflexes; balancing and righting movements; rhythmic contractions of the chest and thorax similar to breathing movements; and a "trotting" reflex involving alternate extension and flexion of the two legs in opposition. It has been suggested that this trotting reflex may underlie such postnatal activities as crawling and walking. There is also evidence of rudimentary learning prior to birth, although investigators disagree as to whether true conditioning can be established in the human before the end of the first month of postnatal life (cf. 8, 19, 74, 88).

Prenatal behavior has likewise been observed in many animal forms. Conditioned reactions have been successfully established in chick embryos prior to emergence from the egg (32, 48). Through an extensive series of observations of the behavior of the chick embryo, Kuo (54) has called attention to mechanical and other forms of stimulation to which the embryo responds, as well as to the many types of muscular responses that are exercised before birth. Similarly, from his study of the fetal cat, Coronios (11) concluded: "Before birth there is a rapid, progressive, and continuous development of behavior. . . . The 'primitive' reactions of breathing, righting, locomotion, and feeding are the products of a long and continuously progressive course of prenatal development" (11, pp. 377–378). Findings such as these sound a note of caution regarding the acceptance of the "sudden emergence" of behavior functions as a criterion of maturation. The sudden appearance of a particular act after birth may in some instances represent a reappearance, in the presence of suitable environmental stimulation, of behavior that has undergone gradual development and exercise prior to birth.

The study of early behavior development has provided extensive evidence of sequential patterning. Uniformities of developmental sequences and an orderly progression of behavior changes seem to be the rule for functions appearing during the prenatal and early postnatal periods. Animal studies have yielded detailed "timetables" of behavior changes to which individual members of each species conform more or less closely. The same type of information has been assembled for human fetal development.

Similarly, Gesell and other child psychologists have been impressed with the regularity of developmental sequences in infancy and early childhood and have emphasized a maturational interpretation of such development (cf. 1, 21, 29, 30, 36, 69, 70). In the development of prehension behavior, for example, the successive stages follow in the same order and at approximately the same ages in different children. Thus the child's reactions toward a small sugar pellet placed in front of him show a characteristic chronological sequence in visual fixation and in hand and finger movements. Use of the entire hand in crude attempts at "palmar prehension," for example, occurs at an earlier age than the use of the thumb in opposition to the palm; this is in turn followed by the use of the thumb and index finger in a more efficient "pincer-like" grasp of the pellet. Such sequential patterning is likewise reported for walking, stair climbing, and most of the sensorimotor development of the first few years.

In further support of the maturation hypothesis, Gesell (30) cites premature and postmature births, i.e., those occurring earlier or later than the normal nine-month gestation period. How does the behavior of a 1-month-old infant who was born prematurely after an eight-month term compare with that of a newborn, normal-term baby? In total age from conception, they are equal. But the premature infant has had the benefit of one month of exposure to postnatal environment, with its many changes in stimulation and increased opportunities for exercising various functions. Gesell maintains that, despite superficial and temporary advantages of the premature child, the basic pattern of behavior development is the same for both.

In summary, maturation appears to play a major part in early behavior development. It is important to take certain facts into account, however, in interpreting the data in this area and in qualifying the generalizations that have been proposed. First, attention must be given to the *total developmental period.* Prenatal exercise of functions may affect the appearance of similar or related functions after birth. The etiology of behavior cannot be understood solely in terms of what happens after birth. Secondly, in the case of functions that develop in later infancy and childhood, we cannot ignore the possible influence of *environmental uniformities.* Gesell's observations, for example, have been limited largely to children reared in middle-class American homes, representing a relatively narrow range of cultural background. It is thus possible that some of the regularity in developmental sequences may have resulted from uniformities in child-rearing practices, as well as from other, unplanned similarities in the physical and psychological milieu of the subjects.

Finally, it is important to realize the *limited nature of the behavior under consideration* in all these studies. The simple sensorimotor functions surveyed in both the animal research and the work on human fetuses and young children are closely linked to structural development. A certain minimum development of receptors, muscles, and connecting nerve cells is an essential prerequisite for the appearance of these functions. It would be unwarranted to generalize from such observations to the development of more complex, symbolical functions involving language or abstract reasoning. The principles formulated from the data on simple sensorimotor functions must be tested anew on more complex functions before they can be accepted as general developmental principles of behavior.

STRUCTURAL FACTORS IN BEHAVIOR DEVELOPMENT

Since any influence which heredity exerts upon behavior must be manifested through "structural" conditions, as defined in Chapter 3, direct study of the part played by structural factors in behavior development represents another approach to the analysis of heredity-environment interactions. This approach has frequently been pursued jointly with one of the other techniques of investigation already discussed. We have seen, for example, that attempts have been made to identify *structural differences between selectively bred strains* and that results to date show glandular conditions to be one of the most promising sources of strain differences.

Similarly, a number of normative developmental studies have included observations on *structural changes which accompany behavior development*. In his work on the salamander, Coghill (10) was the first to trace systematically the anatomical changes in the nervous system which preceded the appearance of such functions as swimming and feeding. A similar but less complete neural basis has been worked out for the earliest behavior development in other animal forms, such as the chick (55) and the rat (cf. 9). Through anatomical and histological studies, the development of sensory structures has likewise been related to the appearance of corresponding behavior functions.

Information regarding the neural changes underlying early human behavior development has been obtained through histological studies of human fetuses after death. Observations of nonmotile fetuses, for instance, have shown that in such cases sensorimotor connections had not yet been established in the nervous system. Through a variety of procedures, data have been gathered which indicate that control of behavior by the cerebral cortex does not begin until some time after birth. Electroencephalograms [2] of human fetuses in the uterus, for example, show little or no evidence of brain activity prior to birth (57).

Even when the gross anatomical connections are present in the nervous system, there is often a lag in the appearance of the corresponding functions. Extensive research has been directed toward the discovery of the additional neural conditions which must be fulfilled prior to the functioning of specific pathways. At one time it was believed that an essential prerequisite condition was myelinization, or the laying down of the fatty myelin sheath which surrounds the nerve fibers. Early investigations pointed to correspondences between the first occurrence of specific behavior functions and myelinization of the appropriate nerve pathways. These findings, however, were not corroborated by subsequent studies, and it is now generally recognized that myelinization is not a prerequisite for the functioning of nerve fibers (cf. 75, p. 267).

Findings regarding myelinization highlight an important point regarding the interpretation of concomitant structural and behavioral development. Myelinization may improve function, or conversely, it may itself be stimulated and accelerated by function, or the two processes may occur at the same time without influencing each other. That correlation does not indicate causation is a familiar truism. It is particularly necessary to bear it in mind when evaluating the role of structural factors in behavior. Today research is still going on in the effort to identify possible histological, chemical, or physical changes which must occur prior to nerve functioning, but no definitive answer has yet been reached.

Another major technique for investigating the relation of structure to behavior consists in the *artificial manipulation of structural factors*. This approach may be illustrated by the surgical removal of portions of the cerebral cortex, the administration of glandular extracts, and the direct stimulation of different parts of the nervous system by electrical or other means. Many of the data of physiological psychology have been gathered by procedures such as these. Through such methods it has been possible to demonstrate the role of specific parts of the nervous system or specific endocrine glands in certain behavior functions. Similarly, it has been established that disruption or loss of particular functions follows the removal of certain neural or glandular structures.

These researches of physiological psychologists have unquestionably added much to our knowledge of the operation of various structures in

---

[2] This technique will be explained in Chapter 5.

behavior. Nevertheless, this approach does not go very far toward clarifying the sources of individual differences in behavior within the normal range of variation. A knowledge of the structural prerequisites of behavior does not necessarily provide an explanation of individual differences among those who meet these prerequisites. It is as though we tried to discover the causes of individual differences in normal speed and style of walking by examining a one-legged man.

From the standpoint of individual differences, a more promising variant of this approach is that which induces physical changes at an early developmental stage. Several of the studies in this category have utilized conditions not too unlike those that might operate in the ordinary course of development. Among the factors whose effect upon subsequent behavior has been investigated at the prenatal level are anoxia (lack of sufficient oxygen), various drugs, nutritional deficiencies, endocrine secretions, and radiation. Recent studies, for example, have reported deficiencies in the learning behavior of rats whose mothers were subjected to X-ray irradiation during pregnancy (26, 56, 81). These effects should not be confused with the production of gene mutations by radiation, discussed in Chapter 3. Mutations are transmissible by heredity; the effects just reported are not.

Finally, mention should be made of the mass of data accumulated on the *relationship between individual differences in physical and psychological traits*. In general, studies in this area have been concerned directly with problems of individual differences. The subjects have usually been adults or older children. A detailed consideration of the physical traits investigated and the results obtained will be reserved for Chapter 5. For the present it will suffice to call attention to certain persistent questions of interpretation and causal analysis. When a significant relationship is established between a particular physical characteristic and a behavioral characteristic, the question of cause and effect is still unanswered. Does the behavior contribute to the structural condition or vice versa? Are they both the result of a third factor? If it can be shown that a particular structural factor affects behavior, what is its *modus operandi*?

The role of physical conditions in behavior may range from that of a relatively irremediable neurological or metabolic deficiency which severely limits behavior development to that represented by a social stereotype which causes differential treatment of persons with certain physical characteristics. Both may affect behavior, but in very different ways. A further question pertains to the manner in which hereditary and environmental factors interact in producing the physical characteristics in question. Then, too, there is the possibility that the physical and psychological traits under consideration are not causally related, in either direction, but that both are affected by a third factor, such as socioeconomic level. For instance, children in an underdeveloped region may show physical handicaps arising from poor diet and medical care, as well as intellectual handicaps resulting from inadequate schooling.

EFFECTS OF PRIOR EXPERIENCE UPON BEHAVIOR

One of the most direct ways of studying the role of maturation and learning in behavior development consists in systematically altering the individual's early experiences and observing the effects upon his subsequent behavior. A large proportion of the research by this method has been carried out on young animals. A few comparable studies have been conducted on human infants and young children. Relevant data have also been accumulated by comparing individuals or groups reared under different conditions, even though the environmental differences were not introduced by the experimenter. Although less well controlled, the latter studies represent a variant of the same basic method.

Animal Experiments. A number of behavior functions commonly regarded as unlearned or "instinctive" have been subjected to experimental control, whereby the animal was prevented from exercising the function until well past the age when such a function normally appears in the species. By such isolation of factors, an attempt is made to determine the extent to which physical maturation of the necessary structures will in itself lead to performance of the given function. Other experimenters have followed the opposite procedure of providing additional stimulation or intensive training in order to determine how far normal behavior development can be accelerated or modified in other ways.

In 1954, Beach and Jaynes (2) surveyed the many studies appearing prior to that time on the effects of early experience upon animal behavior. Interest in this area has continued to be active, as witnessed by the number of new studies published since the Beach and Jaynes review. Among the functions investigated are flying and singing of birds, swimming of frogs, feeding reactions, hoarding of food, reproductive behavior, parental behavior toward the young, grooming, nursing by the young, group formation and preference for members of the same or of different species, perceptual responses in several sense modalities, fighting and other aggressive behavior, wildness, timidity, and other emotional responses. All these functions show some effects of the experimentally introduced conditions, although the extent of such effects varies with the species, the functions, and the nature of the experience provided.

In some situations, the typical species response fails to appear. In others, the response may be altered in various ways. Or the response may be given to stimuli other than those which normally elicit it. An example of the latter is provided by what Lorenz and his associates have called "imprinting" (cf. 2; 84, p. 150). By this is meant that the first stimulus to evoke a given reaction in the very young animal may become the only stimulus that can henceforth arouse it. Thus when newly hatched goslings were isolated from adult geese and allowed to follow the experimenter for some time, they continued to follow him thereafter and showed no inclination to follow adult geese. In the same way, young birds of several species have been found to form attachments to foster parents of other species.

A few representative experiments will serve to illustrate the variety of procedures that have been utilized. Cruze (13) studied the feeding responses of chicks that had been prevented from pecking for varying periods of time. Five equated groups of 25 to 26 chicks each were kept in darkness and hand fed for one, two, three, four, and five days after hatching, respectively. Their subsequent performance when allowed to peck is shown in Figure 29. It will be noted that all groups were about equally poor at the start, regardless of age. However, the older groups advanced faster, and within a few days caught up with those that had begun to peck earlier. Such results indicate the role of maturation, since the chicks that had reached a more advanced stage of physical development were able to profit more from practice than did the younger chicks.

In the second part of Figure 29, the learning curve of Group A, which had unlimited practice after the first day, is compared with that of four other groups which were also allowed to peck after one day, but which had only restricted amounts of daily practice. Group F was permitted only 25 trials a day, and Group G only 12, before being returned to the dark room. Both of these groups showed much less progress than Group A. In fact, Group G revealed almost no improvement after the first day or so. The last group (H) was allowed 12 daily trials for the first ten days, and 25 daily trials thereafter. The performance of Group H was indistinguishable from that of Group G for the first ten days, although Group H quickly outstripped Group G when the daily practice was increased. This experiment thus clearly brings out the joint influence of both maturation and learning in the normal feeding behavior of the chick.

In a similar experiment by Carmichael (4, 5, 6), the swimming of tadpoles which had been kept in drugged water since hatching was compared with that of a control group remaining in fresh water. The drug effectively prevented the exercise of swimming movements until past the age at which tadpoles normally swim. When transferred to fresh water, the animals were observed to swim normally as soon as the effects of the drug wore off.

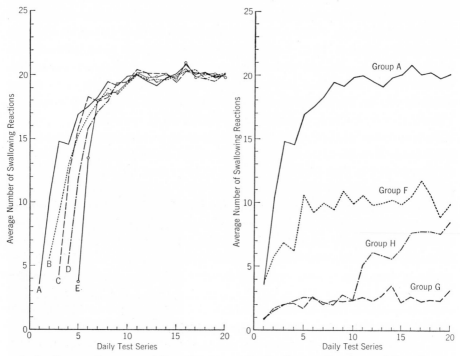

A. Swallowing Reactions of Five Groups of Chicks Prevented from Pecking for 1, 2, 3, 4, and 5 Days, Respectively.

B. Swallowing Reactions of Four Groups of Chicks Allowed Varying Amounts of Daily Practice.

Fig. 29. Effects of Practice on Pecking Performance of Chicks. (From Cruze, 13, pp. 386, 388.)

Maturation would thus seem to account adequately for swimming behavior in this species. In a later experiment, however, another investigator (24) was able to demonstrate a significant advantage of the control animals in speed and distance of swimming. Practice thus plays some part in this function, although the basic motor pattern appears even in the absence of prior activity.

In experiments of the type we are discussing, it is often difficult to be sure that the influence of prior learning has actually been ruled out. This is particularly true of complex behavior patterns which have commonly been called "instincts." For example, female rats reared in isolation nevertheless engage in "nest building" and care for their young in the typical manner of their species. More highly controlled investigations, however, suggest that the rat's previous experience in manipulating materials and in washing and grooming her own body is necessary for the subsequent appearance of such maternal behavior (cf. 62). Female rats reared in cages containing nothing that could be picked up or transported failed to construct nests when materials were made available. Nor did they gather their young into a single area in the customary way. Another group of female rats was fitted with rubber collars which prevented contact of nose or mouth with the lower part of the body. The collars were worn from infancy to sexual maturity. On giving birth, these rats did not clean or groom their young.

Instead of restricting practice, some investigators have provided animals with additional stimulation and training, or with experiences unlike those they normally have. Into this category would fall investigations in which chimpanzees have been reared in a typically human environment. In these cases, the animal is not kept as a pet, but is treated like a human as regards clothing, sleeping and feeding, play activities, and all other aspects of child training. Moreover, the experimenters also had one or more children of their own with whom the ape was reared, and the same treatment was given to ape and human in so far as possible. The first psychologists to undertake such a project systematically and intensively were the Kelloggs (50), who brought a female chimpanzee, Gua, into their home at the age of 7½ months and retained her for a period of nine months. A photograph of Gua displaying some of the typical human behavior which she acquired in this environment is reproduced in Figure 30.

Fig. 30. Gua, a Chimpanzee Reared for Nine Months in a Typically Human Environment. (From Kellogg and Kellogg, 51, p. 226.)

More recently, the Hayes (38, 39, 40, 41) undertook a similar project of longer duration. Viki, another female chimpanzee, was adopted a few days after birth and remained in the experimenter's home until her death from a virus infection six and a half years later. In solving problems involving imitation, Viki proved to be as good as human children of her age and clearly excelled a laboratory-reared chimpanzee. She was able to repeat the experimenter's actions at the command "Do this," and also spontaneously imitated several household activities such as sharpening pencils or prying lids off cans. Viki likewise engaged in spontaneous play with mechanical toys and gadgets as much as did her human companions and proved skillful in the use of tools. On nonverbal tests of intelligence involving form boards, picture puzzles, blocks, and the like, she performed about as well as the human norms for her chronological age. A photograph of Viki, aged 6 years, trying to pull a tooth with pliers and mirror is reproduced in Figure 31.

Fig. 31. Viki, a Six-Year-Old Chimpanzee Reared in a Human Home: Trying to Pull a Loose Tooth with Pliers and Mirror. (From Hayes and Hayes, 41, p. 291.)

Viki's only serious stumbling block proved to be the acquisition of language. With painstaking efforts, the experimenters finally succeeded in teaching her to say three words (mama, papa, cup) and to use them in appropriate situations. For most of her social communication, however, Viki resorted to such practices as pointing, leading persons to the desired object, or imitative movements. Only when other means failed did she resort to vocalization. The experimenters concluded that the chief source of difficulty was to be found in the ape's inadequate drive for vocal play. The babbling and chattering characteristic of human infants was almost completely lacking in the chimpanzee, despite the fact that she was physically able to produce a wide variety of speech sounds. Moreover, although using sounds in emotional expression, Viki appeared to experience serious difficulty in vocalizing voluntarily.

A group of animal experiments of special interest to differential psychology pertain to the effect of early experience upon subsequent learning ability. In their previously cited survey, Beach and Jaynes write: "Many psychologists appear to conceive of learning ability in animals as genetically determined and relatively unmodifiable, but recent findings indicate the untenability of this thesis" (2, p. 255). Extensive research on monkeys and on rats has demonstrated that animals can "learn how to learn"—in other words, they can be "educated."

A number of recent studies on this problem were stimulated by a theory proposed by Hebb (42) to the effect that animals that have had a large amount of perceptual experience early in life will prove to be better learners than those deprived of such experience. Supporting evidence has so far been gathered in studies with rats and dogs (23, 58, 82; cf. also 2). In all these cases, the animals reared under less restrictive conditions performed significantly better in maze learning and problem solving.

Experiments on Human Infants. Experiments that involve interference with the normal course of development in human infants must obviously be limited to relatively mild or otherwise acceptable procedures. In a study by Dennis (16) on the effects of *restricted practice,* two female infants were reared under controlled conditions in the experimenter's home between the ages of 1 and 14 months. During the first seven months of this period, stimulation and activity were rigidly restricted. Opportunities for standing and sitting were eliminated, and opportunities to grasp objects were highly minimized. The nursery was bare of all but essential furnishings. The experimenters had no social contact with the children except for physical care and for a few tests made during this period. They did not smile, frown, speak to, or play with the subjects. The two infants were separated from each other by means of an opaque screen. Beyond the seven months' period, the restrictions on motor exercise and social stimulation were gradually removed.

Throughout the 14 months, the behavior development of the two children was compared with norms established on infants brought up under normal, unrestricted conditions. Functions that normally appear during the first seven months showed no appreciable retardation. Among these were such simple activities as fixating objects; starting, turning the head, or crying at a sound; grasping objects; watching or playing with own hands; and bringing hand or object to mouth. Evidently functions such as these appear, regardless of exercise, when the necessary structural development has occurred. Responses that normally occur beyond the seventh month did, on the whole, show significant retardation, the age at which they appeared in the experimental subjects often falling beyond the range of the normative sample. Even these responses, however, were quickly established when the opportunity for practice was subsequently provided.[3]

A technique that has found more frequent application in child research is known as the *method of co-twin control.* In such experiments, one member of a pair of identical twins is given intensive training in some activity, while the other is retained as a control subject and prevented from exercising the function under investigation. In one of the studies conducted by Gesell and his co-workers (31) by this method, stair climbing and cube behavior (including prehension, manipulation, and constructive play with cubes) were studied in a pair of identical female twins 46 weeks old at the beginning of the experiment. The trained twin (T) was put through a daily 20-minute training period in both types of activity for six weeks. At the end of this period, the control twin (C), who had had no specific training in these functions, proved equal to T in cube behavior.

In stair climbing, a difference was found. Whereas T was a relatively expert climber, her sister could not reach the top of a five-tread staircase even with assistance. Two weeks later, however, still without any training, the control twin was able to climb to the top unassisted. At this age (53 weeks), twin C was herself given a two-week training period, at the end of which she approximated T in her climbing skill. Thus, because of the higher level of maturational development, a two-week training period at 53 weeks of age proved to be nearly as effective as a six-week training period at 46 weeks.

The same pair of identical twins was subsequently put through similar training experiments in other functions, including vocabulary training (44, 80). Beginning at the age of 84 weeks, twin T was given daily, intensive training for five weeks in naming objects, executing simple commissions, and other vocabulary-building techniques. Twin C was deprived of all opportunity to hear language during that period. At the end of the five-week period, when the twins were 89 weeks old, similar training was given to twin C for only four weeks. After this training, twin C had a vocabulary of 30 words. Twin T's vocabulary at the end of her first four weeks of training had been 23 words, although at the end of the total five-week period it rose to 35 words. The investigators emphasize the role of maturation in these results, calling attention to the fact that the twin whose training was begun at the age of 89 weeks progressed more rapidly almost every day and

---

[3] Relatively uncontrolled observations on certain extreme personality disorders resulting from early social and emotional deprivation will be considered in Chapter 9, in connection with the discussion of institutionally reared children.

showed a more mature manner of responding at corresponding stages of training than the one whose training was begun at 84 weeks.

It should be noted in interpreting these results that, first, the difference in rate of learning between the two twins was slight. For example, C's total vocabulary after 27 days of training equalled that of T after 31 days of training (viz., 29 words). Secondly, in vocabulary, pronunciation, and sentence construction, the twin with five weeks of earlier training slightly surpassed the one with four weeks of later training, although this difference had largely disappeared three months later. Finally, it is obvious that a certain amount of structural development in infancy and early childhood facilitates the earliest stages in the acquisition of language. The child cannot produce combinations of sounds resembling those of adults until his auditory and vocal mechanisms permit a certain degree of sound differentiation and control. Thus maturational factors may operate in this purely vocal aspect of language development, while the symbolical or meaningful aspects of linguistic development may depend upon learning.

In interpreting the results of all experiments by the method of co-twin control, it should be borne in mind that the comparison is not actually between learning and maturation. Rather, the comparison is between a specific period of controlled training, on the one hand, and the combined operation of maturation and all the uncontrolled exercise of related functions which the subjects undergo outside the laboratory, on the other. As long as the subjects are not anaesthetized, such uncontrolled exercise goes on. In so far as both twins have equal opportunities for such outside exercise, the difference in their performance in the laboratory-tested functions will be reduced. It would thus seem that, despite its popularity, the method of co-twin control as usually employed fails to yield a clear-cut analysis of contributing factors.

Case Studies of "Wild Children." A sort of "natural experiment" on restricted training is provided by certain well-known cases of children who, when discovered, had presumably been living in isolation or in exclusive contact with animals. Such "wild children" have been described since early historic times. In 1758, Linnaeus included them in his classification of the human species, under the designation of "feral man." An extensive survey of recorded cases has more recently been prepared by Zingg (89, 90). Over forty cases are described, although in a number of them the available information is quite meager or the isolation was only partial. These wild children include a few who had apparently been abandoned or had wandered off and survived in the wild largely through their own efforts, as well as a number who seem to have been reared by such animals as the wolf, bear, goat, pig, sheep, cattle, and leopard. Children who have been confined in isolation from human contacts and have been living under conditions barely sufficient for survival are also included in this category.

One of the most intensively studied cases is that of Victor, the Wild Boy of Aveyron (49). In September 1799 three sportsmen came upon a boy of 11 or 12 in a French forest. The boy was completely naked, unkempt, scarred, unable to talk, and seemed to have been leading a wild, animal-like existence. He was seized by the men as he was climbing a tree to escape their pursuit, and was subsequently brought to civilization, where he finally came under the guidance and observation of the French physician, Itard. A detailed account of this case was published by Itard, describing both the initial reactions of the boy and his progress during five years of intensive training.

The more recently discovered "wolf-children" of Midnapore (27, 50, 72, 76, 79, 89) represent another well-authenticated case. In 1921 two girls, one approximately 2 to 4 years of age and the other 8 or 9, were found living in a cave with wolves in a sparsely settled region of India. They were taken into a local orphanage, where attempts were made to train them. A detailed diary of the girls' activities, kept by the rector of the orphanage, is available in published form (72), together with analyses and comments by several psychologists, a sociologist, a geneticist, and an anthropologist. It proved difficult to keep the girls in good health, particularly because the readjustment to a normal human diet led to weakness and severe skin reactions. The younger girl, Amala, died within a year; the elder, Kamala, lived for about eight years, during which time some progress was made in teaching her to speak and to adopt other human ways.

Mention should also be made of the celebrated and mysterious case of Kaspar Hauser (cf. 72, pp. 277–365), about whom much has been written. Some accounts suggest that this boy was an heir to a princely house and was put out of the way by political enemies. He was apparently confined from early childhood in a dark cell, not large enough for him to stand upright. No clothing or cover was furnished except a shirt and trousers. When he awoke, he was accustomed to find bread and water, but he never saw the person who brought them and he had no knowledge of the existence of other living creatures besides himself. He was released in 1828, when about 17 years of age. At this time he was first discovered wandering aimlessly about the streets of Nuremberg. He could not talk, but repeatedly uttered certain phrases meaninglessly. He is reputed to have had a remarkable sense of smell and a surprising ability to see in the dark. His walking resembled the first efforts of a child. After various vicissitudes, his instruction was undertaken by a skillful and painstaking teacher. Under the latter's tutelage, Kaspar Hauser made rapid progress and soon learned to speak. By this means he was able to communicate what he recalled of his life in the cell, as well as his experiences during his period of instruction. Unlike other cases of children brought into contact with civilization relatively late in life, Kaspar Hauser profited sufficiently from his education to reach and even possibly surpass normal achievement.

Cases of wild children such as these have been of special interest to psychologists because of the possible light they may throw upon the question of how far normal human behavior develops in the absence of normal human stimulation. In his summary of the recorded cases, Zingg (89) concludes that such wild children were, without exception, mute and quadrupedal. No vocalization resembling human speech developed under these circumstances, and the characteristically human, erect locomotion was not found. All had developed some form of locomotion on hands and feet or on hands and knees, and their physical structure had often become modified (by the appearance of calloused pads, etc.) to permit rapid and efficient quadrupedal locomotion.

Characteristic sensory modifications are also reported, the senses of smell, hearing, and sight—especially night vision—often showing an animal-like keenness. Eating habits are markedly unlike those typical of the human. Raw meat is the common diet among children reared by carnivorous animals; wild-living children are described as subsisting largely on bark, roots, grass, herbs, and leaves. One "wild girl" in France had become very adept at swimming for fish and frogs, which constituted her principal food. The pattern of eating behavior is also similar to that of lower animals, including the smelling of food before eating, lowering the mouth to the food, sharpening teeth on bones, and the like. There is no evidence of any tendency to cover the body or to devise "clothing" of any sort. Such children seem to have been relatively insensitive to heat and cold and to have developed no "sense of shame" from nakedness. No crying, tears, or laughter was observed, although other expressions of violent anger or impatience are reported. Expressions of sex interest and activity were either completely absent or present only in the form of diffuse, general, undirected activity. No "consciousness of kind" or gregariousness was evidenced, the children shunning humans and often showing preference for the company of lower animals.

A particularly significant observation—reported for both of the two most thoroughly studied wild children—pertains to the development of space perception. In the case of both the Wild Boy of Aveyron and Kaspar Hauser, a number of deficiencies in the perception of distance, depth, and solidity were noted during the boys' initial contacts with their new surroundings. Itard (49, p. 5) reported that, when first observed, the Wild Boy of Aveyron was unable to distinguish between solid objects and pictures of objects. This was also true of Kaspar Hauser. Similarly, on first looking at a landscape seen through a window, Kaspar Hauser is said to have perceived it as a window shutter splattered with paint of many colors. Difficulties were likewise experienced in judging the size of objects at varying distances (cf. 72, p. 323).

Reports of wild children have been seriously questioned by some psychologists, such as Dennis (18, 20). It is undoubtedly true, as the records themselves show, that in several of the cases summarized by Zingg the association with animals either began after the child had reached an advanced age in human contact, or such association was only partial, the child still remaining in some contact with human adults. It is also true that the data on some of the cases, especially the earlier ones, are so meager and so subject to the inaccuracies and bias of the original observers as to be of doubtful authenticity.

Some psychologists would go further, however, and propose an alternative explanation for *all* cases of wild children. They maintain that such children may have been feebleminded to begin with, which would account for their abandonment in certain cultures. Their lack of typical human behavior, such as language and erect locomotion, as well as their other "animal-like" characteristics, are attributed to their original mental defect. The usual counterargument is to ask: "How, then, could such a feebleminded child have managed to survive in an environment which would tax the ingenuity of even a normal adult?" In answer to this, Dennis (18) has proposed the possibility that the wild children may actually have been abandoned only a short time—perhaps only a few days—before they were found, and that their behavior deficiency was incorrectly interpreted as a sign of prolonged isolation.

In a reply to Dennis' critique, Zingg (90) called attention to the calloused pads and other physical changes following prolonged four-footed locomotion, as well as to the degree of proficiency attained in such locomotion— conditions unlikely to have developed if the child had been living in human society until a short time prior to his discovery. The food preferences of many such cases and the physiological effects of prolonged dietary deficiencies likewise suggest a long separation from human contact. It is improbable that any child—however feebleminded—would have subsisted principally on raw meat if reared by people. This is especially true in India, where many such cases were found and where children are unlikely to have had access to even cooked meat (cf. 73).

The progress in learning human ways made by a number of wild children was also mentioned by Zingg as evidence against the hypothesis of initial feeblemindedness. To be sure, one rarely finds the performance of such subjects after training to equal or even approximate that of normal children of the same age. This is hardly to be expected, however, not only because of the long period of isolation during which opportunities for acquiring normal human behavior were lacking, but also because of the interference or "negative transfer" from other modes of behavior which have been acquired in the wild and which must be "unlearned" before progress can be made. By way of contrast, Zingg referred to one case of a "wolf-boy" of India who was apparently a "true idiot." This boy showed virtually no progress subsequent to his capture, although he lived well into adulthood. The comparatively greater progress made by other wild children suggests that they may have been initially normal and rendered deficient only by their early stimulational deprivation.

Zingg also cited the reports of reliable eyewitnesses indicating that at least two wild children (the wolf-children of Midnapore, described above) had actually been living with wolves for some time prior to their capture. This is emphasized by Zingg in reply to Dennis' argument that no direct evidence is available to show that human children have in fact been reared by animals. Dennis suggests that when children are captured in the company of animals, they may simply have been accidentally brought together by their common efforts to hide from a pursuer. Dennis stresses the importance of this point for the interpretation of the behavior of wild children. He points out that if a child is abandoned before the age of about three, he cannot possibly survive in the wild unless "adopted" and cared for by an animal. On the other hand, if the child was over three at the beginning of his wild existence, then he would already have acquired at least the rudiments of human speech, locomotion, and similar functions, unless he were congenitally defective.

A relevant hypothesis has been proposed by the anthropologist Marian Smith (73). The behavior of wild children may be partly explicable, according to Smith, in terms of the emotional trauma experienced by the child when he is abandoned or removed from his home. This is a more drastic experience than the mere discontinuance of training. Any socialization or acquisition of human behavior which occurred prior to isolation may also fail to persist because it is not reinforced by the child's subsequent experiences. The longer the duration of the wild existence, relative to the earlier period of human nurture, the less likely are the effects of human contact to be discernible. This hypothesis could account for the fact that behavior which may have developed prior to isolation, such as walking or talking, was not observed in any cases of wild children.

The objections raised by Dennis and others must be carefully weighed in interpreting any report on allegedly wild children. It is probable that the objections are valid for the majority of cases discussed by Zingg and others. On the other hand, the available evidence strongly suggests that at least three or four cases represent well-authenticated, genuine instances of prolonged isolation from human contact. The Wild Boy of Aveyron, the wolf-children of Midnapore, Kaspar Hauser, and perhaps one or two others appear to fall into this category. A study of these cases helps to highlight some of the facts of human development established by other, better-controlled procedures.

Cultural Differences in Child-Rearing Practices.   Another sort of "natural experiment" is provided by *infant-cradling practices* prevalent among certain cultures. It was the custom in Albania, for example, as in a number of its neighboring countries, to bandage children tightly to their cradles during the first year of life, so that they could not move their arms or legs. The cradle was kept in a darkened room, and the child had no contact with toys or other objects. The infant was unswathed and bathed once a day, and sometimes less often.

Tests administered to ten such infants between the ages of 4 months and 1 year (cf. 14) showed considerable behavioral retardation. Few reacted spontaneously when given the opportunity to do so. Coordination was decidedly poor, and grasping movements occurred much later than normal. Only one out of the ten infants was able to crawl before the age of 1 year, although all could sit up without support. Social reactions, on the other hand, were found to be advanced, a finding that was attributed to the presence of large families and to the fact that persons were the only familiar type of stimulation in the child's environment. Children over 1 year of age were reported to be normal in social reactions, learning ability, and "mental productivity," but retarded in coordination and expression. Their attitude toward new objects was described as interested and willing, though shy and clumsy, the children frequently depending upon adults for help in novel situations.

Restrictive infant-rearing practices are also to be found among certain American Indian tribes, such as the Navajo and the Hopi. In these groups, the newborn child is bundled tightly in a blanket and tied securely to a stiff board. In such a position, the infant cannot move his arms or legs, or even turn his body. For the first three months he is kept in these wrappings, except for about one hour each day, when he is cleaned and bathed. Later, he spends an increasing amount of time out of the cradle. Dennis (17) reports that, despite this extreme restriction of movement, when Hopi or Navajo children are released they show the same sitting, creeping, and walking behavior—and in the same sequence—as white American children. During the short daily periods when they are freed of their wrappings, moreover, they assume the usual flexed position, reach for objects and carry them to the mouth, reach for their toes and put them into the mouth, and exhibit other characteristic motor behavior of an unrestricted infant. It is also interesting to note that no significant difference was found in this study between the average age of walking of Hopi infants cradled in the traditional manner and other Hopi children who had been cradled in the manner of white American children. In a group of 63 children reared in the Hopi manner, the average age of walking was 14.95 months; for 42 Hopi children reared without binding, the average age of walking was 15.05. This difference is not statistically significant (22).

Similar results were obtained in a study of 110 Japanese and Korean children tested between the ages of 1 month and 3 years (46). On tests of motor development, these children showed no retardation, although they were carried on their mothers' backs in the traditional manner during a considerable part of each day.

The results of these investigations are not in complete agreement, the first suggesting somewhat greater disruption of functions through lack of exercise than do the two latter studies. The specific findings obviously depend upon a number of factors, such as the nature and degree of restriction, as well as the age at which it is discontinued. It is very probable, for example, that motor restriction alone has much less effect than motor restriction coupled with reduction in sensory stimulation and in social contact. The particular functions observed also undoubtedly differ in their dependence upon practice. In general, such studies suggest that certain simple motor functions appearing in early infancy depend almost entirely upon maturation, while many others require relatively brief periods of exercise for their successful performance.

A number of recent studies on cultural differences in child-rearing practices have been concerned with the effects of certain aspects of child training upon subsequent *personality development*. Special attention has been given to the degree of permissiveness or rigor in toilet training, sleeping and feeding habits, and similar functions. An extensive application of this approach is to be found in the survey by Whiting and Child (87). Utilizing data on 75 primitive societies from the Cross-Cultural Files of the Yale Institute of Human Relations, these investigators set out to test a number of hypotheses regarding the relationships between child-rearing practices and personality development. Within our own culture, similar surveys have been concerned with the effects of differences in child-rearing practices among social classes (15). Since all such studies deal with more complex and subtle differences and with more remote effects than did the previously discussed investigations of motor behavior, their findings are more difficult to interpret. The possibility that other, unknown or uncontrolled factors may be crucial in determining the observed group differences in personality traits presents a serious methodological problem. We shall return to a consideration of these studies in later chapters concerned with socioeconomic and other cultural differences (Ch. 15 and 17).

Mention may also be made of the large body of available data on *socioeconomic differences in intellectual functions*, to be discussed in Chapter 15. In so far as the specific class differences observed in such traits as verbal, numerical, spatial, and mechanical aptitudes are traced to corresponding differences in home environment and educational experiences, these studies may be regarded as a further extension of the same approach. Certain recent investigations have been concerned primarily with factors in the home environment which might account for the subsequently observed group differences in test performance. An example is Milner's (59) study of the effects of social class differences in parent–child interaction upon the reading readiness and language development of first-grade school children (cf. Ch. 15).

Training and Individual Differences. Still another type of study concerned with the effects of prior experience upon behavior development is that dealing with training and schooling, to be considered in Chapter 7. These studies include a number of controlled laboratory experiments designed to discover whether individual differences increase or decrease following a period of uniform practice in some simple function. The subjects in these studies have usually been college or graduate students, although some investigations on school children are also available.

A sizable body of data has accumulated on the effects of schooling. Into this category would fall a group of rather controversial studies concerned with the effects of nursery school attendance upon the child's IQ. Some investigators have gathered data on the effectiveness of special training programs in raising the intellectual level of feebleminded subjects. This research will be discussed in Chapter 12, dealing with mental deficiency. Another group of investigations pertains to the relationship between amount of schooling and adult intelligence. A related line of research has been the analysis of long-range trends in the general intellectual level of populations, in relation to educational changes which have occurred over the interval.

STATISTICAL STUDIES OF FAMILY RESEMBLANCE

A fifth and last approach to the analysis of hereditary and environmental factors in behavior is provided by statistical studies of family resemblances, to be discussed in Chapter 9. The interpretation of such resemblances is complicated by the fact that close relatives generally live together. The environment of persons in the same home is certainly more similar than in any other situation outside of an experimental setup. As a result, the two classes of factors, hereditary and environmental, operate jointly to produce greater likeness within the ordinary family than is found among individuals chosen at random. The closer the hereditary relationship, moreover, the greater the environmental proximity. Thus parents and children, and brothers and sisters, usually live in the same home; while more distant relatives, such as uncles and nephews, or cousins, come into less frequent contact. Not only are related individuals exposed to common environmental stimulation because of similarity of living conditions, but they also constitute in part each other's environment and may become more aiike in some respects through such mutual interaction.

In a variety of ways, families offer an excellent example of the operation of environmental influences in the development of behavioral similarities. At the same time, the fact that members of the same family do share a common heredity—in varying degrees—has made family resemblances a favorite source of data for testing hypotheses regarding hereditary factors. It is important to remember in this connection that family resemblance in itself cannot be regarded as evidence for heredity. To demonstrate the operation of hereditary factors, additional analyses and control procedures are required.

Pedigree Studies. The tracing of human family pedigrees with reference to some specific and easily identifiable characteristic may yield valuable data on hereditary factors. As used by geneticists, techniques of pedigree analysis have proved especially productive in the study of simple physical abnormalities such as albinism, web fingers, the presence of extra fingers, clubfoot, and a number of other rarer and more serious malformations or pathological conditions. A few psychological abnormalities also lend themselves to analysis by these techniques.

The application of pedigree analysis to most psychological traits, however, usually meets with well-nigh insurmountable obstacles. A major difficulty arises from the multiplicity of factors contributing to psychological traits. As a result, most pedigree studies in psychology have limited themselves to a demonstration that certain characteristics such as feeblemindedness, insanity, musical genius, or scientific eminence tend to run in families. Such data, which will be examined in Chapter 9, are essentially descriptive and provide little or no basis for explaining the observed similarities.

Correlational Studies of Family Resemblances. The degree of resemblance between related persons may be expressed by means of a correlation coefficient (cf. Ch. 1). For example, a high positive correlation between the intelligence test scores of fathers and sons would indicate that the higher-scoring fathers in the group tend to have the higher-scoring sons, and the lower-scoring fathers tend to have lower-scoring sons. Most correlational studies have been concerned with the degree of relationship between the test scores of parents and children, siblings (a general term for brothers and sisters), and twins. A few have dealt with more remote relations, such as cousins, or grandparents and grandchildren.

In all research on twins, it is important to distinguish between identical and fraternal twins (cf. Ch. 3). Identical twins, it will be recalled, are completely alike in heredity. All differences between such twins must therefore result from environmental factors operating prenatally or postnatally. Fraternal twins, on the other hand, have no more genetic similarity than siblings. Comparisons of the degree of resemblance in psychological traits between identical twins, fraternal twins, and siblings thus provide special opportunities for analyzing the operation of hereditary and environmental factors.

Studies of Special Family Relationships. Some investigators have seen in the study of foster children further opportunities for the isolation of hereditary and environmental influences. Several types of data may be obtained in such investigations. For example, one can study the changes following residence in the foster home, as well as the degree of resemblance of foster children to their own parents and siblings and to their foster parents and foster siblings. A special application of this procedure involves case studies of identical twins reared apart in different foster homes.[4] Children reared in institutions have likewise been investigated from this

---

[4] Stone (78) has suggested the utilization of certain animal forms which normally have multiple progeny of identical heredity. Examples include the clones of unicellular organisms and the multiple births of such vertebrates as the armadillo. Under these circumstances, identical twin experiments could be carried out with many more subjects and better-controlled conditions than would be possible in the case of human subjects.

point of view. Typical results of studies utilizing each of these varied approaches will be reported in Chapter 9.

SUMMARY

In surveying the methods that psychologists have utilized to investigate heredity and environment, it is important to bear in mind the nature of the problem, as discussed in Chapter 3. It is not a question of establishing whether a trait depends upon heredity or environment, or of determining the proportional contribution of heredity and environment. Rather, the object of such research should be to try to identify the specific hereditary and environmental factors involved in the development of each function and the ways in which these factors operate in producing the observed individual differences. The contribution of "structural" or organic conditions to behavior development is relevant to these questions, since it is only through structural characteristics that heredity can affect behavior.

The procedures used in psychological studies on hereditary and environmental factors in behavior can be classified under five major headings: selective breeding, normative developmental studies, structural factors in behavior development, effects of prior experience upon behavior, and statistical studies of family resemblance.

Selective breeding for psychological characteristics has been successfully employed by several investigators working with rats, and a beginning has been made with other species. Rats have been bred for such characteristics as maze learning, amount of spontaneous activity, and emotionality. Further research has suggested that the strain differences in maze learning are probably associated with emotional and motivational rather than with ability differences. Endocrine activity appears to play an important part in behavior differences between strains, a finding that is also supported by comparative behavior studies of existing breeds of dogs.

Normative developmental studies, which chart the normal course of behavior development with age, have been carried out both prenatally and postnatally, on animal and human subjects. In such studies, evidence for maturational factors has been sought largely in the sudden emergence of certain activities without prior practice, as well as in the uniformities of sequential patterning. Results show that, in both humans and animals, considerable behavior development occurs prior to birth. In the light of these observations, some of the evidence for the sudden emergence of behavior after birth becomes suspect. Sequential patterning appears to be the rule in much of the behavior development that takes place during the prenatal and early postnatal periods. In general, these results indicate that maturation is relatively important in the simple sensorimotor development occurring early in life. It is unwarranted, however, to generalize from such observations to the development of more complex, symbolical functions at later ages.

The role of *structural factors in behavior development* has been investigated in a variety of ways. Among these may be listed the comparison of selectively bred strains in various physical characteristics, the observation of physical changes accompanying behavior development, the artificial manipulation of structural factors (as in experimental removal or stimulation of cortical areas), and statistical studies of the relationships between individual differences in physical and psychological traits. So far this approach has yielded little positive information regarding structural differences which can be clearly identified with individual differences in behavior. Moreover, even when correspondences are found, many questions of causal relations remain to be answered. Further discussion of this approach will be found in Chapter 5.

Among studies on the *effects of prior experience upon behavior,* a large number of animal experiments have demonstrated the influence of early experience in modifying many forms of behavior commonly regarded as "instinctive." The ability to learn has itself proved to be susceptible to prior learning. Experimental studies on human infants have been relatively few. Utilizing the method of restricted practice and the method of co-twin control, these studies again suggest the importance of maturational factors in early sensorimotor development, but the data are inconclusive for a number of methodological reasons. Case studies of "wild children" found to be living in isolation or in exclusive contact with animals serve to highlight the extent to which children acquire typically human behavior only through contact with fellow humans. Investigations of cultural differences in infant-cradling practices corroborate other types of studies in showing that restriction of exercise does not in itself affect the appearance of certain simple motor responses in infancy, and that any retardation in other motor functions is quickly overcome when appropriate practice is permitted. Psychologists have also been interested in exploring the possible effects of other cultural differences in child-rearing practices upon subsequent personality and intellectual development. A fuller discussion of these studies is reserved for Chapters 15 and 17. Under the general approach concerned with the effects of prior experience upon behavior should also be included experiments on the influence of practice upon individual differences, as well as the varied research on the effects of schooling, both to be considered in Chapter 7.

The fifth general method covers *statistical studies of family resemblance,* which will be discussed in Chapter 9. This category includes pedigree or family history studies; parental, sibling, and twin correlations in test scores; and research on identical twins reared apart, foster children, and institutional children.

REFERENCES

1. Ames, Louise B. The sequential patterning of prone progression in the human infant. *Genet. Psychol. Monogr.,* 1937, 19, 409–460.
2. Beach, F. A., and Jaynes, J. Effects of early experience upon the behavior of animals. *Psychol. Bull.,* 1954, 51, 239–263.
3. Brody, E. G. Genetic basis of spontaneous activity in the albino rat. *Comp. Psychol. Monogr.,* 1942, 17, No. 5.
4. Carmichael, L. The development of behavior in vertebrates experimentally removed from the influence of external stimulation. *Psychol. Rev.,* 1926, 33, 51–58.
5. Carmichael, L. A further study of the development of behavior in vertebrates experimentally removed from the influence of external stimulation. *Psychol. Rev.,* 1927, 34, 34–47.
6. Carmichael, L. A further experimental study of the development of behavior. *Psychol. Rev.,* 1928, 35, 253–260.
7. Carmichael, L. An experimental study in the prenatal guinea pig of the origin and development of reflexes and patterns of behavior in relation to the stimulation of specific receptor areas during the period of active fetal life. *Genet. Psychol. Monogr.,* 1934, 16, 339–491.
8. Carmichael, L. Ontogenetic development. In S. S. Stevens (Ed.), *Handbook of experimental psychology.* N.Y.: Wiley, 1951. Pp. 281–303.
9. Carmichael, L. The onset and early development of behavior. In L. Carmichael (Ed.), *Manual of child psychology.* (2nd Ed.) N.Y.: Wiley, 1954. Pp. 60–185.
10. Coghill, G. E. *Anatomy and the problem of behavior.* Cambridge: Univer. Press, 1929.
11. Coronios, J. D. Development of behavior in the fetal cat. *Genet. Psychol. Monogr.,* 1933, 14, 283–386.
12. Cruikshank, Ruth M. Animal infancy. In L. Carmichael (Ed.), *Manual of child psychology.* (2nd Ed.) N.Y.: Wiley, 1954. Pp. 186–214.
13. Cruze, W. W. Maturation and learning in chicks. *J. comp. Psychol.,* 1935, 19, 371–409.
14. Danzinger, L., and Frankl, L. Zum Problem der Funktionsreifung. Erster Bericht über Entwicklungsprüfungen en albanischen Kindern. *Z. Kinderforsch.,* 1934, 43, 219–254.
15. Davis, A., and Havighurst, R. J. Social class and color differences in child rearing. *Amer. sociol. Rev.,* 1946, 11, 698–710.

16. Dennis, W. Infant development under conditions of restricted practice and of minimum social stimulation: a preliminary report. *J. genet. Psychol.*, 1938, 53, 149–158.

17. Dennis, W. Does culture appreciably affect patterns of infant behavior? *J. soc. Psychol.*, 1940, 12, 305–317.

18. Dennis, W. The significance of feral man. *Amer. J. Psychol.*, 1941, 54, 425–432.

19. Dennis, W. Is the newborn infant's repertoire learned or instinctive? *Psychol. Rev.*, 1943, 50, 330–337.

20. Dennis, W. A further analysis of reports of wild children. *Child Develpm.*, 1951, 22, 153–158.

21. Dennis, W., and Dennis, Marsena G. Behavioral development in the first year as shown by forty biographies. *Psychol. Rec.*, 1937, 1, 349–361.

22. Dennis, W., and Dennis, Marsena G. The effect of cradling practices upon the onset of walking in Hopi children. *J. genet. Psychol.*, 1940, 56, 77–86.

23. Forgus, R. H. The effect of early perceptual learning on the behavioral organization of adult rats. *J. comp. physiol. Psychol.*, 1954, 47, 331–336.

24. Fromme, A. An experimental study of the factors of maturation and practice in the behavioral development of the embryo of the frog, *Rana pipiens*. *Genet. Psychol. Monogr.*, 1941, 24, 219–256.

25. Fuller, J. L., and Scott, J. P. Heredity and learning ability in infrahuman mammals. *Eugen. Quart.*, 1954, 1, 28–43.

26. Furchtgott, E. Behavioral effects of ionizing radiations. *Psychol. Bull.*, 1956, 53, 320–334.

27. Gesell, A. *Wolf child and human child.* N.Y.: Harper, 1941.

28. Gesell, A. The ontogenesis of infant behavior. In L. Carmichael (Ed.), *Manual of child psychology.* (2nd Ed.) N.Y.: Wiley, 1954. Pp. 335–373.

29. Gesell, A., *et al. The first five years of life.* N.Y.: Harper, 1940.

30. Gesell, A., and Amatruda, Catherine S. *Developmental diagnosis.* (2nd Ed.) N.Y.: Hoeber, 1947.

31. Gesell, A., and Thompson, Helen. Twins T and C from infancy to adolescence: a biogenetic study of individual differences by the method of co-twin control. *Genet. Psychol. Monogr.*, 1941, 24, 3–122.

32. Gos, M. Les réflexes conditionnels chez l'embryon d'oiseau. *Bull. Soc. sci. Liége*, 1935, 4, 194–199, 246–250.

33. Hall, C. S. Emotionality in the rat. *J. comp. Psychol.*, 1934, 18, 385–404; 1936, 22, 61–68, 345–352; 1937, 24, 369–376.

34. Hall, C. S. The genetics of behavior. In S. S. Stevens (Ed.), *Handbook of experimental psychology.* N.Y.: Wiley, 1951. Pp. 304–329.

35. Hall, C. S., and Klein, S. J. Individual differences in aggressiveness in rats. *J. comp. Psychol.*, 1942, 33, 371–383.

36. Halverson, H. M. The acquisition of skill in infancy. *J. genet. Psychol.*, 1933, 43, 3–48.

37. Harris, R. E. An analysis of the maze-learning scores of bright and dull rats with reference to motivational factors. *Psychol. Rec.*, 1940, 4, 130–136.

38. Hayes, Catherine. *The ape in our house.* N.Y.: Harper, 1951.

39. Hayes, K. J., and Hayes, Catherine. The intellectual development of a home-raised chimpanzee. *Proc. Amer. philos. Soc.*, 1951, 95, 105–109.

40. Hayes, K. J., and Hayes, Catherine. Imitation in a home-raised chimpanzee. *J. comp. physiol. Psychol.*, 1952, 45, 450–459.

41. Hayes, K. J., and Hayes, Catherine. The cultural capacity of the chimpanzee. *Human Biol.*, 1954, 26, 288–303.

42. Hebb, D. O. *The organization of behavior.* N.Y.: Wiley, 1949.

43. Heron, W. T. The inheritance of brightness and dullness in maze learning ability in the rat. *J. genet. Psychol.*, 1941, 59, 41–49.

44. Hilgard, J. R. The effect of early and delayed practice of memory and motor performances studied by the method of co-twin control. *Genet. Psychol. Monogr.*, 1933, 14, 493–567.

45. Hirsch, J., and Tryon, R. C. Mass screening and reliable individual measurement in the experimental behavior genetics of lower organisms. *Psychol. Bull.*, 1956, 53, 402–410.

46. Hofstaetter, P. R. Testuntersuchungen an japanischen Kindern und das Reifungsproblem. *Z. Kinderforsch.*, 1937, 46, 71–112.

47. Hooker, D. *The prenatal origin of behavior.* Lawrence: Univer. Kansas Press, 1952.

48. Hunt, E. L. Establishment of conditioned responses in chick embryos. *J. comp. physiol. Psychol.*, 1949, 42, 107–117.

49. Itard, J. M. G. *The wild boy of Aveyron.* (Transl. by G. and M. Humphrey.) N.Y.: Appleton-Century-Crofts, 1932.

50. Kellogg, W. N. A further note on the "wolf children" of India. *Amer. J. Psychol.*, 1934, 46, 149–150.

51. Kellogg, W. N., and Kellogg, Luella A. *The ape and the child.* N.Y.: Whittlesey House, McGraw-Hill, 1933.

52. Kuo, Z. Y. Ontogeny of embryonic behavior in aves: I. The chronology and general nature of the behavior of the chick embryo. *J. exp. Zool.*, 1932, 61, 395–430.

53. Kuo, Z. Y. Ontogeny of embryonic behavior in aves: III. The structure and environmental factors in embryonic behavior. *J. comp. Psychol.*, 1932, 13, 245–272.

54. Kuo, Z. Y. Ontogeny of embryonic behavior in aves: IV. The influence of embryonic movements upon the behavior after hatching. *J. comp. Psychol.*, 1932, 14, 109–122.

55. Kuo, Z. Y. Development of acetylcholine in the chick embryo. *J. Neurophysiol.*, 1939, 2, 488–493.

56. Levinson, B. Effects of fetal radiation on learning. *J. comp. physiol. Psychol.*, 1952, 45, 140–145.

57. Lindsley, D. B. Heart and brain potentials of human fetuses in utero. *Amer. J. Psychol.*, 1942, 55, 412–416.

58. Luchins, A. S., and Forgus, R. H. The effect of differential post-weaning environment on the rigidity of an animal's behavior. *J. genet. Psychol.*, 1955, 86, 51–58.

59. Milner, Esther. A study of the relationships between reading readiness in grade one school children and patterns of parent-child interaction. *Child Develpm.*, 1951, 22, 95–112.

60. Munn, N. L. *The evolution and growth of human behavior.* Boston: Houghton Mifflin, 1955.

61. Pratt, K. C. The neonate. In L. Carmichael (Ed.), *Manual of child psychology.* (2nd Ed.) N.Y.: Wiley, 1954. Pp. 215–291.

62. Riess, B. F. The effect of altered environment and of age on mother-young relationships among animals. *Ann. N. Y. Acad. Sci.,* 1954, 57, 606–610.

63. Rundquist, E. A. Inheritance of spontaneous activity in rats. *J. comp. Psychol.,* 1933, 16, 415–438.

64. Scott, J. P. Genetic differences in the social behavior of inbred strains of mice. *J. Hered.,* 1942, 33, 11–15.

65. Scott, J. P. New directions in the genetic study of personality and intelligence. *Eugen. News,* 1953, 38, 97–101.

66. Scott, J. P., and Charles, Margaret S. Some problems of heredity and social behavior. *J. gen. Psychol.,* 1953, 48, 209–230.

67. Scott, J. P., and Fuller, J. L. Research on genetics and social behavior at the Roscoe B. Jackson Memorial Laboratory, 1946–1951—a progress report. *J. Hered.,* 1951, 42, 191–197.

68. Searle, L. V. The organization of hereditary maze-brightness and maze-dullness. *Genet. Psychol. Monogr.,* 1949, 39, 279–325.

69. Shirley, Mary M. A motor sequence favors the maturation theory. *Psychol. Bull.,* 1931, 28, 204–205.

70. Shirley, Mary M. *The first two years:* Vol. I. *Postural and locomotor development.* Vol. II. *Intellectual development.* Minneapolis: Univer. Minn. Press, 1931, 1933.

71. Silverman, W., Shapiro, F., and Heron, W. T. Brain weight and maze learning in rats. *J. comp. Psychol.,* 1940, 30, 279–282.

72. Singh, J. A. L., and Zingg, R. M. *Wolf-children and feral man.* N.Y.: Harper, 1942.

73. Smith, Marian W. Wild children and the principle of reinforcement. *Child Develpm.,* 1954, 25, 115–123.

74. Spelt, D. K. The conditioning of the human fetus *in utero. J. exp. Psychol.,* 1948, 38, 338–346.

75. Sperry, R. W. Mechanisms of neural maturation. In S. S. Stevens (Ed.), *Handbook of experimental psychology.* N.Y.: Wiley, 1951. Pp. 236–280.

76. Squires, P. C. Wolf children of India. *Amer. J. Psychol.,* 1927, 38, 313–315.

77. Stockard, C. R., Anderson, O. D., and James, W. T. *Genetic and endocrine basis for differences in form and behavior.* Philadelphia: Wistar Inst. Press, 1941.

78. Stone, C. P. Methodological resources for the experimental study of innate behavior as related to environmental factors. *Psychol. Rev.,* 1947, 54, 342–347.

79. Stratton, G. M. Jungle children. *Psychol. Bull.,* 1934, 31, 596–597.

80. Strayer, L. C. Language and growth: the relative efficacy of early and deferred vocabulary training, studied by the method of co-twin control. *Genet. Psychol. Monogr.,* 1930, 8, 209–319.

81. Tait, C. D., Jr., Wall, P. D., Balmuth, Muriel, and Kaplan, S. J. Behavioral changes following radiation. II. Maternal behavior and maze performance. *USAF, Sch. Aviat. Med.,* 1952. Spec. Rep. ii.

82. Thompson, W. R., and Heron, W. The effects of restricting early experience on the problem-solving capacity of dogs. *Canad. J. Psychol.,* 1954, 8, 17–31.

83. Thompson, W. R. The heredity-environment problem. *Bull. Marit. psychol. Ass.,* 1955, 30–40.
84. Tinbergen, N. *The study of instinct.* London: Oxford Univer. Press, 1951.
85. Tryon, R. C. The genetics of learning ability in rats: preliminary report. *Univer. Calif. Publ. Psychol.,* 1929, 4, 71–89.
86. Tryon, R. C. Genetic differences in maze-learning ability in rats. *39th Yearb., Nat. Soc. Stud. Educ.,* 1940, Part I, 111–119.
87. Whiting, J. W. M., and Child, I. L. *Child training and personality: a cross-cultural study.* New Haven: Yale Univer. Press, 1953.
88. Wickens, D. D., and Wickens, Carol. A study of conditioning in the neonate. *J. exp. Psychol.,* 1940, 25, 94–102.
89. Zingg, R. M. Feral man and extreme cases of isolation. *Amer. J. Psychol.,* 1940, 53, 487–517.
90. Zingg, R. M. Reply to Professor Dennis' "The significance of feral man." *Amer. J. Psychol.,* 1941, 54, 432–435.

CHAPTER 5

Physique and Behavior

The psychologist who wishes to study the relationships between physique [1] and behavior may pursue any one of several avenues of investigation. The principal available approaches to this problem, which were outlined in the preceding chapter, include the comparative analysis of physical characteristics in strains selectively bred for behavior traits, the examination of physical changes that parallel behavior development, the artificial alteration of structural conditions, and the investigation of relationships between individual differences in physical and psychological characteristics. It is with the last of these four approaches that the differential psychologist has been primarily concerned. And it is this approach that will be examined more fully in the present chapter.

The study of relationships between physique and behavior is relevant to a number of questions, both theoretical and practical. First, such research should contribute toward an understanding of the etiology of behavior. Not only is the role of structural factors in behavior an important area of investigation in its own right, but its clarification also represents one step toward the identification of hereditary factors in behavior development. It will be recalled that in so far as heredity affects behavior, it must do so through the medium of structural characteristics. Another theoretical question which has stimulated many studies on physique and behavior pertains to the distribution and organization of traits. The research on constitutional types, to be discussed in Chapter 6, falls into this category. From a practical standpoint, interest in the relationship of physique to behavior stems from the possibility of assessing people and predicting behavior on the basis of physical characteristics.

[1] For convenience, the term "physique" is herein used to designate all structural characteristics of the individual, including anatomical, physiological, and biochemical properties.

behavior has been produced. It is not an illusory or overgeneralized association, as in the case of the three types of fallacies discussed above. However, it is important that the origin of such an association be correctly identified. The correlation should not be attributed to hereditary linkages, constitutional factors, and the like.

VARIETIES OF RELATIONSHIP BETWEEN PHYSIQUE AND BEHAVIOR

It is obviously not enough to establish that a correlation exists between certain physical and psychological characteristics. Even when proper methodological controls are applied and a significant correlation is found, it is of paramount importance, both theoretically and practically, to find out what causes the association. In the present section we shall consider the types of relationships that may bring about a significant correlation between physique and behavior.

When any two variables, A and B, are correlated, the causal relations involved may be reduced basically to one of three types, or to some combination of these types: A may cause B, B may cause A, or both A and B may result from a third variable, C. Applying such an analysis to physique and behavior, we may begin by considering the first type of relation, in which *physique influences behavior*. This relationship may itself be manifested in a variety of ways. At one extreme we find neural or glandular abnormalities which set rigid limits to behavior development. Examples are provided by such pathological conditions as the extremely small and defective brain found in certain forms of feeblemindedness or by the underactive thyroid of the cretin. In such cases, the "minimum structural prerequisites" for normal behavior development are absent. It is becoming increasingly apparent, however, that among the large majority of individuals the direct control of behavior by structural factors is not very rigid. Beyond a certain essential minimum, further differences in structural characteristics are not necessarily accompanied by corresponding differences in behavior. To put it differently, the structural equipment of most individuals permits a very wide latitude in behavior development.

A somewhat less direct influence of physique upon behavior is that illustrated by severe sensory or motor handicaps which reduce normal social intercourse and interfere with education. Although these conditions ordinarily impose severe restrictions on intellectual progress and social adjustment, it is nevertheless possible to overcome the limitations in individual cases through suitable adaptations of educational techniques. That such physical handicaps can be circumvented is vividly demonstrated by the career of the deaf-blind Helen Keller and by cases of cerebral palsied students who attain the Ph.D. degree.

Still more indirect are the psychological effects of such conditions as chronic illness or dietary deficiencies which may lead to excessive fatigability, low motivation, and poor endurance. These handicaps tend to retard school progress, interfere seriously with participation in sports, and in other ways limit intellectual and social development. Finally, physique may affect behavior through the operation of social stereotypes. Whether a person is conspicuously tall or short, fat or thin, muscular or puny, blond or brunet— these and many other characteristics may serve as stimuli for the responses of other people toward him. They may influence the attitudes he encounters, the opportunities he is given, and even his own self percept. Through these channels, his behavior may gradually tend to approximate that demanded by the stereotype.

In a survey of certain types of relationship between physique and behavior, Barker *et al.* (7) proposed the term "somatopsychological" for all but the first of the relations described above. They excluded neural and glandular factors, since they were primarily concerned with the relatively indirect, social and psychological influences of physique upon behavior. Their survey covers data on somatopsychological effects associated with normal variations in body size, strength, and physical attractiveness; auditory and visual disabilities; orthopedic conditions; tuberculosis; and acute illness in general. From a methodological angle, Barker and his co-workers point out that the somatopsychological effects of the same physical condition may vary widely from person to person, since each individual may respond differently to his disability or other structural characteristic. Consequently, relationships that are discernible in case studies may tend to be obscured in group trends.

The area of somatopsychological relationships, as defined by Barker *et al.*, is undoubtedly an important one for psychologists to explore further. In considering the ways in which physique may influence behavior, however, we should not lose track of the fact that all categories are arbitrary, since what we actually have is a continuous gradation from the most direct and rigidly limiting type of relation to the most indirect and flexible. We have illustrated four levels in this continuum; and Barker and his associates have coined a useful term for a certain region within the continuum. But examples can easily be found to represent more degrees and varieties of relationships than those cited. It should also be borne in mind that once a certain behavior characteristic has been traced to a physical basis, we may still know nothing about its hereditary or environmental origin. Specific physical characteristics, such as an underdeveloped brain, may themselves be the result of either hereditary or environmental factors.

The second major type of relationship outlined at the opening of this section is that in which *behavior influences physique.* The powerful shoulder muscles of the swimmer and the scholar's stoop both reflect the effects of habitual activity. Smiles and frowns eventually leave their marks upon the human countenance. Investigations on immigrant groups have demonstrated that such characteristics as stature and even skull shape may be influenced by culturally determined experiences (cf. Ch. 16). Additional examples are provided by the many physiological changes occurring during emotional excitement.

Of special interest in this connection are psychosomatic disorders (cf. 5, 21). These are physical disorders in whose development psychological factors are believed to play a contributing or even a determining part. Gastric ulcers, asthma, and allergies are among the most frequently mentioned psychosomatic diseases, although psychological conditions have been considered as possible contributing factors in almost every known illness. So prevalent is the belief that worry, tension, and excessive drive are related to gastric ulcers that this ailment has sometimes been described as "Wall Street stomach." In general, anxiety and emotional stress are the psychological factors associated most commonly with psychosomatic disorders.

Interest in psychosomatic disorders has stimulated the gathering of a mass of data on the personality characteristics of patients suffering from a variety of diseases, including cancer (cf., e.g., 27). The results of many of these studies do not, of course, permit an analysis of causal relations. Longitudinal investigations of individual cases, as well as the recording of changes in physical condition associated with specific emotional experiences and other events in the patient's life, are more likely to shed light upon cause and effect relations (cf. 5). Animal experimentation offers another promising approach, since it has proved possible to induce in animals pathological symptoms similar to some of the psychosomatic disorders observed in humans (10).

The third and last possible type of relation between physique and behavior is that in which the association results from the *common influence of a third factor.* One of the clearest examples of this sort of relationship is to be found in the influence of socioeconomic level. For instance, the child reared in a superior home will have richer opportunities for intellectual development, as well as better diet, hygiene, and medical care, than the child who grows up in a city slum or poor rural area. As a result, some positive correlation would be obtained between intelligence and a number of physical conditions within a group varying widely in socioeconomic background. The correlation may disappear, however, if socioeconomic level is held constant. In evaluating the findings of any study purporting to show a relationship between physical and psychological characteristics, we should be on the lookout for possible "third factors" which may account for the correlation.

In the sections that follow, we shall examine typical findings on the relationships between various aspects of physique and behavior. The data will be considered under the following headings: pathological conditions, physiological factors, sensory handicaps, anatomical dimensions, and developmental relations.

PATHOLOGICAL CONDITIONS

Extreme Behavioral Disorders. There are a number of well-known varieties of intellectual and emotional disorders that are directly traceable to glandular malfunctioning, gross cerebral malformations, the effects of poisons or infections on the central nervous system, and other pathological conditions. The behavior symptoms associated with paresis, delirium tremens, and cretinism, for example, can be clearly related to the physical effects of syphilitic infection, alcohol, and thyroid deficiency, respectively. The underdeveloped and defective brains found in certain forms of feeblemindedness and the severe metabolic disturbances identified in others provide further examples of the psychological effects of extreme physical disorders which interfere with the normal development or functioning of the nervous system. For the largest proportion of feebleminded persons, on the other hand, no physical basis for the intellectual deficiency has yet been discovered. We shall return to a more detailed discussion of the varieties and causes of feeblemindedness in Chapter 12.

In the case of certain disorders, such as schizophrenia, the causal factors are still largely unknown. Considerable evidence has been accumulated to indicate that cerebral malfunctioning of one sort or another is more common among schizophrenics than among normals (13). Such evidence includes deficiencies of certain chemicals in the brain cells, degeneration and miscellaneous abnormalities of cortical neurones, presence of toxic substances in the blood, endocrine dysfunction, and abnormal electroencephalograms.

It is likely that different factors may lead to different forms of schizophrenia, or even that the same symptoms may result from dissimilar causes in different persons. Moreover, experiential or psychological factors may combine with physiological factors or may in some cases be the sole basis for the development of schizophrenia. The fact that schizophrenia is not a single entity, but rather a broad category covering a variety of behavioral disorders, further complicates the picture. Consideration should also be given to the possible physiological effects of emotional stress, degree of activity, nutritional conditions, and other variables related both to psychotic state and to institutional living. Horwitt (38) has pointed out that such factors may exert a marked influence upon certain of the physiological measures in which schizophrenics and normals have been compared. There is thus danger of confusing cause and effect in some of the reported relations.

It is apparent that much more research is required before a definitive statement can be formulated regarding the causes of schizophrenia. Even less has been conclusively established in the case of other psychoses, such as manic-depressive disorders. For at least some patients, it is possible that psychotic symptoms may represent a purely "functional" disorder, with no organic pathology. In other words, there may be no structural abnormality that caused the disorder, although physical disturbances may develop subsequently. On the other hand, some psychologists and psychiatrists are of the opinion that all pronounced personality disturbances have physical bases, although the latter may remain undiscovered so far.

In evaluating the findings of research in this area, the following points should be borne in mind. First, the same symptom may result from different causes in different individuals. Second, severe disorders of the central nervous system always produce major behavioral deviations. At the same time, pronounced behavioral abnormalities need not imply the presence of corresponding structural deficiencies. Third, once a physical basis is identified for a psychological disorder, the problem of tracing the physical condition to a hereditary or environmental origin still remains.

Miscellaneous Physical Defects and Intelligence. A group of early investigations were concerned with the relative frequency of minor physiological disorders among school children differing in intellectual level. The conditions surveyed were those commonly found during routine medical examinations of school children, including such defects as infected tonsils, adenoids, enlarged glands, decayed teeth, malnutrition, and skin diseases. Intellectual level was determined by either intelligence tests or records of school achievement. Some of these surveys failed to reveal any relationship between physical defects and intelligence (55, 76, 86). Others found a small but consistent tendency for nearly every type of defect to occur more often among dull than among normal school children, and more often among the normal than among the intellectually superior (6, 42, 67). In the latter studies, the total number of defects per child also tended to be greatest among the dull and smallest among the bright, while the number of children free from any defect was highest in the bright and lowest in the dull group.

In interpreting these findings, we need to remember that, even when significant group differences were obtained, they were small and left room for many individual exceptions. In any survey, we can find a sizable proportion of dull children who are completely free from physical defects, as well as bright children who suffer from one or more disorders. Then there is the possible effect of socioeconomic factors to be taken into account. Children from poorer homes are more likely to be intellectually duller and to exhibit more physical deficiencies than those from better homes. The extent to which socioeconomic level varied within each survey may be one of the reasons for discrepancies in their findings.

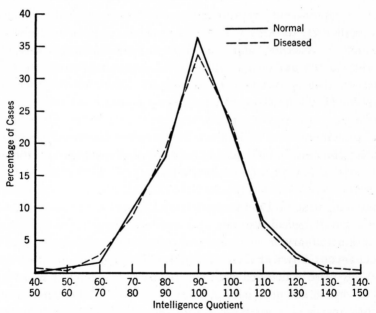

Fig. 32. Percentage Distribution of IQ's of Boys with Normal and with Diseased Tonsils. (Data from Rogers, 66, p. 29.)

In a carefully conducted investigation of the effects of diseased tonsils, Rogers (66) classified boys from a single public school into those with normal tonsils (N = 294) and those with diseased tonsils (N = 236). The mean Stanford-Binet IQ's of the two groups were 95.4 and 94.9, respectively, a difference that is not statistically significant. Moreover, the two distributions showed virtually complete overlapping, as illustrated in Figure 32. It is likely that socioeconomic background was more homogeneous in this group than in those examined in some of the previously cited surveys.

General observations have suggested that children with hookworm infection tend to be intellectually dull, sluggish, and apathetic—a conclusion that has been supported by several studies. A carefully controlled investigation in a typical "hookworm area" in this country was conducted by Smillie and Spencer (73). When the children were classified into five categories on the basis of intensity of infection, the mean IQ varied consistently from 76.3 in the most heavily infected group to 90.2 in the group free from this condition. The correlation between degree of hookworm infestation and IQ among individual children was .30, which is significant at the .01 level (62, p. 196). Socioeconomic factors may again account for much of this association, since hookworm infection is most prevalent where hygienic conditions are poor.

A somewhat more direct approach to the whole problem is provided by "before-and-after" studies, in which the same subjects are retested after treatment for a particular disorder. In such investigations it is important to include a control group suffering from the same disorder and equated with the experimental group in all relevant characteristics, but receiving no treatment. When adequate controls were employed, no significant change in intelligence test scores was observed following treatment for such conditions as dental caries (cf. 62, Ch. 6) or diseased tonsils (36, 52, 65, 66). All in all, available evidence on the type of physiological disorders considered in the present section shows little or no effect of these conditions upon the intellectual level of school children.

Somatopsychological Effects of Illness. Some of the associations found between physiological disorders and intelligence may result from somatopsychological factors (7, 19, 26). Such effects are more likely to be noticeable, however, in the case of highly disabling illnesses. In a study of 101 children who had had poliomyelitis, Stanford-Binet IQ's obtained a year following the illness were compared to pre-polio IQ's taken from the school files (63). A carefully matched control group of children who had not had polio was similarly tested. The results showed a mean drop of 1.5 IQ points in the polio group, in contrast to a mean rise of 2 points in the control group. Although the mean retest IQ differed significantly between the two groups (at the .02 level), it should be noted that neither the gain of the control group nor the loss of the polio group was statistically significant in itself. Such results must therefore be regarded as suggestive rather than conclusive. A special study of 22 cases who sustained large losses in IQ showed these subjects to have had a relatively severe form of the disease. From these data alone, it is of course impossible to determine whether the losses resulted from brain damage or from educational handicap and similar somatopsychological effects of the motor disorder.

A similar problem is encountered in cerebral palsy, where some progress has been made in isolating the two types of effects. There is evidence indicating that in certain cerebral palsied patients the lesion is at the cortical level and intellectual deficiency is of the sort usually associated with organic disorders, while in others the lesion is subcortical and the observed mental retardation results from educational and social handicap (16; 68, Ch. 7).

Reference has already been made to the survey prepared by Barker *et al.* (7) on the somatopsychological effects of physical disabilities. The studies summarized in this survey include both children and adults, and cover a wide variety of orthopedic handicaps, tuberculosis, and the psychological aftermath of prolonged or severe illness in general. Intelligence test data reported in a few of these studies reveal no consistent evidence of intellectual deterioration. The major emphasis of the survey, however, is on emotional and social adjustment. In general, the degree of emotional disturbance found seems to be related, not so much to the nature of the physical condition, as to duration and severity of handicap, cultural background of the patient, and social and personal relations in his home. It should be repeated that different patients' responses to the same illness may vary widely because of other concomitant circumstances. Hence group trends may give an inadequate picture of the full somatopsychological effects.

PHYSIOLOGICAL FACTORS

The search for physiological factors that may be related to individual differences in behavior is being vigorously pursued by psychologists, physiologists, biochemists, and members of other related professions. Several new avenues of investigation have recently been opened. Much has been learned about the role of various physiological factors in behavior pathology. At the same time, attempts to relate behavioral differences within the normal range to physiological characteristics have met with much less success. Consequently, work in the latter area must still be regarded as exploratory and suggestive.

Electroencephalography. A promising and rapidly growing field of brain research centers around the *electroencephalogram* (EEG). a record of the minute changes in electrical potential generated in the brain (22, 28, 51, 59). A special advantage of this technique is that it permits a study of brain function in the living organism. Since many important properties of tissues are lost upon death, post-mortem brain examinations may exclude essential facts. By means of electrodes attached to the scalp, the minute "brain waves," or fluctuations of electrical potential in the brain of the living person, are picked up, magnified, and recorded graphically. Several types of rhythmic changes in electrical potential, differing in frequency and amplitude, have been identified in the adult human brain. Some of the most clear-cut results have been obtained with the *alpha waves,* which have an average frequency of about ten per second and are found in normal children and adults during a relaxed waking state. Fairly consistent age differences have been observed in the frequency and amplitude of these alpha waves, as well as in the percentage of time that the alpha rhythm is present. Between the ages of 3 and 10, for example, there is a progressive increase in the frequency of the alpha rhythm. Sufficient data have been gathered to establish age norms in various aspects of the EEG. Individual differences in EEG have also been observed, the individual characteristics being maintained with considerable consistency on successive retests.

Such findings have led certain investigators to inquire whether the developmental changes in EEG are related primarily to chronological age or to mental age. In studies on several types of feebleminded adults, Kreezer (46, 47) reported a number of significant but generally low correlations between mental age and certain characteristics of the alpha waves. Several points should be noted, however, in interpreting these results. First, the groups studied were usually small and many of the correlations were barely significant. Second, different characteristics of the alpha waves yielded significant correlations in different types of feeblemindedness, suggesting that whatever relationship exists is certainly not a simple one. Third, the significant relationships were confined to types of feeblemindedness having other clearly recognizable physical deficiencies. They were not substantiated in a group of "undifferentiated" feebleminded cases with no observable physical pathology. This suggests that the disturbance in EEG may be associated with the other pathological physical conditions and need have no implications within the normal range of variation. Other investigators have also failed to discover any significant relationship between EEG characteristics and intellectual level among undifferentiated feebleminded subjects (cf. 22, 51).

What little direct evidence is available on the relation of EEG to intellectual level in normal subjects is also negative. In one study on normal

children (45), for example, a significant correlation of .50 was found between alpha frequency and IQ among 48 8-year-olds, but an insignificant
correlation of .12 was obtained among 42 12-year-olds. It is possible that,
among the younger children, individual differences in the level of physical
development within a single year of chronological age may account for the
significant correlation. In a group of 1100 aircrew candidates between the
ages of 18 and 33, no relationship was found between intelligence test score
and alpha frequency (71).

In the area of personality characteristics and emotional abnormalities,
EEG results are inconclusive, with the exception of the extensive body of
data on epilepsy. It has been quite clearly established that epileptics show
characteristic deviations in EEG, and that relatives of epileptics who have
not themselves developed any of the clinical symptoms of epilepsy show
similar disorders in EEG (50, 51). Findings in the case of schizophrenia
have already been referred to in the preceding section. It is also interesting
to note that several studies of children with behavior disorders show abnormalities of the EEG, some of them of an epileptoid form (17, 43, 51, 56).
We can probably attach little significance to the fact that attempts to
correlate personality test scores and EEG characteristics in adults as well as
children have yielded inconsistent and inconclusive results (22, 34, 51). In
such cases, the inadequacy of the personality tests as measures of behavior
characteristics may have been partly responsible for the negative findings.
Saul, Davis, and Davis (69) reported certain correspondences between
EEG patterns and a number of personality characteristics as determined
through psychoanalytic case studies of 136 adult patients. But their results
are suggestive rather than conclusive.

Autonomic Responses. A number of investigations have been concerned
with *autonomic balance,* by which is meant the extent to which the sympathetic or parasympathetic branch of the autonomic nervous system pre-
dominates in the individual's responses. In a series of studies, Wenger (82,
83, 84, 85) developed an index of autonomic balance which exhibited a
fair amount of day-by-day stability within the individual and showed some
relation to personality characteristics. Suggestive positive results were obtained with both children and air force men, although the relationships
between autonomic balance and personality variables were low, and clear-
cut correspondences could be discerned only among subjects at the extremes
of the autonomic balance distribution.

Subsequent research by other investigators suggests greater specialization
of autonomic function than is implied by the concept of general autonomic
balance. Lacey and his co-workers (48, 49) have found evidence of *auto-*

nomic response specificity in subjects' reactions to several types of mild stress. Their data show that, when re-examined under four different stress conditions, subjects tended to manifest the same pattern of autonomic responses significantly more often than would be expected by chance. For example, some subjects would repeatedly give their maximum reaction in palmar conductance (reflecting sweat gland activity), others in heart rate, and so on. Lacey and his associates suggest that, in seeking correlations between autonomic reactivity and personality indices, it may be more fruitful to correlate the individual's maximum autonomic response in any measure with personality variables, rather than to investigate each autonomic measure separately. In support of this recommendation, they cite a correlation of .47 ($P < .02$) between Form-Color Index on the Rorschach test (alleged to be an index of "emotionality") and extent of maximum autonomic reaction in a group of 26 male college students. Use of separate autonomic measures in the same group had yielded insignificant correlations.

Following a different approach, Terry (81) computed intercorrelations among 22 autonomic measures obtained from 85 male college students under conditions of rest and of mild stress. By applying techniques of factor analysis (to be discussed in Chapter 10), he identified three separate factors, which he described as conductance, heart period, and blood pressure.

Biochemical Conditions.   The chemical composition of the blood, which constitutes the internal environment of the organism, is of prime importance in the normal functioning of the individual and in the maintenance of life itself. A large number of investigations have demonstrated pronounced behavior symptoms following changes in such conditions as the temperature, oxygen content, sugar content, or acid-base balance of the blood. One illustration is to be found in the well-known effects of oxygen deprivation—as in high altitudes—which include conspicuous alterations of sensory, motor, intellectual, and emotional responses. There is evidence that some of the blood conditions that produce temporary disturbances of cerebral functioning may lead to irreversible changes in the brain cells and thus effect permanent behavior modifications in the individual. Especially significant are agents of this sort operating in early childhood or during prenatal life. Severe anoxia (oxygen lack) at birth, for example, may produce brain damage leading to motor, intellectual, or emotional disorders throughout life.

A somewhat different question is whether individual differences in blood chemistry among normal adults are in any way related to behavior differences. It should be noted in this connection that the body has a number of regulatory mechanisms which preserve the stability of the internal environment within very narrow limits. The maintenance of this relatively stable state has been termed *"homeostasis."* One of the important regulatory mechanisms is provided by the action of various endocrine glands, which counteract chemical deficits or excesses in the blood composition. Owing to such internal safeguards, the composition of the blood does not vary widely among individuals or within the same individual *under ordinary conditions.* Despite this fact, hypotheses regarding the relationship between individual differences in blood composition and intellectual or personality traits have been plentiful. The study of the behavior correlates of blood chemistry is today an active field of research, but so far the data have been contradictory and disappointing. One of the most widely discussed of these possible relationships is that between emotional stability and homeostasis. There is some evidence (29) which suggests that the more neurotic individuals tend to exhibit greater daily fluctuations in blood composition than the better-adjusted persons. At best, however, the results on blood chemistry and behavior provide interesting leads for future research.

A related approach is illustrated by the biochemical research conducted by Williams and his associates (cf. 88, 89). The gist of their findings is that there are pronounced individual differences in metabolic patterns, as illustrated by the proportion of different constituents in the saliva and urine. Although in two popular books Williams has argued for joint biochemical and behavioral studies and has speculated at length about possible relations between individual differences in psychological and in biochemical characteristics, he has so far presented no data in support of such an association. Moreover, his excursions into psychological topics abound in loose and erroneous statements (cf. 3).

Biochemical correlates of behavior undoubtedly represent a promising area of research. Investigation of certain rare forms of feeblemindedness, for example, has demonstrated the far-reaching psychological effects of certain metabolic disorders (cf. Ch. 12). Whether "biochemical individuality" within the normal range of variation is related to psychological characteristics, however, remains an unanswered question for the present.

Glandular Activity.   It is well known that marked overactivity or underactivity of any of the endocrine glands may have a pronounced effect upon behavior (cf. 9). Within the range of normal variation, however, no significant relationship between glandular functioning and intellectual or emotional characteristics has been conclusively demonstrated. Among the most readily obtained indices of glandular activity is the familiar *basal metabolic rate* (BMR). This is a measure of the rate at which the body uses oxygen, which in turn depends upon the degree of activity of the thyroid gland. An abnormally low BMR can be raised by the administration of thyroid extract. Extreme underactivity of the thyroid results in cretinism, a condition characterized by feeblemindedness as well as by a number of clearly recognizable physical symptoms. Milder variations in BMR among normal adults or adolescents,[2] on the other hand, have consistently shown negligible or zero correlations with intelligence test scores in a number of investigations.

A possible association between mild glandular abnormalities and personality disorders is suggested by the relatively large incidence of glandular disorders among "problem children." In one survey (54) of 1000 children who were classified as behavior problems, 20 per cent showed some glandular defect. In 10 per cent, the glandular condition seemed to be a causal factor in the behavior disorder. That the relationship may not be so direct as these data imply is suggested by the variety of behavior disorders which are associated with the same type of glandular disorder. Conversely, the same kind of behavior disorder is found in children with entirely different glandular defects. As is true of many physical conditions, the relationship with behavior is general and not specific. A plausible hypothesis to account for the observed association between glandular disorders and behavior problems is based upon indirect social consequences of the abnormal physical condition, i.e., upon somatopsychological effects. If the glandular defect handicaps the child or renders him in any way different from other children, the behavior problem may simply represent the child's reaction to this abnormal situation.

Nutritional Factors. Serious food shortages in many countries following World War II gave special impetus to research on the effects of malnutrition. The rapid growth of the young science of nutrition likewise served to focus attention upon the amount and nature of food intake. The question that concerns us now is whether there are psychological effects of diet, apart from the well-known physical effects.

A group of early studies on malnutrition among American and English school children showed slight effects upon intellectual functioning (cf. 41; 62, Ch. 6). These results are ambiguous and inconclusive for several reasons. In some studies, failure to control socioeconomic level made any obtained correlation between nutritional status and intelligence suspect. When the effects of improved diet were investigated, it was often difficult to separate the influence of diet from that of uncontrolled motivational factors associated with the special attention shown the experimental group. Finally—and perhaps most important of all—the degrees of malnutrition studied were

---

[2] Data on BMR in children will be reported in the section on Developmental Relationships.

mild. Hence the results are inapplicable to the severe dietary deficiencies prevalent in many other parts of the world.

One of the few intensive and well-controlled experimental studies of the effects of nutrition upon human behavior is that conducted at the University of Minnesota by Keys and his co-workers (44). Thirty-six men between the ages of 21 and 33, who volunteered for the experiment, were kept for six months on a semistarvation diet described as characteristic of European famine conditions. As a standard, each subject's normal performance during a preliminary three-month period of adequate diet was recorded. Daily intake of calories averaged 3150 during the preliminary normal period and 1755 during the second, or experimental period. Average weight loss of the subjects during the semistarvation period amounted to about 25 per cent.

The clearest behavior change during the experimental period was a decline in strength and endurance in motor tasks, and a less marked but significant loss in motor speed and coordination. On a series of tests of intellectual functions, no change in either speed or level of performance was observed; nor was learning affected. In contrast to this lack of impairment as determined by objective tests, the subjects believed that they had deteriorated sharply. Self-ratings in alertness, concentration, comprehension, and judgment dropped markedly in the course of the experimental period. These differences are probably related to personality changes, which were conspicuous. Personality tests showed a statistically significant increase in depression, hysteria, hypochondria, nervous symptoms, feelings of inadequacy and inferiority, and introversion. Decrease in general activity, social withdrawal, obliteration of sexual drive, constriction of interests, and obsessive preoccupation with thoughts of food were likewise observed. In general, the authors report that their findings corroborate those of field studies on prisoners released from concentration camps and on persons living in communities with severe food shortages.

The third stage in the experiment consisted of a 12-week controlled nutritional rehabilitation period, in which the caloric intake was increased by different amounts in different subgroups. The effects on motor, intellectual, and personality functions paralleled, in reverse, the previous changes during semistarvation. Improvement was large in motor functions and in personality characteristics, but no significant change was found in intellectual functions. This experiment indicates that the behavior changes induced by semistarvation are reversible and remediable. It should be remembered, however, that such a finding applies to a six-month period of inadequate nutrition in adults. What would occur in a child, or following a longer privation period, we cannot infer.

Nutrition research has demonstrated that the *qualitative aspects* of diet are even more important than the quantitative. Animal experiments, as well as clinical observations on humans, have furnished ample evidence that serious physical disorders may result from the lack of one or more essential elements in the diet. Because of the known physiological effects of vitamins of the B-group upon the nervous system, special interest has centered on this group (cf. 44, 74). There is good evidence that a deficiency in B-vitamins reduces physical strength and endurance (12, 15). Clinical reports on patients with vitamin B deficiency have consistently mentioned irritability, moodiness, and lack of cooperation. In cases of more severe deficiency, apathy, depression, and emotional instability are observed. Relatively few well-controlled experimental studies on the effect of vitamin deficiencies upon human behavior are available, and most of the investigations have dealt with too few cases to be conclusive. In general, these studies show no diminution of intellectual functions, but only motor and personality changes (12, 30). Nor has the administration of excess vitamin B to normal individuals shown any consistent effects on behavior.

On the other hand, there is some evidence to suggest that administration of *thiamin* (one of the B-vitamins) to children whose diet has been deficient in vitamins may lead to significant improvements in certain behavior functions. A well-controlled experiment was conducted by Harrell (31) on matched pairs of orphanage children whose normal diet was relatively low in vitamin content. One member of each pair received regular thiamin pills, while the other received a placebo as a control. The procedure was such that neither the children nor any member of the orphanage staff knew which were the experimental and which the control children. Follow-ups over a two-year period showed a significant difference in favor of the thiamin-fed group in such tests as visual acuity, rote memory, and code-learning. The nature of the tests suggests that the advantage of the thiamin-fed group may have resulted largely from greater alertness and better ability to concentrate.

A later study by Harrell *et al.* (32) gave evidence that supplementing the maternal diet with thiamin and other vitamins during pregnancy and lactation may influence the child's subsequent intellectual development. Working with a group of mothers of low socioeconomic level whose normal diets were deficient, the investigators found significantly higher Stanford-Binet IQ's at the ages of three and four years among children whose mothers had received the vitamin supplement than among children whose mothers had been given placebos. The results of this study are consistent with those of experiments on white rats showing the influence of prenatal dietary deficiencies upon learning behavior (cf. 32).

A controversial research area concerns the effects of *glutamic acid* upon the intellectual development of mentally defective children. It is believed that glutamic acid, which is one of the essential amino acids derived from proteins, may influence intellectual development through its effect upon brain metabolism. Zimmerman and his associates (94, 95, 96), who are among the most vigorous exponents of this hypothesis, have reported significant IQ gains in feebleminded children following the administration of glutamic acid. But their results are inconclusive because of various methodological difficulties, and studies by other investigators have yielded inconsistent results (cf. 4, 25, 57). Even if positive results are conclusively established, there is still the question as to whether gains in test scores resulted from specific biochemical effects of glutamic acid on the brain or from more general effects of improved health and alertness. This is the type of question that needs to be asked in the final interpretation of any study on nutritional factors.

SENSORY HANDICAPS

Sensory limitations have a more direct bearing upon behavior than most other kinds of physical deficiency because they cut off environmental stimulation. The individual so handicapped is partially isolated from cultural contacts. For man, visual and auditory defects are obviously the most serious disorders. Since human culture is built to such a large extent upon a foundation of language—a language acquired principally through the eye and the ear—deficiencies in these sense modalities are of basic significance.

An impressive body of research literature on blindness and deafness has accumulated since World War II, and rapid strides have been made in the development of special educational techniques adapted to these handicaps (cf. 7, 11, 19, 61, 93). In line with current trends, there has also been a growing emphasis on improving the emotional and social adjustment of blind and deaf persons.

Any over-all estimate of the average intellectual level of deaf or blind children as a group is bound to be meaningless for a number of reasons. First, both deafness and blindness cover a wide range and variety of handicaps. In fact, no generally acceptable definition or system of classifying these disorders has yet been formulated. Second, most studies have been conducted on children attending either special day classes or residential schools for the deaf or blind. Such groups are likely to include cases of multiple handicaps, among which will be neurological disorders that may severely limit intellectual development. Certain selective factors may also operate in determining admission to these special programs. For example, a bright child with marginal vision or hearing is likely to succeed in a regular school situation, while a dull one with the same amount of deficiency may fail and therefore be enrolled in a special school. For this reason, too, spurious negative relationships may be found between severity of sensory handicap and intellectual level within an institutional population.

Third, those children enrolled in residential schools may show intellectual and emotional characteristics associated with institutional living, quite apart from the direct effects of their sensory handicap. Fourth, the intellectual achievement of deaf and blind children also depends upon the amount and nature of special education that has been available to them. Such training tends to compensate for the sensory isolation by providing necessary contacts with the social environment through other sensory channels. With the marked progress in methods of special instruction, it is to be expected that the mean IQ of children with sensory handicaps is higher today than it was twenty years ago, and that it will be still higher twenty years hence.

Fifth, the age of onset of blindness or deafness is likewise related to intellectual and emotional status, although the relationship is not a simple one. On the one hand, the later the loss occurs, the more opportunity the individual will have had for normal educational experiences. On the other hand, such an individual will have had less time to adjust to the defect, and may encounter more interference in the acquisition of the new reaction systems required by his condition. These two opposing influences probably account for the lack of correspondence often found between age of onset of sensory handicap and intelligence test performance or educational achievement. A sixth factor influencing the intellectual development of the deaf or blind child is his emotional response to the handicap. The attitudes of his family and associates, the general nature of the home milieu, and many other attendant circumstances will determine how effectively the individual adjusts to the handicap and will indirectly affect his educational and intellectual progress.

Visual Handicaps. Like other psychological characteristics, vision tends to follow a normal distribution in the general population. Between the large "normal" group and the totally blind, one finds innumerable degrees of handicap along a virtually continuous scale. Sharply distinguished categories are just as out of place here as in other aspects of individual differences. For practical purposes, a rough threefold classification has been in common use, including persons with correctable defects, the partially seeing, and the blind (87). *Correctable visual defects*, when actually corrected by the use of glasses, have no effect upon intellectual development. If the child

wears glasses from the time when the defect becomes appreciable, no interference with normal environmental contact results. When the defect is not
compensated by means of lenses, however, the child's schoolwork—and
indirectly his intellectual development—usually suffers. Inattention, lack of
interest in school, loss of self-confidence, and inferior performance may
result from unsuspected visual deficiencies.

The term *"partially seeing"* is applied to children whose visual deficiency
is so serious as to necessitate special instructional techniques in sight-saving
classes, where classroom procedures are adapted to a reduced use of vision.
The limits of this category have been set approximately between 20/70 and
20/100 vision in the better eye after maximum correction, although other
factors must also be taken into account. Children in sight-saving classes
represent a very heterogeneous group about whom it is difficult to make
any generalizations. No data are available on the intelligence test performance or academic achievement of a representative sample of such cases. The
somatopsychological picture is complicated by the presence of facial dis-
figurements in a number of these children.

The *blind* have been defined as those who cannot be educated through
visual means. Studies conducted in a large number of schools for the blind
have shown an average retardation of from two to three years in school
progress, but little or no inferiority in average intelligence test performance
(7, 33, 53). In one survey of seventeen schools covering 2372 pupils, the
over-all average IQ was 98.8, the means in different schools ranging from
108.1 to 92 (33). The distributions contained a slightly greater proportion of
very high IQ's and a considerably greater proportion of low IQ's than found
in the general sighted population. The test employed was a special adaptation of the Stanford-Binet prepared by Hayes for the blind. Similar results
have been obtained with adaptations of the Wechsler scales for children and
adults (cf. 8). For the reasons discussed above, these findings can be regarded only as descriptive of the institutional populations surveyed.

There is no evidence for the popular belief that the blind have a finer
discrimination than the sighted in other senses, such as hearing or touch.
The remarkable feats often accomplished by blind persons through the use
of other senses stem from more efficient utilization of sensory cues rather
than from superiority of the senses themselves. Through prolonged training,
an individual may acquire the ability to respond to very slight cues that are
ordinarily ignored. Such seems to be the case among the blind. The so-called
obstacle sense of the blind, which enables them to perceive obstacles in
their path, has been shown to be based primarily upon learned responses
to auditory cues (18, 91, 92).

In personality development, the adjustment made to the visual handicap varies widely with the individual. The range of personality characteristics is fully as wide among the blind as among the sighted. Barker *et al.* (7) and Lowenfeld (53) have analyzed the published data regarding the types of social and emotional problems commonly associated with blindness, as well as the varied ways in which individuals adjust to them. In evaluating the results obtained with most personality tests, it is important to note that many items have different interpretive significance for the blind and the sighted. For this reason, comparisons in terms of specific responses are much more meaningful than total estimates of maladjustment. Above all, it seems fairly clear that it is not the defect itself but its social implications that are at the basis of the insecurity and other emotional difficulties of the blind.

Auditory Handicaps. Contrary to popular belief, hearing deficiencies constitute a more serious handicap to intellectual development than do visual defects. Deafness in early childhood interferes more than blindness with language development and hence with normal social contacts. In the effort to gauge the extent of intellectual handicap resulting from auditory deficiency, we encounter the various methodological problems outlined at the opening of this section, chief among which is the basic question of definition and classification.

A common distinction is that between the hard-of-hearing and the deaf. It seems to be generally agreed that the latter term denotes a more serious handicap than the former—but there the agreement seems to end. Some authorities base the differentiation between the deaf and the hard-of-hearing on whether the loss of hearing occurred before or after the individual had learned to speak (87). According to this view, if the deaf learn to speak at all, they have to do so through nonauditory means. Other authorities have insisted that the only practicable classification is in terms of degree of loss, the deaf being those in whom the sense of hearing is nonfunctional for ordinary purposes, while the hard-of-hearing have functional hearing, with or without a hearing aid (cf. 60, p. 124). In a thorough analysis of the whole problem, Myerson (60) has proposed that all attempts at classification should be replaced by description of individual cases in terms of a number of parameters, including degree of hearing loss with special reference to ability to understand speech, age of onset of defect, type of communication used (speech, lip reading, finger spelling, etc.), and emotional and social adjustment to the handicap.

When we turn to the available studies on auditory deficiencies, however, we find subjects classified into the loosely defined categories given above. In general, investigations on the "hard-of-hearing" have dealt largely with the minor hearing deficiencies found in the ordinary school room; while those on the "deaf" have obtained their subjects from day or residential schools for the deaf, where special instructional methods were employed. It should be recognized that neither group is homogeneous in either the nature or degree of handicap and that there is some overlapping between them.

Among the *hard-of-hearing*, the auditory defect may escape recognition until an audiometric test is administered. The behavior of children with relatively mild auditory deficiencies may be mistaken for carelessness, indifference, rudeness, or dullness. Among the possible effects of such handicaps upon the child may be mentioned poor scholarship, speech defects, loss of interest in school, social withdrawal, and suspiciousness. It is noteworthy that children with hearing defects tend more often to be named by teachers as behavior problems (23). On verbal tests of intelligence, hard-of-hearing children average slightly below the norms. This difference disappears, however, when nonlanguage tests are substituted (cf. 60). In scholastic achievement tests, the hard-of-hearing tend to be retarded when compared with normal-hearing classmates matched in nonlanguage intelligence tests (24, 75).

A number of extensive test surveys have been conducted in schools for the *deaf* (cf. 60). Educationally, such groups have been found to be from three to five years retarded. Their retardation is least in such subjects as arithmetic and spelling, and greatest in language comprehension. On the usual verbal-type intelligence test, the deaf experience considerable difficulty because of their deficient mastery of language and linguistic concepts. So great is this handicap that verbal tests are generally considered inapplicable to deaf children, even though such tests may involve no spoken language. The problem of testing the deaf was, in fact, one of the principal reasons which led Pintner and others to the construction of the early nonlanguage and performance scales.

Even in such tests as the Pintner Non-Language Test, deaf children show retardation, their mean IQ's being of the order of 85 (cf. 60). On individual performance tests involving the manipulation of objects rather than the use of paper-and-pencil materials, the IQ's of deaf children fall closer to the norm, although they vary somewhat with the test. It is likely that some of this variation depends upon the degree to which language concepts aid in performance of the test. Since language serves an important function in so much of our thinking, the linguistic retardation occasioned by deafness may handicap the individual in a fairly broad area of intellectual activity. Also relevant are the results obtained in a well-controlled investigation by

Templin (79, 80), who found deaf children to be from four to eight years retarded in a series of reasoning tests.

It should be borne in mind, of course, that all such findings may change with the further development of special educational techniques. As Myerson has put it, "It is likely that the available data reflect to a far greater degree our ignorance of how to rear children with impaired hearing than they reflect any inherent characteristics of the deaf" (60, p. 139). A case in point is provided by those individuals formerly known as "deaf-mutes." These persons offer a vivid demonstration of the influence of environmental stimulation upon the development of an important behavior function. Never having heard the human voice, the "deaf-mute" is unable to speak, although his vocal organs are perfectly normal. The presence of human vocal organs does not in itself lead to the development of human speech, any more than any other structure ensures the appearance of the function ordinarily associated with it. That the deficiency of the "deaf-mute" is a stimulational one is shown by the fact that, with modern teaching methods based upon the use of other sensory cues, such individuals can be taught to speak.

With regard to personality, the deaf exhibit many of the behavior characteristics observed among other handicapped persons (cf. 7, 60). Test surveys of children in schools for the deaf show more symptoms of maladjustment and more behavior problems than among the normally hearing. Shyness and insecurity are frequently noted. Institutionalized deaf children likewise tend to fall below the norms in social maturity. How much of this difference results from institutionalization and how much from deafness is hard to say. Moreover, as in the case of blind children, some of the responses of deaf children may represent adequate normal reactions to their own life situation. Of special interest are the findings of one survey indicating that deaf children who came from homes in which there were deaf adults tended to be better adjusted than those reared in homes in which all the adults had normal hearing (64). This suggests the dependence of the deaf child's emotional adjustment upon proper adult understanding of the child's problems during his formative years. The presence of one or more other persons who share his handicap would also make the child feel less "different" and isolated.

ANATOMICAL DIMENSIONS

A very different set of factors whose relationships to behavior have been considered from a variety of viewpoints includes such anatomical characteristics as size and shape of head, form of face and of hands, and general body size. Available data on these factors illustrate several of the types of relationship between physical and psychological characteristics outlined at the beginning of this chapter. Such anatomical features have also played a major role in the pseudo-scientific systems of personality analysis exploited by charlatans from time to time.

Head Size and Shape.   Reference has already been made to phrenology which is based on a misinterpretation of the functioning of the cerebral cortex. Beginning with Gall in the eighteenth century, phrenologists have maintained that different areas of the brain control specific behavioral functions, such as mechanical ingenuity, veneration, domestic impulses, and other equally complex and vaguely defined activities. They asserted further that over- or underdevelopment of these traits could be diagnosed by examining the protrusions of the skull. The location of a particular "bump" was taken to mean that the function allegedly controlled by the corresponding cortical area was highly developed in the given individual.

It would seem unnecessary to refute such an obviously untenable doctrine were it not for its durable popularity among the gullible, who make possible its continuing practice by charlatans even today. In the first place, phrenology is founded upon the erroneous assumption that there is a close correspondence between the shape of the skull and that of the brain. Such a correspondence is hardly to be expected, in view of the cerebro-spinal fluid and the several layers of membrane which intervene between brain and skull. It should also be noted that size does not provide a satisfactory index of degree of development within the nervous system. It is the complexity of interrelation of the minute nerve cells and other microscopical characteristics of nerve matter that are more probably related to efficiency of function. Moreover, the type of trait which phrenologists ascribe to different brain areas is quite unlike the functions discovered through investigations of cortical localization. Connections have been demonstrated between certain muscle groups or sense organs and specific brain areas, but this is a far cry from the localization of "literary propensities" or "love of dumb animals" on the cortex!

Turning to less fanciful hypotheses, we find a number of large-scale investigations on the relationship between head size and intelligence, conducted during the first three decades of the present century (cf. 14; 62, Ch. 3). Such measures as head length, width, or height, as well as variously computed estimates of cubic cranial capacity, were correlated with indices of intelligence based upon teachers' ratings, scholastic achievement, or intelligence test performance. Data on college and university students, as well as on elementary and high school pupils, yielded correlations ranging from about .10 to about .20. Although usually significant at the .01 level because of the large number of cases from which they were derived, these correlations indicate a barely perceptible tendency for larger head size to be associated with superior intelligence. Moreover, in so far as head size is related to general body size, the slight degree of relationship found in these surveys may reflect no more than an association of body size with intelligence, to be discussed in a later section.

Some writers have proposed the hypothesis that long-headed persons tend to be more intelligent (cf. 62, pp. 116–121). Others have argued with equal vigor in favor of the opposite hypothesis, namely that broadheadedness is associated with superior intelligence (cf. 62, p. 122). Such hypotheses have been of special interest because of racial differences in head shape, to be considered in Chapter 16. The most widely used measure of head shape is the cephalic index, or ratio of head width to head length:

$$\text{CI} = \frac{\text{head width} \times 100}{\text{head length}}$$

Length of head is measured from the space between the eyebrows to the farthest projection at the back of the head. Head width, or breadth, is the distance from left to right sides, measured at the points of maximal protrusion above each ear. The following is a common classification of cephalic index:

Dolichocephalic (long-headed)	CI below 75
Mesocephalic (medium-headed)	CI between 75 and 80
Brachycephalic (broad-headed)	CI above 80

Investigations on large samples of school children and university students in Europe and America have consistently failed to reveal any significant relationship between cephalic index and intelligence. Neither dolichocephaly nor brachycephaly is indicative of superior intellectual ability.

Face and Hand Shape. A number of characteristics pertaining to facial conformation, hand shape, skin texture, hair and eye color, and the like have been loosely organized in popular systems of "physiognomy" for personality analysis. These systems have no more claim to scientific validity than phrenology. From time to time, however, psychologists have become interested in exploring possible relations between some of these anatomical features and intellectual or personality characteristics. A theoretical rationale which might account for such associations is to be found in endocrine functions. It is well known that extreme under- or overactivity of certain endocrine glands may markedly alter body size and proportions, shape of face and hands, coarseness of skin and hair, and other aspects of appearance. A clear-cut example of the joint effect of endocrine dysfunction on both physique and behavior is provided by cretinism, which results from thyroid under-activity. Such pathological conditions do not, of course, constitute evidence for an association within the normal range of variation. But at least they may suggest plausible hypotheses for investigation.

Several studies conducted under the direction of Hull (39, Ch. 4) were concerned with the relationship between carefully measured dimensions or other characteristics of the face and hands and a number of aptitude and personality variables. Psychological tests and associates' ratings provided the behavior measures. Among the physical traits investigated were convexity of profile, height of forehead, blondness, and a variety of other measures of the face and hands chosen so as to test traditional claims of physiognomists, palmists, and the like. All the relationships investigated yielded insignificant correlations.

More recently, Wolff (90), working in England, has proposed a number of hypotheses regarding hand characteristics and emotional reactions. Although she professes to have found evidence in support of these hypotheses, at least one attempt in this country to verify an alleged relationship between length of thumb and dominance yielded completely negative results (58). Some of the earlier data gathered by one of Hull's students also contradict specific claims made in Wolff's book.

Body Size. Are such gross indices of size as height and weight related to intelligence? That stunted physiques are more common among the feeble-minded than among intellectually normal or superior persons is amply demonstrated by several clinical varieties of feeblemindedness, to be discussed in Chapter 12. If we wish to explore the relationship of physique and intellect in the general population, however, we must exclude these pathological cases, since they would only complicate the picture.

Early studies of the relation of height and weight to indices of academic achievement and to intelligence test scores among college students yielded low and insignificant correlations. Some of these groups, however, were rather small, thus making the results inconclusive. Moreover, college students are much more homogeneous than the general population in intelligence, a fact that would tend to reduce correlations among the former.

A more recent study, conducted during World War II on a sample of 700 American soldiers, revealed consistent differences in mean height and weight among subgroups classified according to scores on the Army General Classification Test (2). Differences between extreme subgroups were large enough to be statistically significant. Similarly, in two random samples of 20-year-old Swedish men examined upon induction into compulsory military service, the correlations between height and intelligence test scores were .22 (N = 2257) and .20 (N = 4061), respectively (40). Both correlations are significant well beyond the .01 level. In a number of similar samples totaling over 7000 cases, the correlations between weight and intelligence test scores averaged .09. Although also significant at the same level, these correlations were much lower than in the case of height. The correlations of height and weight with intelligence remained virtually unchanged when recomputed in samples that were relatively homogeneous in socioeconomic background, such as rural workers. Even in the latter group, however, appreciable variation in socioeconomic level of homes undoubtedly remains. The most plausible explanation of the low but significant correlations found between body size and measures of intelligence would still seem to be that socioeconomic level affects both over-all physical development and opportunities for intellectual stimulation. There is extensive evidence to indicate, for example, that the mean height of the population has increased over successive generations as hygienic, dietary, and medical conditions improved.

Certain theories relate psychological characteristics, not to absolute size, but to body build. Do short, heavy-set people differ in personality from tall, slender individuals? Are bodily proportions related to behavior? Questions of this sort have formed an integral part of the various theories of constitutional types which have been proposed from time to time. Since the typological approach has other important implications for differential psychology, over and above the relationship between physique and behavior, these theories will be reserved for Chapter 6.

DEVELOPMENTAL RELATIONSHIPS

In the case of traits that show appreciable age changes, any correlations found among children should be considered apart from similar correlations obtained in adult groups. A relationship present in the growing organism may disappear when maturity is reached, since it may have resulted simply from developmental influences. It is obvious, of course, that a 10-year-old will excel a 5-year-old in both arithmetic and height. Thus if 10- and 5-year-olds are included within the same group, an artificial correlation will be obtained between arithmetic and height. Such a "spurious" correlation is usually eliminated through the use of relative measures (e.g., IQ) or through comparisons within a single age group. But these procedures do not rule out the entire contribution of developmental differences, since *children of the same chronological age may vary widely in the degree of physical development they have attained.*

There is no consistent relationship between developmental rate and adult status in physical characteristics. Data regarding age of onset of puberty furnish a good illustration of this point. Individuals who reach sexual maturity earlier are generally accelerated in physical development from early childhood (72). The age of onset of puberty is thus one manifestation of the individual's general rate of physical development. During childhood, the earlier-maturing individuals will be taller, heavier, and farther advanced in most physical characteristics than those who reach puberty later. But in adulthood, those who reached puberty earlier are *not* taller or heavier. In fact, a slight tendency has been found for earlier-maturing girls to be somewhat shorter during the late teens (72, 77). The tallest child in a group will not necessarily be the tallest twenty years later. The physical status of a child depends in part upon certain absolute factors which make some individuals, for example, taller than others throughout life, and in part upon individual differences in developmental rate.

In the light of these considerations, it is perhaps not surprising to find that correlations between anatomical or physiological characteristics and intelligence tend to run higher among children than among adults. These correlations are still quite low, rarely exceeding .30, but they are often high enough to indicate a statistically significant relationship (cf. 20, 37, 62). In an extensive study by Abernethy (1), for example, positive correlations were found between various anatomical measures and intelligence at all ages from 8 to 17, but the correlations tended to be lower in the groups that were approaching maturity. In a comparable adult group included in the same study, the correlations were virtually zero. There is also some evidence that "skeletal age," as determined by X-ray photographs of bone structure, is significantly correlated with intelligence in children, and that the correlation diminishes with age (20).

Some startlingly high correlations have been reported by Hinton (35) between basal metabolic rate and IQ in a group of 200 children ranging in age from 6 to 15. These correlations were close to .80 for the 6- to 9-year-old groups; from age 10 on they dropped fairly consistently, reaching a value of about .50 among the 15-year-olds. It will be recalled that investigations on adolescents and adults showed virtually zero correlations between BMR and intelligence. If Hinton's results are confirmed by other studies, they may provide an interesting illustration of age changes in the relationship between bodily conditions and behavior. It is known that the BMR tends to be higher during periods of rapid growth. If BMR is shown to be significantly related to intellectual level in childhood, this may help to explain many of the other correlations.

It has been argued that, in both their physical and psychological development, some individuals may progress at a more rapid rate than others throughout their period of growth. According to this hypothesis, it is these differences in *developmental rate* that may account for the slight positive correlations found between intelligence and certain bodily characteristics among children. It should be remembered, however, that growth does not occur at a uniform or regular rate within the individual, but exhibits many irregular spurts and lags. These temporary fluctuations in rate of growth are quite specific, and no parallelism has been discovered between psychological and physical fluctuations within individual growth curves. Thus the monthly or annual *increments* in structural and in intellectual status are generally uncorrelated (1, 20). Such a finding suggests that whatever relationship exists between bodily and behavioral development is probably an indirect one. For example, the child who is physically accelerated is likely to learn to walk—and possibly talk—earlier, thereby expanding his environmental contacts earlier than the slower-maturing individual. This advantage could account for a slight difference in intellectual development in favor of the earlier-maturing child. On the other hand, the temporary ups and downs in physical and psychological development seem to result from a multitude of unrelated factors, and offer no support to the theory of a "common underlying growth tendency."

The effect of puberty upon behavior development has itself been widely discussed. Contrary to popular belief, there is no evidence that intellectual development is either consistently accelerated or hindered by the onset of sexual maturity (1, 20). Nor is there any relationship between age of sexual maturity and either intellectual or personality characteristics in adulthood, when racial and cultural differences are held constant (1, 77). The onset of puberty does, in general, usher in changes in attitudes, interests, and emotional reactions. In one survey (78), significant differences were found between the personality test responses of prepubertal and postpubertal girls of the same chronological age and comparable socioeconomic and cultural status. Social factors undoubtedly play an important part in bringing about these personality changes, a fact vividly demonstrated by Barker *et al.* (7) in their discussion of somatopsychological effects of puberty.

SUMMARY

Relationships between physical and psychological characteristics are relevant to causal analyses of behavior, to theories of trait organization, and to practical problems of assessing people. Pseudo-scientific systems such as phrenology and physiognomy, as well as a number of popular stereotypes, are based upon alleged relations between physique and intelligence or personality. However erroneous, beliefs of this sort tend to survive because of the common practice of citing selected cases and overlooking negative instances; the tendency to generalize from pathological deviants to normal variations; and the influence of social stereotypes upon the individual's own self percept and upon the way he is perceived by others.

Correlations between physical and psychological traits may indicate that physique influences behavior (e.g., neurological or glandular disorders, somatopsychological effects), or that behavior influences physique (e.g., muscular exercise, psychosomatic disorders), or that both depend upon a third factor (e.g., socioeconomic level).

Pathological conditions may affect behavior in various ways. Severe intellectual or emotional disorders such as cretinism, paresis, and delirium tremens are the direct results of pronounced glandular or cerebral malfunctioning. In the case of other disorders, such as schizophrenia, suggestive evidence of physical correlates has been accumulated, but the causal mechanisms are still unknown. In at least some cases, emotional and intellectual disorders may be purely functional, with no organic pathology.

Surveys on school children have generally revealed a slight tendency for miscellaneous physiological defects to be more common among the duller than among the brighter pupils. There is evidence to suggest that socioeconomic differences may account for all or part of this relation. Prolonged or highly disabling illness, on the other hand, is likely to have somatopsychological effects.

Among the *physiological factors* whose relation to behavior has been explored may be mentioned the EEG, autonomic responses, biochemical conditions, glandular activity, and nutrition. Most of this research has so far yielded little positive information regarding behavior variations within the normal range, although several lines of investigation offer promising leads. The psychological effects of serious dietary deficiencies, as reported in field studies, have been verified under controlled conditions in such investigations as the Minnesota starvation project. Results obtained through the experimental administration of thiamin and glutamic acid are suggestive.

Sensory handicaps, such as deafness and blindness, interfere with intellectual development by limiting environmental contacts. Modern techniques of special education are designed to circumvent these limitations. For the child, deafness is a more serious psychological handicap than blindness because of the important part played by hearing in language development.

The definition and classification of degrees of blindness and deafness are among the unresolved methodological problems that make the available test results in this area ambiguous.

Psychologists have investigated the relation of intellectual and personality traits to a number of *anatomical dimensions* and other characteristics of appearance. Head size and body size show significant but low positive correlations with intelligence. Cephalic index (indicating head shape) is unrelated to ability. Nor is there any support for claims regarding associations between characteristics of the face or hands and personality. Certain correlations found between intelligence and anatomical or physiological traits among children may reflect *developmental relationships* only. In such cases, the correlation disappears when maturity is reached.

In summary, available research on physique and behavior has revealed no well-established relation high enough to be of practical value in assessing abilities or personality through physical signs. Such research has, however, provided causal explanations for a few pathological conditions. And it has opened up promising avenues for investigating causal factors in behavioral differences within the normal range, although no clear-cut relationships have been unequivocally demonstrated to date.

REFERENCES

1. Abernethy, Ethel M. Relationships between mental and physical growth. *Monogr. Soc. Res. Child Developm.*, 1936, 1, No. 7.
2. Altus, W. D. The height and weight of soldiers in association with scores earned on the Army General Classification Test. *J. soc. Psychol.*, 1949, 29, 201–210.
3. Anastasi, Anne. Review of R. J. Williams, "Free and unequal: the biological basis of individual liberty." *Hum. Biol.*, 1955, 27, 243–246.
4. Arbitman, H. D. The present status of glutamic acid therapy for mental deficiency. *Train. Sch. Bull.*, 1952, 48, 187–199.
5. Association for Research in Nervous and Mental Diseases. *Life stress and bodily disease.* Baltimore: Williams & Wilkins, 1950.
6. Ayres, L. P. The effect of physical defects on school progress. *Psychol. Clin.*, 1909–10, 3, 71–77.
7. Barker, R. G., *et al.*, *Adjustment to physical handicap and illness: a survey of the social psychology of physique and disability.* (Rev. Ed.) N.Y.: Soc. Sci. Res. Coun., 1953.
8. Bauman, Mary K., and Hayes, S. P. *A manual for the psychological examination of the adult blind.* N.Y.: Psychol. Corp., 1951.
9. Beach, F. A. *Hormones and behavior; a survey of interrelationships between endocrine secretions and patterns of overt responses.* N.Y.: Hoeber, 1948.
10. Beach, F. A. "Psychosomatic" phenomena in animals. *Psychosom. Med.*, 1952, 14, 261–276.

11. Berlinsky, S. Measurement of the intelligence and personality of the deaf: a review of the literature. *J. Speech Hearing Disorders*, 1952, 17, 39–54.

12. Berryman, G. H., *et al.* Effects upon young men consuming restricted quantities of B-complex vitamins and protein, and changes associated with supplementation. *Amer. J. Physiol.*, 1947, 148, 618–647.

13. Brackbill, G. A. Studies of brain dysfunction in schizophrenia. *Psychol. Bull.*, 1956, 53, 210–226.

14. Broom, M. E. Cranial capacity and intelligence. *Sch. and Soc.*, 1932, 36, 703–704.

15. Brozek, J., Guetzkow, H., Mickelsen, O., and Keys, A. Motor performance of normal young men maintained on restricted intakes of vitamin B complex. *J. appl. Psychol.*, 1946, 30, 359–379.

16. Catalano, F. L. The comparative performance of a group of cerebral palsied children in different intellectual functions. Unpublished doctoral dissertation, Fordham Univer., 1955.

17. Cattell, J. P., and Pacella, B. L. An electroencephalographic and clinical study of children with primary behavior disorders. *Amer. J. Psychiat.*, 1950, 107, 25–33.

18. Cotzin, M., and Dallenbach, K. M. "Facial vision": the role of pitch and loudness in the perception of obstacles by the blind. *Amer. J. Psychol.*, 1950, 63, 485–515.

19. Cruickshank, W. M. (Ed.) *Psychology of exceptional children and youth.* N.Y.: Prentice-Hall, 1955.

20. Dearborn, W. F., and Rothney, J. *Predicting the child's development.* Cambridge, Mass.: Sci-Art Pub., 1941.

21. Dunbar, Flanders. *Emotions and bodily changes.* (4th Ed.) N.Y.: Columbia Univer. Press, 1954.

22. Ellingson, R. J. Brain waves and problems of psychology. *Psychol. Bull.*, 1956, 53, 1–34.

23. Fiedler, Miriam F. Teachers' problems with hard of hearing children. *J. educ. Res.*, 1949, 42, 618–622.

24. Finger, F. W. Hearing deficiency and scholastic deficiency. *Amer. Psychologist*, 1948, 3, 293.

25. Gadson, E. J. Glutamic acid and mental deficiency—a review. *Amer. J. men. Def.*, 1951, 55, 521–528.

26. Garrett, J. F. (Ed.) *Psychological aspects of physical disability.* Washington, D.C.: U.S. Govt. Printing Office, 1952.

27. Gengerelli, J. A., and Kirkner, F. J. (Eds.) *The psychological variables in human cancer.* Berkeley and Los Angeles: Univer. Calif. Press, 1954.

28. Gibbs, F. A., and Gibbs, Erna L. *Atlas of electroencephalography.* (2nd Ed.) Cambridge, Mass.: Addison-Wesley Press, 1950–1952. (Vol. I and II.)

29. Goldstein, H. The biochemical variability of the individual in relation to personality and intelligence. *J. exp. Psychol.*, 1935, 18, 348–371.

30. Guetzkow, H., and Brozek, J. Intellectual functions with restricted intake of B-complex vitamins. *Amer. J. Psychol.*, 1946, 59, 358–381.

31. Harrell, Ruth F. Further effects of added thiamin on learning and other processes. *Teach. Coll., Columbia Univer., Contrib. Educ.*, 1947, No. 928.

32. Harrell, Ruth F., Woodyard, Ella, and Gates, A. I. *The effect of mothers' diets on the intelligence of the offspring.* N.Y.: Teach. Coll. Bur. Publ., 1955.

33. Hayes, S. P. *Contributions to a psychology of blindness.* N.Y.: Amer. Found. Blind, 1941.

34. Henry, C. E., and Knott, J. R. A note on the relationship between personality and the alpha rhythm of the electroencephalogram. *J. exp. Psychol.*, 1941, 28, 362–366.

35. Hinton, R. T. A further study on the role of the basal metabolic rate in the intelligence of children. *J. educ. Psychol.*, 1939, 30, 309–314.

36. Hoefer, C., and Hardy, M. C. The influence of improvement in physical condition on intelligence and educational achievement. *27th Yearb., Nat. Soc. Stud. Educ.*, 1928, Part I, 371–387.

37. Honzik, Marjorie P., and Jones, H. E. Mental-physical relationships during the preschool period. *J. exp. Educ.*, 1937, 6, 139–146.

38. Horwitt, M. K. Fact and artifact in the biology of schizophrenia. *Science*, 1956, 124, 429–430.

39. Hull, C. L. *Aptitude testing.* Yonkers-on-Hudson: World Book Co,. 1928.

40. Husén, T. Undersökningar rörande sambanden mellan somatiska föhållanden och intellektuell prestationsförmåga. *Särtryck ur Tidskrift i militär Hälsovård*, 1951, 76, 41–74. (English summary)

41. Jones, H. E. The environment and mental development. In L. Carmichael (Ed.), *Manual of child psychology.* (2nd Ed.) N.Y.: Wiley, 1954. Pp. 631–696.

42. Kempf, G. A., and Collins, S. D. A study of the relation between mental and physical status of children in two counties of Illinois. *U.S. Publ. Health Rep.* 1929, 44, No. 29, 1743–1784.

43. Kennard, Margaret A. Inheritance of electroencephalogram patterns in children with behavior disorders. *Psychosom. Med.*, 1949, 11, 151–157.

44. Keys, A., *et al. The biology of human starvation.* Minneapolis: Univer. Minn. Press, 1950. 2 vols.

45. Knott, J. R., Friedman, H., and Bardsley, R. Some electroencephalographic correlates of intelligence in eight-year-old and twelve-year-old children. *J. exp. Psychol.*, 1942, 30, 380–391.

46. Kreezer, G. L. The relation of intelligence level and the electroencephalogram. *39th Yearb., Nat. Soc. Stud. Educ.*, 1940, Part I, 130–133.

47. Kreezer, G. L., and Smith, F. W. The relation of the alpha rhythm of the electroencephalogram and intelligence level in the non-differentiated familial type of mental deficiency. *J. Psychol.*, 1950, 29, 47–51.

48. Lacey, J. I., Bateman, Dorothy E., and Van Lehn, Ruth. Autonomic response specificity and Rorschach color responses. *Psychosom. Med.*, 1952, 14, 256–260.

49. Lacey, J. I., Bateman, Dorothy E., and Van Lehn, Ruth. Autonomic response specificity. *Psychosom. Med.*, 1953, 15, 8–21.

50. Lennox, W. G., Gibbs, Erna L., and Gibbs, F. A. Inheritance of cerebral dysrhythmia and epilepsy. In E. A. Strecker, F. G. Ebaugh, and J. R. Ewalt (Eds.), *Practical clinical psychiatry.* Philadelphia: Blakiston, 1947. Pp. 124–125.

51. Lindsley, D. B. Electroencephalography. In J. McV. Hunt (Ed.), *Personality and the behavior disorders.* N.Y.: Ronald, 1944. Vol. 2. Pp. 1033–1103.

52. Lowe, G. M. Mental changes after removing tonsils and adenoids. *Psychol. Clin.,* 1923, 15, 92–100.

53. Lowenfeld, B. Psychological problems of children with impaired vision. In W. M. Cruickshank (Ed.), *Psychology of exceptional children and youth.* N.Y.: Prentice-Hall, 1955. Pp. 214–283.

54. Lurie, L. A. Endocrinology and the understanding and treatment of the exceptional child. *J. Amer. med. Ass.,* 1938, 110, 1531–1536.

55. Mallory, J. N. A study of the relation of some physical defects to achievement in the elementary school. *George Peabody Coll. Teach., Contrib. Educ.,* 1922, No. 9.

56. Miller, C. A., and Lennox, Margaret A. Electroencephalography in behavior problem children. *J. Pediat.,* 1948, 33, 753–761.

57. Milliken, J. R., and Standen, J. L. An investigation into the effects of glutamic acid on human intelligence. *J. Neurol. Neurosurg. Psychiat.* 1951, 14, 47–54.

58. Misiak, H., and Franghiadi, G. J. The thumb and personality. *J. gen. Psychol.,* 1953, 48, 241–244.

59. Morgan, C. F., and Stellar, E. *Physiological psychology.* (Rev. Ed.) N.Y.: McGraw-Hill, 1950.

60. Myerson, L. A psychology of impaired hearing. In W. M. Cruickshank (Ed.), *Psychology of exceptional children and youth.* N.Y.: Prentice-Hall, 1955. Pp. 120–183.

61. Myklebust, H. R. Towards a new understanding of the deaf child. *Amer. Ann. Deaf,* 1953, 98, 345–357.

62. Paterson, D. G. *Physique and intellect.* N.Y.: Appleton-Century-Crofts, 1930.

63. Phillips, E. L., Berman, Isabel R., and Hanson, H. B. Intelligence and personality factors associated with poliomyelitis among school age children. *Monogr. Soc. Res. Child Develpm.,* 1947, 12, No. 2.

64. Pintner, R., and Brunschwig, Lily. Some personality adjustments of deaf children in relation to two different factors. *J. genet. Psychol.,* 1936, 49, 377–388.

65. Richey, A. The effects of diseased tonsils and adenoids on intelligence quotients of 204 children. *J. juv. Res.,* 1934, 18, 1–4.

66. Rogers, Margaret C. Adenoids and diseased tonsils, their effects on general intelligence. *Arch. Psychol.,* 1922, No. 50.

67. Sandwick, R. L. Correlation of physical health and mental efficiency. *J. educ. Res.,* 1920, 1, 199–203.

68. Sarason, S. B. *Psychological problems in mental deficiency.* (Rev. Ed.) N.Y.: Harper, 1953.

69. Saul, L. J., Davis, H., and Davis, P. A. Psychological correlations with the electroencephalogram. *Psychosom. Med.,* 1949, 11, 361–376.

70. Secord, P. F., Dukes, W. F., and Bevan, W. Personalities in faces: I. An experiment in social perceiving. *Genet. Psychol. Monogr.,* 1954, 49, 231–279.

71. Shagass, C. An attempt to correlate the occipital alpha frequency of the electroencephalogram with performance on a mental ability test. *J. exp. Psychol.,* 1946, 36, 88–92.

72. Shuttleworth, F. K. Sexual maturation and the physical growth of girls aged six to nineteen. *Monogr. Soc. Res. Child Develpm.*, 1937, 2, No. 12.

73. Smillie, W. G., and Spencer, Cassie R. Mental retardation in school children infested with hookworms. *J. educ. Psychol.*, 1926, 17, 314–321.

74. Spillane, J. D. *Nutritional disorders of the nervous system.* Baltimore: Williams & Wilkins, 1947.

75. Sprunt, Julie W., and Finger, F. W. Auditory deficiency and academic achievement. *J. Speech Hearing Disorders*, 1949, 14, 26–32.

76. Stalnaker, E., and Roller, R. D., Jr. A study of one hundred non-promoted children. *J. educ. Res.*, 1927, 16, 265–270.

77. Stone, C. P., and Barker, R. G. On the relationships between menarcheal age and certain aspects of personality, intelligence and physique in college women. *J. genet. Psychol.*, 1934, 45, 121–135.

78. Stone, C. P., and Barker, R. G. The attitudes and interests of premenarcheal and postmenarcheal girls. *J. genet. Psychol.*, 1939, 54, 27–71.

79. Templin, Mildred C. *The development of reasoning in children with normal and defective hearing.* Minneapolis: Univer. Minnesota Press, 1950.

80. Templin, Mildred C. A qualitative analysis of explanations of physical causality: I. Comparison of hearing and defective hearing subjects. *Amer. Ann. Deaf*, 1954, 99, 252–269.

81. Terry, R. A. Autonomic balance and temperament. *J. comp. physiol. Psychol.*, 1953, 46, 454–460.

82. Wenger, M. A. The measurement of individual differences in autonomic balance. *Psychosom. Med.*, 1941, 3, 427–434.

83. Wenger, M. A. The stability of measurement of autonomic balance. *Psychosom. Med.*, 1942, 4, 94–95.

84. Wenger, M. A. Preliminary study of the significance of measures of autonomic balance. *Psychosom. Med.*, 1947, 9, 301–309.

85. Wenger, M. A. Studies of autonomic balance in Army Air Forces personnel. *Comp. Psychol. Monogr.*, 1948, 19, 1–111.

86. Wertenberger, E. J. A study of the influence of physical defects upon intelligence and achievement. *Catholic Univer. Amer. Educ. Res. Bull.*, 1927, 2, No. 9.

87. White House Conference on Child Health and Protection. *Special education: the handicapped and the gifted.* N.Y.: Appleton-Century-Crofts, 1931.

88. Williams, R. J. *The human frontier.* N.Y.: Harcourt, Brace, 1946.

89. Williams, R. J. *Free and unequal: the biological basis of individual liberty.* Austin: Univer. Texas Press, 1953.

90. Wolff, Charlotte. *The human hand.* London: Methuen, 1942.

91. Worchel, P., and Dallenbach, K. M. "Facial vision," perception of obstacles by the deaf-blind. *Amer. J. Psychol.*, 1947, 60, 502–553.

92. Worchel, P., and Mauney, J. The effect of practice on the perception of obstacles by the blind. *J. exp. Psychol.*, 1951, 41, 170–176.

93. Zahl, P. A. (Ed.) *Blindness; modern approaches to the unseen environment.* Princeton, N.J.: Princeton Univer. Press, 1950.

94. Zimmerman, F. T., and Burgemeister, Bessie B. Permanency of glutamic acid treatment. *Arch. Neurol. Psychiat.*, 1951, 65, 291–298.

95. Zimmerman, F. T., Burgemeister, Bessie B., and Putnam, T. J. A group study of the effect of glutamic acid upon mental functioning in children and adolescents. *Psychosom. Med.*, 1947, 9, 175–183.

96. Zimmerman, F. T., Burgemeister, Bessie B., and Putnam, T. J. The effect of glutamic acid upon the mental and physical growth of mongols. *Amer. J. Psychiat.*, 1949, 105, 661–668.

CHAPTER 6

Constitutional Types

The relationship between physical and psychological traits has also been considered from the point of view of constitutional types. In the effort to simplify the almost infinite observable variations among individuals, certain basic human types have been proposed. A specific individual can then be described as a more or less close approximation to one of a small number of types. Such constitutional types are offered as a characterization of the individual as a whole, in all his physical, intellectual, and emotional traits, and are not to be envisaged in terms of any isolated qualities of the organism. There is also a strong presumption of an innate or hereditary basis for the development of types. Thus a theory of constitutional types implies a certain degree of conformity among the various characteristics of the individual, these characteristics being ultimately attributed to underlying hereditary factors.

Type theories have a long history. As early as the fifth century B.C., the Greek physician Hippocrates called attention to a connection between body build and susceptibility to different diseases. The early work on typology has been surveyed by Wertheimer and Hesketh (56), Paterson (39, pp. 220–248), and Eysenck (16, Ch. 3). Modern psychological research on constitutional types was greatly stimulated by the publication of Kretschmer's book, whose first English translation appeared in 1925 (33). In this book, Kretschmer outlined in detail a theory of the relationship between body build and personality. More recently, the work of Sheldon has served to revive interest in these problems. The typological systems proposed by Kretschmer and by Sheldon will be considered in the first two sections of the present chapter, together with relevant data.

Basically, all constitutional typologies involve two major concepts. One pertains to the typological as contrasted to the dimensional (or trait) system for describing individual differences. Such a distinction holds whether we are dealing with physical or psychological characteristics. The implications of these two systems and their relative merits will be considered in the third section of this chapter. The other concept is concerned with the relationship between physical and psychological characteristics. All constitutional typologies, such as those of Kretschmer and Sheldon, propose clear-cut associations between body build and personality. In this respect, constitutional typologies represent another approach to the problem of physique and behavior surveyed in Chapter 5. Some of the implications of this aspect of type theories will be examined in the fourth section of the present chapter. It should be emphasized that the two major concepts of constitutional typologies are logically independent. Either could be accepted or rejected without affecting the other.

KRETSCHMER'S TYPOLOGY

Kretschmer (33, 34) classifies body build with reference to four types: pyknic, athletic, leptosome, and dysplastic. The typical *pyknic* is short and thick-set, with relatively large trunk and short legs, round chest, rounded shoulders, and short hands and feet. The *athletic* has a more proportionate development of trunk and limbs, well-developed bones and muscles, wide shoulders, and large hands and feet. The *leptosome* is generally characterized by small body volume in relation to height. He is tall and slender, with relatively narrow chest, long legs, elongated face, and long, narrow hands and feet. In the *dysplastic* category are placed all individuals who present an incompatible mixture of type characteristics in their physical development. Kretschmer suggested a wide variety of physical measures, to be used in conjunction with clinical diagnosis by the experimenter, for differentiating among these bodily types.

The basic contention of Kretschmer's theory is that a relationship exists between the body types he describes and two essentially opposed "temperaments," the cycloid and the schizoid. The *cycloid* individual manifests personality traits which in extreme cases would be classified under the cyclical, or manic-depressive, form of insanity. In this psychosis, the patient typically alternates between extremes of excitement and depression. The *schizoid* tends toward schizophrenia, which is characterized by extreme introversion and lack of interest in one's surroundings. Kretschmer claims that the cycloid is usually pyknic, whereas the schizoid is leptosome or, less frequently, athletic. Although originally applied to different forms of mental disorders, this theory was subsequently extended to include normal individuals who manifest no personality disturbance. The terms "cyclothyme" and "schizo-thyme" were devised to denote these two normal biotypes. The former is described as social, friendly, lively, practical, and realistic; the latter, as quiet and reserved, more solitary, timid, and shut-in. It will be noted that these descriptions correspond quite closely to Jung's extrovert and introvert types.

Evidence to test Kretschmer's hypothesis has been gathered from many sources. Since the theory originated in Kretschmer's observations of psy-chotic patients, many of the data have been obtained from such cases. Surveys by Kretschmer (33, 34) and others (5, 56, 57) have in general re-vealed the predicted correspondence between body build and psychosis. Results obtained in one of these studies on over 8000 cases are summarized

Table 3

PERCENTAGE OF SCHIZOPHRENICS, MANIC-DEPRESSIVES,
AND EPILEPTICS FALLING INTO DIFFERENT
CATEGORIES OF BODY BUILD

(From Westphal, 57, p. 97)

BODY BUILD	SCHIZOPHRENICS ($N = 5233$)	MANIC-DEPRESSIVES ($N = 1361$)	EPILEPTICS ($N = 1505$)
Pyknic	13.7	64.6	5.5
Athletic	16.0	6.7	28.9
Leptosome	50.3	19.2	25.1
Dysplastic	10.5	1.1	29.5
Doubtful	8.6	8.4	11.0

in Table 3. It will be noted that the largest percentage of schizophrenics (50.3) fall into the leptosome category, while 64.6 per cent of the manic-depressives are classified as pyknics. This investigation also included a group of epileptics, who exhibited more scattering of body build. The principal distinguishing features of the epileptic group, as contrasted with the schizo-phrenic and manic-depressive, are its relatively large proportions of athletics and dysplastics.

Interpretation of such results on psychotic cases is complicated by the presence of uncontrolled factors, chief among which is *age*. Schizophrenia is more common among younger persons, while older people are more sus-ceptible to manic-depressive psychoses. It is also a well-established fact, which Kretschmer himself recognized, that older subjects tend more toward the pyknic body build, younger subjects toward the leptosome. To be sure, pyknics may be found among young people, and leptosomes among older groups; and many individuals retain the same type of body build throughout life. But the general trend is sufficiently marked to produce an entirely spurious relationship between body build and psychotic tendencies. For this reason, it is essential that age differences be ruled out in any comparison of the body type of different psychotic groups.

In an investigation by Garvey (21), 130 manic-depressives and 130 schizophrenics were selected so that the two groups were closely matched in age. Only clear cases, classified with complete agreement by the hospital staff (not including the experimenter), were employed. When the patients were divided into heavy and slender types on the basis of general observation, some evidence for Kretschmer's claims was found, although the association was slight. For more precise classification, extensive physical measurements were taken and several ratios between horizontal and vertical bodily dimensions were computed. All showed an *almost complete overlapping* of the two psychotic groups. Not only were the averages closely similar, but also the range and general form of the distribution were practically identical in the two groups.

Another carefully controlled investigation on the relationship between body type and psychosis was conducted by Burchard (5). A total of 407 white male patients from several institutions for the insane were selected for the survey. Of these, 125 were clearly diagnosed as schizophrenics by the hospital staff, and 125 as manic-depressives. The remaining 157 patients manifested a variety of psychotic and neurotic conditions, and were employed as a control group. The subjects in all three groups were classified into pyknics, athletics, and leptosomes by "general impression." Comparisons were also subsequently made in respect to several anthropometric measures and indices. Only seven dysplastics were found in the entire sampling, and these were eliminated from further consideration. All other subjects were retained, any intermediate or mixed types being assigned to the morphological type they resembled most closely. In Table 4 are given the percent-

Table 4

PERCENTAGE OF SCHIZOPHRENIC, MANIC-DEPRESSIVE, AND CONTROL CASES SHOWING PYKNIC, ATHLETIC, AND LEPTOSOME BODY TYPES

(From Burchard, 5, p. 31)

BODY BUILD	MANIC-DEPRESSIVES (N = 125)	SCHIZOPHRENICS (N = 125)	CONTROLS (N = 157)
Pyknic	63.2	36.3	55.6
Athletic	8.8	17.7	11.3
Leptosome	28.0	46.0	33.1

ages of pyknics, athletics, and leptosomes found in the manic-depressive, schizophrenic, and control groups, respectively, when the inspectional method of classification was employed.

The general trend of these figures seems to be in agreement with Kretschmer's theory. Not only are the greatest percentage of manic-depressives pyknic, and the greatest percentage of schizophrenics leptosome, but the control group occupies a position intermediate between these two groups in all percentages. When the schizophrenics and manic-depressives are compared in terms of anthropometric measures, a certain amount of differentiation is also revealed. Reliable differences between the averages of the two groups were found in three out of nine physical measures and in two out of three bodily indices. Nevertheless, the overlapping of the groups in all these measures was very large. This is illustrated in Figure 33, which shows

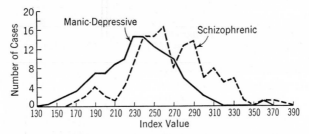

Fig. 33. Frequency Distributions of 125 Manic-Depressives and 125 Schizophrenics on the Wertheimer-Hesketh Index of Body Build. (From Burchard, 5, p. 47.)

the frequency distributions on the Wertheimer-Hesketh index of body build.[1] This index yielded the largest differences between the two groups. It is apparent that, despite the statistically significant differences in averages, schizophrenics can be found who are much more pyknic than certain manic-depressives, and vice versa.

Even the small differences in averages between the two groups may be the result of other uncontrolled factors. Burchard recognized this difficulty and undertook a detailed analysis of his manic-depressive and schizophrenic groups. In regard to racial and national background, occupation, and educational status, no appreciable or consistent differences could be discovered. In age, however, the differences were very large, the average ages of schizophrenic, control, and manic-depressive groups being 30.97, 42.90, and 49.65 years, respectively. Further analysis revealed a definite relationship between

[1] Wertheimer-Hesketh Index (56, p. 415):

$$\frac{\text{leg length} \times 10^3}{\text{transverse chest diameter} \times \text{sagittal chest diameter} \times \text{trunk height}} \times 100$$

age and body build, as indicated in Table 5. This table gives mean Wertheimer-Hesketh indices of subjects falling in successive decades, within the entire sampling as well as within each psychotic group. It is apparent that there is a definite tendency toward a more pyknic body build with advancing age. This is manifested *within each psychotic group,* as well as in the entire group. Further corroboration of this finding is furnished by the correlation of —.256 obtained between age and Wertheimer-Hesketh index in the entire sampling, this correlation being significant at the .01 level.

Table 5

WERTHEIMER-HESKETH INDEX OF BODY BUILD IN RELATION TO AGE AND TYPE OF PSYCHOSIS

(From Burchard, 5, p. 64)

	MEAN WERTHEIMER-HESKETH INDEX			
AGE	ENTIRE GROUP (N = 407)	SCHIZOPHRENIC (N = 125)	MANIC-DEPRESSIVE (N = 125)	CONTROL (N = 157)
15–19	306.11	297.25	262.66	321.00
20–29	275.10	279.77	252.00	273.48
30–39	260.82	272.00	256.33	253.86
40–49	249.34	252.50	246.52	249.41
50–59	253.68	277.50	247.29	257.16
60–69	236.50	243.33	241.67	228.75

Much of the difference observed between the two psychotic groups can therefore be attributed to age. It should be noted, however, that within each decade the schizophrenics have a higher mean index than the manic-depressives, indicating a tendency toward more leptosomic body build. To be sure, the differences are considerably reduced by ruling out age, and the control group no longer retains its intermediate position, but a certain difference in the expected direction remains. This difference could possibly have resulted from other unsuspected factors in which the two psychotic groups may not have been equated. Or it may indicate an actual, although slight, relationship between body build and type of psychosis.

Eysenck (16, p. 85) has pointed out further sources of difficulty in interpreting such data. He notes that the various subgroups of schizophrenics differ from one another in body build almost as much as schizophrenics differ from manic-depressives. It is well known that schizophrenia is a broad psychiatric category, covering a variety of specific syndromes. In his own research on 1000 adult neurotics, Eysenck (16, pp. 89–94) found evidence that the anxious, inhibited type tends to be leptosome, while the hysterical, impulsive group tends to be pyknic. Within the age range covered in his survey, there was no relation between age and body build.

In the effort to check on correspondences between body build and personality among *normals*, several approaches have been followed. A group of early studies on college students were concerned with the relation between height-weight ratio or other more elaborate indices of body build and intelligence test scores, personality inventory scores, or associates' ratings on a number of personality traits (20, 26, 37, 46, 47). All but a few of the correlations proved to be insignificant. Those that did just reach statistical significance were low and may have resulted from an uncontrolled age factor.

Exponents of constitutional typology could argue, however, that such negligible correlations may have resulted from the presence of a large number of individuals of mixed types, in whom no consistent relationship between physique and personality may be apparent. These individuals, who are probably in the majority, would serve to "dilute" any clear-cut relationships among the "pure types." It has also been argued that even when indices are employed in lieu of isolated dimensions, the investigator is not getting a picture of the individual's physique in its totality. And the latter is essential in any concept of constitutional types.

Most of the numerous German investigations on types have proceeded by *selecting* good specimens of each type on the basis of physical measurements or observations and then administering a variety of psychological tests to the groups so obtained. By this method, for example, the conclusions were reached that pyknics are more distractable than leptosomes, that they have a greater perception span, show a better incidental memory, respond "synthetically" rather than "analytically" to a difficult perception, are more sensitive to colors than to forms, are superior in motor tasks except when these require delicacy of movement, and give more extroverted responses. These are among the major differences reported by German investigators.[2]

Many of these studies are open to serious criticism and it is therefore difficult to evaluate their findings. The groups employed were usually small. Averages were reported with no indication of variability within each group or of amount of overlapping between groups. Quantitative data were frequently lacking and only descriptive observations reported. Tests were often inadequate or poorly standardized. The groups themselves, selected chiefly on the basis of physical type, frequently differed in other essential respects.

---

[2] For a survey of the early investigations, see Klineberg *et al.* (31). More recent European work has been summarized by Eysenck (16, 17, 18).

Thus the relative proportion of men and women may not have been constant in all the groups. Or the pyknics may have been older than the leptosomes, in which case this age difference could account for the observed psychological differences. Little or no attempt was made to control this age factor, in some studies the subjects ranging from adolescents to sexagenarians. Social and cultural background may also have affected the results. There is some evidence, for example, that leptosomes are found more commonly among the higher social and educational levels. Since there are also intellectual and possibly emotional differences from one socioeconomic or educational level to another, such factors should be held constant.

In a study by Klineberg, Asch, and Block (31), an attempt was made to compare Kretschmer's body types under more rigidly controlled conditions. The study was limited to college students, so that variations in age and in social and educational level were markedly reduced. The subjects were also very homogeneous in racial and cultural background. From a group of 153 men in a single college, averaging 19 years and 9 months in age, it was possible to select 56 relatively pure pyknics and 59 relatively pure leptosomes. Classification of body type was based upon five indices computed from physical measurements, together with the experimenter's observational diagnosis. That the two chosen groups were clearly differentiated in physique is illustrated by Figure 34. This shows the distributions of the pyknic and leptosome groups in Pignet Index,[3] one of the five criteria of selection employed. It will be noted that overlapping is virtually absent.

In sharp contrast to this distribution is that reproduced in Figure 35, showing the scores of leptosomes and pyknics on one of the psychological tests, viz., cancellation of letters. In this case, the two groups overlap almost completely. Similar results were obtained with all the other tests, which included tests of intelligence and of emotional adjustment, as well as six tests specifically designed to measure alleged characteristics of the two opposed constitutional types. In no case was the difference between the two groups statistically significant. Correlation of measures on 110 subjects confirmed these findings. The correlations between physical indices and test scores were all close to zero. Intercorrelations of the various psychological tests were also negligible. If the underlying conformity implied by type theories were present, a fairly close correspondence should have been found among the various diagnostic tests. Viewed from any angle, the results are completely negative.

A similar investigation of personality traits in relation to physical type was conducted by Klineberg, Fjeld, and Foley (32). The subjects were

---

[3] Pignet Index = height − (weight + chest circumference).

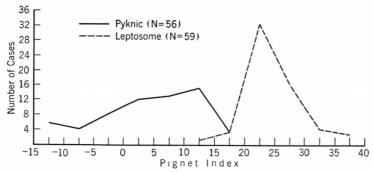

Fig. 34. Distributions of Scores of Leptosomes and Pyknics on the Pignet Index. (From Klineberg, Asch, and Block, 31, p. 180.)

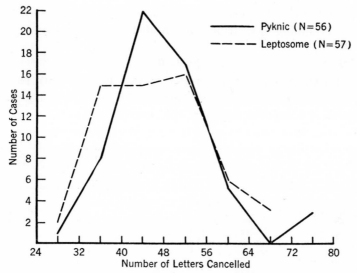

Fig. 35. Distributions of Scores of Leptosomes and Pyknics in Letter Cancellation. (From Klineberg, Asch, and Block, 31, p. 180.)

again students, selected from several colleges in New York City and its environs. A total of 200 men and 229 women were examined. Within each of these groups, the subjects who fell in the upper and those who fell in the lower 25 per cent of the distribution of Pignet Index were selected as leptosomes and pyknics, respectively. This gave 50 leptosomes and 50 pyknics among the men, and 57 leptosomes and 57 pyknics among the women. These contrasted physical types also showed significant differences in nearly all other physical measures and indices obtained in the study, and can safely be regarded as distinctly different in physique. Little or no overlapping was found in any of these measures. All subjects were given the Bernreuter Personality Inventory, the Allport-Vernon Study of Values, and a specially designed test of suggestibility. A large portion of the group also took an honesty test (Maller Test of Sports and Hobbies) and a persistence test (insoluble finger maze).

In Table 6 will be found the mean scores of both male and female leptosomes and pyknics on each test, together with data on the significance of the differences between the means. The results of this carefully controlled study are clearly negative as regards constitutional types. None of the leptosome-pyknic differences is significant at the .01 level. Only 2 of the 30 differences reach significance at the .05 level, a finding that could arise by chance. Moreover, mean scores of all groups fell close to the norms for college men and women in general. A final point to note is that the ranges of the leptosomes and pyknics were nearly identical, showing an almost complete overlapping of distributions on all tests.

Table 6

MEAN SCORES OF LEPTOSOME AND PYKNIC GROUPS ON PERSONALITY TESTS

(From Klineberg, Fjeld, and Foley, 32)

TEST	MALE			FEMALE		
	Leptosome (N = 50)	Pyknic (N = 50)	Critical ratio	Leptosome (N = 57)	Pyknic (N = 57)	Critical ratio
BERNREUTER						
1. B_1N: Neuroticism	−37.50	−39.76	0.14	−40.51	−45.60	0.34
2. B_2S: Self-sufficiency	+34.30	+29.22	0.49	− 0.26	+18.02	1.88
3. B_3I: Introversion	−14.98	−17.88	0.30	−18.47	−27.00	0.95
4. B_4D: Dominance	+39.20	+42.18	0.26	+30.32	+38.54	0.72
5. F_1C: Self-confidence	− 8.54	− 8.46	0.005	+ 4.67	−13.67	1.19
6. F_2S: Sociability	+ 1.22	− 6.66	0.62	−29.79	−18.39	0.97
ALLPORT-VERNON STUDY OF VALUES						
1. Theoretical	31.82	31.46	0.23	28.57	29.32	0.54
2. Economic	28.67	29.98	0.96	27.42	26.71	0.61
3. Aesthetic	27.27	28.40	0.61	34.77	32.91	1.15
4. Social	32.29	31.82	0.39	30.25	32.63	2.22°
5. Political	30.30	31.72	1.08	29.65	29.54	0.09
6. Religious	29.65	26.62	1.47	29.34	28.89	0.28
SUGGESTIBILITY	11.02	10.82	0.23	11.89	11.43	0.56
PERSISTENCE	6.00	10.94	2.22°	6.94	8.71	1.32
HONESTY	97.58	94.77	1.61	99.00	99.14	0.25

° Significant at .05 level.

These studies are of course limited to American college populations. It is possible that other normal populations would show some relationship between body build and psychological characteristics. Other indices of personality might also prove more successful in differentiating between groups. European workers, such as Eysenck, have reported some corroboration of Kretschmer's theory, although the evidence is difficult to interpret because of methodological difficulties. In general, however, it seems clear that even if a significant association should be conclusively established between Kretschmer's body types and personality, the relationship would undoubtedly be very slight.

SHELDON'S TYPOLOGY

A more recent system of constitutional typology is that developed by Sheldon and his co-workers (48, 49, 50, 51). The distinctive feature of this system is that every individual is rated on a 7-point scale in each of the three categories of physique and in each of the three corresponding categories of temperament. Rather than being characterized in terms of the type he most closely resembles, the individual is thus placed along a continuum with respect to each of the three components of physique and of temperament.

The three components of physique were chosen and defined through detailed observations of the photographs of 4000 college men. As shown in Figure 36, each person was photographed in the nude and in a standardized posture, from the frontal, lateral, and dorsal positions. Once the three components had been suggested by this inspectional analysis, suitable anthropometric measures were selected by trial and error. The measurements were made directly on the photographs with needle-point dividers.

A parallel procedure was followed in arriving at the basic components of temperament. First, the authors assembled a list of 650 alleged temperamental "traits" described in the literature, most of them being related to introversion-extroversion. After adding a few from their own observations, arranging, and condensing, they were able to reduce the list to 50 terms which seemed to embody all the essential characteristics. A group of 33 young men, mostly graduate students and instructors, were then rated on a 7-point scale for each of these 50 traits. The ratings were based upon a series of 20 intensive interviews by the experimenter, extending over a period of one year and supplemented by everyday observations. All the 1225 intercorrelations among the ratings of the 50 traits were computed. Inspection of this correlation table suggested to the authors that the traits fell into three principal "clusters," such that the tests within each cluster were positively correlated with one another and negatively correlated with the tests in the other clusters. At this point it was decided to keep only those traits, or items, that had a positive correlation of .60 or more with other items within their cluster and a negative correlation of .30 or more with items outside the cluster. On this basis 22 of the original 50 traits were retained. In the course of subsequent studies on more subjects, the investigators undertook to sharpen and redefine the initial 22 traits and to add others which also satisfied the above correlational criterion. The final scale developed by this technique consisted of 60 traits, 20 in each cluster.

The three components of physique and the corresponding temperamental components may be briefly described as follows:

PHYSIQUE	TEMPERAMENT
1. *Endomorphy*—predominance of soft roundness; relative over-development of digestive viscera	1. *Viscerotonia*—tendency toward relaxation, love of physical comfort, pleasure in eating, sociability
2. *Mesomorphy*—predominance of bone, muscle, and connective tissue; heavy, hard, rectangular physique	2. *Somatotonia*—tendency toward assertiveness, energetic activity, love of power and risk, physical courage
3. *Ectomorphy*—predominance of linearity and fragility; relative to his mass, the ectomorph has greatest sensory exposure and largest brain and nervous system	3. *Cerebrotonia*—tendency toward restraint, introversion, love of privacy and solitude, inhibition

Each individual's *somatotype* consists of three numbers, representing his ratings in endomorphy, mesomorphy, and ectomorphy, respectively. Thus a 7–1–1 represents extreme endomorphy. A 2–6–2 and a 3–6–2 are both highly mesomorphic, but the latter shows more endomorphy than the former. Theoretically, there are 210 somatotype combinations which could be obtained with three components rated on a 7-point scale. But some of these combinations are physically impossible, such as the hypothetical 7–7–7 or 1–1–1. Sheldon (49) describes 88 somatotypes that have been actually observed. The use of a 7-point scale is of course arbitrary and only a matter of convenience. Five, 10, or any other number of steps could be substituted, in which case the total number of somatotypes would decrease or increase.

Sheldon's system was originally developed on men. Extension of the system to women is in progress and it is planned to prepare an *Atlas of Women* to parallel the recently published *Atlas of Men*. Applying the original somatotyping system to women, Sheldon reports that women tend to be more endomorphic than men. Six new somatotypes in the endomorph group, not previously found in male samples, have been identified among women. The most frequent somatotype among the 4000 college women so far surveyed is 5–3–3.

In Figure 36 will be found photographs of four somatotypes, illustrating extremes of endomorphy (7–1–1), mesomorphy (1–7–1), and ectomorphy

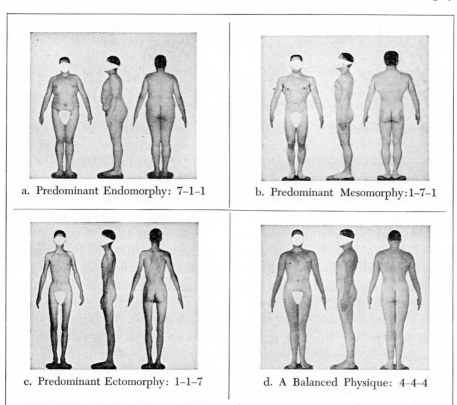

a. Predominant Endomorphy: 7–1–1

b. Predominant Mesomorphy: 1–7–1

c. Predominant Ectomorphy: 1–1–7

d. A Balanced Physique: 4–4–4

Fig. 36.   Examples of Sheldon Somatotypes. (From Sheldon, 49, pp. 37, 66, 225, 325.)

(1–1–7), as well as one physique in which the three components are nearly in balance (4–4–4). The most common physique among the college men who were Sheldon's original subjects was 3–4–4. In somatotyping an individual, the three components are rated in at least five different bodily regions and then averaged. For example, the separate ratings of the 7–1–1 pictured in Figure 36a were 6½–1–1½, 7–1–1, 7–1–1½, 7–1–1, 7–2–1. Resemblance of these somatotypes to Kretschmer's types is apparent. The predominant endomorph in Figure 36 corresponds to Kretschmer's pyknic type, while the predominant mesomorph and ectomorph represent the athletic and leptosome types, respectively. The somatotype reproduced in Figure 36d would be classified as an intermediate or mixed type in Kretschmer's system.

Each of the three temperamental components in Sheldon's system is also rated on a 7-point scale. The primary evidence for the association between somatotype and temperament ratings was derived from a study of 200 university men between the ages of 17 and 31, observed by Sheldon over a five-year period (50). Correlations between corresponding components of physique and temperament in this group were as follows:

Endomorphy and viscerotonia	.79
Mesomorphy and somatotonia	.82
Ectomorphy and cerebrotonia	.83

From a further analysis of the same subjects, the authors suggest the hypothesis that certain *discrepancies* between somatotype and temperamental index may predispose the individual to maladjustment and interfere with his achievement (50, Ch. 7).

The correlations between structural and temperamental components reported by Sheldon are certainly much higher than those found previously. Sheldon and his co-workers attribute this difference to their own reliance upon "essential underlying components" of both physique and temperament, in place of what they regard as the relatively superficial or fragmentary measures of earlier investigators. Sheldon argues, for example, that aptitude or personality tests may not reveal the "deeper and more enduring aspects" of temperament which he claims to have reached through his series of interviews (11, p. 33). For this reason, test scores might not yield such high correlations with somatotype as were found by Sheldon through the use of ratings. A counter-argument is that the well-known "halo effect" may have produced artificially high correspondences between physique and temperamental index, since the same observer assigned both sets of ratings. As the strongest defense against the halo effect, Sheldon offers the fact that the experimenter was aware of its nature and was therefore on guard against it. The effectiveness of such a safeguard is of course debatable.

Subsequent studies by other investigators have failed to corroborate the high degree of association between physique and temperament reported by Sheldon. When ratings were correlated with somatotypes, significant correlations were generally obtained, although they were usually much lower than those found by Sheldon (10, 24, 44, 45). Significant correlations were likewise obtained when scores on the Allport-Vernon Study of Values were compared with somatotypes based on self-ratings for physical qualities

(12). In all such studies, the possibility of spurious correlations resulting from halo effect, social stereotypes, self concepts, and similar factors remains. Those investigations in which independent measures of somatotypes were compared with scores on personality or ability tests, on the other hand, yielded few if any significant correlations (11, 19, 29, 53). In the light of such findings, it can only be concluded that Sheldon's primary claim regarding the association of somatotype and temperament among normal persons remains unproved.

In a further extension of his theory, Sheldon has applied his constitutional classification to psychiatric patients and to delinquents (48, 58). For these purposes, he has devised categories that represent a pathological deficiency in the previously described temperamental components. Utilizing the suffix "-penia" to characterize these negative traits, he proposes the following classification:

> Cerebropenia—lack of inhibition
> Visceropenia—lack of compassion and of relaxed, soft qualities
> Somatopenia—lack of energy and of drive for overt action

At the psychotic level, Sheldon links manic-depressive conditions with cerebropenia, paranoid states with visceropenia, and hebephrenic schizophrenia with somatopenia. Milder forms of the same deficiencies, he maintains, produce the corresponding neuroses, traditionally known as hysteria, psychasthenia, and neurasthenia, respectively.

Some evidence in support of this theory is provided by a study conducted on 167 male patients at Elgin State Hospital (58; 48, pp. 66–78). Significant correlations in the expected directions were found between ratings for psychiatric reaction types, on the one hand, and both somatotype and temperament ratings, on the other. In this investigation, the psychiatric ratings were obtained independently of the somatotype and temperament ratings, so that halo effect was ruled out of the correlations. Some of the association, however, may have resulted from differences in age, socioeconomic level, and other uncontrolled factors among the psychiatric groups. No data on these factors are given in the report of the study.

In a ten-year study of 200 delinquent boys in a rehabilitation home, Sheldon (48) found a predominance of endomorphic mesomorphs. The greatest clustering of somatotypes fell between the mesomorphic and endomorphic extremes, but was distinctly closer to mesomorphy. There was a decided absence of ectomorphy. Sheldon regards these findings as further confirmation of his hypothesis, since the most prevalent somatotype in the delinquent group is that which in his system would be associated with cerebropenia, or lack of inhibition. At the same time, somatotype cannot be regarded as an indicator of delinquency. As Sheldon himself points out, endomorphic mesomorphy is also characteristic of eminent generals, statesmen, and business leaders. Moreover Sutherland (54), in a reanalysis of Sheldon's published data, found no significant association between somatotype and *degree* of criminality as determined from the case histories.

In a somewhat better-controlled study, the Gluecks (22) compared 500 delinquent boys with 500 nondelinquents approximately matched with the delinquents in age, IQ, national origin, and residence in underprivileged neighborhoods. In general, their results on body build confirmed those of Sheldon. There was a significantly larger percentage of mesomorphic and a significantly smaller percentage of ectomorphic physiques among the delinquents than among the controls. Furthermore, one of the largest group differences occurred in the case of endomorphic mesomorphs, who were four times as numerous in the delinquent as in the control group.

The evidence cited by Sheldon in support of his system of classifying personality traits, as well as that purporting to show a close relationship between physique and personality, needs to be carefully examined. The possible operation of halo effect when physique and temperament are rated by the same observer has already been mentioned. Reference has also been made to the presence of such uncontrolled factors as age and socioeconomic level in the study of psychiatric patients.

The original identification of the three temperamental components (viscerotonia, somatotonia, and cerebretonia) can likewise be questioned because of inadequacy of data (cf. 1). Ultimately, the entire structure of evidence for the presence of these particular components stands or falls with the adequacy of the initial experiment on 33 college men. To be sure, subsequent studies were conducted on larger groups. But these studies were designed simply to redefine, sharpen, and expand the originally chosen list of 22 "traits" for measuring the three temperamental components, rather than to check the adequacy of the components themselves. This is clearly indicated by the authors' procedure. The criterion for adding a new trait to the list was that the trait must correlate highly and positively with the traits in one of the original clusters, and negatively with the traits in the other two clusters. Subsequent modification or addition of traits thus depended in a very intimate way upon the results of the initial experiment. The small number and highly unrepresentative nature of the subjects employed in this initial experiment make it ill-suited to play such a fundamental part in the development of the entire schema of temperament classification.

Moreover, the technique of identifying components by *inspection* of a correlation table leaves too much to subjective judgment. In so far as the major contribution of Sheldon's approach is its emphasis upon components rather than types, the best available objective techniques for identifying such components ought to be applied. These techniques, known collectively as "factor analysis," are based upon further statistical analysis of a table of intercorrelations, and will be discussed more fully in Chapter 10. In the present connection it will suffice to note that other investigators have begun to employ these techniques in the analysis of body build as well as personality characteristics, with results that offer little support to Sheldon's tripartite classification. Even more disconcerting is Lubin's (36) finding that, in Sheldon's published table of intercorrelations among temperamental ratings, some of the reported coefficients are arithmetically impossible. It thus appears that the basic data from which the temperamental components were derived contain computational errors!

In reference to the classification of *physique,* it is relevant to note that age (38) and nutritional status (4) do affect the somatotype, despite Sheldon's original claim to the contrary. Sheldon argued, for example, that loss of weight will not change endomorphs into mesomorphs or ectomorphs —"they become simply emaciated endomorphs" (50, p. 8). In more recent writing, he has qualified such assertions somewhat, pointing out that the somatotype is an indication of the individual's body build "under standard conditions of nutrition and in the absence of grossly disturbing pathology" (49, p. 19).

Apart from specific criticisms of the *evidence,* there are more fundamental questions which can be raised regarding Sheldon's whole approach. Is the three-component schema the most efficient system for classifying people in either physique or personality? Are the observed relationships between body build and behavioral characteristics—in so far as reliably established— indications of a basic, hereditary, "constitutional" connection, as Sheldon maintains? Or are there alternative explanations for the obtained correspondences, along some of the lines outlined in Chapter 5? These questions will be considered in the next two sections, with reference not only to Sheldon's theory, but also to constitutional typology in general.

TYPOLOGICAL VERSUS DIMENSIONAL SYSTEMS

Popular notions of "types" imply classification of people into sharply divided categories. They are essentially qualitative schemes, which are incompatible with the continuous, quantitative gradations obtained when any human characteristic is measured. Modern constitutional typologists do not use the term "type" in this popular sense. Sheldon's system was explicitly formulated in terms of components, along which individuals could vary by degree. "Pure" endomorphs (7–1–1), mesomorphs (1–7–1), and ectomorphs (1–1–7) are relatively rare in this schema of classification. Most people occupy intermediate positions in each component. As for Kretschmer's theory, although expressed in reference to extreme type categories, it too recognizes quantitative variations. In his own writings, Kretschmer has repeatedly explained that his "types" are only focal points or turning points in a continuous distribution (34). Individuals may fall anywhere between these focal points. Eysenck (16, 17) and Ekman (14, 15) have both called attention to this aspect of Kretschmer's theory and to its common misunderstanding among American and English psychologists.

Since discontinuity of distribution is not implicit in a typological approach, what then is the chief difference between typological and dimensional systems for classifying people? Essentially, a typology describes each individual by stating his resemblance to a "typical" person. How closely, for example, does the subject approximate the typical pyknic, leptosome, or athletic body build? The principal distinguishing feature of such a system is that its categories are always to some extent mutually exclusive. The closer an individual resembles one type, the less will be his similarity to the others. Categories are so defined that a single individual cannot rate high or low in all. The typological approach utilizes essentially a relative rather than an absolute system of measurement.

Sheldon's system, although superficially expressed in dimensional terms, nevertheless displays this fundamental property of typologies. It will be recalled, for example, that somatotypes represented by 7–7–7, 1–1–1, and many other combinations of ratings are physically impossible owing to the way in which the three components are defined. As the individual's rating in one component rises, his ratings in the others must drop.

A thoroughgoing analysis of the differences between typological and dimensional systems can be found in two articles by Ekman (14, 15), which should be consulted for a full understanding of the problem. Only a few of the major points will be touched upon in the present discussion.

We may begin by considering a simple, hypothetical example, portrayed in Figure 37. Suppose that we want to describe people in terms of two factors, or dimensions (in the statistical sense), namely, height and breadth. Let us assume that we have measured height and that we have a satisfactory measure of breadth—presumably based upon a combination of measurements made at different parts of the body. Each person can then be represented by a point that shows both his height and breadth, six persons having been so indicated in Figure 37. If, now, we replace this dimensional system with a typological system, we can speak of a Short-Broad Type (A) and a Tall-Slender Type (B). Each person will then be described in terms of his closeness to one or the other of these extreme types.

Reference to Figure 37 shows that individual 1 falls close to Type A; individual 2 falls close to Type B; and individuals 3 and 4 represent intermediate or mixed types. All four fall along the line joining Types A and B. But individuals 5 and 6 fall outside the given typological system. The person who is both tall and broad or both short and slender cannot be adequately characterized in terms of the two-type system illustrated. Such a two-type system is fully applicable only when all individuals fall along the line extending from Type A to Type B. The reader familiar with statistics will recognize that this means that the correlation between height and breadth would have to be -1.00. Under these conditions, however, a *single measure* along the line AB would suffice to characterize the individual. Thus if we were to use a dimensional system, only one dimension would be required to do the same job as two types.

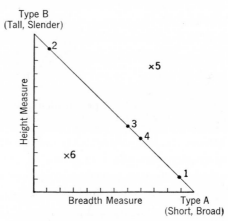

Fig. 37. Schematic Representation of a Typological and a Dimensional System. (Adapted from Ekman, 14, p. 5.)

Ekman (14) has shown that this argument can be generalized to cover all typological systems. For example, in a three-type system, the intercorrelations among the type categories must average $-.50$ for all individuals to fall within the type system.[4] But when this condition is met, two dimensions suffice to identify each individual. In other words, any set of data that can be adequately described by n types, can be described equally well by $n-1$ dimensions. There obviously seems to be no justification for retaining a typological approach under these circumstances.

What of Sheldon's three "components" of physique and personality? Are they types or dimensions? Ekman has demonstrated that Sheldon's system is in effect typological and that a simplified dimensional system can be substituted for it. Using Sheldon's own data on somatotypes, Ekman found the

[4] For n types, the mean correlation among the dimensional variables must be: $-\dfrac{1}{n-1}$

average intercorrelation of the three components to be close to the −.50 required for a three-type system. What this means, of course, is that Sheldon's three components were so defined as to make certain values mutually exclusive.

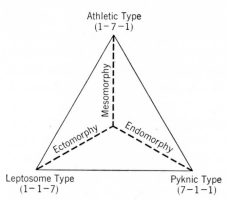

Fig. 38. Schematic Representation of the Typological Systems of Kretschmer and of Sheldon. (From Ekman, 14, p. 18.)

Figure 38 is a schematic representation of the typological systems of both Kretschmer and Sheldon. The figure represents a triangular pyramid, with the base on the plane of the paper. For the data to fit this typological system, all cases must fall within this triangular base. (The typological plane has now replaced the typological line of the two-type system.) Ekman showed that with slight adjustments this condition is met by Sheldon's data. It thus follows that the same data can be adequately described in terms of only two dimensions.

For illustrative purposes, Ekman (15) has worked out a revised somatotype system which includes only endomorphy and mesomorphy. In this system, ectomorphy is represented by a low rating in both endomorphy and mesomorphy. Apart from purely statistical considerations, it appears reasonable to describe the extreme ectomorph (or leptosome) as one who *lacks* the characteristics of both mesomorphs and endomorphs—he is not overendowed with either fat tissue or muscle and bone tissue, being outstanding only in the negative quality of "fragility." Figure 39 gives a schematic representation of this modified two-dimensional classification, showing the position of the Kretschmer and Sheldon types in the new system. Ekman points out that his conversion of Sheldon's system to a two-dimensional schema was intended only as a demonstration of the

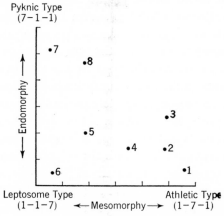

Fig. 39. Schematic Representation of a Three-Type System by Means of a Two-Dimensional System.

formal principles involved. If a dimensional system for adequately describing human physique is to be worked out, the original mesomorphy and endomorphy dimensions will probably have to be refined or reformulated, and possibly other dimensions—not covered by Sheldon's system—should be added. Utilizing a different statistical approach, Humphreys (28) has subsequently corroborated Ekman's conclusions, showing that Sheldon's data provide evidence for only two independent types in either physique or temperament.

While typologists were attracting attention with alluring generalizations, a number of investigators were more quietly pursuing the dimensional approach to body build (6, 7, 8, 18, 23, 25, 27, 35, 40, 41, 42, 43, 52, 55). A summary of much of this research can be found in Eysenck (18, Ch. 5). The usual procedure in these studies is to obtain a number of bodily measures from a large group of men or women and to compute all the intercorrelations among the measures. The complete correlation table is then factor-analyzed (by techniques to be discussed in Chapter 10), in order to identify the dimensions required to describe the given data.

Burt (6, 7, 8) was the first to apply factor analysis to body build, his methodology having been closely followed by other English investigators such as Rees and Eysenck (40, 41, 42, 43). All of these studies agree in finding a general size factor and a second bipolar shape factor corresponding to length versus breadth. The second factor is positively related to longitudinal measures and negatively related to transverse and circumferential measures. An index of body build based on this second factor was found to be normally distributed in groups of men and of women (8, 42). A number of other factors of more restricted scope, such as bone length, size of extremities, and head size, have been identified in specific studies. But such factors usually account for a relatively small part of the common variance among measurements. Of particular interest are two recent studies (25, 52) which tend to confirm Ekman's proposed two-dimensional system. Both investigators identified factors which appear to correspond to the development of fatty tissue and of bone and muscle, respectively.

At this stage, any conclusion regarding the classification of body build would be premature. Most psychologists agree, however, that further progress in this field calls for a dimensional rather than a typological approach.

THE CONSTITUTIONAL HYPOTHESIS

Regardless of the system of measurement employed, all constitutional theories are based upon the propositions that: (1) body build and behavior are significantly related, and (2) this relationship is of a "constitutional" nature. The exact nature of the constitutional relationship has not been spelled out, but it is evident from the writings of constitutional psychologists that they assume a hereditary basis for the association. Moreover, it is also clear that such writers conceive of both body build and personality as resulting from a third, more fundamental set of factors, possibly glandular or neural. It is equally clear that constitutional psychologists have not traditionally attached much importance to the variety of possible psychosomatic and somatopsychological relationships discussed in Chapter 5.

With regard to the first proposition, the evidence so far available on both normal and abnormal subjects suggests that there probably are significant relationships between body build and behavior characteristics, although the correlations are not so high as some constitutional psychologists maintain. The data cited in the earlier sections in reference to the Kretschmer and Sheldon typologies pointed toward such an association. Research by British psychologists using a dimensional approach has likewise indicated the probability that a significant relationship exists between physique and behavior development (cf. 16, 41).

What these relationships mean is a more difficult question to answer. Constitutional psychologists have made little or no attempt to trace the *modus operandi* of the relationships between physique and personality. Most of them have begun with a vaguely expressed assumption of a hereditary connection and have gone no further. It is apparent, however, that alternative explanations do fit the data and merit some consideration.

There is, for example, the likelihood that body build may be partly the result of behavior. Years of strenuous exercise do leave their mark in muscular development. Habitual overeating does lead to the accumulation of fat tissue. It is interesting to note in this connection that recent literature in abnormal psychology as well as in psychosomatic medicine contains many references to "psychological overeating" resulting from frustration and other emotional problems. There are obviously many ways in which the individual's emotional adjustment, interests, and aptitudes can influence the development of his body build. The reader can easily add many other illustrations to those cited.

It can be argued—as some constitutional psychologists have done—that the basic characteristics of body build are determined by heredity and that the changes wrought by habitual activity are minor. If this is the case, the psychosomatic effects mentioned above would be of relatively little importance. There would still remain, however, another set of influences to be considered, namely, the somatopsychological. Barker *et al.* (2) discuss somatopsychological problems of very tall, short, and obese persons, although few direct studies of such individuals are available.

The weakling may cultivate an interest in books or in music because he cannot compete successfully in the more vigorous activities of his age mates. The boy with a strong, muscular body is more likely to engage in sports and to choose an active vocation than he would if he lacked these physical qualifications. Parenthetically, it may also be noted that a sturdy physique is an asset for many of the overtly aggressive acts of the juvenile delinquent —a fact that may provide a simple explanation for the predominance of endomorphic mesomorphs in the delinquent samples surveyed by Sheldon and the Gluecks. True, there are forms of delinquency that do not require physical prowess. But there are also delinquents who are not mesomorphs. The data show only a significantly larger *proportion* of mesomorphic physiques among delinquent than among nondelinquent groups.

At a more subtle level, personality development may reflect the differential social treatment received by individuals of different physiques. In so far as social stereotypes may be identified with physique, they tend to influence the reactions an individual evokes from his associates, as well as his own self percept. This may be especially true in childhood and adolescence, when physical size, muscular prowess and strength, agility, and other characteristics related to physique are more likely to influence social interactions and status. Studies on children and adolescents have repeatedly shown, for instance, that at these ages leaders tend to be taller and heavier than their associates (cf. 30). Moreover, high school leaders are more likely to become leaders in college than those who were not leaders in high school, and the same individuals are also more likely to be community leaders after leaving college (cf. 13, pp. 300–301). The experience gained as school leaders would tend to predispose such individuals to later successful leadership, quite apart from other factors.

There is likewise considerable evidence to suggest that, at least in contemporary American culture, mesomorphy tends to be associated with certain social advantages. Sheldon has repeatedly referred to the mesomorphic build of "successful" men in various walks of life. In a study by Child and Sheldon (11) on college men, one of the highest correlations obtained was that between mesomorphy and dominance. Relevant data are also to be found in an investigation by Cabot (9), which utilized an extensive series of test scores, ratings, and interview data on 212 high school boys. Within this group, 9 boys were clearly and consistently classified as pyknics, 25 as athletics, and 28 as leptosomes. The principal comparisons were made among these three groups. An examination of the personality measures showed that the largest differences occurred between the athletics, on the one hand, and the pyknics and leptosomes, on the other. The athletics tended to be more dominant and extroverted, and more active as social leaders. They were also *rated* higher in creativeness, imagination, responsibility, and influence on their associates. On this basis, Cabot proposed a theory of "socio-biological advantage," according to which a "good" physique (e.g., athletic or mesomorphic) gives the individual certain advantages in his social environment.

This explanation finds some corroboration in a later study by Hanley (24). The Sheldon somatotyping technique was applied to the photographs of 122 young men aged 16 to 20 years, who had been studied four to five years earlier when they were in junior high school. At that time, a sociometric "reputation" test had been employed to discover the traits ascribed to each individual by his classmates. Several significant correlations were found between physique and reputation, some of the highest occurring between mesomorphy and such characterizations as "real boy," "takes chances," "leader," "fights," "grown-up," and "good at games." The author suggests that the traits associated with mesomorphy, taken together, seem to describe the stereotype of the "all-American boy," and recognizes that the presence of this stereotype may account for the association.

A still more direct check on such stereotypes was undertaken by Brodsky (3). The subjects were 125 men, including 75 Negro medical and dental school students and 50 white college students. Five silhouettes were prepared on the basis of Sheldon's photographs to represent the following somatotypes: endomorph, endo-mesomorph, mesomorph, ecto-mesomorph, and ectomorph. These silhouettes were presented to the subjects, together with 50 questions covering the positive and negative aspects of 25 traits, such as: (1) "Which one of this group of five men is most aggressive?" and (2) "Which one of this group of five men is least aggressive?" Since the two groups of subjects yielded no significant differences in frequency of choice of figures, they were combined for further statistical analyses. The choices also appeared to be relatively independent of the subjects' own somatotypes.

The results showed a high degree of consistency in the association of a given somatotype with specific traits. Thus on 45 of the 50 questions, the same figure was chosen by more than 30 per cent of the subjects; on 35 of the questions, 40 per cent or more agreed in choice of a figure; and on 18 of the questions, 50 per cent or more chose a single figure. In general, the endomorph was chosen for predominantly undesirable traits, suggesting the stereotype of a selfish, boorish person. The ectomorph was characterized as essentially friendless and emotionally maladjusted. The mesomorph, on the other hand, was most often designated as a leader and a desirable friend; unfavorable traits of any sort were infrequently attributed to him. The two mixed types received relatively few choices. It is amusing to note, however, that the only question for which the endo-mesomorph was selected by more than 30 per cent of the subjects was that asking who would make "the best university president." This somatotype, it will be recalled, is the one found by Sheldon and the Gluecks to predominate among juvenile delinquents!

SUMMARY

Constitutional typology represents one approach to the relationship between physical and psychological characteristics. Although typological theories have a long history, most of the psychological research pertaining to constitutional types has centered around the current theories of Kretschmer and Sheldon. Kretschmer proposes three principal types—pyknic, athletic, and leptosome—plus mixed and dysplastic categories. He maintains that, in their psychological characteristics, pyknics are inclined to be cyclothymic and leptosomes schizothymic. When applied to psychoses, such an association implies a predominance of pyknics among manic-depressives and a predominance of leptosomes among schizophrenics.

In Sheldon's system, every individual is rated on a 7-point scale on each of three components of physique (endomorphy, mesomorphy, and ectomorphy) and on three corresponding components of temperament (viscerotonia, somatotonia, and cerebrotonia). This system is not essentially different from Kretschmer's. The similarity becomes apparent when we note that, on the one hand, Kretschmer recognizes degrees of resemblance to his focal types, rather than implying sharp distinctions; and on the other hand, Sheldon's system is actually a typology since his components are to some extent mutually exclusive.

Evidence on both normal and abnormal cases suggests that some association between physique and personality exists along the lines specified by Kretschmer and Sheldon, although it is much weaker than was originally supposed. In investigations designed to check on these theories, it is essential to control such factors as age and socioeconomic level.

Constitutional typologies may be examined with regard to two questions, namely, that of typological versus dimensional systems of classification, and that of constitutional versus other kinds of relationship between physique and behavior. In reference to the first, it can be shown that dimensional systems, which describe individuals in terms of factors, traits, or dimensions, are simpler and more generally applicable than typological systems. When the typological systems of Kretschmer and Sheldon are translated into dimensional systems, two dimensions prove adequate for describing the reported individual differences in physique.

The constitutional relationship implies that both physique and behavior result from a common hereditary basis. Alternative hypotheses which may help to explain the significant but low correlations found between body build and psychological characteristics include a variety of psychosomatic and somatopsychological relations. In this connection, the presence of social stereotypes regarding body build must be taken into account. In contemporary American culture—and possibly in some other cultures as well—the athletic, mesomorphic physique is associated with leadership in many fields and tends to evoke favorable social reactions.

REFERENCES

1. Anastasi, Anne. Review of W. H. Sheldon and S. S. Stevens, "The varieties of temperament." *Psychol. Bull.*, 1943, 40, 146–149.
2. Barker, R. G., *et al. Adjustment to physical handicap and illness: a survey of the social psychology of physique and disability.* (Rev. Ed.) N.Y.: Soc. Sci. Res. Coun., 1953.
3. Brodsky, C. M. A study of norms for body form-behavior relationship. *Anthrop. Quart.*, 1954, 27, 91–101.
4. Brozek, J., and Keys, A. Body build and body composition. *Science*, 1952, 116, 140–142.
5. Burchard, E. M. L. Physique and psychosis: an analysis of the postulated relationship between bodily constitution and mental disease syndrome. *Comp. Psychol. Monogr.*, 1936, 13, No. 1.
6. Burt, C. The analysis of temperament. *Brit. J. med. Psychol.*, 1937, 17, 158–188.
7. Burt, C. Factor analysis and physical types. *Psychometrika*, 1947, 12, 171–188.
8. Burt, C., and Banks, C. A factor analysis of body measurements for British adult males. *Ann. Eugen.*, 1947, 13, 238–256.
9. Cabot, P. S. de Q. The relationship between characteristics of personality and physique in adolescents. *Genet. Psychol. Monogr.*, 1938, 20, 3–120.
10. Child, I. L. The relation of somatotype to self-ratings on Sheldon's temperamental traits. *J. Pers.*, 1950, 18, 440–453.
11. Child, I. L., and Sheldon, W. H. The correlation between components of physique and scores on certain psychological tests. *Char. and Pers.*, 1941, 10, 23–34.
12. Coffin, T. E. A three-component theory of leadership. *J. abnorm. soc. Psychol.*, 1944, 39, 63–83.
13. Cole, Luella. *Psychology of adolescence.* (4th Ed.) N.Y.: Rinehart, 1954.
14. Ekman, G. On typological and dimensional systems of reference in describing personality. *Acta psychol.*, 1951, 8, 1–24.

15. Ekman, G. On the number and definition of dimensions in Kretschmer's and Sheldon's constitutional systems. In *Essays in psychology dedicated to David Katz.* Uppsala: Almquist and Wiksells, 1951. Pp. 72–103.
16. Eysenck, H. J. *Dimensions of personality.* London: Routledge & Kegan Paul, 1947.
17. Eysenck, H. J. Personality. *Ann. Rev. Psychol.*, 1952, 3, 151–174.
18. Eysenck, H. J. *The structure of human personality.* N.Y.: Wiley, 1953.
19. Fiske, D. W. A study of relationships to somatotype. *J. appl. Psychol.*, 1944, 28, 504–519.
20. Garrett, H. E., and Kellogg, W. N. The relation of physical constitution to general intelligence, social intelligence, and emotional stability. *J. exp. Psychol.*, 1928, 11, 113–129.
21. Garvey, C. R. Comparative body build of manic-depressive and schizophrenic patients. *Psychol. Bull.*, 1933, 30, 567–568, 739.
22. Glueck, S., and Glueck, Eleanor T. *Unraveling juvenile delinquency.* N.Y.: Commonwealth Fund, 1950.
23. Hammond, W. H. An application of Burt's multiple general factor analysis to the delineation of physical types. *Man*, 1942, 42, 4–11.
24. Hanley, C. Physique and reputation of junior high school boys. *Child Develpm.*, 1951, 22, 247–260.
25. Heath, Helen. A factor analysis of women's measurements taken for garment and pattern construction. *Psychometrika*, 1952, 17, 87–100.
26. Heidbreder, Edna. Intelligence and the height-weight ratio. *J. appl. Psychol.*, 1926, 10, 52–62.
27. Howells, W. W. A factorial study of constitutional types. *Amer. J. phys. Anthrop.*, 1952, 10, 91–118.
28. Humphreys, L. G. Characteristics of type concepts with special reference to Sheldon's typology. *Psychol. Bull.*, 1957, 54, 218–228.
29. Janoff, Irma Z., Beck, L. H., and Child, I. L. The relation of somatotype to reaction time, resistance to pain, and expressive movement. *J. Pers.*, 1950, 18, 454–460.
30. Jenkins, W. O. A review of leadership studies with particular reference to military problems. *Psychol. Bull.*, 1947, 44, 54–79.
31. Klineberg, O., Asch, S. E., and Block, Helen. An experimental study of constitutional types. *Genet. Psychol. Monogr.*, 1934, 16, 140–221.
32. Klineberg, O., Fjeld, Harriet A., and Foley, J. P., Jr. An experimental study of personality differences among constitutional, "racial," and cultural groups. Unpubl. Project Report, 1936.
33. Kretschmer, E. *Physique and character.* (Transl. from 2nd ed. by W. J. H. Sprott.) N.Y.: Harcourt, Brace, 1925.
34. Kretschmer, E. *Körperbau und Charakter.* (20th Ed.) Berlin: Springer, 1951.
35. Lorr, M., and Fields, V. A factorial study of body types. *J. clin. Psychol.*, 1954, 10, 182–185.
36. Lubin, A. A note on Sheldon's table of correlations between temperamental traits. *Brit. J. Psychol., statist. Sect.*, 1950, 3, 186–189.
37. Naccarati, S. The morphologic aspect of intelligence. *Arch. Psychol.*, 1921. No. 45.

38. Newman, R. B. Age changes in body build. *Amer. J. phys. Anthrop.*, 1952, 10, 75–90.
39. Paterson, D. G. *Physique and intellect.* N.Y.: Appleton-Century-Crofts, 1930.
40. Rees, L. The physical constitution and mental illness. *Eugen. Rev.*, 1947, 39, 50–55.
41. Rees, L. Body build, personality and neurosis in women. *J. ment. Sci.*, 1950, 96, 426–434.
42. Rees, L. A factorial study of physical constitution in women. *J. ment. Sci.*, 1950, 96, 619–632.
43. Rees, L., and Eysenck, H. J. A factorial study of some morphological and psychological aspects of human constitution. *J. ment. Sci.*, 1945, 91, 8–21.
44. Sanford, R. N. Physical and physiological correlates of personality structure. In C. Kluckhohn and H. A. Murray (Eds.), *Personality.* (2nd Ed.) N.Y.: Knopf, 1953. Ch. 5.
45. Seltzer, C. C., Wells, F. L., and McTernan, E. B. A relationship between Sheldonian somatotype and psychotype. *J. Pers.*, 1948, 16, 431–436.
46. Sheldon, W. H. Morphologic types and mental ability. *J. personnel Res.*, 1927, 5, 447–451.
47. Sheldon, W. H. Social traits and morphologic types. *J. personnel Res.*, 1927, 6, 47–55.
48. Sheldon, W. H. *Varieties of delinquent youth.* N.Y.: Harper, 1949.
49. Sheldon, W. H. *Atlas of men.* N.Y.: Harper, 1954.
50. Sheldon, W. H., and Stevens, S. S. *The varieties of temperament.* N.Y.: Harper, 1942.
51. Sheldon, W. H., Stevens, S. S., and Tucker, W. B. *The varieties of human physique.* N.Y.: Harper, 1940.
52. Sills, F. D. A factor analysis of somatotypes and of their relationship to achievement in motor skills. *Res. Quart. Amer. Ass. Hlth. phys. Educ.*, 1950, 21, 424–437.
53. Smith, H. C. Psychometric checks on hypotheses derived from Sheldon's work on physique and temperament. *J. Pers.*, 1949, 17, 310–320.
54. Sutherland, E. H. Critique of Sheldon's varieties of delinquent youth. *Amer. sociol. Rev.*, 1951, 16, 10–13.
55. Thurstone, L. L. Factor analysis and body types. *Psychometrika*, 1946, 11, 15–21.
56. Wertheimer, F. I., and Hesketh, F. E. The significance of the physical constitution in mental disease. *Medicine*, 1926, 5, 375–463.
57. Westphal, K. Körperbau und Charakter der Epileptiker. *Nervenartz*, 1931, 4, 96–99.
58. Wittman, Phyllis, Sheldon, W. H., and Katz, C. J. A study of the relationship between constitutional variations and fundamental psychotic behavior reactions. *J. nerv. ment. Dis.*, 1948, 108, 470–476.

CHAPTER 7

Training and
Individual Differences

An important set of questions regarding the origins of individual differences centers around the part played by training in behavior development. When the psychologist speaks of "training," he uses the term in a broader sense than is customary in popular speech and in certain other specialized fields. By "training" the psychologist usually means any activity or series of experiences designed to improve performance. Training may thus range from repetitive exercise of simple motor skills, through complex instructional procedures, to the more intangible phases of education. The process of breaking in a new worker on the assembly line, a course in conversational French, piano lessons, a series of lectures on Greek drama, and a school program aimed at the development of civic responsibility would all come under the heading of training in this sense.

Several types of training research directed toward an analysis of maturational and learning factors in behavior development were surveyed in Chapter 4. Training experiments on animals and human infants were considered in that connection. Examination of another group of training studies, dealing with the rehabilitation of the feebleminded, will be reserved for Chapter 12. In the present chapter, we shall concentrate on certain special training problems that have been investigated with normal adults and school-age children. All of the studies to be discussed have utilized psychological tests of various sorts. Some have investigated the course of learning under controlled laboratory conditions. A large number have been concerned with the effects of formal schooling upon intellectual development.

189

PRACTICE, COACHING, AND TEST SOPHISTICATION

Psychologists have come a long way from the old idea that "the IQ" is a property of the organism, fixed by heredity. It is now generally recognized that an IQ is simply a score on a particular test. As such, it not only varies somewhat with the nature and content of the test, but it is also susceptible to all the influences that affect behavior. For a proper interpretation of any IQ, we therefore need information on: (1) the test from which it was obtained, and (2) the experiential background of the individual, in so far as it may have affected the type of behavior functions sampled by the test.

A more specific group of questions pertains to the individual's previous test-taking experience. To what extent does practice in taking tests improve performance? Can coaching on psychological tests appreciably raise scores? A number of studies provide data on the effects of repeating the *identical test* within periods ranging from a few days to a year (1, 6, 9, 10, 25, 26). Both adults and children and both normal and mentally defective subjects have been employed. Most of the studies have utilized group tests, although some data on individual tests are also available. All agree in showing significant mean gains in score upon retests. Nor is improvement necessarily limited to the initial repetitions. Whether the gains persist or level off in successive administrations seems to depend upon the difficulty of the test and the ability level of the subjects (9, 25, 26).

The implications of such findings are illustrated by the authors of one of these studies, who point out that the meaning of an IQ on a given test may change considerably on repeated retestings. Thus an IQ of 100 might correspond to the 47th percentile of the group if obtained on the first testing, but to the 17th percentile if obtained on a subsequent testing (10, p. 134). In other words, an IQ which on a first test would indicate approximately average ability might signify ability in the lowest quarter of the distribution if obtained on a retest.

It should be noted that repetition may alter the nature of a test, since different *work methods* may be employed before and after practice in solving the same problems. In general, those tests in which work methods change little with repetition show little improvement in score as a result of practice; those in which performance undergoes marked qualitative changes with repetition show large gains. Some evidence for this relationship was provided by a study on college students in which objective test scores were supplemented with qualitative observations of performance and with introspective reports on the methods employed in solving problems (22). In this study, tests measuring speed of simple movements and tests of auditory discrimination showed little or no practice effect. In taking such tests the subjects performed essentially the same functions on initial and later trials. Tests involving precision of movement and those depending upon prior information, such as vocabulary tests, yielded retest gains ranging from 6 to 25 per cent of initial scores. Maze and block design tests, in which a generalized rule could be formulated during the initial test, showed increases of from 76 to 200 per cent. Even greater improvements were found in mechanical aptitude tests in which objects had to be assembled from their constituent parts—in such cases, the earlier solutions could be recalled and reapplied without change in the retest.

Gains in score are also found upon retesting with *parallel forms* of the same test, although such gains tend in general to be smaller. Significant mean gains have been reported when alternate forms of a test were administered in immediate succession (53), at one-day intervals (53), and one month apart (44, 45). Similar results have been obtained with British children (44, 45), normal and intellectually gifted American school children (53), and American high school, college, and graduate students (53). Contemporary test constructors recognize such a practice effect and often make allowances for it. In the Minnesota Preschool Scale, for example, it is suggested that 3 IQ points be deducted as a correction for practice effect when alternate forms are administered within a few weeks (19). Similarly, the manual for the Stanford-Binet reports a mean increase of about 2.5 IQ points when Form L is followed by Form M, or vice versa, within a few days (52).

There is likewise evidence of a more general effect, known as *test sophistication* (26, 47). This simply means that the individual who has had extensive prior experience in taking psychological tests of any sort enjoys a certain advantage in test performance over one who is taking his first test. Part of this advantage stems from having overcome an initial feeling of strangeness, as well as from having developed more self-confidence and better test-taking attitudes. Part is the result of a certain amount of overlap in the type of content and functions covered by many tests. Probably other factors also operate in more subtle and indirect ways. It is particularly important to take test sophistication into account when comparing results from children in different types of schools, where the extent of psychological testing may vary widely.

A number of investigations have been concerned with the effects of *coaching* upon test performance. Several early studies with the Stanford-

Binet demonstrated that children can be taught to perform intelligence test items that they were formerly incapable of executing correctly (5, 23). Large and significant gains in IQ were obtained in one experiment as a result of two hours of coaching on tests the child had failed on a previous administration of the Stanford-Binet (23). Groups coached on material similar but not identical to the test content showed smaller gains. The effects of the coaching declined on successive retests; and at the end of three years, no significant differences remained between the groups coached on identical and on similar material and the control group which had been retested with no intervening coaching. Such a result is to be expected, partly because of forgetting, and partly because the nature of Stanford-Binet items varies at different age levels. The children were therefore being tested on tasks unlike those on which they had been coached.

More recent research on a number of group as well as individual tests has likewise shown that, in general, coaching produces significant gains in mean scores (8, 12, 15, 31, 63, 70, 71, 73). Many of these studies have been conducted by British psychologists, who have been concerned about the effects of practice and coaching upon the tests used in assigning 11-year-old children to different types of secondary schools. As might be expected, the extent of improvement depends upon the ability and earlier educational experiences of the subjects, the nature of the tests, and the amount and type of coaching provided. Subjects with deficient educational backgrounds are more likely to benefit from special coaching than are those who have had superior educational opportunities and are already prepared to do well on the tests. It is obvious, too, that the closer the resemblance between the test content and the coaching material, the greater will be the improvement in test scores. On the other hand, effectiveness of coaching may depend upon the degree to which the subjects are taught principles or types of information which they may be able to apply to a wide variety of situations.

In connection with the last point, some suggestive data have been reported which indicate that large gains in intelligence test scores may result from special training in semantics and in logic (40, 60). Promising results on groups of college students tested before and after such training point to the desirability of other studies along these lines.

A similar approach is represented by special exercises designed to improve children's readiness for first-grade schoolwork and to stimulate the development of various intellectual functions. In one attempt to test the effectiveness of such instruction (28), two kindergarten classes totaling 53 children were put through a 14-week program based on the "Learning to Think" series (57, 58). Before and after this program, the children were given the Thurstone Primary Mental Abilities tests (primary level) and the Wechsler Intelligence Scale for Children. Two control classes of 54 cases took the same pretests and posttests, without the intervening training. All groups improved on the second testing. On the Primary Mental Abilities tests, the trained groups made significantly larger gains than the controls. On the Wechsler, however, all groups improved significantly at the .01 level, the trained groups showing no advantage over the controls. The gains on the Wechsler scale could not, therefore, be attributed to the training program. The results thus suggest that the training provided by the "Learn to Think" series may be specific to the Primary Mental Abilities tests, rather than bringing about a more general improvement. It should be noted in this connection that the training material is closely similar to the test items.

Studies such as the last three cited raise a question as to whether we are dealing with coaching on psychological tests or with general education. The answer to this question depends upon the *breadth of the effect*. If improvement is limited to the specific test items or to closely similar material, then the training would be regarded as coaching. Such coaching would reduce the validity of the test for predictive purposes. On the other hand, if improvement extends to the broader area of behavior which the test is designed to measure, then the training can properly be considered to be education and would in no way invalidate the test. In such a case, the test score still presents an accurate picture of the individual's standing in the abilities under consideration. Obviously, any experience the individual undergoes, either formal or informal, in or out of school, should be reflected in his performance on tests that sample relevant aspects of behavior.

Another point to consider in interpreting individual differences in test scores pertains to the previously mentioned question of work methods. If either practice or coaching on a test leads to the use of different work methods in solving the same problems, then *differences in work methods may also account for individual differences on the initial administration of the test*. For example, individuals whose previous experience includes the solution of many arithmetic problems dealing with amount of money spent and saved out of weekly earnings, or number of pencils that can be bought for a given amount of money, will rely more heavily on memory and routine solutions, and less heavily upon reasoning, in taking a test that consists of such problems. The reverse will be true of individuals without such previous experience. This is even more apparent in such tests as mechanical assembly. On a test of this sort, the initial performance of a person who has frequently taken apart and put together bells, clocks, latches, and other mechanical gadgets may be more nearly comparable to the third-trial performance of a mechanically inexperienced individual than to the latter's first-trial performance.

PRACTICE AND VARIABILITY

A number of interrelated questions have been asked regarding the relation of practice to individual differences. Do individual differences increase or decrease with practice? Do individuals tend to maintain the same relative position in the course of training? To what extent are individual differences attributable to differences in amount of practice? Such questions have both practical and theoretical implications. They have a direct bearing upon personnel selection and placement, vocational and educational counseling, and any other procedure requiring the prediction of how individuals will perform after training. From a theoretical viewpoint, some psychologists have tried to utilize experiments on practice and variability as one approach to the analysis of hereditary and environmental contributions to behavior development.

The answers to these questions, however, have not proved to be so simple as was originally anticipated. Early investigators often obtained conflicting results owing to a number of methodological difficulties.[1] Many of these discrepancies can be shown to arise from the specific ways in which the problems were formulated. One of the differences pertains to the *measure of practice* employed. When we say that two persons have had equal practice, do we mean that they have spent an equal amount of time practicing or that they have done an equal amount of work? For example, have they both spent two hours working on arithmetic problems or have they both solved ten practice problems?

Another difficulty arises from the use of amount or time scores as *measures of progress.* The former are based on the amount of work correctly done during a given time period; the latter, on the time required to complete a given amount of work. Results of practice experiments will also depend upon the choice of *absolute or relative measures of variability,* as described in Chapter 2. Is the extent of individual differences to be expressed in terms of a range, standard deviation, or similar absolute measure, or in terms of a ratio measure such as the coefficient of variation?

A final problem relates to *inequality of units.* In many psychological tests, successive score points do not correspond to equal increments of difficulty.

---

[1] For a survey of this literature and an analysis of the methodological problems, cf. Anastasi (2).

Thus it may be more difficult to add five points to an initial score of 30 than to an initial score of 20. Moreover, changes in work methods that often occur in the course of practice are likely to affect the relative distance between successive score units. If, for example, progress beyond a certain score requires a more complex organization of simple activities, or the development of a more efficient procedure, then score units at this point probably represent larger steps in a scale of difficulty level. Shifts in size of raw-score units may also occur in tasks in which a "physiological limit" is rapidly approached. This is often true in motor tasks and in many tasks in which speed is of primary importance. In such cases, physiological or structurally imposed limitations may make progress beyond a certain point impossible. As this point is approached, it becomes increasingly difficult to improve one's score; the successive score units thus correspond to progressively larger differences in difficulty level. The same effect occurs when progress is artificially limited by the test ceiling. If this ceiling is too low for the subjects being tested, it will have the effect of artifically reducing individual differences in the course of practice, since everyone's progress is arbitrarily cut short at a relatively low level, although a number of individuals could have advanced much farther if given the opportunity.

It can be argued, on both theoretical and practical grounds, that the most meaningful formulation of the problem of practice and variability involves changes in the absolute variability of amount scores following equal amounts of time spent in practice by all subjects (cf. 2). When these conditions are met, most investigations agree in showing an *increase* in individual differences with practice. Typical results can be found in a study by Anastasi (2). Four groups, each comprising from 114 to 200 college students, were given continuous practice in one of the following four tests:

Cancellation: crossing out every "A" in a page of pied type

Symbol-Digit: writing correct number under each symbol, by reference to key

Vocabulary: writing appropriate nonsense syllable next to each given syllable, by reference to key

Hidden Words: underlining all four-letter English words in a page of pied type

Practice consisted of 15 4-minute trials in Hidden Words and 20 2-minute trials in each of the other tests, a different group of subjects being employed for each test. All scores were transmuted into an equal-unit scale previously developed on a single sample of 1000 cases.

Means and standard deviations of the scores on each trial are reproduced in Table 7. It can be readily seen that the standard deviations rise with practice in each test. Although there are minor fluctuations from trial to trial, the trend is unmistakable. On each test, the difference between initial and final SD's is significant at the .01 level. Thus the results indicate that individuals tend to be more *dissimilar* following a period of equal practice than they were at the outset.

Table 7

MEANS AND STANDARD DEVIATIONS OF SCORES OF SUCCESSIVE TRIALS OF EACH OF FOUR TESTS

(From Anastasi, 2, pp. 40–42)

TRIAL	CANCELLATION (N = 200)		SYMBOL-DIGIT (N = 134)		VOCABULARY (N = 123)		HIDDEN WORDS (N = 114)	
	Mean	SD	Mean	SD	Mean	SD	Mean	SD
1	40.63	6.78	41.15	7.58	39.06	6.84	43.58	6.94
2	44.99	6.42	47.63	7.38	46.30	6.03	44.63	6.90
3	47.00	6.60	52.69	7.30	45.22	6.95	49.00	7.52
4	48.00	6.52	54.57	8.04	47.74	5.88	51.25	7.74
5	50.75	6.60	57.90	7.94	49.19	6.86	54.49	7.86
6	50.30	6.68	58.63	8.34	48.80	6.78	55.12	8.24
7	51.68	6.62	61.02	8.66	52.06	7.22	58.18	9.28
8	52.74	7.04	62.25	8.44	48.97	7.89	60.40	8.90
9	53.06	7.28	63.79	8.08	51.59	7.16	61.30	9.10
10	55.83	7.24	64.52	8.36	52.50	8.34	64.40	10.22
11	54.70	7.24	65.22	7.94	53.08	8.90	62.19	10.46
12	55.08	7.22	65.70	9.40	55.35	8.10	63.26	10.96
13	56.09	7.70	67.04	8.06	54.54	7.98	67.02	11.36
14	55.50	7.12	67.51	8.40	54.74	7.26	68.47	12.96
15	57.88	7.54	67.78	8.72	56.02	8.49	69.28	11.44
16	56.67	7.70	69.13	9.78	56.48	8.46		
17	57.01	7.32	68.19	8.92	57.83	8.59		
18	57.62	7.58	68.81	8.80	56.63	9.13		
19	57.08	7.36	69.17	8.40	56.97	8.89		
20	59.60	7.88	70.07	9.98	59.28	8.87		

Mention may also be made in this connection of the evidence suggesting that individual differences tend to increase in the course of *forgetting*. In a survey of data from many published learning experiments, Tilton (59) found a tendency for the standard deviations to rise when subjects were retested after a lapse of time. Differential forgetting thus appears as an additional source of variation in performance.

It has likewise been generally found that, in the course of practice, individuals tend to maintain the *same relative standing* in their group. In a summary of early studies, Kincaid (34) reported that the correlations between scores on initial and final trials were usually over .60. In the previously cited investigation by Anastasi (2), the correlations between initial and final trials were all positive and significant at the .01 level. For the four tests, these correlations were:

Cancellation	.6725
Symbol-Digit	.2981
Vocabulary	.5073
Hidden Words	.8239

Such results indicate that predictions of an individual's posttraining performance from his pretraining score are always better than chance. The accuracy of prediction varies with the nature of the functions and the amount of intervening practice (27). But in the large majority of activities, the correlations are high enough to make prediction practicable.

The fact that individuals tend to maintain their relative status and to diverge rather than converge after a period of equal practice was interpreted by some early writers as evidence for a predominantly hereditary basis of individual differences. It was argued that if initial differences were largely the result of inequalities of past experience, a period of uniform training should drastically reduce such differences. This is a questionable line of reasoning. The influence of environmental factors upon the development of abilities is cumulative. If one individual's prior experience has made him more proficient in a certain task, we should expect him to be better fitted to profit from further training. The initially better performer brings to the task work methods, attitudes, skills, and information which serve also to accelerate his subsequent progress. The more the individual has learned in the past, the better able will he be to learn in the present. Moreover, it should be recognized that "uniform training" may be uniform in a limited sense only. What the individual actually does during such training—and hence what he learns from it—is itself dependent upon his relevant past experiences.

Some investigators have tried to determine the *relative contribution of practice to individual differences.* Suppose we were to administer a Latin examination to the seniors in a particular high school, all of whom have had from one to four years of instruction in Latin. We could then ask, "How much of the total score variability in the entire senior class results from amount of Latin instruction and how much from individual differences within groups that have had the same amount of instruction?" From what we know about the range of performance within a single class in any school subject, we would expect considerable overlapping between the achievement test scores of different instructional groups. For instance, it is not improbable that the best student in the one-year group would do better on the examination than the poorest student in the four-year group. It is certainly obvious that, in the situation described, amount of training in Latin will not prove to be the *only* source of variation in test score. By appropriate statistical analysis, we could determine what proportion of the total variance of Latin test scores in this group is attributable to amount of training and what proportion to individual differences within training groups.[2]

Investigations designed to answer this type of question have utilized both school courses and controlled laboratory practice (16, 24, 41, 42, 54). Some of these studies have tended to create misleading impressions, for a number of reasons. First, some of the published estimates of the proportional contribution of practice and individual differences to total variance are in error because of the use of improper statistical techniques (cf. critiques in 21, p. 162; 24, pp. 5–8). Secondly, as Hamilton (24) has pointed out in a careful analysis of the problem, we cannot attribute to heredity all individual differences which remain when amount of training is held constant. Such an interpretation—proposed by some early writers—ignores the cumulative effects of antecedent environmental factors, which were discussed above. When the training under consideration was obtained in a regular school course, the effect of prior differences in motivation, study habits, and previously acquired information and skills upon the student's course performance is especially important. To this should be added the fact that registration in the same course does not signify the same amount of time spent in learning the subject on the part of different students!

A third and more fundamental objection to most of these studies is that they report what seems to be a generalized estimate of the proportional contribution of practice and individual differences to total variance. That such general estimates are meaningless was clearly demonstrated in a well-planned study by Hamilton (24). Fifth-grade school children were given 20 trials on each of three learning tests—making gates, symbol-digit substitution, and artificial language. Number of cases varied from 22 to 28 for the different tests. The relative contribution of practice to total variance was determined for each test and at different stages of practice. Essentially, this analysis was based on a comparison of the extent of individual differences within single trials with the over-all score changes from trial to trial.

Hamilton's analysis showed that, for each test, the proportional contribution of practice varied widely, depending upon the amount of intervening

---

[2] The technique to be employed for this purpose is based on Fisher's analysis of variance. The variance is the square of the standard deviation, or $\dfrac{\Sigma(X-M)^2}{N}$.

practice. The data reproduced in Table 8 illustrate this point. When average performance on the first two trials was compared with that on the last two, the proportional contribution of practice was consistently larger than that of the other, residual factors making for individual differences within any one trial. On the other hand, when adjacent pairs of trials are compared, it

Table 8

CONTRIBUTION OF PRACTICE TO TOTAL SCORE VARIANCE

(From Hamilton, 24, pp. 32–34)

TEST	TRIALS 1–2 VERSUS 19–20 Percentage of Total Score Variance Attributable to:		TRIALS 1–2 VERSUS 3–4 Percentage of Total Score Variance Attributable to:	
	Practice	Individual Differences	Practice	Individual Differences
Making Gates	84.15	15.85	32.16	67.84
Symbol-Digit	55.65	44.35	25.57	74.43
Artificial Language	71.43	28.57	34.38	65.62

appears that residual individual differences are far more important than practice in determining total score variance. Hamilton concludes that no generalized estimate can be meaningfully presented, since the proportional contribution of practice depends upon: (1) the stage of the learning curve at which individual differences are measured, (2) the amount of practice that intervenes between the trials being compared, (3) the heterogeneity of the groups in regard to other relevant characteristics, and (4) the kind of task or skill under consideration.

The reader may have noticed that this critique of generalized estimates of proportional contribution has a familiar sound. We encountered the same point in Chapter 3, when discussing the interaction of hereditary and environmental factors. It was there pointed out that a different estimate of the proportional contribution of heredity and environment will be obtained in groups that vary in either hereditary or environmental heterogeneity. Thus in a group having relatively uniform environment, hereditary factors have a larger weight in determining individual differences. Conversely, in a group with relatively homogeneous heredity, environmental factors would exert a relatively greater influence in the development of individual differences. It should be noted that the same relationship holds when we determine the relative weights of two different environmental factors or two different hereditary factors. Thus in the Hamilton experiment, if we wish to compare the relative contribution of immediate practice (number of trials or length of training) with the contribution of antecedent factors (environmental and hereditary), the estimate will vary as either present practice or prior conditions vary. For example, if we consider only scores obtained within a single trial, the contribution of practice to score variance would obviously be zero. Similarly, if scores on adjacent trials are compared, the role of practice in producing score differences appears to be relatively small. When, on the other hand, we compare trials that are widely separated, the contribution of practice appears much greater than that of individual differences.

NURSERY SCHOOL STUDIES

Over fifty investigations have been conducted to determine what effect, if any, preschool attendance at a kindergarten or nursery school has upon the child's subsequent intellectual development. Interest in this problem reached a peak in the early 1940's with the publication of a series of studies from the University of Iowa. A lively controversy ensued, with critiques, replies, rejoinders, and counter-rejoinders appearing in the psychological journals. Although preschool studies may have added little to our knowledge of the causes of individual differences, they stimulated a thorough overhauling of the methodology of longitudinal studies. As a by-product of the controversy, attention was focused on the experimental and statistical requirements of such investigations. The net outcome was a positive contribution to the development of sound research methods.

In 1945, Wellman (66) summarized the findings of preschool studies published prior to that time. Because of small samples, lack of control groups, and other limitations, many of these investigations are inconclusive. Some, for example, give only the intelligence test scores of a nursery school group before and after a period of preschool attendance. In such studies it is impossible to determine how much of the change in score may result from retesting or from the time of the year when the tests are given. A control group is essential for this purpose. Another group of studies report only the relative performance in the first grade (or at subsequent scholastic levels) of two groups, one of which had attended preschool while the other had not. The difficulty with this procedure is that nursery school attendance itself may be selective. Even when groups are equated in parental education and occupation, as well as in other broad categories, selection may have occurred within these categories. Thus, among families with the same educational, occupational, and socioeconomic level, those parents who enroll their children in nursery school may still differ in intelligence, personality characteristics, interest in their children, or other subtle and inconspicuous ways. For all these reasons, the most satisfactory procedure involves the testing of a nursery school group before and after nursery school attendance, together with the corresponding testing of a control group over the same interval.

An examination of the extensive and widely quoted investigations of Wellman and her collaborators at the University of Iowa (65) will serve to illustrate the nature of nursery school studies. In one of the Iowa projects, data were gathered from 652 children, aged 18 to 77 months, all of whom were attending either the nursery school or kindergarten conducted by the university. The subjects were given either the Stanford-Binet or the Kuhlmann-Binet in the fall and again in the spring of each year of preschool attendance. During the first year of attendance, the scores showed a mean gain of 6.6 IQ points. Those children who continued in attendance for two or three years showed further mean rises in IQ, although the gains became progressively smaller each year. On the other hand, no significant correlation was found between gain in IQ and actual number of days attended during the year (the latter ranging from 37 to 148 days).

No evaluation of the above findings is possible, of course, without comparable data from a control group. For this purpose, Wellman matched 34 of the preschool children with 34 non-preschool children in chronological age and initial IQ. Between the fall and spring testing, this preschool group gained an average of 7.0 points, while the control group lost an average of 3.9 points. The mean difference of almost 11 points between the two groups on the spring test was statistically significant. At first sight, these findings seem to show a genuine though slight effect of nursery school attendance upon IQ—and they were so interpreted by the Iowa investigators. This conclusion, however, aroused a storm of objections (cf. 17, 18, 37, 38, 68). Some of the more fundamental methodological and interpretive questions raised by these criticisms deserve consideration because of their general implications.

With regard to the continued improvement of children attending nursery school for two or three years, it is likely that the gains in test scores result largely from *practice and test sophistication,* discussed in an earlier section of this chapter. In general, the longer a child remains in nursery school, the more often he is tested. Direct evidence bearing on this question was provided in a study by Jones and Jorgensen (33) at the University of California. These authors found a correlation of .34 between IQ gain and length of nursery school attendance. When number of tests was held constant by a partial correlation technique, however, the correlation between IQ gain and duration of nursery school attendance dropped to a negligible and insignificant value.

Improvement in test performance following preschool attendance may also result in part from better *emotional and motivational adjustment* to the testing situation. In a carefully controlled nursery school study conducted by Goodenough and Maurer (20) at the University of Minnesota, an attempt was made to eliminate this factor by not testing children when they exhibited negativistic behavior. Moreover, if a child continued to show an uncooperative attitude on repeated visits, he was excluded from the study. As a further precaution, none of the examiners was connected with the nursery school. Thus degree of acquaintance between examiner and child was no greater in the nursery than in the non-nursery group. Under these conditions, the nursery group showed negligible gains in mean IQ following nursery school attendance. It might be noted parenthetically that this study may have ruled out too much. In the effort to eliminate specific factors influencing test-taking behavior, the investigators may have overlooked the possibility that nursery school attendance may improve attitudes toward adult-determined tasks in general. Such improvement might in turn facilitate subsequent learning and intellectual development. As in the case of the previously discussed coaching studies, the question is one of breadth or generality of effect.

Further methodological difficulties center around the practice of utilizing *previously differentiated populations,* in which a process of "self-sorting" has occurred. Ideally, matched groups should be chosen in advance by the experimenter, from a single population. In testing the effects of nursery school attendance, for instance, children should first be paired off on the basis of matching characteristics. One member of each pair should then be selected at random for assignment to the nursery school group, the other being assigned to the control group. In actual practice, however, investigations of schooling have had to resort to *a posteriori* matching. Certain children within a community are entered in nursery school on the basis of their parents' decision. Such a decision may itself reflect characteristics which distinguish these parents, their homes, or their children from others in the community. The investigator now steps in and tries to find other children in the community who "match" these nursery children in what he considers to be important characteristics for his study.

With *a posteriori* matching, it is likely that the groups will differ in one or more characteristics whose relevance to the problem under investigation may have been overlooked. If, for example, children from more "intellectually oriented" homes are sent to nursery schools, then the systematic difference in home atmosphere in favor of the nursery group might in time lead to superior development of this group, in contrast to the control group. Or it might happen that children who are inclined to be shy are more often sent to nursery school to enable them to overcome this difficulty. In such a case, the child's shyness might handicap him on his initial intelligence test and lead to an apparent gain on a later test, when the shyness in the unfamiliar situation had decreased. When the experimenter assigns children at random to the nursery and non-nursery groups, any uncontrolled characteristics will tend by chance to be distributed equally in the two groups. But when special factors, such as parents' decision to register their child in nursery school, determine placement in experimental or control group, then the uncontrolled characteristics may vary systematically, piling up an excess of one type of child in only *one* of the groups.

An even more serious objection to the use of matched samples from previously differentiated populations stems from what statisticians call the *"regression effect."* Regression operates whenever comparisons are made between two measures that are imperfectly correlated. This condition applies to any retest, whether the same test is repeated or whether equivalent forms are administered on two occasions. It is well known that no test has a reliability coefficient of 1.00 (cf. Ch. 1). In other words, individuals' scores will generally exhibit some chance variation on a retest. Regression simply means that, through such chance variation, extreme scores tend to "regress" or move toward the mean upon retesting. For example, if children are given Form L of the Stanford-Binet and then retested with Form M six months later, there will be a tendency for those who scored above average on the first test to fall closer to the mean on the second test. Similarly, the low scorers on the first test will tend to rise toward the mean on the second.

Regression results from the presence of uncorrelated, chance factors which affect scores on the two occasions. Some of the individuals receiving high initial scores did so partly because certain chance factors raised their scores on that particular occasion or on that form of the test. Such individuals were thus at an advantage on the initial test. Since, however, such chance factors are uncorrelated on the two tests, these individuals will not be equally favored on the retest and their scores will tend to drop more often than they will rise or remain the same. It is the presence of these chance factors, of course, which keeps the correlation between the two tests from being perfect. In this connection, it is also noteworthy that the reliability of preschool tests tends to be lower than that of tests for older subjects.

Hence chance factors play a larger part in scores obtained at preschool ages and regression effect is relatively great.

A schematic illustration of regression will be found in Figure 40. The upper graph represents the distribution of IQ's on the first testing, the lower graph that on the second testing. Regression is shown in the case of ten persons, each of whom obtained an IQ of 120 on the initial test. Owing to uncorrelated chance factors in the two testings, the scores of these ten persons "fan out" over a wide range on the retest; and the average of the ten retest IQ's (107) is closer to the group mean than was the initial value of 120. It should be added that such regression leaves the total range of the distribution unchanged. Individuals simply trade places, with no reduction in total group variability.

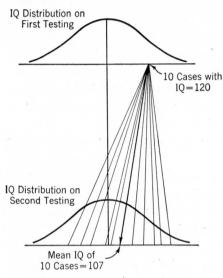

IQ Distribution on First Testing

10 Cases with IQ=120

IQ Distribution on Second Testing

Mean IQ of 10 Cases=107

Fig. 40. "Regression Effect" in Retesting.

How does regression enter into the use of matched samples? Reference to Figure 41 suggests the answer. It is likely, for example, that children attending a university preschool tend to come from superior homes and to have higher IQ's than other children in their community. Thus if we consider the IQ distribution of preschool and non-preschool children as a whole, we may find a situation similar to that represented by population A and population B in Figure 41. If, now, an investigator assembles matched samples from these two populations, he can only do so by choosing children below the mean of population A and above the mean of population B. Upon retesting, therefore, the individuals in sample a (preschool) will tend to regress toward their population mean, i.e., their IQ's will tend to rise. For the same reason, the IQ's of sample b (control) will tend to drop. Thus we have a possible explanation for the mean IQ gain of the preschool group and the mean IQ loss of the control group found in the Iowa study. The final

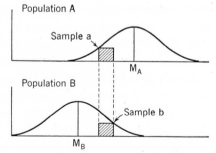

Population A

Sample a

M_A

Population B

Sample b

M_B

Fig. 41. Matched Samples from Dissimilar Populations.

difference in score between the two groups may be no more than a statistical artifact resulting from the way in which the matched samples were chosen.[3]

In the light of the methodological difficulties of the Iowa investigation—and in view of the negative results of other similar studies—it is clear that no effect of nursery school attendance upon IQ has thereby been demonstrated. It should be noted, however, that the Iowa study discussed above was carried out in a university preschool. This was also true of most other preschool studies, including the California and Minnesota projects cited. The fact that children enrolled in such preschools tend, on the whole, to come from superior homes serves to minimize any possible effect of the preschool. If the children are already in an environment that is highly conducive to intellectual development, the additional preschool experience may not represent a noticeable difference. For this reason, investigations with underprivileged children represent a more crucial test of the effect of nursery school attendance.

Suggestive results in this connection are provided by another Iowa study, conducted in an orphanage (67). The children were below average in initial IQ, came from low socioeconomic backgrounds, and were living in a relatively unstimulating institutional environment. Into this setting the investigators introduced a preschool whose activities offered a genuine contrast to routine orphanage life. Moreover, since subjects were assigned by the experimenters to preschool and control groups, there could be no question of either self-sorting or regression effect. Subjects were matched on the basis of IQ, age, sex, nutritional status, and length of orphanage residence. Unfortunately, because of selective dropping out of cases through adoption, the groups did not remain well matched during the three years of the project. When allowances are made for these difficulties, however, the data still indicate a significant effect of preschool attendance upon IQ (39, 67). Among children with 400 days or more of orphanage residence, those attending preschool for 50 per cent or more of the days showed a mean IQ gain of 6.8 points. The final mean IQ of this group was significantly higher than that of the control group.

AMOUNT OF SCHOOLING AND INTELLIGENCE

The effect of schooling upon intellectual development has also been explored through an analysis of the relationship between amount of educa-

---

[3] For a fuller explanation of regression and of its implications for matched-group experiments, the reader is urged to consult the article by Thorndike (55).

tion and intelligence test scores among adults. For example, surveys conducted in the American army during both World Wars yielded correlations of .73 and .74 between intelligence tests (Army Alpha or AGCT) and highest grade reached in school (62, 74). There are, of course, two alternative explanations for such correlations: (1) education raises the intellectual level, and (2) the brighter individuals are more likely to "survive" the increasingly stringent selection of successive educational levels. That the duration of any one individual's education is not entirely dependent upon his ability is fairly obvious. Financial resources, family tradition and attitudes, educational facilities in different localities, and a number of other nonintellectual factors can readily be cited. On the other hand, considerable intellectual selection undoubtedly does occur at successive educational levels beyond the compulsory grades.

Longitudinal studies of the same subjects over a period of years provide a more direct approach to the problem. Lorge (36) reported the results of retesting 131 men who had been tested 20 years earlier while in the eighth grade of New York City public schools. The subjects were first classified in terms of initial test scores, obtained in the eighth grade. Within each class-interval of such initial scores, it was then found that final scores tended to increase as amount of subsequent education increased. For instance, among the 30 men whose initial scores fell between 69 and 78, those who completed only the eighth grade had a final mean score of 20.7, while those who had had graduate training beyond college averaged 38.0.

The comparisons made in the Lorge study were severely limited by the small number of available cases, a fact that made the establishment of significant trends difficult. Moreover, the analysis of data leaves the way open for the operation of regression effect. Thus among subjects receiving the same initial test score, it is probable that those who subsequently continued their education longer had more "negative chance errors" in initial scores, while those who discontinued their schooling earlier had more "positive chance errors." The former would thus be expected to show a rise and the latter a drop in their final scores. As long as the subjects in each subgroup were selected on the basis of initial scores, such a regression effect may be expected.

More recently, however, other longitudinal studies have been conducted with larger samples and better-controlled conditions. In a Swedish investigation, Husén (30) compared the test performance of 722 young men examined upon induction into military service with the scores they had obtained ten years earlier while attending the third grade of primary schools in the city of Malmö.[4] The sample was subdivided into five groups with respect to total amount of education, ranging from the compulsory 7 years of primary school to 12–13 years. Within each group, initial and final IQ's were compared. Relative to the total sample, the lowest educational group dropped by an average of 1.2 IQ points; the other groups showed relative mean gains of 2.1, 3.0, 7.2, and 11.0, respectively. Continuing education was thus associated with larger improvements in test score. The last three mean gains reported were significant at the .01 level. In the same study, amount of schooling correlated .61 with initial test score and .80 with final score (29). The fact that the second correlation is higher provides further evidence of the direct effect of education upon test performance.

Also relevant is an American study by Owens (43) on a more narrowly restricted sample. A group of 127 men were retested with the Army Alpha in 1950, having taken this test 30 years earlier as entering freshmen at Iowa State College. Retest scores showed significant mean gains which increased consistently with amount of college or graduate training received subsequent to the initial test.

The type of analysis employed by both Husén and Owens avoids the regression effect arising from unreliability of test scores, since subjects are not chosen, matched, or grouped on the basis of test performance. Husén, moreover, was able to show that in his data educational differences actually counterbalanced the regression effect (30). Specifically, groups that continued their education longer contained a larger proportion of initially high-scoring subjects than did groups which discontinued their education earlier. On the basis of regression effect, therefore, the better-educated groups should have shown a drop from initial to final score, rather than the relatively large gains which were obtained.

Even this type of experimental design, however, fails to provide a conclusive demonstration of the effects of education upon intellectual development. As long as individuals are permitted to "sort themselves" into groups, it can be argued that: (1) there may have been significant initial differences among them which influenced the sorting; and (2) these initial differences, rather than the varying amounts of intervening education, may account for the group differences in final test scores. It is conceivable, for example, that

---

[4] A similar investigation is under way in Norway, having started in 1953 with the testing of practically all seventh-grade pupils in a region of southern Norway (32). Present plans call for the retesting of the nearly 4000 boys in this sample upon their induction into military service at age 19, approximately five years after the initial testing. Retests will also be made on subgroups of both sexes as they graduate from various secondary schools.

persons who continue their education longer may have stronger motivation to advance, may be more persistent, or may come from homes that are intellectually more stimulating. Factors such as these, rather than the differences in formal education, might account for the proportionately larger gains in test scores made by such persons. To be sure, the same factors should have affected initial scores. But their influence may have been augmented or more conspicuously manifested between the initial and final testing periods.

Nor is it possible to analyze and in some way rule out the influence of *all* such contributing factors, since theoretically we could never be sure that other significant factors might not have been overlooked. In the Husén investigation, for instance, income level and social class were shown to produce smaller changes in IQ than those obtained when amount of education was studied (30). There remain an untold number of other conditions, however, which might account for the IQ changes. Obviously, a conclusive answer can be obtained only with the type of experimental design in which the experimenter decides who shall and who shall not continue his education at each level and assigns the subjects at random to the different educational groups.

It should also be noted that the highest grade reached in school is a rather crude standard for determining amount of education. The same number of years spent in different types of schools do not necessarily represent equivalent amounts of schooling, even when uniform nominal requirements are in effect. Some attempts have been made to investigate the effects of *qualitative educational differences* on intellectual development, although selective factors and other methodological problems make comparisons difficult. Inconclusive or negative results are reported in a few investigations on pupils attending a university elementary school (64) and superior private schools (56), as well as on groups subjected to special curricula (35, 46).

In one study, children enrolled in the first three grades of one-room rural schools were compared with those attending consolidated schools in the same area (72). Stanford-Binet IQ's obtained each fall and spring over a two-year period showed significant gains during the school sessions on the part of the consolidated school children, but only a slight change or a loss in the one-room schools. This difference was not related to family background or to home environment, but was attributed by the author to the superior educational facilities afforded by the consolidated schools. A possible uncontrolled factor in such a study, however, is the relative amount of test-taking experience in the two types of schools.

An observation on Dutch school children is also relevant (11). Intelligence test scores of applicants to an industrial training school in Holland revealed a significant mean drop in IQ during the war years. Knowledge of school conditions during the period of war and occupation suggested that such a decrease in mean IQ may have resulted from inferior schooling. This hypothesis was corroborated by the finding that in the years 1949–51, following the restoration of peacetime educational conditions, the mean IQ's again rose to their prewar level.

LONGITUDINAL STUDIES OF POPULATIONS

The usual application of the longitudinal method in psychological research involves the repeated testing of the same individuals over a period of time. A variant of this procedure is the longitudinal study of populations, whereby different but comparable samples of the same population are examined at corresponding periods in their own development. An outstanding example of this approach is provided by the Scottish surveys (48, 49, 50). In 1932, a group intelligence test was administered to nearly all 11-year-old children in Scotland. The identical test was repeated in 1947, an attempt again being made to reach all Scottish children who were then aged 11. The two samples included 87,498 and 70,805 children, respectively, representing 87 and 88 per cent of the total estimated number of 11-year-olds living in Scotland on the two occasions. The samples are described as complete except for cases whose sensory or motor handicaps precluded valid testing, those school children who were absent on the day of testing, and a few children attending certain private schools for whom the required background data could not be obtained. In both surveys, the Stanford-Binet was also given individually to smaller random samples.

Comparison of mean scores in the 1932 and 1947 Scottish surveys revealed a small but statistically significant improvement over the 15-year interval. This finding was of particular interest since it contradicted a predicted decline in intelligence based on the negative correlations generally reported between intelligence and family size (cf. 3). Such correlations, found in a number of countries, are of the order of −.30. Several writers have argued that, since children from larger families tend to have lower IQ's than those from smaller families, each successive generation should show a slight loss in intellectual level. Further analyses have indicated, however, that the problem is far more complex than was originally supposed and that such predicted declines are highly questionable.[5]

[5] For a discussion of methodological problems and pertinent findings, cf. Anastasi (3).

Although much less extensive and not so well controlled as the Scottish surveys, similar follow-ups have been conducted in England by Burt (4), Cattell (7), and Emmett (13). These studies likewise failed to corroborate the expected drop in test score. It is also noteworthy that a survey of the intelligence test performance of American high school students over a 20-year period suggested that this, too, had improved, despite the marked increase in the proportion of students enrolled in high school (14). Since a larger proportion of the total population was attending high school at the end than at the beginning of this 20-year period, a decrease in mean score would be expected in the high school group unless the total population had improved sufficiently to counteract such a drop.

Chief among the environmental factors which could account for the rise in mean intelligence test scores is the improvement in educational facilities and in general cultural milieu over the intervening years. Increasing familiarity with psychological tests has been suggested as a contributing factor, although there is some evidence in the Scottish surveys that this was not a significant factor (cf. 3, p. 199). In support of an educational interpretation are the relatively large gains in score obtained when schooling and other environmental conditions within a particular community have improved conspicuously. Of special interest is a study conducted on East Tennessee mountain children (69). Group intelligence tests were administered in 1940 to over 3000 children in 40 rural schools. The results were compared with those obtained on children in the same areas and largely from the same families, who had been similarly tested in 1930. During the intervening ten-year period, the economic, social, and educational status of these sections had improved considerably. Paralleling such environmental improvements, a rise in IQ from the first to the second sampling was noted at all ages and all grades, the median IQ's being 82 and 93 in the 1930 and 1940 samplings, respectively. Public school children tested in Honolulu likewise showed large and significant rises in intelligence test scores over a 14-year interval during which considerable progress had been made in educational facilities (51).

Relevant data may also be found in a comparison of the intelligence level of American soldiers in World Wars I and II (61). A group of 768 enlisted men, representative of the entire population of white enlisted soldiers in World War II, were given both the new Army General Classification Test (AGCT) and a revision of the Army Alpha of World War I. The distribution of this group on the AGCT paralleled very closely that of the entire army. On the Alpha, their median score was 104, in contrast to a median of 62 obtained in World War I. The magnitude of this difference can be more clearly envisaged when we consider that the median of the World War II sampling corresponds to the 83rd percentile of World War I. In other words, 83 per cent of the World War I group fell below the median score of the World War II sample. A number of factors may help to account for this marked improvement in intelligence level over the 25 years. Among them are the later group's greater experience in taking tests in school, in industry, and in the army itself. The possible influence of better physical condition, as a result of improvements in public health and in nutrition, should also be considered. The major factor, however, appears to be the higher educational level of the population, together with probable improvements in the quality of instruction, length of school term, and the like. In the World War II sample, the average education was 10.0 years, i.e., two years of high school. The comparable World War I average was 8.0, or elementary school gradua-tion.

SUMMARY

In the present discussion of the relation of training to individual differ-ences, "training" is broadly defined to include any activity or series of experiences designed to improve performance. Certain types of pertinent training research were considered in Chapter 4; others will be examined in Chapter 12. The present chapter was concerned with investigations that have utilized standardized psychological tests and have employed princi-pally normal human adults or school-age children.

Studies with a variety of intelligence tests indicate that significant mean gains in score may be obtained through repetition of either the identical or a parallel form of the test, through coaching on identical or similar material, or through general "test sophistication." In the evaluation of all such effects, a major consideration is breadth of influence, or degree to which the improvement extends beyond the immediate test situation.

To the question, "Do individual differences increase or decrease with practice?" there are different possible answers depending upon the specific formulation of the problem. Results are affected by the definition of equal practice, the use of amount or time scores, the measurement of absolute or relative variability, and the nature of the scale employed. When the ques-tion is formulated so as best to meet both theoretical and practical demands, individual differences usually increase with practice. Persons tend to main-tain the same relative standing throughout training. The relative contribu-tion of practice and of prior individual differences to the total variance of a group depends upon the extent of practice differences in the group, as well as upon the range of prior individual differences. When put in general terms, this is a meaningless and unanswerable question.

Several approaches have been followed in the effort to determine the effect of schooling upon tested intelligence. Studies on nursery school children have been complicated by such methodological problems as test sophistication, the effect of emotional and motivational factors on test performance, the use of previously differentiated populations, and statistical regression. Results on children attending university nursery schools, most of whom come from superior home backgrounds, suggest little or no effect of nursery school attendance upon IQ. Children from underprivileged environments, on the other hand, may show appreciable gains in IQ following nursery school experience.

Among adults, amount of education correlates highly with intelligence test scores. Follow-up studies suggest that at least part of this correlation may be attributed to the direct effect of education upon tested abilities. However, the use of experimental designs involving previously differentiated populations precludes a definitive interpretation of the results of such studies.

Longitudinal investigations of populations over periods ranging from about ten to twenty-five years have revealed a slight but significant trend for intelligence test performance to rise. Such gains may result in part from intervening changes in educational and general cultural facilities. When schooling and other environmental conditions have improved conspicuously within a particular community, relatively large rises in test scores have been observed.

REFERENCES

1. Adkins, Dorothy C. The effects of practice on intelligence test scores. *J. educ. Psychol.*, 1937, 28, 222–231.
2. Anastasi, Anne. Practice and variability. *Psychol. Monogr.*, 1934, 45, No. 5.
3. Anastasi, Anne. Intelligence and family size. *Psychol. Bull.*, 1956, 53, 187–209.
4. Burt, C. *Intelligence and fertility.* London: Hamilton, 1946.
5. Casey, Mary L., Davidson, Helen P., and Harter, Doris I. Three studies on the effect of training in similar and identical material upon Stanford-Binet test scores. *27th Yearb., Nat. Soc. Stud. Educ.*, 1928, Part I, 431–439.
6. Cattell, Psyche. Constant changes in Stanford-Binet IQ. *J. educ. Psychol.*, 1931, 22, 544–550.
7. Cattell, R. B. The fate of national intelligence: a test of a thirteen-year prediction. *Eugen. Rev.*, 1951, 42, 136–148.
8. Cattell, R. B., Feingold, S. N., and Sarason, S. B. A culture-free intelligence test: II. Evaluation of cultural influences on test performance. *J. educ. Psychol.*, 1941, 32, 81–100.

9. Crane, V. R., and Heim, Alice W. The effects of repeated retesting: III. Further experiments and general conclusions. *Quart. J. exp. Psychol.*, 1950, 2, 182–197.

10. Dearborn, W. F., and Rothney, J. *Predicting the child's development.* Cambridge, Mass.: Sci-Art Pub., 1941.

11. de Groot, A. D. War and the intelligence of youth. *J. abnorm. soc. Psychol.*, 1951, 46, 596–597.

12. Dempster, J. J. B. Symposium on the effects of coaching and practice in intelligence tests. III. Southampton investigation and procedure. *Brit. J. educ. Psychol.*, 1954, 24, 1–4.

13. Emmett, W. G. The trend of intelligence in certain districts of England. *Popul. Stud.*, 1950, 3, 324–337.

14. Finch, F. H. Enrollment increases and changes in the mental level. *Appl. Psychol. Monogr.*, 1946, No. 10.

15. French, J. W. An answer to test coaching. *College Board Rev.*, 1955, 27, 5–7.

16. Garrett, H. E. Variability in learning under massed and spaced practice. *J. exp. Psychol.*, 1940, 26, 547–567.

17. Goodenough, Florence L. New evidence on environmental influence on intelligence. *39th Yearb., Nat. Soc. Stud. Educ.*, 1940, Part I, 307–365.

18. Goodenough, Florence L. Some special problems of nature-nurture research. *39th Yearb., Nat. Soc. Stud. Educ.*, 1940, Part I, 367–384.

19. Goodenough, Florence L., Foster, J. G., and Van Wagenen, M. J. *The Minnesota Preschool Tests.* Minneapolis: Educ. Test Bur., 1932.

20. Goodenough, Florence L., and Maurer, Katherine M. The mental development of nursery-school children compared with that of non-nursery school children. *39th Yearb., Nat. Soc. Stud. Educ.*, 1940, Part II, 161–178.

21. Grant, D. A. On "the analysis of variance in psychological research." *Psychol. Bull.*, 1944, 41, 158–166.

22. Greene, E. B. Practice effects on various types of standard tests. *Amer. J. Psychol.*, 1937, 49, 67–75.

23. Greene, Katharine B. The influence of specialized training on tests of general intelligence. *27th Yearb., Nat. Soc. Stud. Educ.*, 1928, Part I, 421–428.

24. Hamilton, Mildred E. The contribution of practice differences to group variability. *Arch. Psychol.*, 1943, No. 278.

25. Heim, Alice W., and Wallace, Jean G. The effects of repeatedly retesting the same group on the same intelligence test. Part I: Normal adults. *Quart. J. exp. Psychol.*, 1949, 1, 151–159.

26. Heim, Alice W., and Wallace, Jean G. The effects of repeatedly retesting the same group on the same intelligence test: II. High grade mental defectives. *Quart. J. exp. Psychol.*, 1950, 2, 19–32.

27. Hertzman, M. Specificity of correlations between initial and final abilities in learning. *Psychol. Rev.*, 1939, 46, 163–175.

28. Holloway, H. D. Effects of training on the SRA Primary Mental Abilities (Primary) and WISC. *Child Develpm.*, 1954, 25, 253–263.

29. Husén, T. *Testresultatens prognosvärde.* Stockholm: Gebers, 1950. (English summary)

30. Husén, T. The influence of schooling upon IQ. *Theoria*, 1951, 17, 61–88.

31. James, W. S. Symposium on the effects of coaching and practice in intelligence tests. II. Coaching for all recommended. *Brit. J. Psychol.*, 1953, 23, 155–162.

32. Jarl, V. Coucheron. Intellectual abilities and schooling as a psychological and social issue. Paper read at Fourteenth Internatl. Congr. Psychol., Montreal, June, 1954.

33. Jones, H. E., and Jorgensen, A. P. Mental growth as related to nursery-school attendance. *39th Yearb., Nat. Soc. Stud. Educ.*, 1940, Part II, 207–222.

34. Kincaid, Margaret. A study of individual differences in learning. *Psychol. Rev.*, 1925, 32, 34–53.

35. Lamson, Edna E. To what extent are intelligence quotients increased by children who participate in a rich, vital school curriculum? *J. educ. Psychol.*, 1938, 29, 67–70.

36. Lorge, I. Schooling makes a difference. *Teach. Coll. Rec.*, 1945, 46, 483–492.

37. McNemar, Q. A critical examination of the University of Iowa studies of environmental influences upon the IQ. *Psychol. Bull.*, 1940, 37, 63–92.

38. McNemar, Q. More on the Iowa IQ studies. *J. Psychol.*, 1940, 10, 237–240.

39. McNemar, Q. Note on Wellman's re-analysis of IQ changes of orphanage preschool children. *J. genet. Psychol.*, 1945, 67, 215–219.

40. Melzer, J. H. Functional logic. *J. higher Educ.*, 1949, 20, 143–146, 170.

41. Owens, W. A., Jr. Intra-individual differences versus inter-individual differences in motor skills. *Educ. psychol. Measmt.*, 1942, 2, 299–314.

42. Owens, W. A., Jr. A new technic in studying the effects of practice upon individual differences. *J. exp. Psychol.*, 1942, 30, 180–183.

43. Owens, W. A., Jr. Age and mental abilities: a longitudinal study. *Genet. Psychol., Monogr.*, 1953, 48, 3–54.

44. Peel, E. A. A note on practice effects in intelligence tests. *Brit. J. educ. Psychol.*, 1951, 21, 122–125.

45. Peel, E. A. Practice effects between three consecutive tests of intelligence. *Brit. J. educ. Psychol.*, 1952, 22, 196–199.

46. Pritchard, Miriam C., Horan, Kathryn M., and Hollingworth, Leta S. The course of mental development in slow learners under an "experience curriculum." *39th Yearb., Nat. Soc. Stud. Educ.*, 1940, Part II, 245–254.

47. Rodger, A. G. The application of six group intelligence tests to the same children, and the effects of practice. *Brit. J. educ. Psychol.*, 1936, 6, 291–305.

48. Scottish Council for Research in Education. *The intelligence of Scottish children: a national survey of an age group.* London: Univer. London Press, 1933.

49. Scottish Council for Research in Education. *The trend of Scottish intelligence.* London: Univer. London Press, 1949.

50. Scottish Council for Research in Education. *Social implications of the 1947 mental survey.* London: Univer. London Press, 1953.

51. Smith, S. Language and non-verbal test performance of racial groups in Honolulu before and after a 14-year interval. *J. gen. Psychol.*, 1942, 26, 51–93.

52. Terman, L. M., and Merrill, Maud A. *Measuring intelligence.* Boston: Houghton Mifflin, 1937.

53. Thorndike, E. L. Practice effects on intelligence tests. *J. exp. Psychol.*, 1922, 5, 101–107.
54. Thorndike, E. L. Heredity and environment. *J. educ. Psychol.*, 1938, 29, 161–166.
55. Thorndike, R. L. Regression fallacies in the matched groups experiment. *Psychometrika*, 1942, 7, 85–102.
56. Thorndike, R. L., *et al.* Retest changes in the IQ in certain superior schools. *39th Yearb., Nat. Soc. Stud. Educ.*, 1940, Part II, 351–361.
57. Thurstone, Thelma G. *Learning to think series. The red book.* Chicago: Science Research Associates, 1948.
58. Thurstone, Thelma G. *Learning to think series. Teacher's manual for play and learn. The red book.* Chicago: Science Research Associates, 1948.
59. Tilton, J. W. The effect of forgetting upon individual differences. *Psychol. Monogr.*, 1936, 47, 173–185.
60. Trainor, J. C. Experimental results of training in general semantics upon intelligence test scores. *Papers from the First American Congress for General Semantics,* Ellensburg, Wash., March, 1935. Pp. 58–67.
61. Tuddenham, R. D. Soldier intelligence in World Wars I and II. *Amer. Psychologist*, 1948, 3, 54–56.
62. United States Army, The Adjutant General's Office, Personnel Research Section. The Army General Classification Test. *Psychol. Bull.*, 1945, 42, 760–768.
63. Vernon, P. E. Symposium on the effects of coaching and practice in intelligence tests: V. Conclusions. *Brit. J. educ. Psychol.*, 1954, 24, 57–63.
64. Wellman, Beth L. Growth in intelligence under differing school environments. *J. exp. Educ.*, 1934–35, 3, 59–83.
65. Wellman, Beth L. Iowa studies on the effects of schooling. *39th Yearb., Nat. Soc. Stud. Educ.*, 1940, Part II, 377–399.
66. Wellman, Beth L. IQ changes of preschool and non-preschool groups during the preschool years: a summary of the literature. *J. Psychol.*, 1945, 20, 347–368.
67. Wellman, Beth L., and Pegram, Edna L. Binet IQ changes of orphanage preschool children: a re-analysis. *J. genet. Psychol.*, 1944, 65, 239–263.
68. Wellman, Beth L., Skeels, H. M., and Skodak, Marie. Review of McNemar's critical examination of Iowa studies. *Psychol. Bull.*, 1940, 37, 93–111.
69. Wheeler, L. R. A comparative study of the intelligence of East Tennessee mountain children. *J. educ. Psychol.*, 1942, 33, 321–334.
70. Wiseman, S. Symposium on the effects of coaching and practice in intelligence tests. IV. The Manchester experiment. *Brit. J. educ. Psychol.*, 1954, 24, 5–8.
71. Wiseman, S., and Wrigley, J. The comparative effects of coaching and practice on the results of verbal intelligence tests. *Brit. J. Psychol.*, 1953, 44, 83–94.
72. Worbois, G. M. Changes in Stanford-Binet IQ for rural consolidated and rural one-room school children. *J. exp. Educ.*, 1942, 11, 210–214.
73. Yates, A. Symposium on the effects of coaching and practice in intelligence tests. *Brit. J. educ. Psychol.*, 1953, 23, 147–154.
74. Yerkes, R. M. (Ed.) Psychological examining in the United States Army. *Mem. Nat. Acad. Sci.*, 1921, 15.

CHAPTER 8

Age Differences

The chronology of behavior within the life span of the individual provides one of the richest sources of data on human variation. Psychological differences between the infant, the teenager, and the octogenarian are fully as striking as the differences in their physical appearance. Much of the psychology of childhood and adolescence has been traditionally devoted to a study of the changes which occur as the individual grows up. Today, the rapid advancement of research on maturity and old age is helping to fill in our knowledge of the entire life cycle.

To the differential psychologist, age changes in abilities and personality traits pose a number of important questions. What part do training and structural growth play in behavior development? To what extent do differences between coexisting age groups reflect general cultural changes? How are gains and losses in test performance over the years related to intervening experiences? How stable is the individual's relative standing within his own age group? Are there basic regularities in the course of development? What bearing do individual differences within single age groups have upon conclusions regarding age differences? Throughout the present chapter, we shall turn repeatedly to questions such as these.

The term "growth" has traditionally been used to designate age changes occurring prior to maturity. When we speak of "growth," we usually think of a definite sequence of developmental stages in the structural characteristics of the individual. As the child grows older, for example, his height increases, his bodily proportions are altered, and many other well-known physical modifications occur. Such changes take place regardless of the specific training the individual may have had.

As structures become altered with age, so we may expect their functions to undergo change. With stronger muscles, the older child can learn to walk, climb stairs, sit up, and perform various other tasks much more readily than his younger brother. It is reasonable to expect that certain types of activity will in general appear at fairly definite stages, since they require a specific degree of structural development for their execution. Very intensive training at an earlier age may produce almost negligible effects when compared with the achievements of an older child with only a minimum of training.

Since such a large share of infant behavior consists in the acquisition of motor skills and sensorimotor coordinations (activities that are closely linked to structural factors), physical growth or maturation rather than practice seems to play the major part in early behavioral development. Evidence cited in Chapter 4 supports such a conclusion. It is quite a different matter, however, to use the concept of growth to describe the intellectual and emotional development of the older child.

When applied to psychological functions, the distinction between investigations of training and those of growth is a superficial one. It is only for convenience that the former were discussed in the preceding chapter and the latter have been reserved for the present one. The data on both topics should be considered together. A few studies, in fact, could be classified in either category. In general, the present chapter will be concerned with studies in which psychological changes with age were observed and charted, with no attempt to alter the normal course of development. There is no implication, of course, that training was lacking during the intervals. Training was simply not introduced or controlled by the experimenter.

CROSS-SECTIONAL AND LONGITUDINAL APPROACHES

Because of the practical difficulty of following up the same individuals year after year, many studies on age differences have resorted to cross-sectional procedures. For example, groups of subjects ranging in age from 10 to 18 years are tested simultaneously and the mean score of each age group is plotted against age. It is assumed that these means indicate the normal course of development and that they approximate closely the scores that would have been obtained if, let us say, the 10-year-olds had been retested annually until they reached age 18.

Such an assumption is open to question for at least some of the groups that have been tested. Different age groups may not be comparable because of the operation of *selective factors*. High school seniors, for instance, are a more highly selected group than high school freshmen, since the poorer students tend to drop out in the course of their high school work. If, as has often been the case, the subjects tested were in school, the higher average score of the older subjects may result in part from this selective dropping out of the less able students. Had the *same* subjects been tested in the freshman and senior year of high school, the mean gain in score might thus have been much smaller.

A further objection to a cross-sectional approach is that the *experiential backgrounds* of different age groups may not be comparable. This is especially evident when comparisons are made between widely disparate age groups. For example, the differences between present-day 40-year-olds and present-day 15-year-olds cannot be attributed entirely to factors associated with age. At the time when today's 40-year-olds were 15, schooling was poorer, opportunities for certain types of activity were less frequent or even nonexistent, and many social attitudes were probably quite different from those current today. Such comparisons are thus complicated by the fact that older and younger groups were brought up under different conditions, owing to general cultural changes which are constantly occurring.

Partly in recognition of the methodological deficiencies of the cross-sectional method and partly because of the availability of better research facilities, increasing use is now being made of the longitudinal approach. Long-range follow-ups of individuals are in progress at a number of research centers. A few examples will serve to indicate the nature and scope of such projects. The most extensive is unquestionably the Stanford University study of gifted children, in which over 1500 California school children selected because of high IQ's have been intensively investigated through repeated follow-ups (91, 92). A large proportion of this group has already been studied through late adulthood. Data are also being accumulated on spouses and offspring of the original subjects, and plans are under way for continuing follow-ups of both generations. A more detailed report of this investigation will be given in Chapter 13, in connection with the discussion of genius.

Two outstanding longitudinal studies conducted at the Institute of Child Welfare of the University of California are the Berkeley Growth Study (8, 9, 10, 11) and the Guidance Study (58). The former began with 61 infants at the age of one month and continued for 25 years, when about half of the original subjects were still available for examination. During the first year, the children were tested monthly with the California First Year Mental Scale; later retests at increasingly longer intervals employed the California Preschool Scale, Stanford-Binet, Terman-McNemar Group Test, and Wechsler-Bellevue Adult Intelligence Scale.

In the Guidance Study, interest centered chiefly around behavior problems rather than intellectual development. The project was initiated in 1929 with the examination of a random sample of 252 Berkeley infants. The subjects were divided into two subsamples of 126 each, matched in a number of socioeconomic, educational, and other parental characteristics. In the case of one of these subsamples, the Guidance Group, the investigators provided intensive discussions with parents on such matters as marital problems, parent-child relations, and child-training procedures. The other subsample served as the Control Group. Identical follow-up data were gathered periodically on both groups by means of physical examinations, intelligence tests, and an open-ended behavior inventory filled out in interviews with the mothers. The first major report of findings, published in 1954, represents an analysis of the frequencies of certain types of behavior problems in the Control Group between the ages of 21 months and 14 years. The principal object of this part of the project was to provide normative data on behavior problems, by age and sex, in a random sample of children.

A still different emphasis is represented by the Harvard Growth Study (21), which collected data on the physical, intellectual, and educational development of approximately 3500 Massachusetts school children. These children were initially tested upon admission to the first grade and were retested annually for twelve years. Mention should likewise be made of the type of project carried out at the Fels Research Institute (86, 87), which is concerned with nearly every phase of the individual's development from conception to maturity. Approximately 300 children and their families who live in the neighboring communities constitute the subjects for the Fels studies. Longitudinal investigations have also been initiated in a number of European countries. A special feature of some of these studies is their provision for the comparative analysis of results obtained in different countries. Of particular interest in this connection is the survey being conducted simultaneously in several countries under the sponsorship of the International Children's Center (25, 26).

It should be noted that the longitudinal method also presents its own peculiar difficulties. When follow-ups cover a period of several years, the number of subjects lost to the study during the interval may be considerable. Consequently, the later follow-ups are often based on a greatly shrunken sample. The participating groups are also likely to be selected with regard to stability of residence and continued cooperation with the investigator. Subjects selected in terms of these conditions may in turn show other characteristics related to cultural level of the home, parent-child relationships, interests, attitudes, and the like. For these reasons, it is likely that the samplings employed in longitudinal studies tend to be somewhat superior to the general population. The reverse may be true in the case of institutional samples, such as orphanage children. In this situation, the superior members may, for example, be more often removed for adoption. The enduring sample would thus represent an inferior selection. In either case, generalizations from a longitudinal sampling to the total population must be made with considerable caution and with due regard for the selective factors which may have operated in the particular situation. At the worst, however, such selection limits the scope of the results, but it does not invalidate them if the population to which they apply is clearly specified.

A further methodological problem pertains to the possible effect which continued participation in the study itself may have upon the subjects' behavior. Practice in taking tests, repeated contacts with the project staff, identification with a special group, and similar conditions associated with the study may influence the subjects' test performance, attitudes, motivation, emotional adjustment, and other characteristics.

Thus it appears that even when time and facilities permit its use, the longitudinal method may not provide a completely satisfactory solution. Under certain conditions, combinations of cross-sectional and longitudinal approaches may be desirable. One proposed procedure involves the cross-sectional testing of different age groups, supplemented by short-range follow-ups (13). For example, 8-year-old and 10-year-old children may be tested three times over a two-year period. Checks on the comparability and continuity of these two age samples are provided by the performance of both groups at age 10, as well as by the trend of retest changes within the two groups. If such comparability is established, data obtained on the two groups over the two-year period can be treated jointly so as to reveal changes between the ages of 8 and 12.

Another experimental design requires the combination of cross-sectional surveys with longitudinal studies of populations (cf. 70). It will be recalled that certain investigations provide data on different but approximately comparable samples of the same population tested after a lapse of several years (cf. Ch. 7). If such a longitudinal study of a population is combined with a cross-sectional survey of different age groups, age changes can be more readily separated from cultural changes. For example, 20-year-olds and 40-year-olds may be tested in 1940 and similar samples of the same ages tested in 1960. Any difference in score between 20-year-olds in 1940 and 20-year-olds in 1960 could be attributed to cultural change. Differences between 20- and 40-year-olds tested simultaneously (in 1940 or 1960) would reflect age changes plus cultural differentials, especially differences in the conditions under which the two age groups were reared. Finally, comparison of 20-year-olds in 1940 with 40-year-olds in 1960 would indicate the joint effects of age and intervening cultural changes which may have modified the subjects' behavior after age 20. It will be noted that even if the same

sample of 20-year-olds tested in 1940 were retested in 1960, intervening cultural changes could not be separated from age changes unless comparable
data were available on groups of the *same age* tested on the two occasions.

GROWTH CURVES

Applications to Psychological Data. Growth curves were first plotted to
show age changes in physical traits, such as height, weight, bodily proportions as indicated by various indices, and the like. As a descriptive technique
for portraying more vividly the course of development of structural characteristics, the growth curve has proved serviceable and intelligible. The
physical data are unambiguous and relatively easy to interpret. By analogy,
however, attempts have been made to plot curves of "mental growth," a
procedure that has led to certain misconceptions. At best these curves are
only a descriptive summary of changes produced by a multiplicity of factors. By lumping all such factors together and giving them a semblance of
systematic growth, the main issues may be obscured.

When applied to test scores and other behavior data, "growth curves"
show the individual's performance at different ages in some standard test
situation. Such a curve does not differ in any essential respect from a
learning curve. In both cases, the subject is tested under similar conditions
at successive intervals and his progress is charted on the curve. Learning
curves, to be sure, usually cover a shorter period of time than growth curves,
although a practice experiment could conceivably extend over several years.
The major difference between learning curves and growth curves seems to
be that in the former the subject is given special training under rigidly
controlled experimental conditions, while in the latter he is left to his own
resources. Most psychological growth curves are essentially learning curves
obtained in the absence of controlled conditions. Such curves reflect the
cumulative effects of the training and experience of everyday life. During
the period of early childhood, sensorimotor and other structural changes
influence the shape of the curve by setting certain limits to behavior development. But it is unlikely that intellectual progress beyond the age of
school entrance is systematically linked with further structural changes.

It follows from this discussion that growth curves may vary with the
cultural milieu in which they are obtained. If the learning conditions differ
from one group to another, the curves of psychological growth may likewise
be expected to differ. Such "growth curves" can still serve a useful purpose
as descriptive devices. As such they may indicate the general course of
development of different functions *under given cultural conditions,* and

would characterize individuals of different age levels *within a specified population.* For such curves, the term "age progress curve" would seem a more accurate designation than "growth curve," since it provides a more realistic description of the type of data from which the curves are derived.

In Figures 42, 43, and 44 will be found examples of some of the most carefully prepared age progress curves for intelligence test performance. The first was plotted by Thurstone and Ackerson (100) from the Stanford-

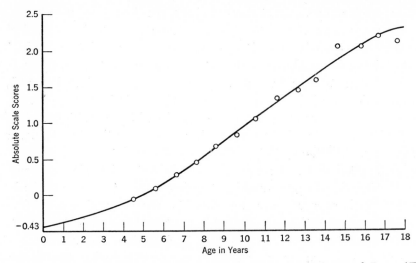

Fig. 42. Age Changes in Stanford-Binet Performance: Cross-Sectional Data. (From Thurstone and Ackerson, 100, p. 576.)

Binet scores of 4208 subjects between the ages of 3 and 18. It will be noted that this curve rises slowly at first, then more rapidly, and then slowly again as the final leveling-off is approached. Such a curve is said to be positively accelerated in the early stages and negatively accelerated later on. The portion of the curve below three years was found by extrapolation, on the basis of the equation derived from the available data. Some empirical confirmation of its shape was provided, however, when the longitudinal data of the Berkeley Growth Study for the first five years were plotted in the same scale units (10, p. 809).

A curve similar in general form to that of Thurstone and Ackerson was found in the Harvard Growth Study (21). Retest scores of 522 children between the ages of 8 and 15 yielded the graph reproduced in Figure 43. The findings of the earlier cross-sectional study are thus confirmed by a longitudinal investigation over a narrower age range. It should be added, however, that a reanalysis of the intelligence test scores obtained in the

Harvard Growth Study revealed marked individual differences in the pattern of age changes (19). The curves fell into four major types (with minor variants), differing principally in the rate of growth during the adolescent years.

Although based on a much smaller sample, the data of the Berkeley Growth Study (10) provide a wider age coverage than either of the other two investigations. The results of this longitudinal study, extending from the

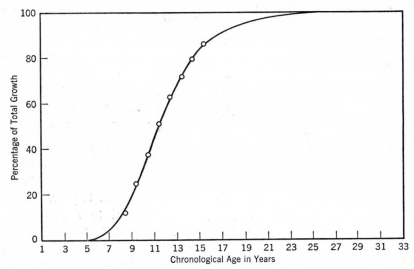

Fig. 43. Age Changes in Intelligence Test Scores in a Group of 522 Children Retested between the Ages of 8 and 15. (From Dearborn and Rothney, 21, p. 215.)

age of one month to 21 years, are given in Figure 44. Again, a curve of the same general shape is obtained. The graph also shows a tendency for individual differences to increase with age, as indicated by the size of the standard deviation.

It should be noted that when short periods of five years or so are studied, especially during middle childhood, the age progress curve for most intelligence tests appears to be approximately a straight line. The form of age progress curves may also be affected by a number of technical and methodological factors, which will be examined in the sections that follow. Familiarity with these points is essential for the proper interpretation of any age curve.

Equality of Scale Units. Unlike physical units such as inches or pounds, scores on psychological tests do not correspond to equal units of ability. Such inequalities in the measuring scale may distort age curves in various ways. Let us suppose, for example, that on a certain test the difference in ability required to improve from a score of 50 to a score of 51 is considerably greater than that required to progress from 20 to 21. Such a discrepancy would tend to make progress *appear* slower at the later ages, since the 50-to-51 step is more likely to fall within the performance range of the older subjects, and the 20-to-21 step within that of the younger subjects.

A special illustration of the influence of test units upon the form of the growth curve is furnished by *mental age* curves. If average mental age is plotted against chronological age, the result will be a straight line. Any divergence from a straight line in such a graph simply indicates dissimilarities between the group under consideration and that on which the particular test was standardized. Age scales are so constructed that the average child will advance one year in mental age for each year of chronological age. The successive mental age units are thus adjusted so as to rule out automatically any differences in amount of improvement from year to year. Such units are unsuited to a study of the course of intellectual development, since the resulting age curve is an artifact of test standardization.

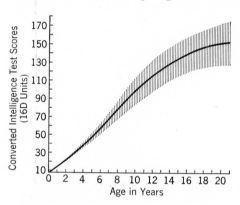

Fig. 44. Age Changes in Intelligence Test Scores in the Berkeley Growth Study. N varied from 61 at age of one month to 33 at 21 years. Shaded area shows increase in variability (SD) with age. (From Bayley, 10, p. 811.)

Different investigators have tried to solve the problem of units in various ways.[1] Thurstone and Ackerson, in plotting the curve reproduced in Figure 42, used a technique known as "absolute scaling," which had been previously developed by Thurstone. The same scaling procedure was employed in the Harvard Growth Study curve, given in Figure 43. The scale utilized in the Berkeley Growth Study curve (Fig. 44), on the other hand, was developed primarily for the purpose of achieving comparability of scores on different tests. The unit chosen was the standard deviation of the 16-year scores on the Wechsler-Bellevue. Scores on all tests and at all ages were expressed in terms of this unit—hence the name 16D scores. Although not designed expressly for equality of units, this scale probably yielded results that approximated closely those which would have been obtained through absolute scaling.

[1] For a discussion of this problem at a more technical level, cf. Shock (79) and Thurstone and Ackerson (100). Explanations of equal-unit scaling procedures can be found in texts on psychological statistics.

Difficulty Level of Test. The form of the age curve is also affected by several characteristics of the test or measuring instrument employed to gauge the amount of progress. Among such factors is the general difficulty level of the test. In a relatively easy task, performance will improve rapidly during the first few years and more slowly later on as a perfect score is approached. In a relatively difficult task, on the other hand, or in a task that requires a certain degree of general information or mastery of techniques before it can be properly executed, progress will be slow at first and much more rapid at the upper age levels. The latter task would thus give a positively rather than a negatively accelerated curve.

Moreover, if the difficulty range of the test is narrow, performance may be artificially cut off at either the upper or lower end, or at both ends. Thus if the *"ceiling"* of the test is too low for the abilities of the older subjects tested, there will not be sufficient items at the difficult end of the scale to permit these subjects to show improvement. Although the subjects' ability may actually increase from, say, 18 to 19 years of age, their scores on such a test may show little or no progress, since their

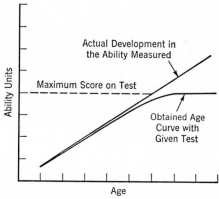

Fig. 45. Effect of Low Test Ceiling upon Form of the Age Progress Curve.

performance is close to a perfect score. The effect this is likely to have on the form of the curve is illustrated schematically in Figure 45. Although the ability that is being measured may continue to increase by equal amounts in successive years (i.e., along a straight line), the scores begin to taper off as they approach the arbitrary test ceiling and will stop rising altogether when the maximum score is reached. An equally artificial slowing down of progress may result at the early ages from the use of a test whose arbitrary *zero point* is too high for the subjects. Thus if a particular test has too few easy items to sample the performance of the younger subjects adequately, the curve will probably rise slowly at first and then rapidly, i.e., it will be a positively accelerated curve.

Changing Composition of "Intelligence" with Age. A major complication in the interpretation of most "growth curves of intelligence" arises from the fact that a different combination of abilities may be measured at various age levels. In long-range follow-up studies, it has usually proved necessary to administer different tests as the subjects grew older. Both the Harvard

Growth Study and the Berkeley Growth Study, for example, followed this practice. If all "intelligence tests" measured a single, underlying function, then the substitution of alternative instruments would be only a minor source of error. But such a view is not borne out by analyses of test scores (8, 10) or by research on the organization of abilities, to be reported in Chapters 10 and 11. There is evidence that what is regarded as "intelligence" and measured by current intelligence tests changes radically in nature with age. One analysis (37) of the Berkeley Growth Study data for the first 18 years suggested that the functions measured during the first 2 years can be described largely as "sensorimotor alertness"; those measured between 2 and 4 years, as "persistence"; and those measured after age 4, as "manipulation of symbols."

Nor does the use of a single intelligence test throughout the age range provide an adequate safeguard against such a changing coverage of abilities. When a complex scale such as the Stanford-Binet is employed, it is likely that different abilities are measured at different age levels. At the upper ages, most intelligence tests are heavily loaded with verbal functions and other abstract and symbolical tasks. At the other extreme, infant tests are largely based upon sensorimotor development. It is also possible that what appears superficially to be a uniform task may call different activities into play at different age levels. For example, the same form board that measures predominantly spatial perception at age 4 may measure chiefly speed of movement at age 10. It is apparent, therefore, that any one age curve may in reality consist of *several overlapping curves for different functions.*

Age Curves for Different Functions.   Even at a single age level, the functions involved in most psychological tests are varied and complex. An individual's score on such a test generally depends upon his abilities in a number of different functions. Even if essentially the same functions are measured by such scores over the age range tested, it is nevertheless true that the resulting curve is a composite of several curves. Each of the contributing functions may develop at a different rate and reach "maturity" at a different age. To be sure, if the composite is consistently and unambiguously defined, age changes in such a composite may be significant in themselves. The growth curve of height, for example, may be analyzed into separate growth curves for limbs and trunk, which develop at different rates. It is still both practically and scientifically useful, however, to measure age changes in total height. But the composite height measures of different investigators have the same composition—a fact that is clearly not true of different intelligence tests. Many psychological tests purporting to be equivalent may thus yield diverse age curves, because of the varying combinations of functions that enter into each test.

Three illustrations of such composite behavior indices will be considered. The first deals with the extent of activity in the human fetus at different prenatal ages. Figure 46 shows average results for 16 fetuses observed during normal gestation (85). The top curve, indicating the percentage of time the fetus is active at different ages, resembles the familiar negatively accelerated growth curve. When, however, the total fetal activity is subdivided into the three commonly observed types, three very different curves are obtained. Small, rhythmic movements show little or no increase with

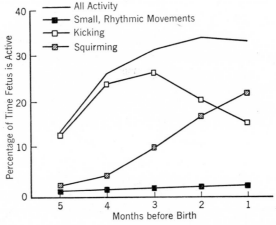

Fig. 46. Age Curves for Different Types of Movement during Prenatal Life. (From Sontag, 85, p. 152.)

age. Kicking shows a sharp rise from 5 to 3 months prior to birth, followed by a drop. Squirming movements, on the other hand, increase in frequency throughout the observation period, rising slowly at first and more rapidly later.

The second illustration concerns the frequency of crying by infants during the first year of life (7). In the Berkeley Growth Study, a record was kept of all instances of crying by the 61 infants in the course of monthly physical and mental examinations. The total figures suggest a general tendency for the amount of crying (frequency and duration) to decline until about 4 months of age, then to increase again, especially after 6 months. The amount of crying drops once more beyond 6 months, but increases slightly toward the end of the first year. On the surface, such a finding might suggest a cyclical development of emotional behavior in the infant. The apparent periodicity, however, may result from the combined effects of a number of

independently varying factors. In the Berkeley Study, crying in response to
different types of stimuli yielded age curves differing in both form and
direction. Three of these curves are reproduced in Figure 47. It will be
noted that "crying as a result of restriction of movement and unaccustomed
position" retains a relatively high frequency throughout the first year, with
no consistent downward or upward trend. "Crying from fatigue" shows a
fairly steady drop from the first to the twelfth month. The reverse trend is

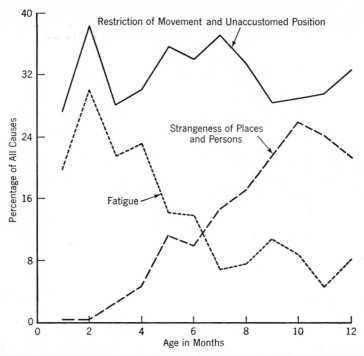

Fig. 47. Age Changes in Crying Behavior in Response to Different Types of Stimuli.
(From Bayley, 7, p. 320.)

evident in "crying because of strangeness of persons or places," which
mounts steeply throughout the year. The apparent periodicity in "emotionality" would thus seem to result from a combination of many specific
emotional responses, each of which follows its own independent course of
development. Such findings suggest that in another investigation a different
trend in the composite crying curve might be produced by altering the
relative frequency of the specific stimuli which evoke crying.

The third illustration is furnished by the scores made by a group of
adolescent boys tested during the standardization of the Minnesota Mechanical Aptitude Battery (cf. 46). Figure 48 shows the age differences in

mean standard scores on two of the tests in this battery, the Spatial Relations and the Assembly tests. It will be noted that the curve for Spatial Relations exhibits a definite negative acceleration, rising more sharply until about age 15 and then slowing down. The curve for the Assembly test, on the other hand, follows almost a straight-line trend, with minor fluctuations.

Similar examples could be cited from the various phases of linguistic growth, age changes in different types of memory tests, and the development of many other functions. It should be evident that the so-called curve of mental growth is not one, but many curves. A few of these curves run

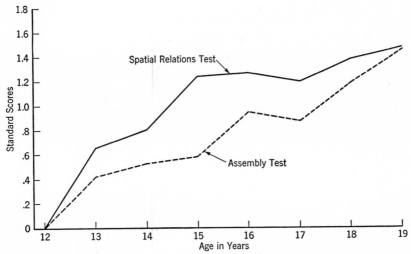

Fig. 48. Age Changes in Two Mechanical Aptitude Tests. (From Jones and Seashore, 46, p. 141.)

parallel, others move along simultaneously but at different rates, while still others succeed one another in overlapping steps.

Average versus Individual Curves. One of the drawbacks of the cross-sectional approach is that it permits the plotting of only average curves. Since different persons are tested at each age level, it is obviously impossible to chart the progress of individual cases. Even when longitudinal data are collected, however, the common practice is to plot the average score for each age. Such a procedure may conceal significant variations from individual to individual. If the development of any particular function varies markedly among different individuals, such differences would probably cancel out in the average curve. The resulting curve might thus be quite unlike the actual course of development for any individual.

A clear-cut illustration of the possible effects of the indiscriminate averaging of individual growth curves is provided by findings on the *prepubertal spurt of growth* (22, 82). Individual growth curves for many physical traits show a spurt or sudden increase in the rate of growth shortly before puberty. Since individuals differ in the age at which they reach puberty, such a spurt of growth falls on different portions of the growth curve for

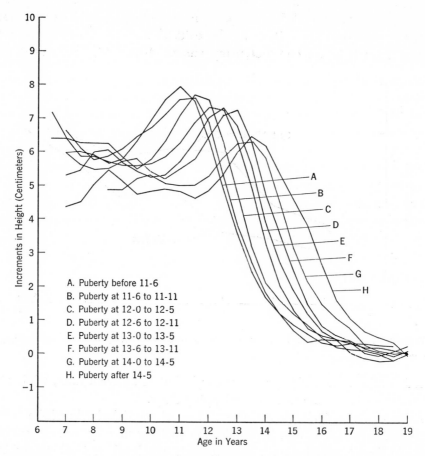

A. Puberty before 11-6
B. Puberty at 11-6 to 11-11
C. Puberty at 12-0 to 12-5
D. Puberty at 12-6 to 12-11
E. Puberty at 13-0 to 13-5
F. Puberty at 13-6 to 13-11
G. Puberty at 14-0 to 14-5
H. Puberty after 14-5

Fig. 49. Mean Annual Increments in Standing Height of Eight Groups of Girls Reaching Puberty at Different Ages. (From Shuttleworth, 82, p. 32.)

different persons. The curve based upon group means would therefore reveal no spurt at any period, since this phenomenon would be completely masked or obscured. When only individuals reaching puberty at the same age are included, however, the prepubescent growth spurt becomes clearly evident, as illustrated in Figure 49. This curve, taken from the Harvard Growth Study, shows the mean annual increase in height of each of eight groups of girls, classified according to age of puberty. The group reaching puberty before 11½ years, for example, has its maximum spurt of growth at age 11. At the other extreme, those reaching puberty after 14½ show their most rapid growth at about 14.

With regard to psychological functions, longitudinal studies have revealed marked individual differences in rates of growth and in the form of the age curves. Cycles of slow or rapid development, spurts, plateaus, and even regressions to lower levels of performance appear in many individual curves, with little or no regularity from person to person (10, 19, 21, 32, 44). Minor irregularities undoubtedly result from test unreliability and other temporary, chance factors. Larger shifts of longer duration, on the other hand, probably reflect changes in environmental influences, in health and emotional adjustment, and in other conditions affecting the child's development. Another source of variation is to be found in changes in the nature of the abilities tested at different ages. Thus a child who is relatively poor in verbal tasks will show slower progress when examined with a predominantly linguistic test. In general, the detailed course of behavior development is influenced by many factors—both structural and experiential— which necessarily vary with the individual.

CONSTANCY OF THE IQ

It will be recalled that one of the questions raised in the preceding chapter, in connection with the effect of practice upon individual differences, pertained to the consistency of the individual's relative standing throughout the course of practice. Did the high scorers on trial one tend to maintain their superiority? Were the poor performers on the initial trial correspondingly poor at the end of practice? The same type of question has been asked regarding age curves. How stable is the individual's status over the years, relative to his age mates? The label "constancy of the IQ" has been historically attached to this question, as a result of early interest in the IQ as a possible index of a unitary, underlying general intelligence. Today, although the label has survived, we recognize that the IQ is only a convenient way of expressing scores on certain types of tests and should be interpreted as such.

It should also be noted at the outset that the traditional question of the "constancy of the IQ" actually involves two separate questions. The first is the purely empirical, practical, actuarial question of *prediction*. We know, for example, that the intellectually gifted school child is likely to develop into a superior adult, and that a feebleminded child will almost certainly fall below average as an adult. Just how precisely can such forecasts be made, and how early in the individual's life? These are the practical questions of prediction, concerned only with observed trends in test scores. The second question is a theoretical one, in which the degree of constancy of the IQ is regarded as an index of *regularity of intellectual development*. The latter question can be investigated through an examination of individual age curves or through an analysis of annual increments in test scores. We shall see that the answer to the first question does not necessarily imply a corresponding answer to the second.

Predictive Value of IQ. Empirically, IQ's have been found to remain sufficiently constant during the elementary school years to make prediction over several years feasible. Among older subjects, intellectual level likewise shows considerable stability, especially when individuals remain in fairly constant environments. Thus the intelligence test scores of college students correlate very highly with the scores obtained by the same individuals in high school or even in the upper elementary school grades (24, 97). In one study, for example, a correlation of .80 was found between scores on the American Council on Education Psychological Examination (ACE) administered at college entrance and intelligence test scores obtained as early as the seventh grade of elementary school (24, p. 476).

In the interpretation of the latter results, it should be noted that only subjects who had continued their education to the college level were included. If the investigators had worked from the other end, by following up a group of elementary school graduates and retesting them after five or six years, the correlations would probably have been lower, since the intervening educational and other experiences of the subjects would have undoubtedly varied much more widely. In a group with comparatively constant educational experiences, individuals tend to maintain the same relative position in intelligence test score over a period of many years. On the other hand, college students represent a highly selected group intellectually and are therefore more homogeneous in intelligence test scores than a random sampling of the general population. This fact tends to lower the correlation between initial and terminal scores in a college group. Data on a much more heterogeneous sample are provided by a Swedish study reported by Husén (41). In this case, a correlation of .72 was found between the test scores of 613 third-grade school boys and the scores obtained by the same subjects ten years later upon their induction into the armed services. During the interval, these subjects had received varying amounts of education.

Retest correlations obviously depend upon the *interval between tests*.

Length of time over which predictions are made affects the accuracy of the forecast. This relationship was clearly demonstrated in Thorndike's analysis of previously published data on school-age children (95). By combining the results from those studies with fairly uniform test-retest intervals and then fitting a curve to these data, Thorndike obtained an equation showing the relationship between time interval and expected correlation. On this basis he estimated, for example, that the test-retest correlation is .90 for an immediate retest, but drops to .70 over a five-year interval. The correlations empirically obtained with school children by subsequent investigators have in general corroborated the values predicted from this curve (cf. 96).

A second factor influencing the accuracy of prediction is *age at which the initial test is administered.* In general, the older the subject the greater will be the constancy of his test scores. Beyond the elementary school years, even relatively long intervals are likely to yield fairly stable results. Thus in the case of tests administered to college students, correlations with earlier tests taken during the freshman year of high school are about as high as those with tests taken during the senior year of high school (97). At the other extreme, preschool tests yield very low correlations with scores obtained during later childhood, as will be seen in the following section.

Finally, it is important to bear in mind that even when retest correlations are high over a given time interval, *large shifts may occur in individual cases.* Repeated corroboration of this fact is provided by both the Berkeley Growth Study (9, 10) and the Guidance Study (58). In an analysis of data on 222 cases from the latter project, Honzik, Macfarlane, and Allen (39) report individual IQ changes of as much as 50 points. Over the period from 6 to 18 years, when retest correlations are generally high, 59 per cent of the subjects changed 15 or more IQ points, 37 per cent changed 20 or more points, and 9 per cent changed 30 or more points.

Nor are most of these individual changes random or erratic in nature. Some children exhibit consistent upward or downward trends over several years. Moreover, changes in score tend to be in the direction of family level, as judged by parental education or socioeconomic status. For example, in the Berkeley Growth Study, the correlation between child's IQ and parents' education rose from approximately zero shortly after birth to .55 at the age of 5 years [2] (10). In the Guidance Study, detailed investigation of home

[2] The mere fact of a rising correlation could theoretically be attributed to either heredity or environment. With increasing age, more opportunities arise for different hereditary factors to be manifested in the child's intellectual development—a situation

conditions, parent-child relationships, and other environmental factors indicated that large upward or downward shifts in IQ were associated with the cultural milieu and emotional climate in which the child was reared. In general, children in underprivileged environments tend to lose and those in superior environments to gain with age, in relation to test norms. And drastic changes in environmental conditions during childhood are likely to result in distinct rises or drops in IQ. Because of the possibility of large shifts in individual scores, the California investigators concluded that single scores—or even two scores—obtained on school-age children need to be interpreted with the utmost caution (39).

Instability of Early IQ's. It is now generally recognized that available preschool tests provide little basis for predicting the individual's later intellectual status. Even with intervals of only a few years, retest correlations are too low for predictive purposes, generally clustering in the .30's. Relevant data are to be found in a number of longitudinal studies (4, 10, 15, 34, 39, 67, 107). In one group of 123 children, for example, performance on the Yale Developmental Examination at 6 months of age correlated only .37 with Merrill-Palmer scores at 2 years (67). In the same group, a correlation of .46 was found between the initial Yale score and Stanford-Binet IQ at the age of 3 years. Even less evidence of predictive validity was found in a more recent study by Wittenborn (107). In an effort to determine the validity of different aspects of the Yale Developmental Examination, a wide variety of criteria were employed, including Stanford-Binet, Arthur Performance Scale, scholastic achievement tests, measures of motor and physical development, and extensive data on personal-social development obtained through interviewing and rating techniques. Predictive validity was checked against 5–6-year performance in a group of 114 children and against 7–9-year performance in a group of 81 children. No significant correlations were found with any of the criterion measures.

On the basis of the Berkeley Growth Study data, Bayley (9, 10) concluded that tests given at 4 years may permit grade school predictions within wide classifications; tests between 2 and 4 years will predict 8- and 9-year performance with some success; but scores obtained before 18 months of age are completely useless in the prediction of abilities during school ages. In this investigation, scores obtained under the age of 18

---

which would produce increasing parent-child resemblance. On the other hand, the observed IQ changes could reflect the continuing influence of parental contacts and of the different sorts of home environments provided by parents of varying intelligence. The correlations alone provide no basis for choosing between these alternative explanations. The results need to be viewed in the light of other, general knowledge regarding the nature and operation of heredity and environment.

months yielded zero and even low negative correlations with later performance.

The Guidance Study likewise demonstrated the low predictive value of early IQ's (38). Initial tests given at 21 months correlated only about .30 with retests at 5 and 6 years of age. Somewhat better prediction was possible with tests administered at the upper preschool ages, but the correlations were still too low for dependable individual forecasts. Essentially the same conclusion was reached by Goodenough and Maurer (34) in follow-ups of over 200 children who had taken the Minnesota Preschool Test before the age of 6. Correlations of these initial scores with Stanford-Binet retests at ages 7 to 12 ranged from .15 to .45. Correlations on smaller groups that were followed into college were also reported. The correlations between preschool tests and scores on the ACE taken upon college entrance were .12 (with tests taken under age 4), .29 (with tests taken between ages 4 and 5), and .39 (with tests between ages 5 and 6).

Even when the same test is administered repeatedly, correlations between preschool IQ's and later scores are low. In a study by Bradway (15), 138 children who had been tested between the ages of 2 and 6, as part of the Stanford-Binet standardization sample, were re-examined ten years later. An analysis of IQ changes led to the conclusion that, although this test "is as good as or better than any other objective index in predicting future intellectual functioning of a preschool child . . . an individual IQ obtained prior to the age of six years must be interpreted with discretion." From the total group of 138 subjects, 50 children showing the largest test-retest changes were selected for special study (16). Results of home visits and interviews with parents in these cases indicated that significant rises or drops in IQ over the ten-year period were related to the various familial and home characteristics investigated. Such findings are similar to those obtained in both the Berkeley Growth Study and the Guidance Study in the case of preschool as well as older children.

Factors Influencing the Stability of Test Scores. A number of conditions may account for the instability of early IQ's and for the growing constancy of scores with age. First, the *standardization samples* on which norms for preschool and infant scales are established are generally smaller and less representative than is the case for older age levels. The norms in terms of which scores are evaluated may thus be less stable. Owing to the nature of tests for very young children, standardization of *testing procedure* may also be less exact.

Another characteristic of the measuring instrument which may produce spurious shifts in score pertains to the *scale of units* employed in the scoring system. Thus two tests may both utilize IQ's; but such IQ's will not be comparable if their standard deviations differ.[3] An IQ of 120 on one test might actually be equivalent to an IQ of 140 on another. Moreover, IQ's are sometimes computed on tests that fail to meet the requirements for the application of this type of score. Consequently, the meaning of an IQ might vary with age even on the same test. On the Merrill-Palmer Scale, for example, an IQ of 114 at one age may indicate the same degree of superiority to the age norm as an IQ of 141 at another age.

A fourth source of variation in early IQ's is to be found in certain characteristics of the behavior of young children which may lower *test reliability*. Establishment of rapport and control of test motivation are certainly more difficult prior to school entrance. The shyness, distractability, negativism, and similar emotional reactions often observed in the behavior of preschool children may lower test scores unduly on a particular occasion.

All of these conditions pertaining to characteristics of the test itself or of its administration and scoring can undoubtedly reduce the predictive value of any test score. Large fluctuations obtained in any individual case should certainly be examined with these factors in mind. On the other hand, in the better-controlled longitudinal studies it seems unlikely that these factors have played a major part. The predictive value of infant tests remains poor even when relatively well-standardized tests are administered and scores are expressed in comparable units. Moreover, some infant and preschool tests yield high reliability coefficients, when such reliability is measured over short intervals (cf. 1, Ch. 11). There is evidence that infant and preschool tests provide a satisfactory index of the child's current status. It is only long-range predictions that fail.

The instability of early IQ's depends only in part upon shortcomings of the measuring instrument. Predictive value of the IQ over periods of more than a year cannot be regarded as synonymous with test reliability in the accepted sense (cf. 1, Ch. 5). If genuine changes in performance level occur during such an interval, the scores on a highly reliable instrument will—and should—change. Body weight at the age of 6 months, for example, may correlate very low with body weight at age 40. Prediction from the former measure to the latter would be hazardous, and yet such measures may have been obtained with scales of nearly perfect reliability. Logically, a test may have high reliability—and validity—at a particular age level, despite the fact that it does not permit accurate long-range predictions. From a practical viewpoint, such a test would still have good diagnostic usefulness, i.e., generalizations could be made from the specific behavior

[3] For an explanation of this point, see Anastasi (1, pp. 73–77).

sample of the test to other behavior of the child at that particular age level.

Further reasons for the instability of early IQ's may be sought in basic characteristics of behavior development itself. Thus it is likely that the individual's level of intellectual functioning is more susceptible to *environmental influences* early in life. The nature of "intelligence," moreover, varies with age—a change reflected in the *content of intelligence tests* for different ages. It is unlikely that the highly verbal and abstract functions sampled by school-age intelligence tests can be accurately predicted by the predominantly sensorimotor tests of infancy and early childhood. Whether it will be possible to devise preschool tests which are sufficiently verbal to correlate highly with later scores remains an unanswered question. It should also be noted that, until they reach school age, most children have not been exposed to a large enough *body of uniform experience*—later furnished by the relatively standardized school curriculum—to permit an adequate sampling of common intellectual tasks for testing purposes. The sharp rise in stability of intelligence test scores following school entrance may be related to this growing pool of common experience.

Finally, an important factor in the increasing constancy of the IQ with age is the *cumulative nature of behavior development.* The individual's behavior equipment at each age includes, in general, all his earlier behavior equipment, plus an increment of new acquisitions. Even if the annual increments bear no relation to one another, a growing consistency of behavior level would appear, simply because earlier acquisitions constitute an increasing proportion of total behavior as age increases. Predictions of IQ from 10 to 16 would thus be more accurate than from 3 to 9 because the scores at 10 include a larger proportion of what is present at 16, while scores at 3 include a smaller proportion of what is present at 9.

Anderson (3) has referred to this relationship between successive scores in his "overlap hypothesis." He writes, "Since the growing individual does not lose what he already has, the constancy of the IQ is in large measure a matter of the part-whole or overlap relation" (3, p. 394). In support of this hypothesis, Anderson computed a series of correlations between initial and terminal "scores" obtained with shuffled cards and random numbers. These correlations, which depended solely upon the extent of overlap between successive measures, agreed closely with test-retest correlations in intelligence test scores found in three published longitudinal studies. In fact, the test scores tended to give somewhat *lower* correlations, a difference attributed by Anderson to such factors as errors of measurement and change in test content with age.

Actuarial Prediction versus Regularity of Development. We may now return to the second question raised at the opening of the present section. Does the "constancy of the IQ," as indicated by the fairly high predictive value of scores obtained during the school years, signify regularity of intellectual development? Anderson's hypothesis of overlap has suggested that it need not do so. Even with no regularity in the amount of annual increments, overlap of scores would permit fairly accurate predictions. Empirical confirmation of this explanation is to be found in an analysis conducted by Roff (74). Using previously published data, Roff correlated the intelligence test performance of children at any one age with their gain in performance after one or more years. These correlations were all close to zero. From such a finding, the author concluded that "the so-called 'constancy of the IQ' is due primarily to the retention by each child of the skills and knowledge which determined his scores in earlier years, and is not due at all to correlation between earlier scores and later gains or increments" (74, p. 385).

In conclusion, the growing individual exhibits an increasing consistency of ability level, not because the "rate of growth" is constant, but because his present accomplishments constitute an ever-increasing portion of his future accomplishment as he grows older. This is tantamount to saying that at age 15 we can make a more accurate prediction of an individual's subsequent behavior than at age 2, because we know more about him at 15. The proportional change in his behavior from age 15 to 16 is less than from age 2 to 3, and certainly much less than from 2 to 16.

INTELLECTUAL FUNCTIONING IN MATURITY AND OLD AGE

The study of maturity and old age is a recent but vigorous branch of contemporary psychology. Interest in the characteristics and problems of older persons has taken many forms. A number of research projects on large groups of adults have been concerned with age changes in general intelligence, special aptitudes, emotional responses, and attitudes. Special efforts have been made to study representative samples at various age levels, in contrast to the rather atypical samples utilized in earlier studies on older persons. Longitudinal approaches are being used increasingly in research on adults. Widespread attention is also being given to the vocational and personal guidance of older people, to retirement problems, and to clinical treatment of maladjustments at these age levels. The importance of this general area of psychological research is evidenced by a rapidly growing body of literature on adult behavior; by the publication of special intelligence tests for adults, such as the Wechsler-Bellevue and the more recent Wechsler Adult Intelligence Scale (WAIS); and by the establishment of a Division on Maturity and Old Age in the American Psychological Association.

The psychologist is by no means alone in his interest in older persons. *Gerontology,* which covers the study of older maturity from many points of view, is today a well-established and thriving branch of science. Practical concern with the problems of advanced age has been heightened by the relatively large number of old persons living today. As medical progress and improvements in living conditions lengthen the life span, the proportion of older persons in the population continues to increase.

The Complete Age Curve for Intelligence. One of the first questions asked about adult intelligence pertained to the *"limit of mental growth."* At what age does the individual reach his peak performance in the sort of functions measured by intelligence tests? What is the mental age of the average adult? Beginning with an estimated adult mental age of 14 based on World War I data, this limit has been pushed progressively higher by subsequent research. In the 1937 revision of the Stanford-Binet, the average adult mental age corresponds to 15 years. On the more recently developed Wechsler-Bellevue—as well as on the still later WAIS—the standardization sample reached its peak scores in the early twenties. Large-scale cross-sectional studies by Jones and Conrad (43) and by Miles and Miles (61), to be discussed below, also revealed improvement in mean score until the late teens or early twenties.

Longitudinal studies have likewise furnished evidence of continuing improvement in intelligence test scores to the age of 20 or beyond (10, 11, 12, 32, 93). In the Berkeley Growth Study, for example, scores continued to improve to age 25 (the last age covered by the survey), and the indications were that the peak had not yet been reached (10, 11). Mention may also be made of retest studies on high school and college students with parallel forms of the ACE Psychological Examination, all of which yielded significant retest gains (6, 40, 55, 81, 98). Without the use of noncollege control groups, it is of course impossible to determine the extent to which such gains are attributable to college training and to other more general conditions. From a purely descriptive viewpoint, however, the fact remains that gains in intelligence test performance were made consistently by these subjects, who ranged in age from the middle teens to the late twenties. There is likewise evidence that individuals who continue their education longer tend to improve in intelligence test performance until a later age and by large amounts (69, 101). Finally, the most recently completed follow-ups suggest that, at least for certain groups, intelligence test scores may continue to improve throughout life (12, 14, 69).

Differences between the results of earlier and later studies undoubtedly reflect both cultural changes and refinements in testing instruments. Early intelligence tests were designed primarily for children and their content was subsequently adapted for adult testing. Today there are more tests appealing to adult interests and providing sufficient ceiling for continued improvement. On the other hand, even when old tests were readministered in recent studies, significant mean rises were observed (e.g., 69). It is

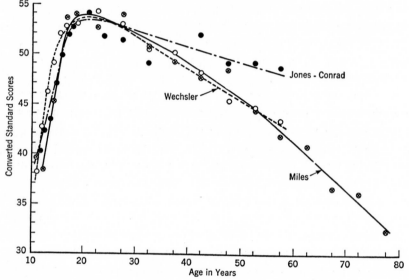

Fig. 50.   Mean Intelligence Test Scores in Relation to Age: A Comparison of Results from Three Cross-Sectional Investigations. (From Jones and Kaplan, 45, p. 72.)

highly probable that educational and other cultural factors contributed to these gains.

Closely related to the question of cessation of intellectual development is that of *onset of decline.* As more data were gathered, in fact, the two questions merged, and it is now apparent that they must be considered together. Depending upon the type of subjects tested and the specific intellectual functions measured, age curves may show continuing rise throughout life, rise followed by a leveling-off with no decline, or rise followed by gradual or steep drop.

Data from three large-scale cross-sectional studies are reproduced in Figure 50. In one of the first systematic surveys of the intelligence of older persons, Jones and Conrad (43) gave the Army Alpha to 1191 subjects between the ages of 10 and 60, constituting nearly the entire population between those ages in 19 rural New England villages. As part of the Stanford Later Maturity Study, Miles and Miles (61) administered a shortened and highly speeded version of the Otis Self-Administering Tests of Mental Ability to 823 subjects ranging in age from 7 to 94. In the effort to obtain roughly comparable samples at different ages, the adult subjects were contacted largely through lodges and social groups.[4] During the standardization of the Wechsler-Bellevue, Wechsler (103) gathered data from 670 children and 1081 adults ranging up to 69 years of age. All subjects in this sample lived in New York State, the adults being selected so that the occupational distribution for each age resembled roughly the corresponding distribution in the national census data.

The three age curves given in Figure 50 have been plotted in terms of standard scores in order to make the data of the three studies comparable. All show a peak in the early twenties, followed by a decline. The rate of decline is less steep in the Jones and Conrad study than in the other two. Such a discrepancy may result in part from sampling irregularities and in part from differences among the tests employed in the three investigations.

In all three studies, individual differences within each age were large, variability tending to increase with age. Although mean scores dropped with age, these differences were small compared to the range of scores within a single age. As a result, even widely separated age groups showed extensive *overlapping* of scores. The brightest persons in the oldest group still performed conspicuously better than the dullest in the younger groups.

That age in itself is a poor guide to ability level is further illustrated by Figure 51, based on an analysis of some of the data from the Stanford Later Maturity Study (61). In this graph, the adult subjects have been classified into four groups in terms of amount of education received, ranging from elementary school to graduate school. Although all four groups show a decline in mean score with age, the four curves neither cross nor meet, the higher educational groups retaining their superiority at all ages. It should also be noted that 70-year-olds who continued their education beyond college averaged higher than 20-year-olds with only elementary or high school education.

Since the three age curves reproduced in Figure 50 were plotted from cross-sectional data, they may have been influenced by cultural changes, as discussed in the first section of this chapter. Owing to the rising educa-

---

[4] As a check on cross-sectional trends, 190 adults between the ages of 25 and 89 were retested after two years. Throughout this age range, approximately the same decline was found over the two-year interval as was expected on the basis of the cross-sectional data (60).

tional level of the population, for example, the 60-year-olds in any of these surveys had undoubtedly received less education as a group than the 20-year-olds with whom they were compared. The suspicion thus arises that at least part of the observed decline in mean test performance may be the result, not of older age, but of less education (2). Some corroboration for this hypothesis is provided by a comparison of the standardization data of the WAIS with those of the older Wechsler-Bellevue (103, 104). Both samples show a decline in score during adulthood which closely parallels the decrease in educational level in the successive age groups. But in the more recently tested WAIS sample, improvement continues longer and decline sets in at a later age than in the Wechsler-Bellevue sample. Such a finding is in line with the educational differences between the two standardization samples and reflects educational changes over the intervening fifteen years. Also relevant are the results obtained by Miner (63) with a vocabulary test administered to a carefully stratified national sample of 1500 persons. Although the total sample showed a slight decline in mean score beyond the 35–44 year level, the age decrements disappeared when subjects were matched in amount of schooling.

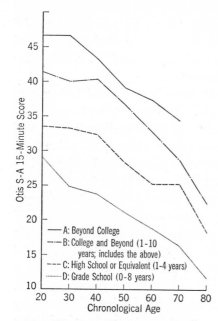

Fig. 51. Age Changes in Intelligence Test Scores at Different Educational Levels. (From Miles and Miles, 61, p. 70.)

Longitudinal data regarding age changes during adulthood are gradually becoming available. Bentz (14) reports results on 208 business executives who had taken the ACE Psychological Examination from 6 to 10 years earlier. Those under 35 years of age at the time of the retest made significant gains; those aged 40 or higher showed a slight loss. In 1950, Owens (69) administered the Army Alpha to 127 men who had taken the identical test 30 years earlier as entering freshmen at Iowa State College. Rather than showing any decline on the retest, the group exhibited a significant mean gain amounting to one-half the standard deviation of the original distribution. Moreover, none of the eight Army Alpha subtests yielded a significant decrease, and five showed a significant rise in mean score.

Continued increases throughout the adult years were likewise found by Bayley and Oden (12) in a follow-up of subjects from the Stanford study of gifted children. In a sample of over a thousand cases, including gifted subjects and their spouses, comparisons were made between two administrations of alternate forms of the Concept Mastery Test, separated by a 12-year interval. Ages on initial test ranged from about 20 to 50 years. All subgroups within this sample, regardless of initial age, showed a significant rise in score.

By combining the data from this analysis with the Army Alpha data from the Owens study and data up to age 21 from the Berkeley Growth Study, Bayley (10) has produced a composite age curve of intelligence. This curve, reproduced in Figure 52, shows a continuing rise, with no decline. The larger gains of the Stanford gifted group may result from the higher ability level of the subjects or from the higher ceiling of the test. Even in the Owens study, of course, the subjects were a

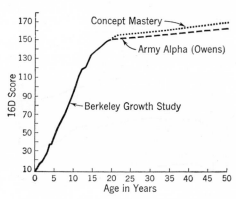

Fig. 52. A Composite Age Curve of Intelligence from Birth to Fifty Years. (From Bayley, 10, p. 816.)

selected sample, since all had been admitted to college. What a longitudinal study of a more nearly random sample would show over this age range cannot be ascertained from the available data.

Functional Specificity of Age Changes. With the growing realization that "intelligence" is a composite of many relatively independent abilities, psychologists have turned increasingly to an analysis of age changes in more specific functions. One manifestation of this trend is to be found in the study of age differences on separate subtests of intelligence tests. Analyses of mean scores obtained by different age groups on the Wechsler-Bellevue subtests, for example, have revealed consistent differences among subtests (20, 31).

Corresponding data from the WAIS standardization samples are reproduced in Figure 53. The age curves show the mean scaled scores of successive age groups on the six verbal and five performance subtests of the WAIS. Results on persons over 60 were obtained from a special "old age sample." Although somewhat different sampling procedures were followed in choosing the "old age sample" and the "national sample" (covering younger ages), the continuity of the age curves for the two samples suggests that they are approximately comparable. All scores are expressed in terms of the mean and standard deviation of the 20–34-year reference group, and these two values are shown to the right of each curve. It can be readily seen that, in general, the performance tests reach their peak earlier and decline more sharply with age than do the verbal tests. Among the latter, Vocabulary shows the least loss. Information, Comprehension, and Arithmetic also reveal relatively little age decrement. Of the performance tests,

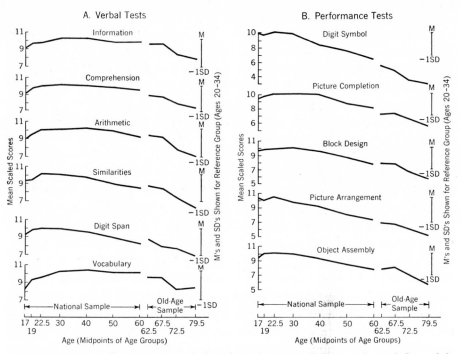

Fig. 53. Age Differences in Verbal and Performance Subtests of Wechsler Adult Intelligence Scale. (From Doppelt and Wallace, 23, p. 322.)

Digit Symbol yields the most pronounced score decrease with age. This test places great emphasis upon speed and visual perception.

These findings obtained with the WAIS (and Wechsler-Bellevue) subtests are in line with the results of a large number of other studies, using many different tests. One of the most consistent of all findings in adult testing is the relative stability of *vocabulary* scores (5, 36, 43, 76, 78, 99, 105). For this reason, it has become common practice to utilize vocabulary scores as a rough index of a person's earlier intellectual level, against which deterioration in other functions may be measured (cf. 1, Ch. 13). Many vocabulary tests are of the multiple-choice variety, in which the subject need only recognize the correct synonym. Vocabulary subtests in individual intelligence tests such as the Stanford-Binet and the Wechsler scales do require the subject to define each word. But any evidence of familiarity with a correct meaning of the word is usually considered acceptable. It is thus possible that a more demanding test of word knowledge might show age decrement. There is some evidence to indicate that, at least in the case of psychotics, ordinary vocabulary scores may reveal no deterioration, while a qualitative analysis of the types of definition given by the subject does indicate significant loss (18, 27).

In tests that emphasize *speed,* older persons are generally handicapped. Some evidence on this point was provided by the Stanford Later Maturity Study (60). When another form of the Otis test was given without time limit to 433 persons who had taken the speeded form, mean age decrement was lower on the unspeeded test up to age 60. Between 60 and 80, however, the drop in score was steep even under unspeeded conditions. A somewhat different procedure was followed by Lorge (56). Three groups of subjects, aged 20 to 25, 27½ to 37½, and 40 to over 70, respectively, were equated on the CAVD, which is a pure power test given with no time limit. When the same subjects were tested with Army Alpha and Otis S-A, mean scores declined progressively from the youngest to the oldest group. It should be noted that in this study regression effect (cf. Ch. 7) may account for some of the obtained group differences in the speeded tests.

Of particular interest is a study by Gurvitz (35), utilizing the Wechsler-Bellevue as well as revisions of the Army Alpha and Army Beta. Gurvitz points out that, in general, the performance tests of the Wechsler are timed, while the verbal tests are untimed. Such a difference could account in part for the greater age decrement found on the performance tests. The Alpha resembles the verbal part of the Wechsler, but is timed; while the Beta is a timed test similar to the performance part of the Wechsler. Comparisons on these three tests were made between large, representative samples of 20–24-year-olds and 45–49-year-olds. The percentages of decline were as follows: Wechsler verbal 11 per cent, Wechsler performance 28 per cent, Beta 23 per cent, Alpha 22 per cent. From these results it would seem that speed is more important than other characteristics of the three tests in determining rate of decline.

That *performance and nonlanguage tests* yield a larger age decrement than verbal tests has been repeatedly demonstrated (29, 30, 68, 73, 76, 105). Nor can the decline be attributed wholly to speed, since significant age losses are also found on such unspeeded tests as Raven's Progressive Matrices (30, 31, 73). In the process of standardization, this test was given to large samples of British children and adults ranging in age up to 65. The test consists of a series of abstract geometrical designs, from each of which a part has been removed. The subject is required to choose the missing part from a set of given alternatives. The easier items require chiefly accuracy of visual perception; the more difficult involve analogies and other logical relationships. Results showed that mean scores on the Progressive Matrices reach their peak at age 14 and begin to decline after 24. On a vocabulary test given to the same subjects, on the other hand, scores increased to age 30 and remained approximately constant to 60. Similar results have been reported for a sample of 600 persons tested in Belgium (68).

Among the largest age decrements are those found in tasks calling for *visual perception* (62, 80, 106). Such a decline is in part associated with general loss of acuity in all senses with increasing age. Even when visual defects are corrected by glasses, however, older persons do more poorly than younger persons on perceptual tasks (62). It has been suggested that part of this deficiency may center around the process of organizing new data and integrating such data with relevant material from past experience (106, p. 146).

In *motor skills*, age decline is less pronounced than is generally supposed. In the Stanford Later Maturity Study, little loss was found until the age of 70 on any of a series of motor tests (62). An exceptionally thorough investigation of age changes in motor skills was conducted by Welford and his co-workers at Cambridge (106). Most of the data were obtained under laboratory conditions, although preliminary studies in industry are also reported. A special feature of this research was the analysis of different aspects of the subjects' motor performance, in order to explore more fully the nature of age changes. Results indicated that the major impairments occurred in the perceptual rather than in the motor aspects of the activities.

Moreover, older subjects tended to change their methods of performing tasks and thus to compensate for their deficiencies. The rigidity or flexibility of the task determines the degree to which such compensatory changes of procedure can be effectively utilized by the subject. Thus Welford *et al.* conclude that, when the task permits a variety of approaches and the method is largely under the subject's control, compensatory changes in performance are likely to occur. Such tasks may show no decline or even an improvement with age owing to overcompensation. On the other hand, "where the performance is narrowly constrained in either form or timing of the constituent reactions, compensation will be virtually impossible" (106, p. 123).

It is also noteworthy that age decrements in *physical strength* are not so large as is commonly believed. Data on industrial workers (28) reveal a peak in the middle twenties followed by a very gradual decline during the next forty years. By the age of 60, the mean is approximately 16.5 per cent below the 20-year-old mean. It would thus seem that older workers are better equipped to cope with moderately heavy work than with relatively light tasks which may demand a high degree of speed and perceptual accuracy.

Can older persons *learn* as well as young people? The notion that "you cannot teach an old dog new tricks" is a common one in popular thinking. Adults frequently deplore their inability to learn a new language or a new motor skill as well as they could in their younger days. Closer observation reveals, however, that the *conditions of learning* are far from comparable at different age levels. Time available for learning, distractions, and motivation to learn are often very different for child and adult. The learning of new skills is frequently undertaken casually and halfheartedly by the adult, while for the child or adolescent it is the core of his serious responsibilties, other activities being "extracurricular."

When older and younger persons learn under comparable conditions in an experimental situation, the differences in their performance are relatively slight. In an early series of investigations with a variety of tasks, E. L. Thorndike (94) concluded that there is an average decline of less than 1 per cent a year in "sheer modifiability" between the ages of 22 and 42. This decline was manifested principally in the more meaningless tests of rote learning, such as drawing lines of given lengths blindfolded, learning a code, or memorizing numbers paired with nonsense syllables. In most other tasks, the older persons could compensate for any loss in learning ability by greater interest, better sustained effort, and a larger fund of relevant experience. For example, in stenography and typewriting, in learning Esperanto, or in university courses, the progress of the older persons equaled and sometimes even excelled that of the younger.

When the new learning runs counter to previous learning, it is reasonable to expect older adults to be handicapped. This may be a simple result of *interference*, or "negative transfer," which need have no necessary connection with age as such. There is some experimental evidence to show that tasks that are hindered by previous experience suffer a larger age decrement than those benefited by such experience. As part of the Stanford Later Maturity Study, Ruch (75) administered learning tests to three groups of 40 subjects each, aged 12–17, 34–59, and 60–82, respectively. The older subjects proved inferior to the younger subjects in the learning of all types of material, although they were *less* inferior on the more meaningful material. For example, the older subjects were least handicapped in learning paired associates which were meaningfully connected, such as nest-owl, soft-chair. Their performance was poorer in learning "nonsense" material, such as $A \times M = B$ or $N \times M = C$, and poorest in memorizing material that conflicted with previous learning, such as $3 \times 4 = 2$ or $3 \times 1 = 1$.

These age differences in learning various types of tasks could be explained on the basis of interference from previously established associations. Or they could result from age differences in interests and motivation. In general, older persons are less likely to exert themselves in tasks which impress them as foolish or meaningless in terms of their experience. Still another alternative explanation may be found in the previously cited hypothesis of Welford, pertaining to the perceptual organization of new data. In discussing their own learning experiments, Welford *et al.* write (106, pp. 121–122):

Indeed, it appeared that sometimes it is difficulty of modifying a pre-existing organization which causes impairment of performance among older people. In the learning experiment, for instance, it was clear that in many cases the main difficulty lay not so much in learning the sequence required, as in unlearning a

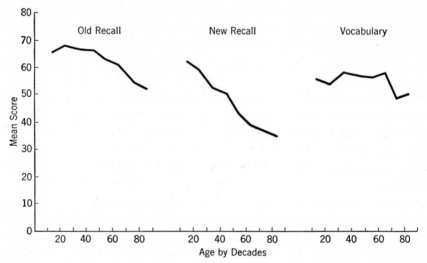

Fig. 54. Age Changes in Memory. (Adapted from Shakow, Dolkart, and Goldman, 77, p. 48.)

sequence which contained a number of errors. Again, in face of the very difficult data presented in the logical-thinking experiment, older subjects showed a much greater tendency than younger to produce answers in terms of past experience and pre-formed opinions, instead of organizing the data itself in the manner required by the instructions.

With regard to *memory,* age decrements have generally been found, although the amount of deficit again varies with the nature of the task. Gilbert (33) administered eleven memory tests to 174 persons aged 60–69 and to an equal number of 20–29-year-olds who had been matched with the older subjects in Stanford-Binet vocabulary scores. All memory tests yielded significant mean differences in favor of the younger group. Differences were smallest, however, on digit span and largest on memory for pairs of unrelated words. It was also found that the brighter old persons tended to show less memory loss than the duller (as determined by vocabulary score).

In another experiment, Shakow *et al.* (77) tested 115 subjects ranging in age from 15 to 90. Three measures were obtained, including vocabulary, ability to recall past events (old recall), and ability to recall recently learned material such as figures, sentences, and ideas presented during the test (new recall). As will be seen in Figure 54, both old and new recall decline with age, although the decline is much steeper in the latter. Vocabulary scores remain virtually constant until about age 70, when they drop sharply.

Age and Creative Achievement. Another approach to the investigation of adult abilities is to be found in the analysis of creative production in such fields as science, literature, music, and art. It can be readily demonstrated, of course, that great contributions to all these fields have been made by individuals of almost any age. Nevertheless, outstanding creative achievements do tend to cluster in certain decades. The photographs of eminent scientists we see in textbooks usually show them to be persons of advanced years. It has been pointed out, however, that such photographs are more likely to be made after the scientist has become an old man and has attained renown (cf. 53, p. 12). A look at the scientist at work—or at the writer, musician, or artist—is likely to reveal a younger man than we had visualized.

Lehman (53) has analyzed a monumental array of published data regarding the ages at which outstanding contributions have been made in many fields of human endeavor. His results show that the peak of creative production falls rather consistently in the decade of the thirties. An example from chemistry will serve to illustrate his procedure and findings. From a dependable published source, Lehman obtained the names of 244 noted chemists (none of whom were still living), together with the dates on which they had made their major contributions. The data were then analyzed so as to show the total number of such contributions made by the entire group within each five-year age interval. In order to allow for the decreasing number of persons as age advanced, Lehman computed the average annual contribution for those members of the group actually living at each age level. These annual averages, expressed as a percentage of the average during the most productive age interval, are given in Figure 55 (solid line).

It will be noted that production rate rises steeply to a maximum in the 30–34-year interval, then declines gradually and steadily. Similar curves were obtained for different sciences and for many kinds of creative work in literature, art, and music. Interesting corroboration of such age curves is provided by longitudinal data on one especially prolific scientist. Figure 56 gives the age at which each of 1086 inventions was patented by Thomas A. Edison. The peak again falls in the mid-thirties.

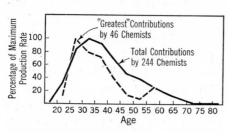

Fig. 55. Age and Creative Production Rate in Chemistry. (From Lehman, 53, p. 7.)

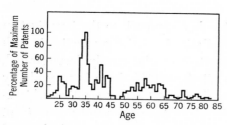

Fig. 56. Age versus Inventions Patented in U.S.A. by Thomas A. Edison. Based on a total of 1086 patents. (From Lehman, 53, p. 11.)

When only output of the highest quality was considered, the peak tended to be reached *earlier* in all creative fields investigated. For the chemists, this is illustrated by the broken-line graph in Figure 55. Another noteworthy observation pertains to changes from generation to generation. In general, creative workers in more recent times have been making their maximum contributions at *younger ages* than was true in earlier periods. Figure 57 illustrates this finding in the case of physicists. The specific *field of activity* seems to have little effect on the age of maximum productivity. In the area of literature, for example, poets reach their peak in the twenties, novelists in the early forties. On the whole, however, the thirties emerge as the "golden decade" of creative achievement.

By contrast, *leaders* in such areas as government and the military services are found to be a more elderly group, the largest clustering of persons occurring between 50 and 70 years. Moreover, the mean age of these groups appears to be increasing rather than decreasing in successive generations. This finding is illustrated in Figure 58, which gives the age distribution of members of the U.S. House of Representatives in the years 1825 and 1925, respectively. It should be noted that social recognition, which is essential for leadership, is more likely to be delayed until a relatively advanced age. The creative worker, on the other hand, can make his contribution prior to and in the absence of recognition by society.

We could speculate at length regarding the reasons for the reported decrement in creative achievement after the thirties. Lehman writes: "As a result of negative transfer, the old generally are more inflexible than the young. This inflexibility may be a handicap to creative work, even though it is dependent on erudition" (53, p. 329). He also recognizes the possible effects of many other factors. Decline in physical vigor, in sensory acuity, and in general health with increasing age undoubtedly reduce productivity in some cases. Interests and motivation may likewise alter with age for a multiplicity of reasons. Financial pressures, domestic responsibilities, and similar extrinsic circumstances may exert varying influences at different ages. Attainment of fame, increase in administrative activities, and other occurrences in one's professional life may also affect the pattern of productivity. Then, too, in a rapidly expanding field, the individual scientist's work is

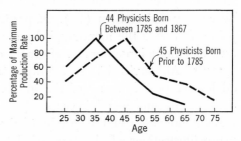

Fig. 57. Age and Creative Production Rate in Physics in Earlier and More Recent Times. (From Lehman, 53, p. 289.)

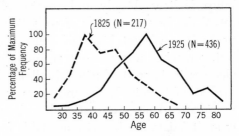

Fig. 58. Age Distribution of Members of U. S. House of Representatives in 1825 and in 1925. (From Lehman, 53, p. 270.)

evaluated against the contribution of an ever increasing number of colleagues. The chances for outstanding achievement are thus reduced for the individual as he grows older. Owing to these and other uncontrolled factors in the data, it is thus apparent that Lehman's results cannot be regarded as conclusive evidence of age decrement in creative ability itself.[5]

AGE AND PERSONALITY

Childhood to Maturity. Descriptions of changes in emotional, motivational, and attitudinal traits which occur as the individual progresses from

[5] For a detailed discussion of spurious factors influencing such data, see the review of Lehman's book by Wayne Dennis (*J. Geront.*, 1956, 11, 331–333).

infancy to adulthood form a major part of standard textbooks on the psychology of childhood and adolescence. Social psychologists, too, have
studied the emergence and development of attitudes, social stereotypes,
self concepts, and various aspects of interpersonal relations in the child
(cf., e.g., 50; 52, Ch. 9 and 10; 72). A summary of much of the research on
personality development in childhood is provided by Jersild (42). An intensive survey covering the entire life span is to be found in the recent book
by Pressey and Kuhlen (71). Of particular interest from a developmental
point of view is the monograph by Shuttleworth (83), in which are gathered together a large number of graphs on physical and psychological development. Although this monograph is specifically concerned with the
adolescent period, many of the graphs extend downward into childhood
and upward into the adult years.

An examination of the graphs in the Shuttleworth monograph provides
many illustrations of the type of data that have been obtained in such
developmental studies. For example, different measures of suggestibility
agree in showing a peak at the ages of 7 and 8 years, after which suggestibility declines sharply and consistently. Studies of children's collections
reveal the largest number of collections in general at age 10, although the
peaks for different kinds of collections fall at different ages. Fingernail
biting reaches a maximum at puberty and then declines. Characteristic
changes in interests during childhood have been investigated through an
analysis of favorite books and magazines, subjects chosen for compositions,
movie attendance, occupational preferences, and the like. Normative developmental data are likewise available for various aspects of social maturity,
self-care, and responsibility. Special mention should be made of the vast
array of data on play and other recreational activities collected by Lehman
and Witty (54). These data were analyzed with reference to age as well as
sex, socioeconomic level, and other factors.

The typical personality changes occurring throughout childhood and
adolescence—and throughout life, for that matter—have frequently been
described in terms of *developmental stages*. Probably the most familiar literary example of this approach is found in Shakespeare's "seven ages of man."
But from time to time psychologists, too, have resorted to such a device and
have proposed their own set of convenient stages for summarizing personality development. As a vivid portrayal of characteristic differences between
age levels, such descriptions have some merit. In the application of such
schemas, however, certain cautions need to be observed. First, it is well to
remember that the transitions between stages are gradual, not sharp.
Secondly, since individuals differ widely in personality development, any

system of stages represents only rough group trends. A third important limitation in the concept of developmental stages arises from the role of cultural factors. The nature, onset, and duration of particular stages may vary widely from culture to culture, or among subgroups within a single culture. Examples of such cultural differences will be given in Chapter 18. A closely related point is that developmental stages need not imply maturational or other structural changes. They may result from culturally determined uniformities in the reactional biographies of individuals.

The Adult Years. The increasing interest of psychologists in the period extending from maturity to senescence is reflected in a growing number of studies of personality changes during adulthood. One of the most extensive of such investigations is Strong's analysis of age changes in interests. The earlier portion of this project (88), conducted as part of the Stanford Later Maturity Study, was based on a cross-sectional analysis of the Strong Vocational Interest Blank responses of 2340 men between the ages of 20 and 60, drawn from eight major occupational fields. Later work by Strong (89) utilized more nearly comparable age samples and supplemented the cross-sectional data by longitudinal follow-ups of the same individuals. In the later investigation, age changes were separately analyzed for the 15- to 25-year period and for the 25- to 55-year period.

In general, Strong's data indicate that similarities in interests among age groups are far greater than differences. Men in different occupations exhibit much more variation in interest patterns than was found between age levels. The major age changes, moreover, occurred between 15 and 25 years. One of these changes was an increase in the number of likes, probably resulting from widening experience. Between 25 and 55, the principal changes included a decrease in liking for activities calling for physical skill and daring, as well as for occupations requiring writing. Significant decrease was also found in liking for activities involving change or interference with established habits. It is interesting to note that liking for change increased from 15 to 25 and then decreased to 55. Thus the least "conservative" age in this respect appears to be the mid-twenties.

In the previously cited survey by Lehman and Witty (54), recreational activities of adults were found to become more traditional and less individualistic with increasing age. The older person's avocational interests thus tended to become channeled in accordance with cultural patterns.

A comparison of responses on the Minnesota Multiphasic Personality Inventory given by college students with those of business and professional men in the 45- to 55-year age range revealed significant differences on many items (17). The answers by the older men indicated diminished physical fitness, decreased interest in strenuous and adventurous activities, and greater tension about work and emotional adjustments, but better social adjustment to family and other relatives. In an experiment on suggestion, older persons proved less susceptible than younger subjects to the influence of either group opinion or expert opinion (59). Again, such a finding could be interpreted as evidence of the greater "conservatism" or relative "inflexibility" of older persons. Specifically it may indicate that the longer one has held an opinion, the less inclined he is to change it.

The extensive surveys by Kinsey and his co-workers on sexual behavior of men (48) and of women (49) provide a mass of data on age differences. Although representing the largest and most carefully collected body of facts on this subject available to date, the findings of the Kinsey investigations have been criticized chiefly on two counts. First, the samplings employed may be atypical, especially since most of the subjects volunteered for the study. Secondly, having been gathered through interviewing procedures, the data are subject to errors of recall, as well as to deliberate exaggerations or other falsifications on the part of subjects. It is likely that these limitations do not affect all results to an equal degree. Relative findings, such as those pertaining to age trends within the samples investigated, are probably among the more dependable facts obtained in these studies.

One of the conclusions that emerges from the Kinsey data is that feelings, attitudes, and other psychological characteristics are not so closely tied up with physiological factors as was formerly supposed. This observation is borne out by data relating to age changes, especially among older persons. Thus the termination of reproductive capacity need not be associated with disruptive psychological changes or loss of sex interests. Other research on the personality of the aged (cf. 51) indicates wide individual differences in the reactions to "change of life" and suggests the importance of psychological factors in determining emotional adjustment during such periods. For that matter, it is being increasingly recognized that the individual's reactions to all aspects of the aging process can be greatly modified by psychological factors. In one review of personality studies of older persons, Kuhlen (51) concludes that "the maintenance of active interests and having sufficient work stand out as of first rank importance" in achieving good adjustment. In a later survey, Watson (102) urges that more research be done on the self concept of older persons and its effect on personality changes. A series of studies on the self concepts of older people and on age stereotypes has been carried out by Lorge and his associates (cf. 57).

Most of the data on adult personality changes have been derived from cross-sectional investigations. Of special interest is a longitudinal study of adult personality conducted by Kelly (47). The project began in the years 1935–38 with the testing of 300 engaged couples in New England. The mean age of the men at that time was 26.7, that of the women 24.7; nearly 90 per cent of the subjects were between the ages of 21 and 30. Approximately twenty years later, 86 per cent of the original subjects were re-examined with the same attitude, interest, and other personality tests and rating scales used in the initial testing.

Analysis of group trends over the interval revealed few significant differences in mean scores, and even these represented small changes. On the Allport-Vernon Study of Values, the men dropped in the Theoretical score, both sexes declined in the Aesthetic, and both rose in the Religious. The last-named change was the largest of the three and was corroborated by a rise in favorable attitude toward the church, as measured by the Remmers Generalized Attitude Scales.[6] Among other significant differences were slightly more favorable attitudes toward child rearing and less favorable attitudes toward housekeeping on the part of both sexes. The men showed a significant rise in favorable attitude toward gardening, as well as significantly higher score on the occupational scale for farmer on the Strong Vocational Interest Blank. Apparently working with the soil gained in popularity with increasing age among the men in this sample!

The Strong test also indicated a significant shift toward more masculine interests on the part of both sexes. As one possible hypothesis to account for this finding, Kelly suggests the increasing mechanization of our culture, as illustrated by the rise in number and variety of mechanical appliances for the home. Such mechanization might produce an increase in the typically "masculine" area of mechanical interests, when scores are evaluated in terms of the original test norms. On the Bernreuter, the only significant change was a rise in self-confidence score on the part of the women. Finally, both sexes rated themselves as less peppy, more careless in dress, having narrower interests, and more ill-natured in temper after the twenty-year interval. Such shifts in self-ratings may reflect a combination of actual personality differences plus changes in insight, self-knowledge, and standards of judgment.

In his evaluation of all these differences, Kelly observes that "each of the significant changes in means is of theoretical interest, but, in the absence of adequate age norms at the two points in time, may be equally well inter-

---

[6] Similar findings were obtained in a study by Nelson (66) in which college students were re-examined after an interval of 14 years.

preted as due to increasing age or cultural change" (47, p. 671). This raises a methodological question which was considered in the opening section of the present chapter.

Data bearing on the general question of cultural change and age differences are to be found in a study by Pressey and Jones (70). In 1953, groups of college students and of adults between the ages of 20 and 60 were given two parts of the Pressey X-O Test. In one of these, the subject is required to cross out all things he considers wrong in a list of 125 items, most of which refer to such "borderline" activities as smoking, drinking, flirting, spitting, giggling, and the like. In the other, he crosses out every item about which he has ever worried or felt anxious. The same test had been given to comparable groups of college students in 1923, 1933, and 1943. The 1923

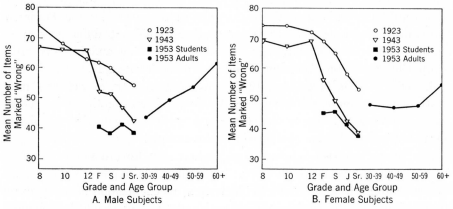

Fig. 59. Responses on the Pressey X-O Test as a Function of Age, Education, and Cultural Change. (Adapted from Pressey and Jones, 70, p. 487.)

testing also included public school children in certain grades of elementary and high school. The data thus permitted cross-sectional comparisons on each of the four years, as well as certain longitudinal comparisons of populations over the four decades.

Some of the results are illustrated in Figure 59. Part A shows the mean number of items marked "wrong" by male subjects in each school grade, college class, and age decade (for adults). Corresponding data for female subjects are given in Part B. Separate graphs have been plotted for results obtained in 1923, 1943, and 1953.[7] Several trends are apparent in these data. First, number of items considered wrong tends to drop somewhat from the eighth to the twelfth grade, and declines much more sharply in the college

---

[7] Although not included in the graphs published by Pressey and Jones, the 1933 data were intermediate between those for 1923 and 1943.

freshman group. Further, smaller decreases occur through the four years of college, except for the 1953 college men, whose scores are uniformly low. The adult groups, on the other hand, considered more items wrong than the students tested during the same year. Moreover, there is a tendency for these scores to rise with age, especially among the men.

Of special interest is the cross-comparison of adults tested in 1953 with students who were in college when these adult groups were in their twenties. Reference to Figure 59 shows that, for example, the 50-year-olds marked about the same number of items wrong as did the college seniors of 30 years before. All other corresponding comparisons yield similar results. It would thus seem that older persons tend to retain the attitudes formed in their youth. Rather than becoming more conservative with age, they merely maintain their earlier position. As a matter of fact, the evidence suggests some movement in the direction of cultural change, since the adult scores were approximately equal to those of *college students* of their generation. In comparison with young people of comparable educational level, these adults would probably have considered fewer things wrong.

Stability of Personality Traits. The results so far considered have dealt with group trends in relation to age and with absolute changes in amount or level. What happens to the individual in the course of such changes? Does he retain the same relative position in the group? It will be recalled that a similar question was asked in connection with training (Ch. 7), as well as in connection with intellectual changes discussed in an earlier section of the present chapter. To answer such questions, we need to turn to longitudinal studies on the same individuals.

Several short-range longitudinal studies on *preschool children* and a few on *school-age children* suggest that, in general, stability of personality traits during childhood is not high, although it is better than would be expected by chance (cf. 42; 64, Ch. 16). Some child psychologists speak of a "nucleus of personality" which persists and can be detected even in infancy. At the same time, available data show that degree of stability varies markedly with the trait and with the individual. It is certainly well established that conspicuous changes in home environment, family relations, "psychological climate" of the home, and other surrounding circumstances do influence the child's subsequent personality development. Moreover, techniques of guidance and therapy *can* bring about measurable improvement in personality characteristics.

An unusual type of longitudinal study is reported by Smith (84), who obtained associates' ratings of five siblings from a single family 50 years after the initial data had been gathered. Personality traits in childhood were rated on the basis of detailed journals which had been kept by the children's mother over a period of 8 years. Analysis of childhood and adult ratings led the investigator to conclude that personality characteristics showed a predominant consistency over the 50 years, the five siblings retaining their original rank in most of the traits. Apart from the limitations in number of cases and the possible influence of subjective factors on these results, it might be noted that the childhood ratings were based on cumulative behavior records over an average period of 6 years per child. It is likely that more reliable predictions of adult personality can be made under these conditions than from single tests or short observation periods.

Available longitudinal evidence on *adults* indicates a relatively high degree of stability of interests, attitudes, and other personality traits over periods of 10 to 20 years (47, 65, 66, 89, 90). Strong's analyses of vocational interests, for example, yielded correlations averaging in the .70's and .80's over intervals of as much as 22 years (90). Kelly's previously described 20-year follow-up (47) showed that vocational interests and values (as measured by the Allport-Vernon) were the most stable traits, with correlations ranging from the .30's to the .60's. Self-ratings and other measures of emotional traits yielded the next highest set of correlations. And attitudes proved to be the least stable of the traits investigated.

Kelly also found that changes tended to be fairly specific to the particular variable. In other words, an individual might be quite stable in one trait and very unstable in another. Analysis of data from marital pairs revealed no evidence for an increasing similarity between spouses over the interval. On the whole, changes in score were not significantly related to the initial score of the subject's marital partner. Marital correlations tended to be positive and significant at the outset and to remain unchanged on the retest. It would thus appear that any observed marital resemblance in these personality traits was a result more of assortative mating than of mutual influence.

SUMMARY

Changes in intellectual and personality characteristics occurring throughout the life span have been investigated by both *cross-sectional* and *longitudinal* methods. In cross-sectional studies, groups may not be comparable because of selective factors and cumulative cultural changes. Increasing use is being made of the longitudinal approach, as evidenced by a number of major ongoing projects on adults as well as children. Certain experimental designs which combine cross-sectional and longitudinal procedures have both practical and theoretical advantages.

When applied to psychological data, *growth curves* can be more properly designated as "age progress curves," since they reflect the combined influence of physical growth and learning. The most carefully constructed age progress curves for intelligence test scores exhibit slow rise in early infancy, followed by more rapid rise and eventual slowing down as maturity is approached. Age progress curves are influenced by a number of technical conditions, such as equality of scale units, difficulty level of test (including test ceiling and test floor), and changing composition of intelligence tests with age. Moreover, since the form of age curves may differ with both the function measured and the individual, composite and average curves may be misleading.

The traditional question of the *constancy of the IQ* pertains to the consistency of the individual's relative standing over a long period of time. Predictive value of intelligence test scores depends upon interval between retests and age at which initial test is administered. Scores increase in stability from childhood to maturity. Tests administered at the preschool and infant levels are virtually worthless as predictors of later achievement. Even in the case of school-age children, large shifts may occur in individual cases. An important factor in the increasing stability of test scores with age is the cumulative nature of behavior development and the consequent "overlap" of scores. There is evidence that the "constancy of the IQ" results from such overlap rather than from regularities of behavior development, since gains are uncorrelated with prior scores.

Studies of *intellectual functioning in maturity and old age* have sought to establish the limit of intellectual growth as well as the onset and rate of decline. It is now evident that intelligence test performance continues to improve at least into the twenties. For superior individuals, especially those with college education or employed in relatively intellectual occupations, such improvement may continue throughout life. Cross-sectional studies of more nearly random samples reveal a decline in score beginning in the late twenties or thirties. Because of cultural changes in amount of education, some of these decrements in test score may reflect educational differences rather than age changes.

The amount of observed age decrement also varies with the nature of the function tested. Vocabulary shows little or no change. Tests involving speed, visual perception, and abstract spatial relations tend to show the sharpest age decline. Loss in motor skills is slight, especially when the subject is free to introduce compensatory changes in method. Older persons can learn nearly as well as younger, but are more seriously handicapped when the task conflicts with well-established habits. Similarly, memory for newly learned material suffers somewhat more impairment with age than does memory for old material.

Creative achievements in art, music, literature, science, and invention may occur at almost any age, but the greatest clustering is found in the thirties. The peak for quality is reached earlier than that for quantity of production. There is also evidence that the peak age for creative achievement has been shifting downward over the generations. On the other hand, the peak for governmental and military leadership falls between 50 and 70 and has been moving upward with time. Owing to the many other contributing factors, observed age differences in outstanding achievement need not signify corresponding changes in creative ability or in other psychological traits.

Research on *age and personality* has provided a wealth of data on characteristic modifications in emotional, motivational, and attitudinal traits from infancy to adulthood. With the growth of gerontology, more and more data are being gathered on personality alterations in later maturity. Apart from decreasing interest in activities requiring physical vigor or involving interference with established habits, changes in interest beyond maturity are slight. The "conservatism" of older persons may reflect cultural change between generations rather than age differences within the individual.

With regard to stability of individual personalities, predictions of future development from preschool or school-age observations are hazardous. At least some individual children will show major shifts in emotional, motivational, or social responses. Beyond the twenties, however, available evidence suggests that most personality traits are fairly stable.

REFERENCES

1. Anastasi, Anne. *Psychological testing*. N.Y.: Macmillan, 1954.
2. Anastasi, Anne. Age changes in adult test performance. *Psychol. Rep.*, 1956, 2, 509.
3. Anderson, J. E. The prediction of terminal intelligence from infant and preschool tests. *39th Yearb., Nat. Soc. Stud. Educ.*, 1940, Part I, 385–403.
4. Anderson, L. D. The predictive value of infancy tests in relation to intelligence at five years. *Child Develpm.*, 1939, 10, 203–212.
5. Babcock, Harriet. An experiment in the measurement of mental deterioration. *Arch. Psychol.*, 1930, No. 117.
6. Barnes, M. W. Gains in the ACE Psychological Examination during the freshman-sophomore years. *Sch. and Soc.*, 1943, 57, 250–252.

7. Bayley, Nancy. A study of the crying of infants during mental and physical tests. *J. genet. Psychol.,* 1932, 40, 306–329.
8. Bayley, Nancy. Mental growth during the first three years: a developmental study of sixty-one children by repeated tests. *Genet. Psychol. Monogr.,* 1933, 14, 1–92.
9. Bayley, Nancy. Consistency and variability in the growth of intelligence from birth to eighteen years. *J. genet. Psychol.,* 1949, 75, 165–196.
10. Bayley, Nancy. On the growth of intelligence. *Amer. Psychologist,* 1955, 10, 805–818.
11. Bayley, Nancy. Data on the growth of intelligence between 16 and 21 years as measured by the Wechsler-Bellevue Scale. *J. genet. Psychol.,* 1957, 90, 3–15.
12. Bayley, Nancy, and Oden, Melita H. The maintenance of intellectual ability in gifted adults. *J. Geront.,* 1955, 10, 91–107.
13. Bell, R. Q. Convergence: an accelerated longitudinal approach. *Child Developm.,* 1953, 24, 145–152.
14. Bentz, V. J. A test-retest experiment on the relationship between age and mental ability. *Amer. Psychologist,* 1953, 8, 319–320.
15. Bradway, K. P. IQ constancy on the Revised Stanford-Binet from the preschool to the junior high school level. *J. genet. Psychol.,* 1944, 65, 197–217.
16. Bradway, K. P. An experimental study of factors associated with Stanford-Binet IQ changes from the preschool to the junior high school. *J. genet. Psychol.,* 1945, 66, 107–128.
17. Brozek, J. Personality changes with age: an item analysis of the Minnesota Multiphasic Personality Inventory. *J. Geront.,* 1955, 10, 194–206.
18. Chodorkoff, B., and Mussen, P. Qualitative aspects of the vocabulary responses of normals and schizophrenics. *J. consult. Psychol.,* 1952, 16, 43–48.
19. Cornell, Ethel L., and Armstrong, C. M. Forms of mental growth patterns revealed by reanalysis of the Harvard growth data. *Child Develpm.,* 1955, 26, 169–204.
20. Corsini, R. J., and Fassett, Katherine K. Intelligence and aging. *J. genet. Psychol.,* 1953, 83, 249–264.
21. Dearborn, W. F., and Rothney, J. *Predicting the child's development.* Cambridge, Mass.: Sci-Art Pub., 1941.
22. Deming, Jean. Application of the Gompertz curve to the observed pattern of growth in length of 48 individual boys and girls during the adolescent cycle of growth. *Hum. Biol.,* 1957, 29, 83–122.
23. Doppelt, J. E., and Wallace, W. L. Standardization of the Wechsler Adult Intelligence Scale for older persons. *J. abnorm. soc. Psychol.,* 1955, 51, 312–330.
24. Embree, R. B. A study of the graduates of University High School from 1921 to 1945, with special reference to their subsequent academic careers. Unpublished doctoral dissertation, Univer. Minn., 1947.
25. Falkner, F. Measurement of somatic growth and development in children. *Courrier* (Centre International de l'Enfance, Paris), 1954, 4, 169–181.
26. Falkner, F. International studies on growth and development. *Children,* 1955, 2, 227–229.

27. Feifel, H. Qualitative differences in the vocabulary responses of normals and abnormals. *Genet. Psychol. Monogr.*, 1949, 39, 151–204.

28. Fisher, M. B., and Birren, J. E. Age and strength. *J. appl. Psychol.*, 1947, 31, 490–497.

29. Foulds, G. A. Variations in the intellectual activities of adults. *Amer. J. Psychol.*, 1949, 62, 238–246.

30. Foulds, G. A., and Raven, J. C. Normal changes in the mental abilities of adults as age advances. *J. ment. Sci.*, 1948, 94, 133–142.

31. Fox, Charlotte, and Birren, J. E. The differential decline of subtest scores of the Wechsler-Bellevue Intelligence scale in 60–69-year-old individuals. *J. genet. Psychol.*, 1950, 77, 313–317.

32. Freeman, F. N., and Flory, C. D. Growth in intellectual ability as measured by repeated tests. *Monogr. Soc. Res. Child Develpm.*, 1937, 2, No. 2.

33. Gilbert, Jean G. Memory loss in senescence. *J. abnorm. soc. Psychol.*, 1941, 36, 73–86.

34. Goodenough, Florence L., and Maurer, Katherine M. *The mental growth of children from two to fourteen years.* Minneapolis: Univer. Minn. Press, 1942.

35. Gurvitz, M. S. Speed as a factor in the decline of performance with age. *Amer. Psychologist*, 1952, 7, 298–299.

36. Heston, J. C., and Connell, C. F. A note on the relation between age and performance of adult subjects on four familiar psychometric tests. *J. appl. Psychol.*, 1941, 25, 415–419.

37. Hofstaetter, P. R. The changing composition of "intelligence": a study of T technique. *J. genet. Psychol.*, 1954, 85, 159–164.

38. Honzik, Marjorie P. The constancy of mental test performance during the preschool period. *J. genet. Psychol.*, 1938, 52, 285–302.

39. Honzik, Marjorie P., Macfarlane, Jean W., and Allen, Lucile. The stability of mental test performance between two and eighteen years. *J. exp. Educ.*, 1948, 17, 309–324.

40. Hunter, E. C. Changes in scores of college students on the American Council Psychological Examination at yearly intervals during the college course. *J. educ. Res.*, 1942, 36, 284–291.

41. Husén, T. The influence of schooling upon IQ. *Theoria*, 1951, 17, 61–88.

42. Jersild, A. T. Emotional development. In L. Carmichael (Ed.), *Manual of child psychology.* N.Y.: Wiley, 1954, Pp. 833–917.

43. Jones, H. E., and Conrad, H. S. The growth and decline of intelligence: a study of a homogeneous group between the ages of ten and sixty. *Genet. Psychol. Monogr.*, 1933, 13, 223–298.

44. Jones, H. E., and Conrad, H. S. Mental development in adolescence. *43rd Yearb., Nat. Soc. Stud. Educ.*, 1944, Part I, 146–163.

45. Jones, H. E., and Kaplan, O. J. Psychological aspects of mental disorders in later life. In O. J. Kaplan (Ed.), *Mental disorders in later life.* Stanford Univer., Calif.: Stanford Univer. Press, 1945. Ch. 4.

46. Jones, H. E., and Seashore, R. H. The development of fine motor and mechanical abilities. *43rd Yearb., Nat. Soc. Stud. Educ.*, 1944, Part I, 123–145.

47. Kelly, E. L. Consistency of the adult personality. *Amer. Psychologist,* 1955, 10, 659–681.

48. Kinsey, A. C., *et al. Sexual behavior in the human male.* Philadelphia: Saunders, 1948.

49. Kinsey, A. C., *et al. Sexual behavior in the human female.* Philadelphia: Saunders, 1953.

50. Koch, Helen L. The social distance between certain racial, nationality, and skin-pigmentation groups in selected populations of American school children. *J. genet. Psychol.,* 1946, 68, 63–95.

51. Kuhlen, R. G. Age differences in personality during adult years. *Psychol. Bull.,* 1945, 42, 333–358.

52. Kuhlen, R. G., and Thompson, G. G. *Psychological studies of human development.* N.Y.: Appleton-Century-Crofts, 1952.

53. Lehman, H. C. *Age and achievement.* Princeton, N.J.: Princeton Univer. Press, 1953.

54. Lehman, H. C., and Witty, P. A. *The psychology of play activities.* N.Y.: Barnes, 1927.

55. Livesay, T. M. Does test intelligence increase at the college level? *J. educ. Psychol.,* 1939, 30, 63–68.

56. Lorge, I. The influence of the test upon the nature of mental decline as a function of age. *J. educ. Psychol.,* 1936, 27, 100–110.

57. Lorge, I. Gerontology (later maturity). *Ann. Rev. Psychol.,* 1956, 7, 349–364.

58. Macfarlane, Jean W., Allen, Lucile, and Honzik, Marjorie P. A developmental study of the behavior problems of normal children between twenty-one months and fourteen years. *Univer. Calif. Publ. Child Develpm.,* 1954, 2, 1–122.

59. Marple, C. H. The comparative susceptibility of three age levels to suggestion of group versus expert opinion. *J. soc. Psychol.,* 1933, 4, 176–186.

60. Miles, Catharine C. Influence of speed and age on intelligence scores of adults. *J. gen. Psychol.,* 1934, 10, 208–210.

61. Miles, Catharine C., and Miles, W. R. The correlation of intelligence scores and chronological age from early to late maturity. *Amer. J. Psychol.,* 1932, 44, 44–78.

62. Miles, W. R. Psychological aspects of aging. In E. V. Cowdry (Ed.), *Problems of ageing.* Baltimore: Williams & Wilkins, 1942. Pp. 756–784.

63. Miner, J. B. *Intelligence in the United States: a survey—with conclusions for manpower utilization in education and employment.* N.Y.: Springer, 1956.

64. Munn, N. L. *The evolution and growth of human behavior.* Boston: Houghton Mifflin, 1955.

65. Nelson, E. N. P. Persistence of attitudes of college students fourteen years later. *Psychol. Monogr.,* 1954, 68, No. 2.

66. Nelson, E. N. P. Patterns of religious attitude shifts from college to fourteen years later. *Psychol. Monogr.,* 1956, 70, No. 17.

67. Nelson, V. L., and Richards, T. W. Studies in mental development: I. Per-

formance on Gesell items at six months and its predictive value for performance at two and three years. *J. genet. Psychol.*, 1938, 52, 303–325.

68. Nyssen, R., and Delys, L. Contribution à l'étude du problème du déclin intellectuel en fonction de l'âge. *Arch. Psychol.*, 1952, 33, 295–310.

69. Owens, W. A., Jr. Age and mental abilities: a longitudinal study. *Genet. Psychol. Monogr.*, 1953, 48, 3–54.

70. Pressey, S. L., and Jones, A. W. 1923–1953 and 20–60 age changes in moral codes, anxieties, and interests, as shown by the "X-O Tests." *J. Psychol.*, 1955, 39, 485–502.

71. Pressey, S. L., and Kuhlen, R. G. *Psychological development through the life span.* N.Y.: Harper, 1957.

72. Radke-Yarrow, Marian, Trager, Helen G., and Davis, Hadassah. Social perceptions and attitudes of children. *Genet. Psychol. Monogr.*, 1949, 40, 327–447.

73. Raven, J. C. The comparative assessment of intellectual ability. *Brit. J. Psychol.*, 1948, 39, 12–19.

74. Roff, M. A statistical study of intelligence test performance. *J. Psychol.*, 1941, 11, 371–386.

75. Ruch, F. M. The differentiative effects of age upon human learning. *J. gen. Psychol.*, 1934, 11, 261–286.

76. Schaie, K. W., Rosenthal, F., and Perlman, R. M. Differential mental deterioration of factorially "pure" functions in later maturity. *J. Geront.*, 1953, 8, 191–196.

77. Shakow, D., Dolkart, M. B., and Goldman, R. The memory function in psychoses of the aged. *Dis. nerv. Syst.*, 1941, 2, 43–48.

78. Shakow, D., and Goldman, R. The effect of age on the Stanford-Binet vocabulary score of adults. *J. educ. Psychol.*, 1938, 31, 241–256.

79. Shock, N. W. Growth curves. In S. S. Stevens (Ed.), *Handbook of experimental psychology.* N.Y.: Wiley, 1951. Pp. 330–346.

80. Shock, N. W. Aging and psychological adjustment. *Rev. educ. Res.*, 1952, 22, 439–458.

81. Shuey, Audrey M. Improvement in scores on the American Council Psychological Examination from freshman to senior year. *J. educ. Psychol.*, 1948, 39, 417–426.

82. Shuttleworth, F. K. Sexual maturation and the physical growth of girls age six to nineteen. *Monogr. Soc. Res. Child Developm.*, 1937, 2, No. 5.

83. Shuttleworth, F. K. The adolescent period: a graphic atlas. *Monogr. Soc. Res. Child Developm.*, 1949, 14, No. 1.

84. Smith, Madorah E. A comparison of certain personality traits as rated in the same individuals in childhood and fifty years later. *Child Developm.*, 1952, 23, 159–180.

85. Sontag, L. W. Differences in modifiability of fetal behavior and physiology. *Psychosomat. Med.*, 1944, 6, 151–154.

86. Sontag, L. W. *The Fels Research Institute for the Study of Human Development.* Yellow Springs, Ohio: Antioch College, 1946.

87. Sontag, L. W. A research institute on child growth and development reports progress. *Child*, 1951, 16, 54–56.

88. Strong, E. K., Jr. *Changes of interest with age.* Stanford Univer., Calif.: Stanford Univer. Press, 1931.
89. Strong, E. K., Jr. *Vocational interests of men and women.* Stanford Univer., Calif.: Stanford Univer. Press, 1943.
90. Strong, E. K., Jr. Permanence of interest scores over 22 years. *J. appl. Psychol.,* 1951, 35, 89–91.
91. Terman, L. M., and Oden, Melita H. *The gifted child grows up.* Stanford Univer., Calif.: Stanford Univer. Press, 1947.
92. Terman, L. M., and Oden, Melita H. *Genetic studies of genius.* Vol. V. Stanford Univer., Calif.: Stanford Univer. Press, 1958.
93. Thorndike, E. L. On the improvement in intelligence scores from thirteen to nineteen. *J. educ. Psychol.,* 1926, 17, 73–76.
94. Thorndike, E. L., *et al. Adult learning.* N.Y.: Macmillian, 1928.
95. Thorndike, R. L. The effect of interval between test and retest on the constancy of the IQ. *J. educ. Psychol.,* 1933, 24, 543–549.
96. Thorndike, R. L. "Constancy" of the IQ. *Psychol. Bull.,* 1940, 37, 167–186.
97. Thorndike, R. L. The prediction of intelligence at college entrance from earlier test. *J. educ. Psychol.,* 1947, 38, 129–148.
98. Thorndike, R. L. Growth of intelligence during adolescence. *J. genet. Psychol.,* 1948, 72, 11–15.
99. Thorndike, R. L., and Gallup, G. H. Verbal intelligence of the American adult. *J. gen. Psychol.,* 1944, 30, 75–85.
100. Thurstone, L. L., and Ackerson, L. The mental growth curve for the Binet tests. *J. educ. Psychol.,* 1929, 20, 569–583.
101. Vernon, P. E. Changes in abilities from 14–20 years. *Advanc. Sci.,* 1948, 5, 138.
102. Watson, R. I. The personality of the aged. A review. *J. Geront.,* 1954, 9, 309–315.
103. Wechsler, D. *The measurement of adult intelligence.* (3rd Ed.) Baltimore: Williams & Wilkins, 1944.
104. Wechsler, D. *Manual for the Wechsler Adult Intelligence Scale.* N.Y.: Psychol. Corp., 1955.
105. Weisenberg, T., Roe, Anne, and McBride, Katharine E. *Adult intelligence.* N.Y.: Commonwealth Fund, 1936.
106. Welford, A. T. *et al. Skill and age; an experimental approach.* London: Oxford Univer. Press, 1951.
107. Wittenborn, J. R., *et al.* A study of adoptive children: II. The predictive validity of the Yale Developmental Examination of Infant Behavior. *Psychol. Monogr.,* 1956, 70, No. 2, 59–92.

CHAPTER 9

Family Resemblance

In popular thought, family resemblances in abilities and personality tend to be viewed as direct manifestations of heredity. The child is described as having his father's business acumen, his aunt's musical talent, "taking after" his grandfather in obstinacy, and perhaps inheriting a keen sense of humor from an Irish grandmother on his father's side! The successful son of an eminent family attributes his accomplishments to the fact that he is well-born. A lecturer's vigor and zeal are explained by his coming from pioneer stock. A boy's ingenuity with mechanical toys is regarded as only natural when one finds that he is descended from a "long line" of boatbuilders and inventors. A number of rather amusing excerpts from biographies of eminent persons, illustrating the common tendency to look for ancestral origins of the individual's talents and defects, have been brought together by Tozzer (117). An example is given below.

The noted Egyptologist, Flinders Petrie, modestly claims little for himself, deriving his entire archaeological equipment from a most assorted collection of ancestral protoplasm from his mother and father, to say nothing of two grandfathers, and a great-grandfather. "Looking back," he writes, "I can now see how much I owe to my forebears; partly carried from my grandfather Petrie's handling of men and material, and his love of drawing; from my great-grandfather Mitton's business ways and banking; from three generations of Flinders surgeons' love of patching up bodies; from my mother's love of history and knowledge of minerals" (117, p. 235).

That such resemblances do not in themselves prove the influence of heredity becomes apparent when we consider family environment. Some of the relevant points were anticipated in Chapter 4. There are a number of ways in which environmental factors may produce similarities between siblings, between parents and children, and—to a lesser degree—among more remote relatives. First, members of the same family tend to have many common

266

features in their environments, such as general economic level, geographical and cultural milieu, and the like. In the case of siblings, such common elements even extend to many features of prenatal environment. Secondly, family interaction provides opportunities for mutual influence. Close relatives thus constitute a part of each other's environment. A third important psychological factor is to be found in social expectancy. The child is often reminded of the special talents and defects of his forebears, and any chance manifestation of similar behavior on his part may be accentuated by such references. Moreover, the fact that people expect him to have inherited his father's administrative ability or his mother's skill in drawing will tend to influence his own self concept. And this in turn is likely to affect his subsequent development.

It should be added that family environment can also account for certain *differences* in psychological traits. Although alike in many fundamental respects, the environments of two brothers reared in the same home are certainly not psychologically identical. For one thing, the environment of one includes an older brother, that of the other contains a younger brother—no small difference in itself! Then, too, parental attitudes toward the two siblings may vary as a result of a multitude of intervening experiences and other events. Similarly, any common occurrence in the home will exert its influence on the two brothers at a different stage in their development. These and many other environmental factors may explain why two siblings exhibit characteristic behavioral differences, just as other aspects of family environment may help us to understand their similarities.

Because of the inevitable mixture of hereditary and environmental factors in family relationships, the mere establishment of family resemblance cannot indicate the reasons for the resemblance. Hence a large amount of the data gathered in this area is only descriptive, indicating degree of familial similarity under existing living conditions. In some investigations, experimental designs have been utilized which permit at least a partial isolation of contributing factors. In the sections that follow, both types of data will be examined.

FAMILY PEDIGREE STUDIES

Eminent Families. The publication of Galton's *Hereditary Genius* (33) in 1869 led the way for a number of statistical surveys of the families of eminent men. The results of such surveys will be discussed in greater detail in Chapter 13, dealing with the superior deviate. An examination of Galton's own study will serve to illustrate the procedure and typical findings. Data were collected on 997 men in 300 families, including judges, statesmen, military leaders, theological scholars and other religious leaders, scientists, poets and other literary men, musicians, and painters. In order to facilitate the tracing of family histories and the location of descendants and other relatives, the study was limited to eminent men who were either English or well known in England. Information was obtained from biographical collections or through direct inquiry among relatives and acquaintances of the men themselves. Galton defined as follows the degree of eminence necessary for inclusion in his survey: "When I speak of an eminent man, I mean one who has achieved a position that is attained by only 250 persons in each million of men, or by one person in each 4000" (33, p. 9). The frequency of such men in the general population is thus .025 of 1 per cent.

That the number of eminent relatives among Galton's group of eminent men was far greater than would be expected by chance was clearly demonstrated by his findings. Within each family, the most eminent man was taken as the point of departure, or index case, and all kinships were expressed in relation to him. Following the name of each index case, Galton appended a list of eminent relatives, together with the nature of their kinship to the index case. From these data, he computed the number of eminent relatives per 100 families, as shown in Table 9. It will be seen that for every 100 families of eminent index cases there were 31 eminent fathers, 41 eminent brothers, and 48 eminent sons. In the case of more distant relatives, the frequencies were smaller but still many times larger than would be expected by chance. These figures certainly show that eminence

Table 9

NUMBER OF EMINENT RELATIVES OF INDEX CASES PER 100 FAMILIES

(From Galton, 33, p. 308)

NATURE OF KINSHIP[*]	NUMBER PER 100 FAMILIES	NATURE OF KINSHIP[*]	NUMBER PER 100 FAMILIES
Father	31	Great-grandfather	3
Brother	41	Great-uncle	5
Son	48	First cousin	13
Grandfather	17	Great-nephew	10
Uncle	18	Great-grandson	3
Nephew	22		
Grandson	14	All more remote	31

[*] No female relatives were included in these summary figures, although the names and achievements of such relatives were given in specific family histories.

tends to run in families. It is quite a different matter, however, to conclude as Galton did that genius is inherited.

Feebleminded Families. The family history method has also been employed by psychologists, sociologists, and geneticists in an effort to analyze the causes of intellectual defect, crime, insanity, and similar conditions (22, 25, 26, 27, 41). Certain families have been discovered which present an overwhelming array of socially inadequate persons over several generations. The same general techniques are used in tracing the history of these families as in the study of eminent groups. Living relatives or descendants are visited and observed, residents of the vicinity are interviewed, and certificates of marriage and birth and similar public records are examined whenever available. These families are usually found in rural districts, often inhabiting the same crude huts built by their ancestors many generations ago. They interbreed extensively, are quite prolific, and may eventually come to constitute their own communities. The most widely known examples of such families are the Jukes and the Kallikaks, these being the pseudonyms given to them by their investigators.

The Jukes first attracted official notice in the course of a prison survey conducted in New York State in 1874, when six members of the same family were found in prison in a single county. This finding initiated a thorough search for other relatives and eventually led to an extensive family history covering seven generations and including 540 persons related by blood and 169 related by marriage or cohabitation (25). In a subsequent follow-up, the family was traced up to 1915 (26). The original Jukes were five sisters whose progeny, legitimate and illegitimate, have been traced for five generations. Two of these sisters married two sons of "Max," a descendant of the early Dutch settlers, who lived as a backwoodsman and is described as a "hunter and fisher, a hard drinker, jolly and companionable, averse to steady toil" (25, p. 14). This man was born in New York State between 1720 and 1740. The genealogy of the Jukes is usually begun with Max, although it is the progeny of the five sisters who have been traced and are shown in the pedigree charts.

The Kallikak family, described by Goddard (41), consists of two branches, one containing normal or superior persons, the other composed largely of defectives. Its history has been traced to the days of the American Revolution. "Martin Kallikak," a 21-year-old youth of good family, who had joined one of the many military companies organized at the time, had sexual relations with a feebleminded girl whom he met at a tavern. The illegitimate child of this union, referred to as "Martin Kallikak, Jr.," was the progenitor of the defective side of the family. At the age of 23, Martin, Sr., married an intellectually superior woman of his own social level and thereby founded a normal family, many of whose members have achieved distinction.

In evaluating the findings on the Kallikak family, Goddard constantly emphasized the role of heredity. Having laid great stress upon the fact that the two groups were branches of the same family, furnishing, "as it were, a natural experiment with a normal branch with which to compare our defective side," he argued that "from this comparison, the conclusion is inevitable that all this degeneracy has come as the result of the defective mentality and bad blood having been brought into the normal family of good blood" (41, pp. 68–69). It seems rather curious that the common descent of the two branches from Martin Kallikak should be regarded as strengthening a hereditary interpretation of the differences between them. The environments of the two groups were in no way equated by this common ancestry. In fact, it is evident that the members of the two branches were reared under widely differing conditions.

Since it first appeared, the Kallikak study was widely criticized both for the inadequacy and crudeness of its data and for its genetic and psychological interpretations (cf. 93). Nevertheless, it is still quoted from time to time as "evidence" for the inheritance of feeblemindedness and other psychological defects. All that these studies show, of course, is that various forms of psychological and social inadequacy, like eminence, tend to run in families. How much of the family resemblance is the result of common environment and how much the result of heredity cannot be determined from such data.

Genetic Analysis of Family Pedigrees.   Under certain circumstances, the study of family pedigrees does provide data concerning the operation of hereditary factors. As used by geneticists, this method involves two major steps: *pedigree analysis* and *gene frequency analysis.* The first step requires data on at least two generations of each of many families, with regard to the presence or absence of the trait under investigation. From an examination of these pedigrees, hypotheses are set up relating to the probable hereditary basis of the trait. As these hypotheses are checked against other pedigrees, some can readily be discarded, while one may be consistent with all the observed pedigrees and is tentatively accepted. The testing of this tentative hypothesis in representative samples of the general population constitutes the second step, or gene frequency analysis.

In animal studies, this is the stage at which selective breeding and cross-breeding would be carried out as a direct test of the chosen hypothesis. Since this is not feasible in human studies, the procedure is to compare the frequency of different phenotypes in the general population with the frequency expected on the basis of the chosen hypothesis. "Phenotypes" refer to the observably different ways in which the characteristic in question is manifested in different individuals. For example, in the case of a characteristic determined by a single pair of dominant-recessive factors, an individual may have received two dominant factors from his two parents, or one dominant and one recessive, or two recessives. Those receiving the dominant-recessive combination, however, manifest the dominant characteristic. Consequently, only two phenotypes are found in this characteristic, in contrast to the three different "genotypes" to which they correspond. If the frequencies of dominant and recessive genes for this characteristic were identical in the general population, then the two phenotypes would occur in the well-known Mendelian ratio of 3:1. Ordinarily, however, the two genes will not be equally common, and the simple 3:1 ratio will not hold. Nevertheless, under these circumstances *certain constant relationships* between the frequencies of different phenotypes will be found. It is these

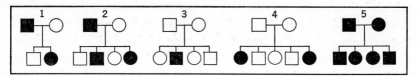

Fig. 60. Selected Pedigrees of Taste Deficiency in Man. Squares designate males, circles females. White indicates a taster, black a nontaster. (From Snyder, 103, p. 482.)

relationships that are employed in the gene frequency analyses. Such relationships can be derived for various types of hereditary mechanisms, such as dominant-recessive or sex-linked characteristics, as well as for characteristics depending upon more than one pair of genes.

The use of family pedigree techniques is well illustrated by the study of taste deficiency in man. Quite accidentally it was discovered that some persons report no taste from the crystals of a certain chemical, phenyl-thio-carbamide (P.T.C.). To most people, these crystals are very bitter. It was soon suspected that this difference might have a genetic basis and investigation of its possible hereditary transmission was begun. Subsequent research has not only confirmed this hypothesis, but has revealed that such taste deficiency extends to a number of other, closely related chemical compounds (cf. 2, 18, 20, 103).

In Figure 60 are reproduced five family pedigrees for taste deficiency, selected from several thousand which were examined (20, 103). The first pedigree leaves the way open for several types of hereditary determination, but different hypotheses can be eliminated successively as each additional family is considered. For example, family No. 3 clearly shows that this taste deficiency cannot be attributed to a dominant factor, since the deficiency appeared in a child both of whose parents were free of it. The suggestion that a single recessive may be involved is borne out by family No. 5, where both parents show the deficiency. In this family, as expected, *all* the offspring are deficient. Other hypotheses, regarding the possibility of sex-linked and sex-influenced factors, can be ruled out by an inspection of the other two pedigrees.

Following the tentative acceptance of the hypothesis of a single pair of dominant-recessive genes, a gene frequency analysis was conducted on a random sample of 800 families. These families included some in which both parents were normal tasters, others in which both were deficient, and still others with one normal and one deficient parent. The proportion of tasters and nontasters among the offspring in each of the three types of families, as well as the proportion of tasters and nontasters in the general population, constitutes the basic data for the gene frequency analysis. If the chosen hypothesis holds, certain relationships are expected among these various proportions. In Table 10 are shown the observed and expected percentages of nontasters among the offspring of each type of family.[1] If taste deficiency depends upon a single recessive factor, all offspring of two nontaster parents should be nontasters. That the obtained percentage is 97.76 rather than 100, owing to the presence of five tasters in this category, need not be regarded as evidence against the hypothesis. The investigators (20) suggest a number of possible reasons to account for these exceptions: the subjective nature of

Table 10

GENE FREQUENCY ANALYSIS OF TASTE DEFICIENCY FOR P.T.C.

(From Cotterman and Snyder, 20, p. 514)

TYPE OF FAMILY	NUMBER OF FAMILIES	TOTAL NUMBER OF OFFSPRING	PERCENTAGE OF NONTASTING OFFSPRING		
			Observed	Expected	Difference
Both parents nontasters	86	223	97.76	100.00	2.24
One parent taster, the other non-taster	289	761	36.53	35.32	1.21 ± 1.76[*]
Both parents tasters	425	1159	12.28	12.47	0.19 ± 1.02[*]

[*] Standard error of the difference.

[1] For an explanation of the computation of the expected percentages, cf. 20, 102.

the taste experience may have led to incorrect diagnoses; parentage may have been incorrectly determined because of unsuspected adoption or illegitimacy; and mutations or unknown factors of a hereditary or environmental nature may have affected the operation of the recessive gene. In the other two types of families, it will be noted that the observed and expected percentages do not differ significantly. The differences are no larger than would be expected from sampling fluctuation. Hence it was concluded that the data verified the hypothesis that taste deficiency is transmitted by a single recessive gene.

When either the pedigrees or the observed frequencies are not consistent with *any* unit-factor hypothesis, other hypotheses can be set up in terms of two or more pairs of factors. For example, with two pairs of dominant-recessive factors, four phenotypes will be found. Even more phenotypes result when there is a lack of dominance in one or more pairs of factors. Under these conditions, the frequency patterns become more complicated, but they are still predictable and therefore amenable to testing. When the number of hereditary factors involved is very large, however, an almost infinite number of quantitative gradations is found, rather than distinct phenotypes. In such cases, the frequency distribution approaches the normal curve.

Apart from the demonstration of a hereditary basis for certain rare forms of feeblemindedness (cf. Ch. 12) and a few other pathological conditions, this type of pedigree analysis has found little use in psychology. Attempts have been made to utilize this method in the investigation of schizophrenia, manic-depressive psychosis, and other severe personality disorders. Analyses of family histories, as well as studies of the incidence of these conditions in relatively isolated populations, have suggested certain hypotheses regarding hereditary predisposing factors (7, 60). There is no general agreement concerning these hypotheses, however; nor is there clear-cut evidence to substantiate them.

One of the obstacles encountered in the application of pedigree analysis to psychological characteristics is the multiplicity of hereditary factors contributing to most behavior functions. If the observed frequencies follow the normal curve, little can be deduced beyond the operation of a very large number of factors. Moreover, the same frequency distribution could result from the combined effect of the innumerable environmental influences to which the developing individual is exposed. Such results certainly do not permit the same clear-cut interpretation that is possible when simpler genetic ratios are involved.

A second disturbing factor in such analyses is the indisputable operation of *assortative mating* in human marriages. Gene frequency analyses are based upon the assumption of random mating with regard to the trait under consideration. This assumption is probably justified in reference to such characteristics as the taste deficiency described above, since most individuals are not even aware of this deficiency in either themselves or their associates. Moreover, this deficiency appears not to be correlated with other characteristics which might enter into assortative mating, such as general appearance, physique, intellectual level, or socioeconomic background. However, most behavior characteristics—and many physical characteristics— either play a direct part in assortative mating or enter indirectly through their association with socioeconomic level, geographical distribution, and the like. Individuals tend to marry within their own groups, economically, nationally, geographically, and intellectually, a practice that produces significant marital correlations in most traits.

A third ever-present difficulty in the genetic analysis of human behavior data is the influence of *environmental factors.* The testing of genetic hypotheses implies either a constant influence of environment or random environmental variation. In actual fact, however, environmental differences among individuals are not random, but tend to go hand in hand with hereditary differences. Thus the child of physically defective or feebleminded parents is also more likely to have low socioeconomic level, poor physical care, and inferior education than is the child of intellectually and physically superior parents.

A further difficulty is presented by the likelihood of *inaccurate and incorrect diagnosis,* especially when information is sought regarding individuals who have been dead for many years. The data collected in retrospect on feebleminded ancestors, for example, are often based upon reports by untrained persons or upon inadequate records. Another difficulty, in the reverse direction, is encountered when gathering information on *characteristics that are not manifested until late in life.* For example, certain psychoses usually occur among older persons. Information on these conditions cannot, therefore, be obtained while the subjects are still young. Moreover, some individuals die before reaching the age when such conditions might have developed.

CORRELATIONAL STUDIES

Parent-Child Resemblance.   Pearson (78, 79) was among the first to apply correlational analysis to parent-child resemblances. Continuing a line of research initiated by Galton (35), he collected measures on parents and offspring in physical traits such as stature, arm span, and forearm length. Parent-child correlations in these traits averaged about .52. The similarity of this correlation to those obtained for bodily characteristics of many animal forms led Pearson and others to suggest that this figure indicates the contribution of hereditary factors to the development of physical traits. Family resemblance in such traits is probably attributable in large part to heredity, although the influence of similar environment, especially in the prenatal stage, should not be overlooked.

More recently, scores obtained by parents and children on *intelligence tests* have been correlated. In the most extensive of these studies, Conrad and Jones (19) administered intelligence tests to 269 family groups, including 977 persons between the ages of 3 and 60. All subjects were native-born, spoke only English at home, and lived in rural districts of New England. Socioeconomic differences within this sampling were small. The younger subjects were tested with the Stanford-Binet, the older with the Army Alpha. For the entire sampling, the total parent-child correlation obtained with these tests was .49. No consistent or significant difference was found between mother-child and father-child correlations, nor did the correlation of sons or daughters with their like-sex parent differ from the correlation with their unlike-sex parent. It might be argued that if environment is important in producing these familial resemblances, then children should resemble their mother more closely than their father. It is true that the mother generally has closer contact with the children than does the father, but it may also be noted that the father's intellectual level probably determines the socioeconomic level of the home more than does that of the mother.

Conrad and Jones demonstrated statistically that the obtained correlation of .49 is consistent with a hereditary interpretation of parent-child resemblance, after allowance is made for assortative mating. They recognized, however, that the results were equally consistent with a purely environmental explanation, or with the combined operation of hereditary and environmental factors. In generalizing from the specific correlation found in this study, it should be borne in mind that parent-child correlations may vary with the nature of the test. Nonverbal functions, for example, tend to yield lower correlations than do the more highly verbal (121). Familial correlations likewise depend upon the degree of homogeneity of home background within the group. Conrad and Jones called attention to the relative homogeneity of their sample, pointing out that the apparent influence of a common home environment within each family is minimized when the differences from home to home are slight. Thus the correlations between parents and children might be much higher if a wider range of homes were sampled.

It should also be noted that the parent-child correlation of approximately .50 in intelligence test scores is not found until the child is about 5 years of age (87). The correlation is considerably lower at earlier ages and approaches zero in infancy. It will be recalled that a similar lack of correlation was found between the individual's score in infancy and his own later performance. The two findings probably have a similar explanation. A principal factor in such an explanation is undoubtedly the difference in behavior functions tested among preschool children and among older children or adults.

Parent-child correlations on *personality tests* likewise tend to be positive and significant, although running lower than intelligence test correlations (21, 88). The correlations vary widely with the particular aspect of personality under consideration. On the whole, parent-child resemblance is lower in emotional characteristics, such as introversion, dominance, or neuroticism, and higher in interests, opinions, and attitudes. In fact, the average parent-child correlation on most attitude scales is approximately as high as on intelligence tests. In connection with the relatively low correlations on tests of emotional characteristics, it is interesting to consider the possible effects of parental personality upon the development of the child's personality. It is likely, for example, that excessive dominance in a parent may foster the opposite type of reaction in the child. The effects of parent-child interaction probably differ widely with the degree of the personality characteristic manifested, as well as with many other attendant circumstances. It is also noteworthy that daughters tend to resemble both parents in attitudes and opinions more than sons do (30, 88). Such a finding suggests that the psychological climate of the home may influence girls more than it does boys in our culture.

Sibling Resemblance. The study of siblings, especially when both are in school, does not present the same practical difficulties met in testing parents. Consequently, investigations on sibling resemblance are more plentiful, over a dozen studies on adequately large samples being on record. With regard to *intelligence tests,* the previously cited study by Conrad and Jones (19) included data on 644 individual siblings in 225 families. The correlation was identical with that found between parents and children in the same study, namely, .49. That the sibling correlation on most intelligence tests is in the neighborhood of .50 has been repeatedly confirmed. The correlation between 384 pairs of siblings tested during the standardization of the 1937 Stanford-Binet (73) was found to be .53. The same sibling correlation was obtained with 1163 children tested in England with a group scale (86). The latter group was especially free from limitations of sampling, since it included all siblings located during a project in which every child born in the city of Bath within specified dates was tested.

Under various conditions, sibling correlations in intelligence test scores may drop as low as .30 or rise to nearly .70 (43). As in the case of parent-child correlations, the more verbal types of tests tend to give higher correlations (121). Heterogeneity of samples is also undoubtedly a factor in producing some of the differences. For example, among college students, who represent a relatively homogeneous group, the sibling correlation in intelligence test scores is closer to .40 than to .50 (113, 114). At the same time, when siblings attending a single school are tested, the influence of common school environment, together with certain selective factors, may tend to raise the sibling correlation. Thus if one member of a sibling pair is attending high school and the other is not, such a pair would automatically be excluded from the study. But these are the very pairs that are likely to show the largest differences in test performance. Their omission would therefore raise the correlation between sibling scores. In one high school sample, for instance, the sibling correlation on an intelligence test was .60 (115). In this case it is probable that selection of sibling pairs, as well as common school environment, had more effect than did the reduction in heterogeneity.

In the Stanford-Binet standardization sample, sibling correlations showed no consistent tendency either to rise or drop with age between 2 and 18 years (73). It is of course true that the older the subjects, the longer will environmental factors have operated upon them. But whether such factors exert a leveling or a differentiating influence upon the development of siblings within any one family obviously depends upon whether the environments of the siblings have remained similar or diverged with age. If, for example, one sibling goes away to boarding school at age 10, while the other remains at home, it would hardly be reasonable to expect environment to make them more alike with age just because they are members of the same family.

The amount of age discrepancy between siblings also appears to have little or no effect upon sibling correlations in intelligence test scores (73, 85). For an interpretation of such findings, much more information is needed regarding the social interaction of siblings with each other and with their parents. A preliminary effort to investigate such social factors, especially as they affect the intelligence test performance of older and younger siblings, is illustrated by an intensive follow-up study of 39 pairs of siblings, conducted as a part of the Fels Growth Study (54). All the sibling pairs consisted of a first-born and a second-born child. The children, ranging in age from 30 months to 12 years, were tested at regular intervals with alternate forms of the Stanford-Binet. With such data, it was possible to compare the performance of first- and second-born siblings in each family on tests administered at the same age. The two siblings in each pair were thus compared on the same test items. Significant differences in the frequency with which first-born and second-born siblings passed certain Stanford-Binet items were found. In general, the first-born siblings tended to excel on relatively abstract, verbal items, while the second-born were superior on a larger number of items, and especially on items involving realistic, concrete tasks. The type of intellectual stimulation received by the first-born child, who is more likely to have adult companionship, is suggested as one possible factor to account for these differences.

Comparisons of test correlations between like-sex and unlike-sex siblings show no consistent differences (19). One might expect a closer resemblance between like-sex siblings because of greater similarity of experience. The interaction and mutual influence of children within the family may be such, however, as to counteract the similarities in the environments of like-sex siblings. When possible sibling rivalries and similar motivational factors are considered, it is apparent that no simple relationship between the development of like-sex and unlike-sex siblings can be predicted.

As is true of parent-child correlations, sibling correlations on *personality tests* are lower, in general, than on intelligence tests. When ratings are employed, as in the pioneer study by Pearson (78), the sibling correlations will be spuriously high because of the rater's tendency to rate two members of the same family alike. Test scores have yielded correlations of the order of .15 in emotional adjustment, introversion, dominance, and similar characteristics (21, 81, 88). On attitude scales, the sibling correlations are higher, clustering between .30 and .40 (21, 88). In their extensive study of character traits among school children, May and Hartshorne (68) compared the performance of 734 pairs of siblings. The sibling correlations on tests of honesty ranged from .21 to .44; in persistence and inhibition, the correlations ranged from .14 to .46, and in cooperativeness and service, from .05 to .40 (cf. 21, 68, 88).

What are the implications of sibling studies for the problem of heredity and environment? Some have pointed out that the intelligence test correlation of approximately .50 found between siblings in the general population falls close to the value expected on the basis of the common heredity of siblings (86). Nevertheless, the fact remains that the obtained correlation lends itself with equal facility to other interpretations, and no one hypothesis can therefore be accepted solely on the basis of such a correlation. Attempts have also been made to compare sibling correlations in psychological and in structural characteristics, in an effort to disentangle the relative contributions of heredity and environment (78, 115). It has been argued, for example, that since the sibling correlation in such traits as height and intelligence is very similar, and since height can be little influenced by environment, then intelligence must be equally independent of environment. This argument begins by assuming that psychological and physical traits are influenced to an equal degree by heredity. Any influence of environment upon psychological traits would then be superimposed upon this common hereditary influence and would be expected to raise the correlation for psychological traits. Such an argument obviously begs the question.

In this connection may also be considered the implications of sibling correlations in animal studies. In an investigation of maze learning in white rats (13), for example, a sibling correlation of .31 was found in the error scores.[2] Since all the rats were living under fairly uniform conditions, this sibling correlation obviously cannot be attributed to environmental differences among the "rat families," but rather indicates the influence of hereditary structural factors upon maze learning. That such factors do operate in maze learning was, of course, indicated in the selective breeding experiments previously discussed (cf. Ch. 4). Does this clearly nonenvironmental sibling correlation in the rat experiments suggest that the sibling correlations in the human studies are likewise determined principally by hereditary factors? Not at all. There is no basis for supposing that the same or similar structural factors which operate in a motor learning situation in white rats also operate in the behavior sampled by human intelligence tests. We cannot generalize from one situation to the other, any more than we could generalize from studies on sensorimotor learning in infants to the learning of calculus by college students, in our earlier discussion of maturation and learning (Ch. 4).

An interesting illustration of the fact that similar correlations may have very different origins is furnished by an investigation on Louisiana public school children in grades 5 to 11 (96). Having located 203 pairs of siblings in these grades, the investigator paired each child with his own sibling and also paired him with an unrelated child of the same age, of similar socio-

---

[2] Because some of the litters classified as independent may have actually been half-siblings, the authors suggest that their group may have been atypically homogeneous and the obtained correlation consequently too low. It is therefore likely that such a sibling correlation should be somewhat higher than .31.

economic background, and attending the same school. The intelligence test scores of these unrelated pairs of children correlated .35, only slightly lower than the correlation found between siblings in the same study. Had the home backgrounds of the unrelated children been paired off more precisely and on the basis of a larger number of characteristics, the correlation between their intelligence test scores might have been even higher.

In conclusion, the study of sibling as well as parent-child correlations in complex intellectual and emotional characterics provides no clues to the origin of family resemblances. Results do suggest the complexity of factors which operate within the usual family milieu. Despite the superficial uniformity of environment, some of the interactions among individuals in the family group may make for similarity of psychological development, while others may produce progressively divergent trends in behavior.

Marital Correlations. Reference has already been made to assortative mating, or the tendency for individuals to choose marital partners exhibiting certain trait similarities (or differences). Husband-wife correlations in physical traits have been found to cluster around .25 (cf. 51, 94). Intelligence tests again yield correlations in the neighborhood of .50, as was found in the case of sibling and parent-child resemblances, although correlations are often lower on tests of separate aptitudes (51, 94, 121). In personality characteristics, correlations vary widely, as would be expected. In the more purely emotional traits, such as emotional stability and social dominance, the correlations are relatively low and sometimes negative, averaging about .15 (21, 88, 94). On tests of attitudes and values, the correlations range from the .20's to the .70's, averaging about .59 (21, 88, 94).

Marital correlations may result in part from common experiences and from mutual influence of the spouses after marriage. It is doubtful, however, whether such factors can account for a large part of the observed correlations, especially since many of the subjects in these studies had not been married long. Data bearing on this question are also provided by the longitudinal study of 300 engaged couples conducted by Kelly (62), cited in the preceding chapter. It will be recalled that tests of attitudes, interests, values, and emotional traits were administered and ratings obtained on a number of characteristics prior to marriage as well as nearly twenty years later. The initial correlations were predominantly positive and ranged from −.02 to +.58. The retest correlations, after approximately twenty years of marriage, were strikingly similar. Few statistically significant shifts were found, and these indicated a slight tendency for the couples to become less similar with time. In commenting upon this finding, Kelly writes, ". . . while we can readily think of many forces tending to promote increasing congruence be-

between mates, we must not overlook the apparently equal impact of forces associated with maintaining the many kinds of role differentiation expected of husbands and wives in our culture" (62, p. 680). The available data thus indicate that "likes tend to marry likes" and provide no support for the popular view that "opposites attract."

TWIN RESEMBLANCE IN PSYCHOLOGICAL TRAITS

Beginning with the pioneer study of Galton in 1875 (cf. 34), twin research has occupied a pre-eminent position in the investigation of hereditary and environmental contributions to psychological development. Today, large-scale twin research programs are in progress in several countries. The discovery of improved techniques for differentiating between identical (monozygous) and fraternal (dizygous) twins has made possible more precise analysis of findings (cf. Ch. 3). Among the most dependable criteria now being used for the diagnosis of zygosity are fingerprints and blood types. Since a large number of blood types have been identified, the comparison of twins in this regard provides a particularly effective index of zygosity.

Psychological Test Performance. Correlations between *intelligence test* scores of identical twins are generally in the .90's, being nearly as high as the reliability coefficients of the tests. In other words, the degree of resemblance between identical twins reared in the same home is about as high as that between test and retest scores of the same individuals. Fraternal twin correlations in intelligence test scores fall between those of identical twins and those of siblings. Such correlations vary more from study to study than almost any other type of familial correlation, probably because of inaccuracies in identification and classification of fraternal twin pairs. Most of these correlations, however, cluster between .60 and .70 (44, 49, 77, 123).

It should be noted that, with regard to heredity, fraternal twins are no more alike than ordinary siblings. Thus the difference between the usual sibling correlation of .50 and the fraternal twin correlation of .60 or .70 must reflect the greater environmental uniformity to which fraternal twins are exposed. Being born at the same time, fraternal twins have a common prenatal environment. Since they are of the same age, moreover, they are subject to more nearly similar experiences throughout childhood than are ordinary siblings. The differences between identical twin and fraternal twin correlations, on the other hand, may result either from hereditary factors or from the still closer similarity in the environments of identical twins. The latter point will be examined more fully in a subsequent section on the environment of twins.

Available data on *special aptitudes* suggest that in these characteristics, too, identical twins are much more alike than fraternals. In both types of twins, however, the resemblance in special aptitudes is much less than in tests of general intelligence. On a series of tests of motor skills given to 46 pairs of fraternal and 47 pairs of identical twins, the correlations averaged .43 for fraternals and .79 for identicals (70). On the Minnesota Spatial Relations Test, a series of form boards measuring primarily spatial perception, a correlation of .28 was found within 33 pairs of fraternal twins, and a correlation of .69 within 29 pairs of identical twins (10).

In *personality tests,* twin correlations tend to be lower than in tests of ability. Identical twins, however, still exhibit closer similarity than do fraternal twins. The degree of twin resemblance in personality characteristics also varies widely with the specific aspect of personality under consideration. All these findings are in line with the results reported in earlier sections on parental and sibling correlations in personality tests.

On the neurotic scale of the Bernreuter Personality Inventory, correlations of .63 for identical and .32 for fraternal twins were obtained (15). Another test in the same general area, the Woodworth-Mathews Personal Data Sheet, gave an identical twin correlation of .54 and a fraternal twin correlation of .36 (46). On tests of other personality characteristics, such as dominance or self-sufficiency, the correlations tend to run lower (15). The Strong Vocational Interest Blank yielded correlations of only .50 for identical twins and .28 for fraternals (15).

From an analysis of scores on the Cattell Junior Personality Quiz obtained by identical and fraternal twins, siblings, unrelated children reared together, and children in the general population, Cattell *et al.* (16) concluded that heredity provides the major cause of variance in some traits, environment in others. Somewhat similar findings were obtained in a second study by Cattell and his associates (17) utilizing objective measures of personality. Owing to the low reliability of test scores in both studies, however, as well as to certain debatable approximations in the statistical analyses, these results must be regarded as highly tentative. Moreover, they were not corroborated in another project employing the Junior Personality Quiz with identical and fraternal twins (118, 119). In a British investigation, Eysenck and his co-workers (28) report correlations of .851 and .217, respectively, for 25 pairs of identical and 25 pairs of like-sexed fraternal twins in a neuroticism score derived from a variety of tests.

Twin resemblances in a number of *expressive reactions* have been investigated by Gedda and his associates at the recently established Gregor Mendel Institute for Medical Genetics and Twin Study, in Rome. For example, in listening to playbacks of their own and their co-twin's voices, 76 per cent of identical twins were unable to choose their co-twin's voice, while only 12 per cent of like-sex fraternals failed to do so (39). In another study (38), facial expressions and postural reactions of identical and fraternal twin pairs were photographed while the subjects were watching humorous or anxiety-producing films. The difference in degree of concordance between identical and fraternal twins was found to be greater in expressive than in postural reactions, and greater in reactions to humor than in anxiety reactions.

Of special interest are two recent twin projects which employed a large and varied battery of tests and utilized precise techniques for the diagnosis of zygosity. One is the study conducted at the Institute of Human Biology of the University of Michigan (118, 119). A total of 45 pairs of identical and 37 pairs of like-sexed fraternal twins of high school age underwent approximately three full days of testing, including verbal, numerical, spatial, memory, reasoning, perceptual, motor, and musical aptitude tests, as well as measures of interests and many tests designed to assess emotional and social traits. In many of the tests, the variance (SD^2) of intra-pair differences was significantly greater for fraternal than for identical twins. In no test was the variance significantly greater for identicals than for fraternals. In other words, it was again demonstrated that in most psychological characteristics identical twins tend to be more alike than fraternal twins.

An extensive battery of equally varied tests was employed in the twin study initiated by Thurstone and his associates (116) at the Psychometric Laboratory of the University of Chicago and continued at the University of North Carolina. The subjects included 48 identical twin pairs and 55 like-sex fraternal twin pairs, all of whom were attending Chicago schools. Mean age of the group was approximately 14 years. An analysis of the distribution of intra-pair differences on each of 53 test scores revealed that small differences predominated among both fraternal and identical twins, the most frequent (or modal) differences being of approximately the same magnitude for both types of twins in many of the tests. The principal difference between the two types of twins was found at the upper end of the distribution of intra-pair differences, large differences being more common in the fraternal group. This finding is illustrated schematically in Figure 61.

For purposes of statistical analysis, the authors designated as "large differences" all differences falling within the upper fifth of the combined distribution of both groups. The proportion of such large differences was found to be significantly greater among the fraternals than among the identicals in 23 of the 53 measures (13 at the .01 level and 10 at the .05 level). It is noteworthy that verbal and spatial tests were among those which differentiated most clearly between fraternal and identical twins, a finding that was corroborated in another study employing some of the same tests (5). Of particular interest, however, is the observation that the majority of fraternal twin pairs were indistinguishable from identical twin pairs in their test performance, the difference between the two types being chiefly a matter of more extreme-deviant pairs among fraternals. An intensive study of these deviant pairs might throw considerable light on the reasons for the large

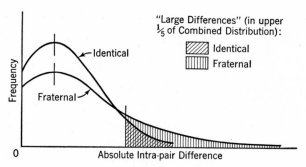

Fig. 61. Schematic Illustration of Distribution of Absolute Intra-pair Differences among Identical and Fraternal Twins. (From Thurstone, Thurstone, and Strandskov, 116.)

intra-pair differences. Were these twins physically more dissimilar than the other fraternals in the group? Were there factors in their environments that might account for their divergent development along specific lines?

Incidence of Psychological Disorders Among Twins. Twins have been widely employed in research on the causes of various psychological disorders. In such studies, the usual procedure involves the identification of individual cases of either monozygous or dizygous twins who manifest a particular disorder. The incidence of the same disorder among their co-twins and other relatives is then investigated. In each family, the individual who serves as the point of departure for the investigation and in terms of whom all family relationships are expressed is usually known as the *index case*. Other terms used to designate such an individual are "propositus" and "proband." When both members of a pair of related persons (twins, siblings, etc.) exhibit the disorder under consideration, they are described as *concordant*. If the disorder is found in only one member, the pair is designated as *discordant*.

An extensive series of investigations of this type has been conducted by

Kallmann and his associates at the New York State Psychiatric Institute (55, 57, 60). The study on schizophrenia, which utilized the largest number of cases, provides the best-established findings. Beginning with 953 twin index cases (268 monozygous and 685 dizygous), all of whom were institutionalized in New York State and diagnosed as schizophrenic, the investigators proceeded to determine which, if any, of the relatives had been similarly diagnosed.

The principal results are summarized in Table 11. It will be noted that 86.2 per cent[3] of the monozygous pairs, but only 14.5 per cent of the dizygous pairs, were concordant. Moreover, the concordance rates for dizygous twins and for full siblings are almost identical. This finding is especially significant, since it will be recalled that the degree of hereditary similarity is the same for dizygous twins and for siblings. Half-siblings yielded a concordance rate of 7.1, and step-siblings, who are not related by heredity, showed a concordance rate which is not appreciably greater than the expectancy of schizophrenia in the general population. The concordance rate for parents of the index cases was 9.3 per cent. Analyzing the data in a slightly different way, Kallmann found that the expectancy of schizophrenia among children of one schizophrenic parent is 16.4 per cent; and among children of two schizophrenic parents, it is 68.1 per cent.

Table 11

CONCORDANCE RATES FOR SCHIZOPHRENIA AS DETERMINED FOR 953 TWIN INDEX CASES IN NEW YORK STATE

(Data from Kallmann, 57, p. 146)

TYPE OF KINSHIP	CONCORDANCE RATE
Monozygous twins	86.2
Dizygous twins	14.5
Full siblings	14.2
Half-siblings	7.1
Step-siblings	1.8
Parents	9.3

Expectancy in general population: 0.7 to 0.9

The much higher concordance rate of schizophrenia among monozygous than among dizygous twin pairs has been corroborated by Slater (101) in England and by other European and American investigators (cf. 57, 101).

[3] The percentages in Table 11 have been corrected for age to allow for the fact that the expectancy rate of schizophrenia varies with age (cf. 57).

In Slater's study, the concordance rate was 76.3 per cent for 41 monozygous pairs and 14.4 per cent for 115 dizygous pairs. On the basis of his own results as well as those of other investigators, Kallmann (57) has proposed a hypothesis in terms of a single recessive gene, possibly producing a metabolic deficiency, which may predispose the individual to schizophrenia. Whether or not schizophrenia actually develops would depend upon other contributing factors of either a genetic or environmental origin.

That certain environmental factors may influence the development of schizophrenia is suggested by a study of mothers of schizophrenics, reported by Mark (67). One hundred mothers of adult male schizophrenics were compared with a control group of mothers of normal men on an attitude questionnaire dealing with child-rearing practices. An examination of the items yielding significant differences between the two groups revealed a tendency for the mothers of schizophrenics to be more restrictive in their control of the child and to exhibit attitudes of both excessive devotion and cool detachment.

Kallmann and his associates have applied the "twin-study method" to the investigation of other psychological disturbances, including manic-depressive, involutional, and senile psychoses (57, 58), childhood schizophrenia (61), feeblemindedness (1), homosexuality (56), and suicide (59), although the number of twin index cases was much smaller in some of these groups than in the major research on adult schizophrenics. With the exception of suicides, all these categories showed a much higher concordance rate among monozygous than among dizygous twins and—when investigated—decreasing expectancy rates among more remote types of kinship. Owing to the smallness of samples, however, some of these findings must be regarded as highly tentative. With regard to the specificity of different psychoses, it is noteworthy that Kallmann reports no twin pair with schizophrenia in one member and manic-depressive psychosis in the other. Nor did his data reveal a single manic-depressive index case with a schizophrenic parent or sibling.

In conclusion, the evidence regarding schizophrenia strongly suggests the operation of hereditary factors, at least in providing a predisposing condition. The exact mechanism whereby such hereditary factors may operate remains to be ascertained. With regard to certain other psychological disorders, there is tentative evidence of the influence of heredity. As Kallmann (e.g., 55) has repeatedly pointed out, the fact that a condition is hereditary in no way indicates that it is incurable. On the contrary, efforts to discover techniques for prevention and therapy should be furthered by a more precise knowledge of causal factors, both hereditary and environmental. Finally, it is important to bear in mind that findings regarding the etiology of pathological conditions need have no implications for the causation of individual differences within the normal range of variation.

THE ENVIRONMENT OF TWINS

There are a number of special circumstances in the environments of twins which may influence their development in various ways. A consideration of these conditions should help to clarify the interpretation of many of the observed twin similarities and differences in psychological traits.

Fraternal versus Identical Twins. All investigators agree in finding identical twins more nearly alike than fraternal twins in abilities, as well as in most other behavior characteristics that have been studied. Identical twins have identical heredity; fraternal twins do not. Can we, then, conclude that the greater resemblance of the former is the result of heredity? It is not so simple as that. The identical twins' closer similarity of heredity is paralleled by a closer similarity of environment. On the basis of extensive field study of twins, for example, Carter (15) argued against the assumption that nurture influences are even approximately the same for identical as for fraternal twins. He wrote:

> Such an assumption seems untenable to anyone who has had much contact with twins in their own social environment, for it is quite evident that the environments of identical twins are on the average more similar than those of fraternal twins. The identical twins obviously like each other better; they obviously have the same friends more often; they obviously spend more time together; and they are obviously treated by their friends, parents, teachers, and acquaintances as if they were more alike than fraternal twins are (15, p. 246).

Many other investigations lend support to such a conclusion (8, 45, 52, 53, 122, 127, 129). It is clear that fraternal twins are often quite unlike in body build, general health, eye and hair color, muscular strength, and many other physical characteristics (108). One twin may be ugly and the other handsome; one sickly and the other hale and vigorous. The effect these physical differences will in turn have upon the twins' relations to their environment may be very far-reaching (45, 125). Each twin will, by virtue of his physical characteristics, automatically "select" different features from the same environment. Actual observation has repeatedly shown that the amount of shared experience of fraternal twins is less than that of identical twins. For example, in a questionnaire (122) answered by 70 pairs of identical twins, 69 pairs of like-sex fraternals, and 55 pairs of unlike-sex fraternals, 43 per cent of the identicals reported that they had never been separated for more than one day. Among the like-sex fraternals, only 26 per cent reported this to be true. Identical twins more often share the same room at home, have the same chum, and are treated more similarly by their families and associates (53). In fact, it is not uncommon for one twin to be mistaken for the other, especially in childhood. All this furnishes an interesting illustration of the indirect influence physical similarities may exert upon behavior. These similarities, which are themselves largely determined by hereditary factors, may in turn alter the individual's environment in such a way as to affect his behavior development.

A word may be added in this connection regarding comparisons between like-sex and unlike-sex fraternals, as well as between fraternal twins and siblings. The greater similarity in test performance generally found for like-sex than for unlike-sex fraternals could result from either hereditary or environmental factors. On the side of heredity, it will be recalled (Ch. 3) that the presence of sex-linked, sex-influenced, and sex-limited factors may introduce a number of hereditary differences between unlike-sex children of the same parents, which are not present in like-sex children. On the side of environment, it is apparent that the effective environments of a boy and a girl are more dissimilar than would be the case for two boys or two girls. Thus the differences in the results obtained with like-sex and unlike-sex fraternals do not lend themselves to unambiguous interpretation. Any differences in degree of resemblance between fraternal twins as a group and siblings as a group, however, can logically be attributed to the greater environmental similarities of the twins. On the basis of heredity, fraternal twins should be no more alike than ordinary siblings. But their environments will tend to be more similar, as was pointed out in an earlier section.

Prenatal and Natal Factors. When identical twins reared in the same home show conspicuous dissimilarities in development, the possible role of prenatal factors or of birth injuries is suggested (83). That prenatal conditions may produce deficiencies in one twin while the other develops normally is quite consistent with what is known regarding the embryology of twinning. During prenatal life, the twins are competitors for the available supply of nourishment. Sometimes one twin loses out completely and fails to survive, while the other develops at his expense. When the inequality is milder, both are born, but one may be weaker than the other.

An example of the possible operation of prenatal and natal factors in producing differences between identical twins is to be found in the occurrence of feeblemindedness. In a survey of several institutions for the feebleminded, Rosanoff *et al.* (89) located 126 persons known to have an identical twin. In the majority of these cases, the other twin was also feebleminded or showed some other abnormal condition such as epilepsy, paralysis, or behavior difficulties. In 11 pairs, however, no defect was found in the other twin. Since the abnormal condition in the defective twin in these pairs appeared early in life, the probability of birth injuries or prenatal factors is strongly indicated.

Some investigators consider cerebral birth injuries to be a relatively common, unsuspected cause of mental deficiency. An injury too mild to attract notice at the time may nevertheless be sufficient to interfere with normal intellectual development later on. This point of view has been expressed by Rosanoff (89), who estimated that conditions favoring birth injuries are about eight times as frequent in the birth records of feebleminded persons as in the general population. Since twins tend on the whole to be born prematurely—when they are relatively small and weak—they are especially subject to birth injuries. The greater prevalence of birth trauma among twins than among single-born children was corroborated by Allen and Kallmann (1) in a recent survey of feebleminded twin index cases.

Intellectual Retardation of Twins. The prenatal and natal hazards surrounding the development of twins have also been cited in explanation of the fact that twins as a whole tend to be intellectually inferior to singletons (single-born children). Such retardation has been repeatedly established in large groups of different age levels studied in several countries. In a survey of nearly 120,000 American high school students with the Henmon Nelson Test of Mental Ability, 412 twin pairs were identified (14). The mean score of these twins fell approximately at the 40th percentile of the entire sample. In a Swedish investigation (49), the mean intelligence test score of 907 male twin pairs examined upon induction into military service was one-fourth of a standard deviation below the mean of the singletons in the same population. An analysis of the distribution of scores indicated that the difference resulted largely from the greater proportion of twins with low IQ's.

The previously cited Scottish surveys, in which a nearly complete sample of 11-year-old children was tested, again revealed a significant mean deficit in the scores of the 974 twins within the sample (95). Similar results were obtained in a survey of 95,237 French school children between the ages of 6 and 12 with a specially constructed pictorial group test of intelligence (111). This sample, which was carefully chosen so as to represent all regions of France, included 750 twins. It should be added that in both the Scottish and French samples, twin inferiority in test scores remained when family size and socioeconomic level were equated.

Further corroboration of the intellectual superiority of singletons is provided by the results of intensive follow-up studies of triplets and quadruplets, as well as by detailed observations of the widely publicized Dionne quintuplets (3, 4, 15, 37). It can be argued that the larger the number of individuals competing for survival in the uterine environment, the more severe the handicaps imposed upon all of them. The observed facts regarding the intellectual development of multiple-birth children appear to lend some support to such a hypothesis. The fact that multiple-birth children are often born prematurely could also account in part for their retardation, since they are actually at an earlier stage of development than their age indicates. It is doubtful, however, whether this factor has a significant effect upon intellectual development in later childhood; its influence is probably limited in large part to early sensory and motor development.

It should be noted that the observed twin retardation is generally most marked in the acquisition of *language*. This linguistic deficiency in turn has an important bearing upon other forms of subsequent intellectual development. The backwardness in language may result at least in part from the presence of two (or more) children of identical age in the same family. It is a common observation that twins frequently form a relatively self-sufficient unit, and consequently have less need for contact and communication with other children and adults. It is just these contacts, however, which provide powerful incentives and opportunities for learning to talk (cf. 69, 127). That twins may be physically retarded or handicapped because of the physiological conditions of twin development seems quite apparent. But that the same conditions provide a sufficient explanation for their intellectual retardation is not conclusively established.

Let us examine some of the specific data on language development among twins. Figure 62 shows the development of the Dionne quintuplets in (1) motor functions, (2) the acquisition of language, and (3) general intelligence. It is apparent that the greatest retardation occurs in language and the least in motor functions. The indices of "general mental development" occupy an intermediate position, probably because of their composite nature. Although the quintuplets were born two months before the normal term, and although the possibility of fetal handicaps exists, it is unlikely that such conditions would produce a more marked retardation in language than in motor development. In his discussion of the linguistic retardation of the quintuplets, Blatz (3) calls attention to a number of likely environmental factors. Since most of their wants were anticipated by ever vigilant attendants, the children had little need to communicate with adults. They

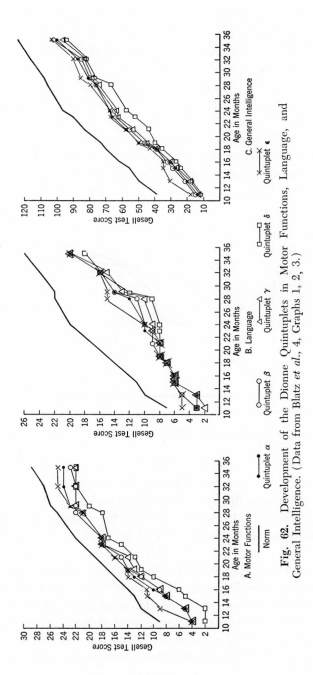

Fig. 62. Development of the Dionne Quintuplets in Motor Functions, Language, and General Intelligence. (Data from Blatz *et al.*, 4, Graphs 1, 2, 3.)

had little to tell each other, since they shared most experiences. By age three, moreover, they had developed a number of mutually intelligible gestures and cries to express their feelings among themselves.

Group surveys of triplets (48) and twins (23, 24, 127) have yielded similar results. Special systems of communication, through gestures and vocal cues, are frequently developed by twins out of their common experiences. The need for acquiring the language of adults is thus reduced. Specific indices of language development, such as length of response or number of different words used during a standard observation period, show consistently more retardation than is found in the total IQ of such children. The extent of this linguistic retardation is illustrated in Figure 63. Bringing

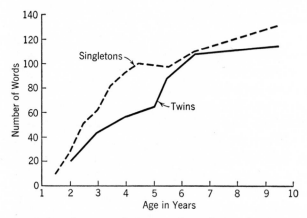

Fig. 63.   Linguistic Development of Twins and Singletons. (From Davis, 23, p. 136.)

together the data of several investigators, this figure shows the average number of different words used during the examination period by twins and singletons between the ages of 1½ and 9½ years.

That the contact of twins with each other may be a major factor in their linguistic retardation is further suggested by the finding that *only-children* are definitely superior to children-with-siblings in every phase of linguistic skill (23). In fact, singletons-with-siblings resemble twins in many phases of their language development more closely than they resemble only-children. In Figure 64 will be found the number of different words used during a test period by twins, singletons-with-siblings, and only-children at the ages of 5½, 6½, and 9½ years. It will be noted that the singletons-with-siblings are somewhat closer to the twins than to the only-children at the first two age levels, and about midway at the third.

Another relevant observation pertains to the *length of the inter-sib inter-*

val. In connection with the previously cited survey of French school children, Tabah and Sutter (111) analyzed the relationship between test score
and age differential between the siblings in 1244 two-sibling families. The
sibling pairs were separated into those with "long" and those with "short"
inter-sib interval. A short interval was defined as one falling at or below
the median interval of approximately two years found for the entire sample; intervals exceeding this amount were classified as long. On the intelligence test, children with long inter-sib intervals obtained a significantly

higher mean score, their superiority persisting within each of the five occupational classes into which the sample was
divided. Moreover, with long inter-sib
intervals, the scores approximated those
of only-children; with short intervals,
the scores were close to those of twins.
Such findings suggest that the more
nearly the sibling relationship approaches that of twins, the greater the
intellectual retardation. The closer the
ages of the two siblings, the greater will
be the chances that the children rely
upon each other's companionship rather
than seeking intellectually more stimulating outside contacts.

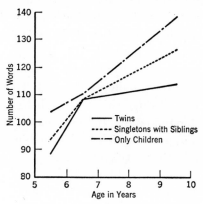

Fig. 64. Comparison of Language
Development of Twins, Singletons
with Siblings, and Only Children.
(From Davis, 23, p. 112.)

More direct evidence regarding the social interaction of siblings tends
further to substantiate this hypothesis. In a carefully designed study by
Koch (63), 384 5- and 6-year-old American children from two-child families
were rated by their teachers on 16 social traits dealing with behavior toward
classmates. A comparison of matched subgroups differing in length of
inter-sib interval revealed a number of significant differences in social
behavior. In explanation of some of these differences, Koch suggests that,

. . . a child's reaching out to peers may be a function in part of his involvement
with, or the degree of satisfyingness of, his sib. When the age difference between
sibs is small, . . . they tend to be more involved with each other (63, p. 23).

In conclusion, the retarding effect of the "twin environment" upon language development seems to be indicated from various sources. Linguistic
retardation in turn has far-reaching implications for all intellectual development. Not only is language necessary as a means of communication in most
human learning, but linguistic symbols themselves play an important part

in problem solving and in the more abstract and complex human intellectual functions.

Social Interaction. The social reactions of twins toward each other provide a promising field of investigation in themselves. Many observers have called attention to the *specialization of "roles"* which twins often seem to work out by a tacit mutual agreement (77, 125, 128). Such a division of labor—observed especially among identical twins—makes for more harmonious relationships and economy of effort. Thus one twin may be the spokesman for the pair in encounters with other persons, showing more interest in people and responding more actively to them. Frequently one twin is the dominant member of the pair, tending more often to lead and to make the decisions for both (24, 125, 128). Such a differentiation of roles may originally arise from slight differences in size and strength, which may have been prenatally established. The parents' efforts to discover and emphasize any distinguishing mark between the twins may be a further source of differentiation. In some cases, minor chance happenings may initiate the difference, which is then willingly accepted and developed by the twins as a matter of convenience.

Such a division of roles, continued and augmented over the years, could account for some of the differences in interests, attitudes, emotional reactions, and abilities sometimes found between twins reared in the same home. Thus in a study of ten pairs of fraternal and two pairs of identical twins located in a college population, tests indicated *less* agreement between twins than between siblings in such characteristics as self-sufficiency, introversion-extroversion, social adjustment, and masculinity-femininity (82). Some evidence was found in the same study that a pair of twins may tend, somewhat more often than siblings, to develop *opposite* trends in dominance and submission.

Such findings are supported by more detailed case studies of individual twins (cf., e.g., 74) and are borne out in very interesting ways by the observations of larger multiple-birth groups. The Dionne quintuplets, for example, although reared under as nearly uniform and controlled conditions as any group of children, nevertheless showed clear-cut personality and ability differences (3, 4). Yet the conclusive demonstration of their monozygosity precludes an explanation of such differences in terms of heredity. In commenting upon these findings, Blatz writes:

It is in the environment, apparently the same for all, that there nevertheless exist subtle yet important differences in the influences bearing on these children—differences of which the social interaction of the five, one upon the other, is the most emphatic yet the most difficult to identify and measure (3, p. 174).

Another vivid demonstration of environmentally determined differences among identical twins is furnished by a set of monozygous female quadruplets studied in America (37). On the Stanford-Binet, one of these quadruplets received an IQ of 110, another 101, while the other two occupied intermediate positions. This relationship was consistently maintained on other tests of intelligence or scholastic ability. On the Stanford Achievement Test, for example, the "bright" quadruplet earned a total score of 124 and the "dull" one 96. Each of the subtests of the Stanford Achievement Test showed the same relationship. Physical and personality differences among the quadruplets closely paralleled these intellectual differences. The dullest quadruplet was also the smallest and had had a poorer health history throughout childhood. The investigators suggest the possibility of differences in fetal blood supply as a basis for both the physical and the psychological dissimilarities. It may well be that the initial, prenatally determined, physical differences led to a subsequent social diversification of roles among the four sisters, which in turn affected their subsequent emotional and intellectual development. The personality differences among the four are reported to be especially conspicuous. The children were characterized by their parents as "the boss," "the clown," "the artist," and "the baby," and the investigators report that an outside observer could readily identify the child fitting each of these labels, even from a brief observation.

TWINS REARED APART

Of considerable interest are the case studies of identical twins who were separated at an early age because of death of parents or other circumstances, and were reared in separated homes. About twenty-five such pairs have been located and carefully studied. The most extensive collection of cases was assembled in an investigation at the University of Chicago, conducted by Newman, Freeman, and Holzinger, a geneticist, psychologist, and statistician, respectively. The principal study (77) covered 19 pairs of identical twins, most of whom had been separated since their first year of life. The actual age of separation in individual cases ranged from two weeks to six years. All the twins had lived apart up to the time of their examination, although in one or two cases they had corresponded or occasionally visited each other. The ages at the time of testing ranged from 11 to 59 years.

Each case was intensively studied through physical measures, psychological and educational tests, and personal interviews. Data were also obtained regarding the foster home and foster parents, educational and vocational history of the twins, health and disease records, and other relevant factors in the subjects' experiential background. A case history illustrating the effects of two fairly dissimilar homes upon a pair of identical twins is summarized below.

Case #4. Mabel and Mary, 29-year-old twins, had been separated at the age of five months and reared by relatives. Mabel had led the life of an active farm woman on a prosperous farm. Mary had lived largely a sedentary life in a small town, clerking in a store during the day and teaching music at night. Mabel had only an elementary school education in a rural school, while Mary had had a complete high school course in an excellent city school. At the time of examination, a vast difference was noted between the twins in intellectual, emotional, and physical traits. Physically, Mabel is described as robust, muscular, and in perfect health, while Mary was underweight, soft-muscled, and in poor general condition; Mabel weighed 138½ lbs., Mary only 110¾ lbs. Intellectually, an equally striking difference was found, but in favor of Mary, whose Stanford-Binet IQ was 106 as compared with 89 for her sister. Even larger differences were obtained in some of the other tests. In personality characteristics, the twins exhibited consistent differences, as determined both by tests and by direct observations. The rural twin tended to be more stolid and stable in emotional reponses, to give fewer neurotic reactions, worry about fewer things, and respond less emotionally to stimuli than did the urban-bred twin. Both the physical differences noted above and the contrast between their psychological environments probably account for these personality differences between the twins (77, pp. 187–195).

To obtain comparative data, Newman, Freeman, and Holzinger tested 50 pairs of *identical twins living together* and 50 pairs of *fraternal twins,* also living together and with their own families. Mean differences as well as correlations in height, weight, and IQ for all three groups are shown in Table 12. It will be noted that the average IQ difference between the separated identicals is 8.2, slightly less than the mean difference between fraternals, but slightly larger than that between nonseparated identicals. Essentially the same relationship is brought out by the correlation coefficients, the separated identicals falling between the nonseperated identicals and the fraternals in closeness of resemblance.

Several writers have tried to draw inferences regarding heredity and environment from a comparison of the degree of resemblance in *physical* and *intellectual* traits in these three groups. In Table 12, the results for height, weight, and IQ are not startlingly different. To be sure, the height and weight correlations for the two groups of identical twins are higher and more nearly alike than are the corresponding intelligence test correlations. But we must bear in mind that measures of height and weight are more reliable than measures of intelligence. Chance errors of measurement in intelligence tests would introduce more fluctuations in score, even in retests of the same individual. Such chance fluctuations tend to lower the correla-

Table 12

A COMPARISON OF IDENTICAL TWINS REARED APART WITH FRATERNAL TWINS AND WITH IDENTICAL TWINS REARED TOGETHER

(Adapted from Newman, Freeman, and Holzinger, 77, pp. 72, 97, 344, 347; and Woodworth, 125, p. 19)

MEASURE	MEAN DIFFERENCE BETWEEN TWINS		
	Fraternal (50 pairs)	Identical Together (50 pairs)	Identical Separated (19 pairs)
Height in cm.	4.4	1.7	1.8
Weight in lb.	10.0	4.1	9.9
Binet IQ	9.9	5.9	8.2

MEASURE	CORRELATIONS * BETWEEN TWINS		
	Fraternal (50 pairs)	Identical Together (50 pairs)	Identical Separated (19 pairs)
Height in cm.	.64	.93	.97
Weight in lb.	.63	.92	.89
Binet IQ	.63	.88	.77

* Certain necessary statistical corrections, for age and for inequalities in IQ range, have been applied to the original correlations given by Newman, Freeman, and Holzinger (77). For further details on these corrections, see 46, 71, and 125.

tions of IQ's and render any differences between such correlations less significant. In other words, we cannot conclude with certainty from the data in Table 12 that the effect of separation was any greater on IQ than it was on height and weight. At the same time, it should be remembered that such comparisons between familial resemblances in physical and in psychological characteristics, although of some interest in themselves, really tell us little about the problem of heredity and environment. Similar correlations *can* result from different factors, and their similarity is therefore no indication that the same influences have operated.

A more crucial approach is provided by an analysis based upon the *extent of environmental differences* between the two twins in each separated pair. The mere separation of twins need not in itself lead to differences. It is conceivable, as a matter of fact, that a particular pair of twins reared apart may be more alike than if they had been reared together. If their respective environments are closely similar—although geographically remote—identical twins should respond with considerable uniformity. Their physical likenesses, based upon a common heredity, would in such a case ensure like responses to like stimulation. Brought up together, on the other hand, the same two twins might show divergent courses of development owing to the specialization of "roles" discussed in the preceding section. Psychologically, environment is not geography.

In Table 13 will be found individual data on each pair of separated identical twins. The original 19 cases of the Chicago study have been augmented with a twentieth case subsequently reported by Gardner and Newman (36). The IQ differences in the last column indicate the excess in favor of whichever twin received the better education. An examination of these IQ differences suggests that, on the whole, they are not random differences such as might result from fortuitous factors, but rather tend to favor the better-educated twin quite consistently. If we restrict our comparisons to the five pairs which present large differences in amount of schooling (first five cases in Table 13), the mean IQ difference in favor of the better-educated twin is 16 points. It will be noted that in the remaining cases the differences in schooling are small or nonexistent. In so far as schooling may affect the IQ, then, these remaining twins would not be expected to differ much. And the differences are, in fact, small.[4] If the cases with similar educational opportunities, where little or no difference is expected, are averaged with those showing clear-cut educational differences, then the possible effects of this environmental factor are diluted and underestimated. A composite figure based upon all these cases, in which specific conditions varied so widely, would only obfuscate the results.

On the basis of the case material, the environments of the separated twins in the Chicago study were rated by five judges for degree of intra-pair difference in educational, social, and physical or "health" advantages, respectively. These ratings, also given in Table 13, show interesting correspondences with the observed differences in intellectual, emotional, and physical characteristics of the twins. Thus a correlation of .79 was found between the discrepancies in educational advantages and the discrepancies in IQ within each pair of twins. Twin discrepancies in body weight correlated .60 with discrepancies in the physical environments. Both of these correlations are significant at the .01 level. When IQ differences were correlated with differences in social and physical environments, with which little relationship would be expected, the correlations were only .51 and .30, respectively. The first of these correlations is significant at the .05 level; the second is not significant.

---

[4] Two cases, 1 and 8, show evidence in their histories of a possible prenatal handicap, which tended to make the twins unlike. If these two cases are omitted, the remaining cases show an insignificant mean difference of less than 2 IQ points.

Table 13

INDIVIDUAL DATA ON TWINS REARED APART

(Adapted from Woodworth, 125, p. 23, with additional data from Newman, Freeman, and Holzinger, 77)

CASE NUMBER	SEX	AGE AT SEPA- RATION	AGE AT TESTING	ENVIRONMENTAL DIFFERENCES				TWIN DIFFER- ENCE IN IQ
				1. In Years of Schooling	2. In Esti- mated Educa- tional Advan- tages †	3. In Esti- mated Social Advan- tages †	4. In Esti- mated Physical Advan- tages †	
11	F	18 mo.	35	14	37	25	22	24
2	F	18 mo.	27	10	32	14	9	12
18	M	1 yr.	27	4	28	31	11	19
4	F	5 mo.	29	4	22	15	23	17
12	F	18 mo.	29	5	19	13	36	7
1	F	18 mo.	19	1	15	27	19	12
17	M	2 yr.	14	0	15	15	15	10
8	F	3 mo.	15	1	14	32	13	15
3	M	2 mo.	23	1	12	15	12	−2
14	F	6 mo.	39	0	12	15	9	−1
5	F	14 mo.	38	1	11	26	23	4
13	M	1 mo.	19	0	11	13	9	1
10	F	1 yr.	12	1	10	15	16	5
15	M	1 yr.	26	2	9	7	8	1
7	M	1 mo.	13	0	9	27	9	−1
19	F	6 yr.	41	0	9	14	22	−9
16	F	2 yr.	11	0	8	12	14	2
6	F	3 yr.	59	0	7	10	22	8
9	M	1 mo.	19	0	7	14	10	6
20*	F	1 mo.	19	0	2	?	?	−3

* The first 19 cases are from Newman, Freeman, and Holzinger (77); case 20 was added later by Gardner and Newman (36).

† Ratings are on a scale of 50 points; the higher the rating, the greater the estimated environmental difference between the twins.

It should be noted that the types of homes into which the twins in any one pair were placed rarely differed very much. If an experiment were being designed to test how far environment may affect, for example, the IQ, the twins would obviously be placed in as different homes as possible. But in the actual placement procedures followed, the reverse tendency usually operates. The placement of children in foster homes tends to be selective, an effort being made to place children with families similar to their own. In a number of twin pairs, the children were adopted by relatives. This would certainly make for greater similarity in socioeconomic, educational, and other characteristics of the two foster homes than would be the case between two families picked at random.

Additional pairs of separated identical twins, studied by other investigators, tend to corroborate the major findings of the Chicago survey (12, 76, 92, 107, 126). Whenever the effective environments differed in any major respect, such differences were reflected in the development of the two twins. An interesting divergence in special aptitudes, for example, was found in a pair of British twins separated at 3 months and reared apart until the age of 16 years (126). Although both had received the same amount of schooling, one twin had a Stanford-Binet IQ of 125, the other of 106. The twin with the lower Stanford-Binet IQ, however, excelled consistently in performance tests and in tests of mechanical aptitude; these differences amounted to as much as two years in mental age and nearly 30 percentile points, respectively, in the two types of tests. Moreover, the twin with the higher Stanford-Binet IQ (and lower mechanical and performance test scores) was inferior to his co-twin in height, weight, and general health. The possible effect of prenatal and postnatal environmental factors upon physique and health, which in turn might influence the divergent development of interests and aptitudes, is suggested by these results.

FOSTER CHILDREN

The development of children reared in foster homes is of considerable interest for practical as well as theoretical reasons. Is there any basis for the popular belief that adopted children "turn out badly"? On the whole the answer appears to be "No," although the contributing factors are too many and too complex to permit a categorical denial. Follow-ups of a group of 910 adopted children indicated that as adults the majority had made a satisfactory vocational and social adjustment (112, 125). A little less than a fourth were judged unsatisfactory in their adjustment because of educational backwardness, shiftlessness and dependency, or delinquency and crime. This proportion is larger than that in the general population, but smaller than would have been expected if the children had been reared in the unfavorable environments from which they were frequently taken. Within the adopted group, a relationship was found between the quality of care and child training provided by the foster home and the number of foster children judged to have made a successful adult adjustment. In the homes rated "excellent" in this regard, 87 per cent of the foster children fell in the satisfactory adult category; in the homes rated "poor," only 66 per cent were so classified.

On intelligence tests, foster children as a group tend to fall somewhat below "own children" brought up in comparable homes (11, 125), but above the average of the general population. At least two factors may account for the latter difference in favor of the foster group. First, placement agencies as well as foster parents tend to choose the most promising children for placement in foster homes, while the more poorly qualified tend to remain under orphanage or boarding-home care. Secondly, the same type of selection occurs with reference to foster homes, the more undesirable homes at the lower end of the distribution being disqualified for adoption purposes. Foster children as a group are thus reared in homes superior to the general average. It is also likely that foster parents, on the whole, have a relatively strong interest in children; otherwise they would not have gone out of their way to adopt one.

Why are foster children less successful—in intelligence test performance as well as in adult achievement—than other children reared in the same type of home? A number of psychologists put the burden of explanation upon unknown "hereditary influences." Presumably this means *genetically determined structural limitations* on behavior development. Such limitations may play a significant part in individual cases, but little or no direct information is available regarding what they are. Part of the explanation, on the other hand, may be provided by *prenatal and natal environmental factors*. Such conditions as diet and medical care of the mother during pregnancy and parturition are probably inferior, in general, for the foster group. That these conditions may affect the structural development—and indirectly the subsequent behavioral development—of the child is being increasingly recognized (104, 110).

When the child has lived with his own family or in an institution for several years prior to adoption, the possible influence of such *early home environment* must also be taken into account. A further factor to consider is the *nature of the family relationship in foster homes*. The attitude of foster parents toward a child may differ in some essential ways from that of own parents. In some cases, the contact of foster parent and child may not be so close or intimate as that of a child and his natural parents. The child himself, when he knows of his adoption, may react differently toward his foster parents than he would toward his own parents. Social expectancy may also complicate the situation. Parents as a rule expect their own children to resemble them in intellectual and emotional development, and this expectation may be manifested in their behavior toward the child, as well as in the attitudes of other relatives and associates. As the child develops, his observers repeatedly call attention to points of family resemblance, real or imagined; he is frequently reminded of ancestral characteristics, which are held up to him as his heritage. Social influences of this sort are absent or greatly minimized in the case of foster children. It would be difficult to estimate what subtle motivational differences may arise as a result of such differences in social expectancy, and what effect the motivational factors may in turn have upon the subsequent course of intellectual development of the child.

To psychologists, foster children have provided one more approach to a possible determination of the contributions of heredity and environment to psychological development, and a number of investigations have been designed especially with this problem in mind. The most extensive projects are those conducted by Burks at Stanford (11), Leahy at Minnesota (65), Freeman and his associates at the University of Chicago (32), and Skodak and Skeels at Iowa (98, 100). A more recent study, stressing personality development, is reported by Wittenborn (124).

The investigations by Burks and Leahy were very similar with regard to procedure and major results. Of the two, Leahy's study is the more recent and better controlled. Leahy (65) administered the Stanford-Binet to 194 foster children and 194 control children living with their own parents. The children in the two groups were individually matched in sex, age, father's occupational level, and father's and mother's schooling.[5] All foster children had been placed for adoption at the age of 6 months or younger and were between 5 and 14 years old when tested. The foster and control parents were examined with the Otis Self-Administering Test.

Correlations between child's Stanford-Binet IQ and parents' Otis scores in both foster and control groups are reproduced below. The correlations between child's IQ and a composite cultural index of the home are also given.

CORRELATION BETWEEN CHILD'S IQ AND:	FOSTER	CONTROL
Father's Otis score	.19	.51
Mother's Otis score	.24	.51
Cultural index of home	.26	.51

Since the correlations in the control group, attributable to heredity plus environment, were consistently higher than those in the foster group, attributable to environment alone, Leahy concluded that heredity is more important than environment in determining individual differences in intelli-

[5] The last three categories apply to own parents in the control group and to foster parents in the experimental group.

gence. This conclusion was similar to that reached by Burks on the basis of the same type of analysis.

In interpreting the correlations reported by Burks and Leahy, a number of factors must be taken into consideration. First, as previously mentioned, intrafamily relationships may not be strictly comparable in foster and own homes. The child's knowledge of adoption may affect his attitude toward his foster parents and foster siblings, as well as his self-confidence and his accomplishment. In Burks' group, 35 per cent of the children knew of their adoption, and in Leahy's group 50 per cent. The parents, of course, always know of the adoption, and their reactions toward the child may be affected by such knowledge in countless ways. Of some relevance in this connection is the finding that two unrelated foster children reared in the same home tend to resemble each other more closely in IQ than an adopted and an own child reared together. To be sure, the obtained differences in correlation are slight and the groups of subjects available for such comparisons too small for conclusive results. But it is interesting to note the consistency of this finding in different studies (11, 32, 65, 99).

A second consideration is the role of natal and prenatal factors, which has also been previously discussed. Such factors, although environmental in nature, would tend to increase the resemblance of children to their own parents, as contrasted with their resemblance to foster parents. Mothers who are intellectually and socially or economically inferior would also be more likely to provide inferior prenatal care through ignorance, irresponsibility, or poverty. It might seem that prenatal environmental factors could not account for resemblance to own fathers. More careful consideration, however, will show that the father's educational, vocational, and economic level will also in part determine the quality of medical, dietary, and other conditions affecting the mother.

A final point pertains to the effect of homogeneity upon correlation coefficients. There are several indications that, despite the care with which Leahy's foster and control groups were matched in parental education and occupation, the cultural levels of the foster and control homes were not truly comparable (120). The foster homes were on the whole superior and *more uniform* than the control homes. Such uniformity would obviously serve to decrease the contribution of home environment to individual differences in IQ. In fact, if home environment plays a significant part in intellectual development, we should expect the foster children to be more alike in IQ than the controls. Such was indeed the case: the IQ's of the foster group had an SD of 12.5, while those of the control group had an SD of 15.4. The greater homogeneity of the foster group in both socioeconomic level and IQ would lead us to expect lower correlations with either variable in the foster than in the control group.

The investigation by Freeman *et al.* (32) utilized a wider variety of approaches but was less well controlled in certain important respects than those by Burks and Leahy. One of its principal weaknesses stemmed from the fact that age of adoption was much higher, averaging four years for the entire sample of 401 cases. The children were again tested with the Stanford-Binet and the foster parents with the Otis test, although additional tests were employed for subsidiary purposes.

Several kinds of analyses were carried out on subgroups of the total sample. A group of 74 children who had been tested prior to adoption and retested after an average interval of four years showed a mean IQ rise from 91.2 to 93.7, the difference being significant at the .05 level. Within this group, those children adopted into the better foster homes (as determined from detailed data on foster parents and cultural level of foster homes) gained an average of 5 IQ points, while those adopted into poorer homes revealed no change over the interval. Similarly, children adopted earlier improved more than those adopted at older ages. It is possible that some of the IQ gains resulted from the fact that the child may have been under emotional stress at the time of the initial test. After several years' residence in the foster home, he would presumably be in a better position to do his best on the test.

The IQ's of 125 sibling pairs reared in different foster homes for periods ranging from 4 to 13 years correlated only .25, in contrast to the correlations of about .50 usually found between siblings in the same home. Moreover, siblings adopted into culturally dissimilar foster homes showed less resemblance than those adopted into similar homes. The correlation between unrelated foster children reared in the same home proved to be .37 ($N = 72$) and that between foster children and own children of the foster parents was .34 ($N = 40$). Within the total sample of 401 cases, a correlation of .48 was found between child's IQ and cultural rating of foster home. This correlation rose to .52 when only children adopted under the age of two years were included. Child's IQ correlated .37 with foster father's Otis score ($N = 180$) and .28 with that of the foster mother ($N = 225$).

In the interpretation of most of these correlations, a major difficulty arises from *selective placement* of foster children. It is a common policy of placement agencies to try to "fit the child to the home" on the basis of any available knowledge about the child himself or his background. Freeman and his co-workers looked into the possibilities of selective placement and were inclined to minimize its effect. But it is likely that selective factors did operate to some extent and thus raised the correlations between children's IQ's and characteristics of their foster parents, siblings, and homes.

A longitudinal study of foster children was conducted by Skodak and Skeels (98, 100). Out of an original sample of 306 children placed for adoption under the age of six months, 100 were followed up for 13 years and periodically retested with the Stanford-Binet. The mean IQ's of the 100 children on each retest were as follows:

Mean Age	2	4	7	13
Mean IQ	117	112	115	117

Skodak and Skeels based their principal conclusion on the fact that these IQ's were considerably higher than would have been anticipated from the family background of the foster children. Available data on educational, occupational, and socioeconomic status of true parents indicated that as a group they were below average. IQ's obtained at the beginning of the study on 80 of the true mothers, described as representative of the entire sample, averaged only 93 (cf. 72, 98). Although the extent of inferiority of the true parents has been a matter of controversy, it seems fairly clear that their over-all intellectual level was below that eventually attained by their children.

Although no data were available on intelligence test performance of foster parents or cultural status of foster homes, Skodak and Skeels found negligible correlations between educational and occupational level of foster parents and foster child's IQ. It is likely that the actual variation in home environment associated with these characteristics of the foster parents was too small in this group to yield significant correlations. On the other hand, the correlation between child's IQ and IQ of true mother ($N = 63$) rose consistently from a value of .00 on the initial test to .44 ($P < .01$) on the last retest.

The latter correlation may indicate parent-child resemblance arising from hereditary factors or from prenatal conditions and other environmental influences. The hereditary interpretation is stressed by Honzik (47), who found that at each age the correlations between foster child's IQ and true parents' intelligence in the Skodak and Skeels study were about as high as those obtained with the California Guidance Study children reared by their own parents. Skodak and Skeels, on the other hand, argue that some resemblance between foster children and true parents may result from selective placement. They present evidence suggesting that the children of relatively bright mothers were placed in homes that were qualitatively superior in many characteristics relevant to child development, while the children of duller mothers were placed in homes deficient in these respects (100, pp. 112–114). It is the investigators' contention that such important qualitative differences in the nature of the foster homes and in the child-rearing practices of the foster parents may have affected selective placement even though they did not show up in such crude indices as occupational level or number of years of schooling of foster parents. Before a conclusive explanation can be established, it is apparent that this foster child–true parent correlation needs to be checked in other groups in which more detailed information on foster home conditions is available.

Data on the relationship between foster home environment and personality development of foster children were gathered in an investigation by Wittenborn (124). The subjects comprised 195 foster children, most of whom had been placed in their adoptive homes under the age of two years. They were divided into a younger group of 114 children aged 5 or 6 years who had not yet entered the first grade at the time of the study and an older group of 81 children who were past the first grade and most of whom were 8 or 9 years old. Children in the first grade were excluded since it was believed that they might be undergoing a period of turmoil following school entrance. Data were obtained through intelligence and achievement tests, physical examinations, a home visit, and intensive interviews with the child and with his foster mother. Analysis of results was concerned chiefly with the relationships between various details of child-rearing practices and the emotional and social behavior of the child. A number of significant correlations were found, the author concluding that "inharmonious, incompatible, and rejective adoptive parents may tend to produce children who are aggressive and fearful" (124, p. 111).

INSTITUTIONAL CHILDREN

Closely related to the analysis of foster family relationships is the study of children reared in institutions. Despite the apparent uniformity of their institutional home, such children generally show nearly as wide individual differences in intelligence as children living in their own homes. Moreover, in one investigation conducted in England (64), correlations in the .20's and .30's were found between the intelligence test scores of orphanage children and the occupational status of their own fathers. It should be noted that these children were placed by the institution in boarding homes until the age of 6. From 6 to 16 they lived at the orphanage, where they attended the same school. Since the occupations of the fathers were known to the orphanage staff, one wonders to what extent selective placement and selective treatment in the institution may have artificially raised the reported correlations. It was also found that, among children admitted to the orphanage before the age of 3, intelligence test scores showed a lower correlation with parental occupational level than in the case of children who remained with their parents after the age of 3. In another British study (50) on orphanage children aged 9 to 16, a similar relationship between child's intelligence and parental occupation was noted. But the intellectual differentiation between occupational classes, as well as the extent of individual differences within any one class, tended to decrease as length of institutional residence increased.

A fairly well-established finding is that orphanage children on the whole have lower IQ's than those reared in their own homes or in either boarding homes or foster homes (29, 40, 42, 66, 97, 125). In itself, such a finding permits of at least two explanations. First, *selective factors* may gradually eliminate the brighter children from an orphanage group, since such children are the most likely to be chosen for adoption. Secondly, *institutional environments* in general may be relatively unstimulating to the developing child. Orphanages vary widely among themselves, of course, in the type of environment they provide. Problems of overcrowding, staffing, space, equipment, and other facilities naturally produce differences in the amount and type of stimulation the child receives. The ratio of adult staff members to children varies in different orphanages from about 1:2 to about 1:25 (cf. 125). To a certain extent, these differences in institutional environments are reflected in the IQ's of the children. Some of the apparently inconsistent results found by investigators in different orphanages are probably attributable in part to such institutional differences.

In a study of infants between the ages of 6 and 12 weeks, Gilliland (40) compared the test performance of over 300 institutional infants with that of an equal number of infants living in their own homes. The IQ's of the institutional infants on the Northwestern Infant Intelligence Test averaged significantly lower than those of the infants in private homes. Of the 40 items in the test, 18 showed a significant difference in favor of infants in private homes. These items dealt with behavior that would be influenced by the nature and extent of the child's contacts with his social and physical environment. Items concerned primarily with maturational changes showed no difference between institutional and noninstitutional groups.

Goldfarb (42) compared a group of children reared from infancy in foster homes with an equated group reared for the first three years of life in an institution and then placed in foster homes. When examined at an average age of twelve years, the continuously home-reared group had a mean

Wechsler IQ of 95.4, while the initially institutionalized group had a mean IQ of 72.4, this difference being significant at the .01 level. Equally significant differences in favor of the home-reared group were found in a number of other tests of aptitudes, school achievement, and emotional and social characteristics.

There is also considerable evidence to show that the retardation of institutional infants is particularly severe in linguistic development (cf. 69). Even before learning to talk, infants reared in a family environment vocalize more—and in a more advanced manner—than infants brought up in institutions (9, 31). At the preschool ages, children reared in their own homes excel orphanage children in size of vocabulary and in the variety of subjects about which they talk (75). Degree and nature of adult contact, as well as number and diversity of other stimuli provided by the environment, are undoubtedly among the important conditions for the acquisition of language. And language in turn represents a major tool for the child's overall intellectual progress.

Data on personality development of institutional children indicate retardation in social maturity and in responsiveness to other persons, as well as poorer emotional adjustment (6, 42, 90, 91). Severe psychiatric disturbances among children reared under conditions of inadequate adult contact have been reported by some writers, notably Ribble (84) and Spitz (105, 106). The latter described a syndrome, which he termed "hospitalism," characterized by depression and withdrawal, extreme retardation in behavior development, and increased susceptibility to disease. According to Spitz, this condition is most likely to occur among infants separated from their mothers and reared in a relatively unstimulating institutional setting during the latter part of the first year of life. It can be relieved by restoring contact with the mother or with another adult who functions in the same role (90, 105). The data reported by Spitz have been criticized because of small number of cases, inadequate control of conditions, and other methodological difficulties (80). Specific conclusions must await further research. In a recent study of Lebanese orphanage children, for example, retardation on infant tests appeared to stem principally from lack of specific learning opportunities.[6] Nevertheless, the general findings of Spitz are in line with those of other types of investigations in suggesting that a close and emotionally warm relationship with one or more adults is an important factor in the child's psychological development (cf. 109).

---

[6] Cf. Dennis, W., and Najarian, P. Infant development under environmental handicap. *Psychol. Monogr.*, 1957, 71, No. 7.

SUMMARY

Because of common family environment, mutual influence of family members, and the persistent operation of social expectancy, family resemblances in psychological traits cannot in themselves demonstrate the contribution of heredity. Analyses of family pedigrees indicate that both outstanding achievement and feeblemindedness tend to run in certain families, but they provide little or no information regarding the relative contribution of hereditary and environmental factors to intellectual development. Family data on psychological traits rarely lend themselves to the well-controlled application of such techniques as pedigree analysis and gene frequency analysis.

Correlations between intelligence test scores of parents and children, as well as between those of siblings, cluster around .50. In personality characteristics, correlations are somewhat lower, especially in such social traits as introversion and dominance. Husband-wife correlations tend to follow a similar pattern. Available evidence indicates that such marital correlations result largely from assortative mating rather than from common experiences and mutual influence of the spouses after marriage.

Identical twin correlations in intelligence tests are generally in the .90's, while fraternal twin correlations fall between .60 and .70. In special aptitudes and in personality traits, twin correlations are usually lower but again reveal closer resemblance between identical than between fraternal twins. There is evidence that in many psychological traits the modal intra-pair difference may be no greater for fraternal than for identical twins, but the frequency of large differences is higher among fraternals. With regard to certain pathological conditions, such as schizophrenia, the percentages of concordance among identical twins, fraternal twins, and siblings are such as to indicate the operation of a hereditary predisposing factor.

In the interpretation of much of the psychological research on twins, the closer similarity in the environments of identical than in those of fraternal twins must be taken into account. Prenatal and natal factors, on the other hand, may produce intra-pair dissimilarities in the case of either identicals or fraternals. Twins are more subject to birth trauma than are singletons, a fact that may account for the greater prevalence of certain forms of feeblemindedness among twins. Intellectual retardation of twins, which is greatest in the linguistic sphere, appears likewise to be associated with the relative self-sufficiency of the twins as a social unit and the consequent reduction in adult contact. Studies on length of inter-sib interval among singletons tend to corroborate this interpretation. Investigations of the social interaction of twins reveal evidence of role specialization, which may in turn influence subsequent intra-pair differentiation in psychological development. Identical twins who have been reared apart since infancy show differences in intelligence test performance which, in general, parallel the differences in their environments.

Research on foster children indicates that, on the whole, such children turn out better than would be anticipated from their family background. There is some evidence to suggest that those placed in superior foster homes improve more than those reared in less favorable foster homes. The data are difficult to interpret, however, owing to selective placement, restriction in range of foster home environments, difficulty of measuring those aspects of home environment most relevant to child development, insufficient information regarding own parents of the foster children, and other methodological limitations. Children reared in institutions tend to be intellectually and emotionally inferior to those reared in family environments, linguistic and social development being most impaired. A major reason for these differences is to be found in the extent and nature of adult contacts available in typical institutional and familial environments.

REFERENCES

1. Allen, G., and Kallmann, F. J. Frequency and types of mental retardation in twins. *Amer. J. hum. Genet.*, 1955, 7, 15–20.
2. Barnicot, N. A., Harris, H., and Kalmus, H. Taste thresholds of further eighteen compounds and their correlation with P.T.C. thresholds. *Ann. Eugen.*, 1951, 16, 119–128.
3. Blatz, W. E. *The five sisters.* N.Y.: Morrow, 1938.
4. Blatz, W. E., *et al.* Collected studies on the Dionne quintuplets. *Univer. Toronto Stud. Child Develpm.*, 1937.
5. Blewett, D. B. An experimental study of the inheritance of intelligence. *J. ment. Sci.*, 1954, 100, 922–933.
6. Bodman, F., MacKinlay, Margaret, and Sykes, Kathleen. The social adaptation of institution children. *Lancet*, 1950, 258, 173–176.
7. Böök, J. A. A genetic and neuropsychiatric investigation of a North-Swedish population, with special regard to schizophrenia and mental deficiency. *Acta genet. statist. Med.*, 1953, 4, 1–100.
8. Bracken, H. v. Mutual intimacy in twins: types of social structure in pairs of identical and fraternal twins. *Char. and Person.*, 1934, 2, 293–309.
9. Brodbeck, A. J., and Irwin, O. C. The speech behavior of infants without families. *Child Develpm.*, 1946, 17, 145–156.
10. Brody, D. Twin resemblances in mechanical ability, with reference to the effects of practice on performance. *Child Develpm.*, 1937, 8, 207–216.

11. Burks, Barbara S. The relative influence of nature and nurture upon mental development; a comparative study of foster parent-foster child resemblance and true parent-true child resemblance. *27th Yearb., Nat. Soc. Stud. Educ.,* 1928, Part I, 219–316.

12. Burks, Barbara S. A study of identical twins reared apart under differing types of family relationships. In Q. McNemar and Maud A. Merrill (Eds.), *Studies in personality.* N.Y.: McGraw-Hill, 1942. Ch. 3.

13. Burlingame, Mildred, and Stone, C. P. Family resemblance in maze-learning ability in white rats. *27th Yearb., Nat. Soc. Stud. Educ.,* 1928, Part I, 89–99.

14. Byrns, Ruth, and Healy, J. The intelligence of twins. *J. genet. Psychol.,* 1936, 49, 474–478.

15. Carter, H. D. Ten years of research on twins: contributions to the nature-nurture problem. *39th Yearb., Nat. Soc. Stud. Educ.,* 1940, Part I, 235–255.

16. Cattell, R. B., Blewett, D. B., and Beloff, J. R. The inheritance of personality. *Amer. J. hum. Genet.,* 1955, 7, 122–146.

17. Cattell, R. B., Stice, G. F., and Kristy, N. F. A first approximation to nature-nurture ratios for eleven primary personality factors in objective tests. *J. abnorm. soc. Psychol.,* 1957, 54, 143–159.

18. Cohen, J., and Ogdon, D. P. Taste blindness to phenyl-thio-carbamide and related compounds. *Psychol. Bull.,* 1949, 46, 490–498.

19. Conrad, H. S., and Jones, H. E. A second study of familial resemblance in intelligence: environmental and genetic implications of parent-child and sibling correlations in the total sample. *39th Yearb., Nat. Soc. Stud. Educ.,* 1940, Part II, 97–141.

20. Cotterman, C. W., and Snyder, L. H. Tests of simple Mendelian inheritance in randomly collected data of one and two generations. *J. Amer. stat. Assoc.,* 1939, 34, 511–523.

21. Crook, M. N. Intra-family relationships in personality test performance. *Psychol. Rec.,* 1937, 1, 479–502.

22. Danielson, F. H., and Davenport, C. B. *The Hill Folk.* Cold Spring Harbor, N.Y.: Eugenics Record Office (Memoir No. 1), 1912.

23. Davis, Edith A. The development of linguistic skill in twins, singletons with siblings, and only children from age five to ten years. *Univer. Minn., Inst. Child Welf., Monogr.,* 1937, No. 14.

24. Day, Ella J. The development of language in twins. *Child Develpm.,* 1932, 3, 179–199, 298–316.

25. Dugdale, R. L. *The Jukes: a study in crime, pauperism, disease, and heredity.* N.Y.: Putnam, 1877.

26. Estabrook, A. H. *The Jukes in 1915.* Washington: Carnegie Institution, 1916.

27. Estabrook, A. H., and Davenport, C. B. *The Nam family.* Cold Spring Harbor, N.Y.: Eugenics Record Office (Memoir No. 2), 1912.

28. Eysenck, H. J., and Prell, D. B. The inheritance of neuroticism: an experimental study. *J. ment. Sci.,* 1951, 97, 441–465.

29. Fischer, Liselotte K. Hospitalism in six-month-old infants. *Amer. J. Orthopsychiat.,* 1952, 22, 522–533.

30. Fisher, Sarah C. *Relationships in attitudes, opinions, and values among family members.* Berkeley, Calif.: Univer. California Press, 1948.

31. Fisichelli, Regina M. An experimental study of the prelinguistic speech development of institutionalized infants. Unpublished doctoral dissertation, Fordham Univer., 1950.

32. Freeman, F. N., Holzinger, K. J., and Mitchell, B. C. The influence of environment on the intelligence, school achievement, and conduct of foster children. *27th Yearb., Nat. Soc. Stud. Educ.*, 1928, Part I, 103–217.

33. Galton, F. *Hereditary genius: an inquiry into its laws and consequences.* London: Macmillan, 1869.

34. Galton, F. *Inquiries into human faculty and its development.* London: Macmillan, 1883.

35. Galton, F. *Natural inheritance.* London: Macmillan, 1889.

36. Gardner, I. C., and Newman, H. H. Mental and physical tests of identical twins reared apart. *J. Hered.*, 1940, 31, 119–126.

37. Gardner, I. C., and Newman, H. H. Studies of quadruplets. VI. The only living one-egg quadruplets. *J. Hered.*, 1943, 34, 259–263.

38. Gedda, L., and Neroni, Lydia. Reazioni posturali e mimiche di 56 coppie di gemelli alla proiezione di film umoristici ed anziogeni. *Acta genet. med. gemellolog.*, 1955, 4, 15–31.

39. Gedda, L., Bianchi, A., and Bianchi-Neroni, Lydia. Voce dei gemelli: I. Prova di identificazione intrageminale della voce in 104 coppie. *Acta genet. med. gemellolog.*, 1955, 4, 121–130.

40. Gilliland, A. R. Environmental influences on infant intelligence test scores, *Harv. educ. Rev.*, 1949, 19, 142–146.

41. Goddard, H. H. *The Kallikak family: a study in the heredity of feeble-mindedness.* N.Y.: Macmillan, 1912.

42. Goldfarb, W. Emotional and intellectual consequences of psychologic deprivation in infancy: a revaluation. In P. H. Hoch and J. Zubin (Eds.), *Psychopathology of childhood.* N.Y.: Grune & Stratton, 1955. Pp. 105–119.

43. Hildreth, Gertrude H. The resemblance of siblings in intelligence and achievement. *Teach. Coll. Contr. Educ.*, 1925, No. 186.

44. Hirsch, N. D. M. *Twins: heredity and environment.* Cambridge: Harvard Univer. Press, 1930.

45. Holmes, S. J. Nature versus nurture in the development of the mind. *Sci. Mon.*, 1930, 31, 245–252.

46. Holzinger, K. J. Reply to special review of "Twins." *Psychol. Bull.*, 1938, 35, 436–444.

47. Honzik, Marjorie P. Developmental studies of parent-child resemblance in intelligence. *Child Develpm.*, 1957, 28, 215–228.

48. Howard, Ruth W. The language development of a group of triplets. *J. genet. Psychol.*, 1934, 69, 181–188.

49. Husén, T. Über die Begabung von Zwillingen. *Psychol. Beitr.*, 1953, 1, 137–145.

50. Jones, D. C., and Carr-Saunders, A. M. The relation between intelligence and social status among orphan children. *Brit. J. Psychol.*, 1926–27, 17, 343–364.

51. Jones, H. E. Homogamy in intellectual abilities. *Amer. J. Sociol.*, 1929–30, 35, 369–382.

52. Jones, H. E. Perceived differences among twins. *Eugen. Quart.*, 1955, 2, 98–102.
53. Jones, H. E., and Wilson, P. T. Reputation differences in like-sex twins. *J. exp. Educ.*, 1932–33, 1, 86–91.
54. Kalhorn, J. Mental test performance of siblings. *Amer. Psychologist*, 1948, 3, 265.
55. Kallmann, F. J. The genetics of psychoses: an analysis of 1232 twin index families. *Amer. J. hum. Genet.*, 1950, 2, 385–390.
56. Kallmann, F. J. Twin and sibship study of overt male homosexuality. *Amer. J. hum. Genet.*, 1952, 4, 136–146.
57. Kallmann, F. J. *Heredity in health and mental disorder: principles of psychiatric genetics in the light of comparative twin studies.* N.Y.: Norton, 1953.
58. Kallmann, F. J. Genetic principles in manic-depressive psychosis. In P. H. Hoch and J. Zubin (Eds.), *Depression.* N.Y.: Grune & Stratton, 1954. Pp. 1–24.
59. Kallmann, F. J., *et al.* Suicide in twins and only children. *Amer. J. hum. Genet.*, 1949, 1, 113–126.
60. Kallmann, F. J., and Baroff, G. S. Abnormalities of behavior. *Ann. Rev. Psychol.*, 1955, 6, 297–326.
61. Kallmann, F. J., and Roth, B. Genetic aspects of preadolescent schizophrenia. *Amer. J. Psychiat.*, 1956, 112, 599–606.
62. Kelly, E. L. Consistency of the adult personality. *Amer. Psychologist*, 1955, 10, 659–681.
63. Koch, Helen L. Attitudes of young children toward their peers as related to certain characteristics of their siblings. *Psychol. Monogr.*, 1956, 70, No. 19, 1–41.
64. Lawrence, E. M. An investigation into the relation between intelligence and inheritance. *Brit. J. Psychol., Monogr. Suppl.*, 1931, 5, No. 16.
65. Leahy, Alice M. Nature-nurture and intelligence. *Genet. Psychol. Monogr.*, 1935, 17, 236–308.
66. Levy, R. J. Effects of institutional versus boarding home care on a group of infants. *J. Pers.*, 1947, 15, 233–241.
67. Mark, J. C. The attitudes of the mothers of male schizophrenics toward child behavior. *J. abnorm. soc. Psychol.*, 1953, 48, 185–189.
68. May, M. A., and Hartshorne, H. Sibling resemblance in deception. *27th Yearb., Nat. Soc. Stud. Educ.*, 1928, Part II, 161–177.
69. McCarthy, Dorothea. Language development in children. In L. Carmichael (Ed.), *Manual of child psychology* (2nd Ed.). N.Y.: Wiley, 1954. Pp. 492–630.
70. McNemar, Q. Twin resemblances in motor skills, and the effect of practice thereon. *J. genet. Psychol.*, 1933, 42, 70–99.
71. McNemar, Q. Special review: Newman, Freeman and Holzinger's Twins: a study of heredity and environment. *Psychol. Bull.*, 1938, 35, 237–249.
72. McNemar, Q. A critical examination of the University of Iowa studies of environmental influences upon the IQ. *Psychol. Bull.*, 1940, 37, 63–92.
73. McNemar, Q. *The revision of the Stanford-Binet Scale: an analysis of the standardization data.* Boston: Houghton Mifflin, 1942.

74. Misbach, L., and Stromberg, R. N. Non-separation as a source of dissimilarities between monozygotic twins: a case report. *J. genet. Psychol.*, 1941, 59, 249–257.

75. Moore, J. K. Speech content of selected groups of orphanage and non-orphanage preschool children. *J. exp. Educ.*, 1947, 16, 122–133.

76. Muller, H. J. Mental traits and heredity. *J. Hered.*, 1925, 16, 433–448.

77. Newman, H. H., Freeman, F. N., and Holzinger, K. J. *Twins: a study of heredity and environment.* Chicago: Univer. Chicago Press, 1937.

78. Pearson, K. On the laws of inheritance in man: II. On the inheritance of the mental and moral characters in man, and its comparison with the inheritance of physical characters. *Biometrika*, 1904, 3, 131–190.

79. Pearson, K., and Lee, A. On the laws of inheritance in man: I. Inheritance of physical characters. *Biometrika*, 1903, 2, 357–462.

80. Pinneau, S. R. The infantile disorders of hospitalism and anaclitic depression. *Psychol. Bull.*, 1955, 52, 429–452.

81. Pintner, R., Forlano, G., and Freedman, H. Sibling resemblances on personality traits. *Sch. and Soc.*, 1939, 49, 190–192.

82. Portenier, Lillian G. Twinning as a factor influencing personality. *J. educ. Psychol.*, 1939, 30, 542–547.

83. Price, B. Primary biases in twin studies; a review of prenatal and natal difference-producing factors in monozygotic pairs. *Amer. J. hum. Genet.*, 1950, 2, 293–352.

84. Ribble, Margaret A. Infantile experience in relation to personality development. In J. McV. Hunt (Ed.), *Personality and the behavior disorders.* N.Y.: Ronald, 1944. Ch. 20.

85. Richardson, S. K. The correlation of intelligence quotients of siblings of the same chronological age levels. *J. juv. Res.*, 1936, 20, 186–198.

86. Roberts, J. A. Fraser. Studies on a child population. V. The resemblance in intelligence between sibs. *Ann. Eugen.*, 1940, 10, 293–312.

87. Roff, M. A statistical study of the development of intelligence test performance. *J. Psychol.*, 1941, 11, 371–386.

88. Roff, M. Intra-family resemblances in personality characteristics. *J. Psychol.*, 1950, 30, 199–227.

89. Rosanoff, A. J., Handy, L. M., and Plesset, I. R. The etiology of mental deficiency with special reference to its occurrence in twins. *Psychol. Monogr.*, 1937, 48, No. 4.

90. Roudinesco, –, and Appel, G. Les répercussions de la stabulation hospitalière sur le développement psycho-moteur des jeunes enfants. *Sem. Hôp.* (Paris), 1950, 26, 2271–2273.

91. Ryan, Sr. Mary I. A comparative study of some personality traits of children living in an orphanage and of children living in a family environment. Unpublished doctoral dissertation, Fordham Univer., 1941.

92. Saudek, R. A British pair of identical twins reared apart. *Char. and Pers.*, 1934, 3, 17–39.

93. Scheinfeld, A. The Kallikaks after thirty years. *J. Hered.*, 1944, 35, 259–264.

94. Schiller, Belle. A quantitative analysis of marriage selection in a small group. *J. soc. Psychol.*, 1932, 3, 297–319.

95. Scottish Council for Research in Education. *Social implications of the 1947 Scottish mental survey.* London: Univer. London Press, 1953.

96. Sims, V. M. The influence of blood relationship and common environment on measured intelligence. *J. educ. Psychol.*, 1931, 22, 56–65.

97. Skeels, H. M., and Dye, H. B. A study of the effect of differential stimulation on mentally retarded children. *Proc. Amer. Assoc. ment. Def.*, 1939, 44, 114–136.

98. Skodak, Marie. Children in foster homes: a study of mental development. *Univer. Iowa Stud. Child Welf.*, 1939, 16, No. 1.

99. Skodak, Marie. Mental growth of adopted children in the same family. *J. genet. Psychol.*, 1950, 77, 3–9.

100. Skodak, Marie, and Skeels, H. M. A final follow-up study of one hundred adopted children. *J. genet. Psychol.*, 1949, 75, 85–125.

101. Slater, E. *Psychotic and neurotic illnesses in twins.* London: H.M. Stationery Office, 1953. (Med. Res. Coun., Spec. Rep. Ser. No. 278)

102. Snyder, L. H. A table to determine the proportion of recessives to be expected in various matings involving a unit character. *Genetics*, 1934, 19, 1–17.

103. Snyder, L. H. *The principles of heredity.* (4th Ed.) Boston: Heath, 1951.

104. Sontag, L. W. Differences in modifiability of fetal behavior and physiology. *Psychosom. Med.*, 1944, 6, 151–154.

105. Spitz, R. A. Hospitalism. An inquiry into the genesis of psychiatric conditions in early childhood. *Psychoanal. Stud. Child*, 1945, 1, 53–74, 113–117.

106. Spitz, R. A. Anaclitic depression. *Psychoanal. Stud. Child*, 1946, 2, 313–342.

107. Stephens, F. E., and Thompson, R. B. The case of Millan and George, identical twins reared apart. *J. Hered.*, 1943, 34, 109–114.

108. Stocks, P. A biometric investigation of twins and their brothers and sisters. *Ann. Eugen.*, 1930, 4, 49–108.

109. Stone, L. J. A critique of studies of infant isolation. *Child Develpm.*, 1954, 25, 9–20.

110. Stuart, H. C. Findings on examination of newborn infants and infants during neonatal period which appear to have a relationship to the diets of their mothers during pregnancy. *Feder. Proc.*, 1945, 4, 271–281.

111. Tabah, L., and Sutter, J. Le niveau intellectuel des enfants d'une même famille. *Ann. hum. Genet.*, 1954, 19, Pt. 2, 120–150.

112. Theis, S. V. *How foster children turn out.* N.Y.: State Charities Aid Assoc., 1924.

113. Thorndike, E. L. The causation of fraternal resemblance. *J. genet. Psychol.*, 1944, 64, 249–264.

114. Thorndike, E. L. The resemblance of siblings in intelligence-test scores. *J. genet. Psychol.*, 1944, 64, 265–267.

115. Thorndike, E. L., and staff. The resemblance of siblings in intelligence. *27th Yearb., Nat. Soc. Stud. Educ.*, 1928, Pt. I, 41–53.

116. Thurstone, Thelma G., Thurstone, L. L., and Strandskov, H. H. A psychological study of twins. 1. Distributions of absolute twin differences for identical and fraternal twins. *Psychometr. Lab., Univer. N. Carolina*, No. 4, 1953.

117. Tozzer, A. M. Biography and biology. In C. Kluckhohn and H. A. Murray

(Eds.), *Personality in nature, society, and culture.* N.Y.: Knopf, 1953. Ch. 13.

118. Vandenberg, S. G. The hereditary abilities study of the University of Michigan. *Eugen. Quart.*, 1956, 3, 94–99.

119. Vandenberg, S. G., and Sutton, H. E. *The Michigan twin study.* Chicago: Univer. Chicago Press (In press).

120. Wallis, W. D. Observations on Dr. Alice M. Leahy's "Nature-nurture and intelligence." *J. genet. Psychol.*, 1936, 49, 315–324.

121. Willoughby, R. R. Family similarities in mental test abilities. *Genet. Psychol. Monogr.*, 1927, 2, 239–277.

122. Wilson, P. T. A study of twins with special reference to heredity as a factor determining differences in environment. *Hum. Biol.*, 1934, 6, 324–354.

123. Wingfield, A. N. *Twins and orphans: the inheritance of intelligence.* London: Dent, 1928.

124. Wittenborn, J. R., *et al.* A study of adoptive children. *Psychol. Monogr.*, 1956, 70, Nos. 1, 2, and 3.

125. Woodworth, R. S. Heredity and environment: a critical survey of recently published material on twins and foster children. *Soc. Sci. Res. Coun. Bull.*, 1941, No. 47.

126. Yates, N., and Brash, H. An investigation of the physical and mental characteristics of a pair of like twins reared apart from infancy. *Ann. Eugen.*, 1941, 11, 89–101.

127. Zazzo, R. Situation gémellaire et développement mental. *J. Psychol. norm. pathol.*, 1952, 45, 208–227.

128. Zazzo, R. Les différences psychologiques des jumeaux identiques et les problèmes de l'individuation. *Bull. Psychol., Groupe Etud. Psychol., Univer. Paris*, 1952, 6 (sp. no.), 111–115.

129. Zazzo, R. Sur le postulat de la comparabilité dans la méthode des jumeaux. *Acta genet. med. gemellolog.*, 1955, 4, 180–191.

CHAPTER 10

Trait Organization:
Theories and Methodology

In preceding chapters, the emphasis has been on *individual variability*, or differences from person to person in any one trait. This and the following chapter, on the other hand, will be concerned chiefly with *trait variability*, or differences from trait to trait within the individual. Investigation of such intra-individual variations in test performance and in other behavioral indices has both practical and theoretical significance. When an individual is classified on the basis of a single global score, such as an IQ, there is still much that remains to be known about his abilities. Two persons attaining the same total score may present very different aptitude "profiles" when their performance along specific lines is analyzed. In planning an educational program for an individual, in helping him to choose a vocation, or in evaluating his qualifications for a particular job, it is of the greatest importance to know his strong and weak points, his special assets and liabilities.

Similarly, in comparative studies of the two sexes and of racial or cultural groups, the use of global scores may obscure or distort differences in separate abilities. Confusion may likewise result from the common tendency to assume that an "IQ" has the same meaning regardless of the test from which it was derived. Some intelligence tests, for example, are almost wholly measures of verbal aptitudes; others draw to a much greater extent upon spatial and perceptual functions. Even different levels of the same test may call into play diverse combinations of abilities, a fact noted in the discussion of age differences (Ch. 8).

317

APPROACHES TO TRAIT VARIABILITY

If the individual's abilities were all more or less on a dead level, a single summary score would be quite adequate. But if appreciable variation in the individual's standing in different traits is the rule, then such a score is crude at best and may sometimes be definitely misleading. It is therefore essential to inquire into the extent of variation within the individual and the way in which different abilities are related and organized.

The study of individual cases displaying *extreme asymmetries of talent* represents one approach to the analysis of trait variability. Are deficiencies along certain lines consistent with intellectual superiority in others? Do special talents in particular fields ever accompany general intellectual backwardness? The occurrence of special talents or defects in a given area would suggest that ability in that area may develop and vary independently of ability in other areas.

We know, for example, that children with high IQ's *can* rate very low in musical aptitude or drawing skill. Conversely, high abilities along these lines may be coupled with mediocre academic aptitudes. Case studies of arithmetic prodigies and "lightning calculators" likewise show that high numerical aptitude can occur in persons of average or inferior "general intelligence" (cf. 6; 8, pp. 11–65). Also relevant are the findings on intellectual decline in old age, as cited in Chapter 8. It will be recalled that the rate of decline varies with different functions, being greatest in perceptual and least in verbal tests. Similarly, psychotic deterioration occurs differentially, some functions showing marked impairment while others remain practically at the prepsychotic level (cf. 5, Ch. 13).

The most spectacular examples of superior development in one function combined with general intellectual deficiency are provided by so-called *idiots savants*. This term, which literally means "wise idiots," is somewhat misleading, since the usual idiot savant is neither particularly wise nor an idiot. He is not usually deficient enough to be classified as an idiot, but is frequently found at the moron or borderline level. And he is "wise" only in a very limited field. In the practical management of his own life he is ordinarily a complete failure.

Like all extreme deviants, idiots savants are rare. Because of their remarkable accomplishments, however, they attract considerable attention, and a number of fairly complete descriptive accounts are available. Most of the earlier cases are summarized in Tredgold and Soddy (58). More recent cases are reported by Rife and Snyder (43), who addressed an inquiry to

55 American institutions for the feebleminded, through which they were able to locate 33 idiots savants. Of these, 8 showed a special talent in music, 8 in mathematics, 7 in drawing, and 10 in miscellaneous areas including mechanics, memory, and motor coordination. A few of these cases manifested skills that were narrowly limited and of dubious psychological significance. On the other hand, a number gave evidence of well-rounded achievement in a fairly broad area. An example of relatively complex numerical talent, appearing early in life, is provided by the case of a 27-year-old man with a mental age of 3 years. In reporting their observations of this case, Rife and Snyder write:

As a small child he would scribble figures on the bathroom tiles or other places whenever he could get hold of a pencil. He never learned to talk, and even now cannot perform such simple requests as pointing to his eyes or ears. In school he could do absolutely nothing, so was sent home, and at sixteen was admitted to the Institution. His hearing is normal. . . . Although he is incapable of carrying on a conversation, or of understanding spoken requests, one may make one's desires along mathematical lines known with a pencil. When a pencil and paper were taken, and the figures 2, 4, and 8 written in a vertical column, the patient immediately continued the series 16, 32, 64, etc. When the series 2, 4, 16 was started, he immediately continued this one, the sixth number being 4,294,967,296. Then 9—3 was written, in the attempt to indicate square root. Under this, several numbers such as 625, 729, and 900 were written. The square root of each was immediately and correctly written. Any problem of multiplication of several digits by several digits was done immediately, only the answer being written (43, pp. 553–554).

In a monograph on idiots savants, Scheerer, Rothman, and Goldstein (44) reported an intensive, five-year study of an 11-year-old boy with a Stanford-Binet IQ of 50, who displayed special talents in music, rote memory, and numerical calculation. They also surveyed various theories which have been advanced to account for idiots savants. Some of these explanations stress motivational factors, others emphasize training and other experiential conditions. Scheerer, Rothman, and Goldstein themselves propose a theory in terms of diminished capacity for abstraction combined with an abnormal exercise of the individual's least impaired function. It is possible, of course, that a number of different causal factors are involved and that the combination may vary in different cases. Whatever the explanation, however, the performance of idiots savants illustrates the extent to which certain intellectual functions may develop independently of others.

A second approach to trait variability consists in the *measurement of intra-individual variability* in large, representative samples of normal subjects. For this purpose, each individual takes a large number of tests and all scores are expressed in comparable units, such as standard scores. It is then possible to compute each individual's variability around his own mean in terms of a standard deviation (SD) or some other measure of variability. Whenever this procedure has been applied, intra-individual variability has proved to be high, the intra-individual SD's averaging from 75 to 80 per cent as large as the SD's of individual differences in single traits. Such results have been obtained on groups of school children, high school and vocational school students, and adults (31, 39).

Amount of intra-individual variability itself varies widely from person to person. In one study, the intra-individual SD's ranged from 4.30 to 9.09 (31). There is some evidence suggesting that duller subjects show greater intra-individual variability, or specialization of abilities, than brighter subjects of the same chronological age (39, 57). A comparison of bright and normal children matched in *mental age*, however, revealed no consistent differences in trait variability between the two groups (17).

Two additional variables whose relationship to trait variability has been studied are *practice* and *age*. In a reanalysis of data collected by several investigators, Preston (41) showed that trait variability tends to decrease with practice and to increase with age. The effect of equal practice is to make the subject more uniform in the various practiced tasks. Age has the opposite effect upon trait variability, the older individual showing more scatter or specialization of ability. It cannot be assumed, of course, that age per se accounts for such changes in trait variability. The groups compared in these investigations also differed in educational level and probably in other respects. It is entirely possible, for example, that education may increase trait variability, even though practice tends to decrease such variability. Education obviously does not consist of "equal practice" in all intellectual functions. Not only does the amount of practice vary in different areas, but motivational changes and other complicating influences are probably introduced in different ways for different individuals. The effects of education on trait variability may thus be quite unlike those obtained in simple practice experiments. Further data on the influence of various conditions upon the specialization of abilities will be considered in the next chapter.

The study of extreme cases of asymmetrical development, as well as the measurement of intra-individual trait variability, suggests that superior talents in one line may be associated with inferior abilities in other respects. It is not to be concluded from this, however, that compensation is the rule. Superior standing in one trait does not *imply* inferiority in another. We have cited only examples in which individuals with a high standing in a certain trait A make a poor showing in a second trait B. We could with equal facility find cases in which the individual is superior in A as well as B, or superior in A and average in B. This, in fact, is what we mean by a low or zero correlation. If various abilities are specific and mutually independent, so that an individual's standing in one tells us nothing about his relative standing in another, we should expect the correlation between such abilities to be zero or very low.

Correlation thus offers another approach to the analysis of trait variability. It should be noted that these are literally alternative approaches or ways of expressing the same facts. Thus the previously cited asymmetries of ability are only extreme cases of trait variability. Similarly, measures of trait variability depend upon the intercorrelations among the traits under consideration, and the one type of measure can be derived from the other (cf. 23, 40). The average trait variability of a group of individuals in a series of tests can be found by the following formula:

$$\overline{V} = 1 - \left(\frac{1}{n} + \frac{\Sigma r}{n^2}\right)$$

in which

$\overline{V}$ is the average variance (SD²) within individuals,

n is the number of tests, and

Σr is the sum of all intercorrelations among the tests, each correlation being entered twice (e.g., r_{12} and r_{21}).

By means of this formula, it can readily be shown that if all the tests were perfectly correlated with one another, trait variability would be zero (40). On the other hand, if all intercorrelations among the tests were zero, the average intra-individual variability would be nearly as high as the variability between individuals, and would approach the latter as the number of tests increases. An examination of correlation coefficients can thus provide the same type of information that is obtained by the measurement of trait variability.

Profile asymmetries can likewise be investigated by the correlational technique. Between what areas of ability are such asymmetries likely to occur? Do certain functions tend to vary together within the individual, so that a deviation in one will be accompanied by a similar deviation in the other? These are the types of questions that are answered by correlation coefficients. Certain functions have long been recognized as "special aptitudes," a designation that carries with it a tacit presupposition of low or zero correlation with other functions. Among the most familiar are musical, artistic, and mechanical aptitudes. It will be recalled that these are some of the areas in which marked asymmetries of talent have been reported. With the continued use of "intelligence" tests, it was also gradually recognized that linguistic (or verbal) scores could be effectively separated from quantitative (or numerical) scores, and it has become common practice for such scores to be independently recorded and evaluated on many intelligence tests. Thus we begin to see faint glimmers of the type of trait distinctions that have emerged from the more refined statistical investigations utilizing the techniques of factor analysis. These techniques, to be considered in a later section, represent further elaborations of the correlational approach.

THEORIES OF TRAIT ORGANIZATION

One of the major outcomes of correlational studies of test scores has been the formulation of theories regarding the organization of psychological traits. In its simplest terms, a trait may be regarded as a *category for the orderly description of the behavior of individuals* (cf. 4). Traits pertain to the interrelationships of behavior. For example, if persons perform about equally well (or equally poorly) on all sorts of verbal tests, such as vocabulary, analogies, and sentence completion, we could obviously substitute a single "verbal score" for all these tests. If, moreover, performance on these verbal tests shows little or no relation to scores on numerical, spatial, or other types of tests, then we can speak of a *verbal trait* representing a distinct category or dimension in terms of which the individual's performance can be described.

Traits are thus identified by measuring varied behavior manifestations of the individual, such as his performance on many different kinds of tests. Traits also refer, as a rule, to relatively enduring characteristics, which have some predictive value. Moreover, they usually cover those characteristics in which individuals differ appreciably from one another. Lastly, a cultural frame of reference is also evident, although not always stated, in most trait classifications. It is those aspects of behavior which are important within a particular culture or environmental setting that are generally identified and described as traits. Even the trait names in our language have a cultural origin and in turn influence our selection and definition of traits (3).

Theories of trait organization are very old. As long as philosophers have discussed the nature of "mind," they have proposed theories regarding the units into which the "mind" was subdivided. It is only since the application of psychological tests and quantitative methods, however, that the relationships among the varied behavior manifestations of the individual could be measured. The more recent theories have been developed as interpretations of specific evidence and thus have a more empirical foundation.

The Two-Factor Theory. The problem of trait organization was first placed upon an empirical basis with the publication of Spearman's 1904 article (45) in which were presented a theory and a new method of investigation. The latter was based upon certain relationships among the intercorrelations of test scores. The analysis was later put on a more systematic basis with the development of the *tetrad criterion*, so called because it deals with tests in sets of four (cf. 46). Even this technique, however, proves unwieldy and inefficient when the number of tests is large. It is also limited in the type of information it can yield regarding the organization of abilities. For these reasons it has now been replaced by the more efficient and flexible methods of factor analysis to be discussed in the following section. Spearman's development of the tetrad criterion nevertheless opened the way for the statistical investigation of trait relationships and made possible a large amount of early research in this area.

On the basis of his analyses of test intercorrelations, Spearman formulated the Two-Factor theory of mental organization (46). According to this theory, all intellectual activities have in common a single *general* factor, or *g*. In addition, each activity has *specific*, or *s*, factors. The *s* factors are considered to be exceedingly numerous and strictly specific to each activity of the individual. No two activities can share specific factors, by definition. Spearman argued that such a theory is consistent with correlation results. Thus the presence of different specifics in every activity would explain the absence of perfect $+ 1.00$ correlations; no two activities, however much they may depend upon the *g* factor, are entirely free from specifics. The fact that most abilities are positively correlated, on the other hand, is attributed to the ubiquitous *g*. Different proportions of *g* and *s* in each activity would produce a wide range of positive correlations, all higher than zero and lower than 1.00.

It follows from the Two-Factor theory that the aim of psychological testing should be to measure the amount of each individual's *g*. If this factor runs through all abilities, it furnishes the only basis for prediction of the subject's performance from one situation to another. It would be futile to measure specific factors, since each operates in only one activity. Accordingly, Spearman proposed that a single test, highly "saturated" with *g*, be substituted for the heterogeneous collection of items in intelligence scales. He suggested that tests dealing with abstract relations, such as the analogies test, are probably the best single measures of *g* and could therefore be

employed for this purpose. A current example of a test constructed to measure the g factor is Raven's Progressive Matrices (42).

In regard to the nature of g, Spearman offered only tentative hypotheses.
He proposed that g may be regarded as the general "mental energy" of the
individual and the s factors as the "engines" through which it operates, or
the specific neurone patterns involved in each activity. This interpretation of
g and s is not, however, an integral part of the Two-Factor theory. It might
be noted that Spearman's g would also furnish a basis for the popular notion
of general intelligence.

Even from the outset, Spearman realized that the Two-Factor theory must
be qualified. When the activities compared are very similar, a certain degree
of correlation may result over and above that attributable to the g factor.
Thus in addition to the general and specific factors, there might be another,
intermediate class of factors, not so universal as g or so strictly specific as the
s factors. Such a factor, which is common to a group of activities but not
to all, has been designated as a *group factor*. In the early formulation of his
theory, Spearman admitted the possibility of very narrow and negligibly
small group factors. Following subsequent investigations by several of his
students, he included much broader group factors such as arithmetic,
mechanical, and linguistic abilities.

Finally, on the basis of a series of studies, additional *general* factors were
suggested. These include p (perseveration), o (oscillation), and w (will),
the last extending the theory to the field of personality traits. It was also
proposed by Spearman (46) that, whereas g represents the total amount
of "mental energy" at the subject's disposal, p may denote the inertia of
such mental energy, and o the unsteadiness of its supply. Thus all the proposed general intellectual factors might be but different manifestations of
the same g factor.

In the later writings of Spearman and his followers, the presence of all
three classes of factors—general, group, and specific—is clearly recognized.
The chief differentiating feature of the later form of the Two-Factor theory
thus seems to be its relative emphasis upon the g factor as a more important
influence than group factors in producing correlation. It should also be
noted that the distinction between general, group, and specific factors is
probably not so fundamental as may at first appear. For example, if the
number or variety of tests in a battery is small, a single "general" factor may
account for all the correlations among them. But when the same tests are
included in a larger battery with a more heterogeneous collection of tests,
the original general factor may now appear to be only a group factor, common to some but not all tests. Similarly, a certain factor may have

occurred in only one of the tests in the original small battery, but may be shared by several tests in the larger battery. Such a factor would have been identified as a specific in the original battery, but would become a group factor in the more comprehensive battery. It is probably more realistic to speak of group factors of varying extent, rather than of sharply differentiated general, group, and specific factors.

Multiple-Factor Theories. The most prevalent contemporary American view of trait organization recognizes a number of moderately broad group factors, each of which may enter with different weights into different tests. For example, the verbal factor may enter with a high weight into a vocabulary test, with a smaller weight into an analogies test, and with a very small weight into an arithmetic reasoning test. Such theories have been variously designated as Multiple-Factor or Weighted Group-Factor theories.

The publication in 1928 of Kelley's *Crossroads in the Mind of Man* (32) paved the way for a large number of studies in quest of particular group factors. After a critical analysis of the methodology and data of Spearman, Kelley contended that the general factor is of relatively minor importance and can usually be attributed to the heterogeneity [1] of the subjects and to the common verbal nature of the tests employed. If a general factor should remain when these influences are ruled out, Kelley maintained that it would probably be small and insignificant. The major relationships among tests he attributed to a relatively small number of broad group factors. Chief among these were manipulation of spatial relationships, facility with numbers, facility with verbal material, memory, and mental speed. This list has been modified and extended by subsequent investigators, employing the more recent methods of factor analysis to be considered in the following section.

One of the leading exponents of the Multiple-Factor theory was Thurstone. On the basis of extensive research by himself and his students, Thurstone proposed about a dozen group factors which he designated as "primary mental abilities." Those most frequently corroborated in the work of Thurstone and of other independent investigators (19, 26, 52, 56) include the following:

V: *verbal comprehension*—the principal factor in such tests as reading, verbal analogies, disarranged sentences, verbal reasoning, and proverb matching. It is most adequately measured by vocabulary tests.

W: *word fluency*—found in such tests as anagrams, rhyming, or naming words in a given category (e.g., boys' names or words with the same initial letter).

---

[1] The influence of heterogeneity upon correlation coefficients will be discussed in the following section.

N: *number*—most closely identified with speed and accuracy of simple arithmetic computations.

S: *space*—it is possible that this factor may represent two distinct factors, one covering the perception of fixed spatial or geometric relations, and the other "manipulatory visualization" in which changed positions or transformations must be visualized.

M: *associative memory*—found principally in tests demanding rote memory for paired associates. The evidence is against the presence of a broader factor through all memory tests. Other restricted memory factors, such as visual or auditory memory, have been suggested by some investigations.

P: *perceptual speed*—quick and accurate grasping of visual details, similarities, and differences. This factor may be the same as the "speed factor" identified by earlier investigators and described as "speed in dealing with very easy material." It may also be restricted to visually presented material.

I (or *R*): *induction* (or *general reasoning*)—the identification of this factor is probably least clear. Thurstone originally proposed an inductive and a deductive factor. The latter was best measured by tests of syllogistic reasoning and the former by tests requiring the subject to find a rule, as in a number series completion test. Evidence for the deductive factor, however, was much more tentative than for the inductive. Moreover, other investigators suggest a general reasoning factor, illustrated by such tests as arithmetic reasoning.

The decades of the 1940's and 1950's witnessed a rapid proliferation of group factors. In the above listing of Thurstone's "primary mental abilities," reference was already made to the identification of more than one space factor and of several memory factors. Later intensive analyses have likewise isolated a number of different factors within the areas of perception (54), reasoning (2, 7, 15, 26, 36), and verbal abilities (12, 26, 34, 49). It appears, for example, that to the original word fluency factor may be added associational fluency, ideational fluency, and expressional fluency (26). In a recent survey of factorial research on aptitudes, Guilford (26) describes some forty intellectual factors and points out gaps in his schema where other likely factors may eventually be identified.

The multiplication of factor studies, each with its sizable array of new factors, presents a bewildering picture. It is often difficult to see how the results of various studies fit together. When different research projects vary in type of subjects, nature of tests, and statistical methodology, the cross-identification of factors from one study to another becomes well-nigh impossible. Are two factors that are given the same or similar names by different investigators really identical? And are all the factors bearing dissimilar names really distinguishable? Do some factors represent subdivisions of broader traits?

In the effort to answer such questions and to introduce some order into the situation, French (19, 20) prepared two surveys, one covering intellectual and the other nonintellectual factors.[2] An explicit object of both surveys was the cross-identification and combination of factors isolated by different investigators who had used sufficiently comparable procedures to make such treatment possible. The final lists include 59 factors based on aptitude and achievement tests and 49 derived from personality measures. On the basis of his interpretation of the evidence, French argues that these factors, although varying in comprehensiveness and frequently overlapping, should nevertheless be regarded as distinct. None of them, he believes, represents merely a subdivision of a broader factor, but each brings something new to the total description of the individual. This interpretation is in sharp contrast to the hierarchical view which will be discussed shortly.

It is apparent that even after these efforts at simplification and coordination, the number of factors remains large. Some psychologists, however, find nothing disconcerting in such results (e.g., 26). Human behavior is varied and complex and it is perhaps unrealistic to expect a half a dozen or a dozen factors to provide an adequate description of it. For specific purposes we can, of course, choose appropriate factors with regard to both nature and breadth. For example, if we are selecting applicants for a difficult and highly specialized mechanical job, we would probably want to measure fairly narrow perceptual and spatial factors which closely match the job requirements. In selecting college students, on the other hand, a few broad factors such as verbal comprehension, numerical facility, and general reasoning would be most relevant. Illustrations of the ways in which factorial results have been utilized in test development will be given in the next chapter.

Hierarchical Theories. An alternative schema for the organization of factors has been proposed by a number of British psychologists, notably Burt (11), Vernon (62), and Eysenck (18). A diagram illustrating Vernon's

[2] In a further effort to systematize both procedure and interpretations of factorial research, the Educational Testing Service, with the help of experts on factor analysis, prepared three tests for each of 16 relatively well-established aptitude factors (21). These 48 tests, most of which were adapted from previously published factorial studies, are available for inclusion in new factor studies as standard reference variables.

application of this system to intellectual traits is reproduced in Figure 65. At the top of the hierarchy, Vernon places Spearman's g factor. At the next level are two broad group factors, corresponding to verbal-educational abilities (v:ed) and to practical-mechanical aptitudes (k:m), respectively. These major factors may be further subdivided. The verbal-educational factor, for example, yields verbal and numerical subfactors. Similarly, the practical-mechanical factor splits into mechanical-information, spatial, and manual subfactors. Still narrower subfactors can be identified by further analysis, let us say, of the verbal tasks. At the lowest level of the hierarchy are the specific factors. Such a hierarchical structure thus resembles a

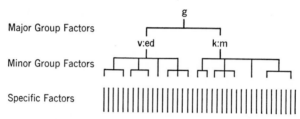

Fig. 65. Diagram Illustrating Hierarchical Theory of Human Abilities. (From Vernon, 62, p. 22.)

genealogical tree, with g at the top, s factors at the bottom, and progressively narrower group factors in between.

The contemporary British approach to the organization of abilities differs from that typical of American psychologists in two principal ways. First, the British schema is essentially multi-level, or hierarchical, while the American factor analysts tend to place all group factors—regardless of breadth—on a single level. Secondly, British psychologists put the prime emphasis on the g factor and try to account for the major part of intertest correlation in terms of g, while American psychologists focus upon group factors and regard g as minor and secondary.

Eysenck (18) has extended the hierarchical arrangement to the description of personality traits. At the top of this hierarchy, which Eysenck calls the "type level," he places three broad factors: introversion, neurosis, and psychosis. Next comes the so-called trait level. Introversion, for example, can be further subdivided into such traits as persistence, rigidity, subjectivity, shyness, and irritability, as illustrated in Figure 66. The next lower level Eysenck terms the "habitual response level." Here he places responses that tend to recur under similar circumstances, as when the same test is repeated. The usual reliability coefficient expresses the sort of behavior consistency measured at this level. The fourth and lowest level is that of specific responses. It should be added that the actual traits identified by Eysenck are based on meager data and must be regarded as tentative until confirmed by further research.

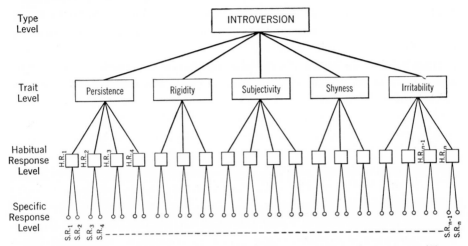

Fig. 66. Diagram Illustrating Hierarchical Theory of Personality Traits. (From Eysenck, 18, p. 13.)

Factors as Operational Unities. That different investigators may arrive at dissimilar schemas of trait organization becomes less perplexing when we recognize that the traits identified through factor analysis are simply an expression of correlation among behavior measures. They are not underlying entities or causal factors, but *descriptive categories*. Hence it is conceivable that different principles of classification may be applicable to the same data.

The concept of factors as descriptive categories is explicit in the writings of Thomson (50, 51), Burt (9, 10), and Vernon (62) in England and those of Tryon (59) in America. Tryon has emphasized the vast multiplicity of behavior components, or determiners. He then argues that correlation between psychological functions results from the overlap among such elementary determiners. As further sources of correlation, he cites possible associations between "environmental fields" or between "gene-blocks." The former would be illustrated by the fact that the individual in an inferior cultural milieu may lack many environmental opportunities for developing *both* linguistic and computational skills. Cultural linkages would thus tend to produce a correlation between these two areas. Correlations between independent gene-blocks could occur through assortative mating. Since individuals tend to marry within their own general socioeconomic and educational level, persons superior in quite different respects are likely to interbreed. Their offspring would thus tend to receive genes for superior develop- ment in a number of initially unrelated characteristics. The same type of selection would operate in the interbreeding of persons of diverse inferiority. Factors identified through correlational studies are thus regarded by Tryon as operational unities among the elementary psychological components, rather than as underlying entities.

Such a view is essentially similar to that represented by Thomson's *Sampling Theory* of trait organization (50, 51). According to this theory, behavior depends upon a very large number of independent elements, which could theoretically correspond to genes, neural elements, stimulus-response bonds, specific experiences, or environmental conditions. Any one activity of the individual, Thomson maintained, depends upon a particular sample or combination of these elements. Correlation results from the overlapping of different samples of elements. Different types of factors may thus be produced, varying from specific, through group factors of differing extent, to a very broad or general factor. Although he originally assumed the sam- pling of elements by different functions to be completely random, Thomson subsequently proposed that the elements are organized into fairly enduring *"subpools of the mind."* These subpools into which the elements are struc- tured or organized would account for the correlations within each area, such as the verbal, numerical, or spatial.

It might be added that other factor analysts have from time to time expressed essential agreement with these interpretations of factors. Thur- stone (53), for instance, suggested that factors are not to be regarded as ultimate psychological entities but rather as "functional unities" or aggre- gates of more elementary components. Such a concept of functional unities appears to resemble quite closely that of Tryon's operational unities and Thomson's subpools of elements. Nevertheless, Thurstone's discussion of factors in other publications and his continued use of the term "primary mental abilities" have tended to foster the impression of factors as under- lying entities.

FACTOR ANALYSIS

The Factor Matrix. The principal object of factor analysis is to simplify the description of data by reducing the number of necessary variables, or "dimensions." Suppose we have administered twenty tests to each of 100 persons. Each individual's performance is thereby described along twenty dimensions, corresponding to the scores on each of the twenty tests. If by factor analysis we find that five factors are sufficient to account for all the common variance covered by these twenty tests, we can substitute these five new dimensions for the original twenty in describing each individual. It should then be possible to construct tests measuring each of these dimensions. The more usual practice is to choose from among the original tests those providing the best measures of each of the final factors. In any event, the number of necessary scores required to cover the behavior domain surveyed by the original test battery would be reduced from twenty to five in the process.

All techniques of factor analysis begin with a complete table of intercorrelations among a set of tests. Such a table is known as a correlation matrix. Every factor analysis ends with a factor matrix, i.e., a table showing the weight or loading of each of the factors in each test. In Table 14 will

Table 14

A FACTOR MATRIX BASED UPON THE INTERCORRELATIONS AMONG THE SCORES OF 437 SCHOOL CHILDREN ON 21 TESTS

(From Thurstone and Thurstone, 56, p. 91)

TESTS	FACTOR LOADINGS							
	P	*N*	*W*	*V*	*S*	*M*	*R*	Residual[*]
1. Identical Numbers	.42	.40	.05	−.02	−.07	−.06	−.06	.08
2. Faces	.45	.17	−.06	.04	.20	.05	.02	−.12
3. Mirror Reading	.36	.09	.19	−.02	.05	−.01	.09	.12
4. First Names	−.02	.09	.02	.00	−.05	.53	.10	.02
5. Figure Recognition	.20	−.10	.02	−.02	.10	.31	.07	−.17
6. Word-Number	.02	.13	−.03	.00	.01	.58	−.04	.04
7. Sentences	.00	.01	−.03	.66	−.08	−.05	.13	.07
8. Vocabulary	−.01	.02	.05	.66	−.04	.02	.02	.05
9. Completion	−.01	.00	−.01	.67	.15	.00	−.01	−.11
10. First Letters	.12	−.03	.63	.03	−.02	.00	−.00	−.08
11. Four-Letter Words	−.02	−.05	.61	−.01	.08	−.01	.04	−.05
12. Suffixes	.04	.03	.45	.18	−.03	.03	−.08	.10
13. Flags	−.04	.05	.03	−.01	.68	.00	.01	−.07
14. Figures	.02	−.06	.01	−.02	.76	−.02	−.02	.07
15. Cards	.07	−.03	−.03	.03	.72	.02	−.03	.13
16. Addition	.01	.64	−.02	.01	.05	.01	−.02	−.03
17. Multiplication	.01	.67	.01	−.03	−.05	.02	.02	.01
18. Three-Higher	−.05	.38	−.01	.06	.20	−.05	.16	−.12
19. Letter Series	−.03	.03	.03	.02	.00	.02	.53	.02
20. Pedigrees	.02	−.05	−.03	.22	−.03	.05	.44	−.02
21. Letter Grouping	.06	.06	.13	−.04	.01	−.06	.42	.06

[*] A residual factor is one that does not have a high enough loading in any variable to permit its psychological identification even on a tentative basis. Usually one or two such residual factors are extracted in the course of a factor analysis, but no attempt is made to interpret them.

be found a factor matrix derived in one of Thurstone's studies from the intercorrelations of 21 tests given to 437 seventh- and eighth-grade school children (56). The seven factors listed across the top of the table correspond to Thurstone's "primary mental abilities," described on pages 325–326, and are indicated by the same letters.

It is clearly beyond the scope of this book to cover the mathematical basis or the computational procedures of factor analysis. A number of different methods for analyzing a set of variables into common factors, or dimensions, have been developed by Kelley (33), Hotelling (30), Burt (9), Holzinger (29), Tryon (60, 61), Thurstone (55), Guttman (27), Wrigley (64), and others. Although differing in their initial postulates, most of these methods yield results that are not too dissimilar. Currently the most widely used techniques are those formulated by Thurstone (55). For brief and relatively simple introductions to such techniques, the student is referred to Guilford (25, Ch. 16) and to Adcock (1). A more detailed treatment of the methodology of factor analysis can be found in Fruchter (22). At a more advanced level, a standard source is Thurstone's *Multiple-Factor Analysis* (55).

An understanding of the results of factor analysis, however, need not be limited to those who have mastered its specialized methodology. Even without knowledge of how the factor loadings are computed, the student will be able to see how a factor matrix is utilized in the interpretation and naming of factors. This step calls for psychological insight rather than statistical training. To learn the nature of a particular factor, we simply examine the tests having high loadings on that factor and we try to discover what psychological processes they have in common. The more tests there are with high loadings on a given factor, the more clearly can we define the nature of the factor.

The process of interpreting factors can be illustrated by reference to Table 14. First we should note that factor loadings are expressed on the same scale as correlation coefficients, i.e., from −1.00 through 0 to +1.00. In fact, factor loadings can be regarded as correlations of each test with a factor (or with what is common to a group of tests). Very low loadings can be ignored since they may represent only chance fluctuations from zero—just as a low correlation may constitute an insignificant deviation from zero. Moreover, even when statistically significant, low factor loadings are of little help in the identification of factors. We cannot readily infer the nature of a factor by scrutinizing a test that has little in common with it.

Accordingly, in interpreting each factor, we consider only those tests whose loadings with that factor exceed some minimum value. In Table 14, all factor loadings of .30 or higher have been italicized. It will be noted that the first factor has loadings over .30 in three tests: Identical Numbers, Faces, and Mirror Reading. These tests require rapid recognition of similarities or differences in simple numerical, pictorial, or verbal material. Hence the factor appears to be the same as the Perceptual Speed (P) factor identified in previous studies. The next factor has its highest loadings in Identical Numbers, Addition, Multiplication, and Three Higher (in which the subject marks every number in a series that exceeds the preceding one by 3). This is obviously a numerical computation factor, although even a test involving the recognition of identical numbers has an appreciable loading on it. By examining the other columns of Table 14 in the same way, we can follow the rationale underlying the naming of the remaining factors as Word Fluency, Verbal Comprehension, Space, Associative Memory, and Reasoning. It is thus apparent that even the statistically unsophisticated reader can study any published table of factor loadings and check the author's interpretation of the factors against his own.

The Reference Axes. For an intelligent reading of reports of factorial research, familiarity with a few other concepts and terms is helpful. It is customary to represent factors geometrically as *reference axes* in terms of which each test can be plotted. Figure 67 illustrates this procedure. In this graph, each of the 21 tests from Table 14 has been plotted against two of

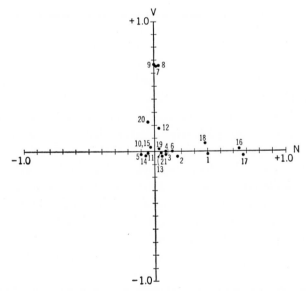

Fig. 67. Factor Loadings of 21 Variables in Table 14 Plotted against Reference Axes *N* (Number Factor) and *V* (Verbal Comprehension).

the factors, namely Number (N) and Verbal Comprehension (V). In similar fashion, the 21 tests can be plotted in terms of every other pair of factors. Each test is represented by a point whose distance along the N and V axes corresponds to the loading of that test with the N and V factors, respectively. To plot Test 1 (Identical Numbers), for example, we move .40 of the way along the N axis and then go down for a distance of $-.02$ along the V axis to locate the point labeled "1." The N and V factor loadings of each of the other tests have been plotted in the same way.

It will be noted that tests 1, 16, 17, and 18 have high loadings on the N axis, while tests 7, 8, and 9 have high loadings on the V axis. All the remaining tests cluster near the zero point, having low or negligible loadings on both of these axes. The high loadings of the latter tests would show up on graphs plotted in terms of other pairs of axes.

An important point to bear in mind is that the position of the reference axes is not fixed by the data. The original correlation table determines only the position of the tests (dots in Figure 67) *in relation to each other*. The same points can be plotted with the reference axes in any position. For this reason, factor analysts usually rotate the axes until they obtain the most satisfactory and easily interpretable pattern. This is a legitimate procedure, somewhat analogous to measuring longitude from, let us say, Chicago rather than Greenwich.

The reference axes used in Table 14 (and Figure 67) have already been rotated in accordance with Thurstone's criteria of "positive manifold" and "simple structure." The former requires the rotation of axes to such a position as to eliminate all significant negative loadings. Most psychologists regard negative loadings as inapplicable to aptitude tests, since such a loading implies that the higher the individual rates in the particular factor, the poorer will be his performance on the test. The criterion of simple structure means that each test shall have loadings on as few factors as possible. Both of these criteria are designed to yield factors that can be most readily and unambiguously interpreted. It will be noted that in Table 14 there are only a few, negligible negative loadings and that most of the tests have appreciable loadings on a single factor only.

Reference axes may be *orthogonal* (at right angles to each other) or *oblique*. When the axes are oblique, it signifies that the factors are correlated with each other. Some factor analysts prefer to work with orthogonal, uncorrelated factors, on the grounds of descriptive simplicity. Others argue that if such criteria as positive manifold and simple structure can be more closely met by oblique axes, the latter should be used. Thurstone (53), for example, has pointed out that there is no reason why psychological factors must be uncorrelated. In measuring physique, height and weight have proved to be useful categories even though they are highly correlated.

When factors are themselves correlated, it is possible to subject the intercorrelations among the factors to the same statistical analyses we employ with intercorrelations among tests. In other words, we can "factorize the factors" and derive *second-order factors*. This process has been followed in a number of studies with both aptitude and personality variables. Certain investigations with aptitude tests have yielded a single, second-order general factor which could be regarded as equivalent to Spearman's *g* (56). In general, American factor analysts have proceeded by accounting for as much of the test intercorrelation as possible through group factors and then identifying *g* as a second-order factor if the data warranted it. British psychologists, on the other hand, usually begin with a *g* factor, to which they attribute the major part of test intercorrelation, and then resort to group factors to account for any remaining correlation. These procedural differences reflect the differences in theoretical emphasis discussed in an earlier section.

Necessary Cautions in the Use of Factor Analysis. Since all techniques of factor analysis begin with intercorrelations, any conditions that affect correlation coefficients will also influence factor loadings. The use of a sufficient *number of persons* to yield stable correlations is of prime importance. Even with 100 cases, a correlation coefficient must be at least .25 to be significantly greater than zero at the .01 level. With smaller groups, correlations may fluctuate so widely from sample to sample as to make any resulting factor loadings quite suspect.

The size of a correlation coefficient is also influenced by the *heterogeneity* of the group. The most obvious example is provided by age heterogeneity. In a group ranging in age from 3 to 15 years, a high positive correlation will be found between even such diverse characteristics as size of great toe and Stanford-Binet mental age, since the older children will tend to have larger toes and higher mental ages. The same two measures would probably yield a zero correlation within a homogeneous age group, such as 10-year-olds. Nor does heterogeneity always raise a correlation. It may lower it, or even produce a negative correlation between variables which are otherwise uncorrelated. Thus if a group composed of Chinese and Scandinavians were rated for height and for proficiency in the use of chopsticks, a fairly high negative correlation would be found between these two measures. The Chinese would, in general, be shorter than the Scandinavians and definitely more adroit in the use of chopsticks. Within either group, however, we should scarcely expect any correlation between the two variables. Groups to be used in factor analyses should be homogeneous in such characteristics as sex, age, racial and national background, socioeconomic level, and the like, unless it can be shown that no significant mean differences exist between subgroups in any of the variables to be correlated.

The tests used in factor analysis should have high *reliability*. Unreliable tests can contribute little to the identification of factors. The different scores that are intercorrelated must also be *experimentally independent*. This means that no two variables in the correlation matrix can be derived from the same set of responses. In such cases, part of the correlation between scores would result from overlap of specific and chance factors in the responses and the resulting factor pattern would thereby be distorted. Examples of experimentally dependent scores include speed and accuracy scores on the same test, scores on such inventories as the Bernreuter or the Strong Vocational Interest Blank in which the same item may be scored on more than one key, and a number of Rorschach indices based on ratios and other combinations of identical responses.

Still another kind of measure unsuited for the usual sort of factor analysis is represented by *ipsative scores*, in which the individual's performance is expressed with reference to his own mean. Scores on the Allport-Vernon-Lindzey Study of Values illustrate this procedure. It is impossible for an individual to obtain high scores on all six parts of this test, or low scores on all six; a high score on one part must be balanced by low scores on other parts. The individual's profile on this test shows his *relative* standing in the six values. If such scores are intercorrelated, some negative correlations will necessarily result simply as an artifact of the scoring system. For the proper application of factor analysis, certain other, more technical conditions must also be met. A discussion of these conditions, together with a more detailed treatment of some of the above points, can be found in McNemar (37) and Guilford (24).

OBVERSE FACTOR ANALYSIS AND OTHER VARIATIONS

In certain applications of factor analysis, an adaptation variously known as "obverse," "inverted," or "transposed" factor analysis has been employed.[3] This technique utilizes correlations in which the usual role of persons and tests has been interchanged. Thus instead of finding the correlation between, let us say, the arithmetic and vocabulary scores of all persons in the group, we compute the correlation between two persons, Smith and Jones, on a

---

[3] Mathematically, the correct term is "transposed," but unfortunately it has not gained wide usage in the psychological literature.

whole series of tests. If such a correlation is high, it means that the pattern of good and poor scores on the various tests is similar for Smith and Jones. In like manner, we can correlate the test scores for every other pair of *persons* in the entire group. These "correlations of persons" can then be factorized by the same methods used with the more familiar "correlations of tests." Obverse factor analysis has been proposed as a means of investigating personality types, since the "group factors for persons" would then represent type factors, or patterns of traits shared by certain individuals. In certain situations, as when an extensive series of measures is available on a relatively small number of persons, obverse factor technique may be desirable. The two approaches should not, however, be regarded as fundamentally different, since substantially the same factors will be found by either procedure (cf. 9).

Cattell (14) presents a composite "co-variation chart" in which he incorporates the correlation of tests and of persons, together with a number of other adaptations. These techniques, which differ only in *what* is correlated, are outlined in Table 15. Each technique is designated by the letter Cattell

Table 15

VARIETIES OF CORRELATIONAL TECHNIQUES AS GIVEN IN CATTELL'S CO-VARIATION CHART

(Adapted from Cattell, 14, p. 109)

(SINGLE OCCASION)	
R—correlation between tests for different persons	Q—correlation between persons for different tests

(SINGLE PERSON)	
P—correlation between tests for different occasions	O—correlation between occasions for different tests

(SINGLE TEST)	
T—correlation between occasions for different persons	S—correlation between persons for different occasions

has associated with it.[4] The two techniques listed in the first row of Table 15, *R* and *Q* techniques, correspond to the previously discussed correlation

---

[4] The use of such letter symbols has become regrettably scrambled in the literature on factorial techniques. In some of the earliest writings on obverse factor analysis, Burt (9) employed the letters *R*, *T*, and *P* with different meanings from those now given them by Cattell. More recently, Cattell (13) and Stephenson (47) have debated their respective rights to the letter *Q*. And Mowrer (38) refers to Cattell's *T* and *S* techniques as the *M* and *N* techniques! Cattell's usage as outlined in Table 15, however, seems to be gaining in general acceptance.

of tests and correlation of persons, respectively. Both utilize scores by different persons on different tests administered on a *single occasion*. The *P* and *O* techniques given in the next row involve a *single person* on whom we have a series of scores or other measures obtained on different occasions. Like *R* and *Q* techniques, *P* and *O* techniques represent the transposes of each other. Dealing with an intensive study of single persons, these techniques are of special interest in clinical psychology (13, 35, 63). Several adaptations of Cattell's *Q* technique have likewise been applied in the clinical area (cf. 16, 38).

The *T* and *S* techniques, found in the last row of Table 15, utilize a *single test* administered on different occasions to different persons, the two techniques again being the transposes of each other. These techniques are useful in research on certain problems in social and in experimental psychology (cf. 38). Another application of *T* technique is illustrated by Hofstaetter's (28) analysis of test scores obtained by the subjects in the Berkeley Growth Study, cited in Chapter 8. By correlating mental ages from birth to maturity and factor analyzing the resulting correlation matrix, Hofstaetter investigated the changing nature of intelligence with age.

Mention should also be made of Stephenson's *Q* technique (48). As far as correlational analysis is concerned, this technique shares certain features with both the *P* and *Q* techniques of Cattell, since correlations may be found between the responses of a single person to a series of stimuli administered under different conditions (as in Cattell's *P* technique) or between the responses of different persons to a series of stimuli administered on a single occasion (as in Cattell's *Q* technique). Stephenson insists, however, that the major difference between his *Q* technique and all other procedures arises from the nature of the basic data utilized in finding the correlations. Briefly, Stephenson presents the subject with a set of trait names, statements, or other kinds of items, with the instructions to sort them into a given number of categories with respect to some criterion, such as how well each trait name describes the subject himself. This process Stephenson calls a "*Q* sort." Other persons can likewise sort the same traits in reference to themselves and the ranks assigned to these traits by different individuals can then be correlated.

A *Q* sort can also be limited to a single individual, the subject being asked to sort the traits in various ways. Thus he may sort them with reference to his own self percept, his percept of an ideal person, the way he believes others perceive him, and so on (cf. 38, 48). This technique has been employed in investigating certain questions in clinical psychology. For example, how closely do the individual's self percept and his ideal percept correlate?

How does this correlation change following therapy or counseling? However obtained, the different Q sorts can be intercorrelated and the correlations can be submitted to a factor analysis by any of the available methods.[5] Stephenson has also proposed other statistical techniques, not involving correlation, which can be used with such data. Thus the common core of his Q technique is to be found, not in its statistical methodology, but in the procedures for gathering the raw data.

SUMMARY

Two persons with the same IQ may have very different aptitude profiles. Data on *intra-individual variability* from trait to trait have been derived from case studies of pronounced asymmetries of talent (of which idiots savants are extreme examples), from measures of the extent of intra-individual variability in large samples, and from correlational studies. The last two approaches provide alternative expressions of the same facts.

Theories of *trait organization* are concerned with the identification of traits, or dimensions, in terms of which the individual's behavior may be most effectively described. The empirical study of trait organization was initiated by Spearman, who first developed a method for analyzing intercorrelations among test scores. On the basis of his research, Spearman proposed a Two-Factor theory, which described intellectual functions in terms of a single g factor and numerous s factors, although narrow group factors were subsequently included.

Among contemporary American psychologists, Multiple-Factor theories are the most prevalent, as illustrated by Thurstone's analysis of intelligence into "primary mental abilities." Recent years have witnessed a proliferation of group factors of varying breadth, as well as some attempts at systematization and coordination of research results. Contemporary British psychologists, such as Burt and Vernon, favor hierarchical theories of trait organization, with the major emphasis on g as a basis for explaining correlation. Broad group factors are recognized, which in turn can be subdivided into narrower group factors, and so on down to specifics. A similar hierarchical pattern has been proposed by Eysenck for personality traits. A number of psychologists have stressed the concept of factors as operational unities rather than underlying entities.

The principal object of *factor analysis* is to simplify the description of

---

[5] Q sorts yield ipsative scores. But as long as correlations are found between persons (or occasions), rather than between traits, no artificial restriction is imposed on the correlations.

data by reducing the number of variables or dimensions. Following computation of the factor matrix and rotation of reference axes, the identification of factors is accomplished by examination of the variables having the highest loadings on each factor. Factors may be orthogonal or oblique. In the latter case, it is possible to compute second-order factors. Proper application of factor analysis requires the observance of certain necessary cautions with reference to number and heterogeneity of subjects, reliability and experimental independence of variables, use of appropriate scores, and other conditions.

For certain purposes, *obverse* (transposed, inverted) *factor analysis* may be employed, in which correlations between persons (Q technique) are substituted for the usual correlations between tests (R technique). Other variations include P, O, T, and S techniques, as well as Stephenson's Q technique. All of these variations differ in *what* is correlated, rather than in the procedures of factor analysis.

REFERENCES

1. Adcock, C. J. *Factorial analysis for non-mathematicians*. Carlton, N. 3, Victoria: Melbourne Univer. Press; N.Y.: Cambridge Univer. Press, 1954.
2. Adkins, Dorothy C., and Lyerly, S. B. *Factor analysis of reasoning tests*. Chapel Hill: Univer. N. Carolina Press, 1952.
3. Allport, G. W., and Odbert, H. S. Trait-names, a psycholexical study. *Psychol. Monogr.*, 1936, 47, No. 1.
4. Anastasi, Anne. The nature of psychological 'traits.' *Psychol. Rev.*, 1948, 55, 127–138.
5. Anastasi, Anne. *Psychological testing*. N.Y.: Macmillan, 1954.
6. Barlow, F. *Mental prodigies*. N.Y.: Philosophical Library, 1952.
7. Botzum, W. A. A factorial study of the reasoning and closure factors. *Psychometrika*, 1951, 16, 361–386.
8. Bryan, W. L., Lindley, E. H., and Harter, N. *On the psychology of learning a life occupation*. Bloomington: Indiana Univer., 1941.
9. Burt, C. *The factors of the mind: an introduction to factor-analysis in psychology*. N.Y.: Macmillan, 1941.
10. Burt, C. Mental abilities and mental factors. *Brit. J. educ. Psychol.*, 1944, 14, 85–89.
11. Burt, C. The structure of the mind; a review of the results of factor analysis. *Brit. J. Psychol.*, 1949, 19, 176–199.
12. Carroll, J. B. A factor analysis of verbal abilities. *Psychometrika*, 1941, 6, 279–308.
13. Cattell, R. B. On the disuse and misuse of P, Q, Qs and O techniques in clinical psychology. *J. clin. Psychol.*, 1951, 7, 203–214.
14. Cattell, R. B. *Factor analysis*. N.Y.: Harper, 1952.
15. Corter, H. M. Factor analysis of some reasoning tests. *Psychol. Monogr.*, 1952, 66, No. 8.

16. Cronbach, L. J. Correlation between persons as a research tool. In O. H. Mowrer (Ed.), *Psychotherapy*. N.Y.: Ronald, 1953. Pp. 376–388.
17. DeVoss, J. C. Specialization of the abilities of gifted children. In L. M. Terman (Ed.), *Genetic studies of genius*. Stanford Univer., Calif.: Stanford Univer. Press, 1925. Vol. I, Ch. 12.
18. Eysenck, H. J. *The structure of human personality*. London: Methuen, 1953.
19. French, J. W. The description of aptitude and achievement tests in terms of rotated factors. *Psychometr. Monogr.*, 1951, No. 5.
20. French, J. W. *The description of personality measurements in terms of rotated factors*. Princeton, N.J.: Educ. Testing Service, 1953.
21. French, J. W. *Manual for kit of selected tests for reference aptitude and achievement factors*. Princeton, N.J.: Educ. Testing Service, 1954.
22. Fruchter, B. *Introduction to factor analysis*. N.Y.: Van Nostrand, 1954.
23. Ghiselli, E. E. Essential conditions in the determination of the extent of trait variability. *J. appl. Psychol.*, 1939, 23, 436–439.
24. Guilford, J. P. When not to factor analyze. *Psychol. Bull.*, 1952, 49, 26–37.
25. Guilford, J. P. *Psychometric methods*. (Rev. Ed.) N.Y.: McGraw-Hill, 1954.
26. Guilford, J. P. The structure of intellect. *Psychol. Bull.*, 1956, 53, 267–293.
27. Guttman, L. A new approach to factor analysis: radex. In P. F. Lazarsfeld (Ed.), *Mathematical thinking in the social sciences*. Glencoe, Ill.: Free Press, 1954. Pp. 258–348.
28. Hofstaetter, P. R. The changing composition of "intelligence": a study in T technique. *J. genet. Psychol.*, 1954, 85, 159–164.
29. Holzinger, K. J., and Harman, H. H. *Factor analysis: a synthesis of factorial methods*. Chicago: Univer. Chicago Press, 1941.
30. Hotelling, H. Analysis of a complex of statistical variables into principal components. *J. educ. Psychol.*, 1933, 24, 417–441, 498–520.
31. Hull, C. L. Variability in amount of different traits possessed by the individual. *J. educ. Psychol.*, 1927, 18, 97–104.
32. Kelley, T. L. *Crossroads in the mind of man: a study of differentiable mental abilities*. Stanford Univer., Calif.: Stanford Univer. Press, 1928.
33. Kelley, T. L. *Essential traits of mental life*. Cambridge: Harvard Univer. Press, 1935.
34. Knoell, D. M., and Harris, C. W. A factor analysis of word fluency. *J. educ. Psychol.*, 1952, 43, 131–148.
35. Luborsky, L. Intra-individual repetitive measurements (P technique) in understanding psychotherapeutic change. In O. H. Mowrer (Ed.), *Psychotherapy*. N.Y.: Ronald, 1953. Pp. 389–413.
36. Matin, L., and Adkins, Dorothy C. A second-order factor analysis of reasoning abilities. *Psychometrika*, 1954, 19, 71–78.
37. McNemar, Q. The factors in factoring behavior. *Psychometrika*, 1951, 16, 353–359.
38. Mowrer, O. H. "Q technique"—description, history, and critique. In O. H. Mowrer (Ed.), *Psychotherapy*. N.Y.: Ronald, 1953. Pp. 316–375.
39. Piéron, H. L'hétérogénéité normale des aptitudes. *Année psychol.*, 1940–41, 41–42, 1–13.
40. Preston, M. G. Concerning the determination of trait variability. *Psychometrika*, 1940, 5, 275–281.

41. Preston, M. G. Trait variability as a function of practice and of age. *J. gen. Psychol.*, 1947, 37, 3–14.

42. Raven, J. C. *Guide to using Progressive Matrices (1938)*. London: Lewis, 1952.

43. Rife, D. C., and Snyder, L. H. Studies in human inheritance. *Hum. Biol.*, 1931, 3, 547–559.

44. Scheerer, M., Rothmann, Eva, and Goldstein, K. A case of "idiot savant": an experimental study of personality organization. *Psychol. Monogr.*, 1945, 58, No. 4.

45. Spearman, C. "General intelligence" objectively determined and measured. *Amer. J. Psychol.*, 1904, 15, 201–293.

46. Spearman, C. *The abilities of man.* N.Y.: Macmillan, 1927.

47. Stephenson, W. A note on Professor R. B. Cattell's methodological adumbrations. *J. clin. Psychol.*, 1952, 8, 206–207.

48. Stephenson, W. *The study of behavior: Q-technique and its methodology.* Chicago: Univer. Chicago Press, 1953.

49. Taylor, C. W. A factorial study of fluency in writing. *Psychometrika*, 1947, 12, 239–262.

50. Thomson, G. H. A hierarchy without a general factor. *Brit. J. Psychol.*, 1916, 8, 271–281.

51. Thomson, G. H. *The factorial analysis of human ability.* (3rd Ed.) Boston: Houghton Mifflin, 1948.

52. Thurstone, L. L. Primary mental abilities. *Psychometr. Monogr.*, 1938, No. 1.

53. Thurstone, L. L. Current issues in factor analysis. *Psychol. Bull.*, 1940, 37, 189–236.

54. Thurstone, L. L. A factorial study of perception. *Psychometr. Monogr.*, 1944, No. 4.

55. Thurstone, L. L. *Multiple-factor analysis.* Chicago: Univer. Chicago Press, 1947.

56. Thurstone, L. L., and Thurstone, Thelma G. Factorial studies of intelligence. *Psychometr. Monogr.*, 1941, No. 2.

57. Tilton, J. W. The relation between IQ and trait differences as measured by group intelligence tests. *J. educ. Psychol.*, 1947, 38, 343–352.

58. Tredgold, R. F., and Soddy, K. *A textbook of mental deficiency.* (9th Ed.) Baltimore: Williams & Wilkins, 1956.

59. Tryon, R. C. A theory of *psychological components*—an alternative to "mathematical factors." *Psychol. Rev.*, 1935, 42, 425–454.

60. Tryon, R. C. *Cluster analysis.* Ann Arbor, Mich.: Edwards, 1939.

61. Tryon, R. C. General dimensions of individual differences: cluster analysis vs. multiple factor analysis. *Educ. psychol. Measmt.*, 1958, 18, 477–495.

62. Vernon, P. E. *The structure of human abilities.* London: Methuen, 1950.

63. Williams, Henrietta V. A. determination of psychosomatic functional unities in personality by means of P-technique. *J. soc. Psychol.*, 1954, 39, 25–45.

64. Wrigley, C. The need for objectivity in factor analysis. *Educ. psychol. Measmt.*, 1958, 18. (In press)

CHAPTER 11

Trait Organization: Major Results

As a research tool, factor analysis is applicable to a wide variety of problems. It has already been utilized in nearly all branches of psychology. Most studies have employed the traditional R technique, but ingenious new applications of P technique, Q technique, and other variants described in the preceding chapter are appearing with increasing frequency. No attempt will be made to survey these miscellaneous factorial studies. References to typical investigations in a few areas can be found in Fruchter (41, Ch. 10), although no comprehensive survey has been published to date. It will be of interest, nevertheless, to take a quick look at the range of problems which have been attacked by such procedures.

Factorial techniques have been used in the classification of emotions and of color sensations; in the evaluation of available tests of visual acuity; and in the identification of common factors in motor skills and in athletic ability. A number of factorial investigations have been concerned with the analysis of body build and with theories of constitutional typology, as discussed in Chapter 6. Traditional psychiatric classifications of psychoses and neuroses have been re-examined and revamped in the light of factorial analyses of symptoms or of patients' test responses. Culture patterns and social change have been explored through factor analyses of the characteristics of nations, states, cities, and neighborhoods. Research on the nature of prejudices and on national stereotypes has likewise made use of factor methods. In business and industrial psychology, we find applications to such problems as advertising readership, job classification, and job evaluation. Nor is the potential usefulness of factor analysis limited to psychology. Although its applications to other fields are still few, they range from an analysis of women's measurements for garment and pattern construction to a study of the voting records of Supreme Court justices!

It is apparent that factor analysis provides a versatile investigative technique. Nevertheless, its chief applications have been in the identification of aptitudes and personality traits and in the development of tests for their measurement. In the sections that follow, we shall consider important developments in test construction and in personality theory which reflect the influence of recent factorial research.

MULTIPLE APTITUDE BATTERIES

In the measurement of abilities, the effect of factor analysis is clearly discernible in the development and increasing use of multiple aptitude batteries (cf. 6, Ch. 14). Rather than yielding a single global measure, such as

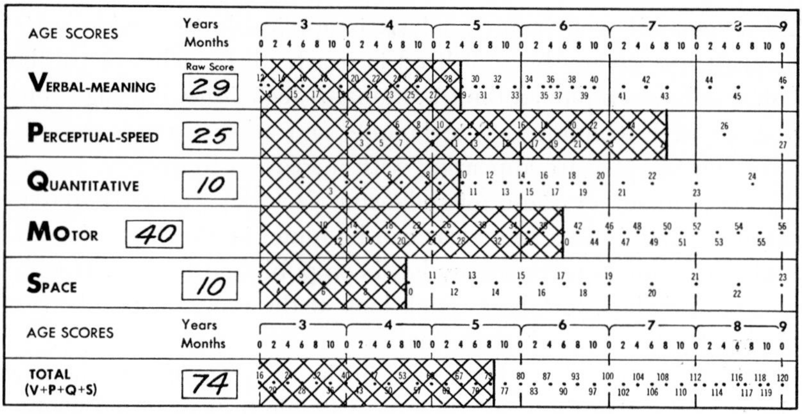

Fig. 68. Profile of a 5-Year-Old Child on the Thurstone Tests of Primary Mental Abilities. (Data from Avakian, 10.)

an IQ, these batteries provide a profile of scores on separate tests, most of which correspond more or less closely to traits identified through factor analysis. The Thurstone tests of Primary Mental Abilities (PMA) represent the first test battery for general use to be constructed as a direct outcome of factorial research. These tests are currently available in three levels, designed for ages 5 to 7, 7 to 11, and 11 to 17, respectively (99).

A profile of scores obtained by a 5-year-old child on the 5-to-7-year form of these tests is reproduced in Figure 68. Mental age scores are reported in verbal-meaning, perceptual-speed, quantitative, motor, and space factors. It is also possible to compute a composite mental age and IQ based on all but the motor tests. Such an IQ corresponds roughly to that obtained on the traditional "intelligence tests." The PMA tests for ages 7 to 11 yield scores in verbal-meaning, number, space, reasoning, and perceptual-speed factors; the form for ages 11 to 17 includes verbal-meaning, word-fluency, number, space, and reasoning factors. It will be noted that the factors measured by the PMA tests are those identified in Thurstone's initial research on multiple aptitude factors, cited in the preceding chapter.

Following the general pattern established by Thurstone, test constructors have been developing multiple-factor batteries for many purposes. Examples include the classification batteries employed by the U.S. Air Force for selecting pilots, navigators, and other aircrew personnel (104). Later an Airman Classification Battery (105) was prepared for testing other air force personnel. In addition to some of the previously established broad factors, these batteries cover a number of relatively specialized factors which were identified in factorial analyses of air force samples. Such factors have particular relevance to the performance of air force jobs. Similar batteries were eventually developed for use in each of the other branches of the U.S. armed services.

Another illustration of multifactor testing is provided by the General Aptitude Test Battery of the U.S. Employment Service (34). Developed for the use of employment counselors in state employment offices, this battery includes tests for verbal, numerical, and spatial abilities, form perception, clerical perception, aiming, motor speed, finger dexterity, and manual dexterity. A "general intelligence" score is also derived from the combined scores on a verbal, a numerical, and a spatial test.

A number of other multiple-factor batteries are available for general use, especially at the high school and college level. Among them may be mentioned the Guilford-Zimmerman Aptitude Survey (53), the Holzinger-Crowder Uni-Factor Tests (58), the Multiple Aptitude Tests (80), the Flanagan Aptitude Classification Tests (39), and the Differential Aptitude Tests (12). The profile of a high school student on the last-named tests is reproduced in Figure 69. Performance on the eight parts of the battery is reported in terms of percentile ranks, the corresponding standard scores also being shown. The type of profile graph employed is known as a *normal percentile chart* (65). In such a chart, distances above and below the median, or 50th percentile, correspond to equal ability units in a normally distributed group. Thus the difference between the 80th and 90th percentiles, for example, is much greater than that between the 50th and 60th, since in a normal curve people cluster more closely in the center and scatter over a wider range as the extremes are approached.

Profiles of test scores on multiple aptitude batteries, such as that reproduced in Figure 69, are finding one of their principal uses in educational and vocational counseling of young people. The student whose profile is given in Figure 69, for example, had planned to enter an engineering school. On a standard intelligence test, his IQ was 115. His mediocre performance on the space test and his poor showing in mechanical comprehension, however, raised doubts about his qualifications for engineering. On the basis of

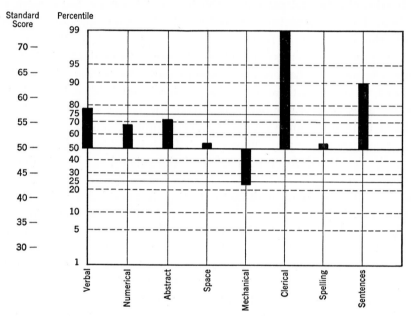

Fig. 69. Profile of a High School Boy on the Differential Aptitude Tests. (From Bennett, Seashore, and Wesman, 12, E8.)

his other scores on the battery and his academic record, the student was advised to enroll in a general college course and to postpone decision regarding a field of specialization.

THE PROFILE APPROACH TO PERSONALITY DESCRIPTION

Factor analysis has also made inroads upon the nonintellectual aspects of personality, especially in the measurement of emotional and social traits (cf. 6, Ch. 20). A number of current personality inventories which yield a profile of trait scores were developed through factorial techniques. One approach is illustrated by the research of Guilford and his co-workers, in which thirteen factors were identified in the personality inventory responses of college students. In this series of studies, as in several others with personality tests, intercorrelations were computed among individual items, rather than among subtests. Such a procedure reflects in part the paucity of definitive knowledge regarding personality organization. The task of statistical analysis would be simpler—and the resulting correlations more stable—if we could group "obviously similar" items into subtests and intercorrelate the scores on such subtests. But it would be difficult to decide in advance just which items to put together. Nothing as clear-cut as the grouping of vocabulary items in one subtest and arithmetic reasoning items in another suggests itself in this area.

The ten most clearly established factors from the Guilford studies were finally incorporated into a single inventory, the Guilford-Zimmerman Temperament Survey (54). This inventory yields separate scores for the following traits, each score being based on 30 items:

G: *General activity*—hurrying, liking for speed, liveliness, vitality, production efficiency vs. slow and deliberate, easily fatigued, inefficient.

R: *Restraint*—serious-minded, deliberate, persistent vs. carefree, impulsive, excitement-loving.

A: *Ascendance*—self-defense, leadership, speaking in public, bluffing vs. submissiveness, hesitation, avoiding conspicuousness.

S: *Sociability*—having many friends, seeking social contacts and limelight vs. few friends and shyness.

E: *Emotional stability*—evenness of moods, optimistic, composure vs. fluctuation of moods, pessimism, daydreaming, excitability, feelings of guilt, worry, loneliness, and ill health.

O: *Objectivity*—thick-skinned vs. hypersensitive, self-centered, suspicious, having ideas of reference, getting into trouble.

F: *Friendliness*—toleration of hostile action, acceptance of domination, respect for others vs. belligerence, hostility, resentment, desire to dominate, and contempt for others.

T: *Thoughtfulness*—reflective, observing of self and others, mental poise vs. interest in overt activity and mental disconcertedness.

P: *Personal relations*—tolerance of people, faith in social institutions vs. fault-finding, critical of institutions, suspicious, self-pitying.

M: *Masculinity*—interest in masculine activities and other emotional responses characteristic of men vs. interest in feminine activities and other emotional responses typical of women.

A reanalysis of Guilford's original data led Thurstone (94) to the conclusion that seven major factors sufficed to account for the obtained intercorrelations. Thurstone thereupon constructed another inventory to measure these seven traits, which he identified as follows: Active, Vigorous, Impulsive, Dominant, Stable, Sociable, and Reflective (93). The inventory, known as the Thurstone Temperament Schedule, contains 20 items for each of the traits.

A somewhat different approach is to be found in the work of Cattell (16). In the effort to arrive at a comprehensive description of personality, Cattell began by assembling all personality trait names occurring in the dictionary (as compiled by Allport and Odbert, 3) and supplemented this list with terms from the psychiatric and psychological literature. By combining synonyms, this list was first reduced to 171 traits. The next step was to obtain ratings for each of these 171 characteristics on 100 subjects of both sexes, all over 25, and varying in occupation from unskilled laborers to artists and business and professional people. Each subject was rated by one person who knew him well, the rating scale containing only two categories for each trait, namely, above average and below average. By correlating these ratings and grouping together all traits that correlated over .45 with each other, 67 clusters were obtained. Through further combination of these clusters, the number was reduced to 35.

Ratings on 208 men by two independent raters were then obtained for these 35 traits. The men averaged 30 years of age and varied widely in occupation. A factor analysis of the intercorrelations of these 35 traits, followed by oblique rotation of axes, led to a further reduction of the number of traits to 12. The latter Cattell designated as "the primary source traits of personality." In later investigations, Cattell and his associates have sought confirmation of these traits in factorial analyses of ratings obtained on college men (17) and on college women (18), as well as in similar analyses of inventory responses and objective tests of personality (20, 21, 23). Cattell has experimented with many objective measures, such as perceptual tests, speed of various types of responses, and physiological indices. Results obtained with *P* technique have likewise been scrutinized to discover whether any of the previously identified factors emerge from intercorrelations among measures of single individuals on different occasions (19).

Although a few factors tend to recur in these various studies, some of the correspondences noted by Cattell appear unconvincing. There is least agreement between the factors derived from objective tests and those based on the analysis of ratings or questionnaire responses. It will be recalled that an element of subjectivity is likely to enter into the identification of factors, since the process depends upon an examination of those measures or items which have the highest loadings on each factor. Hence the cross-identification of factors from investigations using different measures is difficult. All in all, despite the extensive research by Cattell, the traits that he proposes must still be regarded as tentative.

In his most recent summary of relevant research findings, Cattell (21) lists 15 traits found in factorial analysis of ratings, or "life data." These include the original 12 primary source traits (some of which have been renamed) plus three factors identified subsequently. The 15 traits, with their latest descriptions, are given below:

A. Cyclothymia vs. schizothymia
B. Intelligence (defined with emphasis on emotional and motivational aspects, such as perseverance and thoughtfulness)
C. Ego strength vs. proneness to neuroticism
D. Excitability-insecurity
E. Dominance-submissiveness
F. Surgency (i.e., cheerful optimism) vs. desurgency
G. Super-ego strength
H. Parmia [1] (parasympathetic immunity) vs. threctia (threat reactivity)
I. Premsia (protected emotional sensitivity) vs. harria (hard realism)
J. Coasthenia (cultural pressure conflict asthenia, or thinking neurasthenia) vs. zeppia (zestful cooperativeness)
K. Comention (conformity or cultural amenability through good parent self-identification) vs. abcultion (abhorring and rejecting cultural identification)
L. Protension (projection and tension, or paranoid trend) vs. inner relaxation
M. Autia (autonomous, self-absorbed relaxation) vs. praxernia (practical concern, narrowness of interests, incapacity to dissociate feelings of inadequacy)
N. Shrewdness vs. naïveté
O. Guilt-proneness vs. confidence

In addition, Cattell cites the following 8 factors as having emerged only in the analysis of questionnaire responses:

Q_1. Radicalism vs. conservatism
Q_2. Self-sufficiency
Q_3. Self sentiment control
Q_4. Ergic tension (id demand or conflict pressure)
Q_5. Fantasy tendency

---

[1] This and most of the following trait names represent condensations of the trait descriptions given in parentheses.

Q_6. Psychotic tendency (psychoticism)

Q_7. Self-consciousness in public

Q_8. Alert extravert interests

On the basis of their factorial results, Cattell and his associates have prepared two personality inventories. The Sixteen Personality Factor Questionnaire (24), designed for adults, covers the original 12 source traits, together with four factors identified only in factorial analyses of questionnaires. A similar, 12-factor inventory suitable for children between the ages of 10 and 16 years is known as the Junior Personality Quiz (22). Owing to the small number of items used to measure individual factors, the reliability of some of the factor scores is quite low in both inventories, but especially in the children's form. Both instruments clearly require further standardization and validation prior to general use.

Factorial analyses of *interests* and *attitudes* have as yet had little effect on test construction (cf. 6, Ch. 22; 35, Ch. 7). The two most widely used interest tests, the Strong Vocational Interest Blank and the Kuder Preference Record, were not developed by factorial techniques, although their scores have subsequently been subjected to factor analysis. One of the most extensive factorial investigations of interests is that of Guilford *et al.* (50). Based upon the intercorrelations of 95 ten-item interest tests, this study covered an unusually wide range of human interests. The number of subjects was large, including 600 airmen and 720 officer candidates, for whom two separate correlation matrices were computed and analyzed. Of the 24 factors identified for airmen and 23 for officers, 17 were common to both groups. These common factors are given below:

A. Mechanical Interest	J. Need for Diversion
B. Scientific Interest	K. Autistic Thinking
C. Adventure vs. Security	L. Need for Attention
D. Social Welfare	M. Resistance to Restriction
E. Esthetic Appreciation	N. Business Interest
F. Cultural Conformity	O. Outdoor Work Interest
G. Self-reliance vs. Dependence	P. Physical Drive
H. Esthetic Expression	Q. Aggression
I. Clerical Interest	

Several of these factors suggest the role of culture in structuring interest patterns. A number follow traditional occupational categories characteristic of our culture, as illustrated by mechanical, scientific, social-welfare, clerical, and business interests. To a lesser extent this is also true of esthetic appreciation, esthetic expression, and outdoor work interests. Within all such areas, interests may be correlated because they have been learned together.

Other research on interests indicates that, although corresponding scores from different tests of interests and values often correlate highly (30; 35, Ch. 7), there is little correlation between interests and other personality factors (30). Nevertheless, within specific settings, certain interests may be associated with superior or inferior adjustment. For example, in a study with the Kuder Preference Record, neurotic war veterans obtained significantly lower scores than the controls on the mechanical scale and significantly higher scores on the musical and literary scales (84). It appears likely that maladjustments arising in a military situation might be associated with such an interest pattern.

Cattell's recent book (21) extends the description of personality to include what he terms "ergic drive structures" and "sentiment structures." The former, which he presumes to have an innate organic basis, may be illustrated by such drives as sex, gregariousness, parental protectiveness, exploration, escape, and self-assertion. The latter, regarded by Cattell as traits molded by experiential conditions, correspond closely to what others have investigated under the heading of interests. As examples may be mentioned interests related to one's profession, mechanical or material interest, and interest in sports and games.

Psychological studies on *attitudes* have usually been concerned with verbally expressed opinions on social, economic, or political questions. Factor analyses by Ferguson (37) of total scores on ten of the Thurstone attitude scales led to the identification of three factors, which were named Religionism, Humanitarianism, and Nationalism. The first of these factors had its highest loadings (either positive or negative) on the scales for measuring attitude toward God, evolution, and birth control; the second, on those covering attitude toward war, treatment of criminals, and capital punishment; the third, on those dealing with attitude toward patriotism, censorship, law, and communism.

Through factorial analyses of individual items on an attitude questionnaire, Eysenck (35, Ch. 7) isolated two broad attitude factors, which he characterized as Radicalism vs. Conservatism (R) and Tender-mindedness vs. Tough-mindedness (T). To obtain independent corroboration of this classification of attitude items, Eysenck compared the responses of certain criterion groups, representing different political viewpoints or economic levels, to the same items. The results were considered to be consistent with expectation. Thus socialists more frequently endorsed items with a high R loading, while conservatives more often chose items with low R saturations. With regard to the *T* dimension, Eysenck concluded that working-class persons tend to be more tough-minded than middle-class persons, and that both Communists and Fascists tend to fall at the tough-minded end of the scale. Thus Communists are described as radical and tough-minded, Fascists as conservative and tough-minded. Eysenck reports that his findings with British samples have been confirmed in similar surveys on American, Swedish, German, and French samples.

Critical evaluations of Eysenck's publications suggest that his data fail to support many of his conclusions, especially with regard to the Tender-mindedness dimension (26, 72). The major difficulties arise from lack of comparability of samples, peculiarities of the attitude questionnaire and scoring system employed, and questionable statistical analyses. It appears, moreover, that Ferguson's Religionism and Humanitarianism dimensions fit Eysenck's own data better than the two factors he proposes. Although Eysenck's factors have the advantage of corresponding more closely to familiar attitude classifications, it would seem that their acceptance must await further verification.

RESEARCH ON CREATIVITY

A special area of currently active trait research centers around the analysis of creativity. Interest in this problem has been stimulated in part by the practical demands for the identification and maximum utilization of high-level talent in science and engineering. In a general discussion of the question, Thurstone (91, 96) emphasized the fact that creative talent is not synonymous with superior academic intelligence. The possible relation of creative activity to ideational fluency, inductive reasoning, and certain perceptual tendencies was also pointed out by Thurstone. Special attention was given to the nonintellectual, temperamental factors which may be conducive to creativity. Examples include a receptive—as contrasted to a critical—attitude toward novel ideas, as well as relaxed, dispersed attention rather than active concentration on the problem. Thurstone further suggested that research on creativity might profitably be concerned with the nature of the thinking that precedes the moment of insight.

Several studies have approached the problem of creativity through factorial analyses of batteries of tests designed to measure various aspects of creative talent. The most extensive project of this type is one conducted by Guilford and his associates under the auspices of the Office of Naval Research (47, 49, 52, 57, 116). Concerned principally with the aptitudes of high-level personnel, this project set out to explore four areas of thinking, designated as reasoning, creativity, planning, and evaluation. Many new types of tests were developed in the course of the study and were administered, together with tests of the more usual varieties, to groups of air cadets and student officers. Some familiar factors reappeared, including verbal comprehension, numerical facility, spatial visualization, perceptual speed, general reasoning (with heavy loading on arithmetic reasoning tests), and several memory factors. Among the most provocative new factors may be mentioned sensitivity to problems, conceptual foresight, originality, several fluency factors, several flexibility factors, and a number of factors involving the eduction of relations in different types of content.

A number of other similar investigations have been reported in recent years (1, 14, 29, 63). Some correspondences can be discerned between the factors isolated through these different analyses, although the agreement is far from complete (51, 62). The ultimate contribution of such studies, however, can be evaluated only when tests highly loaded with each factor have been constructed and their effectiveness in predicting life achievement has been determined. So far, relatively little progress has been made in relating any of the factors identified in creativity research with external criteria of creative accomplishment.

PERCEPTION AND PERSONALITY

Another large body of contemporary research is concerned with the exploration of new approaches to the organization of personality. It may be noted in this connection that the traditional dichotomy between intellectual and nonintellectual factors seems to be gradually breaking down. This trend is apparent both in the growing number of studies that cut across the two areas and in the nature of some of the new testing techniques. Several large-scale projects on the measurement of basic personality traits have been directed toward the development of objective tests of relatively simple functions, such as sensory, motor, perceptual, learning, and associational activities (cf. 6, pp. 649–658). As examples of this approach may be cited the work of Thurstone (95, 97), MacKinnon (61), Cattell (20), and Eysenck (35).

One type of function which has come to occupy a pre-eminent place in discussions of personality organization is perception. Interest in perceptual functions as a possible approach to the understanding of personality differences antedates research with objective tests and factor analysis. Many projective techniques, such as the Rorschach Inkblot test, are based on an assumed relation between the individual's perceptual responses to relatively

simple stimuli and certain broad personality traits. Projective tests have been
handicapped, however, by inadequate standardization and by the relatively
subjective nature of the scoring and evaluation of responses (cf. 6, Ch. 22).
The latter shortcoming has led some psychologists to suggest that such tests
represent projective instruments for the examiner (and scorer) as much as
for the subject. Some of the current research on more objectively scorable
perceptual tests constitutes an effort to utilize, under better-controlled conditions, certain hypotheses underlying projective techniques.

Also relevant are the various theories of "perceptual types" formulated by
European psychologists, many of which provide the basis for current interpretations of projective test responses.[2] Such theories maintain that individuals exhibit relatively consistent, characteristic modes of perceiving,
which are often related to major personality differences. Among the proposed
perceptual types may be mentioned "form vs. color dominance," as illustrated
by the tendency to perceive and recall forms or colors more readily in
rapidly exposed colored shapes. Another distinction is that between "syn-
thetic" and "analytic" perceivers. When presented with complex visual
material, does the subject tend to perceive an integrated whole with little
detail, or does he concentrate on precise perception of isolated or unrelated
detail?

Several factorial investigations of perception have appeared in recent
years, beginning with Thurstone's (90) factor analysis of about forty perceptual tests in 1944. A by-product of this study was its demonstration that
many familiar perceptual tasks yield wide individual differences in speed and
in other aspects of response. Using 194 university students as subjects, Thurstone identified seven major perceptual factors. Of these, two have proved
most fruitful in subsequent research, especially in relation to personality
variables. Both are concerned with *closure*, or the perception of complete
figures under various stimulus conditions (90, 92). The first closure factor
(Speed of Closure) involves the recognition of a familiar word, object, or
other figure in a relatively unorganized or mutilated visual field. Typical
items from a test highly saturated with this factor (Street Gestalt Completion test) are reproduced in Figure 70. The four pictures represent a dog,
a buggy, a stove, and a horse and rider, respectively.

The second closure factor (Flexibility of Closure) requires the identification of a figure amid distracting and confusing detail in the visual field. Two
items from a test with high loading in this factor (Gottschaldt Figures test)
are given in Figure 71. In each row, the design at the left can be found
concealed or embedded in some of the four drawings at the right. In the

[2] A summary of such theories may be found in Vernon (111, pp. 247–256).

first row, the correct response includes the last two drawings; in the second row, it includes the first and third drawings. It is interesting to note that individuals who do well in tasks calling for the first closure factor do not necessarily excel on those involving the second. Thurstone reports some suggestive data indicating possible relationships of these two factors to personality traits.

Fig. 70. Test Items Illustrating Thurstone's First Closure Factor (Speed of Closure): What does each picture represent? (From Thurstone, 92, p. 7.)

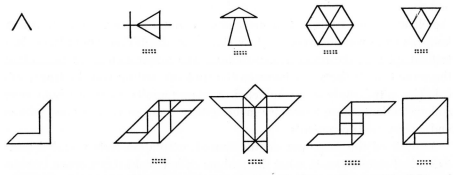

Fig. 71. Test Items Illustrating Thurstone's Second Closure Factor (Flexibility of Closure): Which of the four drawings at the right contain the design at the left? (From Thurstone, 92, p. 7.)

Other recent factorial analyses of perceptual tasks have confirmed some of Thurstone's factors, besides identifying several new factors (42, 71). Of special interest are two studies by Pemberton (66, 67) which provided evidence of a relationship between Thurstone's two closure factors and both cognitive and temperamental characteristics. The second closure factor, flexibility of closure, appeared to be related to reasoning ability, a finding also reported in other investigations on reasoning (14, 49, 66).

Using a number of personality inventories and self-ratings, Pemberton

(67) also demonstrated certain temperamental differences between persons scoring high on the first closure factor and those scoring high on the second. The subjects who excelled on the first factor, speed of closure, tended to rate themselves as sociable, quick in reactions, artistic, self-confident, systematic, neat and precise, and disliking logical and theoretical problems. In contrast, those scoring high on the second factor, flexibility of closure, had high self-ratings on such traits as socially retiring, independent of the good opinions of others, analytical, interested in theoretical and scientific problems, and disliking rigid systematization and routine.

One of the most ambitious projects on perception and personality is the ten-year study of perceptual space orientation conducted by Witkin and his associates (117). Although not utilizing factorial techniques, this study is relevant to the present topic. The principal data were derived from three tests, all dealing with the subject's perception of the upright. In one of these, the rod-and-frame test, the subject sits in a dark room, observing a luminous movable rod which is surrounded by a luminous frame. Both rod and frame can be tilted independently at any angle by the experimenter. The subject must report when the rod appears vertical, ignoring the position of the frame. In the tilting-room-tilting-chair test, both the subject's chair and the room are independently tilted, the subject's task being to straighten the chair in some trials and to straighten the room in others. The third test, known as the rotating room test, is similar to the tilting-room-tilting-chair test except that the room is also rotated. The orientation score on each of the three tests is the angle between the subject's setting and the true vertical. The initial study was conducted on young adults, most of whom were college students. Supplementary investigations were carried out on children and on psychiatric patients.

Analysis of the responses on the spatial orientation tests revealed wide individual differences in what the authors called "field dependence," or the extent to which the subject's perception of the vertical is influenced by the surrounding visual field. Considerable evidence was amassed to indicate that this perceptual trait is a relatively stable, consistent characteristic, having a certain amount of generality. Thus both odd-even and retest reliability coefficients were high, and most of the intercorrelations among the three orientation tests were significant. Of even more interest are the significant correlations between the orientation tests and the Embedded-Figure Test (similar to the previously illustrated Gottschaldt Figures test), which may be regarded as measuring field dependence in a purely visual, paper-and-pencil situation.

On the basis of projective tests and clinical interviews, the investigators also report characteristic personality differences associated with high and low field dependence scores. All of these relationships appear plausible and may open productive approaches to personality analysis. It should be noted, however, that the correlations between personality characteristics and orientation scores obtained in this study may have been contaminated by the examiner's prior knowledge of the subjects' orientation scores. Further verification under more rigidly controlled conditions is thus desirable.

CONDITIONS AFFECTING TRAIT ORGANIZATION

With the application of factor analysis to subjects differing in age, sex, education, occupational background, and other characteristics, certain group differences in factor patterns have come to light. What may at first appear to be a jumble of discordant data should eventually fit into an intelligible picture. Through the comparison of factor patterns in diverse groups, moreover, we may learn something about the nature of trait relationships and how traits develop (5). As early as 1927, Spearman called attention to such group differences, stating, "Another important influence upon the saturation of an ability with g appears to be the class of person at issue" (82, p. 217). At that time he also reported some data suggesting that among older as well as among brighter individuals abilities are more specialized and the general factor plays a relatively small part. It is interesting to note that a large number of the studies by Spearman and his students were conducted on school children, a fact which may partly account for the insistence of these investigators upon the importance of the g factor. Most of the early studies by the American group-factorists, on the other hand, were concerned with college students. Such research yielded little or no evidence of a general factor. Accordingly, the major emphasis was put upon a few broad group factors.

Our understanding of the conditions that influence trait organization may be further advanced by a consideration of factorial research on animal behavior. Similarly, a comparison of findings pertaining to aptitudes with those in the area of personality will provide additional clues to the development of factor patterns. Finally, there are a few studies which indicate changes in factorial organization occurring under experimental conditions. Pertinent results from these various sources will be brought together in the present section.

Age, Educational, and Other Group Differences. A relatively large number of studies have been concerned with *age changes* in the organization of abilities. After surveying the results of research prior to 1946 on groups ranging from five-year-olds to college students, Garrett (44) concluded that "intelligence" is relatively undifferentiated in early childhood and becomes increasingly specialized with age. Relevant data were provided by a comparison of different studies whose subjects varied in age (43, 89, 98), as well as by four studies specifically designed to test the age differentiation hypothesis. In the latter investigations, elementary school children at two or three age levels were examined with the same tests. Three of these studies were cross-sectional (27, 45, 68), one was longitudinal (9).

More recent investigations have raised doubts regarding a simple "differentiation hypothesis." To be sure, studies on children tested shortly after school entrance continue to reveal a large general factor, as evidenced by high correlations among group factors (10, 32). Similarly, the pattern of factor scores exhibits little constancy among children in the first few grades. Thus Tyler (103) reports that the scores of fourth-grade children on the Thurstone tests of Primary Mental Abilities could be predicted as well from the total scores as from the separate factor scores the children had obtained three years earlier.

Other recent studies, however, have yielded results that appear to be inconsistent with the differentiation hypothesis (11, 25, 28, 31, 33, 55, 64, 85, 86). Most of these studies are cross-sectional, only two using a longitudinal approach involving a single retest (64, 86). The ages spanned by the different studies extend from 5½ to 75 years, although no one study covers this whole range. At first sight, the results of the various investigations seem to lead to widely divergent conclusions. In some, the degree of generalization or specialization of abilities seems to remain remarkably uniform with age; in others, abilities appear to become more generalized, the older the individual; and in still others, a trend toward differentiation is evident up to a certain age, followed by a reverse trend toward greater generalization thereafter.

On the other hand Burt (15), who proposed an age differentiation hypothesis as early as 1919, has recently reaffirmed this position following an examination of later published work. He cites his own early longitudinal studies of school children, which demonstrated a decline in the contribution of the general factor and an increase in the contribution of group factors with age. The contradictory findings of other studies he attributes to methodological deficiencies, many of which he discusses in his article. Burt concludes that "between late infancy and early adolescence, there is a definite increase in specialization in ability" (15, p. 85). This specialization he attributes to maturation rather than to educational or other experiential factors, an explanation with which other writers would take issue. With regard to changes beyond adolescence, he notes that evidence for further differentiation of abilities is not easy to find, although specialization of interests is often discernible.

An examination of methodological weaknesses characterizing many studies of age changes in trait organization will help to point up likely pitfalls in this kind of reseach. The *tests* chosen for such a study must be such as to elicit group factors unambiguously. It is thus desirable to have more than one test representing each factor to be identified. For the same reason, most general intelligence tests are unsuited for this type of analysis. Studies using the WISC (55), Wechsler-Bellevue (11), WAIS (28), and Army Alpha (64), for example, are subject to this limitation. Similarly, Hsü (59) has suggested that the alleged *g* factor identified in childhood may be an artifact of the type of test used with children, in which the items are not sufficiently differentiated.

It is also important to make sure that the tests have adequate lower and upper limits, in order to prevent artificial restriction of range among the younger or older subjects, respectively. Another point pertains to test reliability, which is likely to increase with age, especially in the case of young children. Such an increase could spuriously produce an increase in test intercorrelations, with consequent increase in the apparent generalization of abilities with age. Increasing test sophistication with age could likewise add to the contribution of the *g* factor, since test sophistication is likely to affect any one subject's performance on all tests.

With regard to *statistical analysis,* Burt (15) has pointed out that the method of factor analysis chosen should be one suitable for the identification of group factors, rather than one which accounts for most of the correlation in terms of *g*. Several studies have used factorial procedures that he feels are inappropriate for this type of study. Moreover, the general factor identified in some investigations may not be the same at different ages. For example, if the general factor in early childhood is the result of high intercorrelations among separate abilities, while the general factor among older children is a broad verbal factor affecting performance on each of the tests, a direct comparison of the contributions of these two general factors tells us little about the differentiation of abilities with age.

Another set of considerations relates to the choice of *subjects.* In cross-sectional studies (which constitute the large majority of available studies), selective factors may reduce the comparability of different age groups. Especially important is a possible group difference in heterogeneity, since this will affect the size of intercorrelations.[3] College students, for example, are a more homogeneous group with respect to intellectual aptitudes than unselected persons of the same ages. This difference is reflected in data on trait organization. Thus the correlations between tests from the verbal, numerical, and spatial areas are low and negligible among college students. Much higher correlations, on the other hand, have been found among such tests in the case of army and navy personnel within the same age level as the college students (106, 107). The latter groups are more heterogeneous and have received less education, on the average, than the college students. The g factor emerges more prominently in such studies of relatively unselected adults than in investigations of college students.

The age range covered by different investigators is another condition which may lead to discrepant findings. It is quite possible that the direction of change in the organization of abilities may differ in early childhood, later childhood, and adulthood. Hence the results of any one study cannot be generalized beyond the age range covered. Some studies, moreover, may include such a narrow age range that no significant trends can be discerned in the results. Finally, it is essential to ask whether the subjects differed in any important respects besides age. In studies on school children, high school students, and college students, the older subjects have also progressed farther in school. Investigations on older adults usually encounter the opposite trend. Owing to the rising educational level of the population, older persons examined today have received less education, on the whole, than younger persons (cf. Ch. 8). Factorial analyses of the Wechsler-Bellevue (11) and the WAIS (28), for instance, yield age differences in trait organization that may be partly or wholly the result of educational differences.

The effect which varying amount or kind of *education* may have upon trait organization has also received some direct attention. In a study conducted on high school students in Colombia, South America, Fillela (38) found a number of suggestive correspondences between the type of curriculum students had been pursuing and the nature of factors identified through factor analysis of a battery of six tests. Among technical school boys, for instance, the two factors that emerged most clearly were quantitative reasoning and spatial-mechanical reasoning. Among academic high school students, on the other hand, the same tests revealed a verbal and a nonverbal factor. The pattern of test correlations, as well as the resulting factorial

[3] Kelley (60) argued that the major part of the g factor found among children may result from heterogeneity of intellectual maturity within a single age level. Thus the faster-developing child would tend to score higher than the slower-developing child on all tests.

composition of individual tests, thus differed widely from one type of school to the other.

Similar data may be found in Vernon's summary of a number of British studies (112). An early study on the organization of mathematical ability among English school children, for example, revealed wide variations in the correlations among arithmetic, algebra, and geometry scores in different school classes. These variations were found to be related to such conditions as whether or not the three school subjects were taught by the same teacher, or whether the teaching methods emphasized similarities of technique among these three branches of mathematics. In their investigations on British military personnel, Vernon and Parry (113) found technical training to be related to the nature of group factors. There is also evidence of a somewhat different patterning of abilities among high and low school achievers (70) and among students earning high and low total scores on a battery of aptitude tests (79). Such studies suggest that those students who have profited more from the standardized educational experiences provided in school not only score higher on tests but also exhibit a different pattern of intercorrelations among the tests.

Sex differences in ability patterning have been observed as early as the first grade (10, 102), as well as among elementary school children and college students (cf. 5). In a number of these studies, spatial and quantitative factors emerged more clearly as separate abilities among boys than among girls. Although the specific differences found are too complex to summarize briefly, all studies in which sex differences in trait organization have been investigated agree in showing differing factorial compositions for at least some tests in the case of the two sexes. Suggestive data on differences in ability patterning have likewise been reported for persons engaged in certain *occupations* (5, 112), and for members of different *socioeconomic* and *ethnic* groups (69).

A consideration of available data on group differences in trait organization leads to two promising hypotheses. First, persons with different experiential backgrounds, or reactional biographies, show different factor loadings on the same tests. If such a finding is corroborated, it suggests that different persons utilize different work methods in performing the same task (13, 75, 78). One individual may solve by verbal reasoning a problem which for another involves chiefly rote memory and for a third, spatial visualization. This hypothesis points to the need for more research on work methods through direct observation of performance, verbal report by subjects, and other suitable procedures.

A second, related hypothesis pertains to the development of group factors themselves. It may be that the individual's reactional biography tends to shape the very group factors identified by factorial techniques. Such group factors would thus be expected to follow the lines along which educational, vocational, and other life experiences have been organized within a particular culture. Types of tasks that are learned together—in school, on the job, or elsewhere—would as a result tend to become correlated. Data bearing on this hypothesis can be most effectively gathered through longitudinal studies of the same individuals before and after a fairly long period of schooling, job activity, and the like. It would also be of considerable interest to compare factor patterns in widely diverse cultures. Is it likely that we would find a broad, pervasive verbal comprehension factor in a preliterate culture, or a mechanical aptitude factor in a nonindustrial civilization? Perhaps it is too late to find answers to these particular questions today. But at least we can utilize the available range of cultures to answer similar questions on a more limited scale.

Factor Analyses of Animal Behavior. The application of factor analysis to animal behavior is still in an exploratory stage. The number of studies employing such techniques is small and their results must be regarded as tentative. In animal research, it has proved relatively difficult to meet certain methodological requirements of factor analysis, such as high test reliability, sufficient number of experimentally independent variables to permit adequate determination and definition of factors, and enough subjects to yield stable correlations.

Relevant animal studies published prior to 1950 have been summarized by Royce (73). About a dozen early investigations reported correlations between two or more measures of learning. All were concerned with rats, with the exception of one study employing chicks. Correlations were uniformly low, except those between closely similar tasks, such as different mazes. There was no evidence of a general learning factor, or of any sort of group factors beyond a few of very narrow scope. High specificity of performance seemed to be the rule.

The first systematic investigation of animal behavior by means of current procedures of factor analysis is to be found in a study of rat behavior by R. L. Thorndike (88). A total of 32 scores were obtained from seven experimental setups, including mazes, problem boxes, conditioned response apparatus, activity wheel, and an obstruction box for measuring relative strength of different drives. The subjects were 64 albino rats. Factorial analysis yielded three factors, which were identified as docility, transfer of training, and a conditioned response factor. Later, Van Steenberg (108) reanalyzed

Thorndike's data, extracting more factors and rotating the centroid axes for simple structure. This analysis yielded ten factors, five of which the author felt could be interpreted with some confidence. These factors he described as ability to profit from visual cues (common to elevated mazes), adaptability to new situations, speed of movement, ability to learn a right-left alternation, and visual insight or perception of the total stimulus pattern. In another, similar study by Vaughn (110), eight factors were isolated, four of which were tentatively identified as follows: speed, wildness-timidity, associative or insight learning, and transfer.

Other ways in which factor analysis has been applied to the study of animal behavior are illustrated by the work of Searle (77) and Wherry (114, 115). Searle applied obverse factor analysis to rat learning data, correlating rats rather than tests (cf. Ch. 10). Such correlations thus indicated the degree of similarity of score patterns or profiles among different rats. Using rats that were descendants of Tryon's selectively bred maze-bright and maze-dull animals (cf. Ch. 4), Searle obtained 30 behavior measures on each. Intercorrelations and factor analyses of these data verified the hypothesis that the maze-bright and maze-dull rats have different score profiles and constitute two distinct behavior types. The mean correlation of brights with dulls was −.19, while the mean intercorrelation of brights with one another was .59 and that of dulls with one another .53. A detailed examination of the specific measures in which the bright and dull profiles differed led Searle to the descriptions of these two strains cited in Chapter 4. It will be recalled that the major differences were in emotional and motivational characteristics, rather than in general learning or ability factors.

Another variation of factor analysis was utilized by Wherry to study changes in the factorial composition of the same task at different stages of learning. When applied to published data on mazes and other types of learning situations, his analysis yielded remarkably consistent results. In each instance, he identified three factors, one of which predominated in the initial, one in the middle, and one in the final stages of learning. The first seems to correspond to trial and error learning, the second to retracing and uncertain behavior, and the third to the insightful learning of the correct response. It is also interesting to note that an application of this analysis to Tryon's data revealed differences in the relative contribution of these three factors in the bright and dull groups. Among the bright rats, for example, the third factor rose to prominence earlier in the course of learning than among the dulls.

Factorial techniques have recently been employed in connection with a long-range project on genetics and social behavior in dogs (76). Royce (74) factor-analyzed the intercorrelations among 32 physiological, psychological, and social measures of emotionality obtained from 53 dogs. Of the ten factors extracted, those of greatest psychological interest include aggressiveness, activity level, and two timidity factors—one characterized by "freezing" behavior, the other by withdrawal and hyperactivity. In a study of 73 dogs (many of whom were the identical animals used by Royce), Anastasi *et al.* (7) analyzed data on 17 variables derived from various learning situations. Five factors were isolated and tentatively interpreted as follows: activity and impulsiveness, docility or responsiveness to a human trainer, manipulative ability, visual observation, and persistence of positional habits. The results also suggested that the factorial composition of the same task may vary at different stages of training.

In looking over available research results on trait organization in animals, one is impressed, first, with the absence of any broad aptitude factors such as have emerged in human studies. Secondly, the factor structure of the same task may change in the course of training. Thirdly, there appears to be much closer intertwining of intellectual and emotional aspects of behavior than has generally been found with human subjects. Studies on animal learning, for instance, have repeatedly elicited at least some factors which could be best described in emotional and motivational terms. The traditional dichotomy between abilities and personality is certainly not borne out by factorial research on animals. One wonders to what extent this distinction within human behavior may be the result of the classic dichotomy between curricular and extracurricular experiences, between standardized intellectual development and unstandardized emotional development. Of one thing we can be certain: this is a dichotomy to which animals have not been exposed, either in the field or in the laboratory! Probably the most fruitful contribution that animal studies can make to the analysis of trait relationships is the experimental investigation of *how* factor patterns develop under controlled conditions. The opportunities provided by this approach have scarcely been tapped.

Experimentally Produced Changes in Factor Patterns. Too often the trait investigator has asked merely, "*What* is the organization of psychological traits?" or "*Which* are the major human traits?" rather than asking, "*How* does behavior become organized?" and "*How* do psychological traits develop?" The apparent inconsistencies in the findings of trait research on different age, educational, or other groups, point up the need for a more direct investigation of the mechanism by which traits develop—the way in which the specific experiential background of different individuals determines the organization of their behavior into more or less unitary and stable traits.

An exploratory study of this question was conducted by Anastasi (4). The principal aim of the investigation was the *experimental alteration* of a factor pattern through a brief, relevant, interpolated experience. Five tests, including vocabulary, memory span for digits, verbal reasoning of the syllogistic type, code multiplication, and pattern analysis, were administered to 200 sixth-grade school children. All subjects were then given instruction in the use of special techniques or devices which would facilitate performance on the last three tests only. In its general nature. this instruction resembled that received in the course of schoolwork, as, for example, in the teaching of arithmetic operations, short-cuts of computation, and the like. After a lapse of 13 days, parallel forms of all five tests were administered under exactly the same conditions as in the initial testing. Since the entire experiment was of such short duration, age changes were probably negligible and the influence of other, outside conditions relatively slight.

A comparison of the intercorrelations among the five variables in the initial and final testing showed practically no change in the correlation between the two "noninstruction" tests, namely vocabulary and memory span. A slight change was found in the correlations between the "instruction" and "noninstruction" tests, and a marked change in the correlations among the three "instruction" tests. Factor pattern analyses revealed marked differences from the initial to the final testing. An examination of the factor loadings in the five tests before and after instruction suggested that the changes were such as would have been expected from the nature of the interpolated experience. This experiment could thus be regarded as a sort of compressed version of the kind of changes in trait relationships which may occur, at a much slower rate, in the course of ordinary schooling.

Also relevant are studies on the effects of *practice* upon factor patterns. Woodrow (118, 119), for example, found marked changes in the factor loadings of tests following prolonged practice. Nor were these changes a matter of greater reliance upon speed or upon general ability after practice. Similar results were obtained by Greene (48) in a comparison of factor patterns computed for the first and fourth trials of a set of motor and pictorial tests. Many changes occurred in the factorial composition of tests, some of which showed interesting correspondences to changes in observed performance or in subject's reports.

A somewhat different approach was followed by Fleishman and Hempel (40) in an evaluation of practice changes in the Complex Coordination

Test of the U. S. Air Force. This test requires the learning of a complicated psychomotor task involving adjustments of an airplane-type stick and rudder in response to patterns of visual stimuli. Subjects were given 64 trials, from which were derived eight scores corresponding to successive practice stages. These eight scores were factor-analyzed together with scores on 18 tests chosen as reference variables for the identification of different factors. Results indicated systematic, progressive changes in the factorial structure of the Complex Coordination Test with practice. The test became factorially less complex—showing high loadings in fewer factors—as learning progressed. There was also a shift in the nature of the factors contributing to performance at early and late stages of practice.

Such experimental approaches to the development of traits open a way for exploring the mechanism whereby the traits identified in the purely descriptive or cross-sectional studies may have developed. The accumulated effects of education, occupation, and other everyday-life activities upon the organization of behavior may be illuminated by a study of the condensed effects of short-range, experimentally controlled experiences. A provocative theoretical discussion of the way in which traits may become differentiated as a result of transfer of training is given by Ferguson (36).

It could be argued that in these experiments all that may be changed is the *work method* used by the subject in performing the tests. Such an explanation is certainly plausible, but it should be used consistently. For example, when the test scores of subjects of different ages, occupations, or educational levels show diverse factor patterns, such differences, too, may be explicable in terms of different methods of work. Moreover, any *uniformity* of factorial organization among members of a given population may be partly the result of commonly acquired methods of work. Factor pattern analyses show only the organization of behavior as it is found in a group of subjects, but do not indicate the origin of such organization.

If we grant that the "traits" identified by factor analysis are simply functional groupings observable within the subject's behavior, then such traits cannot at the same time be conceived as "underlying abilities" which remain unaffected while the subject's method of doing a task and his objectively observable behavior are profoundly altered. Even the common assumption that certain ultimate limits of performance are set by the individual's sensory, neural, and muscular equipment must be modified in the light of the possible variety of work methods. Changing the method of work may in part overcome some of these physical limitations and thus permit the individual to surpass his previously established "capacity level." The whole process of education is, in one sense, a means of changing work methods.

COMMON VERSUS INDIVIDUAL TRAITS

Some writers on personality have differentiated between "common" and "individual" traits, a distinction most explicitly proposed by Allport (2). Common traits are those characterizing people in general, or at least common to large groups. They are the traits ordinarily identified by factor analysis and measured by standardized tests in which the individual's performance is evaluated in terms of group norms. Individual traits, on the other hand, refer to the sort of trait identified through an analysis of the unique experiences of a particular individual. Such a trait, which mirrors the individual's idiosyncratic behavior organization, is observed through clinical procedures and other intensive, prolonged study of a single individual, as illustrated by Cattell's *P* technique and Stephenson's *Q* technique (Ch. 10). From one point of view, type theories may be regarded as an attempted compromise between the two extremes of common and individual traits. Such theories imply essentially a pattern of behavior relationships shared by a relatively limited group of people—narrower than the groups to which the common traits of factor analysis are ascribed, but including more than a single individual. In general, individual traits and type concepts have flourished principally among writers on personality, while common traits have found more support in the classification of intellectual variables.

It should be remembered that, by whatever procedures identified, a trait is essentially a *pattern of relationships within the individual's behavior.* The so-called common trait, located by studying a group of persons rather than a single individual, is simply a generalized description of a pattern of behavior relationships shared by a group of persons. Why, then, have such common traits found more ready applicability in the description of intellectual rather than emotional and motivational functions?

One reason may be found in the greater *uniformity and standardization of experience* in the intellectual than in the emotional and motivational sphere (cf. 5, 8). An obvious illustration of this point is provided by our system of formal education, in which the standardized content of instruction is directed principally toward intellectual rather than emotional development. Even if the schools were to institute a rigidly standardized "personality curriculum" (a rather depressing thought!), we still would not expect the uniformities of organization characteristic of intellectual development, since much of the individual's emotional development occurs through domestic and recreational activities. Not only courses of study, but also occupations and other traditional areas of activity within any one cultural setting, tend to crystallize and structure intellectual development into relatively uniform patterns. Such patterns become more clearly evident the longer the individual has been exposed to these common experiences. The increasing differentiation of abilities with age and education becomes intelligible in these terms.

A further relevant point is the objection raised by some writers (cf., e.g., 2, 75) that test items may have "private meanings," so to speak, for each individual. Discussions of this point have sometimes led to rather obscurantist criticisms of psychological testing. Actually, this objection is simply another way of saying that the same response may not have the same diagnostic or prognostic significance when made by persons of widely varying experiential backgrounds. Since uniformities and standardization of experience in our culture are more common in the intellectual than in the emotional aspects of behavior, "personality" tests are more subject to such a limitation than are "intelligence" or "aptitude" tests. A further reason for the greater uniformity of intellectual patterns of behavior is found in the degree to which such behavior has been verbalized, as contrasted to emotional responses, which are more largely unverbalized. It may also be relevant to reiterate that the distinction between intellectual and emotional aspects of behavior may itself be culturally determined.

THE CONCEPT OF INTELLIGENCE

Among the many definitions of intelligence which have been proposed by psychologists, two concepts recur most frequently (cf., e.g., 46, 81, 109). First, intelligence has been characterized as the ability to deal with abstract symbols and relationships. Secondly, it has been described as the capacity to adapt to new situations or to profit by experience and is virtually identified with learning ability. Most of these definitions suffer from the weakness that, in their effort to be all-encompassing, they really tell us very little. If, for example, we define intelligence as the capacity for abstraction, we are immediately confronted with the fact that the same individual may deal effectively with abstract verbal concepts but be deficient with quantitative concepts, or vice versa. Similarly, the available evidence offers no support for the view that "learning" is a unitary function (cf., e.g., 56, 118). If intelligence were to be defined in terms of the ability to learn, a legitimate question would be, "To learn what?" In our culture, intelligence has been traditionally identified with *school learning*. Tilton (100), for example, found that intelligence test scores correlate substantially with gains in school achievement tests, when the measuring instruments provide everyone with sufficient room for improvement. Moreover, through factorial analysis of intercorrelations among gains in different school subjects, Tilton (101) also identified a common learning factor within this limited area.

The content of intelligence tests likewise provides clues to the connotations of the term "intelligence" as currently employed. It will be recalled that the original aim of intelligence tests was to sample a large number of different abilities in order to arrive at an estimate of the subject's general level of performance. In so far as the individual's standing in specific functions differs, such a general estimate is unsatisfactory. It is apparent, moreover, that current intelligence tests do not even furnish an adequate estimate of the average ability of the individual, since they are overweighted with certain functions and omit others. Thus in nonlanguage and performance tests of intelligence, spatial and perceptual functions play a major role. Most paper-and-pencil tests, on the other hand, measure chiefly verbal ability and, to a slighter extent, numerical ability. Since the latter type of test is by far the most frequently employed, the term "intelligence" has come to be used almost synonymously with verbal ability. Mental age on the Stanford-Binet, for example, has been found to correlate on the average about .81 with performance on the vocabulary test of the scale (87, p. 302). Within single age groups, this correlation ranges from .65 to .91.

From another angle, most intelligence tests may be regarded as measures of scholastic aptitude, or *ability to succeed in our schools.* This is illustrated particularly well by the procedure commonly followed in validating intelligence tests. The term "validity," it will be recalled, denotes the degree to which a test actually measures what it purports to measure. In the case of most intelligence tests, validity has been checked against school success as a criterion. Scores on the test are correlated with school grades or teachers' estimates of ability, and the higher these correlations the more valid the test is said to be. It should also be noted that tests of intelligence correlate nearly as highly with tests of school achievement as they do with each other.

All in all, it is apparent that most intelligence tests are heavily weighted with certain functions, predominantly verbal aptitude. At the same time, they have proved to be of considerable value as empirical instruments of prediction in a wide variety of practical situations. In forecasting academic promise, aiding in the selection of applicants for most jobs, and assisting the vocational counselor, they are making a significant contribution. That such tests have proved to have empirical validity suggests that the criteria themselves may be "overloaded" with certain aptitudes. If the tests were not overweighted with verbal ability, their validity might drop appreciably, since verbal aptitude undoubtedly plays a predominant role in determining successful achievement in our schools, our vocational pursuits, and other everyday life situations in our culture.

It is thus apparent that "intelligence" can be defined only with reference to a particular setting or environmental milieu. This viewpoint immediately suggests that there are, not one, but many definitions of intelligence (cf. 83). Within our cultural setting, intelligence apparently consists in large part of verbal ability. It will be recalled that the one field from which idiots savants are conspicuously absent is the linguistic one. Success in the practical business of everyday life—for both child and adult—is so closely linked with verbal aptitude that a serious deficiency in this respect will brand the individual as mentally incompetent. Conversely, the person who is especially proficient in verbal functions may thereby compensate for deficiencies along other lines and will rarely, if ever, find his way into an institution for the feebleminded. To define intelligence within our culture is primarily to catalogue those activities made possible by linguistic development.

A comparison of intelligence tests developed within different cultures or subcultures should prove enlightening. To date, the possibilities for making such comparisons are meager, although some pertinent data will be examined in Chapters 15 and 16. Even within our own culture, however, we may observe a tendency for the concept of intelligence to alter as cultural conditions change. Today there is evidence that such factors as the growing mechanization of everyday-living activities, the "do-it-yourself" trend, and especially the rapidly mounting demand for high-level personnel in science and engineering are being reflected in test construction and in a changing definition of intelligence. An increasing amount of research is being devoted to the development of tests for use with adults within industrial and military settings, as contrasted with the earlier tests, which were oriented principally toward school children and college students. New tests include more non-verbal content and put more emphasis on creativity and inventiveness than is true of traditional intelligence tests.

That these developments are beginning to influence the very definition of intelligence is illustrated by Guilford's article on "The Structure of Intellect" (49). Beginning as a large-scale effort to develop tests for high-level personnel, Guilford's research was concentrated largely within the areas of reasoning, creativity, planning, and evaluation, as discussed in an earlier section of this chapter. In a comprehensive re-examination of his own results and those of other factorial investigations, however, Guilford proposes a revised and expanded definition of intelligence as a whole. In contrast to earlier descriptions, this definition gives more weight to spatial content and to creative processes. In conclusion, although intelligence in our culture today is still largely verbal and still primarily concerned with comprehension and retention, there appears to be a trend toward the inclusion of more creative thinking and more nonverbal materials.

SUMMARY

Factor analysis provides a versatile research tool which has already been utilized in nearly all branches of psychology. Its chief applications, however, have been in the identification of aptitudes and personality traits, as well as in the development of tests for their measurement. Multiple aptitude batteries, which yield a profile of scores in different abilities, are a product of factor analysis. In personality research, factor analysis has been employed in a variety of ways, including the analysis of intercorrelations among inventory items, ratings, and objective tests. Some use has also been made of *P* technique based on repeated measures of single individuals. Although a number of personality tests have been constructed to measure the traits isolated through factorial studies, there is as yet relatively little agreement in the factor lists proposed by different investigators. A few traits, such as dominance and emotional stability, do recur in most studies. Factorial investigations of interests and attitudes have yielded suggestive results but have so far had little effect on test development.

An area of growing research activity is the factorial analysis of creative thinking. It is likely that both intellectual and personality characteristics contribute to the individual's creative productivity. Another currently active field of research is concerned with the relation between perception and personality. Both factor analysis and other research techniques are being utilized in such studies. Especially promising are the findings regarding two closure factors, namely, speed of closure and flexibility of closure, as well as the work on "field dependence."

Attention is being turned increasingly from the static description of factor patterns to inquiries into the conditions that bring about or modify trait organization. Suggestive data on age, educational, and other group differences in the organization of abilities are being gathered. Despite apparently conflicting results, the differentiation hypothesis appears to offer the most promising account of age changes in trait organization from infancy to adolescence. Differences in factor patterns between the sexes and between educational, occupational, and other groups suggest that the amount of differentiation and the nature of group factors may be influenced by the subjects' reactional biographies. The data certainly indicate that persons with different experiential backgrounds often use different work methods to perform the same tasks.

The application of factor analysis to animal behavior reveals somewhat greater specificity of aptitudes (with narrower group factors) than has been found in human research. Animal studies likewise indicate close inter-twining of aptitude, emotional, and motivational variables, as well as change in factorial composition of tasks in the course of training. Suggestive data are also provided by human studies on the effects of practice and instruction upon factor patterns. Such studies reproduce in capsule form the sort of influences that operate much more slowly in the course of edu-cation and other life experiences.

The contrast between common and individual traits, proposed by certain writers on personality theory, may reflect the greater standardization of experiences within the intellectual than within the emotional and motiva-tional sphere. Both the identification of common traits and the development of standardized tests have met with more success in the aptitude than in the personality area.

Definitions of intelligence vary widely. Within our culture, intelligence is largely identified with verbal comprehension and has traditionally been evaluated with reference to academic criteria. Recent cultural developments are reflected in a gradual broadening and modification of this concept of intelligence, with growing emphasis on creative thinking and increasing utilization of nonverbal content.

REFERENCES

1. Adkins, Dorothy C., and Lyerly, S. B. *Factor analysis of reasoning tests.* Chapel Hill: Univer. N. Carolina Press, 1952.
2. Allport, G. W. *Personality: a psychological interpretation.* N.Y.: Holt, 1937.
3. Allport, G. W., and Odbert, H. S. Trait-names, a psycholexical study. *Psychol. Monogr.*, 1936, 47, No. 1.
4. Anastasi, Anne. The influence of specific experience upon mental organiza-tion. *Genet. Psychol. Monogr.*, 1936, 18, 245–355.
5. Anastasi, Anne. The nature of psychological "traits." *Psychol. Rev.*, 1948, 55, 127–138.
6. Anastasi, Anne. *Psychological testing.* N.Y.: Macmillan, 1954.
7. Anastasi, Anne, Fuller, J. L., Scott, J. P., and Schmitt, J. R. A factor analysis of the performance of dogs on certain learning tests. *Zoologica*, 1955, 40 (Pt. I), 33–46.
8. Anderson, J. E. Freedom and constraint or potentiality and environment. *Psychol. Bull.*, 1944, 41, 1–29.
9. Asch, S. E. A study of change in mental organization. *Arch. Psychol.*, 1936, No. 195.

10. Avakian, Sonia A. An investigation of trait relationships among six-year-old children. Unpublished doctoral dissertation, Fordham University, 1951.

11. Balinsky, B. An analysis of the mental factors of various age groups from nine to sixty. *Genet. Psychol. Monogr.*, 1941, 23, 191–234.

12. Bennett, G. K., Seashore, H. G., and Wesman, A. G. *Differential Aptitude Tests, Manual.* N.Y.: Psychol. Corp., 1947.

13. Bloom, B. S., and Broder, Lois J. Problem-solving processes of college students. *Suppl. educ. Monogr.*, 1950, No. B.

14. Botzum, W. A. A factorial study of the reasoning and closure factors. *Psychometrika*, 1951, 16, 361–386.

15. Burt, C. The differentiation of intellectual ability. *Brit. J. educ. Psychol.*, 1954, 24, 76–90.

16. Cattell, R. B. *Description and measurement of personality.* Yonkers-on-Hudson, N.Y.: World Book Co., 1946.

17. Cattell, R. B. Confirmation and clarification of the primary personality factors. *Psychometrika*, 1947, 12, 197–220.

18. Cattell, R. B. The primary personality factors in women compared with those in men. *Brit. J. Psychol., statist. Sect.*, 1948, 1, 114–130.

19. Cattell, R. B. The chief invariant psychological and psychophysical functional unities found by P-technique. *J. clin. Psychol.*, 1955, 11, 319–343.

20. Cattell, R. B. The principal replicated factors discovered in objective personality tests. *J. abnorm. soc. Psychol.*, 1955, 50, 291–314.

21. Cattell, R. B. *Personality and motivation structure and measurement.* Yonkers-on-Hudson, N.Y.: World Book Co., 1957.

22. Cattell, R. B., *et al. The IPAT Junior Personality Quiz: Handbook.* Champaign, Ill.: Inst. Pers. Ability Testing, 1953.

23. Cattell, R. B., and Gruen, W. The primary personality factors in 11 year old children, by objective tests. *J. Pers.*, 1955, 23, 460–478.

24. Cattell, R. B., Saunders, D. R., and Stice, G. F. *The Sixteen Personality Factor Questionnaire: Handbook.* Champaign, Ill.: Inst. Pers. Ability Testing, 1950.

25. Chen, T. L., and Chow, H. A factor study of a test battery at different educational levels. *J. genet. Psychol.*, 1948, 73, 187–199.

26. Christie, R. Eysenck's treatment of the personality of communists. *Psychol. Bull.*, 1956, 53, 411–430. (Reply and rejoinder, pp. 431–451)

27. Clark, Mamie P. Changes in primary mental abilities with age. *Arch. Psychol.*, 1944, No. 291.

28. Cohen, J. The factorial structure of the WAIS between early adulthood and old age. *J. consult. Psychol.*, 1957, 21, 283–290.

29. Corter, H. M. Factor analysis of some reasoning tests. *Psychol. Monogr.*, 1952, 66, No. 8.

30. Cottle, W. C. A factorial study of the Multiphasic, Strong, Kuder, and Bell inventories using a population of adult males. *Psychometrika*, 1950, 15, 25–47.

31. Curtis, H. A. A study of the relative effects of age and of test difficulty upon factor patterns. *Genet. Psychol. Monogr.*, 1949, 40, 99–148.

32. Dean, D. A. A factor analysis of the Stanford-Binet and SRA Primary Mental Abilities battery at the first grade level. Unpublished doctoral dissertation, Penn. State College, 1950.

33. Doppelt, J. E. The organization of mental abilities in the age range 13 to 17. *Teach. Coll. Contr. Educ.*, 1950, No. 962.

34. Dvorak, Beatrice J. The new USES General Aptitude Test Battery. *J. appl. Psychol.*, 1947, 31, 372–376.

35. Eysenck, H. J. *The structure of human personality.* London: Methuen, 1953.

36. Ferguson, G. A. On learning and human ability. *Canad. J. Psychol.*, 1954, 8, 95–112.

37. Ferguson, L. W. A revision of the Primary Social Attitude Scales. *J. Psychol.*, 1944, 17, 229–241.

38. Fillela, J. F. Educational and sex differences in the organization of abilities in technical and academic students in Colombia, South America. Unpublished doctoral dissertation, Fordham University, 1957.

39. Flanagan, J. C. *Flanagan Aptitude Classification Tests.* Chicago: Science Research Associates, 1953.

40. Fleishman, E. A., and Hempel, W. E., Jr. Changes in factor structure of a complex psychomotor test as a function of practice. *Psychometrika*, 1954, 19, 239–252.

41. Fruchter, B. *Introduction to factor analysis.* N.Y.: Van Nostrand, 1954.

42. Fruchter, B., and Mahan, W. W. Some perceptual factors measured by motion picture tests. *J. educ. Psychol.*, 1952, 43, 430–435.

43. Garrett, H. E. Differentiable mental traits. *Psychol. Rec.*, 1938, 2, 259–298.

44. Garrett, H. E. A developmental theory of intelligence. *Amer. Psychologist*, 1946, 1, 372–378.

45. Garrett, H. E., Bryan, Alice I., and Perl, Ruth E. The age factor in mental organization. *Arch. Psychol.*, 1935, No. 176.

46. Goddard, H. H. What is intelligence? *J. soc. Psychol.*, 1946, 24, 51–69.

47. Green, R. F., Guilford, J. P., *et al.* A factor analytic study of reasoning abilities. *Psychometrika*, 1953, 18, 135–160.

48. Greene, E. B. An analysis of random and systematic changes with practice. *Psychometrika*, 1943, 8, 37–52.

49. Guilford, J. P. The structure of intellect. *Psychol. Bull.*, 1956, 53, 267–293.

50. Guilford, J. P., *et al.* A factor analysis study of human interests. *Psychol. Monogr.*, 1954, 68, No. 4.

51. Guilford, J. P., *et al.* A factor-analytic study of Navy reasoning tests with the Air Force Aircrew Classification Battery. *Educ. psychol. Measmt.*, 1954, 14, 301–325.

52. Guilford, J. P., *et al.* A factor-analytic study of planning. II. Administration of tests and analysis of results. *Rep. psychol. Lab.*, No. 12. Los Angeles: Univer. Southern Calif., 1955.

53. Guilford, J. P., and Zimmerman, W. S. *The Guilford-Zimmerman Aptitude Survey: Manual.* Beverly Hills, Calif.: Sheridan Supply Co., 1947.

54. Guilford, J. P., and Zimmerman, W. S. *The Guilford-Zimmerman Temperament Survey: Manual.* Beverly Hills, Calif.: Sheridan Supply Co., 1949.

55. Hagen, Elizabeth P. A factor analysis of the Wechsler Intelligence Scale for Children. Unpublished doctoral dissertation, Teachers College, Columbia Univer., 1952.

56. Heese, K. W. A general factor in improvement with practice. *Psychometrika*, 1942, 7, 213–223.

57. Hertzka, A. F., Guilford, J. P., *et al.* A factor-analytic study of evaluative abilities. *Educ. psychol. Measmt.*, 1954, 14, 581–597.

58. Holzinger, K. J., and Crowder, N. A. *Holzinger-Crowder Uni-Factor Tests.* Yonkers-on-Hudson, N.Y.: World Book Co., 1955.

59. Hsü, E. H. Factor analysis, differential bio-process, and mental organization. *J. gen. Psychol.*, 1948, 38, 147–157.

60. Kelley, T. L. *Crossroads in the mind of man: a study of differentiable mental abilities.* Stanford Univer., Calif.: Stanford Univer. Press, 1928.

61. MacKinnon, D. W. Tests for the measurement of personal effectiveness. *Proc., 1951 Conf. Test. Probl., Educ. Test. Serv.*, 1952, 73–81.

62. Marron, J. E. The search for basic reasoning abilities: a review of factor analytic studies. *USAF Hum. Resour. Res. Cent. Res. Bull.*, 1953, No. 53–28.

63. Matin, L., and Adkins, Dorothy C. A second-order factor analysis of reasoning abilities. *Psychometrika*, 1954, 19, 71–78.

64. McHugh, R. B., and Owens, W. A., Jr. Age changes in mental organization—a longitudinal study. *J. Geront.*, 1954, 9, 296–302.

65. Otis, A. S. *Normal percentile chart: manual of directions.* Yonkers-on-Hudson, N.Y.: World Book Co., 1938.

66. Pemberton, Carol L. The closure factors related to other cognitive processes. *Psychometrika*, 1952, 17, 267–288.

67. Pemberton, Carol L. The closure factors related to temperament. *J. Pers.*, 1952, 21, 159–175.

68. Reichard, Suzanne. Mental organization and age level. *Arch. Psychol.*, 1944, No. 295.

69. Roberts, S. O., and Robinson, J. M. Intercorrelations of the Primary Mental Abilities Tests for ten-year-olds by socioeconomic status, sex, and race. *Amer. Psychologist*, 1952, 7, 304–305.

70. Roesslein, C. G. *Differential patterns of intelligence traits between high achieving and low achieving high school boys.* Washington, D.C.: Catholic Univer. Press, 1953.

71. Roff, M. A factorial study of tests in the perceptual area. *Psychometr. Monogr.*, 1952, No. 8.

72. Rokeach, M., and Hanley, C. Eysenck's tender-mindedness dimension: a critique. *Psychol. Bull.*, 1956, 53, 169–176. (Reply and rejoinder, pp. 177–186)

73. Royce, J. R. The factorial analysis of animal behavior. *Psychol. Bull.*, 1950, 47, 235–259.

74. Royce, J. R. A factorial study of emotionality in the dog. *Psychol. Monogr.*, 1955, 69, No. 22.

75. Sargent, S. S. How shall we study individual differences? *Psychol. Rev.*, 1942, 49, 170–181.

76. Scott, J. P., and Fuller, J. L. Research on genetics and social behavior at the Roscoe B. Jackson Memorial Laboratory, 1946–1951—A progress report. *J. Hered.*, 1951, 42, 191–197.

77. Searle, L. V. The organization of hereditary maze-brightness and maze-dullness. *Genet. Psychol. Monogr.*, 1949, 39, 279–325.

78. Seashore, R. H. Work methods—an often neglected factor underlying individual differences. *Psychol. Rev.*, 1939, 46, 123–141.

79. Segel, D. Intellectual abilities in the adolescent period. *Bull. No. 6, Office of Educ., Federal Security Agency,* 1948.
80. Segel, D., and Raskin, Evelyn. *Multiple Aptitude Tests.* Los Angeles: California Test Bur., 1955.
81. Sherman, M. *Intelligence and its deviations.* N.Y.: Ronald, 1945.
82. Spearman, C. *The abilities of man.* N.Y.: Macmillan, 1927.
83. Spiker, C. C., and McCandless, B. R. The concept of intelligence and the philosophy of science. *Psychol. Rev.,* 1954, 61, 255–266.
84. Steinberg, A. The relation of vocational preference to emotional adjustment. *Educ. psychol. Measmt.,* 1952, 12, 96–104.
85. Swineford, Frances. A study in factor analysis: the nature of the general, verbal, and spatial bi-factors. *Suppl. educ. Monogr.,* 1948, No. 67.
86. Swineford, Frances. General, verbal, and spatial bi-factors after three years. *J. educ. Psychol.,* 1949, 40, 353–360.
87. Terman, L. M., and Merrill, Maud A. *Measuring intelligence.* Boston: Houghton Mifflin, 1937.
88. Thorndike, R. L. Organization of behavior in the albino rat. *Genet. Psychol. Monogr.,* 1935, 17, No. 1.
89. Thurstone, L. L. Primary mental abilities. *Psychometr. Monogr.,* 1938, No. 1.
90. Thurstone, L. L. A factorial study of perception. *Psychometr. Monogr.,* 1944, No. 4.
91. Thurstone, L. L. Creative talent. *Proc., 1950 Conf. Test. Probl., Educ. Test. Serv.,* 1951, 55–69.
92. Thurstone, L. L. Some primary abilities in visual thinking. *Psychometr. Lab., Univer. Chicago,* No. 59, August, 1950.
93. Thurstone, L. L. *Thurstone Temperament Schedule: Examiner's Manual.* Chicago: Science Research Associates, 1950.
94. Thurstone, L. L. The dimensions of temperament. *Psychometrika,* 1951, 16, 11–20.
95. Thurstone, L. L. Experimental tests of temperament. In *Essays in psychology dedicated to David Katz.* Uppsala, Sweden: Almquist and Wiksells, 1951. Pp. 248–262.
96. Thurstone, L. L. The scientific study of inventive talent. *Psychometr. Lab., Univer. Chicago,* No. 81, July, 1952.
97. Thurstone, L. L. The development of objective measures of temperament. *Psychometr. Lab., Univer. N. Carolina,* No. 1, April, 1953.
98. Thurstone, L. L., and Thurstone, Thelma G. Factorial studies of intelligence. *Psychometr. Monogr.,* 1941, No. 2.
99. Thurstone, L. L., and Thurstone, Thelma G. SRA *Primary Mental Abilities: Intermediate (11–17); Elementary (7–11); Primary (5–7).* Chicago: Science Research Associates, 1948–1953.
100. Tilton, J. W. Intelligence test scores as indicative of ability to learn. *Educ. psychol. Measmt.,* 1949, 9, 291–296.
101. Tilton, J. W. The intercorrelations between measures of school learning. *J. Psychol.,* 1953, 35, 169–179.
102. Tyler, Leona E. The relationship of interests to abilities and reputation among first-grade children. *Educ. psychol. Measmt.,* 1951, 11, 255–264.

103. Tyler, Leona E. Changes in children's scores on Primary Mental Abilities Tests over a three-year period. *Amer. Psychologist,* 1953, 8, 448–449.
104. U.S. Air Force. *Aviation Psychology Research Reports.* Washington, D.C.: Govt. Printing Office, 1947–48. Rep. No. 1, 5, 11.
105. U.S. Air Force. Development of the Airman Classification Test Battery. *Air Tr. Command Res. Dev. Progr., Res. Bull.,* 48–4, Nov. 1948.
106. U.S. Army, TAGO, Personnel Research Section. Report on statistical studies conducted under Project No. PR-4002; Development of AGCT-3 and Information tests. *P.R.S. Rep. No. 568,* 23 August 1945.
107. U.S. Bureau of Naval Personnel, Training Standards and Curriculum Division, Test and Research Section. Psychological test construction and research in the Bureau of Naval Personnel: Development of the Basic Test Battery for Enlisted Personnel. *Psychol. Bull.,* 1945, 42, 561–571.
108. Van Steenberg, N. J. F. Factors in the learning behavior of the albino rat. *Psychometrika,* 1939, 4, 179–200.
109. Various. Symposium: intelligence and its measurement. *J. educ. Psychol.,* 1921, 12, 123–147, 195–216.
110. Vaughn, C. L. Factors in rat learning: an analysis of the intercorrelations between 34 variables. *Comp. Psychol. Monogr.,* 1937, 14, No. 69.
111. Vernon, Magdalen D. *A further study of visual perception.* Cambridge: Cambridge Univer. Press, 1952.
112. Vernon, P. E. *The structure of human abilities.* London: Methuen, 1950.
113. Vernon, P. E., and Parry, J. B. *Personnel selection in the British Forces.* London: Univer. London Press, 1949.
114. Wherry, R. J. Factorial analysis of learning dynamics in animals. *J. comp. Psychol.,* 1939, 28, 263–272.
115. Wherry, R. J. Determination of the specific components of maze ability for Tryon's bright and dull rats by means of factorial analysis. *J. comp. Psychol.,* 1941, 32, 237–252.
116. Wilson, R. C., Guilford, J. P., *et al.* A factor-analytic study of creative-thinking abilities. *Psychometrika,* 1954, 19, 297–311.
117. Witkin, H. A., *et al. Personality through perception.* N.Y.: Harper, 1954.
118. Woodrow, H. The relation between abilities and improvement with practice. *J. educ. Psychol.,* 1938, 29, 215–230.
119. Woodrow, H. Factors in improvement with practice. *J. Psychol.,* 1939, 7, 55–70.

CHAPTER 12

Mental Deficiency

In its broadest sense, mental deficiency represents the lower end of the distribution of intelligence. It does not refer to a "disease," nor to any single entity, but covers many conditions varying widely in both degree and nature of defect. Moreover, since the distribution of intelligence is continuous, there is no sharp dividing line between normality and mental deficiency. Rather there are many borderline individuals who may be classified into one or the other category depending upon other concomitant circumstances.

The concept of mental deficiency is closely related to the definition of intelligence (cf. Ch. 11). As we examine the various criteria for the identification and classification of mental defectives—to be considered in the following section—it becomes apparent that mental deficiency designates a pronounced inferiority in those abilities that are essential for survival in our cultural milieu. Thus educational progress, vocational adjustment, and performance on traditional intelligence tests have been especially prominent in the definitions of mental deficiency. Moreover, language development and verbal comprehension have formed an integral part of the concept from the outset. As early as 1838, the French physician Esquirol (30) concluded that the individual's use of language provided the most dependable criterion of intellectual level. On this basis, he differentiated between various grades of mental deficiency, ranging from those persons who can use speech readily and easily to those who can only utter monosyllables and cries, and those in whom no language is found at all. Similarly, Binet and Simon (11) wrote: "An idiot is a person who is not able to communicate with his fellows by means of language. He does not talk at all and does not understand."

That linguistic criteria are still implicit in the definition of mental deficiency is evidenced by the continuing use of intelligence tests that are highly saturated with the verbal comprehension factor. At the same time, it is now

378

generally recognized that an IQ should never be the sole basis for the diagnosis of mental deficiency. As will be seen in the next section, many other sources of data must be utilized in reaching a decision regarding any individual case.

An important distinction is that between mental deficiency and emotional or personality disorders. The former refers to intellectual subnormality in a person who has never reached normal intelligence. In the case of personality disorders, there may be intellectual deterioration from a previously higher level. Or the individual may be temporarily handicapped in his intellectual functioning as a result of his emotional difficulties. In either event, however, the person had at one time attained a normal or superior level of intellectual development. In the case of children, this criterion is obviously difficult to apply. Consequently, a number of emotionally disturbed children were heretofore misclassified as mentally deficient. Such conditions, however, can usually be differentiated on the basis of a detailed examination of the child's behavior and case history.

It should also be noted that mental defectives *may* develop personality disorders. The point is simply that there is no necessary connection between the two types of condition. Either may occur without the other.

Personality disorders include *neuroses*—which are relatively mild conditions—as well as more serious disturbances known as *psychoses*. The popular terms "insanity" and "lunacy" correspond roughly to the latter category. The most common psychosis is schizophrenia; another well-known example is manic-depressive psychosis. Since the study of neuroses and psychoses constitutes the principal subject matter of abnormal psychology, these conditions will not be considered in the present book, except in so far as they may be relevant to other topics. Reference has already been made to research on psychotics in connection with family resemblances (Ch. 9) and the role of physiological factors in behavior disorders (Ch. 5). In Chapter 18, the concept of abnormality will be examined with special reference to cultural factors.

CRITERIA AND LEVELS

A number of criteria have been proposed for the identification and classification of mental deficiency, or feeblemindedness. In actual practice, the most common are the *psychometric* and the *legal or sociological*. The former is based upon intelligence test performance and expressed in terms of IQ. According to this definition, the dividing line between normality and mental deficiency is customarily set at an IQ of 70, which corresponds approximately to two standard deviations below the mean on such tests as the 1937 Stanford-Binet and the Wechsler scales. The following classification, first recommended by Terman (89, p. 79) on the basis of the original Stanford-Binet distribution, has been widely adopted:

Dullness, rarely classifiable as feeblemindedness	80–90
Borderline deficiency, sometimes classifiable as dullness, often as feeblemindedness	70–80
Moron	50–70
Imbecile	20–50
Idiot	below 20

In applying this classification, certain cautions need to be observed. First, it should always be borne in mind that the dividing lines between adjacent levels are just as arbitrary as that between normality and mental deficiency. Test performance exhibits a continuous gradation varying only in degree, although the social effects of large aptitude differences may differ qualitatively. Secondly, the given classification was based upon a test whose IQ distribution had a standard deviation of 12 points. IQ's on tests whose standard deviations vary markedly from this value will have a different meaning in terms of the total score distribution. On the current Stanford-Binet and on the Wechsler scales, the standard deviations fall approximately between 15 and 16. On certain other tests yielding IQ's, the standard deviations are as high as 20 or 25 (cf., e.g., 21).

Despite these limitations, the above IQ classification has achieved wide popularity. In a technical report issued in 1954 by a special committee of the World Health Organization, the definition of levels of mental deficiency in terms of these IQ limits was reaffirmed (cf. 10, p. 57). In place of the terms "moron," "imbecile," and "idiot," however, the more innocuous designations of "mild," "moderate," and "severe" subnormality were recommended. It should be added that, when applied to adults, these grades of mental deficiency can be described in terms of mental age attained. Thus mild subnormality (moron) corresponds to mental ages between 8 and 12, moderate (imbecile) to mental ages between 3 and 7, and severe (idiot) to mental ages below 3 years.

Legal and sociological definitions of feeblemindedness stress social inadequacy. British usage has been patterned after the Mental Deficiency Act of 1913 and its subsequent revisions, in which mental deficiency is defined rather loosely as "a condition of arrested or incomplete development of mind existing before the age of eighteen years, whether arising from inherent causes or induced by disease or injury" (cf. 93, p. 5). In the accompanying characterizations of different grades of mental deficiency, the implications of the general definition are more clearly put forth. Thus the idiot is described as one so defective as to be unable to guard against common physical dangers; the imbecile as having a degree of defect which prevents him from managing his affairs; and the feebleminded [1] as one who by reason of his mental deficiency requires care, supervision, or control for his own protection or for the protection of others.

In America, laws pertaining to the identification and treatment of mentally defective persons are the responsibility of the state governments. Hence there is little uniformity in statutory definitions or related practices. In a recent survey of such definitions, Porteus and Corbett (70) call attention to the existing variations and recommend certain standard procedures. For this purpose, they propose that mental defectives be defined as "those persons who by reason of permanently retarded or arrested mental development existing from an early age are incapable of independent self-management and self-support."

In an effort to quantify the assessment of social competence, Doll (27) has developed the Vineland Social Maturity Scale. Consisting of 117 items grouped into year levels, this scale is concerned with the individual's ability to look after his practical needs and to take responsibility. The information required for each item is obtained, not through test situations, but through an interview with an informant or with the subject himself. Based upon what the subject has actually done in his daily living, the items fall into the following eight categories: general self-help, self-help in eating, self-help in dressing, self-direction, occupation, communication, locomotion, and socialization. A social age (SA) and a social quotient (SQ) can be computed from the subject's record on the entire scale.

Correlations between the Vineland Social Maturity Scale and the Stanford-Binet vary widely but are sufficiently low, in general, to indicate that different aspects of behavior are being tapped by the two scales. The Vineland Scale has proved especially helpful to clinicians in reaching decisions regarding institutionalization. Thus an individual who is intellectually deficient in terms of Stanford-Binet IQ may be able to adjust satisfactorily outside of an institution if his social age on the Vineland is adequate.

On the other hand, it would be hazardous to accept a score on the Vineland Social Maturity Scale without considerable knowledge regarding the child's home background. The norms on this scale were established on 620

---

[1] In British usage, the term "feebleminded" designates the highest grade of mental deficiency, corresponding to the American term "moron." In America, "feeblemindedness" is employed as a synonym for "mental deficiency," to cover all grades of intellectual subnormality.

subjects, including 10 males and 10 females at each year from birth to 30 years. The number of cases at each age is thus too small to assure desirable stability of norms. The subjects, moreover, came largely from middle-class American homes. It is apparent that many items, such as those relating to going out alone, use of spending money, and the like, would have a very different significance for children in different socioeconomic levels or in certain minority groups. Cultural differences in child-rearing customs, rather than the child's ability level, might in such cases account for deviations from the norms. Similarly, a considerable number of items are unsuitable for orphanage children.

In recent years, there has been a growing emphasis upon the use of *educational criteria* in the classification of intellectual subnormality. This trend is undoubtedy related to the increasing interest in providing educational facilities for defective children outside of institutions. Among the factors contributing to this movement may be mentioned overcrowding in institutions, recognition of the educability of many intellectually deficient children, progress in the development of special instructional techniques suitable for low intellectual levels, and formation of local and national groups of parents and other interested laymen (such as the National Association for Retarded Children). Educational classifications focus attention upon the higher grades of intellectual defect. In general, such classifications reserve the term "mentally deficient" for children with relatively severe subnormality, while "mentally retarded," "mentally backward," and "mentally handicapped" are applied to children who can be educated in the school system, usually in special classes (18, 49, 78, 95). The majority of such cases fall into the borderline and moron categories in terms of IQ, although other factors must obviously be considered, including physical defects, general health, social maturity, and emotional adjustment.

Lower-grade defectives, requiring custodial care, may be handled either in institutions or at home. Promising results have been obtained in home training programs for low-level mentally deficient children (24, 101). Such programs utilize the services of a specially trained visiting teacher who works with both the child and the parents. The mother is thus enabled to carry on the day-by-day training designed to aid the child in developing simple habits of self-help, speech, muscular coordination, and emotional control.

Some definitions of mental deficiency make *etiology* (or causal factors) an integral part of the concept. Thus Doll (26, p. 215) defined feeblemindedness in terms of the following six criteria: "(1) social incompetence, (2) due to mental subnormality, (3) which has been developmentally arrested, (4) which obtains at maturity, (5) is of constitutional origin, and (6) is essentially incurable." This definition sets up two conditions that would be very difficult to apply to the majority of persons now classified as feebleminded. First, it requires far more knowledge regarding the causes of mental deficiency than is available for most cases. Secondly, it logically calls for a prediction of eventual outcome under all possible forms of training, as well as physical and psychological therapies. These requirements obviously limit the usefulness of the definition and would necessitate the placement of most individuals with low IQ's into an "uncertain" category. Moreover, any form of feeblemindedness now "incurable" may at some future time yield to newly discovered therapeutic techniques.

The attempt to incorporate etiological considerations into the concept of feeblemindedness has also led to the use of a category of "pseudofeebleminded," to include persons who do eventually reach a normal intellectual level as a result of treatment, education, or other environmental changes. This term has done little to clarify the situation and has contributed a certain amount of confusion, since one investigator's "feebleminded subjects" may turn out to be another's "pseudofeebleminded."

It is apparent that the concept of mental deficiency has not been defined with clarity or uniformity. This situation becomes more understandable when we realize that "mental deficiency" is essentially an administrative category. The concept has arisen out of practical demands regarding institutional commitment, admission to special classes, and the like. To some extent, the nature of available facilities influences the classification of a particular case. On one point psychologists are now agreed: decisions regarding any individual should always be based upon *multiple criteria*. These should include an IQ—preferably obtained from more than one intelligence test—as well as some information regarding social maturity as manifested in everyday-life behavior. Detailed knowledge of present physical condition and medical history are essential. All of these facts must be interpreted in the light of background data regarding home environment, family conditions, parental characteristics, educational history, and emotional and motivational factors.

Estimates of the *incidence of mental deficiency* in the general population range widely, but the most careful and comprehensive investigations report frequencies falling between 1 and 2 per cent. The specific percentages found in different surveys vary with the criterion of feeblemindedness employed—whether psychometric, social competence, or others—as well as with the point at which the dividing line is set. Geographical locale also makes a difference, the incidence being much greater in some areas than in others.

Age, too, will affect the estimate, since the relatively short life expectancy of the mentally deficient tends to make their proportion in the population appear larger when the survey is limited to children than when all ages are covered.

Similar difficulties are encountered in attempts to determine the relative frequency of different levels of feeblemindedness. Among institutionalized cases, approximately 15 per cent are idiots, 35 per cent imbeciles, and 50 per cent morons (97). But the proportion of higher-level cases outside of institutions is undoubtedly much larger, since such persons are more likely to shift for themselves or to be cared for at home. The relative proportion of different grades also varies from institution to institution, depending upon the nature of available facilities and admission policies of each institution.

CLINICAL VARIETIES AND ETIOLOGY

Descriptive Categories. Mental defectives have also been classified with respect to clinical variety, on the basis of differentiating physical conditions. Only the most common or most widely known of these categories will be cited in the present discussion. For more comprehensive coverage and more detailed description of each variety, reference can be made to Sarason (77). More medically oriented surveys are provided by Tredgold and Soddy's classic book (93) and by the recent publications of Benda (8, 9, 10). A popular treatment of the subject, directed especially to parents, is given by Heiser (40).

Among the most familiar of the special clinical varieties is *mongolism*, which includes between 5 and 10 per cent of institutionalized cases. This type is characterized by persistence of physical traits which are normal in an early stage of fetal development—hence the name "unfinished child" by which such cases have sometime been described. Among these fetal traits are the slanting orbits and skin fold over the eyes which give such cases a superficial resemblance to members of the Mongolian race. It was these features which originally led to the unfortunate choice of name. There is, of course, no racial connotation whatever in this condition. Authorities have currently proposed other terms, such as "peristatic amentia" (29) or "congenital acromicria" (9), but it may be some time before the term "mongolism" is replaced by a technically more appropriate designation.

Cases of mongolism can be readily identified by a number of other physical characteristics, such as small, round head; smooth, moist, puffy skin; fissured tongue; and short, stubby fingers. Although formerly attributed to nutritional and endocrine deficiencies in the prenatal environment (7, 9), mongolism is now known to be associated with the presence of 47 chromosomes, as contrasted to the normal 46. Recently developed techniques permitting improved observation of chromosomes have revealed that mongoloids possess a particular chromosome in triplicate, rather than in duplicate as found in normal persons.[2] Age of mother is evidently a factor in this chromosomal aberration, since the proportion of mongoloids born to mothers over 40 is much greater than the proportion born to younger mothers.

In connection with the previously cited twin research of Kallmann (reported in Chapter 9), Allen and Baroff (1) analyzed the incidence of mongolism among monozygous and dizygous twins and their siblings. Their findings indicated that the frequency of mongolism among the dizygous twin partners of mongoloids is approximately the same as that among their subsequent siblings. From this they concluded that the pathological factor leading to mongolism is not a transient influence operating during the mongoloid pregnancy, but is to be sought in a relatively permanent change in the mother's reproductive system. The evidence also shows that there are no monozygous twins which are discordant for mongolism. Such a finding would mean that, in order to produce a mongoloid child, the etiological factor must act either on a genetically predisposed embryo or prior to the earliest stage when twinning occurs.

About equal in frequency to mongolism is the type of mental deficiency associated with *cerebral palsy*. As generally used, this category covers brain injuries sustained through instrumental or difficult delivery, premature birth, neonatal anoxia (interruption of oxygen supply), and infectious or toxic factors operating prenatally or in early childhood. Motor disorders of varying nature and degree of severity are the distinguishing characteristic of this clinical variety. It should be noted, however, that these motor symptoms *may* occur in the absence of mental deficiency. A considerable proportion of cerebral palsied cases, in fact, are of normal or superior intelligence. Moreover, in a number of the cerebral palsied patients classified as mentally deficient, the intellectual subnormality may result, not from brain injury, but from the retarding effects of the motor symptoms upon normal educational processes. This type of effect was discussed in Chapter 5, as an example of a somatopsychological influence.

Other clinical varieties of mental deficiency are relatively rare, usually found in less than 1 per cent of the institutionalized population. The *microcephalic* has an abnormally small, pointed skull, with a characteristic "sugarloaf" appearance. The *hydrocephalic* has a very large skull and an excessive accumulation of cerebrospinal fluid in the brain. The *cretin* is easily identified by his stunted physique, coarse thick skin, loss of hair, and other physi-

[2] Cf. Lejeune, J., Turpin, R., and Gautier, Marthe. Le mongolisme, premier exemple d'aberration autosomique humaine. *La Semaine des Hopitaux: Annales de Genetique,* 1959, 1, No. 2, 41–49.

cal characteristics. Thyroid deficiency has been conclusively established as the cause of cretinism. The administration of thyroid extract, if begun early in life, usually effects a considerable improvement in both physical and intellectual condition, although some cases do not respond to this therapy. The causes of microcephaly and hydrocephaly are not so well established, but there is evidence indicating the role of prenatal factors, including maternal nutrition, toxins, infections, and radiation.

Another rare but clearly identifiable clinical type is *phenylpyruvic amentia*. These cases are differentiated by the presence of phenylpyruvic acid in the urine, resulting from a hereditary metabolic disorder. The condition appears to depend upon a single recessive gene, and has never been found in a person of normal intelligence. It is usually accompanied by motor symptoms and is found in association with a severe grade of mental deficiency. Still another hereditary metabolic disorder is *amaurotic idiocy*. This is actually a group of disorders which occur at different ages in childhood and which differ in clinical symptoms and in degree of intellectual subnormality.

Mention may also be made of the suggested role of the *Rh factor* in mental deficiency. Although having no natural antibody in human blood, the Rh factor may provoke the production of antibodies when introduced into the blood of persons lacking in this factor (i.e., Rh negatives). It has been estimated that about 15 per cent of the population are Rh negative and therefore susceptible to the production of such antibodies. Some important implications of this situation for fetal development have been discovered. First, it should be noted that a certain amount of blood transfusion occurs between mother and child during uterine life. If the mother is Rh negative and the child Rh positive, antibodies will be formed in the mother's blood as a result of such a pregnancy. The first-born is not usually affected by this condition, since it takes time for the mother to develop sufficient antibodies. In subsequent Rh positive offspring, however, there may be extensive destruction of fetal blood, leading to a severe physical syndrome known as erythroblastosis fetalis (32).

It has been proposed that in those cases where Rh incompatibility of mother and child does not result in any observable physical disorders, the effect upon the fetal blood may still be sufficient to interfere with normal brain development and thus lead to feeblemindedness. In a study of the blood groups of mentally defective children and their mothers, Yannet and Lieberman (98) found evidence that in a small percentage of institutionalized feebleminded cases not classifiable into any of the known clinical types, the mental deficiency may have resulted from Rh incompatibility. The percentage of Rh positive children with Rh negative mothers in such groups significantly exceeded that found in the general population, as well as that obtained in control groups of mental defectives in other clinical varieties. Further surveys by Yannet and Lieberman (99, 100) indicated that mother-child incompatibility in other major blood groups (A, B, and O) may likewise lead to mental deficiency. On the other hand, later studies by other investigators have yielded conflicting results regarding the contribution of blood-group incompatibility to the development of mental defect (14, 33, 37, 80, 84, 85). Whether or not any cases of mental deficiency can actually be attributed to such etiology must therefore remain an open question until further research provides more conclusive data.

By far the largest proportion of mental defectives—including over half of all institutionalized cases—do not fall into any specific clinical variety. Such individuals are usually indistinguishable from normal persons in appearance, their handicap being manifested only in intellectual subnormality. Their mental deficiency, moreover, is relatively mild, most cases falling into the moron or high-grade imbecile levels. For both of these reasons, such persons are less likely to be institutionalized than are those falling into special clinical varieties. Hence the relative frequency of the former in the general population is probably even higher than would appear from institutional statistics.

Sarason (77) has used the term *"garden-variety mental deficiency"* to refer to this class of defectives. Other common designations are *simple, aclinical,* and *subcultural* feeblemindedness. Some writers distinguish between the *familial* type, in which several cases of simple amentia occur within the family, and the *undifferentiated* or sporadic cases occurring in normal families. The familial category is often employed with the connotation that a hereditary form of feeblemindedness is involved. As was seen in Chapter 9, however, the fact that such mental deficiency tends to "run in families" may be interpreted as evidence for environment just as well as for heredity. In this connection, it is interesting to note that studies that report improvement in intellectual level as a result of special training have found that it is the simple type that responds most readily to such training (45, 46). It is also relevant to observe that simple aments more often come from homes of lower socioeconomic level, while the specific clinical types show a more nearly random distribution of home background (15, 38). The latter occur with greater frequency than the former in families that are normal or superior in intellectual and socioeconomic level. Inferior home environment may be a causal factor in the intellectual retardation of at least some of the simple aments.

Certainly such terms as "simple" or "garden-variety" are more precisely descriptive of our knowledge regarding this type of mental deficiency than are some of the other suggested designations—"unknown" would probably be a more candid characterization. To assume a hereditary basis for just those cases in which no structural deficiencies have yet been demonstrated seems to suggest that feeblemindedness is itself a chemical substance which can be transmitted by the genes! Unless some structural deficiency is demonstrated, *what* is there for these cases to inherit? The evidence for hereditary contributions seems, in fact, to be much clearer in the case of the so-called secondary forms of feeblemindedness. Glandular and metabolic conditions of the mother, blood types, and even maternal body formation which might increase the chances of a difficult birth undoubtedly have a hereditary basis. From one point of view, of course, it may be argued that the feeblemindedness in such cases is only an indirect result of the hereditary condition. But this only serves to point up the artificiality of the heredity-environment distinction, especially as applied to behavior. Of more practical significance is the distinction proposed in Chapter 3 between structurally and functionally determined conditions. The specific clinical varieties of feeblemindedness discussed above are all structurally, or organically, determined and as such would be relatively uninfluenced by training. In these cases, the structural deficiency interferes with the acquisition of normal behavior. Some of the "simple" cases, on the other hand, may be functionally determined and therefore much more responsive to training.

It is highly probable that, as more is learned about the large group of "simple aments," this category will be subdivided into several distinct types with different etiologies. In his post-mortem examinations of simple aments, Benda (10) found evidence of disorders of cell differentiation and other developmental anomalies of the nervous system. From findings such as these, Benda concluded that hereditary neurological disorders always underlie the intellectual deficiency in a subgroup of simple amentia which he designates as "*oligophrenia vera.*" The research of Strauss and his associates (88) on endogenous and exogenous forms of mental deficiency, to be discussed below, likewise suggests an organic basis for the intellectual deficiency in some simple aments.

On the other hand, several writers have called attention to the various environmental factors which may operate in the etiology of simple mental deficiency (57; 77, Ch. 6). The underprivileged homes in which most simple aments are reared are clearly deficient in opportunities for the development of such functions as verbal comprehension and abstract reasoning, which constitute a major part of intelligence in our culture. At the same time, such homes encourage the learning of "self-defeating techniques" (57), such as expectation of failure, low self-esteem, concrete rather than abstract thinking, and suppression of verbalization and of exploratory behavior. In such a social milieu, there is likewise little motivation for school achievement. It should be noted that some psychologists would classify all instances of mental deficiency stemming from such cultural deprivations as "pseudo-feeblemindedness" (cf., e.g., 26, 36, 42, 76). In terms of its psychological manifestations, however, this type of simple amentia is just as "real" as are deficiencies resulting from organic defects.

Etiological Classifications. The concept of pseudofeeblemindedness highlights the efforts that have been made to identify types of mental deficiency on the basis of etiology. In an earlier section, it was noted that etiological considerations form an integral part of certain proposed definitions of mental deficiency as a whole. In a number of schemas for the classification of clinical varieties, etiological concepts have been employed in more specific ways to differentiate among types of mental deficiency. The classification given by Tredgold (93) and widely adopted for many years is essentially etiological. More recently, Benda (9) has proposed another schema based upon causal factors. Benda's system employs three criteria for classifying mental deficiency, namely: (1) hereditary versus environmental causation, (2) nature of pathogenic factor, and (3) time at which the pathogenic factor operates.

With regard to the last-named criterion, Benda makes a major distinction among prenatal, paranatal (during birth), and postnatal disorders. Within the very important prenatal period, furthermore, it is now possible to "date" specific clinical varieties more precisely in the light of the known developmental chronology of the human embryo and fetus. For example, it has been established that mongolism results from developmental disturbances occurring between the sixth and twelfth weeks of gestation. Among the *kinds* of pathogenic factors that have been most clearly identified may be mentioned hereditary metabolic disorders (as in amaurotic and phenylpyruvic amentia); prenatal endocrine and nutritional deficiencies (as in mongolism and cretinism); traumatic factors, such as mechanically caused birth injuries, neonatal anoxia, X-ray exposure, and rubella (German measles) contracted by the mother during pregnancy; and severe infectious diseases of childhood, in so far as they may lead to brain inflammation.

Research on the etiology of mental deficiency is of course of fundamental importance. Consideration of all possible etiological factors operating in any individual case is likewise essential as a basis for proper administrative decisions. Nevertheless, for purposes of classification, etiological criteria prove unsatisfactory for at least two reasons. First, there remain large groups of mental defectives for whom no adequate knowledge of causal factors is yet available. The simple aments are the most conspicuous example, although etiological knowledge regarding other clinical varieties is also far from complete. As more data are accumulated, readjustments have to be made in the classificatory schemas and certain clinical varieties shifted from one category to another. One conclusion that is clearly emerging from current research is that prenatal and paranatal environmental factors play a much greater part in the causation of mental deficiency than was heretofore believed (cf. 10, 50, 55, 68).

A second major difficulty in the application of etiological classifications arises from the fact that pathological conditions which are symptomatically similar *may* have entirely different etiologies. Microcephaly, for instance, results in some cases from traumatic prenatal factors, such as X-ray or rubella. In others, it appears to stem from a hereditary developmental deficiency.

Endogenous versus Exogenous Mental Deficiency.   An etiological distinction which has stimulated extensive research is that between endogenous and exogenous mental deficiency. Briefly, the exogenous are those whose intellectual deficiency is associated with brain injury, while the endogenous exhibit intellectual defect without evidence of any neurological damage. Although the usage of these terms varies among writers on mental deficiency, Strauss and his co-workers (88) employ them in a restricted sense, excluding from consideration all cases of gross neural symptoms, such as are found in the special clinical varieties. Thus as used by Strauss, endogenous and exogenous refer essentially to subdivisions of simple or aclinical amentia. Since relatively mild neurological disorders are involved, the exogenous cases are generally identified through a history of prenatal or postnatal accidents, premature or difficult birth, or infectious diseases in early childhood. As a rule, these cases also come from intellectually normal families, in contrast to the endogenous.

Extensive investigations by Strauss and others suggest that, psychologically, exogenous mental defectives differ in characteristic ways from the endogenous cases (cf. 77, Ch. 5; 88). In their test performance, the brain-injured defectives tend to show disorders of perception and concept formation. They tend also to do better on verbal than on nonverbal tasks, while the reverse is usually true of endogenous mental defectives. In addition, their general behavior is rated significantly more often as erratic, uncontrolled, and uninhibited than that of the endogenous cases.

Some investigators have called attention to the similarities between the behavior of exogenous mental defectives and that of adults who have sustained brain injuries. Resemblances have likewise been noted between the performance of exogenous mental defectives and that of cerebral palsied children, in whom brain injury underlies both the motor and the psychological disorders. All of these findings, corroborated by many investigators working independently, strongly indicate that brain injuries are manifested in a recognizable pattern of psychological disturbances, which contrasts with the over-all deficiency of the endogenous feebleminded. At the same time, it is important to bear in mind that a certain amount of overlapping has always been found between brain-injured and non-brain-injured groups. Some brain-injured cases do not exhibit the expected deficiencies, and some apparently non-brain-injured persons do. Hence it is unwarranted to base a diagnosis of "exogeneity" upon behavior characteristics alone, in the absence of clear evidence of brain injury from neurological examination or case history.

One more point may be noted. Recent research by Knobloch, Pasamanick, and their co-workers (50, 55) suggests that most—if not all—cases of low IQ in infancy are associated with neurological damage. In other words, it is relatively difficult to find endogenous mental defectives early in life. Such a finding leads the investigators to propose that the additional cases of mental deficiency identified at later ages may result from educational and other cultural deprivations operating upon the growing child (50). Although not conclusively established, it is these authors' contention that the number of mental defectives with organic etiology is relatively small, and that among such cases environmentally induced brain injuries play the major part.

Multi-factor versus Uni-factor Subnormality. Another frequent distinction of an etiological nature is that between mental deficiency resulting from a single pathological factor and that arising from a multiplicity of factors. In either case, the factors may be hereditary or environmental, the differentiation referring only to *number* of contributing factors. This distinction, first proposed by Pearson and Jaederholm in 1914, has received its fullest expression in the writings of Fraser Roberts (74). The multi-factor defectives are considered to represent simply the lower end of the distribution of intelligence; the uni-factor, on the other hand, owe their deficiency to the operation of a special pathological condition or accident which leads to mental defect regardless of other concomitant circumstances. Fraser Roberts links this differentiation with *degree of defect.* Thus he maintains that higher-grade cases (including principally morons) have a multiple etiology, while lower-grade cases (chiefly imbeciles and idiots) have a single-factor etiology.

The evidence for the above hypothesis is derived from three main sources. First, large-scale surveys have shown that the distribution of intelligence test scores closely approximates the normal curve when morons are included along with normal and superior persons, but deviates significantly from normality when imbeciles and idiots are added to the group. The number of persons with IQ's below 45 or so is markedly greater than would be expected by chance. This point has already been discussed in Chapter 2. Such a finding is consistent with the hypothesis that, except for the operation of a single pathological factor, most of these low-grade cases would have been distributed at random over the whole range.

A second type of evidence is based upon family resemblances. Low-grade cases come from families of all intellectual levels, while high-grade cases tend to come from intellectually defective families (38, 74). Thus the mean IQ of siblings of morons is *lower* than that of siblings of idiots and imbeciles. Similarly, a number of surveys of the socioeconomic level and occupations of parents of mental defectives have consistently shown that high-grade cases tend to come from low socioeconomic levels, while low-grade cases represent a wide random sampling of the general population in this regard (15, 38, 69, 74).

Rather than basing the distinction upon degree of intellectual defect, other writers have suggested that simple aments may have multiple etiology, while the special clinical varieties result from single pathological factors. Another, slightly different variant, is provided by Lewis' dichotomy into subcultural and pathological cases (54), the latter including *all* cases due to a definite organic abnormality. It is difficult to choose among such bases for differentiation, since the resulting categories overlap to a large extent. Thus most high-grade cases are simple defectives. That some of them may nevertheless have organic pathology is only now being recognized and is still difficult to establish in individual cases, as was seen in the preceding section on endogenous and exogenous etiology. Nevertheless, the distinction between multiple- and single-factor etiology appears promising and the data gathered in support of it should advance our understanding of the causes of mental deficiency.

PHYSICAL CHARACTERISTICS

In general health, susceptibility to disease, and physical development, institutionalized mental defectives *as a group* are clearly below normal. Mortality statistics reveal a much higher death rate and shorter average life span for the feebleminded. In one survey covering 344 idiots and 424 imbeciles, the mean duration of life was 19.0 years for the former and 26.6 for the latter (43). In general, the lower the intellectual level, the shorter the life expectancy. With medical progress and improvement in institutional facilities and care, it is to be expected that such figures will be revised upward. But the fact remains that, under existing conditions, mental defectives are on the average much shorter-lived than the intellectually normal.

Data on height and weight likewise indicate that mental defectives lag behind the general population in physical growth. All surveys of institutionalized mental defectives or of children in special classes for the intellectually retarded have yielded small but significant differences in mean height and weight (34, 65). To be sure, overlapping is extensive as in all such comparisons. Thus in one investigation, 44 per cent of the mentally defective children reached or exceeded the median of normal children in weight and 45 per cent did so in height (65). It will be recalled that complete overlapping is indicated when 50 per cent of one group reach or exceed the median of the other.

At the same time, group trends yield consistent differences, not only between normal and mentally defective samples as a whole, but also among levels of mental deficiency. Goddard (34) collected extensive data on the height and weight of about 11,000 mentally defective persons ranging in age from early infancy to 60 years and living in 19 American institutions for the feebleminded. In Figures 72 and 73 are reproduced curves showing the mean height and weight of successive age groups within each of four intellectual levels: idiot, imbecile, moron, and normal. Data for boys are given in Figure 72, those for girls in Figure 73. It will be noted that the curves for the four intellectual levels exhibit a small but consistent tendency for physical inferiority to parallel intellectual inferiority. This relationship is clearer during the adolescent and adult years than it is at earlier ages. Nevertheless, the same group trends are discernible very early in life. Thus Asher and Fraser Roberts (3) found significantly lower mean birth weights for mental defectives and for children attending special classes for the educationally backward than for the general population.

Miscellaneous physical defects are also more prevalent among feebleminded than among normal persons. Tredgold (93), has surveyed such defects in considerable detail. They range from minor anomalies in head shape, abnormalities of eyes and ears, skin disorders, and susceptibility to pulmonary and infectious diseases to speech defects. The number and

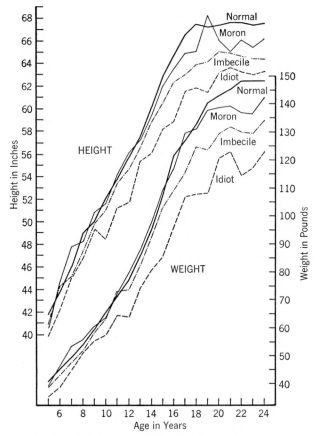

Fig. 72. Mean Height and Weight of Mentally Defective and Normal Boys at Successive Ages. (From Goddard, 34, p. 228.)

severity of such miscellaneous deficiencies tend likewise to be roughly proportional to the degree of intellectual defect. Tredgold and others have seen in these deficiencies evidence of general constitutional weakness resulting from poor heredity and manifesting itself in both physical and intellectual inferiority. That there may be other explanations has probably already occurred to the reader. We shall return to the interpretation of these findings in a moment.

Of particular psychological interest is the greater frequency of total deafness as well as of hearing loss found among institutionalized mental defectives than among the normal population (12, 72). Such findings have important implications for the acquisition of language and for general intellectual development. It is possible that a certain number of simple mental

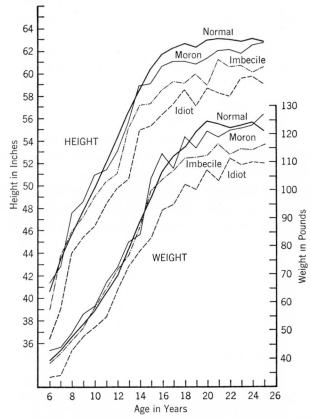

Fig. 73. Mean Height and Weight of Mentally Defective and Normal Girls at Successive Ages. (From Goddard, 34, p. 229.)

defectives may be otherwise normal deaf persons who have failed to receive suitable training to circumvent their sensory handicap. Even relatively minor hearing losses, if undetected, may be enough of a handicap in schoolwork and in other interpersonal contacts to produce mild degrees of mental deficiency.

In the interpretation of the over-all physical deficiency of feebleminded groups, a number of factors must be taken into account. In the first place, persons with physical as well as intellectual defects are more likely to be institutionalized. The mental defective who is physically fit is less often sent to an institution and is more often discharged following training and re-habilitation. Such individuals have a greater chance to succeed in routine occupations requiring strength and a good physique with a minimum of thought and planning. The operation of such a selective factor might in part explain the divergence of Goddard's height and weight curves for different intellectual levels with age. Since only institutional cases were included, the inferiority at the upper ages might have resulted from the fact that the physically strongest and ablest had left the institutions.

Secondly, in a survey extending down to low-grade levels of mental deficiency, it is probable that cases falling into the special clinical varieties are included. The presence of such cases would further lower the average physical measurements of the feebleminded group as a whole. On the other hand, when only simple, aclinical cases are surveyed, it should be remembered that such a group will be below average in socioeconomic background. The sort of home that is deficient in diet, hygiene, and medical care will also tend to be intellectually unstimulating. The common environmental deprivation might thus account for both the mental defect and the physical condition. Finally, some of the physical deficiencies, such as sensory or motor disorders or chronic ill health, may prove to be sufficiently handicapping to exert a seriously retarding effect upon mental development. Such an etiological mechanism will be recognized as an example of the somato-psychological relation between physique and intellect discussed in Chapter 5.

PSYCHOLOGICAL CHARACTERISTICS

Most studies on the psychological characteristics of mental defectives have been conducted on simple aments. Such cases are much more numerous than those representing special clinical varieties; they are likely to be high-grade defectives and hence more readily amenable to testing; and they are of greater psychological interest than the special clinical types, which constitute principally a medical problem. It should be noted, however, that some investigators do not specify the clinical classification of their subjects and it is likely that they are dealing with heterogeneous samples in which simple aments predominate. Moreover, the fact that simple aments themselves may include endogenous and exogenous cases, as well as some unidentified cases belonging to special clinical varieties, further complicates the interpretation of results. Only certain general trends will therefore be considered from the research findings in this area.

One question to which investigators have addressed themselves is that of

IQ changes with age among institutionalized mental defectives. It has been found that in such groups IQ's tend to decrease with age, rather than remaining constant as in normal children and adolescents (52, 82). The mental defectives thus seem to fall farther behind the normal with advancing age. With regard to absolute level of scores, "mental growth" appears to terminate sooner the lower the IQ (52) and the eventual decline begins much earlier than in normal persons (90). All of these findings might indicate a genetically weaker organism. A somewhat more plausible explanation, however, focuses upon the fact of institutionalization itself. Most institutions are set up to provide primarily custodial care, with a minimum of training. This is particularly true in the case of lower-grade cases. Under such conditions, we would not expect much intellectual progress during institutional residence. Selective factors must also be taken into account. Those individuals who make appreciable intellectual progress are more likely to be discharged, leaving the more deteriorated cases in the institutional population.

In the case of certain clinical varieties in which there is progressive organic deterioration, a decrease in IQ would naturally be expected with age. For the majority of simple aments, however, as well as for cases undergoing no further neurological changes, it seems likely that the institutional environment is a major factor in the observed IQ decline. In support of such an explanation are the rises in IQ found in certain institutions with special training programs, as well as the results of rehabilitation studies to be reported in the next section. There is also some evidence suggesting that persons who come from unusually adverse environments show rises in IQ following a period of institutional residence (25). In such cases the institutional environment, limited though it be, nevertheless represents an improvement over the subject's former cultural milieu.

Considerable attention has also been given to the *profile of abilities* of mental defectives. Are such persons equally inferior in all functions? When put in this form, the question can be readily answered in the negative. The idiots savants cited in Chapter 10 represent extreme examples of mental defectives with superior talent along a specific line. At the same time, we must recognize that compensation is not the rule. Feebleminded persons in general do *not* show superior traits which balance their inferiorities. On the contrary, they are usually below average in all intellectual functions, although not uniformly inferior in all.

Because of the predominant role of verbal aptitudes in intelligence tests as well as in the over-all concept of intelligence in our culture, it is to be expected that mental defectives will be most consistently and markedly inferior in these abilities. General findings bear out this expectation. Most simple aments, for example, are poorer on verbal than on performance tests of intelligence. To offset such results, however, it should be recalled that exogenous, or brain-injured, defectives more often exhibit the reverse pattern, being farther below average in perceptual and spatial than in verbal functions. The ability to deal with abstract concepts in any form, however, appears to be one of the most consistent areas of deficiency among mental defectives of all types.

Of special interest because of their possible vocational implications are the results obtained with *motor functions.* In these tasks, mental defectives again fall significantly below the general norms (19, 81, 92), although the distributions reveal extensive overlapping. Thus from the standpoint of individual guidance and rehabilitation, it is noteworthy that a considerable proportion of mental defectives can be found who possess the skills necessary for learning many industrial jobs. But as a group, defectives do not excel in motor functions, any more than they do in more highly intellectual tasks.

A group of studies have been concerned with the relative performance of normals and defectives of the *same mental age,* on individual Stanford-Binet items (53, 56, 58, 73, 91, 94). Are there characteristic ways in which, let us say, the test performance of a 14-year-old with a mental age of 8 differs from that of a normal 8-year-old child? The investigation of Thompson and Magaret (91) represents the most thorough effort to answer this type of question. In this study, the performance of 441 defectives on individual Stanford-Binet items was compared with that of 1326 normals from the standardization sample. All comparisons were made between defectives and normals equated in mental age on the entire scale. Of the 73 items that could be evaluated statistically, 12 significantly favored the defectives and 19 the normals at the .01 level.

Analyses of the nature of the two sets of items showed that they differed most clearly in their *loadings on the "first factor"*—a factor which had been previously identified as common to the entire Stanford-Binet scale (60, Ch. 9). A later comparison of normal, superior, and defective children by the same authors corroborated these findings (56). The superior children significantly surpassed both normals and defectives on items highly saturated with the common factor. Such a result is understandable in view of the fact that the Stanford-Binet scale as a whole is an important criterion in identifying both intellectually defective and superior subjects. Sarason (77, p. 69) points out that the items in which defectives did significantly poorer than normals also included a relatively large number of tasks requiring *oral responses.* He suggested that emotional factors may in part account for the difference, since this type of test is reminiscent of schoolwork and other interpersonal contacts in which defective children have characteristically met with failure and frustration.

Other hypotheses that had been proposed by earlier investigators to explain differences in test performance between normals and defectives were not borne out by Thompson and Magaret's data. It had been suggested, for instance, that defectives, being older, would have an advantage over normal children of the same mental age on items calling for *past experience.* However, when two psychologists were asked by Thompson and Magaret to rate each Stanford-Binet item for its dependence upon past experience, the defectives were found to excel on items *less* dependent upon past experience. It cannot be assumed, of course, that the "past experience" of defectives is the same as that of normal children. In so far as schooling is a major part of such past experience, it is obvious that the two groups would differ in this regard. Stanford-Binet items that are highly dependent upon schoolwork would certainly not be expected to favor defectives.

One respect in which the more advanced chronological age of the defective may provide an advantage over the younger child of the same mental age was illustrated in a study by Sloan and Raskin (83). Through a series of specially designed questions, these investigators found evidence that the defectives were more realistic and practical in their vocational aspirations, wishes, attitudes, and reactions to hypothetical situations. It would appear that the category of "past experience" is too broad to serve effectively in differentiating between defectives and normals. But if we single out more specific aspects of past experience, it is possible to obtain more clear-cut results.

The concept of *rigidity* has likewise been proposed in the attempt to differentiate between defectives and normals. As used by Kounin (51), the term "rigidity" refers chiefly to compartmentalization of functions, which would make it relatively difficult for the defective to relate different activities, objects, or ideas. Kounin's hypothesis was not supported by Thompson and Magaret's data. Those Stanford-Binet items which had been independently rated as more difficult for a "rigid" person in Kounin's sense tended to be easier rather than harder for the defectives. Other writers have used the term "rigidity" to mean stereotypy of behavior (96). Institutionalized morons, for example, will often carry out routine tasks with unswerving precision and with no signs of boredom. Such persons exhibit considerable tolerance for monotonous, repetitive tasks. It is, of course, well known that monotony is a function of the nature of the task, the distracting stimuli, and the characteristics of the worker. The individual with relatively few competing interests and limited ability will find a repetitive task more congenial and satisfying than a task involving many shifts and readjustments. Institutional life itself, with its paucity of activities, may contribute to this condition. Institutionalization may thus be partly responsible both for the greater rigidity of mental defectives in comparison with normals and for the increasing rigidity of institutionalized defectives with age (16).

Another question pertains to the ability of mental defectives to *learn*. As was seen in Chapter 11, this question cannot be answered in general terms since there is no unitary, common learning factor. With regard to school learning, mental defectives are, on the whole, characteristically deficient and their progress is very slow. On the other hand, they *can* learn other functions with varying degrees of effectiveness. A survey of the few published studies on this question suggested that, although a minimum intellectual level is required for learning each type of task, there is little or no relationship between errors or rate of learning and intellectual level beyond that minimum (61). Recent research on the outcomes of rehabilitation programs with mental defectives likewise points up the extent to which such persons may improve with training. These studies will be considered in the following section.

TRAINING AND REHABILITATION

The years since World War II have witnessed a rapid growth in programs for the *vocational and social rehabilitation* of high-grade mental defectives. Several factors have contributed to this development. First, labor shortages made it desirable to tap one more potential source of manpower in the trainable defective. It has been recognized for many years that there are a large number of jobs in our society which can be satisfactorily done by mental defectives, some requiring a minimum mental age as low as six years (6, 17). Secondly, rehabilitation and discharge were seen as one way to help "depopulate" the overcrowded institutions for mental defectives. Finally, in 1943 legislation was enacted by Congress which made it possible to include mental defectives in vocational rehabilitation programs for the handicapped and made federal funds available to the states for this purpose.

Within the late 1940's and early 1950's, a number of states initiated vocational rehabilitation programs for institutionalized mental defectives. Through such efforts, considerable experience has been accumulated regarding the requirements of such programs (cf., e.g., 28, 66). It is generally recognized that for maximum success the program should include careful selection of promising cases, institutional training in self-care and vocational skills, psychotherapy and medical treatment when needed, placement on parole in homes and on jobs selected by counselors, close follow-up and guidance during the adjustment period, and continued counseling facilities after discharge. The common observation that high-grade defectives are particularly deficient in the ability to plan ahead and manage their lives independently makes the availability of counseling services especially crucial for the successful community adjustment of these persons.

A parallel development has been the expansion of educational facilities for trainable mentally defective children within the public school system. *Special classes* for such children have recently been established in many additional localities and considerable attention has been given to improvement of selection procedures, development of suitable curricula and instructional materials, treatment of special disabilities, and other related problems (cf. 49, 75, 95). Of special relevance to differential psychology are the results of *follow-up studies* on mental defectives who have been either paroled from institutions or educated in special classes. To date, a considerable number of such studies have been published, including a wide diversity of training and rehabilitation programs and covering follow-up periods which range from less than a year to over twenty years.[3] With regard to mental level, the subjects fall predominantly in the moron category, although several studies include a few cases at the borderline level and some whose IQ's are low enough to place them within the imbecile group. In so far as can be ascertained, the large majority of cases are simple aments with no gross neurological complications.

The results of these follow-up studies are consistently favorable. Social and vocational adjustment have proved better than had been anticipated and the number of failures is small. When retests were administered, the later IQ's have quite generally shown a rise over the initial level. A few of the more extensive studies will be cited to illustrate procedure and results. Hegge (39) reports a two-year follow-up of 177 young people paroled from a training school for mental defectives in 1941 and 1942. At the time of the survey, 88 per cent were employed, many above the unskilled labor level. Most were earning from $40 to $60 a week, showed a fair amount of job stability, and had secured employment without the assistance of family, friends, or social agencies.

Kennedy (44) conducted a relatively well-controlled follow-up of 256 morons in a Connecticut community, as part of a larger study of the human resources of the state. The IQ's of the group in grade school had ranged

[3] Cf. 2, 4, 5, 13, 20, 23, 31, 39, 44, 45, 59, 62, 63, 67, 71, 79, 87.

from 50 to 75. These subjects, whose mean age at the time of the follow-up was 24 years, were compared with 129 control subjects of normal IQ from the same community, who were matched with the morons in age, sex, age at starting school, race, country of birth, nationality, and father's occupation. That they were not equated in all background variables, however, is indicated by the fact that broken homes and family maladjustments were more prevalent in the moron than in the control group.

In terms of adult outcomes, the morons compared favorably with the normal controls. Thus at the time of the survey, 75.5 per cent of the morons and 68.6 per cent of the controls were classified as self-supporting. The difference is not statistically significant, the results suggesting an equally successful adjustment in this respect in both groups. As a group, the morons were found to be in lower level occupations than the controls. For example, 83 per cent of the morons and 56 per cent of the controls were engaged in manual labor. Fewer morons than normals had clerical, managerial, or professional jobs. Average earnings of the two groups, however, were about the same. In job stability, extent of agency relief, and marital adjustment, there were no significant differences between the two groups. The moron record was slightly poorer with regard to antisocial activity, social participation, and leisure interests. But in this connection it must be recalled that the home backgrounds of the two groups were *not* equated in certain important psychological variables.

The investigation covering the longest period of time was concerned with a group of children with initial IQ's of 70 or less who had attended special classes in the Nebraska public schools. The first follow-up was conducted by Baller (5) in 1936, when the subjects were between the ages of 21 and 34. Of the original group of 206, 196 were located and compared with a high-normal group whose IQ's ranged from 100 to 120. Slightly less than 7 per cent of the original mentally defective group were in institutions for the feebleminded at the time of the follow-up. Educationally, the subnormal group had completed an average of 4 or 5 grades, in contrast to the 12- to 13-grade average of the "normal," control group. The majority of the defectives had no court records, although the proportion with such records exceeded that in the control group: 25 per cent vs. 4 per cent for juvenile court, and 18 per cent vs. 6 per cent for police court. The proportion of mental defectives who had held relatively permanent jobs was 39 per cent, as compared with a proportion in excess of 90 per cent for the control group. Among the subnormal, however, 83 per cent had been at least partially self-supporting for varying periods of time. The proportion of girls who had married was about equal in the two groups, although the subnormal girls tended to marry earlier and to have more children. Among the boys, the percentage who had married was much smaller for the subnormal, probably because of economic reasons. In evaluating all of the findings of this follow-up, we must bear in mind, first, that the control group was above average in IQ and probably not equated with the defectives in many respects, and secondly, that these follow-up data were obtained during a period of economic depression.

In 1953, Charles (23) reported a further follow-up of 151 of Baller's original subjects. At this time, the mean age of the group was 42, with a range from 36 to 49 years. Employment records again showed the group to have made a satisfactory adjustment, on the whole. Thus 82.79 per cent were classified as "usually employed," their jobs ranging from unskilled labor to managerial occupations. Of those gainfully employed, 47.62 per cent had been on the same job for a period of 3 to 20 years. About 80 per cent of the living subjects were married. The large majority of their children are reported as proceeding through school at the normal rate and achieving at least a grade school education. One was a successful college student at the time of the survey. The IQ's of the children ranged from 50 to 138, with a mean of 95.44.

Of particular interest are the retest results obtained by Charles with 20 of the original subjects, whose initial Stanford-Binet IQ's averaged 58.35 and ranged from 41 to 70. The Wechsler-Bellevue retest mean of this group was 81.25, with a range from 60 to 104. Although some of the increase may be due to regression effect, it is unlikely that the entire gain is attributable to this cause. It seems probable that some of the rise indicates a genuine improvement in the functions tested, which paralleled the satisfactory social and vocational adjustment made by many of these subjects in adulthood.

A highly controversial study on the rehabilitation of mental defectives is that reported by Schmidt (79). In this project, 254 boys and girls between the ages of 12 and 14, who had been referred to special classes, were put through a three-year educational program specially designed for them. The average initial Stanford-Binet IQ reported for this group is 52.1, with a range from 27 to 69. The subjects were tested periodically with intelligence, educational achievement, and personality tests during the three-year training period, as well as during a five-year follow-up after the completion of the experimental program. The degree of progress in all aspects of behavior reported in this study far outstrips that found in any other investigation to date. At the completion of the investigation, a mean gain of 40.7 IQ points was observed; 80.7 per cent of the subjects made gains of 30 or more IQ points and 59.6 per cent gained 40 points or more. The larger part of these gains occurred during the three-year experimental period, although in the course of the subsequent five-year follow-up the IQ's showed *continued gains*, rather than dropping toward the initial level.

The progress in educational achievement reported by Schmidt is equally remarkable. Although the average educational performance at the beginning of the experiment fell within the first grade, by the completion of the three-year program it had reached approximately fifth-grade level. Moreover, 79 subjects transferred to the regular elementary school either to qualify for immediate graduation from the eighth grade or to complete the elementary school course in regular classes. During the five-year follow-up period, a large number continued their education in technical, business, or avocational courses, and 27 of the original group had graduated from high school by the termination of the study. Data on subsequent occupational history, socio-economic status, community activities, and the like during the follow-up showed the group to have made a very satisfactory adjustment.

As a control group, Schmidt employed 68 children, also enrolled in special classes for the intellectually deficient but not participating in the experimental program. The control group was approximately equated with an experimental subgroup of 64 cases in initial IQ, educational achievement, and chronological age. The mean gain of this experimental subgroup was 23.8 IQ points, while the control group lost an average of 3.6 points during the same period. Marked differences in educational progress and in subsequent vocational and social adjustment were likewise found between these two groups.

The Schmidt study is difficult to evaluate for several reasons (cf, 35, 47, 64). The presence of a number of minor arithmetic errors and inconsistencies in the published account of the project indicates careless reporting and has aroused skepticism regarding the data as a whole. The procedures employed in the training and rehabilitation program are inadequately described, thus precluding independent corroboration. A study by Hill (41) using presumably similar techniques, for example, revealed only slight gains in IQ. To what extent the procedures followed by Hill were actually comparable to those used in Schmidt's program cannot be ascertained. An examination of Schmidt's report does suggest that at least some of the improvement in test performance and in academic progress may have resulted from the correction of sensory defects, poor health conditions, and language handicap which were initially present in a considerable number of cases. Emotional maladjustments had likewise hampered achievement in several cases and improvement in this respect is reported in the course of the project.

In the instructional procedures themselves, as described by Schmidt, special attention was apparently given to the development of effective work and study habits and to the attainment of minimum levels of performance in reading and language usage. Such techniques should provide for the continuance of improvement after the termination of the experimental period. Similarly, Schmidt emphasizes the stimulation of pupil interest and the adaptation of instruction to the specific needs and deficiencies of each individual. All of these objectives are of course highly desirable in training programs for mental defectives. Whether the specific procedures utilized by Schmidt can be expected to produce gains as large as those claimed, however, must remain an unanswered question for the present. In any event, it appears evident that the effectiveness of many of the techniques would be restricted to certain types of cases.

Mention may be made of another study yielding ambiguous results, as an illustration of further methodological problems. Kephart (45) provided intensive instruction over a period ranging from six months to nearly three years to 16 institutionalized feebleminded boys aged 15 to 18 years at the beginning of the experiment. Utilizing concrete materials, social situations, and abstract problems, the training was designed to stimulate constructive activity and to encourage ingenuity, initiative, and original planning. Following training, mean Stanford-Binet IQ rose from 66.3 to 76.4, in contrast to an insignificant gain of 1.9 points in the control group. All but one of the individual subjects in the trained group showed an improvement in IQ. The chief difficulty in the interpretation of this study arises from the similarity between some of the training materials and the content of the Stanford-Binet. Specifically, some of the training problems involved the recognition of absurdities in stories, a task that has much in common with several Stanford-Binet items. It is thus possible that the improvement may have been restricted to closely similar tasks and would have little effect upon the solution of other kinds of problems. In such a case, the training provided could be regarded as coaching (cf. Ch. 7).

Two recent developments in the training and rehabilitation of mental defectives deserve special attention. One concerns the training of high-grade mental defectives at the *preschool* level. Chamberlain and Moss (22) describe a program of home training designed to prepare such children for school. An investigation of several years' duration on the effectiveness of special preschool training with both an institutional and a community group is reported by Kirk (48). In this study, both training and control groups were tested periodically, the ultimate criterion being the school achievement of the subjects. In general, the results indicated that preschool education *can* increase the rate of intellectual and social development of mentally defective children. Improvement was greater for children from deprived environments than for those with organic disabilities. The trained group, moreover, tended to retain its superiority over the control group during the subsequent school years.

A growing recognition of the value of *psychotherapy* with mental defectives represents a second important trend. A number of investigators have recently applied projective techniques, such as Rorschach inkblots, picture interpretation, spontaneous drawings, and the like, to mentally deficient subjects (cf. 77, Ch. 9). The interpretation of specific findings of these studies is questionable, owing to the unknown validity of scoring procedures and to other technical deficiencies of current projective tests. Nevertheless, such research has served to call attention to the prevalence of emotional problems and anxieties among mental defectives. It is gradually being realized that the difficulties experienced by such persons are not necessarily limited to the intellectual level. Accordingly, the possibilities of utilizing various types of psychotherapy with mental defectives are being explored (77, Ch. 10; 86). In some cases, psychotherapy may help to raise the IQ, in so far as emotional problems may have been interfering with the individual's effective intellectual functioning and development. In others, such therapy may do no more than remove the additional handicap of emotional maladjustments or behavior problems. Even in the latter cases, psychotherapy can play a significant part in the total rehabilitation program.

SUMMARY

In general, the term "mental deficiency" designates a pronounced inferiority in those abilities that are essential for survival within a particular culture. It is thus apparent that the definition of mental deficiency is closely related to the concept of intelligence. In our culture, language development and verbal aptitudes play an important part in the identification of mental defectives. The principal criteria employed in diagnosing and classifying mental defectives are the psychometric (in terms of IQ), the legal or sociological, and the educational. Subdivisions into idiot, imbecile, moron, and borderline levels are also based on these criteria. Proposed definitions of mental deficiency in terms of etiology are difficult to apply since the causes of the deficiency are unknown in a large proportion of cases.

Among the most familiar clinical varieties of mental deficiency are mongolism, cerebral palsy, microcephaly, cretinism, and hydrocephaly. Phenylpyruvic amentia and amaurotic idiocy are relatively rare forms which have been traced to hereditary metabolic disorders. Whether blood-group incompatibility between mother and child is a significant cause of mental deficiency remains an unanswered question at this time. The largest proportion of mental defectives do not fall into any specific clinical varieties. Lacking any gross neurological defects, these cases have been variously described as simple, aclinical, subcultural, familial, undifferentiated, garden-variety, and oligophrenia vera. Some of these terms refer to the entire group, others are restricted to proposed subdivisions. A distinction between endogenous and exogenous (brain-injured) simple aments has stimulated extensive research on the psychological differences between these two types.

Etiologic classifications of clinical varieties take into account hereditary versus environmental causation, nature of pathogenic factor, and time at which the pathogenic factor operates. Current research indicates that prenatal and paranatal environmental factors play a much greater part in the etiology of mental deficiency than was formerly believed. A promising etio-logical distinction is that between multiple-factor and single-factor causation. The former has been applied chiefly to simple aments (and by some to high-grade aments), the latter to the special clinical varieties (or possibly to all organic cases or to low-grade cases regardless of clinical variety).

Mental defectives as a group are below normal in physical development, prevalence of physical and sensory defects, general health, susceptibility to disease, and life span, although overlapping with intellectually normal groups is extensive in all these respects. IQ's of institutionalized defectives tend to decrease with age. At least in the case of some subjects, however, such a decline may be the result of institutionalization itself. Defectives tend to be below average in all functions, although the degree of inferiority varies with the nature of the function. They tend to be most deficient in abstract functions, tasks requiring oral responses, and activities typical of schoolwork. Many exhibit stereotyped behavior and high tolerance for monotonous, repetitive tasks. Although slow in academic learning, defectives make satisfactory progress in learning many other skills suited to their ability level.

There has been rapid expansion in programs for the vocational and social rehabilitation of high-grade mental defectives. An increasing number of defectives are being paroled and discharged from institutions under these programs. Special classes for mentally retarded children conducted within the public school system have likewise shown an upsurge in recent years. Follow-up studies of mental defectives who have been either paroled from institutions or educated in special classes have yielded consistently encouraging results. Some attention is also being given to preschool training programs designed to prepare the backward child for school. There is likewise a growing recognition of the potential value of psychotherapy in the rehabilitation of mental defectives.

REFERENCES

1. Allen, G., and Baroff, G. S. Mongoloid twins and their siblings. *Acta genet. statist. med.,* 1955, 5, 294–326.
2. Anderson, V. V., and Fearing, F. M. *A study of the careers of three hundred twenty-two feebleminded persons.* N.Y.: Nat. Comm. Ment. Hyg., 1923.
3. Asher, Cecile, and Roberts, J. A. Fraser. A study of birthweight and intelligence. *Brit. J. soc. Med.,* 1949, 3, 56–68.
4. Badham, J. N. The outside employment of hospitalized mentally defective patients as a step towards resocialization. *Amer. J. ment. Def.,* 1955, 59, 666–680.
5. Baller, W. R. A study of the present social status of a group of adults who, when they were in elementary schools, were classified as mentally deficient. *Genet. Psychol. Monogr.,* 1936, 18, 165–244.
6. Bell, H. M. *Matching youth and jobs.* Washington, D.C.: Amer. Coun. Educ., 1940.
7. Benda, C. E. *Mongolism and cretinism.* (2nd Ed.) N.Y.: Grune & Stratton, 1949.
8. Benda, C. E. *Developmental disorders of mentation and cerebral palsies.* N.Y.: Grune & Stratton, 1952.
9. Benda, C. E. Psychopathology of childhood. In L. Carmichael (Ed.), *Manual of child psychology.* (Rev. Ed.) N.Y.: Wiley, 1954. Pp. 1115–1161.
10. Benda, C. E., and Farrell, M. J. Psychopathology of mental deficiency in children. In P. H. Hoch and J. Zubin (Eds.), *Psychopathology of childhood.* N.Y.: Grune & Stratton, 1955.
11. Binet, A., and Simon, Th. *The intelligence of the feebleminded.* (Transl. by E. S. Kite.) Vineland, N.J.: Training School Publ., No. 11, 1916.
12. Birch, J. W., and Matthews, J. The hearing of mental defectives: its measurement and characteristics. *Amer. J. ment. Def.,* 1951, 55, 384–393.
13. Bobroff, A. Economic adjustment of 121 adults, formerly students in classes for mental retardates. *Amer. J. ment. Def.,* 1956, 60, 525–535.
14. Böök, J. A., Grubb, R., Engleson, G., and Larson, C. A. Rh-incompatibility and mental deficiency. *Amer. J. hum. Genet.,* 1949, 1, 66–78.
15. Bradway, K. P. Paternal occupational intelligence and mental deficiency. *J. appl. Psychol.,* 1935, 19, 527–542.
16. Brand, H., Benoit, E. P., and Ornstein, G. N. Rigidity and feeblemindedness: an examination of the Kounin-Lewin theory. *J. clin. Psychol.,* 1953, 9, 375–378.
17. Burr, Emily T. The vocational adjustment of mental defectives. *Psychol. Clin.,* 1931, 20, 55–64.
18. Burt, C. *The causes and treatment of backwardness.* N.Y.: Philos. Library, 1953.

19. Cantor, G. N., and Stacey, C. L. Manipulative dexterity in mental defectives. *Amer. J. ment. Def.*, 1951, 56, 401–410.
20. Cassidy, Viola M., and Phelps, H. R. *Postschool adjustment of slow learning children.* Columbus, Ohio: Ohio State Univer. Bur. of Spec. and Adult Educ., 1955.
21. Cattell, R. B. Classical and standard score IQ standardization of the I.P.A.T. Culture-Free Intelligence Scale 2. *J. consult. Psychol.*, 1951, 15, 154–159.
22. Chamberlain, Naomi H., and Moss, Dorothy H. *The three "R's" for the retarded (repetition, relaxation, and routine); a program for training the retarded child at home.* N.Y.: Nat. Assoc. for Retarded Children, 1954.
23. Charles, D. C. Ability and accomplishment of persons earlier judged mentally deficient. *Genet. Psychol. Monogr.*, 1953, 47, 3–71.
24. Cianci, V. Home supervision of mental deficients in New Jersey. *Amer. J. ment. Def.*, 1947, 51, 519–524.
25. Clarke, A. D. B., and Clarke, A. M. Cognitive changes in the feebleminded. *Brit. J. Psychol.*, 1954, 45, 173–179.
26. Doll, E. A. The essentials of an inclusive concept of mental deficiency. *Amer. J. ment. Def.*, 1941, 46, 214–219.
27. Doll, E. A. *The measurement of social competence.* Minneapolis, Minn.: Educ. Test Bur., 1953.
28. Engel, Anna M. Employment of the mentally retarded. *Amer. J. ment. Def.*, 1952, 57, 243–267.
29. Engler, M. *Mongolism (peristatic amentia).* Baltimore: Williams & Wilkins, 1949.
30. Esquirol, J. E. D. *Des maladies mentales considérées sous les rapports médical, hygiénique, et médico-légal.* Paris: Baillière, 1838.
31. Fairbank, R. E. The subnormal child—seventeen years after. *Ment. Hyg.*, 1933, 17, 177–208.
32. Fisher, R. A. The Rhesus factor: a study in scientific method. *Amer. Scient.*, 1947, 35, 94–102, 113.
33. Glasser, F. B., Jacobs, M., and Schain, R. The relation of Rh to mental deficiency. *Psychiat. Quart.*, 1951, 25, 282–287.
34. Goddard, H. H. The height and weight of feebleminded children in American institutions. *J. nerv. ment. Dis.*, 1912, 39, 217–235.
35. Goodenough, Florence L. Review of "Changes in personal, social, and intellectual behavior of children originally classified as feebleminded," by Bernardine G. Schmidt. *J. abnorm. soc. Psychol.*, 1949, 44, 135–139.
36. Guertin, W. H. Differential characteristics of the pseudofeebleminded. *Amer. J. ment. Def.*, 1950, 54, 394–398.
37. Hackel, E. Blood factor incompatibility in the etiology of mental deficiency. *Amer. J. hum. Genet.*, 1954, 6, 224–240.
38. Halperin, S. L. A clinico-genetical study of mental defect. *Amer. J. ment. Def.*, 1945, 50, 8–26.
39. Hegge, T. G. The occupational status of higher-grade mental defectives in the present emergency. *Amer. J. ment. Def.*, 1944, 49, 86–98.
40. Heiser, K. F. *Our backward children.* N.Y.: Norton, 1955.

41. Hill, A. Does special education result in improved intelligence for the slow learner? *J. except. Child.*, 1948, 14, 207–213, 224.

42. Kanner, L. Feeblemindedness: absolute, relative, and apparent. *Nerv. Child,* 1949, 7, 365–397.

43. Kaplan, O. Life expectancy of low-grade mental defectives. *Psychol. Rec.*, 1940, 3, 295–306.

44. Kennedy, Ruby J. R. *The social adjustment of morons in a Connecticut city.* Hartford, Conn.: Mansfield-Southbury Social Service, 1948.

45. Kephart, N. C. The effect of a highly specialized program upon the IQ in high-grade mentally deficient boys. *Proc. Amer. Assoc. ment. Def.*, 1939, 44, 216–221.

46. Kephart, N. C., and Strauss, A. A. A clinical factor influencing variations in the IQ. *Amer. J. Orthopsychiat.*, 1940, 10, 343–350.

47. Kirk, S. A. An evaluation of the study by Bernardine G. Schmidt entitled: "Changes in personal, social, and intellectual behavior of children originally classified as feebleminded." *Psychol. Bull.*, 1948, 45, 321–333.

48. Kirk, S. A., *et al., Early education of the mentally retarded.* Urbana, Ill., Univer. of Illinois Press, 1958.

49. Kirk, S. A., and Johnson, G. O. *Educating the retarded child.* Boston: Houghton Mifflin, 1951.

50. Knobloch, Hilda, and Pasamanick, B. The distribution of intellectual potential in an infant population. Paper read at AAAS, New York City, December, 1956.

51. Kounin, J. S. Experimental studies of rigidity. *Char. and Pers.*, 1941, 9, 254–282.

52. Kuhlmann, F. The results of repeated mental reexaminations of 639 feeble-minded over a period of ten years. *J. appl. Psychol.*, 1921, 5, 195–224.

53. Laycock, S. R., and Clark, S. The comparative performance of a group of old-dull and young-bright children on some items of the Revised Stanford-Binet scale of intelligence, form L. *J. educ. Psychol.*, 1942, 33, 1–12.

54. Lewis, E. D. Types of mental deficiency and their social significance. *J. ment. Sci.*, 1933, 79, 298–304.

55. Lilienfeld, A. M., and Pasamanick, B. The association of maternal and fetal factors with the development of mental deficiency. II. Relationship of maternal age, birth order, previous reproductive loss, and degree of mental deficiency. *Amer. J. ment. Def.*, 1956, 60, 557–569.

56. Magaret, Ann, and Thompson, Clare W. Differential test responses of normal, superior, and mentally defective subjects. *J. abnorm. soc. Psychol.*, 1950, 45, 163–167.

57. McCandless, B. R. Environment and intelligence. *Amer. J. ment. Def.*, 1952, 56, 674–691.

58. McFadden, J. H. Differential responses of normal and feebleminded subjects of equal mental age, on the Kent-Rosanoff free association test and the Stanford revision of the Binet-Simon intelligence test. *Ment. Measmt. Monogr.*, 1931, No. 7.

59. McIntosh, W. J. Follow-up study of one thousand non-academic boys. *J. except. Child.*, 1949, 15, 166–170.

60. McNemar, Q. *The revision of the Stanford-Binet Scale: an analysis of the standardization data.* Boston: Houghton Mifflin, 1942.
61. McPherson, Marian W. A survey of experimental studies of learning in individuals who achieve subnormal ratings on standardized psychometric measures. *Amer. J. ment. Def.*, 1948, 52, 232–254.
62. Muench, G. A. A follow-up of mental defectives after eighteen years. *J. abnorm. soc. Psychol.*, 1944, 39, 407–418.
63. Mullen, F. A. Mentally retarded youth find jobs. *Personnel Guid. J.*, 1952, 31, 20–25.
64. Nolan, W. J. A critique of the evaluations of the study of Bernardine G. Schmidt entitled: "Changes in personal, social, and intellectual behavior of children originally classified as feebleminded." *J. except. Child.*, 1949, 15, 225–234.
65. Norsworthy, Naomi. The psychology of mentally deficient children. *Arch. Psychol.*, 1906, No. 1.
66. O'Brien, Margaret W. A vocational study of a group of institutionalized persons. *Amer. J. ment. Def.*, 1952, 57, 56–62.
67. O'Connor, N. The occupational success of feebleminded adolescents. *Occup. Psychol.* (London), 1953, 27, 157–163.
68. Pasamanick, B., and Lilienfeld, A. M. Association of maternal and fetal factors with development of mental deficiency. 1. Abnormalities in the prenatal and paranatal periods. *J. Amer. med. Assoc.*, 1955, 159, 155–160.
69. Paterson, D. G., and Rundquist, E. A. The occupational background of feeblemindedness. *Amer. J. Psychol.*, 1933, 45, 118–124.
70. Porteus, S. D., and Corbett, G. R. Statutory definitions of feeblemindedness in U. S. A. *J. Psychol.*, 1953, 35, 81–105.
71. Potts, Jane H. Vocational rehabilitation for the mentally retarded in Michigan. *Amer. J. ment. Def.*, 1952, 57, 297–320.
72. Rainier, J. D., and Kallmann, F. J. Genetic and demographic aspects of disordered behavior patterns in a deaf population. Paper read at AAAS, New York City, December, 1956.
73. Rautman, A. L. Relative difficulty of test items of the revised Stanford-Binet: an analysis of records from a low intelligence group. *J. exp. Educ.*, 1942, 10, 183–194.
74. Roberts, J. A. Fraser. The genetics of mental deficiency. *Eugen. Rev.*, 1952, 44, 71–83.
75. Rothstein, J. H. (Comp.) *Bibliography: education of the mentally retarded.* San Francisco, Calif.: San Francisco State College, Division of Education, Special Education Department, 1954.
76. Safian, Debra, and Harms, E. Social and educational impairment wrongly diagnosed as feeblemindedness. *Nerv. Child*, 1949, 7, 416–420.
77. Sarason, S. B. *Psychological problems in mental deficiency.* (3rd Ed.) N.Y.: Harper, 1953.
78. Sarason, S. B. Mentally retarded and mentally defective children: major psychological problems. In W. M. Cruickshank (Ed.), *Psychology of exceptional children and youth.* N.Y.: Prentice-Hall, 1955. Pp. 438–474.
79. Schmidt, Bernardine G. Changes in personal, social, and intellectual be-

havior of children originally classified as feebleminded. *Psychol. Monogr.*, 1946, 60, No. 5.

80. Scholl, M. L., Wheeler, W. E., and Snyder, L. H. Rh antibodies in mothers of feebleminded children. *J. Hered.*, 1947, 38, 253–256.

81. Sloan, W. Motor proficiency and intelligence. *Amer. J. ment. Def.*, 1951, 55, 394–406.

82. Sloan, W., and Harman, H. H. Constancy of IQ in mental defectives. *J. genet. Psychol.*, 1947, 71, 177–185.

83. Sloan, W., and Raskin, A. A study of certain concepts in high grade mental defectives. *Amer. J. ment. Def.*, 1952, 56, 638–642.

84. Snyder, L. H., Schonfeld, M. D., and Offerman, E. M. The Rh factor and feeblemindedness. *J. Hered.*, 1945, 36, 9–10.

85. Snyder, L. H., Schonfeld, M. D., and Offerman, E. M. A further note on the Rh factor and feeblemindedness. *J. Hered.*, 1945, 36, 334.

86. Stacey, C. L., and DeMartino, M. F. (Eds.) *Counseling and psychotherapy with the mentally retarded.* Glencoe, Ill.: The Free Press, 1956.

87. Storrs, J. C. A report on an investigation made of cases discharged from Letchworth Village. *Proc. Amer. Assoc. ment. Def.*, 1934, 58, 220–232.

88. Strauss, A. A., and Lehtinen, L. E. *Psychopathology and education of the brain-injured child.* N.Y.: Grune & Stratton, 1947.

89. Terman, L. M. *The measurement of intelligence.* N.Y.: Houghton Mifflin, 1916.

90. Thompson, Clare W. Decline in limit of performance among adult morons. *Amer. J. Psychol.*, 1951, 64, 203–215.

91. Thompson, Clare W., and Magaret, Ann. Differential test responses of normals and mental defectives. *J. abnorm. soc. Psychol.*, 1947, 42, 285–293.

92. Tizard, J., O'Connor, N., and Crawford, J. M. The abilities of adolescent and adult high-grade male defectives. *J. ment. Sci.*, 1950, 96, 889–907.

93. Tredgold, R. F., and Soddy, K. *A textbook of mental deficiency.* (9th Ed.) Baltimore: Williams & Wilkins, 1956.

94. Wallin, J. E. W. A statistical study of the individual tests in the Stanford-Binet scale. *Ment. Measmt. Monogr.*, 1929, No. 6.

95. Wallin, J. E. W. *Education of mentally handicapped children.* N.Y.: Harper, 1955.

96. Werner, H. The concept of rigidity: a critical evaluation. *Psychol. Rev.*, 1946, 53, 43–52.

97. Whitney, E. A., and Caron, R. E. A brief analysis of recent statistics on mental deficiency. *Amer. J. ment. Def.*, 1947, 51, 713–720.

98. Yannet, H. and Lieberman, Rose. The Rh factor in the etiology of mental deficiency. *Amer. J. ment. Def.*, 1944, 49, 133–137.

99. Yannet, H., and Lieberman, Rose. A and B iso-immunization as a possible factor in the etiology of mental deficiency. *Amer. J. ment. Def.*, 1945, 50, 242–244.

100. Yannet, H., and Lieberman, Rose. Further studies on ABO iso-immunization, secretor status and mental deficiency. *Amer. J. ment. Def.*, 1948, 52, 314–317.

101. Yepsen, L. N., and Cianci, V. Home training for mentally deficient children in New Jersey. *Tr. Sch. Bull.* (Vineland, N.J.), 1946, 43, 21–26.

CHAPTER 13

Genius

In order to be recognized as a genius, the individual must display an unusual degree of the talents demanded by his culture. Since only extreme deviates attract notice, they seem by the very rarity of their attainments to stand off from the rest of mankind and to constitute a distinct group. With the advent of more objective methods of observation and the development of testing techniques, however, the presence of lesser deviates who bridge the gap between the average man and the person of rare gifts has been demonstrated. The popular concept of genius as a separate "species" probably arose in the same fashion as the similar belief regarding the feebleminded, and it is slowly being dispelled by the same methods.

The relationship between genius and eminence is a curious one. Many writers identify the two by the simple expedient of defining genius as the possession of "what it takes" to become eminent in our society. The eminent man is then considered a genius *ipso facto*. There can thus be as many kinds of genius as there are ways of succeeding in the particular society. The successful financier, for example, may be awarded an honorary university degree for his "financial genius," the victorious general for his "military genius." Society often creates a new form of "genius" in order to rationalize its allotment of eminence.

Almost any theory regarding the nature of genius could, of course, be defended by restricting the term "genius" in some arbitrary way. The broadest and most objective definition of genius is that of an individual who excels markedly the average performance in any field. Social evaluation, however, invariably enters into the concept. Genius is defined in terms of specific social criteria and a cultural frame of values. In our society the more abstract and linguistic abilities are considered the "higher" mental processes. Similarly, certain lines of achievement enable the individual to earn the label of genius much more readily than others. Thus academic and scientific

413

work, literature, music, and art are rated higher than, let us say, roller skating or cooking.

To be sure, very exceptional accomplishments in the latter fields might be recognized as genius, after a fashion. An internationally famed roller-skate acrobat or a renowned *chef-de-cuisine* might be called a genius and ranked higher than a mediocre scientist or painter. But in the former instances, the attainments must be proportionately far greater than in the latter in order that the individual may be designated as a genius. And even when the term "genius" is applied to such cases, one feels that it is done only by courtesy and that the word is implicitly enclosed in quotation marks. It is apparent, therefore, that in order to have practical meaning any definition of genius must recognize the *selection of significant talents* which has been made within a given cultural group. To consider the individual apart from the time and place in which he lived is highly artificial.

THEORIES REGARDING THE NATURE OF GENIUS

Genius has been credited with a wide variety of attributes, ranging from divine inspiration and a superhuman "spark" to physical defects and insanity. Among these diverse theories it is possible to identify four underlying viewpoints. These can be designated as the pathological, psychoanalytic, qualitative, and quantitative theories, respectively. The chief differentiating features of each will be considered below.

Pathological Theories. Pathological theories [1] have linked genius with insanity, "racial degeneracy," and even feeblemindedness. Such theories date back to ancient Greece and Rome. Aristotle noted how often eminent men displayed morbid mental symptoms, and Plato distinguished two kinds of delirium: one being ordinary insanity, and the other the "spiritual exhalation" which produces poets, inventors, and prophets. The *furor poeticus* and *amabilis insania* of the Romans had reference to the same phenomenon. Democritus was among those who argued for such a relationship. It was Seneca who inspired Dryden to write his well-known line regarding great wit and madness being near allied. Lamartine spoke of the *"maladie mentale qu'on appelle génie,"* and Pascal maintained that *"l'extrême esprit est voisin de l'extrême folie."* In 1836 Lélut shocked the literary world by declaring that physiological evidence furnished by the life of Socrates left no doubt but that the "father of philosophy" was subject to trances, attacks of catalepsy, and to false perceptions and hallucinations, constituting what Lélut

---

[1] For a survey of this extensive literature, with special reference to literary and artistic genius, cf. Anastasi and Foley, 1, pp. 65 ff.

termed "sensorial or perceptual madness." Ten years later, Lélut reached a similar conclusion about Pascal, calling attention to the latter's religious visions and hallucinations. This early work of Lélut provided an important stimulus for later theories of genius and insanity, as well as for a host of other similar analyses of the pathological traits of eminent men.

The latter half of the nineteenth century was the golden age of pathological theories of genius and witnessed the publication of many weighty tomes on the subject. An outstanding exponent of such a theory was the Italian anthropologist Lombroso, whose book entitled *The Man of Genius* (53) was translated into several languages and read widely at the turn of the present century. Lombroso attributed to the genius certain *physical stigmata*, allegedly indicative of atavistic and degenerative tendencies. Among such stigmata he mentioned short stature, rickets, excessive pallor, emaciation, stammering, left-handedness, and delayed development. He also maintained that there were certain similarities between the creative act of genius and the typical epileptic seizure.

Among modern exponents of pathological theories of genius, the most outstanding are probably Kretschmer (47) and Lange-Eichbaum (48). The former has maintained that for true genius exceptional ability is not enough. He writes, "If we take the psychopathic factor, the ferment of demonic unrest and psychic tension away from the constitution of genius, nothing but an ordinary gifted man would remain" (47, p. 28). In addition, Kretschmer applies his constitutional typology (cf. Ch. 6) to the problem of genius, arguing for a qualitative distinction between the achievements of leptosome and pyknic geniuses. The schizothyme leptosome, he claims, will tend toward subjectivity, as in lyric poetry or expressionist art; the cyclothyme pyknic, on the other hand, allegedly inclines more toward realistic painting, narrative epic poems, and the like.

The most extensive modern contribution to the pathological theory of genius has undoubtedly been made by Lange-Eichbaum (48, 49, 50). In his *Genie, Irrsinn und Ruhm,* published in 1928, he brought together the biographies of 200 men and women of genius from all countries, periods, and fields of endeavor. All these biographies contain references to alleged abnormalities of their subjects. The reports are fully documented with a bibliography of over 1600 references, but vary in length from several pages to the simplest comment such as "for a long time psychotic." Lange-Eichbaum grants that there is not an invariable or necessary association of genius with insanity. At the same time he insists that those geniuses who have not suffered from mental abnormalities are few. Among this small minority he cites Titian, Raphael, Andrea del Sarto, Rubens, Leibnitz, and a few others. From his survey he concluded that, although the proportion of the general population who are psychotic is about 0.5 per cent, among geniuses 12 to 13 per cent have been psychotic at least once during their lifetime. Confining his analysis to the 78 "greatest names" in his list, he finds that more than 10 per cent have been psychotic once in their lifetime. More than 83 per cent have been either psychotic or markedly psychopathic, more than 10 per cent slightly psychopathic, and about 6.5 per cent healthy. When only the 35 names representing "the greatest geniuses of all" were selected, 40 per cent fell into the psychotic category. Over 90 per cent were characterized as either psychopathic or psychotic, and about 8.5 per cent as normal. The conclusions reached in this survey were reaffirmed in a later study by Lange-Eichbaum based on 800 biographies (50).

Lange-Eichbaum's explanation of the association of insanity and genius is threefold. First, the pathological condition is said to increase the strength of the individual's emotions and his responsiveness to minute stimuli, and to decrease his self-control—all of which may result in experiences which "normal" persons do not have. Secondly, Lange-Eichbaum maintains that those suffering from these conditions are likely to experience more unhappiness and feelings of inferiority, which motivate them more strongly. Finally, the tendency to a richer fantasy- and dream-life, associated with some of these disorders, may be conducive to creativity of expression.

It might be noted parenthetically that pathological explanations of genius still play an active part in popular and semi-popular writings on the subject. In a book published in 1952 entitled *The Infirmities of Genius*, Bett (4) relates creativeness to physical weakness or mental instability, illustrating his thesis with the biographies of 15 eminent men of the past.

In evaluating the evidence cited in support of pathological views of genius, several factors must be taken into account. First, in most of the studies, the evidence consists of *selected cases*. Some individuals could, of course, be found to illustrate almost any theory. The real test of the hypothesis must be based on a completely unselected sampling of geniuses. The survey of Lange-Eichbaum is probably less subject to such selective factors than many other such studies, but it is not entirely free from them.

A second point is that many geniuses may become maladjusted in a society built up around the average man and his needs. This is particularly noticeable in the case of a very superior child placed in a class of mediocre school children. It is probably true of superior adults too. In such a case, the maladjustment would be an *indirect result* rather than a cause or an essential component of genius. A different although related consideration is that the genius, by virtue of his superior abilities, may be more *keenly aware* of shortcomings and injustices which he observes and may thus be subjected to more emotional "wear and tear." It has been said that a sensitive and imaginative person cannot live as calmly as a storekeeper (81).

Geniuses, moreover, are often *regarded* as pathological by their fellow men until the practical benefits of their work become tangible. Their undertakings are often misunderstood or ridiculed until their success is demonstrated. The familiar example of Fulton and his steamboat is a case in point. In the past, the genius has at times met with organized and violent opposition or even persecution. Life under such conditions is not conducive to the development of a stable and well-adjusted personality. It should also be noted that, even when the genius is recognized and acclaimed as such, he is likely to be surrounded by such a glare of publicity that all his *actions and idiosyncrasies become common knowledge.* As a result, any behavioral deviation too slight to attract attention in a less outstanding individual is pounced upon, discussed, and elaborated until it may assume the proportions of a neurotic or psychotic symptom. Finally, the *cultural setting* in which the particular man of genius lived must be considered. It is misleading to evaluate the behavior of a thirteenth- or sixteenth-century genius in terms of present criteria of abnormality. Trances and visions, for example, were not so unusual at one time in our history as they are today, nor did they have the same significance.

Psychoanalytic Theories. In common with the more recent modifications of pathological theories, psychoanalytic conceptions of genius emphasize motivational rather than intellectual characteristics (22, 31, 35). Although admitting that a high level of ability is essential, some psychoanalysts regard this aspect of genius as a "psychological riddle" (26) and concentrate upon motivational factors. Others have taken the more extreme position that the genius does not differ in ability from the ordinary man, but differs only in what he does with his ability under strong motivational urges (83). Among the psychoanalytic concepts which have been most frequently applied to an explanation of genius are sublimation, compensation, and "unconscious processes" in creative production (35, 83).

By sublimation is meant that the artistic or scientific achievement serves as a substitute outlet for thwarted drives, often of a sexual nature. The familiar illustration of the poet who composes a love lyric when he is frustrated in love comes to mind. But many of the specific cases to which some psychoanalysts have tried to apply this mechanism are much more far-fetched and seem rather forced. Compensation for real or imagined inferiorities has likewise been proposed as the principal clue to the accomplishments of genius (83). A favorite illustration is that of great orators who, like Demosthenes, developed their talent as a compensation for an initial habit of stammering or a similar speech defect. It has also been suggested that Beethoven composed his greatest works after he became hard of hearing, and that he probably had a hearing defect even in early life. As a result, his interests were allegedly centered upon auditory experiences from an early age and he began a regimen of intensive training which culminated in his outstanding musical achievements (83, p. 119). Like sublimation, compensation can probably help us to understand the motivation of some geniuses, but it should not be applied indiscriminately to all cases.

A number of creative workers, especially artists, have provided accounts of their own creative experiences. Some of these accounts refer to production under trance-like states and to the automatic, apparently uncontrolled appearance of creative ideas. This the psychoanalysts have regarded as evidence for their theory of the importance of "unconscious processes" and the part such processes play in creative work. The number of persons who have written such introspective accounts is, of course, small in comparison with the total number who have achieved eminence in art, science, and other fields of endeavor. Artists, by the very nature of their profession, are more likely to dramatize their own experiences than are other types of creative workers. A sobering contrast to such dramatized accounts is provided by the results of Rossman's inquiry among 710 active and successful American inventors (68). This inquiry, which was supplemented with information obtained from research directors and patent attorneys, covered both the characteristics of inventors and the nature of the inventive process. No part of this study lent any support to the popular notion of invention as a spectacular event. For this group of inventors, the creative experience was on the whole a very methodical, systematic, and matter-of-fact process.

Even among artists, those who have spontaneously written accounts of their own creative experiences may be a rather atypical group. It is likely that the more unstable, pathological individuals have, on the whole, been more interested in recording such observations, just because their experiences were more unusual and newsworthy. The records are far from factual or objective, and any preconceived theories which the individual himself may have had could have colored the original account. Finally, it should be noted that many of the psychoanalytic interpretations of the creative process as well as of the nature of genius are vague and confused, often mixing literal and figurative concepts indiscriminately.

Theories of Qualitative Superiority. According to the doctrine of qualitative superiority, the man of genius is a distinct type differing from the rest of the species in the kind of ability he possesses. Such views can be distinguished from the pathological and the psychoanalytic in that they regard the man of genius as essentially *superior* to the norm. No inferiorities of any sort are implicit in this concept. The achievements of genius, according to these theories, result from some process or condition which is entirely absent in the ordinary man. Such expressions as "the spark of genius" reflect the popular influence of this point of view.

This approach, like the pathological, has a long history (cf. 34). In the ancient world, genius was frequently attributed to divine inspiration. The Greeks spoke of a man's "dæmon" which was supposed to possess divine powers and to furnish the inspiration for his creative work. Among those who discussed genius in these terms are Plato and Socrates. During the Middle Ages, genius was often regarded as the inspiration of a chosen mortal by a divine being or by a devil, the attribution depending upon the use to which the creative talents were put.

Qualitative distinctions are also common in more recent literary and philosophical writings on the subject of genius. Mystic insights and unconscious intuitions have been attributed to the man of genius. In this connection may be mentioned the views of Schopenhauer, Carlyle, and Emerson. In psychological discussions of genius, this point of view is much less common. An example is the theory proposed by Hirsch (34), in which he differentiated three "dimensions" of intelligence. According to this theory, the first dimension is perceptual and cognitive and is shared by man and the lower animals; the second is conceptual and is common to all mankind; the third he designates as "creative intelligence" and attributes only to genius.

Qualitative distinctions appeal to the imagination of the public. The genius whom the layman acclaims differs so greatly from the rest of mankind in his achievements that he seems to belong to another species. A careful analysis of the individual's abilities, however, will reveal no essentially new process. And only a brief unbiased search discloses the presence of intermediate degrees of capacity in all lines.

Theories of Quantitative Superiority. The view that genius involves a quantitative superiority regards the genius as the upper extreme of a continuous distribution of ability. The "special gifts" and "creative powers" of genius are attributed, to a lesser degree, to all mankind. Genius is defined in terms of concrete, measurable behavior rather than in terms of unknown entities. To be sure, the accomplishments of genius are not attributed to any single talent, but to an auspicious combination of various intellectual, motivational, and environmental factors. Moreover, the social effects of exceeding certain critical points in a continuous distribution may be very great. Thus it is possible that quantitative variations in human traits may give rise to qualitatively different results.

A further question which has been vigorously debated is that of *general versus specific genius.* Is the man of genius one who manifests a well-rounded intellectual superiority or one who possesses a highly specialized gift? Some writers (3, 11) have particularly emphasized the role of special aptitudes, such as talent in art, music, or mechanics, in their definition of genius. It follows from what we know about the organization of abilities, however, that this distinction is not a valid one. Since the intercorrelations of diverse abilities are neither highly positive nor highly negative, we should expect all degrees of generality of genius. A few individuals may excel highly in a large number of traits and thus appear to be all-around geniuses, as in the classic example of Leonardo da Vinci. Some will excel in only a few traits, and still others may have a single talent which is sufficiently pronounced to put them in the category of genius.

In the major research on *gifted children,* it has been customary to select subjects on the basis of Stanford-Binet IQ. In Terman's extensive longitudinal project to be discussed in subsequent sections, a minimum IQ of 135 was required for inclusion in the study. Some investigators have extended the limit down as far as 125. On the other hand, Hollingworth (37) pointed out that an IQ of 135 or 140 is certainly far below the "genius level." Such IQ's fall within the upper quarter of college students. In fact, in some of the better colleges, the mean IQ is close to 150. On the basis of her own follow-ups of groups of gifted children, Hollingworth proposed that an *IQ of 180 or higher* is more nearly at the "genius level," equipping the individual for academic and professional distinction, original and creative work, the winning of prizes, and other evidences of eminence.

As a result of current research on the factorial analysis of intelligence (Ch. 11), it is likely that investigations of gifted children and adults will become increasingly concerned with *more clearly defined aptitudes.* The predominantly verbal criterion represented by traditional intelligence tests may be more widely supplemented by tests in the numerical and spatial areas. Moreover, there is clearly apparent a growing interest in the study of *creativity* and *leadership.* It is gradually coming to be recognized that "genius" means not one but many things. The conflicting conclusions reached in some studies of genius can often be reconciled when we realize that there may be several varieties of genius, differing from each other in many ways.

The investigator who selects his subjects through intelligence tests will obtain a group that excels principally in academic abilities. Such subjects will be characterized by rapid learning and good comprehension of abstract material, chiefly of a verbal nature. Studies of research workers, inventors, and artists, on the other hand, are likely to provide a sample that rates high in creativity. And surveys of eminent people who have achieved public recognition will probably include a relatively large proportion of leaders. A minimum level of academic intelligence is undoubtedly essential for outstanding achievement in any area. Nevertheless, an individual may have a high IQ and lack the other qualities required for either creative work or leadership.

With regard to the *origins* of genius, early investigators such as Galton (27, 28), Terman (74), and Hollingworth (36) placed the major emphasis upon hereditary factors. The observation that genius tends to run in families probably gave the greatest impetus to such a hereditary interpretation. As was seen in Chapter 9, however, the many influences stemming from family environment cannot be overlooked.

Today there are indications of a growing interest in ways of *fostering* genius, rather than merely identifying it. More reseach is needed on conditions conducive to the development of high academic intelligence, creativity, and leadership. In a provocative article, Pressey cites data on precocious musicians and precocious athletes to illustrate how favorable environmental factors operating from an early age may lead to outstanding achievement. He concludes that "development of any ability is fostered by a favorable immediate environment, expert instruction, frequent and progressive opportunities for the exercise of ability, social facilitation, and frequent success experiences" (60, p. 124). Some data bearing on environmental qualities favorable for creative achievement are provided by a survey of scientific and technical personnel conducted by Van Zelst and Kerr (79, 80). The more productive persons in the group, as determined by inventions and publications, expressed more individualistic attitudes toward research and exhibited a fundamental dislike for regimentation with regard to choice of problem, working hours, deadlines, and other aspects of the working situation.

METHODS FOR THE STUDY OF GENIUS

Psychological investigations on the nature and development of genius have followed two fundamental approaches, namely, the study of adults who have achieved eminence and the study of gifted children. The specific procedures may be further subdivided into: (1) biographical analysis, (2) case study, (3) statistical survey, (4) historiometry, (5) intelligence test survey, and (6) longitudinal study. Although any one investigator may, and frequently does, combine more than one specific method, we shall consider them independently for clarity of presentation.

In *biographical* studies, all available published material on a given individual is examined in the effort to arrive at an understanding of the nature and origin of his genius. The investigation is limited to a single individual, who is usually chosen from the great men of the past. This method has been employed extensively by psychoanalysts, as well as by the exponents of pathological views of genius. The literature on this method runs to several thousand references (cf. 1, 48, 49, 50). Of special interest as source materials are autobiographies written by eminent men. Outstanding examples are *The Life of Benvenuto Cellini Written by Himself* (17) and the more recent *Ex-prodigy: My Childhood and Youth* by Norbert Wiener (85). The latter gives a detailed and sensitive account of the author's experiences as a typical child prodigy and his development into one of the leading scientists and mathematicians of the twentieth century.

The *case study* method involves intensive testing, interviewing, and observation of single living individuals. Because of the difficulty of subjecting adults to such an investigation, this method was first applied to gifted children. Several such studies of child prodigies, including a number of juvenile authors, were conducted by psychologists during the 1920's and 1930's. Only within the last few years has the case study approach been extended to eminent adults.

The *statistical survey* method, like the biographical, is based upon an analysis of printed records, although differing from the latter method in several essential respects. The purpose of statistical surveys of genius is to discover general trends in a large group, rather than to make an exhaustive analysis of a single case. All available information on a large number of men is obtained from biographical directories, encyclopedias, *Who's Who*, and similar sources. This material is occasionally supplemented from biographies. But the former sources are employed predominantly because of the more objective, reliable, and standardized nature of their data. It will be noted that in this method the criterion of genius is chiefly eminence.

The *historiometry* method makes use of all historical material on an individual or a group of individuals. The data are gathered from a variety of sources, including biographies, directories, and original documents such as letters and diaries. The attempt is made to obtain as complete information as possible, especially on the childhood accomplishments of the great man. This material is then evaluated in terms of a more or less constant standard in order to arrive at an estimate of the individual's traits. This method was employed by Woods (91), in his study of mental and moral heredity in royalty, and by Yoder (93). Terman (70) subsequently suggested an adaptation of historiometry whereby the recorded achievements are evaluated in terms of mental test norms for each age and an IQ is computed. By this method, for example, Terman estimated that the IQ of Francis Galton in childhood was approximately 200.

The *intelligence test survey* involves the direct study of large groups of intellectually superior children by means of mental tests. The subjects are originally selected on the basis of intelligence test performance, and subsequent analyses are made with the aid of standardized intellectual, educational, and personality measures. A relatively recent development is the *longitudinal study,* in which a group of children, originally selected because of high IQ, are followed up into adolescence and adulthood.

Each of these procedures has its own peculiar advantages and disadvantages. No one can be regarded as best or poorest on all counts. The statistical, historiometry, and intelligence test methods can be applied to large groups, and hence disclose general trends. They are also relatively free from selective bias, yielding fairly representative samples. The biographical and case study methods, on the other hand, give a more complete picture of the individual and enable one to note the specific interaction of various conditions in the subject's development. The study of contemporary living geniuses makes direct observation possible and avoids the judgment errors and other inaccuracies which are inevitably present in historical material. At the same time, carefully controlled observation of living geniuses offers many practical difficulties. A further disadvantage in the study of contemporaries is the possibility that the eminence of some may be short-lived and spurious and that others who are laboring in obscurity may be recognized as geniuses by posterity.

Finally, the relative advantages of studying adult geniuses and gifted children may be considered. To investigate intellectually superior children in the effort to discover the characteristics of adult geniuses seems somewhat indirect. Only a small number of such children are likely to develop into adults who can be classified as geniuses. Children, however, are available for prolonged and controlled observation and testing which would be much more difficult with adults. A further advantage of the study of gifted children is that it makes possible a developmental approach to the problem. Such an analysis may go far toward clarifying the origin and nature of genius.

CHARACTERISTICS OF EMINENT MEN

Statistical Surveys.   Investigations of genius through statistical surveys of printed records have been conducted in England by Galton (27, 28), Ellis (25), and Bramwell (8); in France by deCandolle (21), Jacoby (42), and Odin (57); and in America by Cattell (13, 14, 15), Brimhall (9), Clarke (18), Bowerman (6), Visher (82), Davis (20), and Knapp *et al.* (45, 46). Cox (19) gathered data on eminent persons of all countries. Castle (12) conducted a similar survey of eminent women, but the data of this study are very tentative and difficult to interpret. A recently published investigation by Juda (43, 44) covers 294 highly gifted persons born between 1650 and 1900 in the German-speaking areas of Europe. Major findings of these various surveys will be examined briefly.

The *socioeconomic background* of eminent men has generally proved to be distinctly above average. The genius who has been nurtured in a slum is the rare exception. Typical data are provided by Visher's analysis of starred men of science in America (82). Such "starred" men represent the most eminent persons listed in the *Directory of American Men of Science.* Those to be starred in each field of science are chosen on the basis of nominations by scientists who had previously been starred in that field. The original 1000 starred men were selected in 1903, and 250 additions were made in each new quinquennial revision of the directory. Of the 849 starred scientists studied by Visher, nearly half had fathers in the professions. This proportion is far in excess of that found in the general population, the latter falling between 3 and 6 per cent. The entire occupational distribution of the fathers of the starred men is given in Table 16.

A similar occupational distribution is to be found among the fathers of the eminent men and women surveyed by Ellis (25). In Castle's study of

Table 16

OCCUPATIONAL DISTRIBUTION OF FATHERS OF 849 STARRED AMERICAN MEN OF SCIENCE

(Adapted from Visher, 82, p. 533)

OCCUPATIONAL GROUP	PERCENTAGE
Professions	45.5
Business and mercantile	23
Farming	22
Skilled labor	8
Unskilled labor	1

eminent women of all times and nationalities, it was reported that 33.1 per cent had fathers in the "learned professions" (12). Davis' (20) recent survey of 803 native American men listed in *Who's Who in the East* again revealed a marked excess of high-level occupations among the subjects' fathers. The distribution of paternal occupations found by Cox (19) in a group of 282 eminent men and women of all countries is shown in Table 17. In this group, which covered a much earlier period in history (1450–1850), the predominance of high socioeconomic level is even more conspicuous.

Table 17

OCCUPATIONAL DISTRIBUTION OF FATHERS OF 282 EMINENT MEN AND WOMEN OF ALL COUNTRIES

(From Cox, 19, p. 37)

OCCUPATIONAL GROUP	PERCENTAGE
1. Professional and nobility	52.5
2. Semiprofessional, higher business, and gentry	28.7
3. Skilled workmen and lower business	13.1
4. Semiskilled	3.9
5. Unskilled	1.1
No record	0.7

The number of *eminent relatives* may also be considered in this connection. In Galton's survey (27), which was reported in Chapter 9, the 977 eminent men investigated had a total of 739 known relatives who had also achieved eminence. Moreover, the closer the degree of relationship, in general, the more numerous were the eminent relatives. A follow-up of Galton's study, covering three subsequent generations and published in 1948 by Bramwell (8), closely corroborated Galton's findings on the frequency of eminent relatives. Similar results were obtained in Brimhall's investigation (9) of family relationships among American men of science.

Certain interesting trends are suggested by Cattell's analysis of the *place of birth* of American men of science (cf. 13, 15). In his 1906 report, Cattell pointed out that cities contributed a much greater relative proportion of men of science than did rural sections. Even more striking is the comparison of different states which varied widely in their educational facilities. In Table 18 are shown the relative number of scientists born in each of nine states. These states were chosen as the clearest examples of a definite trend which had been operating over an interval of three decades. Corresponding figures are shown for the original group of 1000 scientists selected in the year 1903 and for the group of 250 elected in 1932. All figures have been expressed in terms of 1000 entries to permit direct comparison.

Table 18

PROPORTION OF AMERICAN MEN OF SCIENCE BORN IN EASTERN AND MIDWESTERN STATES

(From Cattell and Cattell, 15, p. 1265)

PLACE OF BIRTH	NUMBER OF CASES (PER 1000 ENTRIES)	
	1903 Group	1932 Group
Massachusetts	134	72
Connecticut	40	16
New York	183	128
Pennsylvania	66	48
Illinois	42	88
Minnesota	4	32
Missouri	14	40
Nebraska	2	20
Kansas	7	32

These data suggest several conclusions which are borne out by the complete results for all parts of the country (cf. 15). In the first place, there are marked discrepancies in the relative number of eminent scientists born in different parts of the country. Secondly, these differences in birthplace correspond closely to differences in educational opportunities in various sections of the country. Thirdly, as educational facilities change, the frequency of scientists shows a corresponding change. Since the turn of the century, for example, there has been rapid and continuing development of education in the midwestern states. The relative quality of education in such states has improved, new universities have been established, the contribution of state and federal funds to higher education has mounted sharply, the number of students in institutions of higher learning has increased rapidly, and a powerful tradition has been built up which fosters intellectual activity. An analysis of the "center of population" of higher education from 1790 to 1920 showed a westward movement at the rate of sixty miles per decade (24). On the basis of such findings alone, we cannot, of course, draw any inferences regarding the relative contributions of hereditary and environmental factors. Whether there has been selective migration of intellectually superior families from New England to the midwestern states, or whether the improved educational facilities have been conducive to the development of more scientists—or whether *both* of these influences have been operating—cannot be conclusively determined from the available data.

A recent survey by Knapp and Goodrich (45) on American scientists was particularly concerned with the types and location of *colleges* in which the subjects had received their undergraduate training. Geographically, the Midwest and the Far West made the largest contribution, with the Northeast and Middle Atlantic states ranking second and the Southern states lowest. It is interesting to note that small liberal arts colleges made a better showing than did large universities. A later survey by Knapp and Greenbaum (46) on the undergraduate background of students receiving the Ph.D. degree and holders of graduate scholarships and fellowships revealed a number of differences in nature and location of colleges attended. For example, the larger, "high-cost" universities contributed a greater proportion of promising scientists than had been true in the earlier survey of established scientists. The authors point to a number of postwar cultural changes which may account for these shifts. However, a few liberal arts colleges characterized by a traditional "hospitality to intellectual values in general" made an exceptionally good showing in *both* surveys. Findings such as these may provide leads for further research on the conditions conducive to the development of high-level talent.

Of interest in connection with pathological theories of genius is the incidence of *insanity* among relatives of eminent men, as well as among the subjects themselves. In all statistical surveys in which cases were not selected to prove a point, the frequency of intellectual and emotional disorders has been found to be consistently smaller among eminent men and their families than in the general population. In the group investigated by Ellis (25, p. 192), less than 2 per cent were reported to have had either insane parents or insane offspring. Among the eminent individuals themselves, Ellis mentions 44 cases of emotional disorder out of a total group of 1030. Of these, only 13 could be definitely classed as insane during the active period of their lives; 19 were either insane for a short period or manifested very mild disorders; and 12 developed senile dementia in old age (cf. 25, pp. 189–190).

Other facts that have been brought to light by these surveys relate to *age of parents at the time of birth of the child, order of birth,* and similar "vital statistics." It has been suggested, for example, that intellectually superior children are more often born of older parents (62). From a somewhat different angle, Lombroso (53) claimed that geniuses are the offspring of aged parents and offered this as further evidence of the pathological nature of genius. The data on this question are difficult to interpret because of the complicating factor of social level. People in the higher social classes, from which geniuses are most frequently recruited, tend to marry later and therefore have children at a later age. They also tend to have fewer children, who thus benefit all the more from educational and other socio-economic advantages. For all these reasons, parental ages are in themselves inconclusive. Among American men of science, Cattell (14: III) found 35 years to be the average age of the father at the time of the subject's birth. For English men of science, Galton (28) found the corresponding figure to be 36 years. Ellis (25) gives 37.1 years for his group of British men and women of eminence. In all these groups, however, the range of parental ages at the time of the subject's birth is extremely wide. In the majority of cases the parents were in the prime of life, contrary to Lombroso's contention.

Somewhat more conclusive is the analysis of order of birth within the family. In general the eminent individual is most often the oldest or first-born child in the family. Next in order of frequency comes the youngest child, intermediate children having the least chance of becoming eminent (cf. 25, 93). These findings are in direct contradiction to the proposed theory that older parents have intellectually more gifted offspring. It would seem that, within the same family, the superior child is most likely to be born when the parents are younger. This finding may have a cultural explanation. The first-born has traditionally enjoyed privileges in our society that his younger siblings may not have had. More is usually expected of the oldest son. If a choice must be made for economic reasons, the oldest child is usually allowed to complete his education, in preference to the younger children. These conditions might be sufficient to produce a slight degree of relationship between birth order and achievement. Motivational factors in sibling relationships may also play a contributing part, as may the fact that the first-born probably receives more adult attention. The latter is particularly true of only children, who would all be classified as "first-born." In connection with vital statistics, mention should also be made of the extensive data gathered by Lehman regarding *age of maximum creativity,* already discussed in Chapter 8.

Historiometry.   The childhood of great men, viewed retrospectively, has been the source of much controversy. There is a popular belief (also proposed by Lombroso) that many geniuses were dull in childhood, a number of favorite examples being cited in support of this contention. Darwin was considered by his teachers to be below average in intellect. Newton was at the bottom of his class. Heine was an academic failure, rebelling against the traditional formalism of the schools of his time. Pasteur, Hume, von

Humboldt, and other equally famous men were unsuccessful in their school-work.

An examination of available biographical material in such cases shows that the intellectual defect was erroneously inferred from the level of scholastic performance within a rather narrowly restricted area. The intellectually superior child may be just as maladjusted in school as the dull or borderline case. Schools adapted to the average child may be unsuited to the highly gifted pupil in many ways. The monotonous drill and rote memorization which constituted such a large part of schoolwork in the days when men like Darwin or Hume attended school would prove particularly irksome to a bright child. Darwin, for instance, seems to have been more interested in his collections of insects than in memorizing Latin declensions, much to the annoyance of his teachers. Thus it is often impossible to accept the recorded opinions of parents or teachers regarding the intellectual status of great men in childhood.

More accurate information can be obtained from factual records of the *specific behavior* of the individual at various ages. An early attempt to conduct such an analysis of the boyhood of great men was made by Yoder (93). Fifty cases, representing a wide variety of occupations or fields of eminence, were selected from the great men of six countries. All subjects were born in the eighteenth or nineteenth centuries, except Newton, Swift, and Voltaire, who were born in the seventeenth. In general, Yoder found that ill health in childhood was often exaggerated by the earlier biographers and that this condition was not so prevalent as is supposed. Feeble or delicate health may, however, offer advantages in some cases by stimulating reading and intellectual pursuits. Dickens was a good example of this. In regard to intellectual status, Yoder reports that excellent memory and vivid imagination were often exhibited by great men from early childhood.

A detailed and comprehensive study of the childhood of great men was conducted by Cox (19), as one part of the *Genetic Studies of Genius* under the general direction of Terman. The technique employed was Terman's adaptation of the historiometry method. Through the examination of several thousand biographical references, information was gathered on the traits of 301 eminent men and women born between 1450 and 1850. Particular attention was given to data on childhood behavior, such as reported age of learning to read, letters and original compositions that had been preserved, and evidences of early interests. Any special circumstances which might have influenced the subject's development were also noted. The material so collected was analyzed and evaluated independently by three trained psychologists. Each investigator estimated the lowest IQ compatible with the given facts for every subject, and the average of these three independent judgments was taken as the final minimum IQ estimate for the given individual.

After allowing for certain inaccuracies in the data, Cox concluded that the average IQ for the group "is not below 155 and probably at least as high as 165" (19, p. 217). The estimated minimum IQ's ranged approximately from 100 to 200. The same geniuses cited by Lombroso and others as instances of early mental inferiority were invariably found to give evidence of high IQ's during childhood. Among these may be mentioned Lord Byron, Sir Walter Scott, and Charles Darwin, whose estimated childhood IQ's proved to be 150, 150, and 135, respectively. Among those receiving IQ's above 180 were Goethe, John Stuart Mill, Macaulay, Pascal, Leibnitz, and Grotius.

Another interesting finding pertains to the average estimated IQ of persons achieving eminence in different fields (71). Philosophers topped the list with a mean IQ of 170; next came poets, dramatists, novelists, and statesmen with 160; scientists had a mean of 155, musicians 145, artists 140, and military leaders 125. This hierarchy probably reflects at least in part the close association of "intelligence" with verbal aptitude in our present standards of evaluation. Those groups with mean IQ's of 160 or over were engaged in activities in which written or spoken language played a predominant role. Farthest from the verbal field in their area of accomplishment are the persons at the bottom of the list: military leaders, artists, and musicians.

In the same survey, 100 geniuses were selected for whom the relevant records were especially full, and ratings were assigned to each person on a number of specific intellectual, emotional, and character traits. These ratings, like the IQ's, were based upon the childhood behavior of the subjects, and the averages of two independent raters were used. As a group, the subjects proved to be unquestionably superior in all traits rated, and were especially outstanding in such characteristics as desire to excel, steadfastness of effort, persistence in the face of obstacles, intellectual work devoted to special pursuits, profoundness of apprehension, and originality and creativeness. Another subgroup of 50 cases, similarly selected because of fullness of data, were rated in a like manner for physical and mental health in childhood. The distribution of the group in these respects is reported to be fairly normal and to show no greater percentage of unfavorable deviants than are found among unselected school children.

Some of the inconsistencies and confusions regarding the association of "genius" and "insanity" may result from the common use of these blanket categories as though they represented single entities (56, 84). If we ask *what kind* of genius and *what kind* of abnormality, we are more likely to get a significant and consistent answer. Reanalyses of the original Cox data, for example, have shown that the incidence of emotional abnormalities is greatest among the "esthetic type" (poets, novelists, artists, musicians) and the "reformer type" (revolutionary statesmen or radical religious leaders). It is least among scientists, soldiers, statesmen, and conservative religious leaders. The more "imaginative" genius is likely to show more psychopathic characteristics than the eminent "man of action." As for specific types of abnormality, analyses of the same group suggest that introversion, emotional excitability, and fanatical self-confidence are the most frequent. Considering how often these geniuses were right in their novel ideas, the last-mentioned symptom seems to be more indicative of fanaticism in the rest of mankind than in the genius!

Other investigators have corroborated these findings regarding the *specificity* of the "genius personality." One survey (61) compared 120 men of science with 123 men of letters, both groups having lived during the nineteenth century. The literary group was limited to poets, novelists, and dramatists; the scientists included only workers in the biological and physical sciences and in mathematics. One interesting difference was found in the socioeconomic backgrounds of the two groups. Though both scientists and literary men came chiefly from the professional class, the two groups differed in that scientists were much more likely than men of letters to come from the farmer and artisan class. For men of letters, the socioeconomic class that ranked second in frequency to the professional was the semiprofessional. On the other hand, actual poverty was more often reported for literary than for scientific men. The scientists as a group were described as more cheerful, modest, and sociable. The literary men excelled in persistence, but were also more emotional, gave more evidence of neurosis, and had a slightly poorer health record both in childhood and adulthood. Also relevant is a later survey (69) of the characteristics of "research workers," conducted by a similar method. Biographical material was examined for 250 research workers ranging from Euclid and Pythagoras to contemporary living scientists. Among the characteristics found most frequently were creativeness, enthusiasm, and aggressiveness; least frequent were religiousness, self-control, and good health.

The results of all these studies have to be accepted with caution because of possible weaknesses in the procedures. Much depends upon the representativeness of the samples, the fullness of the available data, and the objectivity and accuracy with which the recorded behavior items are evaluated by the investigator. When great men of the past are considered, a certain amount of historical perspective is also required, in order to judge the individual against his own cultural setting. On the whole, however, such studies do show that the men and women who achieved eminence tended to come from favorable environments, gave early indication of superior ability, and were not as a group appreciably more unstable than the less gifted. At the same time, it should be clear that "the genius" is not one but many kinds of person.

Case Studies of Living Scientists. During the early 1950's Roe (63, 64, 65, 66, 67) reported a series of clinical studies of small groups of outstanding living American scientists, including 20 biologists, 22 physicists (12 theoretical and 10 experimental), 14 psychologists, and 8 anthropologists. Data were collected by means of specially constructed, high-level tests of verbal, numerical, and spatial aptitudes; Rorschach and Thematic Apperception tests; and detailed interviews. The latter covered life history data as well as the subjects' own accounts of factors relevant to their early development and occupational choices.

Although it is impossible to summarize the multiplicity of details elicited by these procedures, a few general trends may be noted. As in other surveys of eminent men, socioeconomic background was high in these groups. Father's occupation fell into the professional level in the case of 84 per cent of theoretical physicists, 50 per cent of experimental physicists, 45 per cent of biologists, and approximately 50 per cent of psychologists and anthropologists. In most families, a high value was placed upon education, it being usually taken for granted that the subject would attend college even if financial sacrifices were required. The subjects' own educational histories were clearly superior, as evidenced by school acceleration, outstanding grades, fellowships and other academic honors, and the attainment of college and graduate degrees at relatively early ages. Most of the subjects had unquestionably been gifted children. Many were avid readers, showed early talent in the construction of mechanical gadgets, and taught themselves subjects like algebra, calculus, and Latin in their spare time.

On the specially developed aptitude tests, a number of group differences emerged. For example, despite efforts to construct suitable items, the numerical test proved too easy for the physicists and could not be used with this group. The physicists as a whole scored significantly higher than the biologists on the spatial test. And the theoretical physicists did significantly better than the experimental physicists on the verbal test. It is noteworthy, however, that individual differences in score were very wide in each group.

Moreover, once a certain minimum was exceeded, degree of verbal intelligence did not appear to be related to professional success within these groups. Such a finding corroborates the current view that scientific talent cannot be equated with high IQ in the traditional sense.

Analyses of projective test responses (Rorschach and TAT) suggested a number of personality characteristics which differentiated among the groups. The physicists, for example, gave evidence of great intellectual and emotional energy, often not too well controlled. Socially, they were somewhat poorly adjusted. Their responses also indicated independence of parents, with no associated guilt feelings, as well as independence of personal relations generally. Psychologists and anthropologists, by contrast, revealed a tendency toward a dependent parental relationship, associated with feelings of guilt and unhappiness. Responses of the two latter groups likewise evidenced great sensitivity, some aggression, resistance to authoritarianism, and a strong interest in people.

Some of the most interesting data were provided by the subjects' own discussions of their motivation and developmental history. Among the factors recurring most often in these accounts are prestige motivation, personal influence of individual teachers, strong inner drive, sustained effort, and absorption in work to the exclusion of other interests. In the case of at least some physicists and biologists, adverse conditions such as poor health, weak physique, or loss of a parent in childhood contributed to a feeling of "apartness" and tended to foster greater concentration on work interests.

A few other studies of living scientists have utilized procedures similar to some of those employed by Roe, although no intensive case studies were made. In an early study, Rossman (68) surveyed the characteristics of inventors by means of a questionnaire filled out by 710 American inventors, 78 directors of research, and 176 patent attorneys who came in frequent contact with inventors. More recently, Cattell and Drevdahl (16) administered the Sixteen Personality Factor Questionnaire (cited in Chapter 11) to eminent American scientists, including 96 biologists, 91 physicists, and 107 psychologists. Each of the three groups included research workers, teachers, and administrators. Several differences significant at the .01 level were found between scientists and the general population; between scientists and students; and between researchers, teachers, and administrators in the field of science. These results must be regarded as highly tentative, however, owing to the preliminary nature of the test employed.

Mention may also be made of an investigation by Ausubel (2) concerned with the measurement of prestige motivation in a group of children with IQ's over 130. It will be recalled that prestige motivation emerged as an important condition in the case studies reported by Roe. Owing to methodological limitations, Ausubel's study yielded inconclusive results. It is of interest primarily because it focuses attention on a promising area of research, namely personality differences between individuals of the same intellectual level who achieve varying degrees of success. Still another relevant approach is represented by factorial research on the nature of creativity, discussed in Chapter 11.

THE GIFTED CHILD

The "Child Prodigy."   Since geniuses have generally displayed superior talents in childhood, a direct study of gifted children should prove fruitful in an analysis of genius. The original concept of the "child prodigy" was that of a weak, sickly, unsocial, and narrowly specialized individual. His achievements were expected to be of the nature of intellectual "stunts" and to have little or no practical value.

One of the earliest recorded cases of such a child prodigy is that of Christian Henrick Heineken, whose remarkable accomplishments are recorded by his tutor in an old German book (cf. 39, 51). At the age of 14 months, this child had memorized the stories of the Old and New Testaments. At 4 years he could read German, French, and Latin and was a skilled orator in all three languages. At this age, he was also able to perform the fundamental arithmetic operations, and he knew many facts of history and geography. His fame spread throughout Europe and he was summoned to appear before the King of Denmark. True to the traditional stereotype, however, Heineken was a sickly child and died at the age of 4 years and 4 months.

Contrary to popular belief, the case of Christian Henrick Heineken is not at all typical. As an example of a highly gifted child who developed into a healthy and successful adult we may consider the case of Karl Witte (86). Born in Lochau, Prussia, in 1800, this "child prodigy" lived until he was 83, having retained his excellent intellectual powers to the end. Karl was literally educated from the cradle. His father was convinced of the efficacy of early training and undertook to prove this with his son. The child was never taught "baby talk." All the games he played were games of knowledge. When only 8 years old, he read with apparent pleasure the original texts of Homer, Plutarch, Virgil, Cicero, Fénelon, Florian, Metastasio, and Schiller. He matriculated as a regular student at Leipzig at the age of 9. Before his fourteenth birthday he was awarded the Ph.D. degree.

Two years later he became a Doctor of Laws, being at the same time appointed to the teaching staff of the University of Berlin.

Karl Witte's father, in discussing the boy's education, wrote:

. . . he was first of all to be a strong, active, and happy young man, and in this, as everybody knows, I have succeeded. . . . It would have been in the highest degree unpleasant for me to have made of him preeminently a Latin or a Greek scholar or a mathematician. For this reason, I immediately interfered whenever I thought that this or that language or science attracted his attention at too early a time (86, pp. 63–64).

Karl seems not to have been in the least vain or spoiled. He never paraded his knowledge, was modest and unpretentious, and not infrequently tried to learn from his companions what they knew better than he. He had many playmates of his own age and we are told that "he got along so well with them that they invariably became very fond of him and nearly always parted from him with tears in their eyes" (86, p. 187).

Contemporary case studies of gifted children by psychologists likewise lend no support to the view that such children are necessarily inferior in other respects. In 1942 Hollingworth brought together in one book (39) 31 case reports of children whose IQ's were over 180. Such IQ's should occur about once in over a million cases. The accomplishments and adjustment of children in these IQ levels are illustrated by the following cases.

A gifted juvenile author, Elizabeth _____, obtained a Stanford-Binet IQ of 188 when tested at the age of 7 years-10 months (cf. 74; 75; 39, pp. 35–37). She ranked high in all other intellectual and educational tests, but showed special interest and talent for the composition of prose and poetry. This child was reported to be in excellent health and free from physical defects; she was a year or so accelerated in physical development. Elizabeth's superior linguistic abilities were apparent from an early age. At 19 months she could express herself clearly and also knew the alphabet. By her eighth birthday she had read approximately 700 books, including such authors as Burns, Shakespeare, Longfellow, Wordsworth, Scott, and Poe. By this age she had also written over 100 poems and 75 stories. The following is a specimen of her literary products, written at the age of 7 years-11 months and entitled "Fairy Definition":

> Fairies are the fancies of an imaginative brain
> Which wearying of earthly realities aspires to
> Create beings living only in thought
> Endowing the spirits thus created
> With all genius for giving Happiness.

A case that attracted wide attention in the 1920's is that of a boy known in the psychological literature as E____ (39, pp. 134–158). When first tested at the age of 8 years-11 months, E____ obtained a mental age of 15–7, which gave him an IQ of 187. He also excelled on all other tests except those involving manual dexterity. He is reported as being strong and healthy, but not much inclined to indulge in games and sports. At the age of 12 he was admitted to Columbia College. On the Thorndike Intelligence Examination for High School Graduates, he ranked second among 483 competitors. During his freshman year at college all his academic grades were B or better, with the exception of physical education, in which his grade was C. He is described as being a "good sport" and getting along well with the other students. He received the A.B. degree at 15, being also elected to Phi Beta Kappa. At 16 he obtained the M.A. degree, and by 18 had completed practically all requirements toward the Ph.D. degree except the dissertation. On the CAVD Intelligence Examination, his score was 441, which falls approximately in the upper ¼ of 1 per cent of college graduates. Thus, during the period over which he was investigated, E____ showed no tendency to drop below the high intellectual level indicated by his initial IQ.

These cases are typical examples of intellectually superior children. Exceptional talents in childhood are not incompatible with good health, physical vigor, longevity, or a well-rounded personality. To be sure, puny, timid, and sickly children can be found among the gifted, as among the intellectually normal or dull. But such cases are very few and cannot be regarded as representative of the group as a whole.

The highly gifted may, of course, have their own special adjustment problems, especially during childhood and adolescence, by virtue of their exceptional intellectual status. But such maladjustments are an indirect *result* of high intellect, rather than a cause or an intrinsic component of genius (38, 39). Among the possible problems encountered by the child whose IQ is much above 150 are those arising from the fact that he is younger and hence *smaller and weaker than his classmates.* This condition may make him more susceptible to bullying and may interfere with his participation in athletics and active games. A second source of difficulty is the *"isolation"* from contemporaries and from the common activities of others which is likely to result when the individual's interests and abilities are so unlike those of his fellows. *Negativism* toward authority may develop when the child realizes that authority is often irrational or erroneous in its operation. *Intolerance* and unwillingness to "suffer fools gladly" may follow observations of relatively inept thinking on the part of associates. The superior child may also develop habits of *inefficient work and laziness* because ordinary school work offers no challenge to him. Such work habits may carry over into later educational and even vocational activities.

For these reasons, Hollingworth (38, 79) concluded that the optimum IQ from the viewpoint of personal adjustment, leadership, and acceptance by one's fellows—with the "accompanying emoluments and privileges" which such acceptance entails—falls between 130 and 150. Recent case studies of gifted children by Hildreth (32) confirm this conclusion. It might be added that the human relations problems encountered by the highly gifted are only partly the result of their own personality deficiencies. By their very superiority, such individuals are likely to arouse feelings of inferiority and defensive reactions in their associates. Case histories provide a number of instances of acts of rejection and aggression on the part of associates who feel threatened by the exceptional attainments of the gifted child.

On the other hand, the adjustment difficulties of the gifted child are of the sort that can be prevented by proper understanding and a suitable educational environment. Recent case studies of children with very high IQ's point up the role of early identification, educational acceleration, curricular enrichment, and judicious family cooperation in the attainment of favorable outcomes (90). Under the influence of such pioneers as Hollingworth, the special education of the gifted child made rapid strides during the decades of the 1920's and 1930's. For a time, further progress lagged and interest waned. More attention was devoted to the education of mental defectives than to that of the intellectually gifted.

In recent years, however, there has been a resurgence of interest in the gifted child, as witnessed by the formation of several national and local organizations concerned with gifted children. A number of publications appearing in the 1950's deal intensively with the characteristics, problems, and education of gifted children (29, 33, 89). There is also evidence of re-awakened interest in the establishment of special classes for gifted children in the public school system (cf., e.g., 7, 30). The publication, in January 1957, of the first issue of the Newsletter of the recently established National Association for Gifted Children is a further sign of renewed vigor. Among educators and the general public, there is still controversy regarding the wisdom of acceleration and of special classes for gifted children. Psychologists who have worked closely with the gifted, however, have presented strong arguments in favor of both of these practices and have cited convincing evidence in support of their position (54, 59, 72, 76, 92).

Intelligence Test Surveys. The testing of large groups of intellectually superior children has revealed the *continuity* which exists between the average child and the highly gifted "prodigy." In order to include a sufficiently large number of cases in such studies, the standard of selection must be lowered. But by surveying a wider range of superior intellect a more complete picture will be obtained. Since the rise of the mental testing movement, a number of studies on moderately large groups of superior children have appeared. The most extensive project of this sort is that begun in 1921 by Terman and his associates, and reported in the *Genetic Studies of Genius* (cf. 10, 74, 76). Because of the more comprehensive nature of this study and its essential agreement with the findings of other investigations, it will be described in greater detail.

The total group employed in Terman's study (cf. 76, Ch. 1) included 1528 California children, ranging in IQ from 135 to 200 and in age from 3 to 19. These children represent approximately the upper 1 per cent of the school population. Of these, 661 elementary school children constituted the "main experimental group," on which the major findings of the initial test survey were based. This group was compared, in an extensive series of tests and measures, with control groups composed of random samplings of school children. For reasons of expediency, different control groups were employed for various comparisons, the number of cases in such groups ranging from about 600 to 800.

The *socioeconomic level* of the gifted group was decidedly superior. Among the fathers of the gifted children, 31.4 per cent belonged to the professional class, 50 per cent to the semiprofessional or higher business class, 11.8 per cent to the skilled labor class, and 6.8 per cent to the semiskilled or unskilled labor class. The average school grade reached by the parents of the gifted group was 11.8, and by the grandparents 10.0. In comparison to the average person of their generation in the United States, the parents in this group had received from 4 to 5 grades more schooling. Moreover, a third of the fathers and 15.5 per cent of the mothers had graduated from college. The number of eminent relatives and ancestors was also far in excess of that which would be expected by chance, and many of the families had highly distinguished genealogies.

The homes of the gifted children were visited by field workers, and were rated from 0 to 6 on a standardized scale covering necessities, neatness, size, parental conditions, and parental supervision. The average rating of the homes was over 4.5 in each of these five categories, and only 10 per cent of the homes received a total rating which was distinctly poor. Neighborhood ratings and income level were also considerably better than the generality for California.

We may next consider certain *vital statistics* as well as medical and physical data obtained on the gifted children themselves. The frequency of insanity in the family was lower than average. Only 0.4 per cent of the parents and 0.3 per cent of the grandparents and great-grandparents had a record of insanity. As in the studies on adult genius, the gifted group contained a greater proportion of first-born children than the general population. The gifted children developed at a more rapid rate than the normal from early infancy. They walked on the average one month earlier and talked 3½ months earlier than the control groups. The onset of puberty was also somewhat earlier than normal. Physicians' examinations showed superior health and relative freedom from defects in the group as a whole. Similarly, such conditions as "nervousness," stuttering, headaches, general weakness, and poor nutrition were less common in the gifted than in the control groups. In height and weight, physical and muscular development, and strength, the overlapping of gifted and control groups was almost complete. Such differences as did occur, however, favored the gifted group.

The *educational accomplishments* of the gifted group were far in advance of the normal. About 85 per cent of the gifted children were accelerated and none was retarded. The administration of standardized achievement tests in school subjects revealed that the majority of these children had already mastered the subject matter from one to three grades above that in which they were located. Thus with reference to his actual *abilities*, the gifted child is often retarded rather than accelerated in school-grade location. The gifted children as a group tended to excel in all school subjects; onesidedness was not characteristic of these children. Their superiority was greatest, however, in such subjects as language usage, reading, and other "abstract" work, and least in shop training, sewing, cooking, and similar "craft" subjects. It should be pointed out that over-all educational superiority of the gifted group may have resulted partly from the method of selecting subjects for the study. Teachers were asked to name the brightest children as well as the youngest child in each class, and from among these nominees the gifted subjects were chosen by intelligence tests.

The gifted group displayed a wide range of *interests* outside of their schoolwork, as well as an active *play life*. A two-month reading record kept by the children showed that the gifted read more than the control at all ages. At 9 years, the number of books read by the gifted group was three times that of the control. The range of topics covered was also wider and the quality of the books superior in the gifted group. Similarly, the gifted children were more enthusiastic, had more intense interests in general, and reported more hobbies than the control group. Collections were nearly twice as common among the gifted as among the control, and tended also to be larger and more often of a scientific nature. A questionnaire on play information showed that the typical gifted child of 10 knew more about playing and games than the average child of 13. Apart from the fact that the play interests of the gifted children were more mature than those of the control children of their own age, no conspicuous differences were found in their play activities.

In *character and personality development*, the gifted children were also found to be in advance of the normal. This was confirmed both by objective tests and by teachers' and parents' ratings. On a specially devised battery of seven objective personality tests, the differences in favor of the gifted group were large and significant beyond the .01 level in every test (critical ratios ranged from 3.87 to 14.41). From about 60 to 80 per cent of the gifted group equaled or excelled the average of the control group on each of these tests.

The findings of the California study have been closely corroborated by less extensive investigations on similar groups in the Midwest by Witty (87, 88), in New York by Hollingworth (36, 37, 39), in England by Duff (23), and in New Zealand by Parkyn (58). Favorable home and parental background, better-than-average health and physique, outstanding educational achievement, and superior emotional maturity and stability were characteristic of all these gifted groups.

THE GIFTED CHILD GROWS UP

Among the many superstitions entertained in regard to geniuses and child prodigies is that which claims that the gifted child deteriorates as maturity is approached and that his ultimate mental level will be average or even inferior. Prolonged case studies on a few individuals, as well as a number of investigations on groups of gifted children, have quite conclusively disproved this view.

By far the most extensive longitudinal investigation of intellectually superior children is that conducted in the Stanford Gifted Child Study under the direction of Terman. Follow-up data are presented in volumes III, IV, and V of the *Genetic Studies of Genius* (10, 76, 77). An integral part of the plan of this project included periodic follow-ups of the original group of gifted children throughout their lifetime, as well as of their spouses and offspring. Since the initial survey, intensive follow-up studies have been carried out at approximately 12-year intervals, supplemented by intervening follow-ups by mail. Data obtained through 1945, when the majority of the subjects were approximately 35 years old, were summarized by Terman and Oden in *The Gifted Child Grows Up* (76). A fifth volume by the same authors, published in 1959, covered developments through a mean age of 45 years (77). The follow-ups were unusually complete with regard to sample coverage. In the last follow-up to date, conducted 35 years after the initial survey, data were obtained from 98 per cent of the original 1528 cases.

Adult intellectual status was measured by a specially constructed *Concept Mastery Test* consisting of opposites and analogies and covering many fields of information. Through this test it was possible to estimate that the average adult IQ of the gifted group was about 135, representing a drop of 17 points from their childhood average of 152. Terman and McNemar (76, Ch. 11 and 12) conclude that such a drop is no greater than would be expected from regression effect (cf. Ch. 7). Such regression, however, would result not only from errors of measurement in the Stanford-Binet and the Concept Mastery Test, but also from differences in the functions measured by the two tests, as well as from actual behavior changes in the subjects resulting from maturation or learning. In other words, predictions over a twenty-five-year period are subject to considerable chance error, not only because of the unreliability of the tests, but also because much can happen to change the subjects during such a period.

In a subsequent attempt to evaluate the Concept Mastery Test scores of the gifted subjects in terms of general norms, Thorndike (78) utilized other reference groups and arrived at a somewhat lower mean estimate for the gifted group. Owing to the number of approximations which must be made in the process of estimating the change from childhood Stanford-Binet to adult Concept Mastery scores, all such figures must be regarded as tentative. The important point is that as adults the gifted subjects were still well above the mean of the general population, regardless of which estimate is employed. Thorndike (78) reports that, according to his figures, the mean of the gifted group fell slightly above the 95th percentile of the general population.

Educationally, the gifted group excelled in all comparisons. They attended college in much larger numbers, obtained graduate degrees much more often, and received better grades and many more academic honors than any other groups with which comparisons were made. Among the men, 69.5 per cent completed college, and among the women 66.8 per cent. The percentage receiving Ph.D. degrees was over five times as large for the men and over eight times as large for the women in the gifted group as in a representative sample of college graduates. A special study of educational acceleration in the gifted group not only showed acceleration to have been common, but also lent no support to the view that such acceleration may be

Differential Psychology

detrimental. Any slight social handicap suffered by the very accelerated subjects during adolescence seems to have been fully overcome in later years. In fact, whatever differences were found in later achievement or adjustment tended to favor the accelerated group.

Table 19

OCCUPATIONAL CLASSIFICATION OF GIFTED MEN AT MEAN AGE OF 35
IN COMPARISON TO THAT OF ALL EMPLOYED MEN IN CALIFORNIA
(From Terman and Oden, 76, p. 172)

OCCUPATIONAL GROUP	PERCENTAGE OF GIFTED MEN (N = 724)	PERCENTAGE OF EMPLOYED MALES IN CALIFORNIA (1940) (N = 1,878,559)
I. Professional	45.4	5.7
II. Semiprofessional and higher business	25.7	8.1
III. Clerical, skilled trades, retail business	20.7	24.3
IV. Farming and other agricultural pursuits	1.2	12.4
V. Semiskilled trades, minor clerical	6.2	31.6
VI. Slightly skilled trades	0.7 ⎫	17.8
VII. Day laborers: urban and rural	0.0 ⎭	

In occupational level, the gifted group stood far above the average, being represented in the higher professions by eight times its proportional share. In Table 19 will be found the occupational distribution of the gifted men in 1940, together with the corresponding distribution of all employed males in the 1940 California census. At that time, nearly half of the gifted men fell in the professional category, as contrasted to less than 6 per cent of the generality. The corresponding percentages in the semiprofessional and higher business category were 25.7 and 8.1, respectively. On the other hand, only 6.2 per cent of the gifted men were engaged in semiskilled trades, as against 31.6 per cent of the general population. Similarly, less than 1 per cent of the gifted group were employed in the slightly skilled trades and none in the unskilled, as contrasted to 17.8 per cent of the generality in these two classes combined. Even in comparison with groups of male college graduates, the gifted males excelled conspicuously in occupational status. In the 1955 follow-up, the proportion of gifted men engaged in the professions remained approximately the same as in 1940, but the proportion in the semiprofessional and higher business category rose to 40 (77).

The occupational history of the gifted women is much more difficult to interpret, since jobs and careers have a different significance for the two sexes in our culture. Of the entire group of gifted women, 42 per cent were housewives and not gainfully employed at the time of the 1940 follow-up, this percentage rising to 60 in 1955. Among those employed, the largest number were in secretarial or other office work, and the second largest in elementary or high school teaching. Social work, arts, writing, and college teaching and research each claimed from 5 to 7 per cent. Perhaps the most outstanding finding in the comparison of the gifted women with other groups of women college graduates is the smaller proportion of the gifted who chose teaching and the larger proportion who chose office work. The interpretation of any of these results would be hazardous, in view of the multiplicity of factors which influence the occupations of women in our society today. The discussion of sex differences in the next chapter may help to clarify some of these results. At the same time, it is noteworthy that among the "career women" in the gifted group, a number achieved considerable success and recognition. They include several scientists listed in *American Men of Science*, a well-known poet, a biochemist who participated in the development of the Salk vaccine, a highly successful magazine writer, and a prominent college administrator (77).

The mortality rate of the gifted group was below that of the generality, and both physical and mental health remained superior. The incidence of delinquency, alcoholism, and serious maladjustments was less than in the general population, and there was considerable evidence of good emotional and social development and breadth of interests. Participation in extracurricular activities was as conspicuous in college as in high school. Hobbies and avocational interests were well developed and closely resembled those of any contemporary American group. An active interest in political and social matters is suggested by the fact that over 90 per cent of this group reported that they voted in all national elections, in contrast to only about 70 per cent in the general California population. The social and political attitudes of the gifted group showed no marked deviation from the generality. The subjects' war records, in both military and civilian capacities, were also found to be creditable and distinguished.

Of considerable interest are the data on marital status and marital adjustment. The incidence of marriage among both gifted men and gifted women is above that of college graduates of the same age, and is about equal to that in the general population. Intelligence tests of the spouses as well as of the offspring showed both to be quite superior, but below the average of the gifted group itself. On specially designed tests of "marital aptitude" and "marital happiness," the present group was somewhat superior to other groups less highly selected in intelligence. Sexual adjustment was in all respects as normal as in less-gifted groups. Divorce rate was no higher than in the generality of comparable age.

A special study of individuals whose initial IQ's had been 170 or higher showed them to compare favorably with the rest of the gifted group. They were more often accelerated in school, received better grades, and continued their education longer than the average of the entire group. They were as well adjusted emotionally and more successful vocationally than the rest of the group. Thus it seems that this particular group of exceptionally gifted children were, on the whole, able to overcome the special problems and difficulties which their high intellectual level might engender.

Probably one of the most interesting analyses in the entire survey is the comparison of the 150 men rated "most successful" (Group A) with the 150 rated "least successful" (Group C) in adult achievement. Despite the high average accomplishments of the entire gifted group, the adult achievement of individual members ranged from "international eminence to unskilled labor" (76, p. 311). In the effort to clarify some of the correlates of adult achievement, the two contrasted groups A and C were compared on about 200 items of information which had been secured between 1921 and 1941. The most conspicuous differences were the superior educational and vocational level of the parents of the "A" men, as well as the greater "drive to achievement" on the part of the "A" men. For example, over 50 per cent of this group had fathers who were college graduates, in contrast to 15.5 per cent of the "C" men. More than twice as many fathers of the A's were in the professions.

As for the subjects themselves, both self-ratings and ratings by family and associates showed the largest A-C differences to occur in "integration toward goals," "perseverance," and "self-confidence." Significant differences in favor of the "A" men were found in school acceleration, the A group graduating from elementary, high school, and college at younger ages. Initial IQ's also averaged significantly higher for the A group; but this difference was not large, the two averages being 155 and 150. In summary, factors related to home background seemed to play a major role in the adult achievement of these men, all of whom were within the upper levels of intelligence. Among such men, motivational factors—themselves probably traceable to environmental conditions—often made the difference between outstanding achievement and mediocrity.

Another special analysis (73) concerned differences between those who became physical scientists and those specializing in social science, law, or the humanities within a group of approximately 800 men from the total gifted sample. These subjects were followed up in 1950, when their mean age was 40. Out of about 500 items, including test scores, ratings, and biographical data, 108 differentiated between the two groups at the .05

level of significance. Most of the discriminating items dealt with interests, including childhood evidence of scientific interest as well as scores on the Strong Vocational Interest Blank.

Most of the detailed adult data cited above are based on the 1940 follow-up of the Stanford group, conducted when the subjects had reached a mean age of 35 years. The later, 45-year follow-up served largely to confirm the earlier conclusions. In mental and physical health, personal adjustment, vocational achievement, and intellectual status, the gifted group at mid-life retained its position well above the general average. It is interesting to observe that mean performance on the Concept Mastery Test rose significantly, rather than declining, on the 45-year retest. Also noteworthy is the finding that the death rate of the gifted sample at 45 was only about 80 per cent of the normal expectancy for that age group.

Some general corroboration of the California findings, although on a much smaller scale, was provided by follow-ups of the New York (40, 41, 55) and midwestern (88) groups cited previously. These studies, too, indicate that the gifted child, on the whole, grows up to be an intellectually superior and fairly well-adjusted adult.

There is a possibility, however, that the California results may be unduly optimistic regarding the emotional adjustment of children in the highest IQ levels. The method of *selecting the original group* may be partly responsible for such a finding. The major group was chosen on the basis of teachers' recommendations, the children thus recommended being then given intelligence tests for the final selection. As a check on this procedure, the entire population of three schools was tested, following the teacher nominations. The results showed that about 90 per cent of all the children who qualified for the study on the basis of test scores would have been reached by the usual procedure. It is possible that the 10 per cent who were thus lost to the study may have included a disproportionately large number of scholastically and emotionally maladjusted cases. Their exclusion from the study by the method of search might thus lead to an unduly optimistic picture in these two respects. Corroborative evidence is provided by a test survey of over 45,000 children in grades 4 to 8, reported by Lewis (52). Without knowledge of test results, teachers were asked to list each child whom they considered "a distinct problem," "extremely mentally retarded," and "a genius." The influence of the child's classroom adjustment and academic interests and achievement was clearly apparent in the choices for the "genius" category.

The possible effects of *participation in the study* upon the subjects' subsequent development should also be considered. No control subjects were followed up along with the gifted subjects. Not only the knowledge that one is a "gifted child," but the personal interest in each subject which was apparently shown by the field investigators and project directors cannot be completely discounted. The experimental design employed in the study includes no control for this factor.

It should also be noted that gifted children are drawn predominantly from *superior socioeconomic levels*. It may be this aspect of their home background that is largely responsible for their superior personality adjustment. Relevant data are to be found in a study by Bonsall and Stefflre (5), in which 1359 white high school senior boys in a metropolitan area were given the Guilford-Zimmerman Temperament Survey (cf. Ch. 11). Those scoring in the upper 11 per cent of the group on the Thurstone tests of Primary Mental Abilities were designated as "gifted" for the purposes of this study. Parental occupation was used as an index of socioeconomic level. Analysis of results led the authors to conclude that "the previously found superiority of the 'gifted' as regards temperament stems more from the socioeconomic level at which most gifted children are found than from any other difference in 'gifted' children as such."

SUMMARY

Genius represents a superlative degree of those abilities which have high social significance within a particular culture. The principal theories regarding the nature of genius can be subsumed under four headings: pathological, psychoanalytic, qualitative, and quantitative. Genius may exhibit varying degrees of specificity or generality of outstanding abilities. In research on adults, the criterion of genius has usually been that of eminence. Investigations of gifted children, on the other hand, have traditionally employed high IQ as the basis for selecting subjects. It is now recognized, however, that high IQ may be a necessary but not a sufficient condition for outstanding achievement. Increasing emphasis is being placed upon special aptitudes not covered by traditional intelligence tests, and especially upon creativity, leadership, and motivational factors. With regard to the origins of genius, there is likewise a growing interest in ways of fostering genius, rather than merely identifying it.

Methods for the study of genius include biographical analysis, case study, statistical survey, historiometry, intelligence test survey, and longitudinal study. In investigations of *eminent men*, biographical analyses have been utilized chiefly by exponents of pathological and psychoanalytic theories of genius. Case studies have only recently been applied to eminent adults, as illustrated by clinical investigations of small groups of outstanding American physicists, biologists, psychologists, and anthropologists. Statistical surveys of eminent men and women have been conducted in several countries, beginning with the pioneer work of Galton. Their findings consistently show that eminent persons as a group come from relatively high socioeconomic backgrounds, have many eminent relatives, and tend to come from environments with strong intellectual traditions and with superior educational facilities. Contrary to the claims of pathological theories of genius, the incidence of insanity among eminent persons and their relatives tends to be lower than in the general population. Historiometry, which is concerned with the childhood achievements of eminent men, had demonstrated that the large majority were intellectually superior in childhood.

Research on *gifted children* began with individual case studies of "child prodigies." Unlike the popular stereotype, such gifted children tend on the whole to be physically superior and emotionally well adjusted. Children of very high intelligence, however, are subject to special problems of social adjustment by virtue of their conspicuous differences from their age mates. Nevertheless, such problems are not to be regarded as an integral or essential part of high intellect. Rather, they can be avoided by suitable home and school environment. In recent years there has been a resurgence of interest in the gifted child, his problems, and his education.

The outstanding research project on gifted children, combining intelligence test survey and longitudinal methods, is the Stanford study conducted under the direction of Terman. The original sample of 1528 California children with IQ's of 135 or higher was intensively investigated through tests, ratings, questionnaires, home visits, and physical and medical examinations. The subjects are being followed up throughout their own lifetime and data are being gathered on their spouses and offspring. Both the initial study and the follow-ups present an overwhelmingly favorable picture of the educational, social, emotional, and physical status of the intellectually superior child, and of his adult outcome. By way of qualification, it should be noted that maladjusted or educationally unsuccessful gifted children may have been excluded from the study owing to the selection procedures employed. Participation in the study may also have exerted a favorable influence upon the subjects' development. Finally, the fact that the large majority of gifted children, like the majority of eminent men, come from higher socioeconomic levels and tend to have relatively well-educated parents must be recognized as a possible causal factor in both their intellectual development and their social, emotional, and physical superiority.

REFERENCES

1. Anastasi, Anne, and Foley, J. P., Jr. A survey of the literature on artistic behavior in the abnormal: II. Approaches and interrelationships. *Ann. N.Y. Acad. Sci.*, 1941, 42, 1–112.
2. Ausubel, D. P. Prestige motivation of gifted children. *Genet. Psychol. Monogr.*, 1951, 43, 53–117.
3. Bentley, J. E. *Superior children.* N.Y.: Norton, 1937.
4. Bett, W. R. *The infirmities of genius.* N.Y.: Philosophical Library, 1952.
5. Bonsall, Marcella R., and Stefflre, B. The temperament of gifted children. *Calif. J. educ. Res.*, 1955, 6, 162–165.
6. Bowerman, W. G. *Studies in genius.* N.Y.: Philosophical Library, 1947.
7. Bowman, Lillie L. Educational opportunities for gifted children in California. *Calif. J. educ. Res.*, 1955, 6, 195–199.
8. Bramwell, B. S. Galton's "Hereditary genius"; and the three following generations since 1896. *Eugen. Rev.*, 1948, 39, 146–153.
9. Brimhall, D. R. Family resemblances among American men of science. *Amer. Naturalist*, 1922, 56, 504–547; 1923, 57, 74–88, 137–152, 326–344.
10. Burks, Barbara S., Jensen, Dortha W. and Terman, L. M. *The promise of youth: follow-up studies of a thousand gifted children.* Stanford Univer., Calif.: Stanford Univer. Press, 1930.
11. Carroll, H. A. *Genius in the making.* N.Y.: McGraw-Hill, 1940.
12. Castle, Cora S. A statistical study of eminent women. *Arch. Psychol.*, 1913, No. 27.
13. Cattell, J. McK. A statistical study of American men of science: III. *Science,* 1906, N.S., 24, 732–742.
14. Cattell, J. McK. Families of American men of science. I. *Pop. Sci. Mon.,* 1915, 86, 504–515; II. *Sci. Mon.,* 1917, 4, 248–262; III. *Sci. Mon.,* 1917, 5, 368–377.
15. Cattell, J. McK., and Cattell, J. (Eds.) *American men of science.* (5th Ed.) N.Y.: Science Press, 1933.
16. Cattell, R. B., and Drevdahl, J. E. A comparison of the personality profile (16 P.F.) of eminent researchers with that of eminent teachers and administrators and of the general population. *Brit. J. Psychol.*, 1955, 46, 248–261.
17. Cellini, B. *The life of Benvenuto Cellini written by himself.* (Ed. and transl. by J. A. Symonds.) N.Y.: Brentano, 1906.
18. Clarke, E. L. American men of letters. *Stud. in Hist., Econ., and Pub. Law, Columbia Univer.*, 1916, 72, No. 168.
19. Cox, Catharine M. *The early mental traits of three hundred geniuses.* Stanford Univer., Calif.: Stanford Univer. Press, 1926.
20. Davis, B. Eminence and level of social origin. *Amer. J. Sociol.*, 1953, 59, 11–18.
21. deCandolle, A. *Histoire des sciences et des savants depuis deux siècles.* Genève: Georg, 1873.
22. Dooley, L. Psychoanalytic studies of genius. *Amer. J. Psychol.*, 1916, 27, 363–417.

23. Duff, J. F. Children of high intelligence: a follow-up inquiry. *Brit. J. Psychol.*, 1929, 19, 413–439.
24. Eells, W. C. The center of population of higher education. *Sch. and Soc.*, 1926, 24, 339–344.
25. Ellis, H. *A study of British genius.* London: Hurst and Blackett, 1904.
26. Freud, S. *The relation of the poet to day-dreaming. Collected Papers*, Vol. IV. N.Y.: Internat. Psychoanal. Press, 1925.
27. Galton, F. *Hereditary genius.* N.Y.: Macmillan, 1914 (1st Ed., London, 1869).
28. Galton, F. *English men of science.* N.Y.: Appleton, 1875.
29. Gowan, J. C., and Gowan, May S. The gifted child: an annotated bibliography. *Calif. J. educ. Res.*, 1955, 6, 72–94.
30. Hall, T. *Gifted children: the Cleveland story.* Cleveland, Ohio: World Publishing Co., 1956.
31. Herzberg, A. *Psychology of philosophers.* N.Y.: Harcourt, Brace, 1929.
32. Hildreth, Gertrude H. Three gifted children: a developmental study. *J. genet. Psychol.*, 1954, 85, 239–262.
33. Hildreth, Gertrude H., *et al. Educating gifted children at Hunter College Elementary School.* N.Y.: Harper, 1952.
34. Hirsch, N. D. M. *Genius and creative intelligence.* Cambridge, Mass.: Sci-Art, 1931.
35. Hitschmann, E. *Great men: psychoanalytic studies.* N.Y.: International Universities Press, 1956.
36. Hollingworth, Leta S. *Gifted children: their nature and nurture.* N.Y.: Macmillan, 1926.
37. Hollingworth, Leta S. Review of research. *39th Yearb., Nat. Soc. Stud. Educ.*, 1940, Part I, 43–66.
38. Hollingworth, Leta S. Intelligence as an element in personality. *39th Yearb., Nat. Soc. Stud. Educ.*, 1940, Part I, 271–275.
39. Hollingworth, Leta S. *Children above 180 IQ.* N.Y.: World Book Co., 1942.
40. Hollingworth, Leta S., and Kaunitz, Ruth M. The centile status of gifted children at maturity. *J. genet. Psychol.*, 1934, 45, 106–120.
41. Hollingworth, Leta S., and Rust, Metta M. Application of the Bernreuter Inventory of Personality to highly intelligent adolescents. *J. Psychol.*, 1937, 4, 287–293.
42. Jacoby, P. *Études sur la sélection chez l'homme.* Paris: Alcan, 1904 (1st Ed., 1881).
43. Juda, Adele. The relationship between highest mental capacity and psychic abnormalities. *Amer. J. Psychiat.*, 1949, 106, 296–307.
44. Juda, Adele. *Hochstbegabung.* Munich: Urban and Schwarzenberg, 1953.
45. Knapp, R. H., and Goodrich, H. B. *Origins of American scientists.* Chicago: Univer. Chicago Press, 1952.
46. Knapp, R. H., and Greenbaum, J. J. *The younger American scholar: his collegiate origins.* Chicago: Univer. Chicago Press, 1953.
47. Kretschmer, E. *The psychology of men of genius.* N.Y.: Harcourt, Brace, 1931.
48. Lange-Eichbaum, W. *The problem of genius.* (Transl. by E. and C. Paul.) N.Y.: Macmillan, 1932.

49. Lange-Eichbaum, W. *Genie, Irrsinn und Ruhm*. Munich: Reinhardt, 1928.

50. Lange-Eichbaum, W. *Das Genie-Problem; eine Einführung*. Munich: Reinhardt, 1951.

51. Lehndorff, H., and Falkenstein, L. Christian Henrick Heineken: the miracle boy from Lübeck, 1720–1724. *Arch. Pediat.*, 1955, 72, 360–377.

52. Lewis, W. D. Some characteristics of children designated as mentally retarded, as problems, and as geniuses by teachers. *J. genet. Psychol.*, 1947, 70, 29–51.

53. Lombroso, C. *The man of genius*. N.Y.: Scribner's, 1895.

54. Lorge, I. Social gains in the special education of the gifted. *Sch. and Soc.*, 1954, 79 (2024), 4–7.

55. Lorge, I., and Hollingworth, Leta S. Adult status of highly intelligent children. *J. genet. Psychol.*, 1936, 49, 215–226.

56. Miles, Catharine C., and Wolfe, Lillian S. Childhood physical and mental health records of historical geniuses. *Psychol. Monogr.*, 1936, 47, 390–400.

57. Odin, A. *Genèse des grands hommes, gens de lettres français modernes*. Vol. I. Paris: Librairie Universitaire, H. Welter (Ed.), 1895.

58. Parkyn, G. W. *Children of high intelligence, a New Zealand study*. London: Oxford Univer. Press, 1948.

59. Pressey, S. L. Acceleration: basic principles and recent research. *Proc., 1954 Conf. Test. Probl., Educ. Test. Serv.*, 1955, 107–112.

60. Pressey, S. L. Concerning the nature and nurture of genius. *Sci. Mon.*, 1955, 81, 123–129.

61. Raskin, Evelyn. Comparison of scientific and literary ability: a biographical study of eminent scientists and men of letters of the nineteenth century. *J. abnorm. soc. Psychol.*, 1936, 31, 20–35.

62. Redfield, C. L. *Great men and how they are produced*. Chicago: Author, 1915.

63. Roe, Anne. A psychological study of eminent biologists. *Psychol. Monogr.*, 1951, 65, No. 14.

64. Roe, Anne. A psychological study of physical scientists. *Genet. Psychol. Monogr.*, 1951, 43, 121–235.

65. Roe, Anne. A study of imagery in research scientists. *J. Pers.*, 1951, 19, 459–470.

66. Roe, Anne. *The making of a scientist*. N.Y.: Dodd, Mead, 1953.

67. Roe, Anne. A psychological study of eminent psychologists and anthropologists, and a comparison with biological and physical scientists. *Psychol. Monogr.*, 1953, 67, No. 2.

68. Rossman, J. *The psychology of the inventor*. (Rev. Ed.) Washington, D.C.: Inventors Publ. Co., 1931.

69. Shannon, J. R. Traits of research workers. *J. educ. Res.*, 1947, 40, 513–521.

70. Terman, L. M. The intelligence quotient of Francis Galton in childhood. *Amer. J. Psychol.*, 1917, 28, 209–215.

71. Terman, L. M. Psychological approaches to the biography of genius. *Science*, 1940, 92, 293–310.

72. Terman, L. M. The discovery and encouragement of exceptional talent. *Amer. Psychologist*, 1954, 9, 221–230.

73. Terman, L. M. Scientists and non-scientists in a group of 800 gifted men. *Psychol. Monogr.*, 1954, 68, No. 378.

74. Terman, L. M., *et al. Mental and physical traits of a thousand gifted children.* Stanford Univer., Calif.: Stanford Univer. Press, 1925.

75. Terman, L. M., and Fenton, J. C. Preliminary report of a gifted juvenile author. *J. appl. Psychol.*, 1921, 5, 163–178.

76. Terman, L. M., and Oden, Melita H. *The gifted child grows up.* Stanford Univer., Calif.: Stanford Univer. Press, 1947.

77. Terman, L. M., and Oden, Melita H. *The gifted group at midlife.* Stanford Univer., Calif.: Stanford Univer. Press, 1959.

78. Thorndike, R. L. An evaluation of the adult intellectual status of Terman's gifted children. *J. genet. Psychol.*, 1948, 72, 17–27.

79. Van Zelst, R. H., and Kerr, W. A. Some correlates of technical and scientific productivity. *J. abnorm. soc. Psychol.*, 1951, 46, 470–475.

80. Van Zelst, R. H., and Kerr, W. A. A further note on some correlates of scientific and technical productivity. *J. abnorm. soc. Psychol.*, 1952, 47, 129.

81. Vinchon, J. *L'art et la folie.* Paris: Boutelleau (Librairie Stock), 1924.

82. Visher, S. S. *Scientists starred, 1903–1943, in "American Men of Science."* Baltimore, Md.: Johns Hopkins Press, 1947.

83. Wexberg, E. *Individual psychology.* (Transl. by W. B. Wolfe.) N.Y.: Cosmopolitan Book Corp., 1929.

84. White, R. K. Note on the psychopathology of genius. *J. soc. Psychol.*, 1930, 1, 311–315.

85. Wiener, N. *Ex-prodigy: my childhood and youth.* N.Y.: Simon and Schuster, 1953.

86. Witte, K. *The education of Karl Witte.* (Transl. by L. Wiener.) N.Y.: Crowell, 1914.

87. Witty, P. A study of one hundred gifted children. *Kansas State Teach. Coll., Stud. Educ.*, 1930, 1, No. 13.

88. Witty, P. A genetic study of fifty gifted children. *39th Yearb., Nat. Soc. Stud. Educ.*, 1940, Part II, 401–409.

89. Witty, P. (Ed.) *The gifted child.* Boston: Heath, 1951.

90. Witty, P., and Coomer, Anne. A case study of gifted twin boys. *Except. Child.*, 1955, 22, 104–108, 124–125.

91. Woods, F. A. *Mental and moral heredity in royalty.* N.Y.: Holt, 1906.

92. Worcester, D. A. *The education of children of above-average mentality.* Lincoln: Univer. Nebraska Press, 1956.

93. Yoder, A. H. The study of the boyhood of great men. *Ped. Sem.*, 1894–96, 3, 134–156.

CHAPTER 14

Sex Differences

The literature on psychological differences between the sexes is voluminous. Its content ranges from anecdotal observations and speculative discussions to the results of well-designed experiments and performance on standardized tests. Even the investigations reporting objective data from large, representative samples are too numerous to cover within a single chapter. Only general trends can be given, with illustrative studies. By way of preview, it may be stated that several psychological traits—including both aptitudes and personality characteristics—do yield significant mean differences between the sexes. At the same time, individual differences within each sex are extremely wide and the resulting overlapping between distributions is extensive. Moreover, the bulk of available data on sex differences must be regarded as purely *descriptive*. We know a good deal about the ways in which the behavior of men and women differs within a particular culture at a particular time. But we still know very little regarding the origins of such differences. Data from a variety of sources are nevertheless beginning to provide a picture of the operation of biological and cultural factors in the development of behavioral differences between men and women.

METHODOLOGICAL PROBLEMS

In common with other group comparisons, the study of sex differences in behavior presents a number of methodological difficulties. An understanding of these problems is essential for the proper interpretation of the findings of any study. For this reason, we shall begin by considering certain basic questions which must be raised in the evaluation of any data on group differences.

Significance of a Difference. One of the first questions we need to ask regarding any reported group difference in mean score concerns the statistical significance of the difference. This problem was discussed in Chapter 1, as an example of important contributions that statistical method has made to the growth of differential psychology. It will be recalled that the concept of statistical significance deals essentially with the consistency of results from sample to population, as well as their consistency in retests of the same subjects. When we ask whether a mean difference in favor of boys on a mechanical aptitude test is "significant," we actually want to know whether we are justified in *generalizing* beyond the immediate data. How certain can we be that the boys would still average higher than the girls if we were to repeat the test (or a parallel form) on the same subjects at a different time, or on different groups of boys and girls from the same population?

The answer is generally given in the form of a *t* ratio, with its accompanying *P* value. To say that a difference is significant at the .01 level ($P < .01$) means that there is no more than one chance in 100 that a difference as large as or larger than that obtained in our sample could have resulted from chance errors. Hence we can conclude that boys do average higher than girls, with only one chance in 100 that such a conclusion is wrong. If, on the other hand, the obtained difference fails to reach significance at some acceptable level (usually .01 or .05), we cannot conclude that the data have demonstrated any sex difference at all and there is no point in discussing the difference further.

Overlapping. When Samuel Johnson was asked which is more intelligent, man or woman, he replied, "Which man, which woman?" This is a vivid way of expressing the wide individual differences found within each sex, with the consequent overlapping between their distributions. Since in any psychological trait women differ widely from one another, and men likewise vary widely among themselves, any relationship found between group averages will not necessarily hold for individual cases. Even when one group excels another by a large and significant amount, individuals can be found in the "inferior" group who will surpass certain individuals in the "superior" group. Owing to the large extent of individual differences within any one group as contrasted to the relatively small difference between group averages, an individual's membership in a given group furnishes little or no information about his status in most traits.

In most discussions of group differences, attention has been focused primarily upon means or other group characteristics. For a complete picture of the relative standing of the two groups, however, some index of degree of overlapping should be given. The best procedure would be to reproduce

the entire frequency distributions of the two groups. This is often imprac-
ticable, however. A simpler alternative, in the case of normally distributed
samplings, is to state the percentage of subjects in one group who reach or
exceed the median of the other. Complete overlapping is indicated when
50 per cent of one group reach or exceed the median of the other, as illustrated in the first part of Figure 74. The curves will not coincide, of course,
if the *ranges* are unequal. In such a case, complete overlapping is obtained
only in the sense that one distribution is contained entirely within the other.
Moreover, if either distribution is markedly skewed, such a measure of overlap may be misleading.

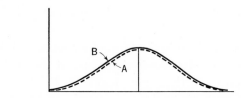

1. 50 Per Cent of Group A Reach or Exceed Median of Group B

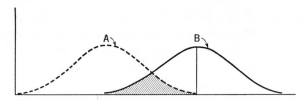

2. Zero Per Cent of Group A Reaches or Exceeds Median of Group B

Fig. 74. Extremes of Overlapping

When more than 50 per cent of group A reach or exceed the median of
group B, then group A is to that extent superior to group B. When less than
50 per cent of A reach or exceed the median of B, group A is inferior to
group B. It should be noted that overlapping is customarily expressed with
reference to the *median* of one group, not with reference to the *lowest* score.
Thus even if zero per cent of group A reaches or exceeds the median of
group B, there are still some individuals in group A who score as well as or
better than certain individuals in group B. This situation is illustrated in the
second part of Figure 74.

That the establishment of a statistically significant difference between
two groups does not preclude the possibility of extensive overlapping between them is illustrated in Figure 75. This figure gives the distribution
curves of 189 boys and 206 girls in the third and fourth elementary school
grades on a test of arithmetic reasoning. The mean score of the boys is

40.39 and that of the girls 35.81. The difference between the means is significant at the .01 level. An examination of the distribution curves, however, reveals extensive overlapping, nearly all individuals in both groups falling within the same range of scores. In terms of the usual measure of overlapping, 28 per cent of the girls reach or exceed the median of the boys.

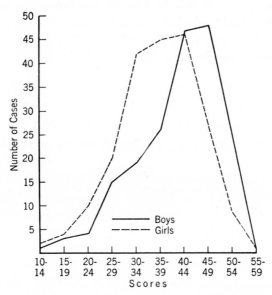

Fig. 75. Distribution of Boys and Girls on a Test of Arithmetic Reasoning: 28 per cent of girls reach or exceed median of boys. (Data from Schiller, 107, p. 67.)

Selective Factors. Samples utilized for group comparisons must be equally representative of their respective populations. Often the operation of selective factors may yield samples that are not truly comparable. Under such circumstances the obtained group difference may result from conditions other than the one under investigation. Thus if a group of college girls were compared with trade school boys, the two samplings would be selected in different ways. Not only is neither group representative of men or women in general, but the one represents the upper end of the female distribution and the other a central or slightly inferior segment of the male distribution with respect to education and correlated variables. In addition to being unrepresentative, these groups are not comparable.

It is unlikely that anyone would seriously attribute differences in test performance between college girls and trade school boys to a sex difference. The lack of comparability of such samples in other respects is too obvious. Sometimes, however, selective factors are more subtle in their operation and may pass unnoticed. We might assume, for example, that high school senior boys and girls represent comparable samples. But this is not the case. Boys whose schoolwork is unsatifactory are more likely than girls to leave school and go to work. Such selective dropping out is borne out by the ratio of boys and girls in successive years of high school, as well as by the school records of those who drop out. As a result, the boys who remain in school constitute a more highly selected group, in terms of academic intelligence, than do the girls. Owing to this differential selection, high school senior boys as a group will excel on the same types of intelligence tests on which girls excelled in the lower grades (16, 98). Such a reversal of sex differences results from the cumulative effects of selective dropping out over the years.

A further example of differential selection is provided by discussions of sex differences in *variability*. Beginning with Havelock Ellis (27), a number

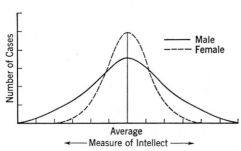

Fig. 76. Hypothetical Distribution of Intelligence among Men and Women According to the Doctrine of Greater Male Variability.

of writers on sex differences have proposed that, although the average ability of men and women may be equal, the range of intelligence is wider among men. Such a possible sex difference in variability is illustrated schematically in Figure 76. According to this doctrine, there should be more geniuses as well as more mental defectives among men than among women. It may be added that the doctrine of greater male variability was regarded by its proponents as a fundamental biological law and was believed to hold for all traits, both physical and psychological. This doctrine enjoyed wide popularity and was adopted by a number of psychologists during the first quarter of the present century (cf., e.g., 21, 134). Nor is it completely absent from contemporary writings, especially popular discussions of sex differences.

The evidence offered in support of the greater intellectual variability of the male was twofold. On the one hand, the statistics on eminence were cited as proof of the greater frequency of superior intellect as well as of the presence of more extreme positive deviants in the male sex. Similar data were presented to establish the wider range of male intelligence at the lower end of the distribution. Surveys of institutions for the feebleminded in several countries revealed a consistent excess of males. The latter finding is now recognized as being largely the result of *differential sex selection in institutional admissions*.

Data bearing upon such an explanation are to be found in a study by Hollingworth (53) on 1000 cases referred for examination to a clinic in New York City, as well as 1142 cases in residence at an institution for mental defectives. In the first place, the males referred for examination, as well as those actually committed, were on the average much younger than the females. Secondly, the IQ's of the females presented for examination were lower than those of the males. This difference in IQ was even greater when the cases actually committed were compared. A survey of the previous occupations and case histories of the subjects suggested that the probable explanation of these findings lies in the uncompetitive nature of many occupations open to women. This makes the detection of feeblemindedness as well as the necessity of commitment less likely among women than among men. A girl of moron level could survive outside of an institution by turning to housework or marriage as a means of livelihood. Families were also more likely to care for a mentally defective girl at home. Boys, on the other hand, were more often forced into industrial work at a relatively early age and soon revealed their mental deficiency in the ensuing competition. Thus, although there is an excess of males in institutions, it would seem that there are more mentally defective women outside of institutions!

A similar differential selection has been found to operate in admissions to special classes for mentally retarded children in the public school system. In a survey conducted in Baltimore (11), results showed that about three times as many boys as girls were enrolled in such special classes. The remaining girls of corresponding ability, however, were found in regular public school classes (cf. also 102). Apparently the differences in social and economic conditions met by the two sexes have led to a "double standard" in the classification of boys and girls as mentally retarded.

The evidence for greater male variability based upon the upper end of the distribution is equally suspect. The excess of males who have achieved eminence may reflect inequalities of opportunities for the attainment of eminence, as well as other cultural factors to be considered in a later section on sex differences in achievement. Of special interest in connection with selective factors, however, are certain findings from surveys of children with very high IQ's. The Stanford Gifted Child Study (cf. Ch. 13) has sometimes been cited in support of the theory of greater male variability, since more gifted boys than girls were located in the survey. The total group included 857 boys and 671 girls. Among the children with IQ's of 170 or over, there were 47 boys and 34 girls. On the other hand, in Hollingworth's compilation of case studies of children with IQ's over 180, 16 girls and 15 boys were found (54). Witty's group of 50 Kansas City children with IQ's of 140 or

higher included 24 girls and 26 boys (148). It will be recalled that the subjects in the Stanford study were located in large part through teachers'
recommendations. Those in Witty's group were found by administering a
group test of intelligence to the entire school population in grades 3 to 7
in Kansas City, Missouri. The Hollingworth cases were identified either
through their conspicuous achievements or through intelligence tests administered for other reasons. It is thus likely that the excess of boys in the
Stanford group resulted from the effect of sex stereotypes on teachers'
judgments. Perhaps a girl with a high IQ was more often regarded by her
teachers simply as a "good pupil," while a boy with the same IQ was judged
to be "brilliant."

Such an explanation in terms of selective factors is supported by the
results of complete school surveys with intelligence tests. In a study in which
a group test was given to all the children in grades 3 to 8 in 22 city schools,
the percentage of boys did not differ significantly from the percentage of
girls in the combined upper and lower 7 per cent of the entire distribution
(103). There were, however, more girls in the upper 7 per cent and more
boys in the lower 7 per cent. In a later survey (74) with the Kuhlmann-
Anderson Intelligence Test, in which approximately 45,000 children in
grades 4 to 8 in 36 states were tested, the upper 10 per cent of the group
likewise included an excess of girls (2676 girls vs. 1853 boys). Among the
highest 2 per cent of the distribution, girls again predominated in the ratio
of 146.3:100. Among the lowest 10 per cent, the reverse tendency was found,
there being 3009 boys and 1618 girls (85). The largely verbal content of
most intelligence tests, as well as their dependence upon schoolwork, probably gives the girls an advantage and accounts for their superior performance. These surveys, however, provide no evidence for greater male variability, nor for greater frequency of boys at the upper IQ levels.

It should be added that more comprehensive surveys dealing with the
entire distribution of each sex have failed to support the doctrine of sex
differences in variability. Karl Pearson (96) was among the first to challenge
the adequacy of studying sex differences in variability by a comparison of
the extremes of the distribution. He called attention to the need for direct
measurement of *variability around the average* in large groups of unselected
subjects. Pearson himself computed coefficients of relative variability for
several classes of data, consisting chiefly of physical and anatomical measurements on adults. He found no evidence of greater male variability, but
rather a slight tendency toward greater female variability. Similarly, Hollingworth and Montague (55) collected a large number of physical measurements on 1000 male and 1000 female infants *at birth*, thus ruling out any

possible effects of differential environment. No consistent sex difference in variability was found.

Later surveys on such physical traits as height, weight, physiological maturity, dentition, and skeletal development, as well as studies with intelligence, special aptitude, and achievement tests, have likewise yielded small and inconsistent differences (77, 87, 101, 103). The relative variability of the two sexes differs with the specific trait under consideration, the age of the subjects, their social and economic level, and even the particular community in which data are obtained. In the case of intelligence tests, moreover, results vary from one test to another.

Special mention may be made of the two Scottish surveys (111, 112), in which nearly complete samples of 11-year-old children were given a group intelligence test. In these investigations, the males exhibited slightly greater variability, the standard deviations being 15.92 versus 15.02 in the 1932 survey and 16.68 versus 15.44 in the 1947 survey. Owing to the very large samples covered, both of these differences are significant at the .01 level. Further analysis revealed, however, that the differences resulted largely from a slight excess of males with very low scores. Several factors may have contributed to such a finding. Since the test was of the usual verbal type, the greater frequency of reading disabilities among boys, as well as their poorer motivation for typical academic tasks, may account for some of the low scores. It was also found that physical handicaps were more prevalent among boys than among girls, and such handicaps may in some cases have interfered with test performance. It is possible that some of these physical handicaps result from sex-linked genetic factors (cf. Ch. 3). Such a hypothesis *could* provide a biological basis for sex differences in variability. Nevertheless, the important point to bear in mind is that in the general population the obtained sex differences in variability are extremely small and usually insignificant.

Ratings and Social Stereotypes. Some of the special methodological problems encountered in group comparisons pertain not to the subjects but to the measuring instruments employed. An example is provided by the use of ratings. A number of investigations on sex differences in personality traits have used ratings by associates. Teachers' ratings of school children have likewise been utilized for both personality characteristics and aptitudes. In all such cases, it is impossible to determine to what extent the ratings reflect the influence of social stereotypes upon the rater's judgment and to what extent they denote the subjects' own characteristics. For example, if teachers expect girls to be more cooperative than boys, the mere fact of being a girl will lead to a higher rating in cooperativeness. In so far as social stereotypes are associated with such categories as sex, race, nationality, or social class, group comparisons based upon ratings will be difficult to interpret.

Intelligence Tests and Global Scores.   Intelligence tests are also unsuited for group comparisons for a number of reasons. First, it should be noted that certain intelligence tests have been deliberately constructed so as to eliminate sex differences in total scores. This is well illustrated by the 1937 Stanford-Binet, which is the revision in current use (86). Items that showed a large sex difference in percentage passing were excluded entirely, on the assumption that sex differences on such items may be specific to the task in question and may simply reflect differences in experience and training. Among the remaining items, those slightly favoring girls were balanced against others which favored boys to an equal degree. The fact that no significant sex difference in IQ was found in the standardization sample of the 1937 Stanford-Binet is therefore an index of the care with which this procedure was followed, and has little or no bearing upon sex differences in intelligence.

A further problem concerns the use of global scores in group comparisons. Group differences in aptitudes may be completely obscured by the comparison of total scores on a composite test. If, for example, boys excel in numerical aptitude and girls in verbal aptitude, and a scale of so-called general intelligence is weighted equally with items from both fields, no significant sex difference in total score will be found. Should the scale be overweighted with items of one type, on the other hand, it will favor the group excelling in that trait, and will indicate an apparent difference in general intelligence. With the development of factor analysis, there has been a growing tendency to look for group differences in separate abilities rather than in "general level of performance." In the study of group differences, it is of the greatest importance to state results in specific terms and to limit conclusions to the particular materials, procedure, and other conditions of each investigation.

Whether boys or girls obtain higher IQ's depends upon the items included in the test. When no deliberate effort has been made to exclude sex differences from the test, there has generally been a tendency to favor girls. This follows from the fact that intelligence tests consist so largely of verbal items, on which girls are superior. In so far as the tests depend upon memory, girls have an additional advantage. Moreover, many intelligence tests are validated against school achievement, in which girls also excel, especially at the elementary school level.[1] It is apparent from this discussion that the question of which is the more "intelligent" sex is somewhat ambig-

---

[1] The evidence for these specific sex differences will be considered in a later section.

uous. In the light of what we now know about trait organization and the nature of intelligence (Ch. 11), this is not surprising. It is much more meaningful to ask what sex differences exist in the more specific functions which make up "intelligence" in our culture.

BIOLOGICAL AND CULTURAL FACTORS

As we examine the major sex differences in aptitude and personality traits to be reported in later sections, we shall repeatedly want to ask, "What is the origin of such differences?" Are they the result of hereditary, biological differences between the sexes, or of social stereotypes, sex roles, and other cultural pressures? Most of the investigations provide little direct data for answering these questions. At the same time, we know that the sexes differ biologically in many ways. And at least some of these physical differences will be reflected in psychological differences, either directly or by way of indirect somatopsychological effects (cf. Ch. 5). Similarly, we know that most cultures provide different psychological environments for the two sexes, and such environmental differences may interact in various ways with biological differences.

Influence of Biological Differences. The different roles males and females play in the *reproductive function* may lead to a number of other sex differences in emotional development, intellectual functioning, and achievement. Some psychoanalysts have emphasized these differences as a basis for wide divergencies in psychological functioning in nearly every phase of living. Several of these psychoanalytic theories regarding sex differences, however, are highly speculative and open to serious question (for critical discussions, cf. 66, 133). At a more objective level, it is evident that the long period of child-bearing and child-rearing, which falls biologically upon the female partner, has important implications for sex differentiation in interests, emotional traits, vocational goals, and achievement in many areas.

The influence of *sex hormones* upon behavior is a direct source of sex differences in psychological traits, over and above the contribution of such hormones to the reproductive function (10). The fact that endocrine secretions are carried to all parts of the body through the blood stream provides an opportunity for very broad behavioral effects. Extensive data from both animal experiments and clinical observations on humans indicate that the presence of male or female sex hormones do influence certain aspects of behavior, such as aggressiveness. At the same time, it should be noted that in terms of sex-hormone production, there is not a sharp contrast between males and females, but the difference is rather one of degree. All males, besides secreting the male sex hormone, androgen, also secrete some female sex hormone, estrogen. Similarly, all females secrete some androgen along with estrogen. It is the relative proportion of the two that determines the degree to which the individual develops masculine or feminine characteristics.

Another possible source of general sex differences is provided by the *sex-determining chromosomes* themselves. It will be recalled (Ch. 3) that every cell in the body receives a complete set of chromosomes. For the female, each body cell contains 23 pairs of chromosomes plus an XX pair; for the male, each body cell contains the same 23 pairs plus an XY pair. In this respect, then, the two sexes differ *in every cell of the body*. This does not mean, of course, that every body cell must necessarily develop differently in men and women, since not all genes may be active in the development of every cell. But these sex differences in gene constitution, repeated in every body cell, may provide a mechanism to account for many of the physical differences between the sexes.

Sex differences have, in fact, been reported for almost every physical variable, including *body build, anatomical characteristics, physiological functioning,* and *biochemical composition* (106, 120, 131). Moreover, the difference in most of these respects increases with age. Thus the human male averages approximately 5 per cent heavier than the female at birth and 20 per cent heavier by age 20; in height, the male excess increases from about 1 or 2 per cent in childhood to about 10 per cent by age 20.[2] Muscular strength shows a consistent difference in favor of males at all ages (61, 106, 131). From early infancy, males likewise exhibit greater "muscular reactivity," as illustrated by a stronger tendency toward restlessness and vigorous overt activity. Of possible relevance to such an excess of muscular reactivity is the greater mean vital capacity of males. (Vital capacity is the total volume of air that can be expelled from the lungs after a maximal inhalation.) This difference is especially significant because vital capacity is an important factor in sustained energy output. In early childhood, the average vital capacity of boys is about 7 per cent higher than that of girls; by adulthood, the male excess reaches about 35 per cent. The vital index, or ratio between vital capacity and body weight, is likewise greater for males at all ages at which measurements have been made. Thus, even in proportion to his body weight, the human male consumes more fuel and produces more energy than the female.

All these physical differences may play an important part in sex differences

---

[2] During a few years in early adolescence, girls are on the average taller and heavier than boys, but this results from the *developmental acceleration* of girls, to be discussed below.

in play activities, interests, and achievement in various fields of work. It is reasonable to expect, for example, that the greater strength and motility of boys increase the likelihood of their manipulating mechanical objects, and thus indirectly facilitate the development of clearer mechanical concepts. Aggressiveness and dominance in social relations may likewise be initially fostered by greater body size, strength, and endurance.

Another important sex difference is to be found in the *developmental acceleration* of girls. Girls not only reach physical maturity earlier, but throughout childhood they are also farther advanced toward their adult status (106, 119, 131). Studies by both cross-sectional and longitudinal methods have shown that, at each age investigated, girls have attained a greater percentage of their adult height and weight than boys (6, 75). Other aspects of physical development show a similar acceleration of the female sex (106). It is well known that girls reach puberty earlier than boys, the difference averaging from 12 to 20 months in various groups. Skeletal development can be measured by the relative degree of ossification, or hardening, of the bones in different parts of the body. In this also, girls have been found to be in advance of boys at every age. A similar difference has been found in dentition. In general, girls shed their deciduous teeth sooner and get their permanent teeth at an earlier age than boys. In the case of certain teeth, these differences amount to one year or over. It is noteworthy that the general developmental acceleration of girls begins *before birth*. Girls are on the average more mature than boys at birth and there is some evidence which indicates that they tend to be born after a shorter gestation period than boys.

The possible psychological significance of sex differences in the rate of physical growth has been emphasized by several writers (cf., e.g., 16, 75, 96, 106). It has been suggested, for example, that girls may be accelerated in intellectual as well as physical development. If this were the case, equated age groups of boys and girls would not be comparable. It would then be necessary to equate the sexes in regard to developmental stage or physical maturity rather than chronological age. But such a procedure would introduce inequalities in amount of training and general environmental stimulation. This problem, of course, arises only in the comparison of children, and does not apply to adults. Children, however, have been the most frequent subjects for surveys on sex differences, both because of their greater accessibility in large numbers and because they have been exposed to relatively more homogeneous environments.

It should be noted that intellectual acceleration of girls has not been directly demonstrated. Its possibility has only been inferred by analogy with physical development. Available data on relationships between psychological and physical traits, however, show the relationships to be far too complex for such a simple correspondence (cf. Ch. 5). The effects of sex differences in developmental rate probably vary widely from trait to trait. For example, the developmental acceleration of girls in infancy may be an important factor in their more rapid progress in the acquisition of language and may give them a head start in verbal development as a whole. In emotional and other personality characteristics, the earlier onset of puberty in girls undoubtedly introduces an uncontrolled factor in sex comparisons at certain ages. Another possible implication of the developmental acceleration of girls is a social one (106). Because of their physical acceleration, adolescent girls tend to associate with boys older than themselves. This probably accounts also for the usual age discrepancy in marriage. Since the girl is generally younger than the boys with whom she associates—and younger than the man she marries—she is surpassed by most of her male associates in education, intellectual development, and general experience. Such a situation may well be at the root of many social attitudes toward the two sexes. A younger individual is likely to have less wisdom, information, and sense of responsibility than an older one, and such an age difference may have been interpreted and fostered as a sex difference.

Another major sex difference pertains to *viability* and *sex-linked defects*. At all ages, the female shows more "viability," or capacity to maintain life, than does the male. The interpretation of mortality statistics in adulthood and even in later childhood, of course, is complicated by differential hazards met by the two sexes in their traditional occupational and recreational activities. That the higher mortality rate of males cannot be explained wholly on this basis, however, is indicated by several facts.

First, prenatal and infant deaths are more common among boys than among girls. It has been estimated that the ratio of male to female conceptions lies between 120:100 and 150:100. The reasons for this excess of male conceptions are not clear. It has been suggested that the male-producing, or Y-bearing, spermatozoon is lighter and more motile than the X-bearing spermatozoon. Another possibility is that the male-producing spermatozoon has a better chance of survival in the uterine environment for either chemical or physical reasons. Whatever the causes, although 20 to 50 per cent more boys are conceived, only 5 to 6 per cent more boys than girls are born. Thus even before birth, death has already taken a much greater toll from the male sex. At every stage of prenatal development, the percentage of male deaths is greater than that of females. Moreover, this difference in viability is not limited to the human, but is true for lower animals as well. Throughout life, the male appears to be biologically more vulnerable in many ways. He is more susceptible to infection and is more often afflicted with physical defects. All but a very small number of defects are more common among males.

One reason for this sex difference in viability and in physical disorders may be found in the sex chromosomes. Since the female receives two X chromosomes, the effect of a defective gene in one of these chromosomes may be counterbalanced by a normal gene in the other. The male, on the other hand, receives only one X chromosome. The Y chromosome contains relatively few genes, and it is doubtful whether any of them are counterparts of X genes. It is thus much more likely that a defective gene in the male will find no normal counterpart to check its effect. This relationship between corresponding genes in each pair of chromosomes can perhaps be best understood when we realize that a defective gene is probably one lacking in certain essential chemical substances. Such a deficit can be overcome by the presence of the same substance in the corresponding normal gene. Color-blindness and hemophilia, both of which are more common in males, represent well-established examples of sex-linked defects (cf. Ch. 3).

We could speculate at length regarding the possible social implications and indirect psychological effects of the greater viability of the female. For example, one result is the increasing excess of women at the upper age levels—a condition that influences the relative opportunity for marriage. A proportional scarcity of males makes marriage a more competitive undertaking for the female than for the male. This situation could in turn be reflected in divergent personality development in the two sexes.

An interesting physiological concept which has received considerable attention in discussions of sex differences is that of *homeostasis,* or the stability of bodily functions. There is evidence that homeostatic mechanisms, which tend to keep the body in its normal condition, operate within narrower limits in the male (131). Thus men show less fluctuation in such measures as body temperature, basal metabolism, acid-base balance of the blood, and level of blood sugar. The observation that females are more subject to flushing and fainting and to various glandular imbalances has likewise been cited as evidence of their greater physiological instability. Experiments have also shown that girls are more reactive than boys to stress situations, but recover more quickly (122).

From these differences in physiological homeostasis, some writers have proposed a parallel sex difference in "mental homeostasis" (60). To this they attribute the greater "psychic unrest" of the female, as evidenced by more frequent emotionality, neurotic tendencies, nervous habits, feelings of inadequacy, and other symptoms of instability. The analogy is interesting, but we must proceed with the utmost caution in making such a transition from physiological to behavior data. Even in physical functions, exceptions can be found to the greater stability of the male sex. Moreover, we cannot *assume* that psychological and physiological homeostasis are necessarily related to a very high degree. It is true, for example, that physiological changes occur during emotional excitement, but it does not follow that individual differences in emotionality are correlated with individual differences in physiological characteristics. Furthermore, the physiological changes themselves may be influenced by the individual's previous experiences, home background, and the like. In fact, the evidence on individual differences in personality development tends to emphasize the role of experiential factors. Such factors may be equally important in determining sex differences in behavior.

Sex Differences in Animals. Since cultural factors often complicate the interpretation of observed sex differences in human behavior, it may be of interest to examine sex differences in subhuman species. It has been argued that, if similar sex differences in behavior are observed at various phyletic levels, such differences are more likely to be directly or indirectly traceable to a structural basis. In maze performance, as well as in other *learning* tasks, sex differences in animals are inconsistent and negligible (93). Although the experimental data on many of the higher forms of animals are quite meager, there seems to be no evidence for a sex difference in ability. What differences have been found pertain rather to emotional characteristics.

There is a considerable body of data—from field studies, the observations of animal breeders and trainers, and the descriptive accounts of laboratory workers—all of which indicate greater *aggressiveness* in the male of most species (19, 47, 106, 116, 149). Fighting, restlessness, and resistance to control have been commonly reported as more characteristic of male than of female animals. That this may be related to the presence of male sex hormones is suggested by a number of experiments involving the removal of gonads, as well as the injection of sex hormones. It is not only reproductive behavior that is affected by such endocrine factors, but also other behavior characteristic of one or the other sex, such as pugnacity or singing in certain species of birds (10, 60, 116).

On the other hand, we must guard against overgeneralizing from such results to sex stereotypes in the human. Animal data that do not fit the familiar human stereotypes can also be found. Carefully controlled studies on *timidity* in rats, for example, showed females to be less timid than males (4). This sex difference persisted, although to a reduced degree, after the removal of gonads from rats of both sexes. Female rats have also been found to be *more active* than males (cf. 93). Also contrary to the traditional human stereotype were observations made on the *mating behavior* of a certain species of monkey (19), in which either sex may initiate the sexual advances preparatory to copulation. There is no indication that the male of this species necessarily takes the initiative in this respect.

All in all, the available findings on sex differences in animal behavior must be interpreted with considerable caution. Such observations may provide leads for the investigation of possible physiological correlates of behavioral characteristics, but it would be premature to make any generalizations regarding universal sex differences in any behavioral function. It should also be borne in mind that, as we ascend the phyletic scale, biological factors tend to become less important and cultural factors more important in determining sex differences in behavior (10, 116).

The Role of Culture. That sex roles and sex stereotypes vary in different times and places is apparent not only from anthropology but from our own cultural history as well. To be sure, a few persistent differences in behavior can be identified. These undoubtedly result from some of the physical differences considered in the preceding section. Thus the widespread prevalence of male dominance in different cultures may be related to sex differences in physique and muscular strength, as well as to sex hormones. But the amount of such sex differences in dominance varies widely from culture to culture, as does the manner in which it is expressed. Moreover, many characteristics associated with the traditional male stereotype in our culture may be absent or reversed in other cultures.

Occupations have traditionally provided one of the principal cultural areas of sex differentiation. In relatively primitive cultures, in which occupations are predominantly physical, a sharp division of labor between the sexes is necessarily observed. Because the female bears and suckles the young, she is likely, in such primitive cultures, to engage in occupations that keep her closer to home, such as the preparation of food and the manufacturing and repair of clothing. Superior muscular strength and endurance cause the men to take over warring, metalwork, hunting, and most of the fishing. But modern occupations do not fit into these primitive categories (106, 116). Even modern warfare is not so much a matter of handling spears and javelins as it is a matter of pushing buttons and designing blueprints. Paradoxically, it is the home that is now one of the principal loci of physical occupations, in contrast to the office, the store, the conference room, or the auditorium. With the development of machinery, the physical demands of more and more occupations are becoming reduced. Our thinking should not, therefore, be hampered by traditional stereotypes, but rather should be guided by the demands of the specific situation and the abilities of the specific individual.

That women have no "natural affinity" for certain tasks, nor men a "natural repugnance" toward their performance, can be amply illustrated. Huxley and Haddon (58, p. 69), in discussing the influence of social pressure upon sex differences in aptitudes, cite the remark of the third century Greek writer, Athenaeus, "Whoever heard of a woman cook?" In the same vein, Mead (89, p. xix) calls attention to "the convention of one Philippine tribe that no man can keep a secret, the Manus assumption that only men enjoy playing with babies, the Toda proscription of almost all domestic work as too sacred for women, or the Arapesh insistence that women's heads are stronger than men's." Other illustrations can be found in the history of our own culture. Most writers on the social history of the Middle Ages, for example, call attention to the "masculine character" of women of that period. Thus Garreau, writing about France at the time of the crusades, has this to say:

A trait peculiar to this epoch is the close resemblance between the manners of men and women. The rule that such and such feelings or acts are permitted to one sex and forbidden to the other was not fairly settled. Men had the right to dissolve in tears, and women that of talking without prudery. . . . If we look at their intellectual level, the women appear distinctly superior. They are more serious; more subtle. With them we do not seem dealing with the rude state of civilization that their husbands belong to. . . . As a rule, women seem to have the habit of weighing their acts; of not yielding to momentary impressions (cf. 2, p. 199).

Play activities of boys and girls have been a subject of frequent discussion. It has been argued, for instance, that girls play with dolls because of a nascent "maternal drive" or some similar innate interest or emotional trait characteristic of their sex. The almost complete absence of this type of play activity among boys has accordingly been regarded as indicative of a fundamental biological diversification in emotional response. An observation made by Mead (88) in her studies on the island of Manus in New Guinea is of interest in this connection. Dolls are ordinarily unknown to the children on this island. But when they were presented for the first time with some wooden statuettes, it was the boys and not the girls who accepted them as dolls, crooning lullabies to them and displaying typical parental behavior. This reaction can be understood in terms of the pattern of adult behavior in Manus. Owing to the traditional division of labor, the women are busy with their various duties throughout the day, while the men have much more leisure time between their activities of hunting and fishing. As a result, the father rather than the mother attends to the children and plays with them. This socially established differentiation of behavior was reflected in the play responses of the boys and girls.

Another vivid illustration of the role of cultural factors in sex differences in behavior is furnished by Mead's description of the traditional emotional characteristics of men and women in three primitive societies in New Guinea (89). The three groups were sharply contrasted in the pattern of male and female personality which they presented. Among the *Arapesh,* both men and women displayed emotional characteristics which in our society would be labeled distinctly feminine. In this group both sexes are trained to be co-operative, unaggressive, gentle, noncompetitive, and responsive to the needs of others. The *Mundugumur* presented a sharply contrasting picture. In that society, both men and women were violent, aggressive, ruthless, and competitive, taking great delight in action and in fighting. Perhaps the most interesting pattern is that of the *Tchambuli,* among whom there appeared to be a reversal of sex attitudes typical of our culture. It was the women who had the position of power in Tchambuli, since they were responsible for the fishing and the manufacturing of mosquito bags, which provided the chief articles of trade for the tribe. The men, on the other hand, engaged predominantly in artistic and other nonutilitarian pursuits, most being skilled in dancing, carving, painting, or other arts. With regard to personality, Tchambuli women were described as impersonal, practical, and efficient, while the men were found to be graceful, artistic, emotionally subservient, timid, and sensitive to the opinions of others.

As in our society, each of these three cultures has its "deviants," its maladjusted individuals whose personality traits clash with the accepted standards. But the deviant in one society often coincides with the traditional ideal of another. Thus the "masculine" woman among the Tchambuli is one who embodies the typically feminine characteristics of our society; the "effeminate" Tchambuli man displays behavior which we would characterize as typically masculine.

In recent years, psychologists, anthropologists, and sociologists have become increasingly interested in studying the differentiation of sex roles within our own contemporary culture (66, 90, 116, 117). From infancy, boys and girls are reared in different "subcultures." They receive differential treatment in a multiplicity of ways from parents, other adults, and playmates. The personalities of the mother and father are themselves important factors in the development of the child's concept of sex roles (91, 100, 114). But there are many other ways in which the boy and girl are made aware of what is expected of them in speech, manners, dress, play activities, and other aspects of behavior.

Even before school entrance, most children have acquired a clear-cut concept of sex roles. There is evidence that working-class children develop an awareness of such roles earlier than middle-class children, and that boys do so earlier than girls (100). Investigations on school children (139, 140) and on college students (32, 118) reveal consistent differences in the traits attributed to the two sexes, as well as in the traits associated with popularity within each sex. It should be added that sex roles may affect the development not only of personality traits but also of aptitudes. Suggestive relationships between aptitude patterns and personality characteristics were found in a study on high school senior boys and girls (138). Boys who excelled in verbal ability and girls who excelled in spatial ability tended to show more personality disturbances than those exhibiting aptitude patterns more consistent with the sex stereotypes prevalent in our culture.

Using a projective test in a developmental study of sex role identification, Brown (17) found that among children aged 5 to 11 years boys show stronger preference for the masculine role than girls do for the feminine role. This finding is consistent with the expressed sex role preferences of adults (cf. 17). Such differences may reflect in part the prestige and other advantages associated with the masculine role in our culture.

In conclusion, cultural factors play an important part in the differentiation of sex roles and in the corresponding sex differences in behavior. Moreover, even when physical differences contribute to sex differences in behavior, the contribution is usually indirect and intricately overlaid with cultural factors. In such cases, it is the *social implications* of such physical differences, rather than the biological sex differences themselves, which lead to divergent personality development in the two sexes.

SEX DIFFERENCES IN APTITUDES

Certain sex differences in aptitudes have been found consistently by different investigators. In such cases, mean differences have been established at a satisfactory level of statistical significance and the differences are large enough to be of practical significance. Nevertheless, we must not lose sight of the extensive *overlapping* which characterizes the distributions of the two sexes in all these aptitudes. Similarly, the results must be regarded as descriptive of sex differences *under existing cultural conditions.*

Motor Skills. On the average, boys surpass girls not only in muscular strength, but also in speed and coordination of *gross bodily movements.*

This difference has been noted from infancy. In extensive observations of children of preschool age, Gesell and his co-workers (36) found that boys were faster and made fewer errors in walking a series of narrow boards. Boys also achieved more accuracy and greater distance in throwing a ball than did girls of the same age. In connection with the latter observation, a study was made of the characteristic ball-throwing pattern of boys and girls. A clear-cut sex differentiation in the typical ball-throwing stance was already apparent among 5- and 6-year-olds. Males of all ages average better than females on such coordination tests as aiming and tracing. Men have also been found to have shorter and more consistent reaction times than women.

In *manual dexterity*, on the other hand, girls generally excel. In early childhood this is exemplified by the fact that girls are usually able to dress themselves at an earlier age and more efficiently than boys (36). Girls' superior control of finger and wrist movements is also indicated in such behavior as hand washing and turning door knobs. In the standardization sample of the Stanford-Binet, more girls than boys passed the tests on buttoning and on tying a bowknot (86). That adult women can perform many manipulatory tasks more quickly and accurately than men has been widely recognized in industry. This fact was especially apparent during World War II, when women were frequently assigned to assembly, inspection, and similar industrial operations. Such an observation is also supported by aptitude test performance. On tests like the O'Connor Finger Dexterity Test, O'Connor Tweezer Dexterity Test, and Purdue Pegboard, the norms for adult women are consistently higher than those for men. Nor are such findings limited to our culture. In an investigation of college students in India, women again surpassed men in dexterity tests, although the sex differences were negligible in a group of industrial workers (132).

Male superiority in gross bodily movements may be largely the result of such structural factors as muscular strength and bodily size and proportions. Female advantage in manual dexterity and speed and control of fine movements, on the other hand, may arise initially from the developmental acceleration of girls. In general, delicate movement follows gross bodily movement within the development of the individual. Girls would thus be expected to develop fine motor coordinations at an earlier age than boys. These initial biologically determined sex differences may affect the acquisition of interests and skills, thereby setting in motion a progressive mechanism of differentiation between the sexes.

Perceptual Processes. In tasks involving the rapid *perception of details* and frequent shifts of attention, women generally excel. This is one of the principal abilities measured by clerical aptitude tests, on which women make a consistently better showing than men. In the norms reported for the Minnesota Clerical Test, for example, only about 16 per cent of male workers in the general population reached or exceeded the median of female workers in checking similarities or differences in lists of names and numbers (5). Moreover, a series of different investigations showed a significant female superiority on this test from the fifth grade through the senior year of high school (5, 108). Similar results have been obtained with other clerical tests, such as the Clerical Speed and Accuracy Test of the Differential Aptitude Tests (14). It should be noted that clerical aptitude tests such as those cited are largely measures of the Perceptual Speed (P) factor identified through factor analysis (cf. Ch. 10). It is thus in this ability that women may be said to excel.

Significant differences in favor of males have been found in another type of perceptual function concerned with *spatial orientation*. In the experiments by Witkin and his associates (147), which were described in Chapter 11, women showed more dependence upon the surrounding visual field than did men. When visual and kinesthetic cues conflicted, as in the tilting-room-tilting-chair test, women made larger errors than men as a result of their inability to disregard the misleading visual cues. With eyes closed, however, women did as well as men in this situation. Women's performance was likewise poorer when a visual stimulus had to be judged independently of its surroundings, as in the rod-and-frame test. Similarly, in the Embedded-Figure Test, women had more difficulty than men in locating the given figure within each complex design.

In an investigation conducted on Swedish university students, a further sex difference in spatial orientation was discovered (105). The task was to point to a tiny illuminated spot in a dark room. Although all subjects experienced considerable difficulty in localizing the luminous point, women made significantly larger errors than men. Women also proved less able to resist stimuli that disrupted their spatial orientation.

Research on sex differences in perceptual functions, as well as on the relationships of such functions to other aspects of behavior, is still in an exploratory stage. It should be recalled in this connection that there is evidence of a possible relation between performance on perceptual orientation tasks and certain broader personality characteristics. The present findings should also be considered in connection with sex differences in various spatial aptitude tests, to be discussed later.

Verbal Functions. Female superiority in verbal or linguistic functions has been noted from infancy to adulthood (83, 131). This difference is found in almost every aspect of language development that has been studied, and has been reported with remarkable consistency by different investigators. Observations on normal as well as on gifted and feebleminded children have shown that on the average girls begin to talk earlier than boys. Similarly, girls of preschool age have a larger vocabulary than boys. In one study (81), the percentage of comprehensible verbal responses was determined for each child. At 18 months, the average percentage was 14 for boys and 38 for girls; at 24 months it was 49 for boys and 78 for girls. Girls likewise begin to use sentences earlier than boys and tend to use longer sentences and more mature sentence structure. In learning to read, girls also make more rapid progress than boys.

Girls reach maturity in articulation at an earlier age than boys. The articulatory patterns of girls in the first school grade are approximately the same as those of boys in the second grade. This developmental difference in the motor aspects of speech may provide a clue to the general female superiority in linguistic functions. The acceleration of girls in physical development probably accounts for their more rapid progress in articulation. This in turn may give them a powerful initial advantage in the mastery of all phases of language. Such a difference in developmental rate may also account in part for the much greater frequency of reading disabilities, stuttering, stammering, and other speech disorders among boys. The ratio of male to female stutterers varies from 2:1 to 10:1 (109, 110). In a survey of 17 groups of reading disability cases (12), the percentage of boys varied from 60 to 100. If in speaking and reading boys are more often held up to standards which they are not structurally ready to meet, they may experience more frustration and confusion in linguistic situations than girls (83, 109, 110). This may be an important factor not only in the development of linguistic disorders but also in the normal individual's subsequent progress in verbal functions. Another hypothesis for the linguistic advantage of girls is based upon sex differences in amount and nature of contact with the mother, who serves as the principal source of early language training (82).

Girls maintain their superiority in many aspects of verbal functioning throughout the elementary and high school level. In a study of language development of children in grades 4 to 12, 472 boys and 514 girls were asked to write a composition on a prescribed topic of interest to both sexes. Within the same time limit, girls produced longer themes than boys, the elementary school boys using on the average 86 per cent as many words as the girls, and the high school boys 83 per cent (68). Girls usually excel in speed of reading and in such tests as opposites, analogies, sentence completion, story completion, and dissected sentences. Relevant data are provided by investigations using separate verbal tests, as well as by the analysis of subtest scores on intelligence tests. The over-all superiority of girls on a number of common intelligence tests results in part from the predominance of verbal content in such tests.

With the more recently developed multiple-factor batteries, it has proved possible to analyze sex differences in verbal functions somewhat more precisely. Studies of high-school-age groups with the Thurstone tests of Primary Mental Abilities showed a significant difference in favor of girls in Word Fluency (W), but not in Verbal Comprehension (V), in which sex differences tended to be negligible and inconsistent (46, 49, 52). Similarly, in the normative sample of the Differential Aptitude Tests, girls excelled significantly in Language Usage, but the Verbal Reasoning test yielded small, negligible differences in favor of boys (14, 144). It should be borne in mind, of course, that high school boys are a more select group than high school girls—a difference which would affect the results of some of the above investigations. Nevertheless, it is evident that girls do relatively better in word fluency and in tasks involving mastery of the mechanics of language than they do in vocabulary, verbal comprehension, and verbal reasoning tests.

Memory. Girls also excel in tests of memory, although the differences are neither so large nor so consistent in this respect as they are on verbal tests. In the standardization sample of the 1937 Stanford-Binet (86), a significantly greater percentage of girls passed the tests of picture memories and copying a bead chain from memory. No significant difference in favor of either sex was found on other memory tests in the scale. Group tests of intelligence also tend to show superior female performance on subtests involving memory. In digit span and in memory for geometric forms, however, sex differences are negligible and inconsistent. In memory for narratives, the direction of sex differences often depends upon the relative appeal of the content for the two sexes.

In general, however, when the content favors neither sex, girls tend to excel more consistently in logical than in rote memory. This may result from the greater dependence of logical memory tests upon reading ability. It is possible, in fact, that the female superiority in many memory tests is attributable to the role of verbal functions in facilitating retention and recall of most types of material. Another relevant observation is that women seem to have more vivid mental imagery than men in every sense modality. To what extent such a difference may be the result of sex differences in occupations and other traditional activities cannot be ascertained from the data.

Spatial and Mechanical Aptitudes. A difference in favor of males has been repeatedly observed in tests of spatial and mechanical aptitudes. The possibility that this difference has a predominantly cultural basis, however, is suggested by several facts. Thus male superiority is more pronounced and consistent in tests depending upon mechanical information than in the more abstract tests of spatial relations, which may be equally unfamiliar to both sexes. Moreover, male superiority in this area is not evidenced as early as is female superiority in verbal aptitude. For example, in the extensive observations by Gesell and his associates at Yale, no significant or consistent sex differences were found during the first five years of life in tests involving block building, form boards, and form recognition (36).

Among children of school age, on the other hand, a clear-cut sex differentiation on mechanical tests is apparent. On the Stanford-Binet, boys were found to excel significantly in block counting from pictures, directional orientation, and plan of search, all of which probably involve spatial abilities (86). On such tests as form boards, puzzle boxes, assembling objects, and slot mazes, boys also score much higher than girls in both speed and accuracy. A similar male superiority was found by Porteus (97) in his graded paper-and-pencil mazes. Boys clearly excelled on these mazes, when compared with girls of the same Stanford-Binet IQ's.

Table 20

CRITICAL RATIOS OF THE DIFFERENCES BETWEEN MALE
AND FEMALE AVERAGES ON THE MINNESOTA
MECHANICAL APTITUDE TESTS

(From Paterson *et al.*, 95, p. 274)

| | CRITICAL RATIO $(\text{diff.}/\sigma_{\text{diff.}})$ [*] | |
TEST	seventh grade pupils	college sophomores
Assembly	12.1	10.4
Paper Form Board	2.0	2.4
Spatial Relations	−3.2	2.4
Block Packing	−5.0	1.4
Card Sorting	−8.9	−0.6

[*] In this table, a minus sign indicates a difference in favor of the girls. A critical ratio of 2.58 or higher represents significance at the .01 level.

In the standardization of the Minnesota Mechanical Aptitude Tests (95), sex differences were investigated among seventh-grade children and college sophomores. In Table 20 will be found the critical ratios of the differences between male and female means on these tests. The largest sex difference is that on the Assembly Test, which requires the assembling of a number of common objects, such as a bottle stopper or a spark plug, from the given parts. The greater experience of boys with mechanical objects undoubtedly gives them an advantage on such a test. The Paper Form Board Test, involving more abstract spatial visualization, shows a male superiority which falls short of that required at the .01 level of significance. The Spatial Relations Test calls for the insertion of numerous irregularly shaped pieces in their appropriate recesses as rapidly as possible. This test, together with Block Packing and Card Sorting, favors girls in accordance with the commonly reported sex difference in manual dexterity and perceptual discrimination. It should be noted, however, that the female advantage on these tests disappears in the college sampling, either because of selective factors or because of intervening experiential differences.

On tests of mechanical comprehension, women score lower than men, as would be expected on the basis of sex differences in mechanical information and experience. This is illustrated by the results of a survey with the Bennett Test of Mechanical Comprehension (Form AA), given to 390 females and 338 males of comparable age and education, including high school and adult groups (13). The males averaged much higher than the females on this test, the critical ratios of the differences ranging from 7.2 to 10.5 in different groups. Although the sex difference varied considerably from problem to problem, the females as a group made more errors than the males on every item.

Mention may also be made of sex differences on performance tests of "intelligence," many of which depend largely upon spatial rather than verbal aptitudes. Such tests generally favor boys. For example, in a complete sampling of 11-year-old children examined in one of the Scottish surveys, a battery of eight performance tests selected from well-known intelligence scales was administered in addition to the Stanford-Binet (77). The total performance score showed a significant difference in favor of the boys, although Stanford-Binet IQ yielded no significant sex difference in the same sample. On multiple aptitude batteries, boys consistently excel on spatial factors (14, 46, 49, 52, 144).

Numerical Aptitudes. On numerical tests, the largest differences again favor boys. Such a male advantage fails to appear, however, until the children are well into the elementary school period. Gesell's observations on preschool children show either negligible sex differences or a slight superiority of girls in the early development of numerical concepts (36). Surveys on kindergarten and first-grade children have also yielded no significant sex difference in arithmetic abilities (cf. 131). At the lower levels of the Stanford-Binet, sex differences on tests involving counting and number concepts are likewise negligible or inconsistent.

Among elementary school children as well as older subjects, *computation tests* show either no sex difference or, more often, a difference in favor of girls (131). On arithmetic problems and other *numerical reasoning tests,* on the other hand, males excel quite consistently (131). In the 1937 Stanford-Binet (86), boys excel significantly on the tests of arithmetic reasoning, ingenuity (a more difficult type of numerical reasoning problem), and induction (in which a generalized numerical rule must be found). On most group tests of intelligence at the elementary, high school, and college levels, boys excel on such tests as arithmetic reasoning and number series completion. In the case of multiple factor batteries, girls tend to surpass boys on tests of the Number factor (N), which measure speed and accuracy in the mechanics of computation (46), while boys usually score higher on numerical reasoning tests (14, 144).

A few studies throw additional light upon sex differences in problem solving in general. Their findings may thus help to clarify some of the observed sex differences in numerical reasoning, as well as in the solution of reasoning problems in other areas. Working with college students, Sweeney (125) found males significantly superior on problems that called for "restructuring," that is, discarding the first approach and reorganizing facts in new ways. This sex difference remained even when groups were equated for general intelligence, verbal and mathematical aptitudes, relevant knowledge, and a number of background factors.

In a study on high school seniors, Kostik (67) found that boys excelled in their ability to transfer, or apply skill and knowledge to new situations. Again, relevant factors such as intelligence, previous knowledge, reading ability, practice effect, and certain personality traits were controlled. Male superiority in transfer of training has also been confirmed in other studies on high school and college students (cf. 50). All of these investigations provide promising leads for further research on sex differences, especially when considered in conjunction with recent work on the nature of creative and reasoning processes (cf. Ch. 11). The extent to which these sex differences may result from problem-solving attitudes that may be amenable to training should also be explored.

Artistic and Musical Aptitudes. Among preschool children, girls generally include more details in their drawings than do boys (36). This is true in their spontaneous drawings as well as in various controlled drawing tests, such as drawing a man or completing figures. Differences in developmental rate, as well as in the traditional play activities of boys and girls, may account for such findings. In later childhood and adulthood, sex differences in artistic production and appreciation are even more difficult to evaluate because of obvious differences in relevant training and experience. On such tests of art appreciation as the McAdory and the Meier Art Judgment Test, women exceed men in average scores by small but significant amounts [3] (7, 30).

In the Seashore Measures of Musical Talents, which measure relatively simple auditory discrimination and memory, no significant sex differences have been found (31). On more complex tests, placing greater emphasis upon esthetic appreciation, the scores generally favor women. An interesting clue to the probable origin of some of these differences is provided by an investigation of college students with the Kwalwasser-Dykema music tests (37). Comparisons were made between men and women within a group of 1000 students in twelve eastern colleges. In the total undifferentiated groups, women excelled in average score. But when only subjects who had received no musical training were compared, the sex difference disappeared. These findings thus suggest that the sex differences ordinarily reported on such tests may result from differential amounts of training received by the two sexes.

SEX DIFFERENCES IN PERSONALITY

Interests and Attitudes. That conspicuous personality differences exist between adult men and women in our society is clearly apparent from everyday observation. In many emotional and social characteristics, this differentiation is noticeable from an early age. An important aspect of personality development in which traditional sex differences are manifested includes interests, preferences, ideals, attitudes, and personal sense of values. Because of their relatively subtle and persistent nature, these characteristics often exert an unsuspected influence, not only upon the development of emotional and character traits, but also upon the individual's achievements and effective abilities.

Data on sex differences in interests and attitudes are available from a wide variety of sources. Especially plentiful is the information gathered on *children* (cf. 131). The preferences of boys and girls have been compared in such areas as play activities, spontaneous drawings, the choice of topics

---

[3] In a study by Prothro and Perry (99), no significant sex difference on the Meier Art Test was found in a combined sample of Negro and white high school and college students. However, females scored slightly higher among whites and males slightly higher among Negroes.

for written compositions, collections, reading, movies, radio programs, favorite characters in fiction or in public life, vocational choices, and general life goals. Fairly clear-cut and consistent male and female interest patterns have emerged from these varied studies.

A few examples will suffice to show the trend of results. Extensive surveys of *play activities* (72, 128) have shown that boys engage more often in active, vigorous play, in activities involving muscular dexterity and skill, and in highly organized and competitive games. The play of girls tends to be more sedentary, conservative, and restrained in range of action. In a study by Honzik (56) on 252 children from the Berkeley Growth Study, the subjects were given different types of play materials and told to construct an imaginary scene from a moving picture. Boys used more blocks and vehicles in carrying out this task, while girls utilized more furniture and family figures. A reanalysis of the same data by Erikson (29) showed that boys tended more often to represent high structures, ruins, and objects in arrested motion; girls were more likely to construct predominantly static scenes and to use blocks to mark off enclosures such as rooms.

In *reading, movies,* and *radio programs,* boys prefer adventure, travel, and exploration; among girls, stories about love and romance, children, and family life rank highest. A survey of reading preferences among Swiss children corroborated these findings (8). *Vocational choices* of high school students suggest that boys desire jobs offering power, profit, and independence, while girls place higher value upon interesting job experiences and social service (121). In a comparison of the *"areas of life concern"* which high school students ranked highest for discussion and reading in school, certain sex differences were found which increased in late adolescence (126). The boys gave the highest ranks to discussions of physical health, safety, and money, and showed a more openly expressed interest in sex. The girls were more concerned about personal attractiveness, personal philosophy, planning the daily schedule, mental health, manners, personal qualities, and home and family relationships.

Research with *adult groups* by a variety of techniques reveals similar sex differences in interests and attitudes. A number of investigators have systematically analyzed snatches of *conversation* by men and women overheard in different locales in New York City (18, 92, 143) and in a midwestern college town (70), as well as on two busy London streets (69). Although the locale does to a certain extent determine the topics of conversation, the principal sex differences are quite consistent. Money, business affairs, and sports are more common in conversations between men; other women and clothes are more common in conversations between women. Moreover, women converse to a significantly greater degree than men about people. The conversations of mixed groups tend to be dominated by topics either of equal interest to both sexes or of little interest to either.

Sex differences have likewise been found on such *interest tests* as the Kuder Preference Record (135, 137), designed especially as measures of vocational preferences. On the average, males show stronger preferences for mechanical, persuasive, computational, and scientific work. Female averages indicate greater interest in the literary, musical, artistic, social service, and clerical areas. Similar differences between men and women in general have been found on the Strong Vocational Interest Blank (123). On the other

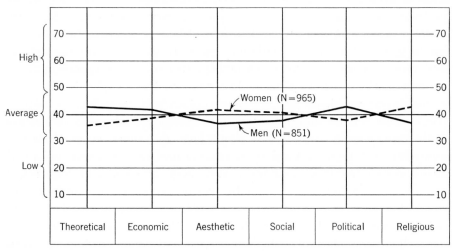

Fig. 77. Mean Profiles of Male and Female College Students on the Allport-Vernon-Lindzey Study of Values. (Data from Allport, Vernon, and Lindzey, 3, p. 9.)

hand, groups of men and women engaged in the *same occupations* showed very similar interest patterns (115). Thus women physicians or life insurance saleswomen resemble men physicians or life insurance salesmen much more closely in their interests than they did housewives. Significant sex differences have also been obtained on the Allport-Vernon-Lindzey *Study of Values* (3). As can be seen in Figure 77, women's responses rate highest in the esthetic, social, and religious values. This suggests that the immediate enjoyment of artistic experiences, a concern for the welfare of other people, and an emphasis upon spiritual values may be relatively important in the life goals of women. The men's profile shows peaks in the theoretical, economic, and political values. Such a profile indicates an interest in abstract knowledge and understanding, a drive for practical success, and a desire for prestige and power over others. Although all statistically significant, these sex differences are not large, and the overlapping is considerable. As in the case of the Strong VIB, far larger differences have been found between different occupational groups of the same sex than between men and women in general.

Throughout this survey of sex differences in interests, preferences, attitudes, and values, we have encountered repeated evidence of the greater *social orientation* of women. This sex difference appears early in life and continues into old age. One possible factor in the greater social interest and social orientation of girls may be their earlier language development. Their more rapid mastery of speech would certainly give girls an advantage in communicating with other children as well as with adults, and would thus encourage activities of a social nature. Of prime importance, however, are the subtle social pressures which probably begin to operate much earlier than is generally realized. Traditional sex roles and sex stereotypes are almost certain to be reflected in the attitudes of parents and others toward the child almost from the time of his birth.

Throughout childhood, sex differences in sociality have been noted in a wide variety of situations (60, 131). In the play activities of nursery school children, boys show more concern with things, girls with personal relationships. Similarly, girls manifest more responsibility and "motherly behavior" toward other children than do boys. At all ages, girls engage more often in "social" games involving other children; they read more books about people and more frequently express interest in occupations dealing with people. The girls' greater concern with questions of appearance and manners is indirectly an indication of more interest in what others will think of them. Parents' tabulations of the questions children asked in their presence showed a significantly greater proportion of questions about social relations asked by girls. Nicknames of an affectionate form are more common among girls, those based on physical peculiarities more common among boys. Girls are more frequently angered by situations affecting their social prestige, and also experience more jealousy. Their wishes, fears, daydreams, and pleasant and unpleasant memories more often concern people. Even studies of children's dreams have shown that girls more often than boys dream about people of various sorts, as well as about their own family and home.

Both sex differences in memory and a stronger interest in people probably account for the superior performance of women in associating names with faces. In one investigation on 210 college students, highly significant differences in favor of women were found in the case of both a pictorial test and a miniature social situation in which spoken names were identified with individual persons (63). It is likewise interesting to note that in a study of persons aged from 70 to 90, sociability showed a high positive correlation with happiness in females, but an insignificant correlation in males (cf. 60).

There is also evidence from a number of sources which suggests a sex difference in *achievement motivation*. Males in our culture appear to have a stronger drive to achieve and to advance than do females. This difference is illustrated by the previously cited vocational choices of high school students and by the results obtained with the *Study of Values*. The occupational histories of the subjects participating in the Stanford Gifted Child Study, as reported in Chapter 13, also bear out this point. It will be recalled that, despite their high intellectual level, the majority of employed women in this group had chosen occupations of a fairly routine nature, such as office work.

Experiments on the "level of aspiration" of boys and girls corroborate these general observations. In such experiments, the subject is required to state in advance what score he will try to reach on each trial. The discrepancy between anticipated goal and actual performance is an indication of the individual's aspiration level. In an investigation on boys and girls in the fourth, sixth, eighth, and twelfth grades, girls were found to have lower goal discrepancy scores than boys (142). Using a different approach, McClelland and his co-workers (84) again found large sex differences in achievement drive. In this study, subjects wrote stories in response to pictures before and after they had taken an "intelligence" test under conditions designed to stimulate achievement needs. The stories, which were scored for expressions of achievement motivation, showed significant changes following the testing experience in males, but not in females. Through supplementary experiments it was shown, however, that when the intervening experience provided a challenge to social rather than to intellectual acceptability, the achievement motivation scores changed significantly in females but not in males. Such results again highlight the predominant social orientation of women in our culture and indicate that sex differences in achievement motivation must be considered with reference to type of goal.

Sexual Behavior.   Differences in the orientation and attitudes of men and women are also reflected in their sexual behavior. The most extensive source of information on this subject is provided by the research of Kinsey and his associates (64, 65). In these investigations, data were gathered through intensive, two-hour interviews of 5300 white American men and 5940 white American women. The second volume (65), reporting the data for women, also contains comparisons of results for the two sexes. Methodologically, the Kinsey research has been criticized chiefly on two grounds. First, the data are based on what subjects recall and report regarding their sexual experiences. Although the interviewers were highly skilled and good cooperation was apparently obtained from subjects, there is an unknown source of error in this regard.

A second and more serious criticism concerns what has been called "volunteer error." Since most subjects were volunteers, it is likely that they differed in systematic ways from those not reached by the study. There is some evidence that volunteers for any investigation differ significantly in personality characteristics from nonvolunteers (104). Even more relevant is the finding by Maslow and Sakoda (79) that college students who volunteered for the Kinsey interviews rated significantly higher than their classmates on a self-esteem inventory. In a previous study, Maslow (78) had found a high positive correlation between self-esteem score and unconventional sex attitudes. Such findings suggest that the volunteer error in the Kinsey data may operate in the direction of exaggerating the frequency of unconventional sexual behavior in the general population.

Another sampling difficulty concerns the lack of comparability of total male and female samples, especially with regard to education. It should be added, however, that when equated subgroups of men and women were compared, the major sex differences found in the total sample persisted. For further methodological analyses, the reader is referred to reviews of the two volumes by Terman (127) and by Hyman and Barmack (59), respectively. More extensive critiques, together with discussions of the implications of the findings from various points of view, can be found in recent books edited by Ellis (26), by Geddes (35), and by Himelhoch and Fava (51).

With regard to *sex differences,* the major and best-established finding of the Kinsey research is that males are sexually aroused by a *wider variety of symbolic stimuli,* such as pictures or verbal accounts of sexual activity, nude figures, and objects associated with the opposite sex. Since similar sex differences have been reported for animals, there is probably some biological basis for such a finding. Nevertheless, the explanation proposed by Kinsey *et al.* in terms of sex differences in the cerebral cortex appears highly questionable. In the human, moreover, any existing biological differences are undoubtedly overlaid with manifold cultural factors. Of possible relevance is the finding that in the case of certain stimuli, such as romantic motion pictures, women reported sexual arousal more frequently than men. The greater social acceptability of such stimuli may be related to the sex difference in response. It should also be noted that the range of individual differences within each sex was found to be extremely wide and overlapping was extensive. Thus about one third of the females in the Kinsey study were aroused by symbolic stimuli as often as or oftener than the average of the males. Similarly, 2 to 3 per cent of the females responded sexually to a wider variety of factors than any males in the sample.

Emotional Adjustment.   A major personality area in which large sex differences have been reported is that of *emotional instability* or *neuroticism.* Among preschool and elementary school children, girls report more fears and worries than boys and manifest more "nervous habits," such as nail-biting and thumb-sucking (cf. 131). On the other hand, "behavior problems" are more common among boys. The total amount of instability may thus be no different in the two sexes at these age levels. Girls may simply resort to milder and less violent ways of expressing maladjustment than boys, because of differences in sex roles and socially imposed restrictions. In the California Guidance Study (76), described in Chapter 8, significant sex differences were found in the incidence of different *kinds* of problem behavior in children between the ages of 3 and 13 years. Boys more often exhibited overactivity, attention-demanding behavior, jealousy, competitiveness, lying, selfishness in sharing, temper tantrums, and stealing. Girls were more likely to suck their thumbs; be excessively reserved; fuss about their food; be timid, shy, fearful, oversensitive, and somber; and have mood swings.

On neurotic inventories, clear-cut sex differences in emotional instability do not appear until the adolescent years. This finding was corroborated in a number of investigations with adaptations of the Woodworth Personal Data Sheet, specially designed for use with children and adolescents (44, 80, 128, 131). An interesting illustration of age changes in this respect is shown in Figure 78, based upon the scores of 575 boys and 558 girls be-

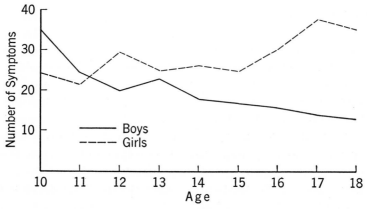

Fig. 78.   Median Number of Symptoms Reported by Boys and Girls on the Woodworth-Mathews Test of Emotional Instability. (From Mathews, 80, p. 21.)

tween the ages of 9 and 19. At age 10, the boys reported a larger median number of neurotic symptoms than the girls on the Woodworth-Mathews Test. With increasing age, the median number of symptoms tends to rise among the girls, but drops among the boys. Beyond age 14, the sex difference is statistically significant and consistently in favor of boys. The increasing differentiation of social pressures with age is one hypothesis that is obviously suggested by such data.

Among adult groups, sex differences on adjustment inventories are large and consistent. On the Bernreuter Personality Inventory, for instance, women college students report significantly more neurotic symptoms than men, as can be seen in Table 21. On the same inventory, men scored significantly more *dominant, self-sufficient,* and *self-confident.* The significantly higher *introversion* mean of women must be interpreted with reservations,

Table 21

SEX DIFFERENCES AMONG COLLEGE STUDENTS ON THE BERNREUTER PERSONALITY INVENTORY

(Data adapted from Bernreuter, 15)

SCALE	MALE AVERAGE	FEMALE AVERAGE	CRITICAL RATIO [*]	DIRECTION OF DIFFERENCE
B_1N: Neuroticism	−57.3	−42.8	3.15	Women more neurotic
B_2S: Self-sufficiency	27.0	6.8	5.89	Men more self-sufficient
B_3I: Introversion	−25.6	−14.7	3.50	Women more introverted
B_4D: Dominance	45.9	30.6	3.77	Men more dominant
F_1C: Confidence	−51.5	8.7	9.62	Men more self-confident
F_2S: Sociability	−25.9	−31.1	0.88	No significant difference

[*] Computed by the writer from published norms. Ratios of 2.58 or higher indicate significance at the .01 level.

since other studies yield inconsistent results. It appears that women show more introversion along certain lines, men more introversion along others (48). The lack of sex difference in the *sociability* scale may result from the fact that the items in this scale cover both social orientation and social participation. From an analysis of data on 3000 college students, Johnson and Terman (60) concluded that women do not actually behave more socially than men, although they desire more strongly to be social. The overt expression of social interests in the female is more often inhibited by timidity and lack of self-confidence, as well as by more specific culturally imposed restrictions.

The sex difference in number of neurotic responses has been corroborated with other personality inventories (40, 43). That such differences are not limited to questionnaire replies is suggested by a study of a college group (23). Students who had taken a personality inventory were subsequently interviewed by two experienced counselors. The excess of maladjustment among the women, as revealed by the interviews, was even greater than that indicated by the test scores.

In their analysis of the relevant literature, Johnson and Terman (60) emphasized constitutional rather than cultural factors as a basis for the greater emotional imbalance of the female. Among the types of evidence cited in support of such a conclusion were: (1) the early age at which sex differences in nervous habits appear; (2) the persistence of sex differences in neuroticism today, despite the trend toward equalization of social pressures; (3) the fact that sex differences in emotionality are as great or greater among institutionalized blind, deaf, or orphaned children, despite the relative uniformity of the institutional environments; and (4) the fact that peaks of "nervous" behavior often coincide with such physiological changes as puberty and the menopause.

All these lines of evidence permit alternative explanations. Puberty and the menopause are periods of acute social crises in our society, as well as periods of physiological upsets. Institutional environments are far from uniform for boys and girls. In fact, there is no reason to suppose that sex stereotypes are any different among institutional personnel than among any other members of our culture. The persistence of sex differences in neuroticism in contemporary society is not surprising. The greater equalization of education and the sporadic admission of women to certain predominantly "masculine" occupations, without the removal of other sources of frustration and discrimination, may increase rather than decrease conflict and maladjustment. As for the excess of nervous habits among female children, it has already been pointed out that nervous habits may be an insufficient index of emotionality. The evidence does not conclusively show that the female is the more "emotional" sex in childhood, even if we were to grant that the environments of boys and girls were equated.

Aggressiveness and Dominance.   One of the most persistent sex differences is to be found in the greater *aggressiveness* of the male. The origins of this sex difference are probably partly cultural and partly biological. It will be recalled, for example, that a similar sex difference in aggression and fighting has been observed in many species of animals. The greater size and muscular strength of the male is undoubtedly one contributing factor, and the male sex hormone is another. The part played by the latter is demonstrated by the conspicuous changes in aggressive behavior following gonadal transplants in animals.

Within our culture, sex differences in aggressiveness are manifested from early childhood. Studies on nursery and preschool children, using either teachers' reports or direct observations, have repeatedly demonstrated that boys display more anger, aggression, destructiveness, and quarrelsome behavior than girls (45, 94, 131). In an investigation of 150 preschool children, Sears (113) observed doll play in which dolls represented family members in typical home settings. These play materials were thus utilized as a "projective technique," providing children with an opportunity to act out their feelings. In this situation, boys not only showed significantly more aggression than girls, but they were also more likely to manifest aggression in terms of physical harm, while girls resorted more often to verbal and other symbolic forms of aggression. Sex differences in the urge to destroy were likewise found in an analysis of questionnaire data based upon college students' recall of incidents of childhood destructiveness (22).

Sex differences in aggressiveness may also account for the excess of boys referred to child guidance clinics as *behavior problems* (1, 38). A recent survey of 2500 cases taken from one year's files of the principal child guidance centers in four large American cities showed an excess of boys over girls in the ratio of 2½ to 1 (38). When only cases referred for aggressive and anti-social behavior were considered, the ratio rose to almost 4 to 1. Additional data are furnished by a number of extensive school surveys in which teachers were asked to supply information about the problem children in their classes. The results of all these surveys are in close agreement (131). In one investigation covering ten cities, the ratio of boys to girls in the problem group was 4:1 (146). Among the undesirable types of behavior reported much more frequently for boys than for girls are: truancy, destruction of property, stealing, profanity, disobedience, defiance, cruelty, bullying, and rudeness (145). Moreover, a larger number of undesirable behavior manifestations per child are reported for boys than for girls (145). To what extent these sex differences may be a reflection of teachers' attitudes toward boys and girls, and to what extent they represent real behavior differences, is difficult to determine. That the differences are at least partly the result of a "sex halo" in teachers' ratings is suggested by a number of investigations of such ratings (cf. 131).

Also relevant are statistics on *crime and delinquency*. Such records must, of course, be interpreted with considerable caution, since opportunities for crime are very different for the two sexes. Moreover, the differential treatment of the two sexes by the courts is clearly apparent. For most crimes, the available statistics probably underestimate the frequency of occurrence among women. The one exception is sex delinquency, which is judged with less leniency for women than for men. Whatever the reasons, however, the discrepancy between the crime records of the two sexes is tremendous. During a typical year, the men sent to federal and state prisons and reformatories outnumbered the women in the ratio of nearly 25:1 (cf. 106, p. 245). A similar ratio was found between male and female convictions in New York State within a one-year period. But when the number of arrests was considered, the ratio dropped to 19:1 (106, p. 248). The latter finding illustrates the differential treatment of men and women by the courts. Statistics on juvenile delinquency vary widely from one report to another, owing to such factors as the criterion of delinquency and differences in local conditions and practices. All agree, however, in showing a much greater proportion of delinquent boys than girls (131).

The administration of personality inventories has revealed similar sex differences in *ascendance* or *dominance*. Although the latter trait as measured by such inventories is not the same as aggression, there is much in common between them. On such inventories as the Bernreuter (15), Gordon (40), and Guilford-Zimmerman (43), males obtain significantly higher dominance scores than females in high school, college, and miscellaneous adult groups.

Masculinity-Femininity Tests of Personality.   An approach to sex differences that has been used increasingly in recent years is the comparison of men and women in those responses which have proved to be most characteristic of each sex in our contemporary culture. Test items are chosen on the basis of their ability to discriminate between the responses of the sexes. Thus if 30 per cent of the men and 29 per cent of the women were to report that they like modern art, the item would be discarded because it does not differentiate between the sexes. Only those items marked by a significantly different proportion of men and women are retained. The resulting test provides an index of "masculinity-femininity" in the sense that it reflects the characteristic male and female responses in our culture. This approach is illustrated by the Attitude-Interest Analysis developed by Terman and Miles, as well as by the masculinity-femininity scores on such tests as the Strong Vocational Interest Blank, the Minnesota Multiphasic Personality Inventory, the Guilford-Zimmerman Temperament Survey, and the Gough Femininity Scale (42). Recently attempts have also been made to develop projective tests of masculinity-femininity for use with children (17, 29, 56) and with adults (34).

It should be noted that such tests are deliberately designed so as to exaggerate sex differences, in the same way that such intelligence tests as the Stanford-Binet are designed to exclude or minimize sex differences. The behavior of men and women undoubtedly shows many similarities. These tests, however, concentrate on the differences, since it is their purpose to measure the differences between men and women as fully as possible. For any person taking such a test, the M-F (masculinity-femininity) index indicates the degree to which his responses agree with those most characteristic of men or of women in our culture.

The most extensive investigation of characteristic sex differences in personality is that conducted by Terman and Miles (129). After an exhaustive survey of the literature and prolonged research, items were chosen that revealed the most pronounced differences between representative samplings of men and women in our society. Data were gathered on many hundreds of persons, including elementary school, high school, college, and graduate students; unselected adults; members of several occupations; and specially selected groups such as athletes, juvenile delinquents, and adult homosexuals. The Attitude-Interest Analysis, constructed as a result of this research, consists of seven parts: Word Association, Inkblot Association, Information, Emotional and Ethical Attitudes, Interests, Opinions, and Introvertive Response.

This scale proved very successful in differentiating between the responses of male and female groups. Significant sex differences in total score were obtained at all age levels, from teenagers to octogenarians. The critical ratios of these differences ranged from 7.2 to 39.9. Overlapping of male and female distributions was also relatively slight. The test thus achieved its purpose of selecting those behavior characteristics which differentiate most clearly between the sexes.

An intensive analysis of the male and female responses on each part of the test brought to light those aspects of the personalities of the two sexes which are most clearly differentiated in our culture. Terman and Miles summarize these differences as follows:

From whatever angle we have examined them the males included in the standardization groups evinced a distinctive interest in exploit and adventure, in outdoor and physically strenuous occupations, in machinery and tools, in science, physical phenomena, and inventions; and, from rather occasional evidence, in business and commerce. On the other hand, the females of our groups have evinced a distinctive interest in domestic affairs and in æsthetic objects and occupations; they have distinctly preferred more sedentary and indoor occupations, and occupations more directly ministrative, particularly to the young, the helpless, the distressed. Supporting and supplementing these are the more subjective differences—those in emotional disposition and direction. The males directly or indirectly manifest the greater self-assertion and aggressiveness; they express more hardihood and fearlessness, and more roughness of manners, language, and sentiments. The females express themselves as more compassionate and sympathetic, more timid, more fastidious, and æsthetically sensitive, more emotional in general (or at least more expressive of the four emotions considered), severer moralists, yet admit in themselves weaknesses in emotional control and (less noticeably) in physique (129, pp. 447–448).

In regard to the *origin* of such sex differences in personality, there are several lines of evidence which suggest the greater contribution of cultural than biological influences. One source of relevant data is to be found in some of the group profile comparisons reported by Terman and Miles (129, pp. 570–579). These profiles, showing the subtest averages of various male and female groups, strongly suggest the *specificity* of differences in masculinity-femininity. Groups with the same mean total score may achieve such a score in very different ways. For example, among the most "masculine" groups in terms of M-F index are high school boys and engineers. Both obtained identical mean total scores, but the high masculinity of the high school boys resulted largely from their interests and information, while that of the engineers was primarily due to their emotional and ethical attitudes. On the latter test, the high school boys were actually more feminine than the general male population.

These discrepancies become understandable when we consider the results of a factor analysis of part scores on the Terman-Miles test, conducted on ninth-grade boys and girls (33). Two factors were identified, the first being predominantly emotional and described as "toughness" or "insensitivity" for the boys and "sensitivity" for the girls. The second was an interest factor. In the girls' data, there was also some evidence of a third factor related to the acceptance of a feminine social role.

Correlations between M-F scores and *physical characteristics* have been generally low and insignificant (9; 39; 129, Ch. 5). Such correlations as have been found are probably the result of the social effects of certain conspicuous physical characteristics, rather than the result of underlying biological factors. For example, a slight tendency has been found for taller men (129) and for men with deeper voices (39) to obtain a more masculine M-F index. Such a correlation may simply reflect the influence of social stereotypes upon the development of the individual's personality. Studies of male homosexuals (129, Chs. 11–13) have also indicated that experiential rather than structural factors were primarily responsible for the development of homosexual behavior. Especially important were early home environment and parental attitude toward the individual.

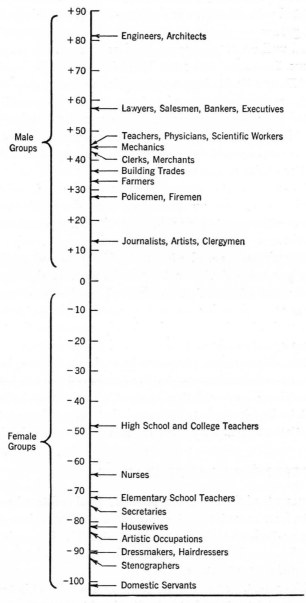

Fig. 79. Mean M-F Index of Men and Women in Various Occupations. The positive end of the scale indicates the more masculine scores, the negative end the more feminine scores. (Data from Terman and Miles, 129, pp. 159, 179.)

In the general population, the M-F index has been found to be significantly associated with *education* and *occupation* (129). Illustrative data on occupational groups are shown in Figure 79. It was also found that highly intelligent and well-educated women tend to score more "masculine" than their sex norms. For example, women listed in *Who's Who*, as well as those holding an M.D. or a Ph.D. degree, average more "masculine" in total score than any of the occupational groups shown in Figure 79. Similarly, men who have cultivated avocational interests of an artistic or cultural nature tend to obtain more "feminine" scores. Thus the equalizing influence of specific training or experience seems to bring about a convergence of the temperamental qualities of the two sexes.

The M-F index seems also to depend upon the *domestic milieu* in which the individual was brought up. Such factors as the death of one parent, excessive or exclusive association with one or the other parent, and predominance of brothers or of sisters among the siblings are much more closely related to M-F score than are physical traits (129). Moreover, there is some evidence to suggest that deviation toward the norm of the opposite sex in both men and women is associated with unpleasant and undesirable childhood experiences, broken homes, and parental maladjustment (117). A pleasant, happy childhood, on the other hand, encourages the individual to accept the appropriate male or female model of behavior presented by his culture. That sex differences as measured by such tests may be largely determined by *culture patterns* is suggested by results obtained in Holland (57). The administration of a translation of the Terman-Miles Attitude-Interest Analysis Test to Dutch subjects indicated that only a few of the original items differentiated significantly between men and women in that country.

SEX DIFFERENCES IN ACHIEVEMENT

The achievements of the two sexes, both in school and in subsequent vocational pursuits, bear some interesting and often complex relationships to sex differences in aptitudes and in personality traits. The far-reaching implications of sex roles can also be discerned in the relative achievements of the two sexes in different situations.

School Achievement. In academic work as a whole, girls tend to excel. Nevertheless, administration of *standardized achievement tests* reveals sex differences in separate school subjects that correspond closely to those found on intelligence and aptitude tests. On such batteries as the Stanford Achievement Test, given to many thousands of elementary school children in several different surveys, boys score significantly higher in science, social studies, and arithmetic reasoning; girls, in spelling, language usage, and (less consistently) arithmetic computation (cf. 131, 136). Some of the largest sex differences have been reported on science tests administered at the high school (62) and college (71) levels. Equally striking differences have been found in connection with the annual Science Talent Search (24, 25). Although two to three times as many boys as girls apply for this competition each year—and the girls would thus be expected to be a more highly selected sample—large, significant differences are regularly obtained in favor of the boys.

In general, girls surpass boys in those school subjects depending largely upon verbal abilities, memory, and perceptual speed and accuracy. Boys excel in those subjects that call into play numerical reasoning and spatial aptitudes, as well as in certain "information" subjects such as history, geography, and science. This is in agreement with the common superiority of boys on tests of general information included in intelligence scales, and probably results from the less restricted and more heterogeneous environment to which boys are exposed, as well as from their wider range of reading interests. Terman (128), for example, in his survey of the reading habits of gifted children, reports that girls read imaginative and emotional fiction as well as stories of school and home life far more often than boys, while the latter showed a predominant interest in books on science, history, biography, travel, and informational fiction and adventure tales. It is also noteworthy that sex differences in science and mathematics increase markedly with age. Moreover, studies at the preschool and primary levels have revealed no sex difference in functions related to quantitative and scientific thinking, such as the development of number concepts or the solution of problems involving causal relations.

With regard to *school progress*, girls are consistently more successful than boys. They are less frequently retarded, more frequently accelerated, and promoted in larger numbers than boys (75). Similarly, in *school grades* girls excel throughout, even in those subjects that favor boys on achievement tests. Thus a comparison of grades in arithmetic, history, or any other subject in which boys obtain higher achievement test scores shows a sex difference in favor of girls. The advantage enjoyed by girls in school grades was made particularly vivid in an investigation (73) on 202 boys and 188 girls in grades 2 to 6, all of whom were given the Stanford Achievement Test. The girls were found to excel in school grades, *when compared with boys receiving the same achievement test scores*. Thus the grades showed a iar greater female superiority than seemed to be warranted by performance on objective achievement tests.

In high school, girls generally obtain better grades than boys, even though the latter are a more select group and make a better showing on achievement tests. There is likewise evidence that at the college level girls adjust better than boys to the academic environment. In an analysis of the records of 1818 students entering a coeducational college during a single year, women accounted for a relatively small proportion of scholastic failures, inferior students, and nonparticipants in college activities, and for a relatively large proportion of superior students (124). Also relevant is the finding that in air force technical schools women obtain better grades than men with the same Aptitude Index (41).

One reason for the greater scholastic success of girls may be found in their superior *linguistic aptitudes*, which probably play an important part in most school learning. Current methods of instruction, as well as methods of testing, are predominantly verbal. Another possible factor, especially in the early school grades, is the neatness and general superiority of girls' *handwriting*, which may affect grades on written work. In investigations on both elementary and high school groups, girls have been found to excel markedly in the quality of their handwriting (cf. 75, 150). Both the developmental acceleration of girls and their superiority in manual dexterity undoubtedly contribute to their greater handwriting skill.

It is likely that *personality differences* between boys and girls also influence the assignment of grades. Girls are generally more docile, quieter, not so subject to out-of-school distractions, and less resistant to school discipline than boys. These personality differences may affect grades both through the amount of material actually learned and, more directly, through the impression created on the teacher.

The effect of *sex stereotypes* themselves needs to be taken into account. That such stereotypes do influence the judgments of both teachers and classmates is illustrated by the findings of Hartshorne, May, and Maller (44). In this investigation of elementary school pupils, girls received significantly higher ratings in service, persistence, and inhibition, although objective tests yielded a significant difference only in inhibition. Mention should also be made of the predominance of *women teachers* in the elementary grades. Not only can girls identify more readily than boys with a woman teacher, but it is also possible that in subtle ways teaching methods and other classroom procedures are better adapted to the needs of girls. As a result, girls may develop a more favorable attitude toward school at the outset, and this attitude may carry over to all classroom situations.

Vocational Achievement. Examination of any biographical directory shows a far greater number of men than women to have achieved eminence. And of the few women listed in such compendiums, many acquired fame through special circumstances, such as royal birth, rather than through the possession of exceptional talent. In Ellis' study (28) of British genius, only 55 women were included in the total group of 1030 subjects. Nor did the standard of eminence seem to be higher for women than for men. On the contrary, Ellis claims that many of the women in his group had become famous "on the strength of achievements which would not have allowed a man to play a similarly large part." Cattell's (21) compilation of the 1000 most eminent persons in the world listed only 32 women. Of these, 11 were hereditary sovereigns and 8 became famous through other fortuitous circumstances.

Similar results were obtained by Castle (20) in her statistical study of eminent women. A total of 868 names of women were collected, representing 42 nations and covering a wide range of epochs from the seventh century B.C. to the nineteenth century. The *largest number* of women (38 per cent) had achieved eminence in literature. However, the *highest degree of eminence,* as indicated by the number of lines allotted to the individual in standard biographical directories, was obtained by women as sovereigns, political leaders, mothers of eminent men, and mistresses. Among other nonintellectual ways by which women had achieved fame were marriage, religion, birth, philanthropy, tragic fate, beauty, and being "immortalized in literature." In more recent times, the discrepancy in number of men and women who have distinguished themselves in intellectual pursuits is still large, although steadily diminishing. In the Directory of American Men of Science, for instance, only 50 women are included in a total of 2607 scientists "starred" between 1903 and 1943 (141).

The interpretation of such achievement data is obviously complicated by the many factors besides ability which determine eminence. The recorded differences in achievement *could* be fully accounted for in terms of environmental conditions. Many types of *occupations* have been completely closed to women until recently. Even today, competition is not on an equal basis for men and women in many fields. *Educational opportunities* have likewise been dissimilar in the past, although currently the environments of the two sexes are more nearly equated in this respect than in any other. Although America was in advance of most other countries in the education of women, until nearly the middle of the nineteenth century there was not a single institution of collegiate rank in this country which admitted women. Professional and postgraduate education was not available until a much later date. Even in the elementary and secondary schools, the traditional curriculum of girls was different from that of boys, including much less science and more literature, art, and other "genteel" subjects.

Another important source of sex differences in achievement is to be found in *sex roles and stereotypes.* These represent pervasive and enduring social influences operating from early childhood. What is expected of an individual is a powerful element in the development of his own self concept. When such expectation has the force of cultural tradition behind it and is repeatedly corroborated in nearly all encounters with family, teachers, age mates, and other associates, it is difficult not to succumb to it. As a result, the individual himself becomes convinced that he possesses the traits ascribed to him.

Perhaps the follow-up studies of gifted children discussed in the preceding chapter may offer a clue to adult sex differences in achievement. In the Stanford Gifted Child Study (130), the adult occupations of the women were on the whole quite undistinguished. The number of women engaged in university teaching, research, art, or writing was small. The reported sex differences in adult vocational activities are especially noteworthy when we remember that the men and women in this group had been so selected as to fall within *the same IQ range in childhood.* Moreover, initial IQ showed a fairly close relationship to occupational level among the men, but virtually no relationship among the women. In fact, two-thirds of the women with IQ's of 170 or above were housewives or office workers.

The statistics on higher education also favored the men in this group. Although the percentages graduating from college were closely similar for the two sexes, many more men than women took graduate degrees, especially at the doctoral level. Moreover, in the follow-up testing at both adolescent and adult levels, women showed a larger mean drop in IQ than men. It is possible that, with increasing exposure to traditional activities and social pressures, the intellectually superior boy will continue to improve in intellectual functions, while the equally superior girl is more likely to be steered into less intellectual pursuits. Such sex differences in educational, vocational, and avocational activities would in turn be reflected in an increasing divergence of intelligence test scores with age.

SUMMARY

For the proper evaluation of data on sex differences—or on any other group differences—we need to inquire about statistical significance of differences, extent of overlapping between groups, and comparability of samples.

The use of ratings and of IQ's or other global scores may prove particularly misleading in group comparisons.

Both biological and cultural factors contribute to the development of sex differences in aptitudes and personality traits. The influence of biological factors may be relatively direct, as in the effect of male sex hormone upon aggressive behavior. Or it may be indirect, as in the social and educational effects of the developmental acceleration of girls. The contribution of culture is highlighted by the wide variations in sex roles found in different cultures and in different periods of our own history. Recent research has focused attention upon sex roles in our own culture—their acquisition in childhood, their effect upon behavior development, and their relation to personality adjustment.

From a purely descriptive point of view, certain sex differences in aptitudes and in personality traits have been reliably established under existing cultural conditions. Males tend to excel in speed and coordination of gross bodily movements, spatial orientation and other spatial aptitudes, mechanical comprehension, and arithmetic reasoning. Females tend to surpass males in manual dexterity, perceptual speed and accuracy, memory, numerical computation, verbal fluency, and other tasks involving the mechanics of language. Many sex differences in interests and attitudes have been found in studies conducted on both children and adults by a wide variety of methods. All of these differences reflect the traditional sex roles of our culture. Of particular interest are sex differences in social orientation and in achievement motivation. Other important personality differences have been reported in sexual behavior, emotional adjustment, and aggressiveness. Available masculinity-femininity tests provide an index of the degree to which the individual's personality resembles the personality typical of men or of women in our culture.

In school achievement, girls consistently excel. They seem in many ways to be more successful than boys in a typical academic situation. In later vocational activities, on the other hand, men achieve distinction in much greater numbers and to a much higher degree than women. Both of these apparently inconsistent findings may reflect a complex interaction of sex differences in aptitudes and personality, sex roles, and other cultural conditions.

From all that has been said, it is apparent that we cannot speak of inferiority and superiority, but only of *specific differences* in aptitudes or personality between the sexes. These differences are largely the result of *cultural and other experiential factors*, although certain physical sex differences undoubtedly influence behavior development, either directly or through their social effects. Lastly, the overlapping in all psychological characteristics is such that we need to consider men and women as *individuals,* rather than in terms of group stereotypes. These three points will prove to be useful "rules" to observe in understanding other group differences to be considered in the chapters that follow.

REFERENCES

1. Ackerson, L. *Children's behavior problems.* Chicago: Univer. Chicago Press, 1931.
2. Adams, H. *Mont-Saint-Michel and Chartres.* Boston: Houghton Mifflin, 1913.
3. Allport, G. W., Vernon, P. E., and Lindzey, G. *Study of Values* (Rev. Ed.): *Manual of directions.* Boston: Houghton Mifflin, 1951.
4. Anderson, E. E. Sex differences in timidity in normal and gonadectomized rats. *J. genet. Psychol.,* 1941, 59, 139–153.
5. Andrew, Dorothy M., and Paterson, D. G. *Minnesota Clerical Test: Manual.* N.Y.: Psychol. Corp., 1946.
6. Baldwin, B. T. The physical growth of children from birth to maturity. *Univer. Iowa Stud. Child Welf.,* 1921, 1.
7. Barrett, H. O. Sex differences in art ability. *J. educ. Res.,* 1950, 43, 391–393.
8. Baumgarten-Tramer, Franziska. Zur Frage der psychischen Geschlectsunterschiede bei Schulkindern. *Criança portug.,* 1945–46, 5, 261–269.
9. Bayley, Nancy. Some psychological correlates of somatic androgyny. *Child Develpm.,* 1951, 22, 47–60.
10. Beach, F. A. *Hormones and behavior.* N.Y.: Hoeber, 1948.
11. Bennett, A. A comparative study of subnormal children in elementary schools. *Teach. Coll. Contr. Educ.,* 1932, No. 510.
12. Bennett, C. C. An inquiry into the genesis of poor reading. *Teach. Coll. Contr. Educ.,* 1938, No. 755.
13. Bennett, G. K., and Cruikshank, Ruth M. Sex differences in the understanding of mechanical problems. *J. appl. Psychol.,* 1942, 26, 121–127.
14. Bennett, G. K., Seashore, H. G., and Wesman, A. G. *Differential Aptitude Tests: Manual.* (2nd Ed.) N.Y.: Psychol. Corp., 1952.
15. Bernreuter, R. G. *The Personality Inventory: Percentile Norms.* Stanford Univer., Calif.: Stanford Univer. Press, 1938.
16. Book, W. F., and Meadows, J. L. Sex differences in 5925 high school seniors in ten psychological tests. *J. appl. Psychol.,* 1928, 12, 56–81.
17. Brown, D. G. Masculinity-femininity development in children. *J. consult. Psychol.,* 1957, 21, 197–202.
18. Carlson, J. S., Cook, S. W., and Stromberg, E. L. Sex differences in conversation. *J. appl. Psychol.,* 1936, 20, 727–735.
19. Carpenter, C. R. A field study of the behavior and social relations of howling monkeys. *Comp. Psychol. Monogr.,* 1934, 10, No. 42.
20. Castle, Cora S. A statistical study of eminent women. *Arch. Psychol.,* 1913, No. 27.
21. Cattell, J. McK. A statistical study of eminent men. *Pop. Sci. Mon.,* 1903, 62, 359–377.

22. Clark, W. H. Sex differences and motivation in the urge to destroy. *J. soc. Psychol.*, 1952, 36, 167–177.
23. Darley, J. G. Tested maladjustment related to clinically diagnosed maladjustment. *J. appl. Psychol.*, 1937, 21, 632–642.
24. Edgerton, H. A., and Britt, S. H. Sex differences in the Science Talent Test. *Science*, 1944, 100, 192–193.
25. Edgerton, H. A., and Britt, S. H. Technical aspects of the Fourth Annual Science Talent Search. *Educ. psychol. Measmt.*, 1947, 7, 3–21.
26. Ellis, A. (Ed.) *Sex life of the American woman and the Kinsey Report.* N.Y.: Greenberg, 1954.
27. Ellis, H. *Man and woman: a study of human secondary sexual characters.* N.Y.: Scribner's, 1904.
28. Ellis, H. *A study of British genius.* London: Hurst and Blackett, 1904.
29. Erikson, E. H. Sex differences in the play configurations of pre-adolescents. *Amer. J. Orthopsychiat.*, 1951, 21, 667–692.
30. Eurich, A. C., and Carroll, H. A. Group differences in art judgment. *Sch. and Soc.*, 1931, 34, 204–206.
31. Farnsworth, P. R. An historical, critical, and experimental study of the Seashore-Kwalwasser Test Battery. *Genet. Psychol. Monogr.*, 1931, 9, No. 5, 291–393.
32. Fernberger, S. W. Persistence of stereotypes concerning sex differences. *J. abnorm. soc. Psychol.*, 1948, 43, 97–101.
33. Ford, C., Jr., and Tyler, Leona E. A factor analysis of Terman and Miles' M-F Test. *J. appl. Psychol.*, 1952, 36, 251–253.
34. Franck, Kate, and Rosen, E. A projective test of masculinity-femininity. *J. consult. Psychol.*, 1949, 13, 247–256.
35. Geddes, D. P. *An analysis of the Kinsey reports on sexual behavior in the human male and female.* N.Y.: Dutton, 1954.
36. Gesell, A., *et al. The first five years of life.* N.Y.: Harper, 1940.
37. Gilbert, G. M. Sex differences in musical aptitude and training. *J. gen. Psychol.*, 1942, 26, 19–33.
38. Gilbert, G. M. A survey of "referral problems" in metropolitan child guidance centers. *J. clin. Psychol.*, 1957, 13, 37–42.
39. Gilkinson, H. Masculine temperament and secondary sex characteristics: a study of the relationship between psychological and physical measures of masculinity. *Genet. Psychol. Monogr.*, 1937, 19, 105–154.
40. Gordon, L. V. *Gordon Personal Profile: Manual.* Yonkers-on-Hudson, N.Y.: World Book Co., 1953.
41. Gordon, Mary A. A study in the applicability of the same minimum qualifying scores for technical schools to white males, WAF, and Negro males. *HRRC, Air Res. Develpm. Command, Tech. Rep.* 53–34, 1953.
42. Gough, H. G. Identifying psychological femininity. *Educ. psychol. Measmt.*, 1952, 12, 427–439.
43. Guilford, J. P., and Zimmerman, W. S. *The Guilford-Zimmerman Temperament Survey: Manual.* Beverly Hills, Calif.: Sheridan Supply Co., 1949.
44. Hartshorne, H., May, M. A., and Maller, J. B. *Studies in the nature of character.* Vol. II. *Studies in service and self-control.* N.Y.: Macmillan, 1929.

45. Hattwick, Laberta A. Sex differences in behavior of nursery school children. *Child Develpm.*, 1937, 8, 343–355.

46. Havighurst, R. J., and Breese, Fay H. Relation between ability and social status in a midwestern community: III. primary mental abilities. *J. educ. Psychol.*, 1947, 38, 241–247.

47. Hebb, D. O. Behavioral differences between male and female chimpanzees. *Bull. Canad. psychol. Assoc.*, 1946, 6, 56–58.

48. Heidbreder, Edna. Introversion and extroversion in men and women. *J. abnorm. soc. Psychol.*, 1927, 22, 52–61.

49. Herzberg, F., and Lapkin, M. A study of sex differences on the Primary Mental Abilities test. *Educ. psychol. Measmt.*, 1954, 14, 687–689.

50. Hilgard, E. R., Edgren, R. D., and Irvine, R. P. Errors in transfer following learning with understanding: further studies with Katona's card-trick experiments. *J. exp. Psychol.*, 1954, 47, 457–464.

51. Himelhoch, J., and Fava, Sylvia F. (Eds.) *Sexual behavior in American society; an appraisal of the first two Kinsey reports.* N.Y.: Norton, 1955.

52. Hobson, J. R. Sex differences in primary mental abilities. *J. educ. Res.*, 1947, 41, 126–132.

53. Hollingworth, Leta S. Differential action upon the sexes of forces which tend to segregate the feebleminded. *J. abnorm. Psychol.*, 1922, 17, 35–57.

54. Hollingworth, Leta S. *Children above 180 IQ.* Yonkers-on-Hudson, N.Y.: World Book Co., 1942.

55. Hollingworth, Leta S., and Montague, Helen. The comparative variability of the sexes at birth. *Amer. J. Sociol.*, 1914–15, 20, 335–370.

56. Honzik, Marjorie P. Sex differences in the occurrence of materials in the play constructions of pre-adolescents. *Child Develpm.*, 1951, 22, 15–36.

57. Houwink, R. H. (The Attitude-Interest Analysis Test of Terman and Miles and a specimen revision for the Netherlands.) *Ned. Tijdschr. Psychol.*, 1950, 5, 242–262.

58. Huxley, J. S., and Haddon, A. C. *We Europeans.* N.Y.: Harper, 1936.

59. Hyman, H., and Barmack, J. E. Special review: Sexual behavior in the human female. *Psychol. Bull.*, 1954, 51, 418–432.

60. Johnson, Winifred B., and Terman, L. M. Some highlights in the literature of psychological sex differences published since 1920. *J. Psychol.*, 1940, 9, 327–336.

61. Jones, H. E. Sex differences in physical abilities. *Hum. Biol.*, 1947, 19, 12–25.

62. Jordan, A. M. Sex differences in mental traits. *High Sch. J.*, 1937, 20, 254–261.

63. Kaess, W. A., and Witryol, S. L. Memory for names and faces: a characteristic of social intelligence? *J. appl. Psychol.*, 1955, 39, 457–462.

64. Kinsey, A. C., *et al. Sexual behavior in the human male.* Philadelphia: Saunders, 1948.

65. Kinsey, A. C., *et al. Sexual behavior in the human female.* Philadelphia: Saunders, 1953.

66. Komarovsky, Mirra. *Women in the modern world: their education and their dilemmas.* Boston: Little, Brown, 1953.

67. Kostik, M. M. A study of transfer: sex differences in the reasoning process. *J. educ. Psychol.,* 1954, 45, 449–458.

68. LaBrant, L. L. A study of certain language developments of children in grades four to twelve inclusive. *Genet. Psychol. Monogr.,* 1933, 14, 387–491.

69. Landis, C. National differences in conversations. *J. abnorm. soc. Psychol.,* 1927, 21, 354–357.

70. Landis, M. H., and Burtt, H. E. A study of conversations. *J. comp. Psychol.,* 1924, 4, 81–89.

71. Learned, W. S., and Wood, B. D. The student and his knowledge. *Carnegie Found. Adv. Teach. Bull.,* 1938, No. 29.

72. Lehman, H. C., and Witty, P. A. *The psychology of play activities.* N.Y.: Barnes, 1927.

73. Lentz, T. F. Sex differences in school marks with achievement test scores constant. *Sch. and Soc.,* 1929, 29, 65–68.

74. Lewis, W. D. Sex distribution of intelligence among inferior and superior children. *J. genet. Psychol.,* 1945, 67, 67–75.

75. Lincoln, E. A. *Sex differences in the growth of American school children.* Baltimore: Warwick and York, 1927.

76. Macfarlane, Jean W., Allen, Lucile, and Honzik, Marjorie P. A developmental study of the behavior problems of normal children between twenty-one months and fourteen years. *Univer. Calif. Publ. Child Develpm.,* 1954, 2, 1–122.

77. Macmeeken, Agnes M. *The intelligence of a representative group of Scottish children.* London: Univer. London Press, 1939.

78. Maslow, A. H. Self-esteem (dominance-feeling) and sexuality in women. *J. soc. Psychol.,* 1942, 16, 259–294.

79. Maslow, A. H., and Sakoda, J. M. Volunteer-error in the Kinsey study. *J. abnorm. soc. Psychol.,* 1952, 47, 259–262.

80. Mathews, Ellen. A study of emotional stability in children. *J. Delinqu.* 1923, 8, 1–40.

81. McCarthy, Dorothea. The language development of the preschool child. *Univer. Minn. Inst. Child Welf. Monogr.,* 1930, 4.

82. McCarthy, Dorothea. Some possible explanations of sex differences in language development and disorders. *J. Psychol.,* 1953, 35, 155–160.

83. McCarthy, Dorothea. Language development in children. In L. Carmichael (Ed.), *Manual of child psychology.* (2nd Ed.) N.Y.: Wiley, 1954. Pp. 492–630.

84. McClelland, D., et al. *The achievement motive.* N.Y.: Appleton-Century-Crofts, 1953.

85. McGehee, W. A study of retarded children in the elementary school. *Peabody Coll. Contr. Educ.,* 1939, No. 246.

86. McNemar, Q. *The revision of the Stanford-Binet Scale: an analysis of the standardization data.* Boston: Houghton Mifflin, 1942.

87. McNemar, Q., and Terman, L. M. Sex differences in variational tendency. *Genet. Psychol. Monogr.,* 1936, 18, No. 1.

88. Mead, Margaret. *Growing up in New Guinea.* N.Y.: Morrow, 1930.

89. Mead, Margaret. *Sex and temperament in three primitive societies.* N.Y.: Morrow, 1935.

90. Mead, Margaret. *Male and female, a study of the sexes in a changing world.* N.Y.: Morrow, 1949.

91. Milner, Esther. Effects of sex role and social status on the early adolescent personality. *Genet. Psychol. Monogr.,* 1949, 40, 231–325.

92. Moore, H. T. Further data concerning sex differences. *J. abnorm. soc. Psychol.,* 1922, 17, 210–214.

93. Munn, N. L. *Handbook of psychological research on the rat.* Boston: Houghton Mifflin, 1950.

94. Muste, Myra J., and Sharpe, Doris F. Some influential factors in the determination of aggressive behavior in preschool children. *Child Develpm.,* 1947, 18, 11–28.

95. Paterson, D. G., *et al. Minnesota Mechanical Ability Tests.* Minneapolis: Univer. Minn. Press, 1930.

96. Pearson, K. *The chances of death and other studies in evolution.* London: Arnold, 1897. Vol. I.

97. Porteus, S. D. The measurement of intelligence: 643 children examined by the Binet and Porteus tests. *J. educ. Psychol.,* 1918, 9, 13–31.

98. Pressey, L. W. Sex differences shown by 2544 school children on a group scale of intelligence, with special reference to variability. *J. appl. Psychol.,* 1918, 2, 323–340.

99. Prothro, E. T., and Perry, H. T. Group differences in performance on the Meier Art Test. *J. appl. Psychol.,* 1950, 34, 96–97.

100. Rabban, M. Sex-role identification in young children in two diverse social groups. *Genet. Psychol. Monogr.,* 1950, 42, 81–158.

101. Rhinehart, J. B. Sex differences in dispersion at the high school and college levels. *Psychol. Monogr.,* 1947, 61, No. 282.

102. Rigg, M. G. The use and abuse of the ungraded room. *Educ. Admin. Super.,* 1936, 22, 389–391.

103. Rigg, M. G. The relative variability in intelligence of boys and girls. *J. genet. Psychol.,* 1940, 56, 211–214.

104. Riggs, Margaret M., and Kaess, W. Personality differences between volunteers and nonvolunteers. *J. Psychol.,* 1955, 40, 229–245.

105. Sandström, C. I. Sex differences in localization and orientation. *Acta Psychol.,* 1953, 9, 82–96.

106. Scheinfeld, A. *Women and men.* N.Y.: Harcourt, Brace, 1943.

107. Schiller, Belle. Verbal, numerical, and spatial abilities of young children. *Arch. Psychol.,* 1934, No. 161.

108. Schneidler, Gwendolen R., and Paterson, D. G. Sex differences in clerical aptitude. *J. educ. Psychol.,* 1942, 33, 303–309.

109. Schnell, H. Sex differences in relation to stuttering: Part I. *J. Speech Disorders,* 1946, 11, 277–298.

110. Schnell, H. Sex differences in relation to stuttering: Part II. *J. Speech Disorders,* 1947, 12, 23–38.

111. Scottish Council for Research in Education. *The intelligence of a representative group of Scottish children.* London: Univer. London Press, 1939.

112. Scottish Council for Research in Education. *The trend of Scottish intelligence.* London: Univer. London Press, 1949.

113. Sears, Pauline S. Doll play aggression in normal young children: influence of sex, age, sibling status, father's absence. *Psychol. Monogr.*, 1951, 65, No. 6.

114. Sears, R. R., Pintler, M. H., and Sears, Pauline S. Effect of father separation on preschool children's doll play aggression. *Child Develpm.*, 1946, 17, 219–243.

115. Seder, M. A. The vocational interests of professional women. *J. appl. Psychol.*, 1940, 24, 130–143, 265–272.

116. Seward, Georgene H. *Sex and the social order.* N.Y.: McGraw-Hill, 1946.

117. Seward, Georgene H. *Psychotherapy and culture conflict.* N.Y.: Ronald, 1956.

118. Sherriffs, A. C., and Jarrett, R. F. Sex differences in attitudes about sex differences. *J. Psychol.*, 1953, 35, 161–168.

119. Shuttleworth, F. K. Physical and mental growth of boys and girls ages six through nineteen in relation to age of maximum growth. *Monogr. Soc. Res. Child Develpm.*, 1939, 4, No. 3.

120. Shuttleworth, F. K. The adolescent period: a graphic atlas. *Monogr. Soc. Res. Child Develpm.*, 1949, 14, No. 1.

121. Singer, S. L., and Stefflre, B. Sex differences in job values and desires. *Personnel Guid. J.*, 1954, 32, 483–484.

122. Sontag, L. W. Physiological factors and personality in children. *Child Develpm.*, 1947, 18, 185–189.

123. Strong, E. K., Jr. *Vocational interests of men and women.* Stanford Univer., Calif.: Stanford Univer. Press, 1943.

124. Summerskill, J., and Darling, C. D. Sex differences in adjustment to college. *J. educ. Psychol.*, 1955, 46, 355–361.

125. Sweeney, E. J. Sex differences in problem solving. *Stanford Univer., Dept. Psychol., Tech. Rep.* No. 1, Dec. 1, 1953.

126. Symonds, P. M. Changes in sex differences in problems and interests of adolescents with increasing age. *J. genet. Psychol.*, 1937, 50, 83–89.

127. Terman, L. M. Kinsey's "Sexual behavior in the human male": some comments and criticisms. *Psychol. Bull.*, 1948, 45, 443–459.

128. Terman, L. M., et al. *Genetic studies of genius.* Vol. I. Stanford Univer., Calif.: Stanford Univer. Press, 1925.

129. Terman, L. M., and Miles, Catharine C. *Sex and personality: studies in masculinity and femininity.* N.Y.: McGraw-Hill, 1936.

130. Terman, L. M., and Oden, Melita H. *The gifted child grows up.* Stanford Univer., Calif.: Stanford Univer. Press, 1947.

131. Terman, L. M., and Tyler, Leona E. Psychological sex differences. In L. Carmichael (Ed.), *Manual of child psychology.* (2nd Ed.) N.Y.: Wiley, 1954. Pp. 1064–1114.

132. Thanga, M. N. An experimental study of sex differences in manual dexterity. *J. Educ. and Psychol., Baroda*, 1955, 13, 77–86.

133. Thompson, Clara. Cultural pressures in the psychology of women. In

P. Mullahy (Ed.), *A study of interpersonal relations.* N.Y.: Hermitage Press, 1949. Pp. 130–146.

134. Thorndike, E. L. *Educational psychology.* N.Y.: Teachers Coll., Columbia Univer., 1914. Vol. III.

135. Traxler, A. E., and McCall, W. C. Some data on the Kuder Preference Record. *Educ. psychol. Measmt.,* 1941, 1, 253–268.

136. Traxler, A. E., and Spaulding, Geraldine. Sex differences in achievement of independent school pupils as measured by Stanford Achievement Test, Form K. *Educ. Rec. Bull.,* 1954, No. 63, 69–80.

137. Triggs, Frances O. A study of the relation of the Kuder Preference Record scores to various other measures. *Educ. psychol. Measmt.,* 1943, 3, 341–354.

138. Trumbull, R. A study in relationships between factors of personality and intelligence. *J. soc. Psychol.,* 1953, 38, 161–173.

139. Tuddenham, R. D. Studies in reputation: III. Correlates of popularity among elementary school children. *J. educ. Psychol.,* 1951, 42, 257–276.

140. Tuddenham, R. D. Studies in reputation. I. Sex and grade differences in school children's evaluations of their peers. *Psychol. Monogr.,* 1952, 66, No. 1.

141. Visher, S. S. *Scientists starred, 1903–1943, in "American men of science."* Baltimore: Johns Hopkins Press, 1947.

142. Walter, L. M., and Marzolf, S. S. The relation of sex, age, and school achievement to levels of aspiration. *J. educ. Psychol.,* 1951, 42, 285–292.

143. Watson, Jeanne, Breed, W., and Posman, H. A study in urban conversation: sample of 1001 remarks overheard in Manhattan. *J. soc. Psychol.,* 1948, 28, 121–123.

144. Wesman, A. G. Separation of sex groups in test reporting. *J. educ. Psychol.,* 1949, 40, 223–229.

145. Wickman, E. K. *Children's behavior and teachers' attitudes.* N.Y.: Commonwealth Fund, 1928.

146. Williams, H. D. A survey of predelinquent children in ten middle western cities. *J. juv. Res.,* 1933, 17, 163–174.

147. Witkin, H. A., *et al. Personality through perception.* N.Y.: Harper, 1954.

148. Witty, P. A genetic study of fifty gifted children. *39th Yearb., Nat. Soc. Stud. Educ.,* 1940, Part II, 401–409.

149. Yerkes, R. M. *Chimpanzees: a laboratory colony.* New Haven, Conn.: Yale Univer. Press, 1943.

150. Zazzo, R. Première contribution des psychologues scolaires à la psychologie différentielle des sexes. *Enfance,* 1948, 1, 168–175.

CHAPTER **15**

Social Class Differences

Within a single nation, there are usually classes of people or subcultures, each with its distinctive traditions, ways of life, emotional responses, and aptitude patterns. In America, for example, the differences between such regions as New England, the South, the Midwest, and the West are familiar in fact as in fiction. Similarly, the distinction between city and country dweller is a common one. In effect this is not a twofold classification, but covers a variety of recognizable groups. From the large metropolis, through the medium-sized city, the small town, the village with its general store and post office, to the isolated mountain outpost, there are major differences in the psychological as well as the physical environment.

A particularly important cultural differentiation is that represented by social classes. Recent research in American communities has demonstrated not only the prevalence of such social stratification, but also the profound effect which the individual's class membership may have upon his behavior development. The chief difference between a rigid "caste system" and the class systems found in a democracy such as that of the United States is the greater degree of "social mobility" possible in the latter. Thus it is possible for the individual in a lower social class to rise to a higher status through his own efforts. It is this possibility that is at the root of many of the characteristic motivations and attitudes of the "middle class," with its emphasis upon hard work, self-improvement, and achievement.

SOCIAL CLASS STRUCTURE

The class differentiation of American society has been intensively analyzed in a number of studies of American communities, most of them conducted under the general direction of W. Lloyd Warner. Typical towns

505

in different parts of the country have been described under such pseudonyms as *Yankee City* in New England (115), *Old City* in the South (24), and *Jonesville* in the Midwest (116). Other parts of the Midwest are represented by *Middletown* (63, 64) and *Plainville, U.S.A.* (117). The methods employed in these investigation are an adaptation of the observational procedures utilized by anthropologists in their field studies of primitive cultures. In general, the investigators live in the community for an extended period of time, taking part in its social activities and interviewing local informants —persons from different social levels whose activities bring them into contact with many community members. By such techniques, information is obtained not only on the over-all class structure of the community but also on

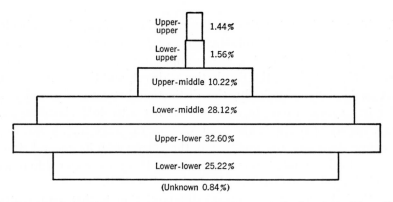

Fig. 80. Social Stratification in an American Community: Yankee City. (From Warner and Lunt, 115, p. 88.)

the class membership of individual persons. A major consideration in the class identification of individuals centers about the amount and nature of their participation in social activities with members of a particular class.

The results of such surveys reveal a stratification into six classes, designated as upper-upper, lower-upper, upper-middle, lower-middle, upper-lower, and lower-lower. Figure 80 shows the percentage of persons falling into each of these classes in a sample of 16,785 cases studied in *Yankee City*. These percentages did not differ substantially in the other communities investigated. The distinction between upper-upper and lower-upper in the New England and southern towns was based primarily on family background, the upper-uppers representing the "old aristocracy" and the lower-uppers the "newly rich." In the midwestern communities, this distinction was not generally made, there being only one "upper" class comprising the wealthiest and most prominent families. The upper-middle class consisted principally of business and professional people, the "pillars of society," while the lower-middle class included small tradesmen, "white collar workers," and some skilled labor. The upper-lowers, comprising largely semiskilled and unskilled workers, were often described by middle-class persons as "poor but respectable" and "hardworking people." In contrast, the lower-lowers were characterized as shiftless and disorderly. The lower-middle and upper-lower classes, which together include over 60 per cent of the population, constitute the level of the "common man" (116) and the "core culture."

Warner and his associates refer to the observational procedures described above as the Method of Evaluated Participation (E.P.). This is a direct but laborious and time-consuming technique for determining the individual's social class membership. A simpler and shorter procedure, yielding an Index of Status Characteristics (I.S.C.), was subsequently developed by Warner and his co-workers (116). The I.S.C. for each individual is computed by rating him on a seven-point scale on each of four factors, namely, Occupation, Source of Income, House Type, and Dwelling Area, and then finding a weighted sum of the four ratings. Detailed procedures for arriving at this index are described by Warner *et al.* in *Social Class in America* (116). The authors also report data indicating good agreement between social status as determined by the E.P. and the I.S.C. methods. Since occupational level receives a relatively large weight in the computation of I.S.C., besides being correlated with the other three characteristics, it can itself provide a fair approximation of social status as defined in the Warner surveys. Hence the large body of available data on the relationship between occupational level and intelligence, to be discussed in a subsequent section, may be fitted in the picture of class differentiation built up by sociological research.

Another approach to the investigation of class structure is represented by the work by Tryon (111). Using cluster analysis (a variation of factor analysis), Tryon studied the intercorrelations among 33 kinds of census data for 243 neighborhoods in the San Francisco Bay Area. An advantage of this procedure is that it requires only objective data available in public records. The analysis yielded three factors or dimensions. The first is a Family Life (*F*) dimension, characterized by single-family dwellings, large families, and nonworking housewives. The second, Assimilation (*A*), refers primarily to proportion of native-born, white residents in a neighborhood, although it also has significant loadings on certain occupational variables. The third factor is identified as Socioeconomic Independence (*S*) and includes such variables as high occupational and educational level, high-quality homes, and employment of domestic servants. Tryon points out that what is usually designated as socioeconomic level, as well as the social status measured by the Warner techniques, represents a combination of his Socioeconomic Independence and Assimilation factors.

Still another simplified technique for determining an individual's social class is provided by the SCI Occupational Rating Scale developed by Sims (97, 98). In this scale, the subject is presented with a list of 42 occupational titles, ranging from U. S. ambassador to garbage collector, but arranged in random order. These occupations were chosen from a much longer list through preliminary research on the prestige ratings of the various occupations. For each given occupation, the subject indicates whether he feels that the people in that occupation belong in the *same* social class as himself and his family, or in a *higher* or *lower* class. If he is not sufficiently familiar with a particular occupation, he may mark it "doubtful." The subject's score, from which his class membership is determined, is based upon the number of occupations marked "lower" and half of those marked "same." In effect, this scale is a device for finding the social level with which the individual *identifies* himself, although its results correlate highly with such objective factors as income level and occupation. On the other hand, discrepancies between objective and perceived status in individual cases may be of considerable psychological interest.

CLASS DIFFERENCES IN PSYCHOLOGICAL DEVELOPMENT

Of special interest to the differential psychologist are the effects which social class membership may have upon the individual's emotional and intellectual development. Although social mobility is common and distinctions between social classes are not sharp in our society, such classes nevertheless represent distinct subcultures. The nature and extent of social interaction between members of different classes is limited. Moreover, class stratification is reflected in conspicuous differences in home life, education, recreational outlets, and community activities.

Child Rearing. Several writers have placed particular emphasis upon class differences in child-rearing practices and the possible implications of such differences for psychological development (21, 22, 25, 65, 74). Davis and Havighurst (25) studied this question by means of intensive interviews of upper-middle and upper-lower class families in Chicago. The interviews covered such matters as feeding schedules, toilet training, daytime naps, going out alone, hour at which child is required to be home at night, and age at which the child is expected to assume various responsibilities. Several statistically significant differences were found within both the white and

Negro groups studied. The differences were such as to suggest that middle-class parents tend to be more rigorous in their child-training practices, frustrate the child more in feeding and cleanliness training, and expect children to take responsibility earlier.

Other studies have suggested that children in the "core culture" (lower-middle and upper-lower classes) tend to be reared under conditions that are unduly restrictive and demanding of conformity, as contrasted to the greater freedom enjoyed by children in the lowest social class (cf., e.g., 74). That such a conclusion needs to be qualified, however, is indicated by the findings of Maas (65), who interviewed boys and girls between the ages of 10 and 15 belonging to the core culture. Maas concluded that, although physically more restricted and more rigidly reared with regard to weaning, toilet training, and other infant-rearing practices, the core culture child has more freedom to communicate with both parents and experiences less fear of parents and less parental rejection than the lower-class child.

Corroborative evidence is provided by Milner (75) in a study of first-grade children. First, a close relationship was demonstrated between Warner's Index of Social Characteristics and the reading readiness and linguistic development of the children. Two subgroups of high and low language scorers were then selected for intensive study through interviews of the children and of their mothers. The results revealed a number of sharp differences between the two subgroups, which also differed in socioeconomic level. Milner concluded that, upon entering school, the lower-class child seems to lack chiefly two advantages of the middle-class child. The first is "a warm positive family atmosphere or adult-relationship pattern which is more and more being recognized as a motivational prerequisite for any kind of adult-controlled learning." The lower-class children in Milner's study perceived adults as predominantly hostile. The second advantage is described as "an extensive opportunity to interact verbally with adults of high personal value to the child who possess adequate speech patterns." The latter point is illustrated by a radically different atmosphere around the meal table. In the homes of the high scorers, there was more spontaneous mealtime conversation between adults and children. In contrast, parents of the low scorers tended to prohibit or discourage conversation by children during meals. There is ample evidence from other studies of both preschool and school-age children indicating a close relation between language development and socioeconomic level (cf. 70). Milner's study throws some light on the possible causal mechanisms underlying this relationship.

On the basis of interview data obtained from over 600 English boys aged

13 to 14 years, Himmelweit (45) likewise found more favorable parent-child relationships in middle-class than in lower-class homes. Despite the stronger pressure for conformity to which middle-class children were subjected, there was no evidence of greater over-all anxiety or tension. As a possible explanation, the author suggests the greater "child-centeredness" of the middle-class home. In such homes, children feel more accepted and can discuss matters with their parents and confide in them.

It would seem that generalizations regarding restrictiveness or freedom of child-rearing practices in relation to social level must be carefully scrutinized. Homes that are more permissive in some respects may be more rigid in others (cf., e.g., 93). More detailed studies of child-rearing practices, with larger samples, are undoubtedly needed. Perhaps some of the points will be clarified by the application of the intensive observational techniques developed by Barker and Wright (8, 9). Calling their approach "psychological ecology," these investigators provide a full description of the child's everyday activities, social interactions, and psychological "habitat." As yet the method has only been utilized in a small midwestern community with relatively narrow socioeconomic range and little social class segregation.

In so far as can be determined from available data, middle-class and core culture parents tend to demand more conformity than lower-class parents and may thereby induce frustration and stifle initiative and creativity in some cases. On the other hand, certain aspects of lower-class family life tend to undermine the child's self-confidence and emotional security and to discourage intellectual development. These differences are reflected in the poorer emotional adjustment and inferior school achievement of lower-class children.

Class differences in behavior are further augmented by the "peer culture" consisting of the child's own age mates. There is evidence that the prestige value of behavior traits varies with socioeconomic level (3, 80). Thus among boys and girls of higher socioeconomic level, more value is put on conformity to adult standards and conventional rules of conduct, while self-assertion and aggression receive a higher premium among those of lower socioeconomic status. Class differentiation has likewise been observed in the nature and extent of children's leisure activities (66).

Social class differences are also manifested in the school, in both academic and extracurricular activities. Davis (21, 22) has argued that public schools are primarily adapted to the middle-class culture, since educational personnel is recruited principally from the middle class. This situation, according to Davis, makes the curriculum, type of incentives, and other aspects of the educational experience provided by the schools unsuited to lower-class children. He suggests that this may be an important reason for the frequent school maladjustment and educational backwardness of these children.

The evidence does show that school achievement is positively related to social status (36, 37, 38, 47, 114). Nor can the differences be explained simply in terms of intellectual level. In one survey of pupils with IQ's of 110 or above, conducted in the 1930's, comparisons were made between subgroups of higher and lower socioeconomic status (cf. 114, pp. 51 ff.). In the upper social group, 93 per cent graduated from high school and 57 per cent attended college; in the lower, 72 per cent graduated from high school and 13 per cent attended college. With the rapid expansion of scholarship programs in recent years, these discrepancies have undoubtedly been reduced. Nevertheless, there is evidence that class differences in attitude toward education are an important factor (43, 45, 47, 103). Studies of both the children themselves and their parents indicate that higher-status children are taught to respond favorably to the competitive situations represented by schoolwork and intelligence tests; and that they are more strongly motivated for personal achievement and academic advancement. The expectations and attitudes of teachers and school administrators may also contribute to the superior scholastic attainments of higher-status children (47).

Sexual Behavior. The research of Kinsey and his associates (53, 54) on sexual behavior of American men and women, cited in Chapter 14, also provides data on socioeconomic differences. For this purpose, socioeconomic level was determined on the basis of the subject's educational and occupational level and the occupational level of his parents. The investigators were strongly impressed by the relationship between male sexual behavior and social level. Lower social class males, for example, reported a higher incidence of premarital and extramarital sexual relations than did higher social class males; but masturbation was more frequently reported in the higher social levels. Upper-class males also respond erotically to a wider range of stimuli than do lower-class males. The investigators themselves regarded such socioeconomic differences as one of the basic findings of their survey. They wrote:

The data now available show that patterns of sexual behavior may be strikingly different for the different social levels that exist in the same city or town, and sometimes in immediately adjacent sections of a single community. The data show that divergencies in the sexual patterns of such social groups may be as great as those which anthropologists have found between the sexual patterns of different racial groups in remote parts of the world. There is no American pattern of sexual behavior, but scores of patterns, each of which is confined to a particular segment of our society (53, p. 329).

To be sure, these results may reflect no more than the degree of willing-ness or reluctance of American men in different socioeconomic classes to *report* certain sexual activities. Even if this is the case, however, the data would indicate socioeconomic differences in *attitudes* toward various forms of sexual behavior. In sharp contrast to the results for males, social factors were found to be of minor significance in determining patterns of sexual behavior in the female. Little or no relation was observed between the nature or extent of sexual activity of women and either their educational level or the occupational level of their parents.

Emotional Adjustment.   Surveys by means of personality inventories and other types of personality tests have tended to substantiate the class differ-ences which would be expected on the basis of known cultural differentials. School children of lower social status show significantly more neuroticism, emotional insecurity, and irritability; they report a larger number of worries and obtain poorer scores on the Vineland Social Maturity Scale (6, 78). Sims (99) found that among high school and college students, his index of Social Class Identification was positively correlated with social adjustment as measured by the Bell Adjustment Inventory. On the Bernreuter Per-sonality Inventory, high social status men were found to be significantly less neurotic, more self-sufficient, and more dominant than low social status men (cf. 6). An investigation of small samples of Harvard students with projective techniques suggested characteristic differences between upper-class and middle-class personalities (69).[1]

Gough (37, 38, 39) has constructed a social status personality scale by the same procedures employed in the development of masculinity-femininity tests (cf. Ch. 14). Within a group of 223 high school seniors in a midwestern city, two extreme social status samples were chosen in terms of objective environmental characteristics. An item analysis, based on the responses of these two samples on the 550 items of the Minnesota Multiphasic Personal-ity Inventory, revealed 34 items which yielded significant socioeconomic differences (37). An examination of these items suggests that students of higher socioeconomic level show stronger literary and artistic interests; have more social poise, security, and confidence in themselves and others; report fewer fears and anxieties; display more "emancipated" and "frank" attitudes in moral, religious, and sexual matters; and are inclined to be more positive, dogmatic, and self-righteous in their opinions.

[1] In certain studies of highly selected samples, such as college students or intellectually gifted children, no significant relationships were found between personality and socio-economic level, probably because of the restricted range of the groups in both social status and other characteristics (cf. 6).

The 34 differentiating items were grouped into a "status scale," from which the personality status scores of a new sample of 263 students were computed. These status scores correlated .50 with objective status scores based on characteristics of home background. Moreover, the correlations of the personality status scores with each of a number of other variables closely paralleled the pattern of correlations of home status with the same variables. The variables with which each of these two types of status scores were correlated included each of the other scales of the Minnesota Multiphasic Personality Inventory, as well as other personality tests, intelligence and achievement tests, and academic grades (38). These correlations further suggested that students of higher social status show more satisfactory social adjustment, less insecurity, and less social introversion than do lower-status students.

The comparison of personality status and objective status scores suggests interesting possibilities for the prediction of social mobility in individual cases (39). Thus discrepancies between the personality status score and objective status score may be related to the individual's tendency to rise or drop in the social hierarchy. For example, an individual with low objective status score but high personality status score might be more likely to go to college than one with low status scores in both respects. If this hypothesis is verified, it might help to explain the relatively small personality test differences between socioeconomic groups which are found when selected populations are compared, as in the case of certain college groups.

It is also noteworthy that large-scale surveys show the *incidence of psychoses* to be greater the lower the socioeconomic level. Clark (19) analyzed 12,168 male first-admissions to psychiatric hospitals in the Chicago area. Among white patients, age-adjusted admission rate correlated −.83 with income level and −.75 with prestige level of the subject's occupation. Among Negroes, the corresponding correlations were −.53 and −.60. In a later study conducted in New Haven, Connecticut, Redlich *et al.* (85) considered all patients receiving psychiatric treatment on December 1, 1950 as their experimental population. The group thus included patients in public and private hospitals, as well as persons receiving treatment in physicians' offices. Results again revealed an increasing number of psychiatric disorders with lower socioeconomic level. Moreover, neuroses were much more common than psychoses at the upper social levels, while the reverse was true at the lower levels. Part of this difference is undoubtedly due to the fact that upper-class persons are more likely than lower-class persons to recognize neurotic conditions and can more often afford treatment for such relatively mild disorders. The fact remains, however, that mental disorders as a whole were much more prevalent in lower than in higher socioeconomic levels.

Interests and Attitudes. It is now well established that occupational groups exhibit characteristic differences in *interests,* not only in strictly vocational matters, but in almost all areas of everyday activity. These differences are, in fact, the basis upon which such tests as the Strong Vocational Interest Blank have been constructed. An even more relevant finding reported by Strong (106) pertains to the marked differences in interest pattern found between different occupational *levels.* Strong has devised a special scoring key for measuring the occupational level (O.L.) of the individual's interests. This was done by selecting those items that differentiated most clearly between the interests of unskilled laborers and those of business and professional men. Not only does this score differ with the position of the individual's occupation in the socioeconomic hierarchy, but within any one occupation it tends to be higher for those men whose work is of a managerial character.

Some of the largest and most consistent class differences have been found in *attitude surveys.* Nation-wide polling studies, as well as more intensive investigations in local areas (50, 71), agree in finding higher socioeconomic level to be associated with more conservative attitudes, and lower socioeconomic level with more radical attitudes. As one might expect, individuals who already occupy a more favored position in the social ladder tend to favor the preservation of the *status quo.* In general, too, middle-class persons are more concerned with advancement along vocational and other lines, while the lower classes emphasize security (71).

One of the most carefully controlled surveys on the attitudes of different social classes was conducted by Centers (16). Through interviews of 1100 persons, chosen as a representative sample of the adult white male population, attitudes on major economic and social issues were explored. On the basis of their replies to certain questions, individuals were classified into five categories in reference to expressed conservatism-radicalism. In Figure 81 will be found the relative frequency of these five response categories among individuals of different occupational levels. Separate results are given for urban and rural samplings. The occupational differences are large and clearcut, the author concluding that such differences leave little doubt that people's politicoeconomic orientations are closely associated with their socioeconomic statuses. Another interesting observation was that, within any single occupational category, those persons who subjectively identified themselves with the "working class" expressed more radical attitudes than those who classified themselves in the "middle class." In a later study of high school students, a similar relationship was found between expressed radicalism-conservatism and parental occupational level (17). The findings with regard to class identification were likewise corroborated.

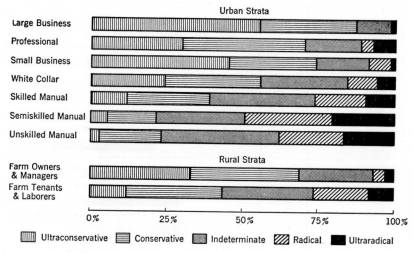

Fig. 81. Attitude Differences of Occupational Strata with Reference to Politico-economic Conservatism-Radicalism. (From Centers, 16, p. 58.)

SOCIOECONOMIC STATUS AND INTELLIGENCE

Occupational Hierarchy. There is a large body of data indicating a positive relation between occupational level and intelligence test performance. Analyses of scores obtained by American soldiers on the Army Alpha during World War I (31) and on the AGCT during World War II (104) provide large-scale corroboration of this relationship. Illustrative data on fifteen common occupations, selected from different levels of the hierarchy, are reproduced in Figure 82. In the complete analysis, similar data are available for 227 occupations which were represented in sufficiently large numbers to yield reliable means. The results were based on the AGCT scores of a representative sample of 81,553 white enlisted men.

Because of selective factors operating in deferments, rejections, and discharges, such army samplings cannot be regarded as representative of adult civilian populations. Moreover, no officers were included in the occupational survey, thus further restricting the distribution at the upper levels. The representation of professional groups is especially limited by these factors. Data on doctors and engineers, for example, are virtually nonexistent in such tabulations. Despite these limitations, it is clear that the intelligence test scores followed the general occupational hierarchy, paralleling the socioeconomic status of the various groups. Although overlapping is large and mean differences between adjacent groups are slight,

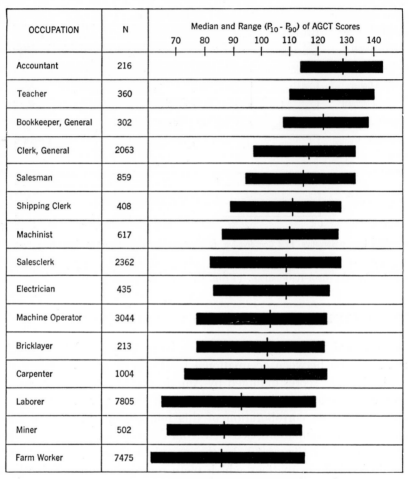

Fig. 82. AGCT Score in Relation to Civilian Occupation. (Data from Stewart, 104, pp. 5–13.)

the test scores of groups from different parts of the occupational hierarchy differ by large and statistically significant amounts.

Similar results have been obtained with the Wechsler-Bellevue in a sample of 1753 gainfully employed adults drawn chiefly from the New York metropolitan area (96). A vocabulary test administered to a stratified national sample of 1500 persons aged 10 years and up likewise yielded significant differences between broad occupational levels (76). Using the Raven Progressive Matrices with the employees of a single large company in Great Britain, Foulds and Raven (30) observed the same type of occupational differences in mean scores. In Sweden, large and significant differences in test scores were found between two groups of conscripts for military service, representing higher (N = 267) and lower (N = 660) occupational levels, respectively (14).

Social Status and Intelligence of Children. The correspondence between intelligence test performance and occupational level is not limited to adults but persists when children are classified according to *paternal occupation.* Thus the relationship cannot be explained entirely in terms of differences in vocational experiences and amount of formal schooling. More general conditions must be involved, which characterize not only the men in different occupations, but also their families. In Table 22 will be found an occupational analysis of data collected during the standardization of the Stanford-Binet (73). On the more recently developed Wechsler Intelligence Scale for Children (WISC), mean IQ's varied from 110.9 for children of professional and semiprofessional men to 94.6 for children of urban and rural laborers and farm foremen (92). Similar findings have been obtained in a large number of investigations, from the preschool to the college level (cf. 62, 77). In general, there seems to be a difference of about 20 points between the mean IQ's of the children of professional men and those of the children of unskilled laborers.

TABLE 22

MEAN STANFORD-BINET IQ'S OF 2757 CHILDREN CLASSIFIED
ACCORDING TO PATERNAL OCCUPATION

(From McNemar, 73, p. 38)

FATHER'S OCCUPATION	CHRONOLOGICAL AGE OF CHILD			
	2–5½	6–9	10–14	15–18
I. Professional	114.8	114.9	117.5	116.4
II. Semiprofessional and managerial	112.4	107.3	112.2	116.7
III. Clerical, skilled trades, and retail business	108.8	104.9	107.4	109.6
IV. Rural owners	97.8	94.6	92.4	94.3
V. Semiskilled, minor clerical, and minor business	104.3	104.6	103.4	106.7
VI. Slightly skilled	97.2	100.0	100.6	96.2
VII. Day labor, urban and rural	93.8	96.0	97.2	97.6

Nor have such findings been limited to American samples. In the 1947 Scottish Survey, a close correspondence was found between father's occupational class and mean test score of children (90). Similar differences were revealed in a nation-wide survey of French school children between the ages of 6 and 12 (44, Ch. 5). In this study, a pictorial group test was administered to over 95,000 children, chosen so as to provide a representative cross-section of the elementary school population of France. Investigations conducted on a smaller scale in several other countries have likewise corroborated the relationship between parental occupation and child intelligence (15, 26, 27, 61, 72, 79, 81, 100).

A number of investigators have employed *scales for rating home conditions,* thus permitting the computation of correlations between intelligence test score and social level. Several scales have been developed for this purpose (cf. 58, 62), one of the most comprehensive being the Minnesota Home Status Index devised by Leahy (58). Most of the scales utilize information obtained through home visits and interviews with parents. Some investigators have attempted to prepare scales emphasizing the psychologically more significant aspects of the child's environment, such as parent-child relations and opportunities for various kinds of activity (102, 113). A weakness of the latter scales stems from the relatively subjective nature of the original choice of variables, as well as of the ratings themselves. However, such scales open up interesting possibilities for further research.

As would be expected, the correlations between home ratings and intelligence vary with the content of the home-rating scales, the nature of the test used to measure intelligence, and the characteristics of the sampling tested. In general, the correlations found between the ages of 3 and 18 years cluster around .40, although they range from .20 to slightly over .50 (cf. 62, 77). The correlations show no consistent age trend within these age limits. Below age 3, however, the correlations drop, and between birth and 18 months they are generally zero or slightly negative. It should be recalled that psychological tests for infants are largely measures of simple sensorimotor development. As the child grows older, the tests become increasingly verbal and abstract in content. Since different functions are tested, there is thus no real inconsistency between the correlations obtained on infants and those on older children. On the whole, studies employing the correlation technique have corroborated the results obtained by the comparison of occupational groups.

Still another approach involves the relation between test scores and the individual's *social class membership* as determined by the Warner techniques. In a series of studies by Havighurst and his co-workers (41, 42, 49), tests were administered to nearly complete samples of 10-, 13-, and 16-year-olds in a midwestern city. The 13-year group was given the Thurstone tests of Primary Mental Abilities. The other two age groups were examined with well-known verbal and performance tests of intelligence, as well as with special tests of reading and of spatial and mechanical aptitudes. Each subject was classified into one of five status groups, ranging from A (upper) to E (lower-lower).

Mean scores of the different status groups on each test are presented in Tables 23, 24, and 25. Despite the small number of cases (especially at the higher levels), nearly all tests show a tendency for scores to rise with social status within each sample. When extreme social groups are compared, most of the differences are statistically significant. The clearest exception to this trend is provided by the performance of the 16-year-old boys on the Minnesota Mechanical Assembly Test (Table 25). Mean scores on this test showed no consistent relation to social status, and the highest mean was obtained by the lowest social group. A possible reason for these results is that the

Table 23

MEAN TEST SCORES OBTAINED BY 10-YEAR-OLDS IN DIFFERENT SOCIAL STATUS GROUPS

(Adapted from Havighurst and Janke, 42, p. 363)

SOCIAL STATUS	N	STANFORD-BINET IQ	CORNELL-COXE IQ	DRAW-A-MAN IQ	IOWA SILENT READING QUOTIENT	PAPER FORM BOARD	PORTEUS MAZE MA	MINN. MECH. ASSEM. T-SCORE (BOYS)	CHICAGO MECH. ASSEM. T-SCORE (GIRLS)
C.	26	114	116	107	99	22.5	12.7	52.5	56.0
D.	68	110	110	102	99	21.3	12.8	49.2	49.5
E.	16	91	96	91	88	15.7	10.4	46.9	41.3

Table 24

MEAN SCORES ON THURSTONE TESTS OF PRIMARY MENTAL ABILITIES OBTAINED BY 13-YEAR-OLDS IN DIFFERENT SOCIAL STATUS GROUPS

(Adapted from Havighurst and Breese, 41, p. 244)

SOCIAL STATUS	N	NUMBER (N)	VERBAL COMPREHENSION (V)	SPACE (S)	WORD-FLUENCY (W)	REASONING (R)	MEMORY (M)
C.	21	52.7	55.6	52.5	53.4	53.8	52.5
D.	58	51.6	50.0	50.3	50.4	49.9	50.0
E.	11	36.4	39.4	43.0	40.1	43.4	44.1

lower-status boys may have had more experience in dealing with mechanical objects and may thus have been more familiar with the tasks involved in the test. It is also noteworthy that class differences tended to be larger on the Stanford-Binet than on performance tests. The Draw-a-Man test yielded the smallest difference, a finding that has been corroborated in another similar study (11).

Table 25

**MEAN TEST SCORES OBTAINED BY 16-YEAR-OLDS IN DIFFERENT
SOCIAL STATUS GROUPS**

(Adapted from Janke and Havighurst, 49, pp. 503–504)

SOCIAL STATUS	N	STANFORD-BINET IQ	WECHSLER-BELLEVUE PERF. IQ	IOWA SILENT READING T-SCORE	PAPER FORM BOARD	MINN. MECH. ASSEM. T-SCORE (BOYS)	CHICAGO MECH. ASSEM. T-SCORE (GIRLS)
A & B	9	128	118	58.0	44	46.8	62.1
C.	44	112	109	51.0	40	51.6	52.0
D.	49	104	102	48.9	31	48.8	48.5
E.	13	98	103	45.6	31	53.0	45.3

In the tests of Primary Mental Abilities administered to the 13-year-olds, it is again apparent that status differences vary with the function tested. Number, Verbal Comprehension, and Word Fluency yield larger mean differences than Space, Reasoning, and Memory. The same trend is shown by the correlations with the Index of Status Characteristics, which were as follows:

Number	.32	Word Fluency	.30
Verbal Comprehension	.42	Reasoning	.23
Space	.25	Memory	.21

The highest correlation is obtained in the case of Verbal Comprehension; Number and Word Fluency give somewhat lower correlations; and the values are still lower for Space, Reasoning, and Memory. The investigators suggest that the correlations with social status are higher in those abilities that tend to be favored by a superior social environment. This question will be considered more fully in a later section dealing with the specificity of class differences.

Some investigations have demonstrated a correspondence between the socioeconomic ratings of a whole *community* and the mean IQ of its children. In a study of over 300 neighborhoods in New York City, each with a population of about 23,000, Maller (67) found a correlation of .50 between economic status of the neighborhood (based on value of home rentals) and mean IQ of its school children. Working with even broader units, E. L. Thorndike and Woodyard (109) obtained very high correlations between mean intelligence test scores of sixth-grade pupils and various social indices for each of 30 cities. For example, intelligence test scores correlated .78 with the index of per capita income for each city, and they correlated .86 with a composite index of the general "goodness" of community life, based on a variety of criteria. In a more recent nation-wide survey by R. L. Thorndike (110), community variables correlated higher with intelligence than with achievement tests. Among the possible reasons suggested for this finding was the fact that education is relatively standardized in America and it is primarily in nonschool factors that communities differ. Hence educational achievement would be less responsive to community variables than would more general indices such as intelligence test scores.

The observed relationships between socioeconomic factors and intelligence lend themselves to several *interpretations*. It can be argued that the intellectual differences found today among social classes result from a gradual hereditary differentiation which has been going on through selection. Thus the more intelligent individuals would gradually work their way up to the more demanding but more desirable positions, each person tending eventually to "find his level." Since intellectually superior parents tend to have intellectually superior offspring, the children in the higher social strata would be more intelligent, on the whole, than those from the lower social levels. A second hypothesis would explain the intellectual development of the child in terms of the cultural level in which he is reared. The child who grows up in the home of an unskilled laborer does not have the same opportunities for intellectual development—and consequently will not reach the same ability level—as a child of equal initial capacity brought up in the home of a professional man. A third possible hypothesis is that both socioeconomic and intellectual variables may be related through some other factor, such as personality characteristics, national origin, or family size.

We cannot choose among these explanations without probing further into the particular circumstances in each case. Some investigators have been impressed with the finding that class differences in intelligence test performance appear so early in life and are practically as large among 3-year-olds as among 18-year-olds. This has sometimes been regarded as evidence for a hereditary interpretation of class differences, on the grounds that environmentally produced differences should increase with age, as environmental factors have more time to operate. Under certain conditions, however, the trend may be reversed. If the environmental differences continue to an equal degree or increase with age, then we should expect their differentiating effects on behavior also to increase. But if any equalizing influences are introduced into the environment at certain ages, as at the time of school entrance, these might counteract the divergence of behavior development otherwise expected.

In all comparisons of intellectual and socioeconomic variables, we must not lose sight of the wide range of individual differences within each social level, nor of the overlapping between levels. It is also well to bear in mind that the total number of persons in the lower social classes is larger than that in the higher classes. Consequently, if we begin with intellectual rather than with social categories, we may find that a larger percentage of intellectually superior persons come from the lower than from the upper social classes. For example, among Wisconsin high school seniors who fell above the group median in intelligence test scores, only 7.9 per cent had fathers in the professions, while 17.4 per cent had fathers in skilled labor (12). This was true despite the fact that the median percentile score of all subjects with professional fathers was 68.5 and that of all subjects with fathers in skilled labor was 51.1. These findings are by no means peculiar to this study. Similar results would be obtained in most studies if the data were expressed in the same form. This simply means that the lower social classes may contribute a larger absolute number of intellectually superior persons than the upper classes, although relative to the total number of persons in each class, the contribution of the higher classes is greater. Beyond a certain point, the larger numbers in the lower classes would no longer suffice to counteract the shrinking proportional contribution. This occurred, for instance, in the Stanford Gifted Child Study, in which 31.4 per cent of the subjects had fathers in the professions, as compared to 11.8 per cent with fathers in the skilled labor class (cf. Ch. 13).

INTELLECTUAL DEVELOPMENT OF ISOLATED GROUPS

Certain groups have been of special interest to the differential psychologist because of their relative isolation from outside social contacts. Gordon (35) investigated the educational achievement and intelligence test performance of a group of English *canal-boat children*. It was estimated that these children attended school for only about 5 per cent of the regular school year. Special schools were maintained for them, which they could attend when the boats were tied up for loading or discharging. Their home environment also provided little intellectual stimulation, many of the parents being illiterate and contacts with persons outside the family being few. The mean Stanford-Binet IQ of the entire group of 76 canal-boat children was 69.6. Taken at face value, this would suggest at best a borderline group, with a few distinctly feebleminded individuals. Further analysis of the data, however, brought out the fact that IQ *declined sharply with age* within the group, the 4- to 6-year-olds obtaining an average IQ of 90, while the oldest group (12 to 22 years) averaged only 60. The correlation between IQ and age was −.755. Even when children in the same family were compared, a consistent drop in IQ from the youngest to the eldest sibling was noted.

In another part of the same survey, Gordon studied 82 *gypsy children* living in England. The mean Stanford-Binet IQ of this group was 74.5, and the correlation between age and IQ was −.430. Thus both the total inferiority and the age decrement in intelligence were less pronounced in this group than in the canal-boat group. Corresponding to these findings is the fact that the school attendance of the gypsy children averaged considerably higher than that of the canal-boat children, being 34.9 per cent of the total number of possible school days. The gypsy families led a nomadic existence, the children attending school only during the few winter months when they had a fixed abode. Although their living conditions were crude and primitive, these gypsy children had more social contacts outside of their immediate family, and were thus less isolated than the canal-boat children. It is also noteworthy that within the gypsy group, IQ showed a significant positive correlation of .368 with amount of school attendance for each child.

Of special interest is the age decrement reported by Gordon for both canal-boat and gypsy children, but not found in surveys of more privileged groups. One possible explanation for such a decrement is that the intellectual needs of the younger child can be satisfied almost as well in the restricted environment of the canal boat or gypsy camp as in a prosperous urban home. As the child grows older, however, the differential effects of poorer home environment and of deficient schooling become increasingly apparent. Another factor which undoubtedly enters into the obtained results is the well-known difference in the functions measured by intelligence tests at the lower and upper age levels. The increasing emphasis upon verbal and other abstract functions at the older ages may present a progressively greater handicap to children whose environments do not encourage the development of these abilities.

Gordon's findings have been corroborated by several studies of *mountain children* in America. Because of poor roads and general inaccessibility, the inhabitants of these mountainous regions lived in virtual isolation during a large part of the year. The groups were also characterized by low standard of living and high degree of inbreeding. Practically all persons in the areas studied were of British descent, their families having lived in this country for many generations. Intelligence test surveys of children living in such isolated mountain communities have been conducted in Kentucky (5, 46), Tennessee (18, 118, 119), Georgia (28), and the Blue Ridge Mountains (94). Results are quite consistent. Mean IQ is clearly below the national norms; inferiority is greater on verbal tests than on nonlanguage and per- formance tests; and scores tend to decline with age. Mention should also be made of the 10-year follow-up conducted by Wheeler (119) in a Tennes- see mountain community, which was reported in Chapter 7. It will be re- called that a significant rise in mean IQ of this child population paralleled the improved socioeconomic level of the community.

Typical findings from a study conducted by Sherman and Key (94) are shown in Table 26. The subjects included 102 mountain children from four hollows in the Blue Ridge Mountains, approximately one hundred miles from Washington, D.C., as well as 81 children living in a small village situated at the base of the Blue Ridge. Racially, the inhabitants of the five communities were quite homogeneous, all being descended from a com- mon ancestral stock. It will be noted that both village and mountain children average below 100 IQ on nearly all tests. The inferiority is less, however, among the village children, who had better schooling facilities. Both groups show a fairly consistent age decrement, which is also less marked in the village group. In the case of the mountain children, mean IQ's tended to be lower on the verbal than on the nonverbal and performance tests.

Table 26
MEAN IQ OF MOUNTAIN AND VILLAGE CHILDREN IN RELATION TO AGE
(From Sherman and Key, 94, p. 287)

AGE	PINTNER-CUNNINGHAM TEST		NATIONAL INTELLIGENCE TEST		GOODENOUGH DRAW-A-MAN TEST		PINTNER-PATERSON PERFORMANCE TESTS	
	Mt.	Vill.	Mt.	Vill.	Mt.	Vill.	Mt.	Vill.
6– 8	84	94			80	93	89	
8–10	70	91		117	66	82	76	93
10–12	53	76	66	101	71	69	70	87
12–14			67	91	69	73	83	
14–16			52	87	49	70	73	

It might be added that age decrement is not limited to the relatively unusual groups of children discussed in the present section, but has also been reported for other underprivileged groups. This decrement is especially apparent where educational facilities are deficient. Among the groups for which such a drop in IQ with age has been found may be mentioned: southern mill-town children of low socioeconomic level (52); children reared in a high delinquency area in a large city (60); and children admitted to an orphanage after varying periods of residence in their own, very inferior homes (101). Such age decrements have also been noted in investigations on rural children, to be discussed in the following section.

URBAN-RURAL AND OTHER REGIONAL DIFFERENCES

Urban-Rural Differences in Test Scores. The fact that rural children as a group average significantly lower than urban children on current intelligence tests has been repeatedly demonstrated.[2] Typical results are given in Table 27, based upon the standardization sample of the Stanford-Binet

Table 27

MEAN STANFORD-BINET IQ'S OF URBAN, SUBURBAN,
AND RURAL CHILDREN

(From McNemar, 73, p. 37)

	AGE RANGE IN YEARS					
LOCALITY	2–5½		6–14		15–18	
	N	Mean	N	Mean	N	Mean
Urban	354	106.3	864	105.8	204	107.9
Suburban	158	105.0	537	104.5	112	106.9
Rural	144	100.6	422	95.4	103	95.7

(73). Separate means for urban and suburban groups are included, but as would be expected, these groups did not differ appreciably. Suburban communities are within commuting distance of large cities, and they share most of the benefits of urban centers. The rural children, on the other hand, average about 10 IQ points lower than the urban during school age (6–18), and about 5 points lower during the preschool period (2–5½). It is noteworthy, too, that there was a slight tendency for rural IQ's to drop at the beginning of the school period, no such tendency having been found among urban children (107). On the more recently standardized WISC, rural

[2] For a good summary of early studies, cf. Shimberg (95).

children again averaged significantly lower than urban children, the difference being somewhat larger on the Verbal than on the Performance Scale (92).

That age is an important factor in the amount of urban-rural difference was demonstrated in the thorough and comprehensive investigation conducted by Baldwin, Fillmore, and Hadley (7) in Iowa. Children in four rural communities were compared with Iowa City children, as well as with test norms, on a variety of intelligence tests suitable for the different age levels. Results showed that among the rural infants there was no noticeable inferiority. In the preschool group, rural inferiority appeared at the 5- and 6-year levels, no significant differences having been found at the younger ages. The rural school children, however, showed definite intellectual retardation, which increased as they progressed through school. This deficiency was also more pronounced in one-room than in consolidated schools.

An analysis of the rural children's performance on different tests or parts of tests revealed their greater handicap on verbal materials. In regard to the performance tests, it is interesting to note that the farm children excelled on the Mare-and-Foal Test, a picture completion test portraying a farm scene. On all other performance tests which involved *speed,* the rural subjects were deficient, their movements tending to be slow and deliberate. The usual instructions to work rapidly did not seem to provide sufficient incentive for these children. The rate of movement could, however, be increased if other appeals were added. The investigators suggested that "the children's apparent lack of comprehension of the meaning of hurry is to be expected as a consequence of some of the influences that surround them" (7, p. 254).

Rural children tend to do even more poorly on group tests than on individual tests (82). The country child's performance on a group test may be handicapped by his shyness with strangers, a difficulty that would be partly overcome by the examiner's efforts to establish rapport in the administration of an individual test. Intelligence test scores have also been found to be related to the quality of the soil, children living on good farm land averaging higher than those in hilly areas with inferior soil (83). These differences are undoubtedly related to the fact that areas with better farm land are more prosperous and have superior educational facilities.

Urban-rural differences in test scores have likewise been reported for a number of European countries. Klineberg (55) administered an abbreviated form of the Pintner-Paterson Performance Scale to 10–12-year-old boys in Paris, Hamburg, and Rome, as well as in rural areas in each of the three countries. Large, significant differences in mean scores were found in favor of the city groups, these differences being much greater than those between the three nations. When the entire urban and rural samples were compared, only 30.12 per cent of the rural children reached or exceeded the urban median. Studies conducted in Sweden (13), in Rumania (84, 86), and in Ceylon (105) have likewise revealed significant urban-rural differences.

Investigations in Great Britain have tended to show less urban-rural differentiation in intelligence test performance than has been found in America or in other European countries. Especially is this true of the more remote rural districts of Great Britain, which frequently show no inferiority to the urban areas (10, 108). An illustration of this finding is provided by the first Scottish Survey, in which the Stanford-Binet was given to a complete sampling of children born in Scotland on a particular day (88). In Table 28 will be found mean IQ's for the four cities, the in-

Table 28

MEAN IQ'S OF CHILDREN IN URBAN AND RURAL AREAS OF SCOTLAND

(From Rusk, 88, p. 272)

AREA	NUMBER OF CASES	MEAN IQ	SD
The four cities	319	100.86	15.29
Industrial belt	393	99.19	16.18
Entire rural area	162	100.92	14.52
Highlands and islands	47	101.79	13.13

dustrial belt, the entire rural area, and a subdivision of the rural area comprising the highlands and islands, which represent the more isolated rural districts. Not only are there no significant differences between the mean IQ's of any of these groups, but also the highest mean and the smallest variability are found in the highlands and islands. The relative performance of urban and rural groups in this survey was closely corroborated by the more extensive survey with group tests.[3] In partial explanation of these findings, the investigator observed that "perhaps nowhere has scholastic opportunity been more evenly equated than in Scotland" (88, p. 273). It should also be noted that rural living is relatively more desirable and enjoys greater prestige in the British culture than in many other countries.

Factors Contributing to Regional Differences. The distinction between

[3] In the second Scottish Survey, children in the four cities obtained a significantly higher mean than children in predominantly rural areas, but the difference was too small to be of practical importance (90, Ch. 8).

urban and rural populations is partly one of occupation, but it also involves other important aspects of physical and social environment. Most of the differences are such as to handicap the rural child in academic progress and in the type of abilities sampled by intelligence tests. Educational facilities are usually poorer in rural than in urban areas. The length of the school term is often shortened in rural communities because of impassable road conditions at certain times of the year, or because the children are needed to help with farm duties in busy seasons, or for other reasons of a local nature. In some cases the school term lasts only six months. Similarly, the difference in type and amount of instruction received in consolidated and one-room schools is a very real one. In the latter type of school, in which pupils of all ages and grades are taught by a single teacher and in a single classroom, progress must necessarily be very halting. Differences in the availability of books and other supplies, as well as in teacher training, are also important.

The general cultural milieu of different localities likewise presents striking contrasts. Libraries, museums, and other community facilities are far more accessible and better developed in urban than in rural districts. Recreational activities of rural children are quite different from those of urban children, as shown, for example, in the extensive survey of play activities conducted by Lehman and Witty (59). These investigators concluded that the differences are "directly traceable to environmental opportunities," and that such differences may in turn influence the direction of the child's intellectual development. The extent and variety of social contacts also differentiate city and country groups. Between the cosmopolitan associations of the large metropolis, with its diversity of customs, manners, and peoples, and the relatively homogeneous and sparse contacts of the rural village or open country there exist tremendous differences in social stimulation.

A few investigators have tried to analyze the relative contribution of various environmental factors to regional differences in test performance. It has been well known for some time, for example, that intelligence test scores vary significantly among states. Relevant data were provided by analyses of Army Alpha scores from World War I (1, 120) and AGCT scores from World War II (104). In general, mean scores tended to be lower for southern than for northern states, the differences persisting even when men in the same occupations were compared across states (104). Similar state differences were found in both white and Negro populations. In a special analysis of World War I scores, a correlation of .72 was found between mean Alpha score of each state and its rating in educational efficiency (1). The latter was derived from records of percentage of daily school attendance, percentage of children attending high school, per capita expenditure for education, and teacher salaries.

A more intensive analysis was carried out by Davenport and Remmers (20) with qualifying examination scores of applicants for special educational programs conducted by the Navy during World War II. The mean scores obtained by men from each state were correlated with 12 socio-economic variables and the resulting correlation matrix was factor-analyzed. Three factors having significant loadings in the test scores were identified as income level, urbanization, and geographic location (North versus South). Of the three, however, income level had by far the largest weight.

In a Swedish investigation, Carlsson (13) compared the mean test scores of over 38,000 19-year-old conscripts from the 22 military registration districts of Sweden. Large, significant differences were found, the more highly urbanized districts tending to have the highest means. When educational and occupational level were ruled out, however, the regional differences were so greatly reduced as to be negligible for practical purposes. The remaining small but statistically significant differences were explained as probably resulting from differences in the quality of education (which could not be controlled in the analysis), as well as other cultural advantages of urban life. Carlsson also cites an earlier analysis of regional differences by Husén, in which education proved to be the most important factor, occupation the next most important, and degree of urbanization the least important. It should be noted that there is no necessary inconsistency between these findings and those of Davenport and Remmers, since regional differences in income level may influence test performance chiefly through their effect on educational expenditures.

Current research in farming areas in the United States reveals that the urban-rural gap in intelligence test performance is rapidly shrinking.[4] Such a change may result partly from population shifts and partly from major improvements in the rural environment. Among the contributing factors may be mentioned the gradual disappearance of small farms and the replacement of farm laborers by machinery, as well as the sharp increase in facilities for education, communication, and transportation available to the rural population.

Selective Migration. One of the explanations proposed for urban-rural differences in test performance is that of selective migration. According to this hypothesis, the more intelligent persons are attracted to urban centers, while the duller and less ambitious tend to remain in the country. The operation of such a selective process for several generations would even-

---

[4] Personal communication from Dr. John E. Anderson, May 1957.

tually lead to an inferior rural stock. It is probably true that in certain localities migration may have drained the country of its most able families. In other situations, however, it may be the shiftless and dull who migrate because they are unable to succeed at home. The forces of selection are too difficult to disentangle, unless the specific history and conditions of the district under consideration are known. No single generalization can be applied to all migrations.

The most direct test of the selective migration hypothesis is through a study of the migrants themselves. Such a procedure was followed in a number of studies by Klineberg (56, 57). In one of these, an intelligence test was administered to 12-year-old school boys in three southern cities. When migrants were classified according to length of urban residence, mean scores rose from 38.3 for the one-year group to 68.7 for those who had lived in the city for 7 years or longer. A city-born group tested for comparative purposes averaged 74.6.

Another study by Klineberg (57) dealt with migrants from rural New Jersey to urban centers in the same general area. It was possible to examine the records of 597 migrant children who had taken intelligence tests in rural schools prior to their urban migration. These children were found to average slightly *below* the nonmigrants in the same rural schools. The results of both of these studies suggest that the migrating populations did not represent an initially superior selection, but that they gradually improved *after* moving to the superior urban environment.

It should be noted that both of these studies were concerned with *children*, who did not themselves initiate the migration but simply moved with their families. Somewhat different results have been reported in studies on *adult migrants*. In such cases, the individuals studied are usually the ones who made the decision to migrate. In this respect, these studies might be said to be more direct. At the same time, it might be noted that from the viewpoint of long-range effects over a period of several generations the data on the children of migrants are actually more relevant.

In general, studies on adults do show a tendency for migrants from rural to urban areas to constitute a superior sampling of the rural population (34, 48, 68, 89). In the most extensive of these studies, Gist and Clark (34) followed up a sample of 2544 high school students in forty rural communities in Kansas, all of whom had taken the same intelligence test at a median age of 16 years. Residence data were obtained when the group had reached a median age of 29. Comparisons among various migrating and nonmigrating groups revealed statistically significant differences in initial IQ. Thus migrants to urban centers excelled both nonmigrants and migrants to other rural areas; those who had moved to larger, cosmopolitan centers surpassed those who had moved to smaller cities; and those who had left the state averaged significantly higher than those who had remained in Kansas.

Two points should be borne in mind in interpreting these results. First, since the original sampling consisted of high school students, no information is provided regarding the lower levels of the population. There is some evidence to suggest that migrants may be drawn from the extremes of the distribution (32, 121). Thus among moderately successful persons, it may be that the more alert, ambitious, and intelligent are attracted by the superior opportunities offered by the cities. But at the lowest socioeconomic levels, it may be the more hopeless and destitute who are more likely to migrate. A second point is that selective migration does not imply a hereditary interpretation of urban-rural differences. If it should be demonstrated conclusively that the superior families tend to migrate to cities, such families may be superior because of environmental factors within their original surroundings, and their offspring may in turn be superior because they are reared in a relatively favorable family milieu.

SPECIFICITY OF SOCIAL CLASS DIFFERENCES

Among investigations cited earlier in this chapter, we have already seen evidence that the amount of difference in favor of urban groups and upper social classes varies with the nature of the test. On certain types of tests, group differences may disappear or may even be reversed. In this connection, mention may be made of results obtained with performance as contrasted to verbal tests of intelligence, with mechanical aptitude tests, and with the various tests of primary mental abilities.

Certain studies provide more detailed analyses of socioeconomic group differences in specific functions. In an investigation by Jones, Conrad, and Blanchard (51), the performance of rural children was compared to that of the standardization sample on individual Stanford-Binet items. The subjects were 351 children between the ages of 4 and 14 years, all living in rural areas of Massachusetts and Vermont. In terms of total IQ, the rural group was clearly inferior. The items showing the greatest rural inferiority were: those involving the use of paper and pencil, as in copying a square; those depending upon specific experiences more common in an urban environment, such as familiarity with coins, streetcars, and the like; and distinctly verbal tests, such as vocabulary and definition of abstract terms. Further analysis revealed an increasing urban-rural difference with age in such tests as vocabulary, dissected sentences, naming words, and word definitions. On the other hand, urban-rural differences decreased with age on such predominantly nonverbal tests as ball-and-field, giving the number of fingers on the two hands, and counting thirteen pennies.

Results obtained with four Pintner-Paterson Performance tests, administered to the same subjects, are also of interest. On Digit-Symbol Substitution (a paper-and-pencil test), the rural children were very inferior. They were slightly below average on Knox Cube and Five-Figure Form Board. On the

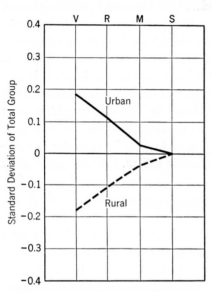

Mare-and-Foal, however, they surpassed the norms, as was also true of the Iowa farm children tested by Baldwin, Fillmore, and Hadley.

A special analysis of the WISC standardization sample provides data on the percentage of subjects in various groups who obtained a higher IQ on the Verbal Scale and the percentage who obtained a higher IQ on the Performance Scale (91). When children were classified according to parental occupation, the only significant deviation from chance distribution occurred in the professional and semiprofessional group, in which 62 per cent had a higher Verbal than Performance IQ. Among urban children as a whole, there was a slight tendency in the same direction, while rural children more often earned a

Fig. 83. Urban-Rural Differences in Verbal, Reading, Mathematical, and Scientific Parts of Army-Navy College Qualifying Test. (From Turnbull, 112, p. 31.)

higher Performance than Verbal IQ. Although statistically significant, this urban-rural difference was much smaller than that between occupational classes.

Relevant data are also provided by Turnbull (112) in an analysis of scores on the Army-Navy College Qualifying Test. This test included four parts: verbal, scientific, reading, and mathematical. In Figure 83 will be found the mean scores obtained by two samples of 2000 cases each, chosen on the basis of community size to represent urban and rural groups, respectively. The group difference was very large on the verbal part, slightly smaller on the reading part, and much smaller on the mathematical. On the scientific part, the two groups were equal. It should be noted that the scientific portion of the test consisted of items of the "common sense" type, depending more on scientific interest and alert observation than on technical information. Within each part of the test, the relative difficulty of individual items also varied significantly from urban to rural sample, a finding that suggests the influence of specific environmental conditions.

Intelligence tests have been standardized predominantly on urban populations, since such groups are more readily accessible in large numbers. Even in the more carefully developed tests, in which a proportional representation of rural groups has been sought, the urban subjects still greatly outnumber the rural in the standardization sample, as they do in the general population. Consequently such tests are probably overweighted with items that favor the city dweller, and they may fail to sample adequately those abilities in which rural subjects excel. Intelligence tests have likewise been validated against such criteria as school achievement, which tends to favor middle-class children. In general, those abilities that are important in any culture or subculture tend to improve with age; others will not. This may account for the declining IQ of rural and other isolated groups on tests developed within an urban middle-class subculture.

Suppose the procedure were reversed and a test developed on a rural population were administered to urban and rural groups—what would the results show? A direct attack on this question is to be found in a study by Shimberg (95). The basic plan was to construct one form of a test on urban children and another on rural children. The procedures were in every other way parallel. Items for each form were selected from a larger initial pool on the basis of percentage of children in the urban and rural samples, respectively, who answered each item correctly. By this method, two 25-item scaled tests were prepared, in which successive items represented approximately equal increments in difficulty. When these two forms were administered to new samples of urban and rural children, the urban group excelled significantly on the urban form; but on the rural form, a large significant difference was found in favor of the rural group.

A similar approach with regard to social class differences is illustrated by some of the research of the Committee on Human Development of the University of Chicago, under the direction of Allison Davis. In the effort to study "cultural differentials" in intelligence test performance, the investigators administered eight widely used group intelligence tests to nearly all children aged 9, 10, 13, and 14 years in a midwestern city (29). By means of the Index of Status Characteristics, a high-status group and a low-status group were chosen for comparison. Wide differences in the relative superiority of the high-status group were found, not only between tests, but also from item to item within a single test. For example, an item based upon an understanding of the term "sonata" was passed by 74 per cent of high-status children and only 29 per cent of low-status children, while an item involving the classification of cutting tools was passed by 71 per cent of high-status and 74 per cent of low-status cases. The large majority of items, however, favored the high-status group; differences in favor of the low-status group were rare. In another study conducted as part of the same research project, Haggard (40) investigated the relative effect of such factors as practice, motivation, testing conditions, and item form upon the test performance of high-status and low-status subjects.

As a result of these studies, a test designed to be relatively free from "social class bias" has been developed. Known as the Davis-Eells Games (23), this test requires no reading, all instructions being given orally. The content is entirely pictorial, consisting of problems chosen from the every-day-life experiences of children in the urban American culture. All parts of the test are presented as games, efforts being made to induce a comfortable and relaxed atmosphere. Praise and encouragement are also freely given to increase motivation. Several items portray humorous situations, introduced as a further appeal to the interests of children. The contribution of speed is reduced to a minimum.

Recent studies have cast doubt upon the success of the Davis-Eells Games in eliminating social class differentials from test performance (4, 33, 87). There is evidence indicating that even on this test high-status children significantly excel low-status children, and that low-status children may do no better on this test than on standard intelligence tests such as the Binet and WISC. A more basic objection to this approach to test construction concerns validity. If a test is designed to predict criteria that are themselves culturally weighted, the elimination of cultural differentials from the test would only lower its validity (cf. 2). For example, if a middle-class environment fosters the development of behavior characteristics leading to superior school achievement, then any test which validly predicts school achievement will necessarily favor the middle-class child. In so far as class differences and other cultural factors affect behavior, these differences will be reflected in test performance, since the latter is nothing more than a sample of behavior. It is not so much that tests are unfair to lower-status groups, as that lower-class environment is not conducive to the effective development of "intelligence" as defined in our culture.

SUMMARY

Studies of American cities using either the Method of Evaluated Participation or the Index of Status Characteristics have revealed a stratification into six social classes, although in certain regions the differentiation between the two upper classes is absent. Class structure has also been investigated by cluster analysis and by techniques based on the individual's class identification. Psychological studies have revealed class differences in child-rearing practices, sexual behavior, emotional adjustment, interests, and attitudes.

Even prior to the investigation of class differentiation, occupational differences in intelligence test performance were found both in the case of adults engaged in different kinds of work and in the case of children classified according to parental occupation. Significant correlations with intelligence test scores have likewise been obtained with scales for rating home conditions and with the Index of Status Characteristics. Mean IQ's of children in different communities are also correlated with socioeconomic variables.

Investigations of isolated groups, such as canal-boat, gypsy, and mountain children, reveal an age decrement in mean IQ. Such a decline may result in part from changes in the nature of the functions tested at different ages and in part from the increasing influence of environmental deprivation.

Urban-rural comparisons, both in America and elsewhere, have consistently favored urban subjects. In this case, too, the differences tend to increase with age. Analyses of test scores by states or by other major regions indicate that socioeconomic factors, and especially educational expenditures, are of prime importance. With regard to selective migration, there is some evidence to suggest that adults who move from rural to urban areas tend to be intellectually superior to nonmigrants, but that the children of migrant families do not excel those who remain in a rural area. Moreover, test scores of migrant children tend to increase with length of residence in an urban community.

Intellectual differences between social classes and between regions are specific to the functions tested. Each subculture fosters the development of its own characteristic pattern of aptitudes and personality traits. Tests constructed within one subculture thus tend to favor individuals reared in that subculture. No one test measures "intelligence" or "personality adjustment" in the abstract, but each must be interpreted in terms of the criteria against which it was validated.

REFERENCES

1. Alexander, H. B. A comparison of the ranks of American states in Army Alpha and in social-economic status. *Sch. and Soc.,* 1922, 16, 388–392.
2. Anastasi, Anne. Some implications of cultural factors for test construction. *Proc., 1949 Conf. Test. Probl., Educ. Test. Serv.,* 1950, 13–17.
3. Anastasi, Anne, and Miller, Shirley. Adolescent prestige factors in relation to academic and socio-economic variables. *J. soc. Psychol.,* 1949, 29, 43–50.

4. Angelino, H., and Shedd, C. L. An initial report of a validation study of the Davis-Eells Test of General Intelligence or Problem-Solving Ability. *J. Psychol.*, 1955, 40, 35–38.
5. Asher, E. J. The inadequacy of current intelligence tests for testing Kentucky mountain children. *J. genet. Psychol.*, 1935, 46, 480–486.
6. Auld, F., Jr. Influence of social class on personality test responses. *Psychol. Bull.*, 1952, 49, 318–332.
7. Baldwin, B. T., Fillmore, Eva A., and Hadley, L. *Farm children.* N.Y.: Appleton-Century-Crofts, 1930.
8. Barker, R. G., and Wright, H. F. *One boy's day.* N.Y.: Harper, 1951.
9. Barker, R. G., and Wright, H. F. *Midwest and its children: the psychological ecology of an American town.* Evanston, Ill.: Row, Peterson, 1955.
10. Bickersteth, M. E. Application of mental tests to children of various ages. *Brit. J. Psychol.*, 1917, 9, 23–73.
11. Britton, J. H. Influence of social class upon performance on the Draw-A-Man Test. *J. educ. Psychol.*, 1954, 45, 44–51.
12. Byrns, Ruth, and Henmon, V. A. C. Parental occupation and mental ability. *J. educ. Psychol.*, 1936, 27, 284–291.
13. Carlsson, G. The regional distribution of intelligence. *Stat. Rev.* (Sweden), 1954, 3, 313–323.
14. Carlsson, G. Social class, intelligence, and the verbal factor. *Acta psychol.*, 1955, 11, 269–278.
15. Cattell, R. B. Occupational norms of intelligence, and the standardization of an adult intelligence test. *Brit. J. Psychol.*, 1934–35, 25, 1–28.
16. Centers, R. *The psychology of social classes.* Princeton, N.J.: Princeton Univer. Press, 1949.
17. Centers, R. Children of the New Deal: social stratification and adolescent attitudes. *Int. J. Opin. Attitude Res.*, 1950, 4, 315–335.
18. Chapanis, A., and Williams, W. C. Results of a mental survey with the Kuhlmann-Anderson intelligence tests in Williamson County, Tennessee. *J. genet. Psychol.*, 1945, 67, 27–55.
19. Clark, R. E. Psychoses, income and occupational prestige. *Amer. J. Sociol.*, 1949, 54, 433–440.
20. Davenport, K. S., and Remmers, H. H. Factors in state characteristics related to average A-12 and V-12 test scores. *J. educ. Psychol.*, 1950, 41, 110–115.
21. Davis, A. American status systems and the socialization of the child. *Amer. sociol. Rev.*, 1941, 6, 345–354.
22. Davis, A. Socialization and adolescent personality. *43rd Yearb., Nat. Soc. Stud. Educ.*, 1944, Part I, 198–216.
23. Davis, A., and Eells, K. *Davis-Eells Games: Davis-Eells Test of General Intelligence or Problem-Solving Ability, Manual.* Yonkers-on-Hudson, N.Y.: World Book Co., 1953.
24. Davis, A., Gardner, B. B., and Gardner, Mary R. *Deep South: a social anthropological study of caste and class.* Chicago: Univer. Chicago Press, 1941.
25. Davis, A., and Havighurst, R. J. Social class and color differences in child rearing. *Amer. sociol. Rev.*, 1946, 11, 698–710.

26. Dubnoff, Belle. A comparative study of mental development in infancy. *J. genet. Psychol.*, 1938, 53, 67–73.

27. Duff, J. F., and Thomson, G. H. The social and geographical distribution of intelligence in Northumberland. *Brit. J. Psychol.*, 1923, 14, 192–198.

28. Edwards, A. S., and Jones, L. An experimental and field study of North Georgia mountaineers. *J. soc. Psychol.*, 1938, 9, 317–333.

29. Eells, K., Davis, A., Havighurst, R. J., Herrick, V. E., and Tyler, R. W. *Intelligence and cultural differences.* Chicago: Univer. Chicago Press, 1951.

30. Foulds, G. A., and Raven, J. C. Intellectual ability and occupational grade. *Occup. Psychol., Lond.*, 1948, 22, 197–203.

31. Fryer, D. Occupational intelligence standards. *Sch. and Soc.*, 1922, 16, 273–277.

32. Gee, W., and Corson, J. J. Rural depopulation in certain Tidewater and Piedmont areas of Virginia. *Univer. Virginia soc. Sci. Monogr.*, 1929, No. 3.

33. Geist, H. Evaluation of culture-free intelligence. *Calif. J. educ. Res.*, 1954, 5, 209–214.

34. Gist, N. P., and Clark, C. D. Intelligence as a selective factor in urban-rural migration. *Amer. J. Sociol.*, 1938, 44, 36–58.

35. Gordon, H. *Mental and scholastic tests among retarded children.* London: Bd. Educ., Educ. Pamphlet no. 44, 1923.

36. Gough, H. G. The relationship of socio-economic status to personality inventory and achievement test scores. *J. educ. Psychol.*, 1946, 37, 527–540.

37. Gough, H. G. A new dimension of status. I. Development of a personality scale. *Amer. sociol. Rev.*, 1948, 13, 401–409.

38. Gough, H. G. A new dimension of status. II. Relationship of the St scale to other variables. *Amer. sociol. Rev.*, 1948, 13, 534–537.

39. Gough, H. G. A new dimension of status. III. Discrepancies between the St scale and "objective status." *Amer. sociol. Rev.*, 1949, 14, 275–281.

40. Haggard, E. A. Social-status and intelligence: an experimental study of certain cultural determinants of measured intelligence. *Genet. Psychol. Monogr.*, 1954, 49, 141–186.

41. Havighurst, R. J., and Breese, F. H. Relation between ability and social status in a midwestern community: III. Primary Mental Abilities. *J. educ. Psychol.*, 1947, 38, 241–247.

42. Havighurst, R. J., and Janke, L. L. Relation between ability and social status in a midwestern community: I. ten-year-old children. *J. educ. Psychol.*, 1944, 35, 357–368.

43. Havighurst, R. J., and Taba, Hilda. *Adolescent character and personality.* N.Y.: Wiley, 1949.

44. Heuyer, G., *et al.* Le niveau intellectuel des enfants d'âge scolaire. *Inst. nat. d'études démographiques: Travaux et documents*, Cahier 13, 1950.

45. Himmelweit, Hilde T. Socio-economic background and personality. *Int. soc. Sci. Bull.*, 1955, 7, 29–35.

46. Hirsch, N. D. M. An experimental study of the East Kentucky mountaineers. *Genet. Psychol. Monogr.*, 1928, 3, 183–244.

47. Hollingshead, A. B. *Elmtown's youth: the impact of social classes on adolescents.* N.Y.: Wiley, 1949.

48. Husén, T. (Concerning the problem of selective migration on the basis of intellectual differences.) *Studia Psychol. Paedagog., Lund,* 1948, 2, 30–63.
49. Janke, L. L., and Havighurst, R. J. Relations between ability and social status in a midwestern community: II. sixteen-year-old boys and girls. *J. educ. Psychol.,* 1945, 36, 499–509.
50. Jones, A. W. *Life, liberty, and property.* Philadelphia: Lippincott, 1941.
51. Jones, H. E., Conrad, H. S., and Blanchard, M. B. Environmental handicap in mental test performance. *Univer. Calif. Publ. Psychol.,* 1932, 5, No. 3, 63–99.
52. Jordan, A. M. Parental occupation and children's intelligence scores. *J. appl. Psychol.,* 1933, 17, 103–119.
53. Kinsey, A. C., *et al. Sexual behavior in the human male.* Philadelphia: Saunders, 1948.
54. Kinsey, A. C., *et al. Sexual behavior in the human female.* Philadelphia: Saunders, 1953.
55. Klineberg, O. A study of psychological differences between "racial" and national groups in Europe. *Arch. Psychol.,* 1931, No. 132.
56. Klineberg, O. *Negro intelligence and selective migration.* N.Y.: Columbia Univer. Press, 1935.
57. Klineberg, O. The intelligence of migrants. *Amer. sociol. Rev.,* 1938, 3, 218–224.
58. Leahy, Alice M. *The measurement of urban environment.* Minneapolis, Minn.: Univer. Minn. Press, 1936.
59. Lehman, H. C., and Witty, P. A. *The psychology of play activities.* N.Y.: Barnes, 1927.
60. Lichtenstein, M., and Brown, A. W. Intelligence and achievement of children in a delinquency area. *J. juv. Res.,* 1938, 22, 1–25.
61. Livesay, T. M. Relation of economic status to "intelligence" and to racial derivation of high school seniors in Hawaii. *Amer. J. Psychol.,* 1944, 57, 77–82.
62. Loevinger, Jane. Intelligence as related to socio-economic factors. *39th Yearb., Nat. Soc. Stud. Educ.,* 1940, Part I, 159–210.
63. Lynd, R. S., and Lynd, Helen M. *Middletown.* N.Y.: Harcourt, Brace, 1929.
64. Lynd, R. S., and Lynd, Helen M. *Middletown in transition.* N.Y.: Harcourt, Brace, 1937.
65. Maas, H. S. Some social class differences in the family systems and group relations of pre- and early adolescents. *Child Develpm.,* 1951, 22, 145–152.
66. MacDonald, Margherita, McGuire, Carson, and Havighurst, R. J. Leisure activities and the socioeconomic status of children. *Amer. J. Sociol.,* 1949, 54, 505–519.
67. Maller, J. B. Mental ability and its relation to physical health and social economic status. *Psychol. Clinic,* 1933, 22, 101–107.
68. Mauldin, W. P. Selective migration from small towns. *Amer. sociol. Rev.,* 1940, 5, 748–758.
69. McArthur, C. Personality differences between middle and upper classes. *J. abnorm. soc. Psychol.,* 1955, 50, 247–254.
70. McCarthy, Dorothea. Language development in children. In L. Carmichael

(Ed.), *Manual of child psychology.* (2nd Ed.) N.Y.: Wiley, 1954, Pp. 492–630.

71. McConnell, J. W. *The evolution of social classes.* Washington, D.C.: Amer. Coun. Pub. Affairs, 1942.

72. McDonald, H. The social distribution of intelligence in the Isle of Wight. *Brit. J. Psychol.,* 1925, 16, 123–129.

73. McNemar, Q. *The revision of the Stanford-Binet Scale.* Boston. Houghton Mifflin, 1942.

74. Milner, Esther. Effects of sex role and social status on the early adolescent personality. *Genet. Psychol. Monogr.,* 1949, 40, 231–325.

75. Milner, Esther. A study of the relationships between reading readiness in grade one school children and patterns of parent-child interaction. *Child Develpm.,* 1951, 22, 95–112.

76. Miner, J. B. *Intelligence in the United States: a survey—with conclusions for manpower utilization in education and employment.* N.Y.: Springer, 1956.

77. Neff, W. S. Socio-economic status and intelligence: a critical survey. *Psychol. Bull.,* 1938, 35, 727–757.

78. Phillips, E. L. Intellectual and personality factors associated with social class attitudes among junior high school children. *J. genet. Psychol.,* 1950, 77, 61–72.

79. Pieter, J. (Intelligence quotient and environment.) *Kwart. Psychol.,* 1939, 11, 265–322.

80. Pope, B. Socio-economic contrasts in children's peer culture prestige values. *Genet. Psychol. Monogr.,* 1953, 48, 157–220.

81. Preda, G., and Mates, E. (The relation between children's intelligence and father's occupation). *Bul. Soc. Psihol. med. Sibiu,* 1939, 6, 33–39.

82. Pressey, L. W. The influence of inadequate schooling and poor environment upon results with tests of intelligence. *J. appl. Psychol.,* 1920, 4, 91–96.

83. Pressey, S. L., and Thomas, J. B. A study of country children in a good and a poor farming district by means of a group scale of intelligence. *J. appl. Psychol.,* 1919, 3, 283–286.

84. Rădulescu-Motru, C., and Nestor, I. M. (Experimental researches on the intelligence of the Rumanians.) *Acad. Română,* 1948, 50 p. (cf. *Psychol. Abstr.,* 1950, No. 160)

85. Redlich, F. C., *et al.* Social structure and psychiatric disorders. *Amer. J. Psychiat.,* 1953, 109, 729–734.

86. Rosca, A. (Intelligence in rural and urban communities). *Rev. Psihol.,* 1939, 2, 131–141.

87. Rosenblum, S., Keller, J. E., and Papania, N. Davis-Eells ("culture-fair") test performance of lower-class retarded children. *J. consult. Psychol.,* 1955, 19, 51–54.

88. Rusk, R. R. The intelligence of Scottish children. *39th Yearb., Nat. Soc. Stud. Educ.,* 1940, Part II, 269–273.

89. Sanford, G. A. Selective migration in a rural Alabama community. *Amer. sociol. Rev.,* 1940, 5, 759–766.

90. Scottish Council for Research in Education. *Social implications of the 1947 Scottish mental survey.* London: Univer. London Press, 1953.

91. Seashore, H. G. Differences between verbal and performance IQ's on the Wechsler Intelligence Scale for Children. *J. consult. Psychol.*, 1951, 15, 62–67.

92. Seashore, H., Wesman, A., and Doppelt, J. The standardization of the Wechsler Intelligence Scale for Children. *J. consult. Psychol.*, 1950, 14, 99–110.

93. Sewell, W. H., Mussen, P. H., and Harris, C. W. Relationships among child training practices. *Amer. sociol. Rev.*, 1955, 20, 137–148.

94. Sherman, M., and Key, Cora B. The intelligence of isolated mountain children. *Child Develpm.*, 1932, 3, 279–290.

95. Shimberg, Myra E. An investigation into the validity of norms with special reference to urban and rural groups. *Arch. Psychol.*, 1929, No. 104.

96. Simon, L. M., and Levitt, E. A. The relation between Wechsler-Bellevue IQ scores and occupational area. *Occupations*, 1950, 29, 23–25.

97. Sims, V. M. A technique for measuring social class identification. *Educ. psychol. Measmt.*, 1951, 11, 541–548.

98. Sims, V. M. *Sims SCI Occupational Rating Scale: Manual of directions.* Yonkers-on-Hudson, N.Y.: World Book Co., 1952.

99. Sims, V. M. Relations between the social class identification and personality adjustment of a group of high school and college students. *J. soc. Psychol.*, 1954, 40, 323–327.

100. Sirkin, M. The relation between intelligence, age, and home environment of elementary school pupils. *Sch. and Soc.*, 1929, 30, 304–308.

101. Skeels, H. M., and Fillmore, Eva A. Mental development of children from underprivileged homes. *J. genet. Psychol.*, 1937, 50, 427–439.

102. Skodak, Marie. Children in foster homes: a study of mental development. *Univer. Iowa Stud. Child Welf.*, 1939, 16, No. 1.

103. Stendler, Celia B. Social class differences in parental attitudes toward school at grade-I level. *Child Develpm.*, 1951, 22, 36–46.

104. Stewart, Naomi. A.G.C.T. scores of army personnel grouped by occupation. *Occupations*, 1947, 26, 5–41.

105. Straus, M. A. Subcultural variation in Ceylonese mental ability: a study in national character. *J. soc. Psychol.*, 1954, 39, 129–141.

106. Strong, E. K., Jr. *Vocational interests of men and women.* Stanford Univer., Calif.: Stanford Univer. Press, 1943.

107. Terman, L. M., and Merrill, Maud A. *Measuring intelligence.* N.Y.: Houghton Mifflin, 1937.

108. Thomson, G. H. The Northumberland mental tests. *Brit. J. Psychol.*, 1921, 12, 201–222.

109. Thorndike, E. L., and Woodyard, Ella. Differences within and between communities in the intelligence of children. *J. educ. Psychol.*, 1942, 33, 641–656.

110. Thorndike, R. L. Community variables as predictors of intelligence and academic achievement. *J. educ. Psychol.*, 1951, 42, 321–338.

111. Tryon, R. C. Identification of social areas by cluster analysis. *Univer. Calif. Publ. Psychol.*, 1955, 8, No. 1.

112. Turnbull, W. W. Influence of cultural background on predictive test scores. *Proc., 1949 Conf. Test. Probl., Educ. Test. Serv.*, 1950, 29–34.

113. Van Alstyne, Dorothy. The environment of three-year-old children: factors related to intelligence and vocabulary tests. *Teach. Coll. Contr. Educ.*, 1929, No. 366.

114. Warner, W. L., Havighurst, R. J., and Loeb, M. B. *Who shall be educated?* N.Y.: Harper, 1944.

115. Warner, W. L., and Lunt, P. S. *The social life of the modern community.* New Haven, Conn.: Yale Univer. Press, 1941.

116. Warner, W. L., Meeker, Marchia, and Eells, K. *Social class in America: a manual of procedure for the measurement of social status.* Chicago: Science Research Associates, 1949.

117. West, J. *Plainville, U.S.A.* N.Y.: Columbia Univer. Press, 1945.

118. Wheeler, L. R. The intelligence of East Tennessee mountain children. *J. educ. Psychol.*, 1932, 23, 351–370.

119. Wheeler, L. R. A comparative study of the intelligence of East Tennessee mountain children. *J. educ. Psychol.*, 1942, 33, 321–334.

120. Yerkes, R. M. (Ed.) Psychological examining in the United States Army. *Mem. nat. Acad. Sci.*, 1921, 15.

121. Zimmerman, C. C. The migration to towns and cities. *Amer. J. Sociol.*, 1926, 32, 450–455; 1927, 33, 105–109.

CHAPTER 16

Race Differences:
Methodological Problems

The comparative evaluation of the races of man has long been a subject of common concern and lively controversy. It is an interesting commentary upon human thought that nearly all theories of racial inequality proclaim the superiority of the particular race of their respective exponents. Thus Aristotle (cf. 74, pp. 318–320) tried to show that the intellectual leadership of the Greeks must of necessity follow from their favorable geographical location. He argued that the peoples inhabiting the colder regions of northern Europe, although outstanding for bravery and physical prowess, were intellectually incapable of a high degree of political organization or leadership. Similarly, the Asiatics, although intellectually keen and inventive, lacked spirit. The Greeks alone, being geographically intermediate, were endowed with the proper balance of these traits and were thus by nature fitted to rule the earth. Similar claims have been made for such groups as the Arabians, the Romans, the French, the Anglo-Saxon, the "white" race as distinguished from those having a different skin pigmentation, the Nordics, the Alpines, the Mediterraneans, and various others (cf. 9).

Particularly influential in popular thinking was the theory proposed a little over a century ago by de Gobineau (30). In his *Essay on the Inequality of Human Races*, de Gobineau tried to give a scientific foundation for the current race prejudices of his culture. Later writers carried this process further in their efforts to establish the superiority of the white race, and especially of its Nordic subdivision (cf., e.g., 22). The Nazi racial doctrines promulgated during World War II represent an especially flagrant example of the misinterpretation and perversion of scientific data for political purposes.

542

Since race relations have provided some particularly violent chapters in human history, discussions of race differences are likely to arouse strong emotions. Under such conditions, unbiased and objective analysis of facts proves difficult. It is one of the earmarks of prejudice to ignore the limitations of available data and to draw unwarranted inferences. In view of the prevalence of racial stereotypes and of emotionally toned views about race differences, conclusions need to be carefully evaluated and supporting data scrutinized. It is therefore of prime importance to have a knowledge of methodological and interpretive problems in this area.

THE CONCEPT OF RACE

Race is a biological concept referring to subdivisions of a species. It corresponds to such classifications as breed, stock, and strain in animals. Modern geneticists emphasize the *process* of race formation or diversification, as well as the reverse process of race mixture or hybridization, both of which are continually occurring (cf. 33, 34, 35, 36). They point out that the evidence is against the existence of distinctly differentiated "pure races" of man, either now or at any time in the past. Genetic differences between human races are not absolute but relative. *Human races are populations that differ in the relative frequency of certain genes.* As a result, any racial group will exhibit variation in hereditary physical characteristics and will overlap with other populations in such characteristics. For example, Nordics as a group have a greater frequency of blue eyes than do Mediterraneans. But some Mediterraneans have blue eyes and some Nordics have brown eyes. Although the presence of such "nonconformist" individuals might be due to migration or race mixture, geneticists now stress the fact that such cases are to be expected in the ordinary process of race formation. Their existence simply indicates that racial diversification, or the sorting out of genes into different populations, has not proceeded far enough to eliminate such variants.

Races are formed whenever a particular group of people becomes relatively isolated, for either geographic or social reasons, so that marriage among its members is more frequent than marriage with outsiders. Major geographical barriers such as the Sahara Desert or the Himalayas have for centuries separated Europeans from African Negroes and from Asiatic Mongoloids, respectively—a condition that has lead to a relatively high degree of racial differentiation in certain regions. In areas lacking such barriers, intermediate types and gradual transitions are prevalent.

The number of racial categories into which mankind is classified is largely

a matter of convenience, since all degrees of differences between populations can be identified. The racial distinction between European whites and
central African Negroes is a large one; that between Norwegians and
Spaniards is smaller; and that between the inhabitants of two French
villages, still smaller. But regardless of its order of magnitude, the nature
of the distinction is fundamentally the same, the examples cited representing different stages of race formation. How far down the scale the term
"race" is applied is an arbitrary decision. Hence it is not surprising to find
wide variation in the number of races and subraces proposed by different
anthropologists. A well-known classification is that of Kroeber (63), which
includes three major races—Caucasian, Mongoloid, and Negroid—plus a
doubtful category of small populations which are difficult to classify. Each
of the three major races is further subdivided into three to four subraces.
Thus the Caucasian race is broken down into Nordic, Alpine, Mediterranean, and Hindu groups. A somewhat different schema, comprising thirty
races, is provided by Coon *et al.* (24).

Popular discussions of race are further confused by the use of national
and linguistic categories as though they referred to distinct racial groups.
A nation is a political unit, which does not necessarily represent either
cultural or racial homogeneity. Through historical and geographical reasons,
members of the same nation may be racially more dissimilar than members
of different nations. Under most circumstances, however, national boundaries tend to foster race formation, since marriages are more likely to
occur within than across such boundaries. There is little or no justification,
on the other hand, for the use of such expressions as "Latin race" or "Aryan
race," since these categories refer to large groups of languages spoken by
peoples varying both culturally and genetically.

In their efforts to identify and define races, anthropologists and biologists
have utilized a number of inherited physical characteristics as criteria of
race. Among the most common are skin color, eye color, hair color and texture (straight, wavy, or woolly), height, and such facial characteristics as
nose width and lip thickness. Extensive use has also been made of the
cephalic index, or ratio between head width and head length (front to
back). Some populations are characteristically dolichocephalic, or long-
headed, others are brachycephalic, or broad-headed. There is now some
question, however, regarding the extent to which these differences can be
attributed to hereditary racial characteristics. Evidence from several investigations indicates that the cephalic index may be drastically modified
by cultural factors, especially cradling and related infant-rearing practices
(cf. 11, 12, 41).

A major limitation of most of the traditional criteria of race stems from their complex genetic basis. Each depends not upon one but upon many genes. As a result, their mode of inheritance is not clearly established. Moreover, the same characteristic may arise from a different gene combination in different persons. For these reasons, geneticists have been turning their attention increasingly to traits with simpler and better-established hereditary mechanisms, such as the blood groups, PTC taste reactions, and fingerprint patterns (cf. 34).

It should also be noted that the physical traits used to classify races are independently distributed. Blood groups, stature, and skin color, for example, are not highly correlated from population to population. The application of any one of these criteria thus yields a different classification of mankind than is obtained with other criteria. For instance, some Negro populations are characteristically very tall, others very short. Some groups are dark-skinned and straight-haired, others are equally dark-skinned and woolly-haired.

Difficulties of classification will arise whether we begin with single criteria or with combinations of criteria. If, on the other hand, we begin with certain major geographical groups, which because of proximity have functioned as genetic communities, we can proceed to describe the physical characteristics of each population. Any population can be uniquely described in terms of the *frequencies* of certain inherited physical traits. In some of the separate traits, each population may resemble other populations. But the relative frequencies, as well as the combination of traits, will differentiate it from other groups.

Thus "racial criteria" can be meaningfully employed to describe existing *populations*. But their application to the racial identification of *individuals* may lead to confusions and misclassifications (cf. 33). Persons sharing a certain combination of physical characteristics are not necessarily members of the same racial group. Thus Germans and Italians exhibiting the typical "Alpine" coloring and body build are not members of the same subrace, unless it can be established that the particular individuals had recently migrated, or that their ancestors had migrated and refrained from intermarrying with the local population. Otherwise their physical resemblance may merely indicate the range of variation existing within the gene pools of their respective populations. In such a case, the individuals selected from the two populations may differ widely in other traits; and even the traits in which they resemble each other may arise from different gene combinations.

Many popular ideas about race are based on a misunderstanding of the operation of heredity. It is beyond the scope of the present discussion to explain the genetic mechanisms whereby racial differentiation in physical traits, such as skin color or blood groups, takes place. A particularly clear exposition of these processes can be found in Dobzhansky (33). For our present purposes, it will suffice to note that, in view of available genetic knowledge, it appears improbable that racial differentiation in such physical traits was accompanied by differentiation with regard to genes affecting intellectual or personality development. It is theoretically much more likely that *behavioral* differences between human populations result from cultural than from racial factors (28, 33, 35).

SELECTIVE FACTORS

As in all group comparisons, one of the methodological problems in psychological studies of race differences concerns the operation of selective factors in sampling. Many early studies with psychological tests, for example, were conducted on *immigrant* groups in the United States. Such groups cannot be assumed to be representative samples of their home populations. They are not drawn proportionately from all educational and occupational levels, but usually constitute a selected group. Moreover, selective factors may operate differently in each country. As a result, immigrant groups from different nations are *neither fair samplings of their home populations nor comparable among themselves.* If it could be shown, for instance, that immigrants from all nations were drawn consistently from lower socioeconomic levels, then such groups would at least be comparable with each other. But it is well known that, through purely historical reasons, immigrants from some nations may represent a relatively inferior sampling of their population, from others a more nearly random or average sampling, and from still others a relatively superior sampling. Moreover, the nature of the sampling from a given country may change markedly from time to time.

It has been suggested, for example, that the superior performance of Chinese and Japanese children in America on many of our intelligence tests may be the result of selective factors, only the more progressive families emigrating from these countries (cf., e.g., 27, 84). Many of the immigrants from southern Europe, on the other hand, are probably an inferior sampling of their own national population. In one investigation (43), groups of Danish and Italian girls in the United States and in Europe were examined with a nonlanguage group test of intelligence. Although the Danish samplings in this country excelled the Italian, no significant difference was found between the groups tested in Copenhagen and in Rome.

A type of selective sampling that complicates certain comparisons among racial or national groups results from differential social selection. We have already seen an example of such differential selection in the admission of men and women to institutions for mental defectives (Ch. 14). Similar factors may operate with respect to various minority groups living within the same country. In evaluating any results on special groups, such as college students, army inductees, or institutional populations, we need to be on the alert for possible spurious effects resulting from such selective factors. For example, comparisons of the test performance of Negro and white *soldiers* in World War II were complicated by the fact that Selective Service screening standards were apparently different for the two groups (58).

Another illustration of differential selective factors is provided by comparisons of Negro and white *college students.* In one investigation (39), Negro college girls were found to be significantly more "self-sufficient" as indicated by the Bernreuter Personality Inventory, the remaining scores on this test yielding no significant differences between the two groups. Does such a finding demonstrate that Negroes are more self-sufficient than whites? Obviously not, since only college girls were tested. Does it indicate that in the upper intellectual levels Negro girls are more self-sufficient than white girls? Not necessarily, because Negro girls who go to college may represent a selected sampling not only with respect to intellectual level, but also with respect to a number of personality traits. It may have *required* more self-sufficiency for a Negro girl to continue her education than it did for a white girl, because of the relatively greater economic and social obstacles which the former had to overcome. Any personality difference between the two groups may thus do no more than reflect these differences in the operation of selective factors. Of course, we must also consider the possibility that going to college may itself be a factor in increasing the self-sufficiency of a Negro girl. The realization that one has successfully surmounted obstacles is probably an important condition in the development of feelings of self-sufficiency.

Statistics on *crime* and *insanity* are especially subject to differential selective factors. Statements have often been made regarding the "predisposition" of various racial groups to crime. The large percentage of crime in the United States has been attributed by some to the influx of certain classes of immigrants into our country. Statistics have been cited to show the greater frequency of crime among Negroes and among immigrants from eastern and southern Europe than among the native-born white population.

Figures *can* lie, and in the interpretation of crime statistics it is particularly difficult to disentangle the many uncontrolled factors which confuse the issue. Among such factors may be mentioned the inequality in arrests and convictions among various groups. Negroes and "foreigners," for example, are more readily arrested "on suspicion" and on less grounds than is generally required for native-born whites. The fact that most foreigners are adults would also give them a disproportionate percentage of crime if they are compared with the figures for native-born persons of *all* ages. Similarly, foreigners are more often city dwellers and live under poorer social and economic conditions than native-born Americans—all of which is conducive to crime. The foreigner, furthermore, may have brought with him traditions and folkways which happen to conflict with the accepted behavior in our country. Mexicans in the United States, for example, show a relatively large number of arrests for carrying concealed weapons (95). In this they may simply be continuing habits that they acquired in their own country in a perfectly legitimate way. Despite the many factors that load the dice against the foreign-born in crime statistics, careful analyses of the data on native and foreign-born persons *over 18 years of age* have failed to reveal a higher rate of arrests, convictions, or commitments among the latter (95).

Most of the conditions that render the evaluation of crime statistics difficult also affect the data on insanity. In addition may be mentioned the factor of hospitalization. Institutional subjects may not be a representative sampling of the actual cases of mental disorder in different groups, since the available facilities for hospital care are not equal in different parts of the country. On the other hand, because of economic conditions, certain groups are better able to care for the mentally disordered persons at home, thus eliminating the necessity for hospitalization. It is interesting to note that, although the uncorrected hospital statistics show about twice as many cases of insanity among the foreign-born as among the native-born, the difference virtually disappears when various corrections are made for sampling inequalities (65). Even when nonhospitalized cases under psychiatric treatment are included, selective factors may still operate as a result of group differences in the recognition of mental illness and in the acceptance of psychiatric treatment (81).

GROUP DIFFERENCES AND THE INDIVIDUAL

It will be recalled that two important questions to consider in interpreting the results of any group comparison are those of *significant difference* and *overlapping*. Both were discussed in connection with sex differences (Ch. 14). The first deals essentially with the applicability of sample results to the larger population from which the sample was drawn. The latter is concerned with the opposite process, that of applying group findings to individuals. Because groups overlap, the differences found between group means may disappear or be reversed in comparisons between individuals.

Although overlapping of distributions has already been illustrated in the chapter on sex differences, the question is of sufficient importance in the evaluation of race difference data to bear repetition and elaboration. In Figure 84 will be seen two schematic distributions showing what is often loosely described as "30 per cent overlap." This means that 30 per cent of

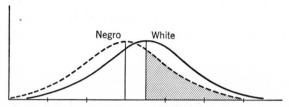

Fig. 84. Schematic Distributions Illustrating "30 Per Cent Overlap."

one group reach or exceed the median of the other, as indicated by the shaded area. Such a degree of overlap is close to that usually found between psychological test scores of Negroes and whites in the United States.

One implication of such overlap is that if a Negro is chosen at random from his group, the chances are 30 out of 100 that his score will reach or exceed that of the average white. Thus if we were to assume that a Negro is inferior to the white median, under these conditions, we would be in error 30 out of 100 times. Such an error ratio may be compared with the ".01 level of significance" customarily required before accepting a conclusion as established in scientific research. In that case, the chances of being in error are only one out of 100. It is thus apparent that, owing to the extensive overlapping of test scores, a knowledge of the individual's group membership does not permit us to predict his relative test performance at an acceptable probability level.

Another noteworthy point concerns the total amount of overlapping of the distributions. If 30 per cent of the Negroes reach or exceed the white median, the percentage who reach or exceed the lowest score of the white group will be approximately 99. Under these conditions, therefore, the ranges will overlap almost completely. It would thus be likely that the best performers in both groups would obtain scores that are equally high, and the poorest in both groups would score equally low. The above estimate is based on the assumptions that both distributions are normal and that their SD's are equal. In actual practice, of course, the total amount of overlap can be determined by examining the obtained distributions of scores. It will be recalled in this connection that, in the example cited in Chapter 14, in which 28 per cent of the girls reached or exceeded the boys' median, the range of scores was virtually the same in the two groups.

The implications of overlapping make it abundantly clear that differences between group means, even when statistically significant, may be of little practical value for dealing with individuals. Mean differences between groups are always far smaller than differences among individuals within each group. There is no short-cut to the understanding of people, no possibility of learning the peculiarities of a few broad groups into which individuals may then be conveniently pigeonholed. In the study of individuals, the only proper unit is the individual.

CULTURAL DIFFERENCES

The interpretation of behavioral differences between racial groups is complicated by the fact that such groups also differ in culture. The geographical and social isolation which leads to race formation is very likely to be associated with cultural diversification. Cultural factors often account for group isolation in the first place; and any form of isolation tends to preserve and augment cultural differentiation. The perennial question that confronts the investigator of psychological race differences is: to what extent could cultural factors have produced the obtained differences? In the present section, we shall examine some of the principal ways in which cultural differences between racial groups may be reflected in psychological test results.

General Cultural Milieu.   The particular culture in which the individual is reared may influence his behavioral development through many channels. The operation of environmental forces is not limited to the extent and quality of educational opportunities available in the school, the home, and the neighborhood. The question is not only one of amount, but of kind. The experiences of people living in different cultures may vary in such a way as to lead to basically different perceptual responses, lend a different meaning to their actions, stimulate the development of totally different interests, and furnish diverse ideals and standards of behavior.

Field investigators have recorded some striking examples of the influence of *traditions and customs* upon test performance. Porteus (79), in his testing of Australian aborigines, found it difficult to convince his subjects that they were to solve the problems individually and without assistance. In explanation of this behavior, he writes:

. . . the aborigine is used to concerted thinking. Not only is every problem in tribal life debated and settled by the council of elders, but it is always discussed until a unanimous decision is reached. On many occasions the subject of a test was evidently extremely puzzled by the fact that I would render him no assistance, especially when, as happened in the centre, I was testing some men who were reputedly my tribal brothers. This was a matter which caused considerable delay as, again and again, the subject would pause for approval or assistance in the task (79, p. 308).

Similarly, Klineberg (62) reports that among the Dakota Indians it is considered bad form to answer a question in the presence of someone else who does not know the answer. This creates a particularly difficult situation in school, where teachers find it difficult to induce children to recite in class. In the same group, custom forbids one to answer a question unless he is absolutely sure of the answer. The effect this would have upon intelligence tests, in which the subject is advised to "guess" when not sure and is urged to "try his best" on a difficult problem, can be readily foreseen. The child who refuses to give any answer unless he is certain of its correctness will lose many points that he might have earned through partial credits and chance successes.

Mention should likewise be made of the important role of *speed* in most intelligence tests and of the widely varying emphasis placed upon speed in different cultures. An investigation by Klineberg (61) on Indian, Negro, and white school boys illustrates the operation of this factor. Several of the tests in the Pintner-Paterson Performance Scale were administered to the following groups:

136 Indians attending Haskell Institute in Kansas
120 Indians at the Yakima Reservation in Washington
107 whites in rural Washington, near the Indian reservation
139 Negroes in a rural district of West Virginia
 25 whites in the same district of West Virginia
200 Negroes in New York City
100 whites in New York City

In *accuracy* of performance, as measured by the number of errors on each test, the Indians excelled the whites, and the Negroes were either equal or slightly superior to the whites. All measures of *speed,* on the other hand, favored the whites. A comparison of groups *of the same race but living in different environments* suggested that these differences in speed were cultural rather than biological. Thus the New York City Negroes clearly excelled the West Virginia Negroes in every comparison. Similarly, the Haskell Institute Indians were consistently faster than those tested on the Yakima Reservation. A further division of the Haskell group into those who had previously lived on a reservation and those who had lived among whites in a town or city showed the latter to excel in speed.

In explanation of these results, Klineberg called attention to the relatively insignificant part that speed played in the life of the reservation Indian or the rural southern Negro. Time was of little or no concern in the daily activities of the Indian. He could see no reason for hurrying through a task, especially if he found it congenial and interesting. Thus in so far as the examiner aroused the child's interest in the test, he made the necessity of speeding appear even more absurd. At Haskell Institute, on the other hand, time was much more important than on the reservation. The students were constantly kept busy with a variety of tasks and the entire day was carefully scheduled. The white teachers, too, fostered the attitude that it is desirable to finish things as quickly as possible. Similarly, the New York City Negroes had been exposed to the bustle of life in a big metropolis, whereas the rural Negroes were adapted to a much slower tempo of activity.

The importance of *motivation and interest* in intelligence test performance has been repeatedly emphasized. Yet it is apparent that many of the tests in current use cannot arouse the same emotional reaction in other cultures as they do in our own. Thus for the middle-class white American child the usual intelligence test bears a close resemblance to his everyday schoolwork, which is probably the most serious business of his life at the time. He is therefore easily spurred on to exert his best efforts and to try to excel his fellows. For an American Indian child, on the other hand, the same test cannot have such significance. This type of activity has no place in the traditional behavior of his family or tribe. Similarly, many investigators have noted that among Negro children interest in intelligence tests is not as keen as among white children, and that the former seem not to be so strongly motivated as the latter. It will be recalled that differences in the drive to achieve—on tests, in school, and in other situations—were also found among social classes (Ch. 15).

Such motivational differences may be directly related to membership in underprivileged groups. Several theories have been proposed, for example, regarding the reaction of the American Negro and other minority groups to socially imposed frustrations. Dollard (37) has suggested that the Negro may assume an attitude of stupidity and lethargy as a defense mechanism against frustration and oppression. Such an attitude would provide a sort of revenge and enable the individual to avoid disagreeable responsibilities. Similarly, Brown (16) has argued that the linguistic development of the Negro may be hindered by social pressures which inhibit verbalization. Inarticulateness reduces the possibility of incurring the hostility of the dominant social group, and might thus be "cultivated" as a measure of discretion.

A subtle but powerful influence in the individual's psychological environment is that of *social expectancy*. Reference has already been made to this factor in connection with physique and behavior (Ch. 5), family resemblances (Ch. 9), and sex roles (Ch. 14). Perhaps its most pervasive effects, however, are to be found in the case of racial minority groups. Extensive research has been done on the nature of racial and national stereotypes (cf. 1, 19, 50, 54). From an early age, the minority group member becomes aware of the characteristic behavior traits associated with his racial or national stereotype. In his daily contacts with family, playmates, teachers, and other adults, he finds constant reminders of what is expected of him. Gradually these expectations become part of his own self concept, which in turn affects his motivation and achievement. By these means, what is expected of an individual tends to determine what he becomes—a tendency that has come to be known as the "self-fulfilling prophecy" (cf. 1, 54, 72).

Culture Conflicts. Persons exposed to the inconsistent and often incompatible mores, goals, and social pressures represented by different cultures are likely to develop personality difficulties of varying degrees of severity. Emotional maladjustments occurring under these conditions cannot therefore be interpreted as evidence of inferior racial background, deleterious effects of race mixture, or other unfavorable hereditary factors. It is now recognized, moreover, that emotional disorders may interfere with intellectual development and impair the effective functioning of the individual in many areas.

Studies of immigrant groups must take into account the problems associated with adjustment to a new culture. The confusion of standards and the shifting reference points contingent upon such an adjustment cannot fail to have an effect upon the subject's behavioral development. The point has frequently been made that the maladjustment is greatest, not in the case of the immigrating generation who retain their customs to a large extent, nor in the case of the third and succeeding generations where adaptation and assimilation is virtually complete, but in the case of the offspring of the immigrants—or second generation—who are caught in the maelstrom occasioned by two different frames of reference.

On personality inventories, for example, children of immigrant parents report more neurotic symptoms, on the average, than do children of native-born parents (68). Crime and delinquency rates also tend to be higher among American-born children of foreign parentage, especially in the more highly urbanized and industralized communities where conflicts with old-world values are more acute (17, 47, 48, 94). Clinical and sociological investigations have likewise revealed many areas of emotional conflict, with resulting personality maladjustments, among second-generation Americans (17, 85, 94). The problems are particularly severe in the case of immigrants from southern Europe and from the Orient, whose cultures differ in important respects from that prevalent in America. Disruptive effects of culture conflicts have likewise been observed in a number of American Indian groups, when tribal customs clash with the needs and demands of the surrounding American culture (85, Ch. 10; 93).

Socioeconomic Level. In the contemporary American culture, membership in minority groups tends to be associated with low socioeconomic status. The homes in which were reared the children of immigrants, Negroes, or American Indians have on the whole been far below the native white standard in many respects. Whether we consider occupational and educational level of parents, income, degree of overcrowding of homes, facilities for health and physical comfort, opportunities for intellectual and recreational facilities, or parent-child relations, we find clear evidence of underprivileged status.

In view of the relation between socioeconomic level and both intellectual and personality development, discussed in the preceding chapter, the predominance of lower-class membership in minority groups must be taken into account in interpreting their test results. In a series of early studies of many different American Indian groups, for example, Garth (45) found a close correspondence between mean intelligence test score of children and socioeconomic level of group. To a certain extent, these differences in socioeconomic level also represent degree of assimilation of the white culture. Such assimilation would of course provide an advantage in performance on tests developed within that culture (53).

Several investigations on the relationship between socioeconomic factors and IQ among American Negroes have contributed toward a clarification of the nature of this relationship. First, it should be noted that the differences in intelligence test scores among occupational classes tend to be *smaller* for Negro than for white children. Thus in a survey of third-grade Negro school children in Washington, D.C., Robinson and Meenes (82) found a 13- to 14-point difference in mean IQ between the children of laborers and the children of professional men. Among white children, this difference is generally about 20 points (cf. Ch. 15). Moreover, the mean

IQ's do not follow the occupational hierarchy so closely among Negro as among white children, but tend rather to fall into a dichotomy, with clerical, business, and professional occupations in the upper category, and skilled and unskilled labor in the lower (21, 77, 82).

It is likely that the socioeconomic level of Negro homes is less closely related to occupational class than is true of white homes. The range or heterogeneity of white homes is undoubtedly much greater than that of Negro homes. The difference between the remuneration of a Negro in business or professional work and one in the skilled trades is probably much smaller than that between whites in the corresponding occupational categories. Restricted vocational opportunities would also mean that at least some Negroes with sufficient ability and education to hold a higher-level job might be engaged in lower-level occupations. All these conditions would tend to reduce the differences in the IQ's of Negro children from different occupational classes.

Some corroborative evidence for these interpretations is provided by the previously mentioned study of Robinson and Meenes (82). The Kuhlmann-Anderson IQ's of 444 third-grade Negro children attending Washington, D.C., public schools in 1938–39 were compared with those of 491 Negro children in the third grade of the same schools in 1945–46. In the latter year, when vocational opportunities for Negroes were better, a closer correspondence between paternal occupation and child's IQ was found. Moreover, the mean IQ of the entire group was higher in 1945–46 than in 1938–39. The latter finding may likewise be related to the improved socioeconomic status of the second group. High correlations were also found between the mean IQ of children in each of the schools in the survey and such factors as average rental or frequency of radios in the community.

Not only intelligence, but also emotional adjustment and other personality characteristics may be related to socioeconomic factors. For example, surveys of children's play activities have shown that Negro children tend to engage in group play relatively more often than white children (66). Before attributing such a finding to a greater "sociability" of the Negro race, it is well to consider that crowded housing and inadequate facilities for many other types of play may account for part or all of such a difference.

In a personality inventory survey of 1647 children between the ages of 9 and 15, Brown (14) compared the scores of several subgroups, including: urban and rural; low, middle, and high socioeconomic levels; and Jewish, Slovak, and native American non-Jewish. Adjustment scores proved to be much more closely related to socioeconomic level than to either racial group or urban-rural residence. Statistically significant differences in such scores were found between the different socioeconomic groups, but the differences among the other types of groups investigated were consistently small and insignificant.

Education.   It is now generally recognized that differences in the amount and nature of schooling are reflected in intelligence test performance (cf. Ch. 7). Yet in this respect, too, marked differences exist between various racial groups that have been compared in test scores. The quality of instruction available in segregated Negro and Indian schools is usually far inferior to that in white schools. Regularity of attendance, length of school term, and total number of years attended likewise differ among such groups. Not only have educational facilities been unequal for some of these groups, but the motivation to do well in school or to continue one's education is much weaker for persons who see little probability that they can utilize such education for vocational advancement or life adjustment. In this respect, the situation is similar to that described with reference to lower social classes—except that it is even more extreme in minority group members because of greater obstacles to upward mobility.

In the case of adults, intelligence test scores are highly correlated with total amount of schooling, among Negroes as among whites. This relationship was demonstrated in analyses of intelligence test scores of American soldiers during both World Wars (44, 96). When comparisons were made between mean test scores of Negroes and whites within the same educational level, however, the white means still excelled significantly. Such a finding is to be expected in view of the differences in quality of education, as well as in other uncontrolled factors such as socioeconomic level.

Studies of "Equated Groups."   It is apparent that holding number of years of schooling constant in the comparison of Negro and white adults in our culture does not rule out environmental differences between the groups. A few investigators have endeavored to control other variables in the effort to obtain equated samples of the two races. Their results consistently show that significant Negro-white differences in test performance remain under these conditions. An examination of these studies reveals that, although superficially equated, the groups still differed in a number of important respects.

In a study conducted in Canada, Tanser (92) compared Negro and white children attending the same schools. Educational facilities were thus controlled. Nevertheless significant differences were found in the socioeconomic level of the two groups. Moreover, it is reported that the white children attended school more regularly than the Negro, a difference often associated with social class differences. Thus within the entire sample of white children tested, school attendance averaged 93.38 per cent; within the Negro sample, it averaged 84.77 per cent. Bruce (18) tested Negro and white children in a poor rural district in Virginia, attempting to control both educational and socioeconomic variables. Education, however, was equated only by choosing Negro and white schools with the same teacher-pupil ratio, other differences between these schools remaining uncontrolled. In the same study, subgroups of 49 Negro and 49 white children were matched in Sims socioeconomic ratings. But the author admitted that this scale was unsuited to the groups studied because it does not discriminate adequately at the lower socioeconomic levels, where most of the subjects fell.

A more recent investigation by McGurk (70, 71) was again designed to control both educational and socioeconomic factors. The subjects were Negro and white high school seniors in Pennsylvania and New Jersey. The 213 Negro and 213 white subjects chosen for study were attending the same schools and enrolled in the same curricula. In addition, the Negroes and whites were matched on the basis of eleven items from the Sims Score Card for Socioeconomic Status. Again it appears unlikely that the items on this scale can have the same meaning when applied to Negroes and whites. Among the items, for example, is father's occupational level, classified into two categories: professional, business, and clerical versus skilled and un-skilled labor. It is highly probable that relatively more Negroes than whites fell near the bottom of each of these very broad categories. Even if specific occupations had been matched, of course, it is well known that the home of an average Negro doctor and an average white doctor, for example, are likely to differ widely in income level and in many other characteristics. Another important uncontrolled factor in this, as in the other studies cited, is that of social expectancy and related motivational differences.

Still another methodological problem which needs to be considered in evaluating such equated-group studies pertains to regression [1] (cf. Ch. 7). Since the total Negro and white populations from which the samples were drawn differ in socioeconomic level, regression will operate. Thus if eleven indices of socioeconomic level were employed as a basis for choosing matched Negro and white samples, it is to be expected that in other cultural characteristics (whose correlations with the given indices would certainly fall below 1.00) these samples will regress toward their respective population means. The effect will be to increase the differences between

---

[1] This point was brought to the writer's attention by Dr. John W. French, of Educational Testing Service.

the matched samples in all uncontrolled background variables. This is just another example of the inapplicability of matched-group experimental designs to dissimilar populations.

BILINGUALISM

It is obvious that in the comparison of groups speaking different languages, verbal tests cannot be employed. Nonlanguage and performance tests have been devised for this purpose. It is not to be concluded, however, that the same traits are being measured by all these tests. As was shown in Chapter 11, tests included under the heading of "intelligence" call into play widely different abilities. Thus when unfamiliarity with the language makes the application of verbal tests impossible in a given group, the range of processes which can be measured in that group is thereby narrowed. There is no substitute for verbal tests. It is a psychological impossibility to eliminate the verbal content of a test without altering the intellectual processes involved.

The actual effect of language handicap upon test performance is likely to be most serious, however, when such a handicap is present *to a mild degree.* If the individual has a moderate understanding of English, it is usually deemed unnecessary to give him a nonverbal test. But such an individual may lack the facility in the use of English or the range of vocabulary required to compete fairly on a verbal test. It has been shown, for example, that the reaction time of bilinguals is faster when instructions are given in the language they know better (64). Similar differences have been found in the rapidity with which words are given by free association in the two languages (60, 64).

Bilingualism is often encountered among immigrants who have lived in America for many years, or in their children, who may speak a foreign language at home and English in school. American Indian children frequently present the same problem. Investigations have also been conducted on bilingual children in other countries, such as Wales, Ireland, South Africa, and Hawaii. The rather extensive literature on this problem has been surveyed by Arsenian (6) and by Darcy (26). A few typical studies will be examined, to illustrate the major findings.

When children in American schools are examined with the usual verbal intelligence tests, those from foreign-speaking homes generally make a poorer showing as a group. In an analysis of data secured independently by different investigators, Goodenough (49) found a high correlation between the mean IQ of children in various immigrant groups and the proportion of parents in each group who had adopted English as the language spoken at home. There are, of course, two possible explanations for such a finding. On the one hand, the lower intelligence test scores of some groups may result directly from their greater language handicap. On the other hand, those national groups in which English is not commonly adopted may be less intelligent and less progressive from the outset. Their failure to learn English would thus be the result of lower intelligence and poorer adaptability.

Neither interpretation can be selected solely on the basis of the correlation between the two factors. Other data, however, suggest that the former is the more probable one. It is quite likely, for example, that because of the *greater similarity of some languages to English* it is easier for individuals from certain countries to learn English, quite apart from their intellectual level. Another factor of possible relevance is to be found in the reasons for which immigrants from various countries come to America. Those from some countries may come largely with the intention of settling permanently; those from other countries may traditionally retain a vague hope of returning to their home country after "making their fortune." Such *impermanence* is likely to be reflected in their halfhearted attempts to master the English language or to see that their children master it. A further question is whether the immigrants come into a *community of their own compatriots,* as found in the foreign neighborhoods of some of our larger cities, or whether they are scattered in predominantly American communities. In the case of certain national groups, represented by relatively small numbers of immigrants and not concentrated in any one area, the individual has little choice but to learn English.

The most crucial argument regarding the role of language handicap, however, is provided by the finding that the inferiority of the bilingual groups is greatly diminished and may disappear entirely when *nonlanguage tests* are employed. This has been repeatedly demonstrated with many groups. In a carefully controlled study, Arsenian (5) administered the Pintner Non-Language Test to 1152 American-born children of Italian parents and 1196 American-born children of Jewish parents, ranging in age from 9 to 14. Degree of bilingualism was ascertained by means of a written questionnaire. The results showed no significant correlation between extent of bilingualism and intelligence test score in either group, the correlations being $-.079$ and $-.193$ in the Italian and Jewish groups, respectively.

Similar results were obtained by Darcy (25) at the preschool level. Two groups of nursery school children, one bilingual and the other monoglot, were matched in age, sex, and paternal occupation. The second language was Italian in all cases. The two groups, each consisting of 106 children, were given the Stanford-Binet and a performance test, the Atkins Object-Fitting Test. The bilinguals were significantly inferior to the monoglots on the Stanford-Binet, but significantly superior to the monoglots on the object-fitting test. Studies on American Indian children (46, 53, 59) and on American-born Japanese children (27) have likewise revealed little or no inferiority on performance and nonlanguage tests, in contrast to significant inferiorities on verbal tests. Various analyses of the data strongly indicated the role of language handicap in the observed test deficiencies.

It should be noted that bilingualism often leads to handicap in both languages. When a child speaks one language at home and another at school, his mastery of *both* languages may be retarded as a result. This has been found in studies of preschool Chinese children in Honolulu (86, 87), Puerto Rican school children in New York City (4), and Welsh-speaking and English-speaking children in Wales (7). Such a result is not surprising. If we consider the acquisition of vocabulary as an example, it is apparent that, when a child speaks a different language at home and at school, he will learn a somewhat different set of words in the two situations and his vocabulary in each language will thereby be curtailed.

A further point to bear in mind, however, is that bilingualism as such does not necessarily result in language handicap. Under certain circumstances, bilingualism may produce no handicap in one or both languages, and in such cases we would not expect it to depress intelligence test performance. For example, Pintner and Arsenian (78) found no relationship between degree of bilingualism and scores on a verbal intelligence test in a group of 469 native-born Jewish school children in New York City. It has been a general finding, in fact, that Jewish school children, as well as college students, do especially well on verbal tests. Thus the bilingualism of the Jewish child is not such as to interfere with his mastery of English. One reason for this may be found in the attitude of the Jewish group toward the two languages, as contrasted with the attitude of other foreign-language groups. The Jewish child in America will eventually have to make his way in an English-speaking society, and English is therefore of prime importance to him. On the other hand, those national groups which are in large part oriented toward the possibility of returning to their country of origin may regard English more as a temporary expedient. Another important factor is undoubtedly the strong educational tradition in the Jewish culture and the parental insistence that the child do well in school, especially in the relatively abstract academic subjects (cf. 62).

Whether or not bilingualism in childhood proves to be a handicap apparently depends upon a number of factors. Some investigators have concluded that it is inadvisable to introduce a second language at the preschool years except in the case of linguistically superior children (86). The way in which the two languages are taught and related to each other is undoubtedly an important aspect of the situation. Introducing the second language as a school subject under certain circumstances seems to produce favorable results (69, 89). There is also evidence suggesting the role of emotional factors. In an investigation of bilingual and monolingual college students, Spoerl (88) found more maladjustment among the bilinguals, as determined by interviews, academic records, and personality test scores. In general, such maladjustment seemed to result chiefly from the culture conflict experienced by members of the "second generation." Their bilingualism, however, tended to make the maladjustment more acute, since it served as a symbol of the conflict.

In summary, bilingualism per se need not handicap a child. Bilingualism as it occurs in a large proportion of the immigrant population, however, is such as to reduce the child's mastery of *either* language, because one language is restricted largely to one set of situations in the child's life, and the other language restricted to another set. What the child needs is to learn to express himself in at least one language in all types of situations. It is not the interference of the two languages, so much as the restriction in the learning of one or both to limited areas, that produces a handicap.

CROSS-CULTURAL TESTING

"Culture-Free Tests." The use of psychological tests in comparative studies of persons reared in different cultures or subcultures presents many problems besides that of language. Even nonlanguage and performance tests generally require information that may be unavailable in certain cultures. To meet these difficulties, several attempts have been made to construct so-called culture-free tests. Among the best-known current examples are the Leiter International Performance Scale, the Cattell Culture-Free Test of Intelligence, and the Raven Progressive Matrices.[2] It should be noted that no test can be truly culture-free. Tests cannot be designed in a cultural vacuum. Nevertheless it is theoretically possible to construct a test which presupposes only experiences that are common to different cultures. Although not *free* from cultural influences, such a test would utilize

[2] For relevant references, as well as for a fuller discussion of the problems and techniques of cross-cultural testing, cf. Anastasi, 3, pp. 255–268.

only elements *common* to all cultures. This is what the available "culture-free" tests have undertaken to do.

In actual practice, however, such tests fall short of their objective in many respects. No existing test is entirely unrestricted in its cultural reference. The difference between "culture-free" and other tests is one of degree. The mere use of paper and pencil or the presentation of abstract tasks which have no immediate practical significance will favor some cultural groups and handicap others. Pictures are likewise unsuitable in cultures unaccustomed to representative drawing. A two-dimensional reproduction of an object is not a perfect replica of the original; it simply presents certain cues which, as a result of past experience, lead to the perception of the object. If the cues are highly reduced, as in a simplified or schematic drawing, and if the necessary past experience is absent, the correct perception may not follow. Other relevant factors which differ from culture to culture include intrinsic interest of test content, rapport with the examiner, drive to do well on a test, desire to excel others, and past habits of solving problems individually or cooperatively.

There is also evidence that the presence of an examiner of a different racial or cultural group may interfere with rapport during test administration and thus lower the subjects' test performance. In a study by Canady (20), Negro and white school children were given the Stanford-Binet by both Negro and white examiners. Some of the subjects in each racial group were tested by the white examiner first, and some by the Negro examiner first. In both white and Negro groups, the mean IQ was about six points higher when the subjects were tested by an examiner of their own race. A similar effect was demonstrated in a different way in a longitudinal study of Negro preschool children by Pasamanick and Knobloch (75). On successive retests with the Yale Developmental Examination during the first two years, the Negro children showed a significant decline in developmental quotient within the language area, in contrast to their continued acceleration in the motor area. Further analysis revealed, however, that the retardation was limited to items involving verbal responsiveness during the examination, while comprehension of speech and reported language behavior showed no such decline. In explanation of these findings, the authors suggest that the presence of the white examiner may have served to inhibit the child's verbal responsiveness in the test situation.

The sort of misinterpretations that may arise when test content is categorically described as "culture-free" or "noncultural" is illustrated in the previously cited study by McGurk (70, 71). The Negro and white high school seniors examined in this investigation were given two sets of test questions, equated in difficulty but differing in cultural content as determined by judges' ratings. Each judge was left free to define "cultural" as he chose. A comparison of the questions in the "cultural" and the "noncultural" sets indicates that "cultural" was closely identified with verbal content and with dependence upon schooling. Yet these are not the principal ways in which the cultural backgrounds of the Negro and white subjects differed. Since all were high school seniors enrolled in the same classes, schooling was presumably more uniform than home background. Moreover, the American Negro is not bilingual, and his linguistic deficiency should be no greater than that in other intellectual functions, especially when no oral responses are required. The so-called noncultural questions, on the other hand, made relatively heavy demands on perceptual and spatial aptitudes, in which other investigations have shown the Negro to be relatively deficient. In view of these characteristics of the items, it is not surprising to find that the Negro students scored significantly poorer on the "noncultural" than on the "cultural" items in this study.

Specificity of Group Differences. As in the case of social class and urban-rural differences, racial and national differences in psychological traits have proved to be specific, not general. Groups differ in their relative standing in different functions. Each culture or subculture fosters the development of a different *pattern* of abilities. Data on a wide variety of cultures support such a conclusion. Among the groups examined by Porteus (80) in Hawaii, the Japanese excelled the Chinese in the Porteus Maze Test and in all performance and mechanical aptitude tests; but the Chinese surpassed the Japanese in tests of the Binet type and in auditory memory span. Similarly, Japanese children tested in America scored significantly higher than the white American norms in tests involving sustained attention, visual perception, or spatial orientation, while falling behind on verbal and arithmetic tests (27).

In a study of Ceylonese university students by Straus (90, 91), the Ceylonese group greatly surpassed the American norms on the language part of the California Test of Mental Maturity, while falling far below the norms on the nonlanguage part. This difference is the reverse of what might have been anticipated in the case of a bilingual population such as the Ceylonese. Straus attributes the results to the value systems of the upper-class Ceylonese culture, which include rejection of manual tasks and attachment of high prestige to verbal scholarship. The nature of the Ceylonese educational system, with its emphasis upon feats of memory and upon learning by precept and rote, is also cited as a possible contributing influence.

American Indian children, on the other hand, usually average about as high as the American white on performance tests, but fall below on language tests. On the Goodenough Draw-a-Man test, several American Indian groups significantly excel the white norms (31, 52, 83). In a study of Hopi school children, Dennis (31) obtained an interesting sex difference on this test, which appears to be related to cultural factors. The girls received a mean IQ of 99.5, the boys 116.6. Dennis attributed this sex difference to the fact that in the Hopi culture graphic art is traditionally a masculine concern, and consequently boys develop more interest in art and have more practice in it than girls. A similar sex difference in the Draw-a-Man test has been observed in other Indian communities which foster such a traditional sex distinction in artistic pursuits (52).

Differences in specific traits have likewise been found in comparisons among European immigrant groups in this country. Jewish children, for example, usually excel on verbal tests and fall behind in problems dealing with concrete objects and spatial relations. In a study conducted with kindergarten children in the Minneapolis public schools, the Stanford-Binet was administered to groups of Jewish and Scandinavian children equated in age, sex ratio, and socioeconomic status (15). The Jewish children were found to be superior on tests based upon general information and verbal comprehension, while the Scandinavian children excelled on tests requiring spatial orientation and sensorimotor coordination. Similarly, in an analysis of the scores of Jewish and non-Jewish college freshmen on the American Council on Education Psychological Examination, the Jewish students did relatively better on the linguistic than on the quantitative parts of the test, while the reverse was true of the non-Jewish students (56). In contrast to such findings, surveys of American-born children of Italian parentage have generally shown that these children do relatively well on performance tests and relatively poorly when examined with abstract or linguistic materials (10).

Such differences in intelligence test performance among various immigrant groups may, of course, be accounted for partly on the basis of the differential language handicaps discussed in an earlier section. Cultural traditions, however, undoubtedly play a major part in producing these group differences in intellectual development. In Jewish families, there is a characteristically marked emphasis upon the formal aspects of education and upon abstract intelligence, to the almost total neglect of mechanical intelligence and manual dexterity. Italians, on the other hand, have a traditional admiration for manipulative arts and crafts, while placing relatively little emphasis upon the more abstract types of talent.

Investigations on the American Negro have revealed a relatively large inferiority on perceptual and spatial functions, in comparison to most types of verbal tasks. Negro children do particularly poorly on such tests as the Chicago Non-Verbal Examination (73) and the Minnesota Paper Form Board (8). On the California Test of Mental Maturity, Negroes score higher on the language than on the nonlanguage part (51). When Negro and white boys were matched on Stanford-Binet IQ and their performance on individual items was compared, the Negroes excelled on disarranged sentences, memory for sentences, and vocabulary, but were inferior on arithmetic reasoning, repeating digits backwards, and detecting absurdities in pictures (23). In several studies of special groups by means of the Wechsler-Bellevue, Negroes proved to be significantly poorer in Block Design, Digit Symbol, and Arithmetic than in most of the verbal tests (29, 32, 42). It is also interesting to note that a difference in the same direction is found in comparisons of northern and southern Negroes. When northern-reared and southern-reared Negroes were matched on two of the verbal tests of the Wechsler-Bellevue, the southern-reared Negroes were most inferior to the northern Negroes on Digit Symbol, Block Design, and Picture Arrangement (67).

Several factors in the cultural background of the American Negro may help to explain such findings. Performance tests usually put more premium on speed than do verbal tests. And the typical environment of the American Negro—especially in the South—provides little inducement for developing habits of rapid work. A second contributing factor may be found in the Negro attitude of passive compliance as contrasted to active exploration. Such an attitude is more conducive to rote verbal learning than to perceptual manipulation of stimuli and problem solving. Still another possible explanation is provided by Hebb's hypothesis that early perceptual learning influences subsequent intellectual development (55). This hypothesis, together with corroborative data from animal reseach, was cited in Chapter 4. It is likely that impoverishment of early perceptual experience in the Negro child may have retarded the development of certain intellectual functions.

Some supporting evidence is available in comparative studies of the effects of perceptual training on Negro and white performance. Eagleson (40) gave 50 white and 50 Negro high school students special training in visual discrimination of length. Although the whites excelled initially, the Negroes benefited more from training and the differences between the two groups diminished with training. Even more relevant is an experiment by Boger (13) with Negro and white primary school children. Group intelligence tests were administered in January and in May. During the intervening period, one half of the Negro and one half of the white children received practice with problems involving visual perception, discrimination, and spatial relations. The intelligence tests showed significant increases following such training, the Negro children making larger gains than the whites. The improvement remained on a later retest in October. Moreover, Negro gains were greater on the nonlanguage than on the language tests.

Cultural Evaluation of Behavior Functions. It might be argued that, despite their multi-dimensional differences, racial groups could still be arranged in a rank-order of ability if we considered only those functions which play a major part in the concept of "intelligence." As was indicated in Chapter 11, however, the concept of intelligence may itself be culturally conditioned. Intelligence tests might be very different if they had been constructed among American Indians or Australian aborigines rather than in American cities. The criterion employed in validating intelligence tests has nearly always been success in our social system. Scores on the test are correlated with school achievement or perhaps with some more general measure of success in our society. If such correlations are high, it is concluded that the test is a good measure of "intelligence." The age criterion is based on the same principle. If scores on a given test show a progressive increase with age, it may simply mean that the test is measuring those traits which our culture imparts to the individual. The older the subject, the more opportunity he will have had, in general, to acquire such aptitudes.

Thus it would seem that our intelligence tests measure only the ability to succeed in our particular culture. Each culture, partly through the physical conditions of its environment and partly through social tradition, "selects" certain activities as the most significant. These it encourages and stimulates; others it neglects or actively suppresses. The relative standing of different cultural groups in "intelligence" is a function of the traits included under the concept of intelligence, or, to state the same point differently, it is a function of the particular culture in which the test was constructed.

Since current intelligence tests are a characteristic American development and since the testing of racial groups has been conducted largely by American psychologists, intergroup comparisons have generally been made with tests standardized within our culture. On such tests it is not surprising that most comparisons favor American subjects. What would happen if a test were constructed in a different culture by a procedure analogous to that followed in the preparation of our own tests? The instances in which this has been attempted are rare, but the results are enlightening. DuBois (38) standardized a Draw-a-Horse Test on Indian children, following closely the procedure of the Goodenough Draw-a-Man Test. In terms of age-grade placement and other criteria of "intelligence," the horse test proved to be more valid than the man test for these children. Moreover, when both tests were administered to white and Indian children, the whites excelled on the man-drawing and the Indians on the horse-drawing test. On the basis of the latter test, the 11-year-old white boys tested in this study would have obtained an average "IQ" of 74!

Porteus (79) tried a similar experiment while working among the Australian aborigines. Having been impressed with the remarkable tracking skill of these people, he constructed a test with photographs of footprints, the task being to match the two prints made by the same foot. On this test, the Australians did practically as well as a group of 120 white high school students in Hawaii who were tested for comparison. In commenting upon these results, Porteus remarks:

Allowing for their unfamiliarity with photographs we may say, then, that with test material with which they are familiar the aborigines' ability to discriminate form and spatial relationships is at least equal to that of whites of high school standards of education and of better than average social standing (79, p. 401).

What has been said regarding specificity of group differences applies equally well to personality traits as to abilities. It is just as futile to try to measure "adjustment" in the abstract as to try to measure "intelligence" in the abstract. A response indicative of neuroticism in one culture may represent successful adjustment in another. If an upper-middle-class white man reports on a personality inventory that he is usually discriminated against in social contacts, it may be diagnostic of paranoid tendencies. But the same response on the part of a lower-class southern Negro may show a realistic awareness of existing conditions. A testing instrument designed within one culture cannot be used to compare the "personality adjustment" of different cultures—any more than it can be used to compare their "intelligence."

A convincing demonstration of this fact is provided by Hsü (57), who administered a neurotic inventory to Chinese students in China and in America. The group living in China obtained a much higher "neurotic" score than the Chinese group in America. Within the latter group, moreover, neurotic score decreased with increasing length of American residence. The author carried the analysis further, however, comparing performance on each item and utilizing his knowledge of Chinese culture to interpret the observed differences in terms of background factors. The items were classified under such headings as sex tabu and morality, self-depreciation and modesty, family conflict and tradition, anger and courage, and care of health and filial duty. In reference to the last-named category, it was pointed out that according to Chinese culture, since the body is received from the parents, its care is considered a part of filial duty. In connection with responses indicating excessive modesty and withdrawal, mention was made of such Chinese proverbs as "Great wisdom appears like stupidity," and "The taller tree will fall first in storms." Other quotations from Chinese classics as well as popular proverbs were utilized to show the cultural basis of many apparently neurotic responses.

LEVELS OF CULTURAL DIFFERENTIALS

Cultural differentials may operate in a variety of ways to bring about group differences in behavior. The level at which such cultural influences are manifested varies along a continuum extending from superficial and temporary effects to those which are basic, permanent, and far-reaching. From both a practical and a theoretical viewpoint, it is important to inquire at what level of this continuum any observed behavioral difference falls. At one extreme, we find cultural differences that may affect only responses on a particular test and thus reduce its validity for certain groups. There are undoubtedly test items that have no diagnostic value when applied to persons from certain cultures because of lack of familiarity with specific objects or other relatively trivial differences in experience.

On the other hand, most cultural factors that affect test responses are also likely to influence the broader area of behavior which the test is designed to sample (cf. 2). For example, inadequate mastery of English may handicap a child not only on an intelligence test but also in his school-work, contact with associates, play activities, and other situations of daily life. Such a condition would thus interfere with the child's subsequent intellectual and emotional development and would have practical implications that extend far beyond immediate test performance. At the same time, deficiencies of this sort can be remedied without too much difficulty. Suitable language training *can* bring such individuals up to an effective functioning level within a relatively short period. The intensive educational programs successfully employed with illiterates in the armed forces of the United States during World War II represent another illustration of the remediable nature of fairly severe cultural handicaps. Similarly, many conditions arising from inferior environmental backgrounds can be ameliorated through such means as remedial reading work, educational and vocational counseling, and psychotherapy.

To be sure, the longer the deleterious factors or privations have been operating in the individual's lifetime, the less likely it becomes that their effects can be overcome. And it should be clearly recognized that conditions which are environmentally determined are not necessarily remediable. Adverse experiential factors operating over many years may very well produce intellectual or emotional damage which can no longer be eliminated at the time when remedial measures are introduced. It is also important to bear in mind, however, that the permanence or irremediability of a psychological condition is no proof of hereditary origin.

A vivid illustration of the fact that cultural differentials may produce permanent effects upon individual behavior is provided by recent research of Pasamanick and his associates (76) upon complications of pregnancy and parturition. In a series of studies on large samples of Negroes and whites in Baltimore, these investigators showed that prenatal and paranatal disorders are significantly related to mental defect and behavior disorders in the offspring. An important source of such irregularities in the process of childbearing and birth is to be found in deficiencies of maternal nutrition and other conditions associated with low socioeconomic status. Analysis of the data revealed a much higher frequency of all such medical complications in lower than in higher socioeconomic levels, and a higher frequency among Negroes than among whites. Here then is an example of cultural differentials producing structural deficiencies which in turn lead to behavioral inadequacies or disorders. The effects of this sort of cultural differential cannot be remedied within the lifetime of the individual, but require more than one generation for their elimination. Again it needs to be emphasized, however, that such a situation does not imply hereditary defect, nor does it provide any justification for failure to improve the environmental conditions of underprivileged groups.

SUMMARY

Biologically, human races are populations differing in the relative frequency of certain genes. They are formed as a result of varying degrees of geographic or cultural isolation from other groups. Racial classifications should not be confused with national or linguistic categories. Existing *populations* can be differentiated in terms of the distribution of certain physical traits, such as skin color or blood groups. But when applied to *individuals*, such racial criteria may lead to misclassification.

Samples of different races or nationalities available for study may not be comparable because of the differential operation of selective factors. This difficulty is encountered in investigations of such groups as immigrants, college students, or military inductees, as well as in the statistics on crime and insanity. As in all group comparisons, data on race differences must be interpreted in terms of statistical significance of differences and overlapping of distributions. The latter is especially important as a safeguard against the unwarranted application of group trends to the evaluation of individuals.

The fact that racial groups also differ in culture complicates the interpretation of observed race differences in intellectual or personality traits. Among the cultural factors that may affect performance on psychological tests are included general traditions and customs, relative emphasis placed upon speed in different cultures, motivation to excel on the sort of tasks sampled by intelligence tests, and social expectancy. Emotional maladjustments—which in turn may interfere with effective intellectual functioning—are a frequent result of culture conflict, as seen in the case of the children of immigrants. Minority group membership tends also to be associated with low socioeconomic status and inferior education. Attempts to compare "equated groups" from different races are handicapped chiefly by failure to rule out all important cultural differences and by the regression effect which operates when matched samples are selected from dissimilar populations.

Bilingualism as it occurs among children of immigrant groups frequently serves to reduce the child's proficiency in both languages and seriously interferes with test performance. Under certain conditions, however, children may learn a second language without handicap. In so-called culture-free tests, an attempt is made to utilize content common to all cultures. Nevertheless, such tests still tend to favor certain cultures in a variety of ways.

Groups differ in specific ways. They cannot be arranged in a hierarchy with respect to general intelligence or over-all personality adjustment. Each culture tends to select and foster certain abilities and certain ways of behaving. Any test developed within a particular culture reflects such a selection and tends to favor individuals reared in that culture.

Cultural differentials may operate at many levels. At one extreme they may render individual test items "unfair" for certain groups. At the other, they may produce far-reaching organic defects leading to mental deficiency or behavior disorders. Some of the effects of cultural differences are remediable within the individual's lifetime; others call for long-range programs involving more than one generation.

REFERENCES

1. Allport, G. W. *The nature of prejudice.* Cambridge, Mass.: Addison-Wesley, 1954.

2. Anastasi, Anne. The concept of validity in the interpretation of test scores. *Educ. psychol. Measmt.*, 1950, 10, 67–78.
3. Anastasi, Anne. *Psychological testing.* N.Y.: Macmillan, 1954.
4. Anastasi, Anne, and Cordova, F. A. Some effects of bilingualism upon the intelligence test performance of Puerto Rican children in New York City. *J. educ. Psychol.*, 1953, 44, 1–19.
5. Arsenian, S. Bilingualism and mental development. *Teach. Coll. Contr. Educ.*, 1937, No. 712.
6. Arsenian, S. Bilingualism in the post-war world. *Psychol. Bull.*, 1945, 42, 65–86.
7. Barke, Ethel M., and Williams, D. E. P. A further study of the comparative intelligence in certain bilingual and monoglot schools in South Wales. *Brit. J. educ. Psychol.*, 1938, 8, 63–77.
8. Bean, K. L. Negro responses to verbal and non-verbal test material. *J. Psychol.*, 1942, 13, 343–353.
9. Benedict, Ruth. *Race: science and politics.* N.Y.: Modern Age, 1940.
10. Bere, M. A. Comparative study of mental capacity of children of foreign parentage. *Teach. Coll. Contr. Educ.*, 1924, No. 154.
11. Boas, F. *Abstract of the report on changes in bodily form of descendants of immigrants.* Washington, D.C.: Govt. Printing Office, 1911.
12. Boas, F. *Race, language, and culture.* N.Y.: Macmillan, 1940.
13. Boger, J. H. An experimental study of the effects of perceptual training on group IQ test scores. *J. educ. Res.*, 1952, 46, 43–52.
14. Brown, F. A comparative study of the influence of race and locale upon emotional stability of children. *J. genet. Psychol.*, 1936, 49, 325–342.
15. Brown, F. A comparative study of the intelligence of Jewish and Scandinavian kindergarten children. *J. genet. Psychol.*, 1944, 64, 67–92.
16. Brown, F. An experimental and critical study of the intelligence of Negro and white kindergarten children. *J. genet. Psychol.*, 1944, 65, 161–175.
17. Brown, F. J., and Roucek, J. S. (Eds.) *One America: the historical contributions and present problems of our racial and national minorities.* N.Y.: Prentice-Hall, 1952.
18. Bruce, Myrtle. Factors affecting intelligence test performance of whites and Negroes. *Arch. Psychol.*, 1940, No. 252.
19. Buchanan, W., and Cantril, H. *How nations see each other; a study in public opinion.* Urbana, Ill.: Univer. Illinois Press, 1953.
20. Canady, H. G. The effect of "rapport" on the IQ: a new approach to the problem of racial psychology. *J. Negro Educ.*, 1936, 5, 209–219.
21. Canady, H. G. The intelligence of Negro college students and parental occupation. *Amer. J. Sociol.*, 1936, 42, 388–389.
22. Chamberlain, H. S. *Die Grundlagen des neunzehnten Jahrhunderts.* München: Bruckman, 1901.
23. Clarke, D. P. Stanford-Binet Scale L response patterns in matched racial groups. *J. Negro Educ.*, 1941, 10, 230–238.
24. Coon, C. S., Garn, S. M., and Birdsell, J. B. *Races; a study of race formation in man.* Springfield, Ill.: Thomas, 1950.
25. Darcy, Natalie T. The effect of bilingualism upon the measurement of the intelligence of children of preschool age. *J. educ. Psychol.*, 1946, 37, 21–44.

26. Darcy, Natalie T. A review of the literature on the effects of bilingualism upon the measurement of intelligence. *J. genet. Psychol.*, 1953, 82, 21–57.

27. Darsie, M. L. Mental capacity of American-born Japanese children. *Comp. Psychol. Monogr.*, 1926, 15, No. 3.

28. David, P. R., and Snyder, L. H. Genetic variability and human behavior. In J. H. Rohrer and M. Sherif (Eds.), *Social psychology at the crossroads*. N.Y.: Harper, 1951, Pp. 53–82.

29. Davidson, K. S., *et al.* A preliminary study of Negro and white differences on Form I of the Wechsler-Bellevue Scale. *J. consult. Psychol.*, 1950, 14, 489–492.

30. De Gobineau, A. J. *Essai sur l'inégalité des races humaines*. Paris: Firmin-Didot, 1853.

31. Dennis, W. The performance of Hopi children on the Goodenough Draw-a-Man Test. *J. comp. Psychol.*, 1942, 34, 341–348.

32. DeStephens, W. P. Are criminals morons? *J. soc. Psychol.*, 1953, 38, 187–199.

33. Dobzhansky, T. The genetic nature of differences among men. In S. Persons (Ed.), *Evolutionary thought in America*. New Haven, Conn.: Yale Univer. Press, 1950, Pp. 86–155.

34. Dobzhansky, T. Human diversity and adaptation. *Cold Spring Harbor Symposia on Quantitative Biology*, 1951, 15, 385–400.

35. Dobzhansky, T. Human races in the light of genetics. *Int. soc. Sci. Bull. (UNESCO)*, 1951, 3, 660–663.

36. Dobzhansky, T. Mendelian populations and their evolution. In L. C. Dunn (Ed.), *Genetics in the twentieth century*. N.Y.: Macmillan, 1951. Pp. 573–589.

37. Dollard, J. *Caste and class in a southern town*. (2nd Ed.) N.Y.: Harper, 1949.

38. DuBois, P. H. A test standardized on Pueblo Indian children. *Psychol. Bull.*, 1939, 36, 523.

39. Eagleson, O. W. A racial comparison of personality traits. *J. appl. Psychol.*, 1938, 22, 271–274.

40. Eagleson, O. W. Comparative studies of white and Negro subjects in learning to discriminate visual magnitude. *J. Psychol.*, 1937, 4, 167–197.

41. Ewing, J. F. Hyperbrachycephaly as influenced by cultural conditioning. *Pap. Peabody Mus.*, 1950, 23 (2).

42. Franklin, J. C. Discriminative value and patterns of the Wechsler-Bellevue Scales in the examination of delinquent Negro boys. *Educ. psychol. Measmt.*, 1945, 5, 71–85.

43. Franzblau, Rose N. Race differences in mental and physical traits studied in different environments. *Arch. Psychol.*, 1935, No. 177.

44. Fulk, B. E., and Harrell, T. W. Negro-white Army test scores and last school grade. *J. appl. Psychol.*, 1952, 36, 34–35.

45. Garth, T. R. A comparison of the intelligence of Mexican and mixed and full blood Indian children. *Psychol. Rev.*, 1923, 30, 388–401.

46. Garth, T. R., and Smith, O. D. The performance of full-blood Indians on language and non-language intelligence tests. *J. abnorm. soc. Psychol.*, 1937, 32, 376–381.

47. Glueck, Eleanor T. Culture conflict and delinquency. *Ment. Hyg.*, 1937, 21, 46–66.
48. Glueck, S., and Glueck, Eleanor T. *One thousand juvenile delinquents.* Cambridge, Mass.: Harvard Univer. Press, 1934.
49. Goodenough, Florence L. Racial differences in intelligence of school children. *J. exp. Psychol.*, 1926, 9, 388–397.
50. Goodman, Mary E. *Race awareness in young children.* Cambridge, Mass: Addison-Wesley, 1952.
51. Hammer, E. F. Comparison of the performances of Negro children and adolescents on two tests of intelligence, one an emergency scale. *J. genet. Psychol.*, 1954, 84, 85–93.
52. Havighurst, R. J., Gunther, Minna K., and Pratt, Inez E. Environment and the Draw-a-Man Test: the performance of Indian children. *J. abnorm. soc. Psychol.*, 1946, 41, 50–63.
53. Havighurst, R. J., and Hilkevitch, Rhea R. The intelligence of Indian children as measured by a performance scale. *J. abnorm. soc. Psychol.*, 1944, 39, 419–433.
54. Hayakawa, S. I. The semantics of being Negro. *Etc. Rev. gen. Semant.*, 1953, 10, 163–175.
55. Hebb, D. O. *The organization of behavior.* N.Y.: Wiley, 1949.
56. Held, O. C. A comparative study of the performance of Jewish and gentile college students on the American Council Psychological Examination. *J. soc. Psychol.*, 1941, 13, 407–411.
57. Hsü, E. H. The neurotic score as a function of culture. *J. soc. Psychol.*, 1951, 34, 3–30.
58. Hunt, W. A. Negro-white differences in intelligence in World War II—a note of caution. *J. abnorm. soc. Psychol.*, 1947, 42, 254–255.
59. Jamieson, E., and Sandiford, P. The mental capacity of Southern Ontario Indians. *J. educ. Psychol.*, 1928, 19, 536–551.
60. Johnson, G. B., Jr. Bilingualism as measured by a reaction-time technique and the relationship between a language and a non-language intelligence quotient. *J. genet. Psychol.*, 1953, 82, 3–9.
61. Klineberg, O. An experimental study of speed and other factors in "racial" differences. *Arch. Psychol.*, 1928, No. 93.
62. Klineberg, O. *Race differences.* N.Y.: Harper, 1935.
63. Kroeber, A. L. *Anthropology.* (2nd Ed.) N.Y.: Harcourt, Brace, 1948.
64. Lambert, W. E. Measurement of the linguistic dominance of bilinguals. *J. abnorm. soc. Psychol.*, 1955, 50, 197–200.
65. Landis, C., and Bolles, M. Marjorie. *Textbook of abnormal psychology.* (2nd Ed.) N.Y.: Macmillan, 1950.
66. Lehman, H. C., and Witty, P. A. The Negro child's index of more social participation. *J. appl. Psychol.*, 1926, 10, 462–469.
67. Machover, S. Cultural and racial variations in patterns of intellect. *Teach. Coll. Contr. Educ.*, 1943, No. 875.
68. Mathews, Ellen. A study of emotional instability in children. *J. Delinqu.*, 1923, 8, 1–40.
69. McConkey, W. G. An experiment in bilingual education. *J. soc. Res., Pretoria*, 1951, 2, 29–42.

70. McGurk, F. C. J. *Comparison of the performance of Negro and white high school seniors on cultural and non-cultural psychological test questions.* Washington, D.C.: Catholic Univer. Press, 1951. (microcard)

71. McGurk, F. C. J. On white and Negro test performance and socioeconomic factors. *J. abnorm. soc. Psychol.,* 1953, 48, 448–450.

72. Merton, R. K. The self-fulfilling prophecy. *Antioch Rev.,* 1948, 8, 193–210.

73. Newland, T. E., and Lawrence, W. C. Chicago Non-Verbal Examination results on an East Tennessee Negro population. *J. clin. Psychol.,* 1953, 9, 44–46.

74. Newman, W. L. (Ed.) *The politics of Aristotle.* Oxford: Clarendon Press, 1887, Vol. I.

75. Pasamanick, B., and Knobloch, Hilda. Early language behavior in Negro children and the testing of intelligence. *J. abnorm. soc. Psychol.,* 1955, 50, 401–402.

76. Pasamanick, B., Knobloch, Hilda, and Lilienfeld, A. M. Socioeconomic status and some precursors of neuropsychiatric disorder. *Amer. J. Orthopsychiat.,* 1956, 26, 594–601.

77. Peterson, J., and Lanier, L. H. Studies in the comparative abilities of whites and Negroes. *Ment. Measmt. Monogr.,* 1929, No. 5.

78. Pintner, R., and Arsenian, S. The relation of bilingualism to verbal intelligence and to school adjustment. *J. educ. Res.,* 1937, 31, 255–263.

79. Porteus, S. D. *The psychology of a primitive people.* N.Y.: Longmans, Green, 1931.

80. Porteus, S. D. Racial group differences in mentality. *Tabul. biol., Haag,* 1939, 18, 66–75.

81. Roberts, B. H., and Myers, J. K. Religion, national origin, immigration, and mental illness. *Amer. J. Psychiat.,* 1954, 110, 759–764.

82. Robinson, Mary L., and Meenes, M. The relationship between test intelligence of third grade Negro children and the occupations of their parents. *J. Negro Educ.,* 1947, 16, 136–141.

83. Russell, R. W. The spontaneous and instructed drawings of Zuñi children. *J. comp. Psychol.,* 1943, 35, 11–15.

84. Sandiford, P., and Kerr, Ruby. Intelligence of Chinese and Japanese children. *J. educ. Psychol.,* 1926, 17, 361–367.

85. Seward, Georgene. *Psychotherapy and culture conflict.* N.Y.: Ronald, 1956.

86. Smith, Madorah E. Measurement of vocabularies of young bilingual children in both of the languages used. *J. genet. Psychol.,* 1949, 74, 305–310.

87. Smith, Madorah E. Word variety as a measure of bilingualism in preschool children. *J. genet. Psychol.,* 1957, 90, 143–150.

88. Spoerl, Dorothy T. Bilinguality and emotional adjustment. *J. abnorm. soc. Psychol.,* 1943, 38, 37–57.

89. Stark, W. A. The effect of bilingualism on general intelligence: an investigation carried out in certain Dublin primary schools. *Brit. J. educ. Psychol.,* 1940, 10, 78–79.

90. Straus, M. A. Mental ability and cultural needs: a psychocultural interpretation of the intelligence test performance of Ceylon University entrants. *Amer. sociol. Rev.,* 1951, 16, 371–375.

91. Straus, M. A. Subcultural variation in Ceylonese mental ability: a study in national character. *J. soc. Psychol.*, 1954, 39, 129–141.
92. Tanser, H. A. *The settlement of Negroes in Kent County, Ontario.* Chatham, Ontario: H. A. Tanser, 1939.
93. Thompson, Laura. *Culture in crisis: a study of the Hopi Indians.* N.Y.: Harper, 1950.
94. Warner, W. L., and Srole, L. *The social systems of American ethnic groups.* New Haven, Conn.: Yale Univer. Press, 1945.
95. Wickersham, G. W., *et al. Report on crime and the foreign born.* (U.S. Nat. Comm. on Law Observ. and Enforc., Rep. No. 10.) Washington, D.C.: Govt. Printing Office, 1933.
96. Yerkes, R. M. (Ed.) Psychological examining in the United States Army. *Mem. nat. Acad. Sci.*, 1921, 15.

CHAPTER 17

Race Differences:
Major Results

There is an ambiguity in the term "race differences" which has added to the confusion and controversy in discussions of race. To find that racial groups differ in behavior may be regarded as demonstrating the existence of "race differences" but not necessarily differences *resulting* from race. The latter imply hereditary etiology traceable to genes that are more frequent in one racial group than in another. The vast majority of investigations on race differences provide only descriptive data, with no evidence regarding the causes of the observed group differences. Whether we examine the comparative achievements of different races as revealed by historical and anthropological records, or whether we consider psychological test results, the influence of the many environmental differences discussed in the preceding chapter cannot be ignored. It is only when special experimental designs have been employed that some progress could be made toward tracing causal factors. Such designs will be illustrated in the present chapter with research on hybrid groups, infants and preschool children, regional differences and migration, cross-comparisons of cultural and biological groups, and culture and personality.

DESCRIPTIVE SURVEYS OF RACE DIFFERENCES

The wide differences in the contributions of different races to science, literature, art, and other cultural developments have sometimes been cited as evidence of hereditary psychological differences between races (cf., e.g., 30). It is thus argued that differences in cultural level among races might be a result rather than a cause of behavioral differences. According to such

576

a view, individuals of a given race may be handicapped by poor facilities for intellectual development just because their predecessors lacked the capacity or energy to produce a more "favorable" environment.

There are several lines of evidence, however, which tend to negate such an interpretation. First, achievement and cultural level are frequently found to vary not with race but with environmental factors. Thus a group that is characterized by a given achievement level may be racially very hetero-geneous and may constitute a unit only in terms of a common experiential background. Secondly, the relative achievements of a given group are influ-enced by a number of factors which cannot themselves be attributed to racial capacity without stretching the point unduly. The characteristics of the physical environment, the degree of contact with other groups, the discovery of new routes of travel and communication, and historical events within *other* groups—and thus not within the control of the group under consideration—have played an important part in the cultural development of many societies. Thirdly, the relative cultural status of racial groups changes with time. Civilizations rise and fall, often in the absence of any known change in racial composition.

In connection with the comparative achievements of different races, mention should also be made of the theory that "primitive" man excels in sensory capacities, in contrast to "civilized" man's "superior intellectual equipment." This theory has been especially proposed as an explanation of the remarkable feats of primitive persons in such tasks as the recognition of birds or animals concealed among foliage, the interpretation of footprints, the use of olfactory cues in finding one's way or in identifying animals, and the like. Considerable evidence has been accumulated, however, to show that such achievements are not attributable to superior sensory equipment. Rather do they result from the individual's having *learned* to respond to very slight cues and to discriminate small differences. The situation is roughly similar to that underlying the blind person's skill in responding to auditory and tactual cues. The needs of life in a primitive environment are such as to encourage the learning of appropriate responses to slight sensory cues which may spell danger, food, or other urgent matters. That such achievements result from learning rather than from race differences in acuity is suggested by the fact that persons from "civilized" countries have proved able to learn similar responses when put in situations that demanded them.

Objective tests of sensory acuity have likewise lent no support to the view that primitive man's achievements result from sensory superiority. As early as 1904, at the St. Louis World's Fair, Woodworth (97) and Bruner (13) applied what few tests were then available to such groups as American Indians, Negritos from the Philippine Islands, Malayan Filipinos, Ainus from Japan, Africans, Eskimos, Patagonians, and others. White visitors to the exposition were similarly tested. On such controlled tests of sensory acuity, the primitive groups did no better than the white norms. Subsequent investigations on many different groups have corroborated these findings.

A similar explanation in terms of learning rather than sensory differences seems to hold for alleged racial differences in musical achievements. The esthetic intricacies of certain American Indian dances have led many observers to ascribe a superior musical sensitivity to that race. Even more familiar is the traditional musical talent of the American Negro, whose achievements in this respect have become an important element of American music. That cultural rather than racial factors account for these accomplishments is suggested by extensive surveys with the Seashore Measures of Musical Talents. In the discrimination of pitch, intensity, time, and rhythm, as well as in the other simple tests in this well-known series, no significant superiority in favor of Indians or Negroes has been found (7, 31).

Many surveys of different racial groups have been conducted with tests of "general intelligence," special aptitudes, and personality traits. The large majority indicate no more than the relative performance of various groups on specific tests constructed within a particular culture. In view of the many problems encountered in cross-cultural testing and the multiplicity of levels at which cultural differentials may affect test scores (cf. Ch. 16), there is little to be gained from a mere summary of the findings of such investigations. Moreover, the literature on this topic is too extensive to cover within the scope of the present book. Major portions of this literature have been reported by Garth (31), Klineberg (51, 53, 54), and Mann (65). Special surveys of psychological studies on the American Negro have also been prepared (14, 55). The present chapter will be concerned with only a few types of studies, chosen because they illustrate promising experimental designs or because they represent current research trends.

PSYCHOLOGICAL STUDIES OF RACE MIXTURE

Investigations on the psychological effects of race mixture are complicated by the fact that such mixtures are often selective. Thus hybrids may come predominantly from certain socioeconomic or educational levels within one or both racial groups. Such selective factors are particularly evident in cultures where race mixture is opposed by laws, customs, or social attitudes. Another difficulty in the way of interpretation arises from the possible correlation between race mixture and cultural assimilation. The hybrid is likely to have had more contact with the dominant culture and tends to be accepted more readily into that culture. On the other hand, in the case of certain groups such as the American Negro, an individual with any discernible amount of Negro ancestry is classified socially as a Negro, even though biologically he may be much closer to the white than to the Negro race.

One claim sometimes made regarding race mixture is that hybrids tend to be inferior to either parent stock and that race mixture in itself is detrimental. Such an assertion is contrary to the findings of both biology and psychology (10, 23, 84, 86). Cross-breeding experiments with animals, for example, have generally provided evidence for what biologists call hybrid vigor, or "heterosis." Far from being inferior, hybrids tend to manifest greater biological strength. Both historical and anthropological studies of human populations likewise lend no support to the belief that race mixture leads to deterioration. On the contrary, there is evidence that the rise of great civilizations has often been preceded by a mingling of two or more racial stocks. Such a finding may, however, reflect the expansion of cultural contacts rather than the operation of biological factors.

According to another, relatively common view of race mixture, hybrid groups should fall between the parent stocks in mental level. It is argued that, if one race is genetically superior to the other, the mixed offspring of both races will be intermediate in intelligence. Furthermore, the greater the proportion of the superior race in his ancestry, the higher should be the individual's intelligence. It should be noted that this hypothesis implies complete linkage, with no crossing over, between those genes determining skin color or other racial criteria and those determining "intelligence." With incomplete linkage, any correlation between racial characteristics and intelligence would disappear within a few generations of cross-breeding.

Most of the studies on the relation between race mixture and intelligence test performance have been conducted either on American Indians or American Negroes. The earlier studies on American Indians seemed to support the above hypothesis, since correlations in the .40's were found between amount of white admixture, as determined by ancestry records, and scores on verbal group intelligence tests (32, 42). However, the subjects of these studies were drawn from a large number of different Indian tribes, varying in both amount of white mixture and, concomitantly, in their familiarity with English and in their general assimilation of the white culture. That the tribal differences in cultural assimilation, rather than the race mixture, accounted for the correlation was later demonstrated by two types of findings. First, the correlation is highest on verbal and information tests, and disappears when nonverbal and performance tests are employed (89). Secondly, the correlation drops to zero on *both* verbal and nonverbal tests when comparisons are made within a single tribe which is relatively homogeneous in its degree of assimilation of the white culture (48, 80).

Similarly, no relation between degree of white ancestry and intelligence test performance is found among American Negroes, when precise measures and reliable indicators of race mixture are employed. Such results have been reported for both school children and college students (41, 48, 76). Further corroboration is provided by a survey of a group of gifted Negro children, with Stanford-Binet IQ's ranging from 125 to 200 (96). The children were classified into four categories of race mixture on the basis of genealogical data secured from the parents. In Table 29 will be found the percentage of children falling into each of these categories for the entire group of 63 cases, as well as for a subgroup of 28 with IQ's of 140 or higher. For comparative

Table 29

PROPORTION OF WHITE ANCESTRY AMONG NEGRO SCHOOL CHILDREN WITH IQ'S OF 125 OR HIGHER

(Adapted from Witty and Jenkins, 96, pp. 189–190)

DEGREE OF WHITE MIXTURE	PERCENTAGE IN GENERAL NEGRO POPULATION	PERCENTAGE AMONG GIFTED NEGRO CHILDREN	
		IQ 125 or Higher (N = 63)	IQ 140 or Higher (N = 28)
No white ancestry *	28.3	22.2	21.4
More Negro than white	31.7	46.1	42.8
About equal	25.2	15.9	21.4
More white than Negro	14.8	15.9	14.3

* Less than one-sixteenth of mother's and of father's ancestry reported to be white.

purposes, the corresponding percentages for the general Negro population are also given. It will be seen that there is no consistent tendency for the proportion of white ancestry to be greater in the gifted groups than in the general Negro population. It is also interesting to note that the highest IQ in the group, 200, was obtained by a Negro girl whose ancestry showed no evidence of white mixture (90, 96).

GROUP COMPARISONS AT INFANT AND PRESCHOOL LEVEL

In Chapter 15 it was noted that among relatively isolated and culturally restricted groups, such as canal-boat, gypsy, and mountain children, intelligence test performance tends to decline with age relative to the test norms. A similar but less pronounced decrement has been found in most rural communities. It will be recalled that one hypothesis for such age decline was based upon the changing nature of intelligence tests with age. The Stanford-Binet, for example, becomes increasingly verbal at the upper age levels. Age decrements have also been observed, however, when exclusively verbal tests were employed at different ages, or when a single highly homogeneous test like the Goodenough Draw-a-Man Test was administered over a wide age range. In such cases, the age decrement is probably attributable to the cumulative effects of poor environment.

Although such age differentials have not been investigated as extensively among racial groups as among rural and culturally isolated communities, some data are available which suggest that at the infant and preschool level racial differences may be highly reduced or may disappear altogether. In a study of 53 Negro infants in New Haven, Pasamanick and Knobloch (58, 74) found no significant inferiority to the white norms on the Yale Developmental Examination. The initial examination was conducted at a mean age of 26 weeks. Follow-up of 40 cases at an average age of approximately two years again revealed no retardation. Mean quotients at this age on different parts of the examination ranged from 101 in language development to 124 in gross motor development.

A more detailed analysis of language performance, already cited in Chapter 16, indicated that the children were significantly better on items requiring verbal comprehension than on those calling for oral responsiveness (58, 75). Among the factors to be considered in explanation of this finding are the influence of a white examiner, social pressures tending to inhibit verbalization in Negro children, and possibly a dawning awareness of racial stereotypes. In gross motor development, the Negro children were accelerated with reference to white norms, and their performance was significantly better than in the language area. The investigators hypothesized that such acceleration results from the greater "permissiveness" of the lower-class homes in which the large majority of the Negro children were being reared. Corroborative data for this explanation were provided in a study of Negro children in Washington, D.C., by Williams and Scott (95), in which lower-class children scored significantly higher than middle-class children in the motor area. Interviews with parents likewise revealed greater permissiveness of infant-rearing practices in the lower-class Negro homes. When the homes were classified with respect to the latter variable, children in the more permissive homes scored significantly higher than those in the more rigid homes.

Comparisons of Negro and white infants in the Chicago area by Gilliland (34) supported the general findings of Pasamanick and Knobloch. In this study, 113 Negro infants were compared with 533 white infants on the Northwestern Infant Intelligence Tests and the Cattell Infant Intelligence Scale. All were under the age of 26 weeks. In none of the comparisons was there a significant difference between Negro and white means. The Cattell Scale was developed as a downward extension of the Stanford-Binet. The Northwestern Tests, designed specially for the ages of 4 to 36 weeks, emphasize adaptation to environment rather than physical growth and sensori-motor development. Although revealing no significant difference between Negro and white infants, it is noteworthy that the Northwestern Tests do discriminate effectively at the early age levels, as indicated by wide individual differences and by a significant inferiority in the performance of orphanage children as compared to children reared in their own homes.

The results of Gilliland, as well as those of Pasamanick and Knobloch, are in sharp contrast to those of an earlier study by McGraw (67), published in 1931. Working with Negro and white infants in Florida, McGraw found that the whites excelled significantly on the Bühler Babytests. These tests cover a wide variety of functions but place somewhat more emphasis upon social behavior and problem solving than is the case in most other infant scales. In explanation of McGraw's discrepant findings, Pasamanick and Knobloch (58, 74) point out that the white infants tested by McGraw were also taller and heavier than the Negro infants. Such a difference in physical development may have resulted from inequalities in prenatal and postnatal care and nutrition. Differences in maternal diet are particularly important in this connection, as was demonstrated by the investigation of Harrell *et al.* cited in Chapter 5. In the New Haven group examined by Pasamanick and Knobloch, the heights and weights of the Negro infants exceeded those found by McGraw and approached the white norms. Owing to economic and social reasons, the diet of Florida Negroes in the late 1920's was undoubtedly inferior to that of New Haven Negroes in the early 1940's. Such a nutritional difference may account for both the physical and behavioral retardation of the former group. Another possible contributing factor in the McGraw study may be found in the relatively large number of items involving social interaction with a white examiner.

Tests of Negro preschool children have likewise revealed no significant inferiority to white norms. In a group of 91 Negro kindergarten children in Minneapolis, Brown (12) found a mean Stanford-Binet IQ of 100.78. The same author points out, however, that by the sixth and seventh grade, Negro children in Minneapolis public schools usually declined to the IQ level reported by other investigators. It might be added that a group of 341 white kindergarten children tested by Brown in the same study obtained a mean Stanford-Binet IQ of 107.06, which was significantly higher than that of the Negro children. However, the two groups differed extensively in fathers' occupational level, the whites representing a random sample of the general population in this respect, while the Negroes came largely from the skilled and unskilled labor classes. When the Negro children were compared with white children in the corresponding occupational levels, no significant difference in mean IQ remained.

In a study conducted in New York City by Anastasi and D'Angelo (3), measures of language development and Goodenough Draw-a-Man IQ were obtained on 100 5-year-old Negro and white children attending Department of Welfare Day Care Centers. The subjects included 25 Negroes and 25 whites living in segregated neighborhoods and 25 Negroes and 25 whites living in interracial neighborhoods. Sex ratio was approximately the same in each subgroup. Socioeconomic and other background factors were relatively uniform in all groups. No significant race difference was found in Draw-a-Man IQ. Analysis of spontaneous speech samples, in terms of both sentence length and maturity of sentence structure, revealed a number of significant differences favoring whites in segregated neighborhoods, but only one significant difference in the same direction in interracial neighborhoods. In the interpretation of relative findings with the Draw-a-Man test and the spontaneous speech samples, it should again be borne in mind that all measures were obtained by a white examiner.

Mention may also be made of a study of New York City Puerto Rican children, many of whom represent Negro-white mixtures of varying degrees (4). The subjects included 25 Puerto Rican boys and 25 Puerto Rican girls attending day nurseries. Goodenough Draw-a-Man IQ and measures of language development were again obtained for each child. All testing was done by a Spanish-speaking Puerto Rican examiner, although the subjects' speech was recorded in Spanish or English, as given by the child. Approximately 93 per cent of all sentences recorded for the group were spoken entirely in Spanish, 6 per cent employed a mixture of Spanish and English, and 1 per cent were entirely English. On the Goodenough test, the mean IQ of the group was 95.70, a value that did not differ significantly from either the Negro or white means found by Anastasi and D'Angelo. Emotional resistance to the drawing task was encountered in a number of the Puerto Rican children, a fact which may account for their slightly inferior performance. In many of the language measures, however, the Puerto Rican group significantly exceeded the white norms for their age. The greater extent of adult contact in the family environment of these Puerto Rican children is cited as a possible explanatory factor. It should be added that, as in the case of other underprivileged minority groups, the test performance of older Puerto Rican school children tested in the same New York City area from which the preschool sample was drawn fell considerably below test norms (2).

REGIONAL DIFFERENCES AND MIGRATION

That test performance varies among states or other major regions has already been discused in Chapter 15. Such differences have been found among both whites and Negroes. Reference may also be made to a study by Klineberg (48), cited in Chapter 16, in which the performance test scores of New York City Negro boys excelled those of West Virginia rural Negro boys; and Indian boys living at a government school surpassed the group tested on an Indian reservation. Such intraracial differences—between groups reared in diverse cultural settings—often exceed interracial differences within the same area.

One of the findings of the army testing during World War I was that the median Alpha scores of Negroes from Illinois, New York, Ohio, and Pennsylvania were higher than the median Alpha scores of whites from Arkansas, Georgia, Kentucky, and Mississippi. The relative standing of these groups follows from the fact that there were large regional differences among both Negroes and whites. The data provide a vivid illustration of the extent of overlapping between the white and Negro distributions. Not only could many individuals be found in the lower (Negro) distribution who excelled individuals in the higher (white) distribution, but also local groups could be found in the lower-scoring population which excelled other local groups in the higher-scoring population.

Of special interest in studies on the American Negro are comparisons between northern and southern Negroes. Differences between such groups undoubtedly result partly from the same socioeconomic and educational differences that account for differences between whites from northern and southern states. But they probably also reflect, to a certain extent, differences in the relative social position of the Negro in the North and the South. The superior test performance of northern Negroes has been repeatedly demonstrated with varied samples, including draftees in both World Wars (18, 98), college students (78), and school children (76). Such regional differences persist when comparisons are made between groups matched in occupational level.

In explanation of regional differences in intelligence test performance, two contrasting hypotheses have been proposed: one in terms of *environmental handicap,* the other in terms of *selective migration.* The former attributes the regional differences to inequalities in home conditions, educational facilities, and other opportunities for advancement. The latter proposes that the more intelligent and progressive individuals, who have more initiative and are better able to adjust to new surroundings, are more likely to migrate to the more desirable areas. The one hypothesis maintains that superior ability is a *result* of migration to a more favored area, the other that the migrating individuals were superior to begin with. Although the selective migration hypothesis is commonly coupled with a hereditary interpretation of regional differences in ability, it should be noted that this does not necessarily follow. Thus it is likely that persons of superior educational and socioeconomic level are more often aware of the opportunities offered by migration to a better area. This would be true regardless of whether hereditary or environmental factors were initially responsible for the higher educational and socioeconomic status of such individuals. These persons may in turn have more intelligent offspring, not necessarily because of better "genetic stock," but because they provide their children with a more stimulating home environment. Logically, therefore, the selective migration hypothesis is equally consistent with a predominantly hereditary or a predominantly environmental determination of individual differences. If, on the other hand, regional differences can be shown to have developed *after* migration, then they can be explained only in environmental terms.

A number of investigations have been specifically designed to test the selective migration hypothesis with reference to northern and southern Negroes. In one survey on several thousand Negro school children in Washington, D.C., Long (63) found significant differences in mean IQ in favor of Washington-born children. In other words, the children who had migrated to Washington—in most cases from inferior southern communities— were not as intelligent as those born and reared in Washington. In a more intensive study of a random sample of the migrant children, a significant positive correlation was found between length of residence in Washington and IQ.

A series of studies conducted under the direction of Klineberg (50) approached the problem of selective migration in two ways. First, the school records of 562 Negro children who had transferred from southern to northern schools were examined. The grades obtained by these children in the southern schools, prior to migration, showed the group to be a typical cross-section of their school population. Mean grades did not differ significantly between migrants and nonmigrants. Hence the migrating group was not initially superior to those who had remained in the southern schools.

A second approach followed in the same series of investigations involved the comparison of intelligence test scores obtained by groups of Negro school children who had lived in New York City for different periods of time. Over 3000 10- to 12-year-old Negro children in the Harlem district of New York City were examined with a variety of individual and group tests. The subjects in the different residence groups were equated for age and sex; they attended the same schools and were approximately equal in socioeconomic background, the only important difference between them being the number of years spent in New York City. A group of Negro school children born in New York City was also included for comparison. Special checks were employed to demonstrate that the differences between the vari-

Table 30

RELATION BETWEEN LENGTH OF RESIDENCE IN NEW YORK CITY AND INTELLIGENCE TEST SCORES OF NEGRO SCHOOL CHILDREN

(Adapted from Klineberg, 50)

NATIONAL INTELLIGENCE TEST			STANFORD-BINET		
Years of Residence	Number of Cases	Mean Score	Years of Residence	Number of Cases	Mean IQ
1–2	150	72	Less than 1	42	81.4
3–4	125	76	1–2	40	84.2
5–6	136	84	2–3	40	84.5
7–8	112	90	3–4	46	85.5*
Over 8	157	94	Over 4	47	87.4
Northern-born	1017	92	New York-born	99	87.3

MINNESOTA PAPER FORM BOARD			PINTNER-PATERSON		
Years of Residence	Number of Cases	Median Score	Years of Residence	Number of Cases	Mean Point Score
1–2	27	39.00	Less than 2	20	142.5
3–4	25	26.67	2–5	20	139.8
5–6	30	31.88	Over 5	20	152.1
7–8	23	37.50			
9–10	25	37.50	Northern-born	50	164.5
Over 10	41	37.50			
New York-born	223	41.61			

* This figure is misprinted as 88.5 in the Klineberg monograph (50, p. 46).

ous residence groups could not be attributed to differences in the proportion of white mixture, nor to a progressive decline in the quality of migrants coming to New York in successive years.

In Table 30 will be found the mean scores of each residence group on the National Intelligence Test, the Stanford-Binet, the Minnesota Paper Form Board, and an abbreviated form of the Pintner-Paterson Performance Scale. On the three "intelligence tests," there is a tendency for mean scores to rise with increasing length of New York City residence. The gains are large on the National Intelligence Test, a predominantly verbal, group test which would be most likely to reflect differences in schooling. The Pintner-Paterson shows large differences when extreme residence groups are compared, probably because of its dependence upon speed of performance. Differences are small on the Stanford-Binet and they are inconsistent and negligible on the Minnesota Paper Form Board. It should be noted that the individual subgroups among which comparisons are made are often small and the results must therefore be regarded as tentative.

More conclusive evidence of the relationship between intelligence test score and length of time spent in northern schools is provided by a later study by Lee (61). Working with Negro children in Philadelphia, Lee employed larger samples than were used in the various Klineberg studies and analyzed retest scores of the *same children* after varying periods of northern residence. Within a group of Philadelphia-born Negro children, comparisons were also made between those who had and those who had not attended kindergarten. The principal instrument employed was the Philadelphia Tests of Mental and Verbal Ability, a series of group intelligence tests standardized on Philadelphia school children.

In Table 31 will be found the mean IQ's of each group of Negro children on initial tests and subsequent retests. It will be noted, first, that the group which had attended kindergarten averaged consistently higher than the group which entered the first grade with no preschool experience. These differences, significant at the .01 level, appeared in the first grade and remained on all retests. The advantage of the kindergarten group may result from selective factors in kindergarten enrollment, or from the effect of early perceptual and other relevant training in kindergarten, or from a combination of both types of causes. Within each of the Philadelphia-born groups, there is no consistent tendency for scores to rise upon retesting, the successive means exhibiting only chance fluctuations.

This finding contrasts sharply with the results obtained with southern-born Negro children who had migrated to Philadelphia. In each of the latter groups, there is a significant tendency for mean scores to improve with

Table 31

**MEAN IQ'S OF NEGRO CHILDREN ON THE PHILADELPHIA TESTS
OF MENTAL AND VERBAL ABILITY**

(From Lee, 61, p. 231)

GROUP	N	MEAN SCORE AT GRADE INDICATED				
		1A	2B	4B	6B	9A
Philadelphia-born, with kindergarten	212	96.7	95.9	97.2	97.5	96.6
Philadelphia-born, without kindergarten	424	92.1	93.4	94.7	94.0	93.7
Southern-born, entering Philadelphia schools in grade:						
1A	182	86.5	89.3	91.8	93.3	92.8
1B–2B	109		86.7	88.6	90.9	90.5
3A–4B	199			86.3	87.2	89.4
5A–6B	221				88.2	90.2
7A–9A	219					87.4

increasing length of northern residence. Thus the group entering Philadelphia schools in 1A rises from 86.5 upon school entrance to 92.8 in grade 9A; the group transferring to Philadelphia schools in 1B–2B rises from 86.7 to 90.5, and so on for the other southern-born groups. It is also noteworthy that the earlier the children had entered a northern school, the higher their IQ in any one grade. This can be seen by reading down each grade column in Table 31. Corroborative data for all the above findings were also obtained with the tests of Primary Mental Abilities (PMA) and the Minnesota Paper Form Board, which were administered to some or all of the subjects in this study. With the exception of the PMA Memory Test, in which no significant group differences were found, all tests showed rising mean scores with increasing length of northern residence, as well as significant superiority of the group which had attended kindergarten.

CROSS-COMPARISONS OF CULTURAL AND BIOLOGICAL GROUPS

A promising approach to the analysis of group differences in behavior involves cross-comparisons of cultural and biological groups. The basic experimental design calls for the reclassification of the same individuals with reference to more than one criterion, such as nationality, physical type, schooling, or sex. One of the earliest systematic applications of this research design is to be found in a study by Klineberg (49). An abbreviated form of the Pintner-Paterson Performance Scale was administered to 700 10- to 12-year-old school boys in rural areas of France, Germany, and Italy. The samples were taken from regions known to have a predominance of pure Nordics, Alpines, and Mediterraneans, respectively. In addition, only those subjects were selected who met the specifications of their respective racial type with regard to eye color, hair color, and cephalic index.

Table 32

PERFORMANCE TEST SCORES OF EUROPEAN BOYS CLASSIFIED ACCORDING TO NATIONALITY AND PHYSICAL TYPE

(From Klineberg, 49, pp. 27, 30, 31.)

GROUP (N = 100 in each)	PROVINCE	NUMBER OF VILLAGES COVERED	PERFORMANCE SCALE SCORE		
			Mean	Median	Range
German Nordic	Hanover	17	198.2	197.6	69–289
French Mediterranean	Eastern Pyrenees	12	197.4	204.4	71–271
German Alpine	Baden	10	193.6	199.0	80–211
Italian Alpine	Piedmont	10	188.8	186.3	69–306
French Alpine	Auvergne and Velay	19	180.2	185.3	72–296
French Nordic	Flanders	13	178.8	183.3	63–314
Italian Mediterranean	Sicily	9	173.0	172.7	69–308

COMBINED GROUP MEANS			
German	195.9	Nordic	188.5
French	185.7	Alpine	187.5
Italian	180.9	Mediterranean	185.2

Table 32 gives a list of the specific groups examined, their location, and their test performance. When all subjects were classified with respect to nationality, two of the three mean differences in test scores were significant at the .01 level. When they were reclassified into Nordic, Alpine, and Mediterranean, without reference to nationality, none of the mean differences was significant. Whatever differences were found, therefore, were associated with the predominantly cultural category of nationality, rather than with physical type. Examination of specific subgroup performance likewise fails to support the popular stereotype of a Nordic-Alpine-Mediterranean hierarchy. Although the highest mean score is obtained by a Nordic group, the highest median is found in a Mediterranean group. Similarly, the rank-order of the racial groups *within* any one nation is inconsistent. Thus in France the Mediterranean group is best, the Alpine intermediate, and the Nordic poorest; whereas in Germany the Nordic is superior to the Alpine sampling, and in Italy the Alpine is superior to the Mediterranean. The marked *overlapping* of groups, as indicated by the range, should likewise be noted. Also relevant to a cultural interpretation of group differences is the fact that the largest mean differences in this study were found between the rural groups and three urban samples tested in Paris, Hamburg, and Rome. These differences greatly exceeded the national differences cited above.

Certain limitations of this study should be borne in mind. First, the tests employed are restricted in the functions they measure. Moreover, the scores depend to a large extent upon speed, since the tests are relatively easy for subjects within the age range covered. Finally, it should be recognized that the investigator was actually testing the popular concept of race, whereby an individual is classified on the basis of physical characteristics without consideration of his ancestry or of the genetic population to which he belongs. The investigation was thus concerned with the relation between physical type and intelligence test performance, rather than with race differences as such. It will be recalled from the discussion of race in Chapter 16 that French and German Nordics, for example, do not constitute a single racial group in the genetic sense.

Mention should also be made of an investigation of personality traits conducted by Klineberg, Fjeld, and Foley (56) which represents another test of the popular stereotypes associated with Nordics, Alpines, and Mediterraneans. Over 400 male and female students attending eight colleges in the greater New York area were given a series of personality tests including Bernreuter Personality Inventory, Allport-Vernon Study of Values, an honesty test (Maller Test of Sports and Hobbies), and two specially constructed tests designed to measure suggestibility and persistence, respectively. The subjects were classified as Nordic, Alpine, and Mediterranean on the basis of cephalic index, eye color, hair color, and skin color. Although most of the scores yielded statistically significant differences between *colleges*, none of the differences between Nordic, Alpine, and Mediterranean types proved to be significant.[1] Physical type again proved to be unrelated to psychological characteristics.

[1] There were two exceptions, the religious and esthetic scores on the Study of Values yielding significant differences between physical types. These differences, however, seem to result from a marked predominance of a single physical type in certain colleges. The data with regard to these particular comparisons are therefore inconclusive owing to the presence of confounding factors.

In popular thinking, group differences in gestures, postures, and speed and tempo of bodily movement have been closely associated with alleged racial differences in personality. Available evidence, however, fails to support a racial interpretation of gesture patterns (25, 59). An exploratory study into the role of cultural as contrasted to biological factors in gestural behavior was conducted by Efron and Foley (26). The subjects included: (1) "traditional" Italians living in one of the Italian neighborhoods of New York City; (2) "traditional" Jews living in New York's lower East Side; and (3) "assimilated" Italians and Jews living in Americanized environments. Gestural behavior was investigated by direct observation and verbal description, sketches made by an artist, and motion pictures. All three observational techniques were employed with gesticulation occurring in ordinary everyday-life situations, the subjects being unaware of the fact that they were being observed. The motion picture film was further analyzed by projecting it frame by frame upon coordinate paper and plotting the successive positions of motile parts as shown in Figure 85. The numbers in this figure

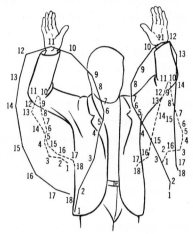

Fig. 85. Graphic Technique Employed in the Analysis of Gestures. (From Efron and Foley, 26, p. 154.)

indicate the direction of movement of right and left wrists and right and left elbows, respectively.

Both the quantitative and qualitative data gathered in this study led to two principal conclusions. First, the gesture patterns of traditional Italians and Jews could be clearly differentiated in terms of such characteristics as part of the body utilized, form of movement, laterality and symmetry, radius, direction, rhythm, and tempo. Jewish gestures tended also to be symbolic, whereas Italian gestures were characteristically pictorial or pantomimic. The second major finding, however, was that traditional gesture patterns were absent in the assimilated groups. Gesticulation as a whole was much less frequent in such assimilated groups, and the gestures that were employed closely resembled in nature those typical of American groups.

Another illustration of the type of experimental design under consideration is provided by Mann's reanalysis of Maze Test scores obtained by Porteus from several groups of South African and Australian aboriginals (65). Mann noted that some of the tribes had had access to either mission or government schools, while others had no schooling facilities. When the tribes were classified first with regard to race (African or Australian) and secondly with regard to schooling (presence or absence of schools), the racial difference in mean score was small and insignificant, while that associated with schooling was significant beyond the .01 level. Performance on this relatively "culture-free" test was thus more closely related to the availability of educational facilities than to racial origin.

From the standpoint of methodology, it should be noted that *analysis of variance* is especially well suited to experimental designs in which the same subjects are reclassified with reference to different criteria. With this statistical technique, it is possible to identify significant effects of each of the separate factors, as well as the interaction between them. The meaning of interaction in this context can be illustrated by considering the previously cited study of Negro and white preschool children conducted by Anastasi and D'Angelo (3). The data on language development revealed a significant interaction between sex and race. This arose from the fact that among whites girls surpassed boys, while among Negroes boys excelled. These findings were consistent with the results of separate studies on both whites (cf. 66) and Negroes (4, 12). It is interesting to note that a similar sex difference in favor of boys has been reported in studies on early language development of Chinese children in Hawaii (85). There is no obvious explanation for such a reversal of sex differences. It may be the result of social pressures which give boys in certain cultures more opportunities or motivation for linguistic development, while girls enjoy the advantage in other cultures. Whatever the reasons, the fact of significant interaction between sex and race in language development suggests a fruitful starting point for further cross-cultural research. It also points to the desirability of making more use of analysis of variance in such cross-cultural investigations than has heretofore been done.

RESEARCH ON CULTURE AND PERSONALITY

The past two decades have witnessed a rapid growth in studies on the relation between culture and personality development. Rather than ranking existing populations in a hierarchy with respect to standards of intelligence or personal adjustment formulated within a single culture, these studies concentrate upon a description of the multi-dimensional differences between groups. This approach also includes a search for cultural factors which may account for the observed group differences in behavior. Major emphasis is placed upon emotional and motivational development, although the indirect effects of such traits upon intellectual functioning and achievement have also received attention. From the standpoint of methodology, this research is characterized by the use of a wide variety of data-gathering procedures, the cooperation of specialists from many fields in joint projects, and increasing attempts to enlist the services of trained personnel within the cultures under investigation.

Procedures for the Study of "National Character." Students of culture and personality have frequently employed the term "national character." It must be borne in mind that this term is used in a cultural rather than a biological sense. Moreover, there is no implication that every individual within a nation conforms to the given description of national character. Rather, national character represents the modal, or most frequent, personality pattern within a culture. Around this mode, individuals and subgroups may exhibit varying degrees of deviation. Regional differences may be considerable within certain cultures (cf., e.g., 29). In fact, the extent of heterogeneity of personality patterns within a culture may itself be regarded as an important aspect of national character. It should also be recognized that national character is subject to change as cultural conditions change.

The many methods which have been employed to study national character may be conveniently grouped under seven headings.[2] One approach is illustrated by the innumerable *descriptive accounts* of individual cultures prepared by anthropologists, psychiatrists, psychoanalysts, journalists, and other writers. These reports vary widely in their objectivity, fullness, and sources of information. Well-known examples include the descriptions of the American culture by Gorer (36) and by Mead (68), as well as Benedict's account of the traditional Japanese culture (8). When a foreign observer describes a culture, it is possible that an analysis of his description may provide some cues regarding his own culture, since the latter would be reflected in his perceptions. On the other hand, common features that recur in the descriptions by observers from different countries are more likely to refer to distinctive characteristics of the culture observed. Such a compilation of the reactions of different observers is illustrated by Commager's book (17) on the American people, which includes excerpts from 35 writers representing 13 nations.

Descriptive accounts of national character are subject to many limitations. They are likely to present an oversimplified view of a national culture, with insufficient attention to regional and other subgroup differences. The data may be unrepresentative both with regard to subjects and with regard

[2] For fuller discussions and critical evaluations of such methods, cf. 27; 43; 52, Ch. 2; 54, Ch. 14; 70.

to aspects of behavior chosen for description. Moreover, interpretations of individual motivation in terms of traditional behavior patterns may prove misleading. Dennis (20), for example, found that, although overt displays of rivalry and competition are traditionally infrequent in the Hopi culture, nevertheless in test situations Hopi children expressed competitive attitudes as often as or oftener than white American children.

A second method consists in the comparative analysis of *vital and social statistics*, such as incidence of crime, psychosis, and psychosomatic disorders. A special application of this procedure is illustrated by Cattell's factorial analysis of 80 demographic, economic, and geographic variables for 69 countries (15). *Content analysis* of cultural products represents a third type of procedure. Such materials as movies, plays, books, and magazines are examined for recurrent and characteristic themes. Some investigators have even used the occurrence in one language of terms not found in other languages as a basis for speculations about national character.

A fourth source of data regarding national character is provided by *community studies*, such as those of Middletown and Yankee City reported in Chapter 15. Studies of this sort have also been conducted in Chinese, Japanese, and Mexican villages (cf. 52, p. 61). It is of course important to consider how representative the particular community may be of the entire culture under investigation. *Public opinion and attitude surveys* have likewise been employed in investigations of national character. Examples are provided by Rodnick's research in Norway (79), Murphy's survey of attitudes and tensions in India (72), and Gillespie and Allport's comparative study of the attitudes of college students in ten countries (33). In any generalizations about national differences from such data, attention must be given to the comparability of samples. College students in America and in Egypt, for example, do not represent comparable samples of the youth of the respective nations, since a much larger proportion of young people attend college in America than in Egypt.

A sixth approach involves the observation of *child-rearing practices* in different cultures, together with an attempt to relate characteristics of adult personality to certain features of these practices. Thus it is maintained that adult behavior reflects the degree to which childhood experiences were characterized by austerity, rigidity, aloofness, informality, emotional warmth, and the like. Psychoanalytic theories are frequently drawn upon in formulating these hypotheses. Reference to this approach was made in Chapter 4, where the research of Whiting and Child (94) on available data from 75 primitive societies was cited. This analysis was followed up by field observations of child-rearing practices in India, Mexico, Okinawa, the

Philippines, and the New England section of the United States (93). Although providing a source of hypotheses for further research, interpretations of national character in terms of child-rearing practices must be regarded as highly tentative (cf. 43, 52, 73).

The last type of method to be considered is of particular interest to psychologists, since it utilizes *intensive studies of individuals* by means of interviews or psychological tests. In this connection, particular use has been made of projective techniques, including Rorschach inkblots, Thematic Apperception Test, Rosenzweig Picture-Frustration, sentence completion, drawings, and various toy tests (cf. 1, 37). Responses of subjects in standardized experimental situations have also been analyzed in such studies. Examples of these procedures will be cited in the following sections.

Cross-Cultural Investigations. Two examples will serve to illustrate current cross-cultural investigations. One of the most comprehensive research programs on national character was initiated during World War II under the auspices of the United States Office of Naval Research and other cooperating organizations. Originally designed to provide knowledge regarding the customs, attitudes, and other psychological characteristics of both allies and enemy nations, this research was followed during the postwar period by similar studies in several European and Asiatic cultures. One phase of this program, the Columbia University Research in Contemporary Cultures (9, 60, 69) included projects on pre-Soviet Russian, contemporary Soviet, Czech, Polish, Eastern European Jewish, French, Syrian, and Chinese cultures. Another, the Coordinated Investigation of Micronesian Anthropology (35, 45, 71) was concerned with intensive studies of the native cultures on several South Pacific archipelagos.

Each project utilized a number of data-gathering techniques, such as interviews and autobiographical reports; intelligence, aptitude, and personality tests; projective techniques; analysis of cultural products; and investigations of child-rearing practices. Observations in foreign countries were often supplemented with studies of immigrant groups in America. Most of the projects involved the joint efforts of anthropologists and psychologists, although the primary emphasis throughout was anthropological.

Another major illustration of cross-cultural research is provided by the work of the Organization for Comparative Social Research (24). This organization was composed of cooperating teams of social scientists in seven European nations, namely, Belgium, England, France, Holland, Norway, Sweden, and Western Germany. The research program included a series of coordinated projects conducted simultaneously in the seven countries. The hypotheses under investigation were concerned principally with the behavior of group members under conditions of threat. Both experimental and survey procedures were utilized.

The experimental situation (81, 82) was presented in the guise of a first meeting of a boys' aviation club. In each group, the subjects had a twenty-minute discussion, which was observed by two investigators. A competition was announced, in which groups building the best model airplanes would receive a reward. Each group could choose among five models, including four attractive, motor-driven planes and a fifth uninteresting, glider model. One member of each group was a "stooge" who always chose the glider, while the other members nearly always chose one of the other models. The reactions of the group members to the deviant, who threatened the achievement of the desired group goal, were investigated by means of two sociometric-type measures.

Survey procedures (6) were employed in another part of the project dealing with the attitudes of teachers in the same seven nations. Samples of 300 primary and 100 secondary school teachers were interviewed in each country. The interviews were especially designed to explore the respondents' perception of threat in the current international situation.

Intensive Studies of Single Cultures. Current research on group differences also includes intensive investigations of personality development within single cultures. From a practical point of view, such studies contribute to the improvement of intergroup relations and bring to light adverse environmental conditions requiring correction. At the same time, this type of research advances psychological knowledge by providing an opportunity to investigate cause-effect relations in behavior development within different cultural settings. Generalizations regarding human behavior which were derived within a single culture may have to be modified or even rejected when tested in a dissimilar culture, as will be illustrated in the following chapter. Any study of behavior development within a culture unlike our own adds to our knowledge of psychological principles, especially when the behavior data can be related to concomitant cultural factors.

An outstanding example of the type of investigation under consideration is to be found in the Indian Personality and Administration Research (38, 39, 40, 46, 57, 62, 64, 91). This was a long-range interdisciplinary project sponsored jointly by the United States Office of Indian Affairs and the University of Chicago Committee on Human Development. Its aim was to study American Indians in terms of both individual personality development and tribal structure, in order to recommend ways of improving the Indian Service and of developing responsible local autonomy. The project covered eleven communities in five Indian tribes, namely, Hopi, Navaho, Papago,

Sioux, and Zuñi. Utilizing the services of specialists in anthropology, psychology, psychiatry, pedagogy, public administration, linguistics, and ecology, the research provided a comprehensive view of life in each community. Field work was concerned largely with an investigation of the personalities of a representative sample of children between the ages of 6 and 18 in the social context of each of the chosen communities. Data were gathered through interviews, participant observation, medical examinations, and a battery of eight psychological tests. In this battery were included the Arthur Performance Scale, Goodenough Draw-a-Man Test, Rorschach, and other personality tests of a projective or guided-interview type.

Research on the American Negro by a variety of techniques has likewise contributed to a better understanding of the role of cultural factors in shaping personality. A series of books published in the early 1940's reported the results of extensive investigations of Negro youth conducted under the auspices of the American Youth Commission of the American Council on Education (5, 19, 28, 44, 77, 88, 92). Although primarily sociological in approach, these studies contained a wealth of psychological material. Data were gathered on several thousand Negro adolescents in many parts of the United States. Community studies, intensive interviews, case studies, and psychological testing were among the methods employed in different parts of the project.

Several more recent investigations have employed such projective techniques as the Rorschach, Thematic Apperception Test, Rosenzweig Picture-Frustration, and drawing tests. The results of these studies have thrown some light on the characteristic anxieties, emotional conflicts, frustrations, aggressions, and apathy induced by the cultural conditions under which American Negroes generally live (cf. 83, pp. 133–137). Further data on the emotional problems of American Negroes at different socioeconomic levels are provided by Kardiner and Ovesey (47). A major part of the latter study consists in detailed case reports of 25 Negro men and women, selected to represent lower, middle, and upper classes. Each case was studied through psychoanalytic interviews, ranging in number from 10 to over 100. The average subject was investigated over a period of four to six months. About half of the subjects were interviewed in the course of psychotherapy, the rest participating in the study as volunteers or for pay.

Mention may also be made of recent research on the Japanese, including samples living in Japan and in America. The attitudes of postwar Japanese youths in various sections of Japan were investigated by Stoetzel (87) through a questionnaire supplemented by a projective picture test and autobiographies. In a later study conducted with the collaboration of

Japanese colleagues, De Vos (22) analyzed responses to three projective techniques administered to nearly 1000 subjects in two cities and three villages in central Japan. Several investigations conducted in America have been specifically concerned with the problems and effects of acculturation in the case of Japanese-Americans (11, 16, 21).

SUMMARY

The large majority of studies on race differences provide only descriptive data, with no information regarding the causes of the observed behavioral differences. The historical contributions of different races to science, literature, art, and other cultural developments can be more readily explained in terms of environmental conditions than in terms of biological differences between populations. Primitive man's skill in responding to slight sensory cues is attributable to learning rather than to sensory superiority. Most investigations reporting race differences on intelligence, special aptitude, or personality tests are difficult to interpret because of the complex operation of cultural differentials. The present chapter covered only certain types of studies on race differences, chosen either to illustrate promising experimental designs or to highlight current research trends.

Surveys of *hybrid populations* lend no support to claims that race mixture is biologically detrimental. Moreover, research on American Indians and American Negroes indicates that intelligence test performance is related to degree of cultural assimilation rather than to proportion of white ancestry. Psychological tests administered at the *infant and preschool level* have in general revealed no significant difference between Negroes and whites in over-all behavioral development. Certain specific differences in, for example, oral responsiveness and motor development, can be related to known cultural factors. Prenatal nutritional deficiencies which retard physical development may also cause behavioral retardation in certain underprivileged groups.

Large *regional differences* in test performance have been established among Negroes as well as among whites in America. Available evidence indicates that—at least for the American Negro in the North and the South— these differences result from educational and other environmental inequalities rather than from selective migration. *Cross-comparisons* of the same individuals classified with respect to cultural and biological criteria have so far favored a cultural interpretation of group differences in intellectual and personality factors.

Research on *culture and personality* is a characteristic development of the past two decades. Concentrating on existing differences among populations, this research seeks to identify specific conditions within each culture which lead to the development of typical personality patterns. Such studies of "national character" have followed a variety of procedures, including descriptive accounts of entire cultures prepared by anthropologists, psychiatrists, and other observers; analyses of vital and social statistics; content analysis; community studies; public opinion and attitude surveys; observations of child-rearing practices; and intensive studies of individuals by means of interviews or psychological tests. A number of comprehensive research programs on national character have been conducted since the end of World War II. Intensive interdisciplinary studies of certain populations, such as the American Indian, have also advanced our knowledge of the role of culture in behavior development.

REFERENCES

1. Abel, Theodora M. The Rorschach test in the study of culture. *Rorschach Res. Exch.*, 1948, 12, 79–93.
2. Anastasi, Anne, and Cordova, F. A. Some effects of bilingualism upon the intelligence test performance of Puerto Rican children in New York City. *J. educ. Psychol.*, 1953, 44, 1–19.
3. Anastasi, Anne, and D'Angelo, Rita Y. A comparison of Negro and white preschool children in language development and Goodenough Draw-a-Man IQ. *J. genet. Psychol.*, 1952, 81, 147–165.
4. Anastasi, Anne, and deJesús, C. Language development and Goodenough Draw-a-Man IQ of Puerto Rican preschool children in New York City. *J. abnorm. soc. Psychol.*, 1953, 48, 357–366.
5. Atwood, J. H., *et al. Thus be their destiny; the personality development of Negro youth in three communities.* Washington, D.C.: Amer. Coun. Educ., 1941.
6. Aubert, V., Fisher, B. R., and Rokkan, S. A comparative study of teachers' attitudes to international problems and policies: preliminary review of relationships in interview data from seven western European countries. *Proc., Int. Congr. Psychol., Montreal*, June 1954, 210–211.
7. Beach, K. L. The musical talent of southern Negroes as measured with the Seashore tests. *J. genet. Psychol.*, 1936, 49, 244–249.
8. Benedict, Ruth. *The chrysanthemum and the sword; patterns of Japanese culture.* Boston: Houghton Mifflin, 1946.
9. Benedict, Ruth. Child rearing in certain European countries. *Amer. J. Orthopsychiat.*, 1949, 19, 342–350.
10. Böök, J. A. Race mixture. *Acta genet. Stat. med.*, 1954, 5, 3–12.
11. Briggs, D. L. Social adaptation among Japanese-American youth: a comparative study. *Sociol. soc. Res.*, 1954, 38, 283–300.
12. Brown, F. An experimental and critical study of the intelligence of Negro and white kindergarten children. *J. genet. Psychol.*, 1944, 65, 161–175.

13. Bruner, F. G. The hearing of primitive peoples. *Arch. Psychol.*, 1908, No. 11.

14. Canady, H. G. The psychology of the Negro. In P. L. Harriman (Ed.), *Encyclopedia of psychology*. N.Y.: Philos. Lib., 1946. Pp. 407–416.

15. Cattell, R. B. The principal culture patterns discoverable in the syntal dimensions of existing nations. *J. soc. Psychol.*, 1950, 32, 215–253.

16. Caudill, W. Japanese-American personality and acculturation. *Genet. Psychol. Monogr.*, 1952, 45, 3–102.

17. Commager, H. S. *America in perspective: the United States through foreign eyes*. N.Y.: Random House, 1947.

18. Davenport, R. K. Implications of military selection and classification in relation to universal military training. *J. Negro Educ.*, 1946, 15, 585–594.

19. Davis, A., and Dollard, J. *Children of bondage: the personality development of Negro youth in the urban South*. Washington, D.C.: Amer. Coun. Educ., 1940.

20. Dennis, W. Are Hopi children noncompetitive? *J. abnorm. soc. Psychol.*, 1955, 50, 99–100.

21. De Vos, G. A. A comparison of the personality differences in two generations of Japanese Americans by means of the Rorschach test. *Nagoya J. med. Sci.*, 1954, 17, 153–265.

22. De Vos, G. A. Japanese value-attitudes assessed by application of Sargent's Insight Test method. *Amer. Psychologist*, 1956, 11, 410.

23. Dickinson, A. Race mixture: a social or a biological problem? *Eugen. Rev.*, 1949, 41, 81–85.

24. Duyker, H. C. J. Cross-national research: theoretical and practical considerations. *Proc., Int. Congr. Psychol., Montreal,* June 1954, 206–207.

25. Efron, D. *Gesture and environment*. N.Y.: Kings Crown Press, 1941.

26. Efron, D., and Foley, J. P., Jr. A comparative investigation of gestural behavior patterns in Italian and Jewish groups living under different as well as similar environmental conditions. *Z. Sozialforsch.*, 1937, 6, 151–159. Reprinted in T. M. Newcomb and E. L. Hartley (Eds.), *Readings in social psychology*. N.Y.: Holt, 1947. Pp. 33–40.

27. Farber, M. L. The problem of national character: a methodological analysis. *J. Psychol.*, 1950, 30, 307–316.

28. Frazier, E. F. *Negro youth at the crossways*. Washington, D.C.: Amer. Coun. Educ., 1940.

29. Fried, M. H. Chinese society: class as subculture. *Trans. N.Y. Acad. Sci.*, 1952, 14, 331–336.

30. Galton, F. *Hereditary genius: an inquiry into its laws and consequences*. London: Macmillan, 1914. (1st Ed. 1869)

31. Garth, T. R. *Race psychology: a study of racial mental differences*. N.Y.: McGraw-Hill, 1931.

32. Garth, T. R., Schuelke, N., and Abell, W. The intelligence of mixed-blood Indians. *J. appl. Psychol.*, 1927, 11, 268–275.

33. Gillespie, J. M., and Allport, G. W. *Youth's outlook on the future*. Garden City, N.Y.: Doubleday, 1955.

34. Gilliland, A. R. Socioeconomic status and race as factors in infant intelligence test scores. *Child Develpm.*, 1951, 22, 271–273.

35. Gladwin, T., and Sarason, S. B. *Truk: man in paradise.* N.Y.: Wenner-Gren Foundation, 1953.

36. Gorer, G. *The American people; a study in national character.* N.Y.: Norton, 1948.

37. Hallowell, A. I. The use of projective techniques in the study of the socio-psychological aspects of acculturation. *J. proj. Tech.,* 1951, 15, 27–44.

38. Havighurst, R. J., Gunther, Minna K., and Pratt, Inez E. Environment and the Draw-a-Man test: the performance of Indian children. *J. abnorm. soc. Psychol.,* 1946, 41, 50–63.

39. Havighurst, R. J., and Hilkevitch, Rhea R. The intelligence of Indian children as measured by a performance scale. *J. abnorm. soc. Psychol.,* 1944, 39, 419–433.

40. Havighurst, R. J., and Neugarten, B. L. *American Indian and white children; a sociopsychological investigation.* Chicago: Univer. Chicago Press, 1955.

41. Herskovits, M. J. On the relation between Negro-white mixture and standing in intelligence tests. *J. genet. Psychol.,* 1926, 33, 30–42.

42. Hunter, W. S., and Sommermier, E. The relation of degree of Indian blood to score on the Otis intelligence test. *J. comp. Psychol.,* 1922, 2, 257–277.

43. Inkeles, A., and Levinson, D. J. National character: the study of modal personality and sociocultural systems. In G. Lindzey (Ed.), *Handbook of social psychology.* Cambridge, Mass.: Addison-Wesley, 1954, vol. II. Pp. 977–1020.

44. Johnson, C. S. *Growing up in the black belt.* Washington, D.C.: Amer. Coun. Educ., 1941.

45. Joseph, Alice, and Murray, Veronica F. *Chamorros and Carolinians of Saipan.* Cambridge, Mass.: Harvard Univer. Press, 1951.

46. Joseph, Alice, Spicer, Rosamund B., and Chesky, Jane. *The desert people; a study of the Papago Indians.* Chicago: Univer. Chicago Press, 1949.

47. Kardiner, A., and Ovesey, L. *The mark of oppression; a psychological study of the American Negro.* N.Y.: Norton, 1951.

48. Klineberg, O. An experimental study of speed and other factors in "racial" differences. *Arch. Psychol.,* 1928, No. 93.

49. Klineberg, O. A study of psychological differences between "racial" and national groups in Europe. *Arch. Psychol.,* 1931, No. 132.

50. Klineberg, O. *Negro intelligence and selective migration.* N.Y.: Columbia Univer. Press, 1935.

51. Klineberg, O. *Race differences.* N.Y.: Harper, 1935.

52. Klineberg, O. *Tensions affecting international understanding; a survey of research.* N.Y.: Soc. Sci. Res. Coun., 1950. (SSRC Bull., 62)

53. Klineberg, O. *Race and psychology.* Paris: UNESCO, 1951.

54. Klineberg, O. *Social psychology.* (2nd Ed.) N.Y.: Holt, 1954.

55. Klineberg, O. (Ed.) *Characteristics of the American Negro.* N.Y.: Harper, 1944.

56. Klineberg, O., Fjeld, Harriet A., and Foley, J. P., Jr. An experimental study of personality differences among constitutional, "racial," and cultural groups. (Unpubl. Project Report, 1936)

57. Kluckhohn, C., and Leighton, Dorothea G. *The Navaho.* Cambridge, Mass.: Harvard Univer. Press, 1946.

58. Knobloch, Hilda, and Pasamanick, B. Further observations on the behavioral development of Negro children. *J. genet. Psychol.*, 1953, 83, 137–157.

59. La Barre, W. The cultural basis of emotions and gestures. *J. Pers.*, 1947, 16, 49–68.

60. La Barre, W. Columbia University research in contemporary culture. *Sci. Mon.*, 1948, 67, 239–240.

61. Lee, E. S. Negro intelligence and selective migration: a Philadelphia test of the Klineberg hypothesis. *Amer. sociol. Rev.*, 1951, 16, 227–233.

62. Leighton, Dorothea C., and Kluckhohn, C. *Children of the people: the Navaho individual and his development.* Cambridge, Mass.: Harvard Univer. Press, 1947.

63. Long, H. H. The intelligence of colored elementary pupils in Washington, D.C. *J. Negro Educ.*, 1934, 3, 205–222.

64. MacGregor, G. *Warriors without weapons: a study of the society and personality development of the Pine Ridge Sioux.* Chicago: Univer. Chicago Press, 1946.

65. Mann, C. W. Mental measurements in primitive communities. *Psychol. Bull.*, 1940, 37, 366–395.

66. McCarthy, Dorothea. Language development in children. In L. Carmichael (Ed.), *Manual of child psychology.* (Rev. Ed.) N.Y.: Wiley, 1954. Pp. 492–630.

67. McGraw, Myrtle B. A comparative study of a group of southern white and Negro infants. *Genet. Psychol. Monogr.*, 1931, 10, 1–105.

68. Mead, Margaret. *And keep your powder dry.* N.Y.: Morrow, 1942.

69. Mead, Margaret. Research in contemporary cultures. In H. Guetzkow (Ed.), *Groups, leadership and men; research in human relations.* Pittsburgh, Pa.: Carnegie Press, 1951. Pp. 106–118.

70. Mead, Margaret. Research on primitive children. In L. Carmichael (Ed.), *Manual of child psychology.* (Rev. Ed.) N.Y.: Wiley, 1954. Pp. 735–780.

71. Murdock, G. P. New light on the peoples of Micronesia. *Science*, 1948, 108, 423–425.

72. Murphy, G. *In the minds of men.* N.Y.: Basic Books, 1953.

73. Orlansky, H. Infant care and personality. *Psychol. Bull.*, 1949, 46, 1–48.

74. Pasamanick, B. A comparative study of the behavioral development of Negro infants. *J. genet. Psychol.*, 1946, 69, 3–44.

75. Pasamanick, B., and Knobloch, Hilda. Early language behavior in Negro children and the testing of intelligence. *J. abnorm. soc. Psychol.*, 1955, 50, 401–402.

76. Peterson, J., and Lanier, L. H. Studies in the comparative abilities of whites and Negroes. *Ment. Measmt. Monogr.*, 1929, No. 5.

77. Reid, I. DeA. *In a minor key.* Washington, D.C.: Amer. Coun. Educ., 1940.

78. Roberts, S. O. Socioeconomic status and performance on the ACE of Negro freshman college veterans and non-veterans, from the North and South. *Amer. Psychologist*, 1948, 3, 266.

79. Rodnick, D. *The Norwegians; a study in national culture.* Washington, D.C.: Public Affairs Press, 1955.

80. Rohrer, J. H. The test intelligence of Osage Indians. *J. soc. Psychol.*, 1942, 16, 99–105

81. Schacter, S. Methodological problems and factual findings in an international study in group behavior. *Proc., Int. Congr. Psychol., Montreal,* June 1954, 208–210.

82. Schacter, S., *et al.* Cross-cultural experiments on threat and rejection. *Hum. Relat.,* 1954, 7, 403–440.

83. Seward, Georgene. *Psychotherapy and culture conflict.* N.Y.: Ronald, 1956.

84. Shapiro, H. L. *Race mixture.* Paris: UNESCO, 1953.

85. Smith, Madorah E. Measurement of vocabularies of young bilingual children in both of the languages used. *J. genet. Psychol.,* 1949, 74, 305–310.

86. Snell, G. D. Hybrids and history. The role of race and ethnic crossing in individual and national achievement. *Quart. Rev. Biol.,* 1951, 26, 331–347.

87. Stoetzel, Jean. *Without the chrysanthemum and the sword; a study of the attitudes of youth in post-war Japan.* N.Y.: Columbia Univer. Press, 1955.

88. Sutherland, R. L. *Color, class, and personality.* Washington, D.C.: Amer. Coun. Educ., 1942.

89. Telford, C. W. Comparative studies of full and mixed blood North Dakota Indians. *Psychol. Monogr.,* 1938, 50, No. 5, 116–129.

90. Theman, V., and Witty, P. A. Case studies and genetic records of two gifted Negroes. *J. Psychol.,* 1943, 15, 165–181.

91. Thompson, Laura. *Culture in crisis: a study of the Hopi Indians.* N.Y.: Harper, 1950.

92. Warner, W. L., Junker, B. H., and Adams, W. A. *Color and human nature: Negro personality development in a northern city.* Washington, D.C.: Amer. Coun. Educ., 1941.

93. Whiting, J. W. M., *et al. Field guide for a study of socialization in five societies.* Cambridge, Mass., 1954. (mimeographed)

94. Whiting, J. W. M., and Child, I. L. *Child training and personality: a cross-cultural study.* New Haven, Conn.: Yale Univer. Press, 1953.

95. Williams, Judith R., and Scott, R. B. Growth and development of Negro infants: IV. Motor development and its relationship to child rearing practices in two groups of Negro infants. *Child Develpm.,* 1953, 24 (2), 103–121.

96. Witty, P. A., and Jenkins, M. D. Intra-race testing and Negro intelligence. *J. Psychol.,* 1936, 1, 179–192.

97. Woodworth, R. S. Race differences in mental traits. *Science,* 1910, 31, 171–186.

98. Yerkes, R. M. (Ed.) Psychological examining in the United States Army. *Mem. nat. Acad. Sci.,* 1921, 15.

CHAPTER 18

Culture and the Individual

In its broadest sense, differential psychology is concerned with all variations in behavior phenomena among individuals and among groups. The observation and measurement of such differences have led to the accumulation of a vast body of descriptive material which has proved scientifically interesting and practically useful. Examples of such material have been given throughout the present book. The fundamental aim of differential psychology is not, however, the collection of descriptive material. Its aim is similar to that of all psychology, namely, the *understanding of behavior*. Differential psychology approaches this problem through a comparative analysis of behavior under varying environmental and biological conditions. By relating the observed differences in behavior to other known concomitant phenomena, it should be possible to tease out the relative contribution of different factors to behavioral development. If we can determine why one person reacts differently from another, we shall know what makes people react as they do.

The unit of differential psychology is the individual, conceived as a reacting organism; our interest in groups is only secondary. Many traditional groupings, furthermore, have proved to be arbitrary and ill-defined. From the standpoint of behavioral development, the effective groupings are stimulational and not biological. It is not the race, or sex, or physical "type" to which the individual belongs by heredity that determines his psychological make-up, but the cultural group in which he was reared, the traditions, attitudes, and points of view impressed upon him, and the type of abilities fostered and encouraged. Even when behavioral differences are found to be associated with physically defined groups, it is usually the indirect social effects of such groupings, rather than their biological characteristics, which influence behavior development.

Since all types of behavior are influenced by the subject's stimulational background, it follows that psychological data obtained within any one cultural group cannot be generalized to cover all human behavior. Many statements offered under the heading of general psychology are not general at all, but are based upon human behavior as it develops within a single culture (cf. 22, 42, 69). This limitation has sometimes been described as a "community-centrism" which pervades much of our psychological information. It has been suggested that many textbooks of "general psychology" might be more accurately characterized as dealing with "the psychology of Americans and Western Europeans of the late eighteenth and early nineteenth centuries."

In a somewhat similar vein, Dollard (20, p. 17) stresses the importance of considering the cultural setting in which behavioral observations are made. He ventures to suggest that "to the social psychologist, the three most indispensable letters in the alphabet are I.O.C. (in our culture)," and points out that these qualifying letters should be regarded as implicit in all descriptions of behavior within our cultural setting. Such cultural restrictions undoubtedly apply to much of the *descriptive* and *factual* content of psychology. This does not, however, preclude the possibility that when the specific behavior is studied against the individual's stimulational background, the same *principles* of behavior will be found to operate (cf. 24, 26). Such a study of group and individual differences in behavior should, in fact, help to clarify the common underlying principles of behavior development.

CULTURAL FRAMES OF REFERENCE

The observations of psychologists and anthropologists in various cultures provide innumerable illustrations of the influence of cultural "frames of reference" upon behavior (cf. 42, 43, 44, 69, 70). What is often regarded as a "natural" response to a particular stimulus may be "natural" only because of the social norms and standards which we have acquired in our own cultural setting. Our very conception of the world about us is influenced by our own specific reactional history. A purely "impartial" or "objective" observer is a psychological impossibility. Each individual's observation and description of any fact is conditioned by his special past experiences as well as by the more general traditions and customs inculcated by his group. In this connection, one may regard the instruments and techniques of science as a means of reducing or minimizing the effect of the observer's idiosyncrasies.

Even the simplest *perceptual responses* may be influenced by cultural frames of reference. Whether we perceive an object as light or heavy, long or short, hot or cold, pleasant or unpleasant may depend in part upon our previous, socially determined experiences. An interesting illustration is provided by the perception of family resemblances and differences in certain primitive cultures. Among the Trobrianders, for example, resemblance to the father is considered natural, whereas the child is never said to resemble the mother or any of the maternal relatives (52). The existence of the latter types of resemblance is vigorously disclaimed. Resemblances between brothers are likewise denied, although the resemblance of each brother to the father is granted! It is, of course, difficult to determine to what extent these reactions represent a refusal to admit the proscribed resemblance, and to what extent they indicate a failure to perceive the similarities of appearance. The results of many experiments on the effects of expectation and "set" upon perception, however, make it appear entirely plausible that the Trobrianders only notice those familial resemblances which have been institutionalized by their culture.

It is well known that preferences for tastes and odors, as well as likes and dislikes for foods, vary widely from one culture to another. Among certain African tribes, cologne and scented soap evoked loathing and disgust (cf. 43, p. 214). On the other hand, odors that we find very unpleasant have at other times or places been used as perfumes.

Popular conceptions of time and space, although commonly taken for granted, can be shown to be culturally influenced (33, 43, 69, 76). The concern with precise estimation of the time of occurrence and duration of events, so characteristic of our culture, is quite lacking in others. The indifference to time found among many primitive groups is illustrated by the prevalent lack of knowledge about one's own age, and by the inability to indicate how long ago an event occurred if a period of several years has intervened. Other differences are to be found in the way in which time is reckoned. The use of astronomical events as a framework for the measurement of time is by no means universal, many other familiar and recurrent events serving this purpose among different peoples. Thus in Madagascar the natives refer to "a rice-cooking" when they wish to indicate an interval of about an hour, and to "the frying of a locust" to designate a much shorter lapse of time. In the Andaman Islands, it is possible to identify a succession of characteristic odors during the year, as different plants come to bloom. Odors also play an important part in the magic of the Andamanese. It is not surprising, therefore, to find that these people have "adopted an original method of marking the different periods of the year by means of the odoriferous flowers that are in bloom at different times. Their calendar is a calendar of scents" (66, p. 311).

Space concepts are equally dependent upon culturally determined frames of reference. That individuals' conceptions of distance and geography are largely colored by their own experiences is at the basis of the waggish "maps" of the United States which have been prepared to portray, for example, a Bostonian's or a New Yorker's idea of the country. Like most caricatures, these "maps" undoubtedly reflect some bona fide perceptual differences resulting from the different interests, traditions, and knowledge of persons reared in different parts of the country. Other examples could easily be cited from everyday observation. The seasoned air traveler has a very different conception of distances than does the farmer who has never ventured farther than the village store.

In a relatively isolated Turkish village described by Sherif and Sherif (70, pp. 693–696), distances up to three or four kilometers were described as "within a bullet's reach" or "as far as my voice can go." More remote points were indicated in terms of the time required to reach them on foot. Confusions and misconceptions would arise on the few occasions when such persons traveled by train or bus, since they had no basis for translating the time spent in transit into their familiar frame of reference. A similar use of such "psychological units" to express distance has been observed among the Saulteaux Indians, who estimate distance in terms of the number of "sleeps," or nights spent on the road (34).

Even the familiar designation of directions in terms of north, south, east, and west, although prevailing over a large part of the world, is not a universal system. Thus among the natives of Dobu, space was conceived as a large garden clearing, such as the individual encountered in the daily life of his community. "Just as the garden has its inland border *kaikai*, its seaward border *kunnkumwana*, and its sides *nana*, so also has space in its widest extension" (29, p. 131).

The individual's *memory* for events he has observed or facts he has been told is likewise colored by his cultural background. This is particularly well illustrated by the observations and tests of Bartlett (4, 5) and Nadel (59, 60). Both investigators, working with South African tribes, have shown the important part played by cultural patterns in the "restructuralization" and distortions of recall. For example, when repeating a European story, individuals in these groups tended to cast it with characters typical of their tribal folklore. They likewise rearranged sequences and introduced twists of plot characteristic of their native stories.

An especially clear illustration of the effect of cultural milieu upon behavior is furnished by *esthetic preferences* and artistic "taste." The evolution of styles in music, painting, sculpture, architecture, and other arts testifies to the shifting demands of "taste." Styles that are derided as harsh, barbaric, and uncouth by one generation have often been accepted as masterpieces by the next. Any artistic innovation which clashes too vigorously with familiar and traditional forms of artistic expression requires a period of gradual habituation. It is an unfortunate but psychologically understandable fact that great art leaders who are subsequently hailed as initiators of new movements may suffer ridicule and derision during their lifetime. This follows from the fact that they often come at a time when adequate experiential background for the enjoyment of their products is lacking.

The question of the sophisticated and the naïve observer is also relevant to this point. The trained critic or the sophisticated observer has had certain specific experiences which enable him to enjoy artistic products that may appear meaningless, indifferent, or even unpleasant to others. Psychologically, there is no "naïve observer"; such an individual is naïve only from the standpoint of a specific class of experiences. His judgments are, however, directly influenced by other experiences which he has had. His artistic reactions will be largely dictated by common everyday observations and popular fashions. Thus the observer may enjoy realistic art because he is more familiar with photographic reproductions of objects; or he may reflect some traditional artistic conception which has been inculcated in him from early childhood. But in no case is his judgment made independently of experience. The essential difference between the sophisticated and the naïve observer is in the *kind* of past experience which they have had.

It is a familiar observation that Occidentals who hear Chinese music for the first time find it not only discordant and harsh, but also unpleasantly loud. At the same time, it has been reported that the Chinese find American jazz and Wagnerian brasses disturbingly loud upon their first exposure to such music (cf. 43, p. 213). The history of Western music likewise reveals marked changes in musical preferences. Music that is pleasing to one generation may sound dull and uninteresting to another. What is at one time rejected as dissonant and ugly may be later acclaimed as esthetically satisfying. In a classic experiment, Moore (57) found that repeated exposure to dissonant intervals in musical passages increased esthetic preference for such intervals. Moore explained these results in terms of a progressive shift in the perception of consonance. A later experiment, however, demonstrated that increasing appreciation for dissonant music is not correlated with a proportionate transformation of dissonances into consonances (13). With repetition, the subjects may simply learn to like dissonances, while still perceiving them as such.

Another relevant experiment is that conducted by Foley (25, 27) on occupational differences in preferential auditory tempo. The subjects were young women enrolled in the following trade school courses: power machine sewing, hand sewing, beauty culture, typewriting, and domestic occupations (waitress training, home nursing, nursery education, etc.). The five groups were approximately comparable in age, intellectual level, education, socioeconomic level, and racial and national background. When asked to report preferences for auditory tempos ranging from 56 to 200 metronome beats per minute, the subjects in the typewriting and machine sewing courses selected significantly faster tempos than those in the other three courses. These group differences were more marked in the advanced than in the beginning classes. Further analyses likewise indicated that the group differences were associated with the nature of vocational training experience rather than with initial selective factors. Thus the subjects who had become accustomed to hearing the rapid, repetitive noises of the typewriters and sewing machines exhibited a shift in the frame of reference in terms of which their preferential judgments were made.

We need not go beyond everyday observations in our own culture to find further evidence of shifting frames of reference in preferential responses. A vivid illustration is provided by the response to changing fashions in women's wear. A style that appears beautiful to most observers when it is at the height of fashion will probably look dull and unattractive within a season, and positively ludicrous if viewed ten years later. These rapid changes in "taste" come as no surprise to fashion leaders, since the fashion industry deliberately provides the stimulation which brings about the change in response. Upon the introduction of a new style, the buying public is exposed to a carefully planned and coordinated campaign designed to prepare it for the acceptance of such a style. The new fashion is pictured in magazines and newspapers; attractive models wear it on the street and in theatres, restaurants, and other public places; window displays feature it conspicuously. Through these and similar techniques, the public is rapidly "sensitized" to the new style in much the same manner that Moore's subjects were habituated to the unfamiliar, discordant combinations of notes. If the fashion is too "discordant" and clashes too violently with the previous experience of the public, the sensitizing process may fail and the fashion will be rejected. Similarly, the successful fashion leader keeps well posted on current developments in other areas—social, economic, political, artistic—in order to coordinate his innovations with the more general frame of reference of his consumer public.

DEVELOPMENTAL STAGES AND THE CULTURAL SETTING

Theories of developmental stages furnish numerous illustrations of the tendency to overgeneralize from observations within a single culture. Child psychology is replete with such theories. Much interesting material has been gathered, for example, on *concept formation*. The child's ideas about the physical world, his consciousness of self, his interpretation of dreams, and similar conceptions have been analyzed into definite developmental sequences. Outstanding in this field are the theories of the Swiss psychologist Piaget (63, 64, 65).

In an extensive series of investigations, Piaget arrived at the conclusion that the thinking of the child is animistic and that the transition from this initial animism to the adult's conception of the world is made through four major stages. For children between the ages of 4 and 6, everything active is alive. Since children of this age are also anthropocentric, "activity" is regarded as synonymous with usefulness to man. Thus the sun is active because it gives warmth, stones are active because you can throw them. At this first stage, therefore, all objects that are unbroken and in good condition are considered to be alive and "conscious." In the next stage (6–7 years), only movable objects are believed to be alive. In the third stage (8–10 years), life is attributed only to things that can move spontaneously. Thus the sun and a river are alive, but an automobile is not. In the final stage (11 years on), life is restricted to animals and plants, or sometimes to animals only.

Such stages have been commonly accepted as an inevitable or natural development through which the child must pass. There are a number of factors within the experience of a child in our society, however, which might account for such animistic tendencies. The language that the child is taught encourages him to form an animistic conception of the world. Thus he hears the sun referred to as "he" and the moon or a ship as "she." Figurative expressions, such as the "rising" and "setting" of celestial bodies, the "running" brook, and the "howling" wind, are not conducive to an impersonal conception of natural phenomena. If to this are added the fancies of poetry, fairy tales, and other imaginative literature, it is apparent that the child's experience has a strongly animistic flavor. It is not until he has had the opportunity to accumulate a certain amount of information from direct observation of cause and effect in everyday situations that such a child can arrive at a realistic notion of the world.

Data supporting such an experiential interpretation of the development of children's concepts are to be found in studies on children in different cultures. Mead's observations on the island of Manus in New Guinea led her to conclude that animism is absent in the thinking of Manus children (56). In both the spontaneous remarks of these children and in their replies to questions, she found evidence of a very realistic conception of natural objects and events. Mead attributed this realistic attitude to the type of training which such children receive. From early childhood they are forced to make a correct adjustment to the physical demands of their environment. The responsibility for a mishap is never shifted to an inanimate object, as in blaming the log if the child trips over it. If the child hurts himself, he is told that it is the result of his own clumsiness. It is interesting to note that, in certain respects, the adults are more animistic than the children in this culture, since they explain sickness, death, and other misfortunes as the activity of "spirits."

In a subsequent investigation by Dennis (16), designed as a more direct check of Piaget's theories, Hopi children were studied through standardized individual interviews and a group questionnaire. The survey dealt with (1) animism in the more restricted sense, i.e., being alive; (2) the attribution of "consciousness" to things; and (3) "moral realism," as in the explanation that "the bridge fell because the boys crossing it had stolen apples." In all three respects, the Hopi children were found to be more animistic and less realistic in their replies than white children of the same ages tested in other investigations. Dennis attributed these differences to the many dissimilarities in the social environments of Hopi children and white American children.

In a further discussion of Piaget's work, Dennis (17) points out that Piaget's observations actually show that from an early age the child's perception of the world is permeated with culturally imposed values and categories. Moreover, Piaget does not have comparative data on adults. In his own research, Dennis (18) has found evidence of considerable animistic thinking among adults in our society.

Emotional development has also been analyzed from the point of view of "stages." The most widely discussed of such stages is probably the period of "storm and stress" characteristic of the adolescent. Many writers on child psychology ascribe emotional upheavals, personality changes, conflicts, and maladjustments to this age. There is evidence, however, to show that this is not a universal phenomenon. In certain societies (cf., e.g., 54, 55), the adolescent assumes his altered status, both physical and social, without emotional disturbance. His tasks are cut out for him by tradition; there are no momentous choices and decisions to be made; no mystery attaches to his position; and no trace of embarrassment is encountered.

There is much in our society, on the other hand, which fosters adolescent maladjustments. Thus the individual is placed in an ambiguous and ill-defined position, being treated neither as a child nor as an adult. Restrictions upon his actions are frequently increased, while at the same time he is expected to be more self-reliant than he had formerly been. Embarrassment and a general atmosphere of mystery are often directly induced by adults through their attitudes, remarks, and actions. In view of the many experiential factors in our society which might lead to adolescent maladjustments, there seems to be no need to posit an innate or physiological basis to the storm and stress of this period, nor to regard such emotional upheaval as a necessary developmental stage.

Another aspect of child behavior to which the concept of developmental stages has been widely applied is *drawing*. Children's drawings have been collected in large numbers and submitted to detailed analyses, in the hope that they might furnish a clue to the child's mentality. The best-known example of such a use of children's drawings is provided by the Goodenough Draw-a-Man Test, with its carefully standardized scoring and extensive age norms. The voluminous literature on children's drawings reveals a traditional emphasis upon maturational interpretations of age changes (cf. 2, 31).

Comparative studies of children's drawings in different cultures, however, suggest that both the subject matter and the technique of the drawings reflect cultural factors at least as much as they do age differences (2, 3, 15, 68). Whether the child draws broad panoramic views or scenes at close range, isolated objects or organized pictures, imaginative themes or realistic portrayals seems to depend in large measure upon his specific environmental milieu. In certain groups, the drawings are full of action, in others stationary objects and figures predominate. The organization of the picture likewise differs from one group to another. In some groups, a single unified scene is most often presented, in others a sequence of events, in still others isolated objects. The degree to which color is employed, as well as the choice of specific hues, usually reflects the influence of both physical environment and social traditions. Amount and kind of detail portrayed likewise differ from one culture to another.

Stylized representations and special cultural attributes are also discernible in the drawings by children in certain cultures, becoming increasingly apparent with age (cf. 2, 3, 15). In a study of Hopi children with the Goodenough Draw-a-Man Test, the younger children tended to draw generalized human figures, while approximately one-third of the 10-year-olds drew figures in which special characteristics of the Indian culture could be recognized (15). A similar tendency has been noted among Indian children of the Northwest Coast of Canada. In response to the instructions to draw

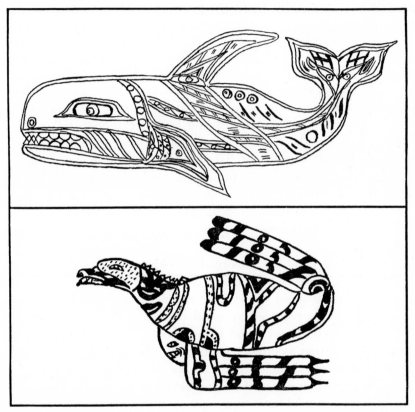

Fig. 86. Drawings by Indian Children of the Northwest Pacific Coast, in Response to Directions to Draw an Animal. (From Anastasi and Foley, 3, p. 369.)

an animal, a number of these children produced stylized representations of the killer whale, sea lion, thunder bird, and mythical double-headed serpent. The highly conventionalized technique of these drawings can be seen in Figure 86, showing the killer whale and sea lion. Such stylized drawings were not only more common among older than among younger children, but also more frequent among boys than among girls (17 per cent versus 7 per cent). This sex difference is probably related to the fact that painting and carving are exclusively male activities in these tribes. In the light of results in different cultures, it would seem hazardous to regard the richness of detail, general technique, or any other feature of children's drawings as an index of developmental level, unless such features are considered in reference to the child's cultural background.

ABNORMALITY AND CULTURE

The term "abnormal," which means literally "away from the norm," has been used to cover at least three distinct concepts (cf. 23, 38, 58). First we may consider the *anti-normative* view which regards as abnormal any deviation from the ideal or perfect condition. The norm [1] in such a case is a goal or desideratum to be approximated by existing conditions. To be "normal," according to this view, would be the exception rather than the rule. Such a use of the terms "normal" and "abnormal" is illustrated by a number of common expressions. To say that a person is one of the "lucky few" who have a normal skin or normal teeth, for example, implies an identification of normality with freedom from defects or other imperfections. Or to assert that few can remain normal under the stress and strain of modern life suggests that normality is an ideal state of perfect composure and stability.

A second view identifies abnormality with *pathological* or dangerous conditions. This usage is particularly common in medicine. To be classed as abnormal in this sense would have distinctly undesirable connotations. Such a view may be regarded as an adaptation of the anti-normative concept to meet practical and social requirements. The abnormal still represents a deviation from a perfect condition, but the deviation is now so great as to present practical difficulties. The condition requires action of some sort for the protection either of the individual or of society. Thus a person who exhibits a few mild neurotic symptoms, such as a compulsion to avoid stepping on the cracks in the sidewalk or a slight twitching of the forehead, may elicit the remark: "a bit queer, yes—but not serious—nothing *really abnormal* about him." But let such an individual become so depressed over an imagined or exaggerated wrong that his work must be discontinued, or let him threaten a suspected enemy with physical violence, and he will immediately earn the label of "abnormal." According to this view, only a

---

[1] This use of the term "norm" should not be confused with the concept of empirical norm prevalent in psychological testing. In its present sense, "norm" refers to a standard of value. This is the sense in which logicians employ the term "norm" when speaking of ethics and esthetics as normative disciplines (cf., e.g., 11).

very small number of individuals are abnormal, the large majority being indiscriminately classified as normal.

Both of the above views necessitate an arbitrary norm or standard. In the first, the norm is a theoretical ideal; in the latter, a practical criterion of individual and social survival. A more objective and empirical approach to the problem is provided by a purely *statistical* concept of abnormality. The norm in this case is the average. It is the usual and most common condition. The abnormal is the unusual, the relatively infrequent. The more infrequent a condition, furthermore, the more abnormal it is considered. Many conditions classed as abnormal in the pathological sense would also be regarded as statistically abnormal because of their relative rarity. On the other hand, the majority of those individuals classed as abnormal according to the anti-normative view would be considered normal, since they constitute the large, intermediate, and most representative segment of the population. Similarly, those who approximate the ideal or perfect state too closely would now be regarded as abnormal, since they deviate significantly from the ordinary, average individual.

It is apparent that this is the only sense in which abnormality can be objectively determined and measured. Such a statistical concept of abnormality need not imply complacence and acceptance of existing ills as has been occasionally claimed. It is "normal" for a 4-year-old child to be illiterate; yet we teach children to read and write. It is "normal" for American adults to have a few dental cavities; yet we go to the dentist to have our cavities filled, and we do our best to prevent their development. If a large majority of people display behavior which we consider undesirable, labeling it abnormal will not lead to improvement. The statistical concept of abnormality represents no more than a realistic and objective recognition of facts.

It follows from the statistical view that the abnormal may be *either inferior or superior* to the normal. The abnormal corresponds simply to the two ends of a continuous distribution curve. Since the distribution is roughly symmetrical, the superior deviate is just as abnormal as the inferior, in the sense that he is equally far from the norm. In the present section, we shall consider ways in which culture may influence both the differentiation between normality and abnormality and the evaluation of superiority and inferiority.

Varieties of Normality. Psychologically, all behavior follows normally from its antecedent conditions—there is no essential distinction between the mechanisms or psychological principles of normal and abnormal behavior. Abnormality is the normal consequence of certain stimulating conditions and structural characteristics. Behavior is abnormal only in the sense that it deviates from a norm. This norm is determined by the specific conditions of life within a given group. Thus it follows that behavior which is considered abnormal in one culture may be normal in another.

Cultural standards enter into the definition of normality in at least two ways (23). First, the *position of the norm* and the line of demarcation between normality and abnormality may differ from one group to another. As a result, any given behavioral manifestation may occupy a very different place in different distributions of behavior. To take an illustration from physical traits, if we ask whether a man is tall or short, we may obtain very different answers when different groups are employed as standards. The same individual might be abnormally tall when referred to the distribution of height in the Japanese and very short when referred to the Scandinavian distribution. Similarly, in certain groups violent displays of emotion are the rule and stolidity would be abnormal. In others, the reverse is true. The range of variation over which normal behavior may occur can also differ. Thus two cultures having the same norm may differ in the degree of deviation from this norm which is possible without maladjustment. In one, rigid adherence to a narrowly defined behavioral norm may be required, either because of tradition or because of the exigencies of the physical environment. In another, wider latitude and larger individual differences may be acceptable as "normal."

In the second place, culturally established standards may determine *which end of the distribution is superior and which subnormal.* Comparative anthropology provides many examples of behavioral deviations which are regarded as unadaptive, pathological, insane, or mentally deficient in one culture and are admired or revered in another. Such behavior may be abnormal in both cases, in the statistical sense, but its social evaluation and practical value in the different cultures place it at opposite ends of the scale. This point was clearly expressed by Benedict (8), who wrote:

> . . . it is probable that about the same range of individual temperaments are found in any group, but the group has already made its cultural choice of those human endowments and peculiarities it will put to use . . . the misfit is the person whose disposition is not capitalized by his culture. . . . It is clear that there is not possible any generalized description of "the" deviant—he is the representative of that arc of human capacities that is not capitalized in his culture (p. 24).

The same point of view was further elaborated in a later article (9) by Benedict as follows:

One of these problems relates to the customary normal-abnormal categories and our conclusions regarding them. In how far are such categories culturally determined, or in how far can we with assurance regard them as absolute? In how far can we regard inability to function socially as diagnostic of abnormality, or in how far is it necessary to regard this as a function of the culture?

As a matter of fact, one of the most striking facts that emerge from a study of widely varying cultures is the ease with which our abnormals function in other cultures. It does not matter what kind of "abnormality" we choose for illustration, those which indicate extreme instability, or those which are more in the nature of character traits like sadism or delusions of grandeur or of persecution, there are well described cultures in which these abnormals function at ease and with honor, and apparently without danger or difficulty to the society (p. 60).

Among the natives of Dobu, an island in Melanesia, fear, suspicion, and mutual distrust characterize the attitudes of the entire group (29). They take constant precautions against being poisoned or having their property removed by sorcery or trickery. Within our culture such behavior would be described as paranoid, but it represents a normal adjustment to the Dobuan culture. Illustrations can easily be multiplied (10, 42, 43, 46). The cataleptic seizures constituting an important part of the behavior of the Siberian shaman and the homosexual practices common in many American Indian and Siberian communities represent other illustrations. Trance states are a normal part of the behavior repertory of certain American Indian groups, and it is the individual who is unable to experience the trance who is the deviant. Epileptic seizures, excessive daydreaming, and withdrawal characterize the superior deviant in certain cultures, rather than being a source of maladjustment.

To be sure, the specific etiological mechanism as well as the significance of such behavior for the individual differs from that in our culture. But this is just what we mean by saying it is normal in one culture and abnormal in another. In one case the individual is behaving in a manner that is sanctioned and explicitly encouraged by his culture; he is conforming to the accepted and institutionalized pattern. In the other case he is not. Wegrocki (75) has argued against the cultural and statistical concept of abnormality on the grounds that the same overt behavior symptoms may be indicative of severe maladjustment in one culture and of good adjustment in another. Far from being a criticism of the cultural concept of abnormality, this follows directly from it.

Varieties of Abnormality. All cultures have their deviants and their maladjustments. But the form which such maladjustments take may vary widely with the cultural setting (7, 10, 21, 32, 42, 43, 48, 50, 78). In the *windigo psychosis* among the Ojibwa Indians, the individual believes he has been transformed into a windigo, a mythical cannibalistic giant made of ice (49). The condition usually begins with a state of depression and often develops into violence and compulsive cannibalism, in which the individual may kill and eat the members of his own family. Other familiar examples include *arctic hysteria* (1), found in northern Siberia, in which the individual shows a high degree of suggestibility and compulsively imitates the words and actions of those in his vicinity. A similar condition found among the people of Malay is known as *latah* (1). Also characteristic of the Malayan culture is *amok*. The person who "runs amok" attacks in a blind rage everyone he meets, frequently injuring or killing many before he is stopped.

The influence of cultural factors upon the specific nature of deviant or maladjusted behavior was also illustrated by a survey of the neuroses observed among native African troops during World War II (61). The relative frequency of certain types of symptoms, such as phobias and hysterical symptoms of a motor or sensory nature, and the almost complete absence of other conditions, such as anxiety states, could best be understood in terms of the particular tribal beliefs and traditions. In some cultures, the incidence of certain forms of psychiatric disorders may be lessened because opportunities for the normal expression of certain behavior tendencies are available. In a survey conducted in Bombay, for example, schizophrenia was comparatively rare and manic-depressive psychosis more common (19). The reverse is true in America. Klineberg (43, p. 398) suggests that in the Indian culture the individual who is inclined to "escape from reality" may find normal channels for such extreme introvertive behavior in mystical religious experiences, an opportunity not so readily available in Western culture. Klineberg cites informal observations in a psychopathic hospital in Peking which tended to support this hypothesis.

Illustrations of "fashions in abnormality" can likewise be found in our own cultural history (cf. 43). The dancing manias which swept over entire villages during the Middle Ages represent a form of neurotic behavior having no counterpart today. Many of the manifestations of witchcraft provide additional instances of culturally determined symptoms. The trance states and the hysterical anesthesias, such as the "devil's claw" (an insensitive spot on the skin often used as evidence in witchcraft trials), were all part of a clinical picture which fitted into the culture of its time. As a further example, mention may be made of the delicate, languishing type of illness of unknown origin which was so common among Victorian gentlewomen.

Also relevant is an investigation of two groups of schizophrenics in a veteran's hospital in the New York metropolitan area (72). While closely equated in age, education, socioeconomic level, religion, and number of American generations, one group was of Irish and the other of Italian extraction. Both personality test performance and ratings of ward behavior revealed significant group differences in the nature of schizophrenic symptoms. The Irish-Americans showed a greater tendency to imaginative and fantasy behavior and more inhibition of motor expression, while the Italian-Americans were more overtly aggressive and impulsive. The investigators relate these findings to subcultural differences in child-rearing practices and family constellation, as well as to other cultural factors.

It should be noted, of course, that the establishment of cultural and subcultural variations in the nature of psychiatric symptoms does not imply the absence of biological factors in their etiology. Neurological and biochemical findings (Ch. 5), as well as data on the possible role of hereditary factors (Ch. 9), must be considered along with cultural conditions in any analysis of the development of specific psychiatric disorders.

LANGUAGE AS A CULTURAL FACTOR IN BEHAVIOR

The data of comparative linguistics and anthropology—and more recently the writings of the semanticists—have suggested the important part which the nature of a people's language may play in their conceptions of the world about them, their attitudes, and other behavior characteristics (cf., 14, 35, 36, 37, 43, 45, 62, 67, 77). In a very fundamental sense, language provides the tools for much of our thinking. The relationship between language and thought has been vividly expressed by Whorf (77, p. 212), who points out that each particular language "is not merely a reproducing instrument for voicing ideas but rather is itself the shaper of ideas, the program and guide for the individual's mental activity, for his analysis of impressions, for his synthesis of his mental stock in trade." As he further states, "We dissect nature along lines laid down by our native languages." In a similar vein, Mauthner (53, p. 4) wrote, "If Aristotle had spoken Chinese or Dacotan, he would have had to adopt an entirely different logic, or at any rate an entirely different theory of categories."

Language influences the type of distinctions and discriminations which we make in observing our surroundings. Objects and events in nature do not, of course, occur in the distinct categories to which we have become accustomed. Such categories have generally been developed to fit specific purposes and to facilitate our dealings with objects. Once objects are put into a specific category, or "named," however, our attention is thereby focused upon their similarities or common characteristics, and we tend to ignore differences among members of the class. Thus what we notice and what we overlook in our environment depend in part upon our particular linguistic system. When the conditions existing within a given culture have made certain distinctions important, we are likely to find separate words corresponding to such differentiations.

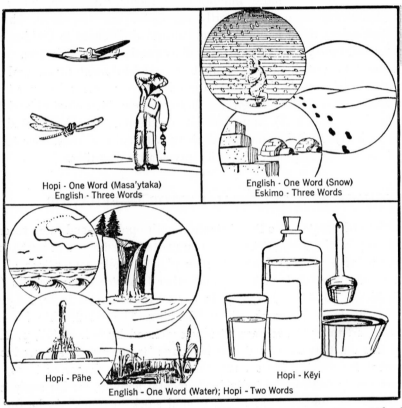

Hopi - One Word (Masa'ytaka)
English - Three Words

English - One Word (Snow)
Eskimo - Three Words

Hopi - Pāhe

Hopi - Kēyi

English - One Word (Water); Hopi - Two Words

Fig. 87. The Classification of Objects in Different Languages. (From Whorf, 77, p. 210.)

This is illustrated in Figure 87, in which certain words in the Eskimo and Hopi languages are compared with their English equivalents. Thus to correspond to our one word, "snow," Eskimos have several words, indicating "falling snow," "slushy snow," "hard-packed snow," and so on. On the other hand, the Hopi use a single word to designate "anything which flies, exclusive of birds." An insect, an airplane, and even a pilot would be called by this single name, the context determining which was meant. For our one word, "water," however, the Hopi have two words, one referring to "flowing water" and the other to "water in one place, held within a container."

Examples could easily be multiplied. In Arabic, the number of different words relating to "camel" is said to be about six thousand (73). There are terms to refer to riding camels, milk camels, and slaughter camels; other terms to indicate the pedigree and geographical origin of the camel; and still others to differentiate camels in different stages of pregnancy and to specify innumerable other characteristics important to a people so dependent upon camels in their daily life.

A particularly interesting example of the role of language in the classification of observed phenomena is provided by *color terminology*. The way in which hues are grouped varies in different languages, and probably in turn affects the type of color discriminations that are customarily made in each particular culture. In certain modern European languages, there are different words for "light blue" and "dark blue," just as in English we have the terms "pink" and "red." The Ashantis of the African Gold Coast have color names for black, red, and white: the term "black" is used for any dark color, such as blue, purple, or brown; while "red" also covers pink, orange, and yellow (74). In the same group, gray is expressed by the word for "wood ashes," and green by the term for "tree" or "leaf" (74). The terms for "blue" and "green" are often combined in primitive languages. We cannot, of course, conclude from these linguistic classifications that the color sensitivity of such peoples is inferior to or different from ours. Objective tests of color-blindness have demonstrated a normal ability for color discrimination, despite the lack of differentiating terminology (cf., e.g., 71). It is apparently the specific conditions of the particular culture that determined the type of classification developed in each case.

Not only vocabulary, but also the formal aspects of language, show characteristic differences from one culture to another. Thus in the Hopi language there are no temporal references in verbs, but special forms are employed to indicate the nature of the statement, such as immediate observation, memory, or generalization (cf. 77, p. 217). Similarly, among the Hupa Indians of California, a suffix is used to designate the source of information, such as hearing, sight, or conjecture from circumstantial evidence (30). Our distinction between nouns and verbs is not so fundamental or universal as might be supposed. To take another illustration from the Hopi language, such terms as "lightning," "wave," "meteor," "puff of smoke," and "pulsation" are verbs, as are all events of necessarily brief duration (cf. 77, p. 216). In some languages, the distinction between verbs and nouns is nonexistent, all terms corresponding most nearly to our verbs. Thus "it burns" would signify a flame, and "a house occurs" or "it houses" would refer to our noun "house" (cf. 77, pp. 216–217).

In an analysis of the extensive data collected by Malinowski on the Trobriand Islanders, Lee (51) proposed a provocative theory regarding the language of these people and its role in their other behavior. The Trobriand language, according to Lee, shows a focusing of attention upon disparate elements or acts, considered independently, rather than upon relationships among events. Their sentences are composed of essentially unrelated words. The comparative and superlative degree are absent, as are pure adjectival concepts; adjectives in this language refer to specific classes of objects and cannot be abstracted from them. Cause-and-effect relationships are not conventionally expressed. When questioned regarding such causal relations, the individual Trobriander does not have ready-made answers provided by his culture. Each individual must think out his own answer, the replies showing confusion and disagreements. Chronological sequences are likewise unimportant to them. "The past is not an ordered series, but rather a chaotic repository of unrelated events, which, at best, are remembered as anecdotes" (51, p. 360).

A frequently reported observation is the relative scarcity of abstract terms in most primitive languages. Such a condition, of course, makes abstract thought much more difficult. It need not, however, imply an inability to carry on abstract thinking, any more than color-blindness is implied by the color terminologies discussed above. The presence or absence of abstract terms in a particular language may simply reflect the conditions of life within that culture. There is some evidence suggesting that terms of a higher level of abstraction can often be developed by such peoples when a situation is presented that requires such terms (cf. 43, p. 51).

Finally, it should be borne in mind that language is, essentially, *behavior* (cf. 40). It is not an independent entity, as philologists are sometimes inclined to regard it. At the same time, language serves as a potent cultural influence. The particular system of linguistic terms and forms institutionalized by a given culture represents an important part of the total complex of stimulation to which each individual is exposed. Regardless of how such linguistic behavior originally evolved in the group, it assumes a major role in shaping the psychological development of the individual.

"HUMAN NATURE" IN DIFFERENT CULTURES

Certain ways of acting have long been popularly regarded as "natural." This designation usually implies that the behavior in question is "normal" as well as innate and biologically predetermined. Closely related to this concept are those of "perversion" and "reversion." The former refers to behavior which is considered "unnatural"; the latter implies a revival or reinstatement of a more "primitive" and less "artificial" type of behavior. Thus if one type of behavior is assumed to be *natural,* then any environmentally produced variation of such behavior is considered a *perversion.* Similarly, if a "civilized" person be put in a "primitive" environment, the behavioral changes which may ensue are regarded as a *reversion* to a natural state. The latter is implicitly assumed to have existed all along, but to have been held in abeyance, so to speak, by conditions in a civilized community. It is apparent that the concepts of perversion and reversion have meaning only as long as one specific way of behaving is assumed to be the "natural" way.

It has been repeatedly demonstrated, however, that no one form of behavior is any more natural than another in the sense of being predetermined by innate constitution. The data on this question are derived chiefly from two sources. The first is the *experimental production* of behavioral variations. A number of such experiments on infrahuman organisms have been reported in Chapter 4. The import of their results was to show that different types of behavior will follow as a natural result of varying environmental conditions. Much so-called instinctive behavior has been shown to be natural only under given environmental conditions.

The same point has been demonstrated by *intercultural comparisons.* Many forms of behavior which have been labeled "instincts" and "fundamental drives" are found to differ significantly from one cultural group to another (cf. 43, Ch. 5–6; 69, Ch. 8). Thus the role of cultural factors in the expression of the *maternal drive* is illustrated by the widespread custom of adopting children, which is practiced among several Melanesian, South African, and American Indian groups. In certain tribes, children are so infrequently reared by their own parents that it is very difficult to obtain genealogies. Similarly, in ancient China the social concept of maternity was distinct from biological maternity. Thus all offspring of "secondary wives" within the family unit were considered to be children of the "first wife." The latter was the only person in the role of mother, the other wives being indiscriminately regarded as "aunts" by their own as well as other children in the family (cf. 43).

Aggressiveness and *fighting,* popularly considered to be among primitive man's natural impulses, are unknown among several groups. In a few tribes, for example, no weapons or implements of warfare are to be found. That men should attack each other seems inconceivable to individuals reared in such cultural groups. Similarly, *acquisitiveness* and the desire for personal property are not a universal phenomenon (6). A striking demonstration of this fact is provided by the social institution of the *potlatch,* as found among the Indians of the Canadian Northwest Coast. In this culture, social prestige is achieved through the distribution or giving-away of personal property, rather than through its acquisition.

The manifestations of the *sex drive,* with its attendant feelings such as love and jealousy, likewise exhibit wide intercultural variations. The diverse customs and conventions associated with mating behavior in different groups have been extensively described by anthropologists and many are undoubtedly familiar to the reader (cf. 28). It will be recalled that similar differences in the typical manifestations of sex behavior were found by Kinsey *et al.* (41) in their comparisons of different socioeconomic classes within our own culture.

Cultural influences are also discernible in the *motor habits* of different peoples. The gait and tempo of walking, as well as the characteristic standing, sitting, and sleeping postures, vary widely from one culture to another. The carved ivory and wooden headrests of Africa which are preserved in our art museums impress the American observer as a most uncomfortable sleeping aid! Most primitive peoples sit in a squatting posture; Eskimos, as well as many American Indian groups, habitually sit on their heels (cf. 12).

The role of cultural factors in the development of gestures has already been discussed in the preceding chapter. A typical illustration of the cultural conditioning of a response often assumed to be "natural" and universal is to be found in gestures of negation and affirmation. Nodding to signify assent is by no means shared by all peoples, nor is the lateral turning of the head a universal sign of negation. The Semang, a pygmy tribe of interior Malaya, say "yes" by thrusting the head sharply forward, and "no" by lowering the eyes (47). The Dyaks of Borneo raise their eyebrows for "yes," and contract them slightly for "no." For the Maori, raising the head and chin signifies "yes"; among the Sicilians, the same gesture means "no" (42, p. 282). The use of the fingers in pointing is likewise restricted to certain cultures. Among several American Indian groups, for example, pointing is executed with the lips (47).

Closely related to such observations of gesture is the comparative study of *emotional expression* in different cultures. A rich body of data is available in this area, indicating differences in extent of emotional display, occasions on which emotional behavior is manifested, specific patterning of emotional responses, and degree of control the individual is able to exert over such behavior (cf. 43, Ch. 7; 47). The manner of greeting employed by different peoples would in itself constitute a fertile field for such intercultural comparisons. The practice of kissing, as a friendly greeting or as a sexual response, varies widely in different cultures and is totally absent in a number of primitive societies. It is interesting to note in this connection that Kinsey and his associates (41) found similar differences between social classes within our own culture. Among persons of lower socioeconomic level, kissing as a sexual response was relatively infrequent and was even regarded by many as unhygienic. The latter attitude was particularly interesting in view of the fact that it was frequently expressed by persons who habitually used common drinking cups and followed other practices considered insanitary in higher socioeconomic levels.

Many instances have been recorded of the ceremonial control of certain emotional reactions, such as weeping, to a degree that appears surprising to persons reared in our culture. Ritual shedding of tears on a variety of prescribed occasions has been observed in such countries as China and Montenegro, in a number of American Indian tribes, and among the Maori, Andaman Islanders, and other primitive cultures (43, Ch. 7).

THE INDIVIDUAL AS A MEMBER OF MULTIPLE GROUPS

Psychologically the individual belongs to every group with which he shares behavior.[2] From this point of view, group membership is to be defined in terms of behavioral rather than biological categories. The effective grouping is not based upon the individual's race or sex or body build, but upon his experiential background. Thus if the individual is reared as a member of a certain national group with its own traditions and cultural background and its own peculiar complex of stimulating conditions, he will display the behavioral characteristics of that group regardless of his racial origin. It should be understood, of course, that mere physical presence does not constitute group membership in a psychological sense. If a Negro child were brought up in a community composed exclusively of whites, he would not necessarily receive the same social stimulation as a white child. Similarly, a boy who is brought up exclusively by female relatives will not develop the personality traits of a girl. A psychological group is based solely upon shared behavior and not upon geographical proximity or biological resemblance.

It follows from such a concept of group that any one individual is effec-

[2] This criterion of a psychological group is essentially that formulated by Kantor (39), who seems to have been the first to discuss social behavior in terms of *shared responses* to objects having common stimulus functions.

tively a member of a large and varied set of groups. A *multiplicity of behavioral groups,* large and small, cut across each other in the individual's background. Some of the most important of these groups have already been discussed in earlier chapters. The individual is born into a broad cultural division such as, for example, "Western civilization," with its characteristic sources of stimulation. He will develop certain aptitudes, emotional traits, attitudes, and beliefs as a result of his affiliation with this group. He is also a member of a given national group with its more specific traditional ways of acting.

If the individual displays certain physical characteristics, such as a particular skin color, facial conformation, and body build, he may be classified as a member of a given "racial" group which occupies a distinct position within the broader national division. In so far as his racial background leads to certain social distinctions and culturally imposed differentiations of behavior, it will operate as an effective grouping. The same may be said of sex. If, within a given society, traditional beliefs in regard to sex differences exist so that the sexes are exposed to dissimilar psychological stimulation, then the individual's sex will in part determine his behavioral characteristics.

There are a number of other behavioral groupings which, although less frequently recognized and less clearly defined, may be equally influential in the individual's development. Thus it will be recalled that important psychological differences are usually found between the city-bred and country-bred child, as well as between different social classes (cf. Ch. 15). Similarly, the particular state, province, or other major division of a nation in which the individual is reared, and even the specific town and neighborhood in which he lives, will exert significant influences upon his intellectual and emotional development.

Other groups with which an individual identifies himself behaviorally include his occupational class, his religion, his political party, his club, his educational institution. That such groupings represent clear-cut cultural distinctions is readily illustrated by the stereotypes which have become attached to many of these groups. To people within our society, a distinct picture will be suggested by the mention of such designations as country doctor, business man, Roman Catholic, Orthodox Jew, Republican, Rotarian, Harvard man. These groups influence the individual's behavior in two ways. First, they directly stimulate and foster certain ways of acting. Secondly, the reactions of other people to the individual are influenced by their knowledge of his group affiliation. The social attitudes and "social expectancy" which the individual encounters will in turn affect his behavior.

Family groupings, with their characteristic activities and traditions, constitute another important part of the individual's psychological environment. The degenerate Jukes and Kallikaks, eminent families such as the Huxleys and the Darwins, and many other striking examples testify to the cultural influence of family membership. Cutting across such family groupings are age distinctions. "Stages" are socially imposed upon the continuous life activities of the individual and he is treated more or less differently at each period. The individual may also look upon himself as belonging to a particular generation—he may be a member of the "older generation," the "young married set," the "teenagers," and so forth. Even such apparently minor factors as one's hobbies and recreations will in turn affect the individual's subsequent behavior. Psychological membership in many new groups may result from a newly developed interest in bowling, stamp collecting, or early American pressed glass. The number of behavioral groupings could easily be multiplied. These examples will suffice to illustrate the nature of such groupings and their effect upon behavior development.

The individual may be regarded partly as a resultant of his multiple group memberships. To be sure, each individual also undergoes experiences that are absolutely unique to himself. Such experiences are probably less significant, however, in shaping the more basic aspects of his personality than is his shared behavior. The experiences that are common to a group of individuals have a certain degree of permanence in the sense that they will tend to be repeated more often and to be corroborated or reenforced by other similar experiences. In general, the more highly organized the group, the more consistent and systematic will be the experiences its members undergo. This will tend to make the shared experiences on the whole more effective than the purely individual. Moreover, even the individual's idiosyncratic experiences will generally have certain cultural features which differentiate them from the idiosyncratic experiences of persons in other cultures. Thus an individual may compose a poem which is unique in its totality and to this extent unlike any poem ever written by any other person; but the fact that the poem is a political satire, that it is composed in the English language and in iambic pentameter, and that it is written with a ball-point pen are among the many distinctly cultural features of such an activity.

In view of the pronounced effect of such shared or common behavior upon the individual's development, it may appear surprising that individuals are no more alike in their behavior repertoire than we ordinarily find them to be. The extent of individual differences within any one group is extremely large. In fact, the variations among individuals have always proved to be more marked than the differences from one group to another. How can the "individuality" of each person be explained in terms of his shared experiential background?

The key to this problem seems to lie in the *multiplicity* of overlapping groups with which the individual may be behaviorally identified. The number of such groups is so great that the *specific combination* is unique for each individual. Not only does this furnish a stimulational basis for the existence of wide individual differences, but it also suggests a mechanism whereby the individual may "rise above" his group. There are many examples of individuals who have broken away from the customs and traditional ways of acting of their group. Through such situations, modifications of the group itself may also be effected.

In these cases the individual is not reacting contrary to his past experience, as might at first appear. This would be psychologically impossible. His behavior is the result of psychological membership in various *conflicting* groups. Many group memberships can exist side by side in a composite behavioral adjustment. But in certain cases two or more groups may foster different ways of reacting to the same situation. This enables the individual to become aware of the arbitrariness of the restrictions and traditions of each group, to evaluate them critically, and to regard them more "objectively." Membership in many diverse groups frees the individual from the intellectual and other limitations of each group and makes possible the fullest development of "individuality."

SUMMARY

The fundamental aim of differential psychology is the understanding of behavior and its ultimate unit is the individual. By relating the facts of individual differences to concomitant circumstances, we can advance our knowledge regarding the nature of human behavior. Many psychological generalizations are based upon data obtained within a single culture. Such community-centrism can be corrected by testing hypotheses in different cultures.

Observations by psychologists and anthropologists provide examples of the operation of cultural frames of reference in many kinds of behavior involving perception, memory, and esthetic judgment. Our concepts of time and space, our food preferences, and our appreciation of music and art all reveal the influence of experiential background. The developmental stages through which the individual passes in the process of reaching maturity may vary from culture to culture. Such variations can be illustrated with reference to concept formation, emotional development, and children's drawings.

Cultural factors are also reflected in the distinction between normal and abnormal behavior. The term "abnormal" has been used in an anti-normative, a pathological, and a statistical sense. The statistical concept of abnormality recognizes the continuous distribution of behavioral differences, in which individuals may deviate in either direction from the empirical norm or modal behavior. It follows that the psychologically abnormal or deviate individual cannot be properly identified without reference to a particular cultural norm. Behavior that is abnormal in one culture may be normal in another. The inferior deviate of one culture may be the superior deviate of another. Culture may determine the position of the norm, the social evaluation of a particular form of behavior, the prevalence of psychiatric disorders, and the specific ways in which maladjustment will be expressed.

An important source of cultural differences is to be found in the characteristics of the languages spoken by different peoples. Language provides the tools for much of our thinking. It gives us the categories in terms of which we perceive objects, observe similarities and differences, and construct concepts.

Much of the behavior commonly ascribed to "human nature" proves to be neither universal nor natural when checked in different cultures. Pronounced cultural differences have been found in a number of so-called fundamental drives, as illustrated by maternal reactions toward offspring, aggressiveness and fighting behavior, acquisitiveness and the desire for personal possessions, and sexual behavior. The influence of culture is also clearly discernible in basic motor habits, such as gait and tempo of walking; characteristic standing, sitting, and sleeping postures; and the gestures employed to convey various meanings. Comparative studies of emotional expression in different cultures likewise reveal differences in the extent of emotional display, occasions on which emotions are manifested, nature of emotional expression, and degree of control that can be exerted over emotional responses.

Psychologically, the individual belongs to every group with which he shares behavior. In this sense, any one person is a member of a vast number of overlapping groups, which may be identified in terms of national, racial, sex, age, geographical, educational, vocational, religious, familial, and many other categories. The multiplicity of such groups, the uniqueness of their specific combinations, and the conflicting behavior sometimes fostered by different groups, all contribute to the distinctive "individuality" of each person's behavior development.

REFERENCES

1. Aberle, D. F. "Arctic hysteria" and latah in Mongolia. *Trans. N. Y. Acad. Sci.*, 1952, 14, 291–297.
2. Anastasi, Anne, and Foley, J. P., Jr. An analysis of spontaneous drawings by children in different cultures. *J. appl. Psychol.*, 1936, 20, 689–726.
3. Anastasi, Anne, and Foley, J. P., Jr. A study of animal drawings by Indian children of the North Pacific Coast. *J. soc. Psychol.*, 1938, 9, 363–374.
4. Bartlett, F. C. *Remembering: a study in experimental and social psychology.* London: Cambridge Univer. Press, 1932.
5. Bartlett, F. C. Psychological methods and anthropological problems. *Africa*, 1937, 10, 400–420.
6. Beaglehole, E. *Property: a study in social psychology.* N.Y.: Macmillan, 1932.
7. Benedict, P. K., and Jacks, I. Mental illness in primitive societies. *Psychiatry*, 1954, 17, 377–389.
8. Benedict, Ruth, Configurations of culture in North America. *Amer. Anthr.*, 1932, N. S. 34, 1–27.
9. Benedict, Ruth. Anthropology and the abnormal. *J. gen. Psychol.*, 1934, 10, 59–82.
10. Benedict, Ruth. *Patterns of culture.* Boston: Houghton Mifflin, 1934.
11. Benjamin, A. C. *An introduction to the philosophy of science.* N.Y.: Macmillan, 1937.
12. Boas, F. *The mind of primitive man.* (Rev. Ed.) N.Y.: Macmillan, 1938.
13. Bugg, E. G., and Thompson, A. S. An experimental test of the genetic theory of consonance. *J. gen. Psychol.*, 1952, 47, 71–90.
14. Chase, S. *The tyranny of words.* N.Y.: Harcourt, Brace, 1938.
15. Dennis, W. The performance of Hopi Indian children on the Goodenough Draw-a-Man test. *J. comp. Psychol.*, 1942, 34, 341–348.
16. Dennis, W. Animism and related tendencies in Hopi children. *J. abnorm. soc. Psychol.*, 1943, 38, 21–36.
17. Dennis, W. Cultural and developmental factors in perception. In R. R. Blake and G. V. Ramsey (Eds.), *Perception; an approach to personality.* N.Y.: Ronald, 1951. Pp. 148–169.
18. Dennis, W. Animistic thinking among college and university students. *Sci. Mon.*, 1953, 76, 247–249.
19. Dhunjibhoy, J. E. A brief résumé of the types of insanity commonly met with in India. *J. ment. Sci.*, 1930, 76, 254–264.
20. Dollard, J. *Criteria for the life history—with analysis of six notable documents.* New Haven: Yale Univer. Press, 1935.
21. Eaton, J. W., and Weil, R. J. *Culture and mental disorders.* Glencoe, Ill.: Free Press, 1955.
22. Foley, J. P., Jr. The comparative approach to psychological phenomena. *Psychol. Rev.*, 1935, 42, 480–490.

23. Foley, J. P., Jr. The criterion of abnormality. *J. abnorm. soc. Psychol.*, 1935, 30, 279–291.

24. Foley, J. P., Jr. Psychological "ultimates": a note on psychological "fact" versus psychological "law." *J. gen. Psychol.*, 1936, 15, 455–458.

25. Foley, J. P., Jr. An experimental study of the effect of occupational experience upon motor speed and preferential tempo. *Arch. Psychol.*, 1937, No. 219.

26. Foley, J. P., Jr. The scientific psychology of individual and group differences. *J. soc. Psychol.*, 1938, 9, 375–377.

27. Foley, J. P., Jr. The occupational conditioning of preferential auditory tempo: a contribution toward an empirical theory of aesthetics. *J. soc. Psychol.*, 1940, 12, 121–129.

28. Ford, C. S., and Beach, F. A. *Patterns of sexual behavior.* N.Y.: Harper, 1951.

29. Fortune, R. F. *Sorcerers of Dobu.* London: Routledge, 1932.

30. Goddard, P. E. Life and culture of the Hupa. *Univer. Calif. Publ. Amer. Archeol. Ethnol.*, 1903, 1, 1–88.

31. Goodenough, Florence L., and Harris, D. B. Studies in the psychology of children's drawings: II. 1928–1949. *Psychol. Bull.*, 1950, 47, 369–433.

32. Grygier, T. Psychiatric observations in the Arctic. *Brit. J. Psychol.*, 1948, 39, 84–96.

33. Hallowell, A. I. Temporal orientation in western civilization and in a preliterate society. *Amer. Anthr.*, 1937, 39, 647–670.

34. Hallowell, A. I. Some psychological aspects of measurements among the Saulteaux. *Amer. Anthr.*, 1942, 44, 62–67.

35. Hayakawa, S. I. *Language in thought and action.* N.Y.: Harcourt, Brace, 1949.

36. Hayakawa, S. I. (Ed.) *Language, meaning, and maturity.* N.Y.: Harper, 1954.

37. Hoijer, H. (Ed.) *Language in culture; conference on the interrelations of language and other aspects of culture.* Chicago: Univer. Chicago Press, 1954.

38. Hollingworth, H. L. *Abnormal psychology: its concepts and theories.* N.Y.: Ronald, 1930.

39. Kantor, J. R. *An outline of social psychology.* Chicago: Follett, 1929.

40. Kantor, J. R. *An objective psychology of grammar.* Bloomington, Ind.: Indiana Univer. Publ. (Science Series, No. 1), 1936.

41. Kinsey, A. C., Pomeroy, W. B., and Martin, C. E. *Sexual behavior in the human male.* Philadelphia: Saunders, 1948.

42. Klineberg, O. *Race differences.* N.Y.: Harper, 1935.

43. Klineberg, O. *Social psychology.* (2nd Ed.) N.Y.: Holt, 1954.

44. Kluckhohn, C. Culture and behavior. In G. Lindzey (Ed.), *Handbook of social psychology.* Cambridge, Mass.: Addison-Wesley, 1954. Pp. 921–976.

45. Korzybski, A. *Science and sanity.* (2nd Ed.) Lancaster, Pa.: Science Press, 1941.

46. Kroeber, A. L. Psychosis or social sanction. *Char. and Pers.*, 1940, 8, 204–215.

47. La Barre, W. The cultural basis of emotions and gestures. *J. Pers.*, 1947, 16, 49–68.

48. Lambe, T. A. The role of cultural factors in paranoid psychosis among the Yoruba tribe. *J. ment. Sci.*, 1955, 101, 239–266.
49. Landes, R. The abnormal among the Ojibwa Indians. *J. abnorm. soc. Psychol.*, 1938, 33, 14–33.
50. Landis, C., and Bolles, M. Marjorie. *Textbook of abnormal psychology.* (Rev. Ed.) N.Y.: Macmillan, 1950.
51. Lee, D. D. A primitive system of values. *Philos. Sci.*, 1940, 7, 355–378.
52. Malinowski, B. *The father in primitive society.* N.Y.: Norton, 1927.
53. Mauthner, F. *Beiträge zu einer Kritik der Sprache.* (2nd Ed.) Stuttgart: Cotta, 1913. Vol. III.
54. Mead, Margaret. *Coming of age in Samoa.* N.Y.: Morrow, 1928.
55. Mead, Margaret. *Growing up in New Guinea.* N.Y.: Morrow, 1930.
56. Mead, Margaret. An investigation of the thought of primitive children with special reference to animism. *J. roy. anthr. Inst.*, 1932, 62, 173–190.
57. Moore, H. T. The genetic aspect of consonance and dissonance. *Psychol. Monogr.*, 1914, 17, No. 73.
58. Mowrer, O. H. What is normal behavior? In L. A. Pennington and I. A. Berg (Eds.), *An introduction to clinical psychology.* (2nd Ed.) N.Y.: Ronald, 1954. Pp. 58–88.
59. Nadel, S. F. Experiments on culture psychology. *Africa*, 1937, 10, 421–435.
60. Nadel, S. F. A field experiment in racial psychology. *Brit. J. Psychol.*, 1937–38, 28, 195–211.
61. Nichols, L. A. Neuroses in native African troops. *J. ment. Sci.*, 1944, 90, 862–868.
62. Ogden, C. K., and Richards, I. A. *The meaning of meaning.* (6th Ed.) N.Y.: Harcourt, Brace, 1944.
63. Piaget, J. *The child's conception of the world.* N.Y.: Harcourt, Brace, 1929.
64. Piaget, J. *The child's conception of physical causality.* N.Y.: Harcourt, Brace, 1930.
65. Piaget, J. *The moral judgment of the child.* N.Y.: Harcourt, Brace, 1932.
66. Radcliffe-Brown, A. *The Andaman Islanders: a study in social anthropology.* London: Cambridge Univer. Press, 1922.
67. Sapir, E. Language. *Encycl. soc. Sci.*, 1933, 9, 155–169.
68. Schubert, A. Drawings of Orotchen children and young people. *J. genet. Psychol.*, 1930, 37, 232–244.
69. Sherif, M. *The psychology of social norms.* N.Y.: Harper, 1936.
70. Sherif, M., and Sherif, Carolyn W. *An outline of social psychology.* (Rev. Ed.) N.Y.: Harper, 1956.
71. Simon, K. Color vision of Buganda Africans. *E. Afr. med. J.*, 1951, 28 (2), 75–79.
72. Singer, J. L., and Opler, M. K. Contrasting patterns of fantasy and motility in Irish and Italian schizophrenics. *J. abnorm. soc. Psychol.*, 1956, 53, 42–47.
73. Thomas, W. I. *Primitive behavior, an introduction to the social sciences.* N.Y.: McGraw-Hill, 1937.
74. Wallis, W. D. *An introduction to anthropology.* N.Y.: Harper, 1926.
75. Wegrocki, H. J. A critique of cultural and statistical concepts of abnormality. *J. abnorm. soc. Psychol.*, 1939, 34, 166–178.

76. Werner, H. *Comparative psychology of mental development.* (Rev. Ed.) N.Y.: Follett, 1948.
77. Whorf, B. L. *Language, thought, and reality: selected writings of* . . . . (Ed. by J. B. Carroll.) Cambridge, Mass.: Technology Press, M.I.T.; N.Y.: Wiley, 1956.
78. Yap, P. M. Mental diseases peculiar to certain cultures: a survey of comparative psychiatry. *J. ment. Sci.,* 1951, 97, 313–327.

Author Index

In order not to crowd the text with names of investigators, relatively few authors' names have been directly cited in the discussion, the majority of references being reported by number only. All these references, however, have been included in the Author Index. When looking up such a reference, the reader should find the author's name in the bibliography at the end of the particular chapter, note the number of the reference, and then locate that number on the given page of the text. References to bibliographies have been set in italics in the Author Index.

Subject Index

DATE DUE

JE 7 - '64			
FE 18 '65			
JA 23 '67			
MR 21 '67			
MY 2 '67			
MY 17 '67			
NO 27 '67			
MAR 15 '69			
APR 14 '69			
DE 16 '69			
AP 23 '76			
DEC 19 '85			
GAYLORD			PRINTED IN U.S.A.